ISC
COMMERCE
Class XI

Written in strict conformity with the latest syllabus of the Council for the Indian School Certificate Examination for ISC Examination to be held in and after 2018

ISC COMMERCE

Class XI

S Mukherjee MSc (London)
Chairman of the Board of Studies [Deptt. of Com.]
St. Xavier's College, Kolkata [Autonomous] [Retd.]

D Datta MA (Cal)
General Manager, IDBI Bank, Mumbai (Retd.)

C D Gupta MBA (Ahmedabad)
Global Innovation Manager, UL Ltd, Singapore

New Central Book Agency (P) Ltd
LONDON
HYDERABAD ERNAKULAM BHUBANESWAR
NEW DELHI KOLKATA PUNE GUWAHATI

NCBA

REGD OFFICE
8/1 Chintamoni Das Lane, Kolkata 700 009, India
email: ncbapvtltd@eth.net

OVERSEAS
NCBA (UK) Ltd, 149 Park Avenue North, Northampton, NN3 2HY, UK
email: ncbauk@yahoo.com

EXPORT
NCBA Exports Pvt. Ltd, 212 Shahpur Jat, New Delhi 110 049
email: ncbaexports@ncbapvtltd.com

BRANCHES

2/27 Ansari Road, 1st Floor
Daryaganj, **New Delhi** 110 002
email: ncbadel@ncbapvtltd.com

Shop Nos. 3 & 4, Vinayak Towers
681/B Budhwar Peth, Appa Balwant Chowk
Pune 411 002
email: ncbapune@ncbapvtltd.com

Shop No. 15, Bharati Towers, Ground Floor
Forest Park
Bhubaneswar 751 001
email: ncbabub@ncbapvtltd.com

House No. 3-1-315, 1st Floor
Nimboliadda, Kachiguda, **Hyderabad** 500 027
email: ncbahydb@ncbapvtltd.com

GSS Shopping Complex, 1st Floor
Opposite College Post Office, Convent Road
Ernakulam 682 035
0484-4021054 / 53

Radhamayee Complex (Second Floor)
Opp. SBI, Panbazar, Jaswanta Road
Guwahati 781 001
email: ncbaguwahati@ncbapvtltd.com

ISC COMMERCE [XI] • S Mukherjee, D Datta and C D Gupta

First Published: 2017

PUBLISHER AND TYPESETTER
New Central Book Agency (P) Ltd
8/1 Chintamoni Das Lane, Kolkata 700 009

PRINTER
New Central Book Agency (P) Ltd
Web-Offset Division, Dhulagarh, Sankrail, Howrah

PROJECT TEAM
Swapan Sarkar, Pradip Biswas and Prodip Baidya

ISBN: 978 93 5255 069 2

Price ₹ 350.00

CONTENTS

PREFACE

The title has been written by following the latest syllabus of ISC Commerce (XI). To be honest, the syllabus has been carefully and meticulously followed. The noble features of the title which separate it from the competing ones are the following:

1. A completely student-friendly approach has been followed.
2. Every topic has been treated in a concise way without compromising with quality and coverage (contents) of the syllabus.
3. Simple sentences with easy language have been used throughout the text.
4. Certain irrelevant topics discussed in other books have been totally omitted.
5. A comprehensive glossary has been added to enable the students to be familiar with the vocabulary of commerce since every subject has its own language and nomenclature.
6. The title includes various case studies which are likely to generate creativity among students and enhance their comprehensive power.

A serious note for subject teachers:

In the syllabus only two sectors of the economy have been erroneously highlighted, viz., the primary sector and the secondary sector under the broad heading industrial sector. Also note that there is a third sector of the economy, viz., the tertiary sector. It has been omitted from the syllabus. This sounds like a paradox more so in view of the fact that in recent past, there has occurred slow growth of commodity producing (primary and secondary) sectors and a much faster growth of the services (tertiary) sector. This is also observable in India's globalised economy. And the production of any good (tangible item) is not complete unless and until it reaches the final buyer. Keeping this strategic issue in mind, the syllabus makers should have included this topic in the main curriculum but they have dropped it for reasons which are not quite transparent to the author. What appears to be really subversive, if not paradoxical is that the assignment given under the first project work makes pointed reference to the tertiary sector by giving an explicit specification of the three sectors which conjointly constitutes a modern economy. Keeping this point in view, the authors have included the tertiary sector in Chapter 2. Also note that what is broadly called 'commerce' falls under the tertiary (service-generating and not commodity-producing) sector. In fact, many topics included in the syllabus such as banking and finance, insurance, foreign (export-import) trade and domestic trade (wholesaling and retailing) fall under the tertiary sector. So the exclusion of this topic is no doubt a serious omission and it is high time that syllabus makers took note of this dream reality and came down to earth.

Acknowledgements

In completing the project, the authors have benefited from the support and cooperation received from a cross section of people. Thanks go to the following persons:

Siladitya Sinha Roy	*Banita Banerjee*	*Arun Kabri*	*Mayur Tanna*
U. N. Panda	*K. K. Nehra*	*Prakash Das*	*Suman Chakraborty*
Subir Biswas	*Prabhat Jas*	*Soumen Paul*	*Swapan Sarkar*

Special thanks go to S. S. Roy for his extended endeavour to help the authors in all possible ways and to Sougata Das for doing the pain-staking job of doing computer entry of the entire handwritten manuscript and for helping the publisher for transforming an ugly caterpillar to a beautiful butterfly. Finally, the authors' heartfelt thanks go to the publisher for bearing with them during their protracted period of intellectual pregnancy. The authors welcome opinions and comments on the title and suggestions for its further improvements from subject teachers and of course students. Their commendable effort will help to make the title less imperfect and faulty than it is in its first print and render a useful service to the students of our invisible schools who remains scattered throughout the country and abroad.

S Mukherjee, D Datta and C D Gupta

A FEW WORDS OF ADVICE FOR THE STUDENTS

Dear students,

I am trying to achieve my goal through this open letter which will help you all to be a successful candidate in the exam. Besides hard work, there are some other techniques which can be adopted for excellent results. It is very common to notice that many brilliant students fail to score good marks in the exam. in spite of devoting a number of midnights in studies. But the important thing is that you need to know the method of studying. Being in teaching profession for so many years, I feel like sharing my personal experience with the help of the following instructions:

1. Be regular in class. You need to study for hours daily what has been taught in the class. It will help you to implant the topic in your mind.
2. Jot down the important points while you are studying and make short notes on the topics. Key words and key terms will help you to do this task. The previous years' questions may help you to know the type of questions you are about to face.
3. Go through the self-prepared notes before the day of your exam.
4. You must be careful enough while choosing the questions among several alternatives during the exam. So it is necessary to read the question paper and other instructions given by the examiner throughly.
5. Frame your answers according to the questions. Answers must be to the point.
6. Write all the answers point-wise in separate paragraphs.
7. It must be clear to the examiner from the introduction of your answer that you have understood the question.
8. Conclusion to each answer is a must. It should include your opinion/view which might strike the examiner to give you more marks.
9. You should divide time equally for each answer as they carry equal marks. Time management is important during exam. So don't give too much emphasis on a particular question.
10. In some cases, when you are asked to write a controversial answer, give your views both in favour of and against the topic and then evaluate your judgement.
11. Avoid using first person in your answers.
12. Check your roll number and other relevant information in your answer script and revise your paper before you submit it finally.

I hope all these advices will make you energetic, courageous and conscious before the examination. Feel free to send me your opinions or suggestions to help me improve the text in the next editions of the book.

Wish you success in exam.

Authors

SYLLABUS

AIMS

1. To develop an interest in the theory and practice of business, trade and industry.
2. To familiarise candidates with theoretical foundations organising, managing and handling operations of a business firm.
3. To provide a study of the more important aspects of the commercial world.
4. To provide knowledge of the activities of commerce in the marketing of goods and services.

*There will be **two** papers in the subject.*

Paper I – *Theory: 3 hours ... 80 marks*

Paper II – *Project Work ... 20 marks*

PAPER I – THEORY – 80 Marks

***Part I (20 marks)** will consist of compulsory short answer questions testing knowledge, application and skills relating to elementary/fundamental aspects of the entire syllabus.*

***Part II (60 marks)** will consist of **eight** questions out of which candidates will be required to answer five questions, each carrying 12 marks.*

1. Nature and Purpose of Business

(i) Classification of human activities – economic and non-economic.

Classification of human activities – economic and non-economic. Types of economic activities.

Distinction between business, profession and employment.

(ii) Definition and concept of business; classification of business activities.

Definition of business. Characteristics of business. Classification of business activities:

(a) *Industry: types of industries on the basis of activity (primary and secondary) and on the basis of size (micro, small, medium and large).*

Role of small businesses in India.

(b) *Commerce: branches of Commerce. Commerce — its nature and functions; importance of Commerce. Branches of Commerce — trade and aids to trade. Relationship between commerce, trade and industry.*

(iii) Business objectives.

Business objectives: economic; social; human and national. Role of Profit in business.

2. Forms of Business Organisations

(i) Introduction to business organisations.

Meaning, characteristics, types (private sector, public sector, Public Private Partnerships (PPPs)/Joint Sector). Comparison between different types of organisations.

(ii) Sole trader — objectives; formation; merits and demerits.

Meaning and definition of sole trader; characteristics and objectives of sole trader; merits and demerits.

(iii) Partnership

(a) Meaning, features; types of partners and partnership firms.

Meaning and definition of partnership; features of partnership firms; types of partners and partnerships.

(b) Registration of Partnership firms.

Formation, meaning and contents of partnership deed; registration and consequences of non-registration.

(c) Evaluation of partnership; merits and demerits.

Self-explanatory.

(d) Comparison of sole proprietorship and partnership.

Self-explanatory.

(iv) Corporate Organisations

(a) *Joint Stock Company: meaning, features, merits, demerits and objectives.*

(b) *Stages of Formation of a Company.*

(c) *Promotion, meaning, role and types of promoters.*

(d) *Incorporation of a company — Meaning and steps of incorporation (including filing of documents), certificate of incorporation.*

(e) *Memorandum of Association and Articles of Association (excluding alterations) and distinction between the two documents.*

Meaning and contents of MOA and AOA. Distinction between the MOA and AOA.

(f) *Commencement of business.*

Steps, Certificate of Commencement.

(g) *Prospectus and statement in lieu of prospectus — meaning and contents only.*

(h) *Types of companies — Classification of companies on the basis of mode of incorporation, liability of members, public interest, ownership, control and nationality.*

Public and private companies and their comparative studies, privileges of private companies.

(i) *Global enterprises — Meaning, characteristics, merits and demerits of Global Enterprises.*

(v) Public Sector Undertakings

(a) *Meaning; characteristics, objectives, role and forms of Public Sector Undertakings (Departmental Undertakings, Public Corporations and Government Companies).*

Public Sector Undertakings — meaning; characteristics, objectives, role and criticisms. Forms of Public Sector Undertakings (Departmental undertakings; Public Corporation and Government companies — definitions, features, merits and demerits).

(b) *Public Private Partnerships.*
Meaning and features of PPPs.

(vi) *Cooperative organisations* — meaning; characteristics and types.
Cooperative organisations — meaning; characteristics, advantages and disadvantages; Types of cooperative organisations, distinction between joint stock companies and cooperative organisation.

3. Social Responsibility of Business and Business Ethics

Concept and need for social responsibility.

Responsibility towards owners, investors, consumers, employees, government and community; Responsibility of business towards protection of environment; Meaning and importance of Business ethics.

4. Emerging Modes of Business

(i) E-business.
Scope and benefits, Resources required for successful e-business implementation, online transaction, payment mechanisms, security and safety of business transactions.

(ii) Outsourcing.
Concept, need and scope of BPO and KPO.

(iii) Smart cards.
Meaning and utility

5. Stock Exchange

(i) Meaning and importance
(ii) Functions and services
(iii) Major Stock Exchanges in India (BSE, NSE, DSE, ASE) — types and locations.
(iv) Types of operators — Brokers, Jobbers, Bulls and Bears.
(v) Terms used in Stock Exchange — ex-dividend, cum dividend, spot delivery, forward delivery.
(vi) SEBI — functions and objectives.
Self-explanatory

6. Trade

(i) Wholesalers.
Meaning and services of wholesaler to retailer, customer and producer:

(ii) (a) Retail trade — Meaning and characteristics.
Retail trade — meaning, characteristics of retail trade. Distinction between wholesale and retail trade.

(b) Types of retail trade — Itinerant and small scale fixed shops: departmental store, chain store, mail order houses, tele shopping, franchise, consumer cooperative stores, hypermarkets and automatic vending machines.
Meaning, features, merits and demerits to be covered.

(c) Documents used in home trade.

Documents and procedure used in home trade — inquiry; quotation; catalogues; order; invoice; debit note; credit note.

Price quotations — cash discount and trade discount.

(iii) Role of Chambers of Commerce and Industry and Trade Associations.

Meaning and functions of Chamber of Commerce and trade associations

7. Foreign Trade

(i) Meaning, difference between internal trade and external trade.

Meaning and characteristics of international trade; problems of international trade; advantages and disadvantages of international trade.

(ii) Export trade: Meaning, objectives and procedure of export trade.

Self-explanatory.

(iii) Import trade — Meaning, objectives, purpose and procedure.

Meaning and functions of import trade; objectives, purpose and procedure.

(iv) Documents involved in international trade.

Documents involved in export trade, such as: indent, letter of credit, shipping order, shipping bill, mate's receipt, bill of lading, certificate of origin, consular invoice, documentary bill of exchange (DA/DP), all need to be explained.

Documents involved in import trade, such as: import licence, indent, letter of credit, documentary bill of exchange, bill of entry, bill of sight, port trust dues receipt, application to import, advice note, bill of lading, all need to be explained.

(v) World Trade Organisation.

WTO — meaning and objectives.

8. Insurance

(i) Insurance — Meaning, objectives and purpose

Meaning, objectives and purpose of insurance; Concept of re-insurance and double insurance.

(ii) Risks in business — insurable and non-insurable.

Risks in business — insurance and non-insurable — meaning and examples of both. Characteristics of insurable risks.

(iii) Principle of insurance.

Fundamental principles to be explained: utmost good faith; insurable interest; indemnity; contribution; doctrine of subrogation; causa proxima, mitigation of loss.

(iv) Types of insurance: life and non-life.

Types of insurance — life, health, fire, marine, motor, social and fidelity insurance (Meaning and importance only).

PAPER II – PROJECT WORK – 20 Marks

Candidates will be expected to have completed **two** projects from any topic covered in Theory. Mark allocation for each Project (10 marks):

Overall format	1 mark
Content	4 marks
Findings	2 marks
Viva voce based on the Project	3 marks

A list of suggested Projects is given below:

1. Select a daily use consumer product. Trace its origin right from the primary industry through the secondary and tertiary industries. Draw a flow chart to include all the business activities in its path from the producer to the consumer.
2. Assume you are starting a partnership firm with your friend/friends. Develop a business plan covering the following aspects:
   - Formation of this partnership firm – rules and steps that would be followed including the partnership deed.
   - Choice of types of partners involved and your justification for the same.
3. Select two infrastructure projects of public sector undertakings that have been recently commissioned.

   Analyse each project in terms of:
   - Objective
   - Profitability
   - Adherence to the time schedule for project completion.
   - Social utility
   - Conclusion.
4. Identify two Public Private Partnership projects.

   Find out:
   - The equity participation of both the partners.
   - Objectives of the partnership
   - Strengths both partners bring into the venture.
5. Select one consumer cooperative and one housing cooperative.

   For each of the cooperatives.
   - State the objectives.
   - The organisational structure.
   - Details of surplus distribution and the form of government support.
6. Study real life cases in which organisations did not show responsibility towards investors/consumers/employees/government/community. Take at least two such cases. For each case prepare a report based on the following:
   - A brief about the case.
   - Different issues involved in the case.
   - Who was at fault and why?
   - What should the company have done to stand by the business ethics?
   - Do you agree with the company's view point? Give reasons.

7. Document and analyse the Corporate Social Responsibility activities of a pharmaceutical company and a five-star hotel.
   Comment on the changing role assumed by Corporates towards business ethics and social responsibility in the last two decades.
8. Identify any trade association and chamber of commerce headquartered in your town/city.
   Study each in terms of:
   - Its objectives.
   - Services provided to members.
   - Help given to the business community.
9. Contact an insurance agent and collect information about 5 different types of life insurance policies provided by different companies. Include information as per details given below for every insurance plan and make a comparative analysis.
   - Premium of insurance
   - Terms of inclusions and exclusions of each policy
   - Term of the policy
   - Withdrawal of money from the insurance scheme (surrender/foreclosure)
   - Advantages/disadvantages of the plan.
10. Study the BPO and KPO industry in India. Collect newspapers/magazine articles on BPOs and KPOs.
    Prepare a report highlighting:
    - Their contribution to the business community and the nation.
    - Their growth over the past 10 years in India.

    Comment on the social cost of such organisation.
11. Visit a company that is involved in e-business (which offers online services) or a consultancy, which helps in developing websites for such companies.
    Study different aspects they keep in mind while preparing business plans for e-business. Include information regarding the payment mechanisms, security and safety of business transactions. The risks involved in e-business should also be covered. Also include the steps they follow while implementing the plan and starting the business.

1 CLASSIFICATION OF HUMAN ACTIVITIES — ECONOMIC AND NON-ECONOMIC

SYLLABUS

- *Classification of human activities—economic and non-economic.*
- *Types of economic activities.*
- *Distinction between business, profession and employment.*

> *At its core business is, and always has been, about survival and surplus – about the advancement of self and of society.*
>
> — D. K.: *The Business Book*

LEARNING OUTCOMES

On completion of this chapter, you will be able to understand the following:

1.1 Historical Background of Business
1.2 Human Activities
1.3 Meaning of Human Activities
1.4 Nature of Economic Activity
1.5 Most Notable Features of Business, Profession and Employment
1.6 Distinction among Business, Profession and Employment

1.1 HISTORICAL BACKGROUND OF BUSINESS

With the dawn of civilisation, as goods and services began to be traded, people started thinking about business. It is a basic human activity in general and economic activity in particular since it is connected with money earning and money spending. The emergence of specialist producers and the use of money as a medium of exchange were methods by which individuals and societies could, in modern terms, gain a 'business edge'.

The lessons of early traders resonate even today. Specialism revealed the benefits of economies of scale — that cost per unit falls as more items are produced. Money gave rise to the concept of 'value added' — selling an item at more than its cost to produce.

However, the study of business as a human (or an economic) activity in its own right emerged quite recently. The post-war period saw the growth of big firms (monopolies and multinational corporations) — businesses with multiple and diverse interests all over the world. In truth, if business thinking has shifted, so too has the nature of business itself. Once a firm was constrained by its locality; today the opportunities are truly global (See Chapter 8).

More recent thinking about business has brought to the fore diverse corporate ethics and social responsibilities (See Chapter 5).

Business is a fascinating subject. It surrounds us and affects us every day. A walk down in a main street, a visit to any supermarket or Big Bazaar, an Internet search on almost any topic will reveal 'commerce' at its many and varied forms. At its core business is, and always has been, about survival and surplus generation by making as much value addition as possible. It is about the advancement of self and of society. As the world continues to open up, and as opportunities for enterprises multiply, an interest in business will grow and business itself will become more exciting and challenging. Moreover, for those with entrepreneurial zeal (spirit) business is likely to become more gainful or rewarding. It is against this backdrop that we study the subject, called 'commerce' which is the main component of the broad subject, called business.

1.2 HUMAN ACTIVITIES

Human activities are of two main types: (i) economic activities (connected with money-earning and money-spending) and (ii) non-economic activities. See Fig.1.1. Economic activities are of three broad types, viz., business, profession and paid employment. Non-economic activities include personal, family, social and religious activities which are not related to earning or spending of money in any way. However, in this chapter, we restrict ourselves to a study of the meaning and features of only economic activities, simply because these can be measured in terms of money (i.e., income earned and/or income spent.)

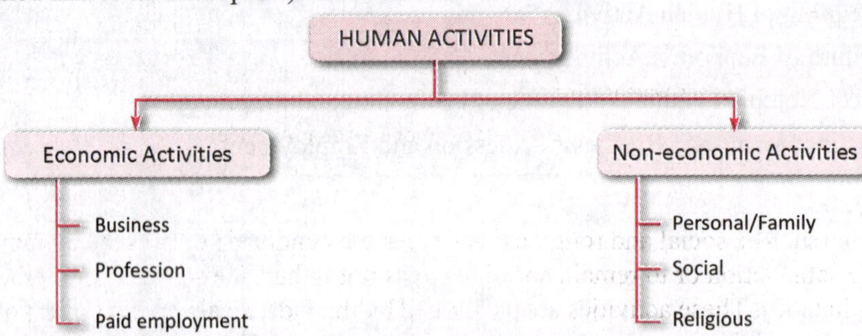

FIGURE 1.1: Main Types of Human Activities

1.2.1 Economic Activities

Two main purposes of conducting an economic activity are making a living and accumulating wealth.

Anything connected with money-earning and money-spending is an economic activity. Three such activities are production, exchange and distribution of goods and rendering of paid services. Economic activities are undertaken by economic units such as households and business people to make a living as also to accumulate wealth. A manufacturer, a trader, a farmer, a street hawker, a doctor, a teacher, a lawyer and a worker are all economic units and engaged in one type of economic activity or another. Through the conduct of such activities people earn income to satisfy their unlimited wants and needs such as those food, clothing, shelter, recreation, education, health care and so on. For example, a business person makes profits, a doctor charges fee for his medical advice and an employee earns wages (or salaries) by selling his services (labour power).

1.2.2 Types of Economic Activities

Economic activities are of the following three categories:

(i) *Business:* Producing and distributing goods and services on a regular basis for making profits.

(ii) *Profession:* Any activity requiring a recognised set of skills, knowledge and experience such as the ones possessed by chartered accountants, doctors, lawyers, business consultants, etc. These attributes qualify them to practise a certain occupation.

(iii) *Employment:* Working for others against receipt of wages and salaries — both in cash and in kind. For example, a worker, a salesperson, a foreman, a supervisor and a manager are all employed persons. We present a list of activities related to business, profession and employment in Fig. 1.2.

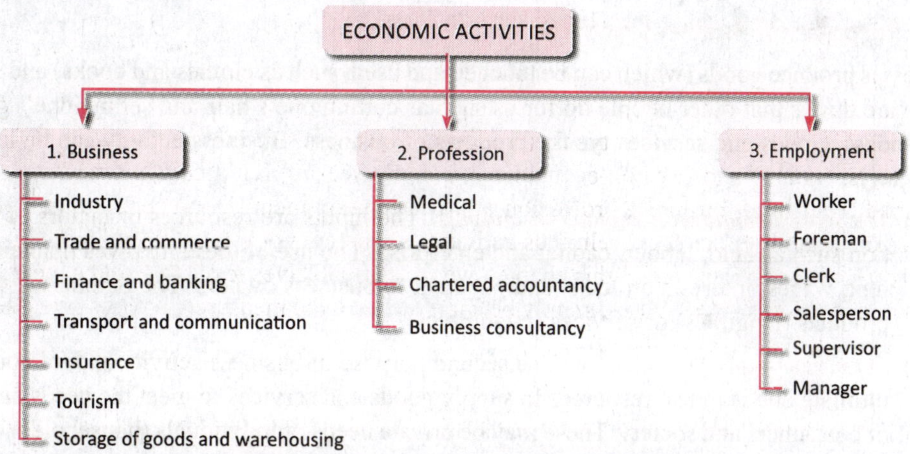

FIGURE 1.2: Different Types of Economic Activities

1.2.3 Non-economic Activities

Non-economic (such as social and religious) activities are conducted or pursued by human beings to get psychic satisfaction or to remain sociable (so as not to hurt the sentiments of others by, say, not believing in God). These activities are performed by the individuals on their own volition (discretion) without receiving any payment or reward in exchange. For example, a housewife cooks food for her family, a holy person remains engaged in a religious activity, and a benevolent person serves society by being associated with an orphanage or a non-government organisation.

1.3 MEANING OF HUMAN ACTIVITIES

People perform or conduct different types of activities for making a living. Such activities are called human activities. Human activities are of two main types – economic and non-economic. And perhaps the most important economic activity is business.

The term 'business' refers to a commercial enterprise, profession or trade operated for the purpose of earning a profit by providing a product (good) or service. Businesses are created by entrepreneurs who put money at risk to promote a particular venture for the purpose of making a profit. They vary in size from one-person sole proprietorship to an international corporation having billions of dollars in assets and thousands of employees.

The aim of all businesses is to combine factors of production to make products — both goods like food, cars and shoes as also services such as tourism, insurance and banking — to satisfy people's wants and make profit. After all, business is a money-earning activity.

In today's world most people work in one job for a daily or monthly wage. With this money, they are able to purchase a wide range and variety of goods and services produced by many different businesses. Business activity therefore:

(i) combines scarce factors of production in order to produce saleable goods and services;

(ii) produces those goods and services which are needed to satisfy the unlimited wants and desires of people; and

(iii) employs people as workers and pays them wages to allow them to consume products made by other people through recurring exchange.

1.3.1 Purposes of Business Activity

Businesses produce goods (which can be touched and used, such as clothes and books) and services (which are things that other people do for us such as cutting one's hair and selling one's goods in retail shops). Goods and services are the products of business. Business activity can be looked at in two ways:

(i) *The transformation of inputs into outputs:* The inputs are resources or factors of production such as land, labour, capital and enterprise. The use of these involves financial costs: rent, wages, interests on loans and payment to business owners. The outputs are physical products (tangibles) or services (intangibles).

(ii) *Supply of goods and services:* The second purpose of business activity and, of course, the ultimate one is to use resources to supply goods and services to meet the needs and wants of consumers and society. These may be private needs of individuals (households) or social needs like medical services, transport, communication and education.

As these activities are performed, jobs and incomes are created, goods and services are produced. As a result the levels of living of individuals and societies are improved.

1.3.2 Stages of Production and the Concept of Value Added

When transformation of inputs into output takes place to produce different goods and services, a number of stages is involved. And business activity at all stages involves adding value to resources such as raw materials and semi-finished goods and making them more desirable to — and thus valued by — the final purchasers of them. Without business activity we would all be entirely dependent on goods which we can make or grow ourselves.

It has to be noted that each stage of production is more valuable than the previous one due to economic value addition. This value will also be added value which consumers place on a finished product (market value added). Let us explain and illustrate this key concept.

As the transformation — or production — process proceeds through various stages, value addition is made to raw materials and semi-finished goods (or bought-in components) at each stage. This is because the work carried out increases the value of the parts and raw materials used. When the product is finished, its value and price at which it is sold is more than the value of the factors of production used to make the product.

Therefore, the amount of value added to a finished product is the difference between the sales value of the product and the cost of all resources to produce it. See Fig. 1.3. [Note that added value is not the same as profit.]

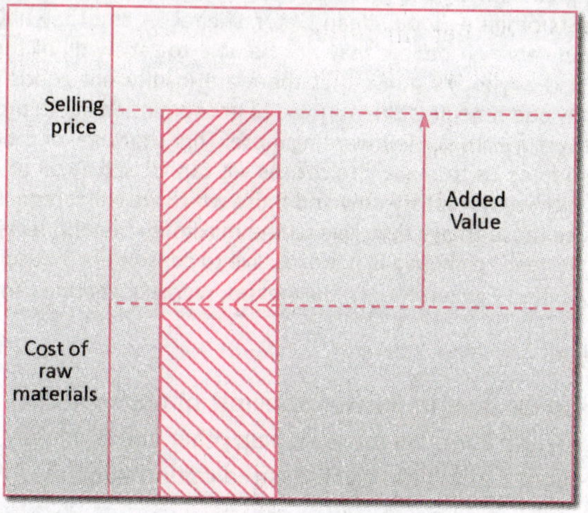

FIGURE 1.3: Added Value

> **SYNOPSIS FOR LEARNING: THE PURPOSE OF BUSINESS ACTIVITY**
>
> Businesses are organisations which have been set up to produce goods and services. They supply these goods and services to individuals and other businesses which need them either for further production or for final use.

1.3.3 Types of Businesses

There are many different types of business organisations. Some are major international businesses such as Kuwait Petroleum Corporation or Coca-Cola. Others are smaller businesses which operate within their own country or even locality.

> **CASE STUDY: KUWAIT PETROLEUM CORPORATION (KPC)**
>
> Kuwait Petroleum Corporation (KPC) is one of the world's largest oil companies. The company makes products such as petrol and diesel from crude oil. Crude oil is oil in its raw or natural state. It occurs naturally in deposits within the earth. To produce the petrol that people buy from garages. KPC must first extract the crude oil from the earth. The company does this by drilling oil wells, many of which are under the sea. KPC then transports the crude oil to oil refineries where it is turned into petrol or other oil products that customers want.

1.4 NATURE OF ECONOMIC ACTIVITY

Economic activity means taking decisions about the transformation of input into output and always involves choices. This is because resources are always scarce (limited in relation to human needs and wants). Individuals, businesses and society generally always want more than they can afford. So choices must be made. Any rational choice is associated with a key concept — known as opportunity cost.

Opportunity cost is the real cost of making a decision about using resources. The real cost of something is what is given up when one chooses it. Businesses need to be aware of the opportunity cost of any action before making final decisions.

COMMENTARY: ECONOMIC ACTIVITY AND THE PROBLEM OF CHOICE

We live in a world of great wealth and great scarcity. Very poor people are unable to obtain the very basic requirements of life — food, clean water, shelter — and they have many unsatisfied needs and wants. Even very rich people may not be able to satisfy all of their wants for luxury goods and services. It is anybody's guess that there are insufficient goods to satisfy all of our needs and wants at any one time. It is the purpose of economic activity to provide for as many of our wants as possible; yet we are still left wanting more. This 'shortage' of products and resources needed to make them force us to make choices. As we cannot satisfy all of our wants, then we must choose those which we will satisfy now and those which we will forego. If we are careful and rational, we will choose those things that give us the maximum benefit, leaving out those things of less value to us. This need to choose is not exclusive to consumers (households). All economic units have to make choices — governments, businesses, workers, charities and so on.

1.4.1 Opportunity Cost

The need to choose leads to the next important principle of our subject — opportunity cost. In deciding to purchase or obtain one item, we must give up other goods as they cannot all be purchased. Opportunity cost is the benefit of the next most desired option which is given up.

Examples: With limited resources if consumers choose to buy the MP3 player, then the sports shoes become the opportunity cost. With limited resources, if government chooses to build the fighter plane, then the hospital becomes the opportunity cost.

BUSINESS FOCUS —
THE NATURE OF ECONOMIC ACTIVITY, THE PROBLEM OF CHOICE AND OPPORTUNITY COST

Economic activity means taking decisions about the transformation of inputs to outputs and it always involves choices. This is because resources are always limited in relation to needs and wants. Individuals, businesses and society generally always want more than they can afford. So choices must be made. Opportunity cost is the real cost of making a decision about using resources. The real cost of something is what is given up when one chooses it. See Table 1.1.

TABLE 1.1: Examples of Opportunity Cost

Individual examples	Opportunity cost
Studying a leveis	Not taking a job
Taking a holiday by the sea	Not visiting mountains
Buying a shirt	Not buying some
Business examples	**Opportunity cost**
Buying a new computer network	Not buying new lorries
Spending on research and development	Not increasing advertising
Hiring some workers	Not being able to buy a machine
Society examples	**Opportunity cost**
More hospitals	Fewer soldiers and weapons
Powerful cars	Safer roads
Lower taxes	Less government spending on education

Note: Businesses need to be aware of the opportunity cost of any action before they make final decisions.

1.5 MOST NOTABLE FEATURES OF BUSINESS, PROFESSION AND EMPLOYMENT

In the real world of business we find three main economic activities, namely, (i) business, (ii) profession, and (iii) employment. These are no doubt different from one another, but they are interrelated and interdependent in the modern world. So we now study these three concepts one by one as also their basic common features.

1.5.1 Meaning and Features of Business

As noted above business includes any economic activity concerned with the production and sale of goods or services for making profit. The main business activities are manufacturing, trading (wholesaling and retailing), mining and quarrying, finance and banking, storage and warehousing, transportation, and insurance. There are nine basic features of business. See Box below.

SYNOPSIS FOR LEARNING: NINE NOTABLE FEATURES OF BUSINESS

1. *Economic activity:* Business, being an economic activity, is concerned with monetary transactions in pursuit of profits.
2. *Production and procurement:* Business is concerned with both production (manufacturing) and procurement of goods and services for final sale (trading). Therefore it involves two main activities, viz., production and exchange.
3. *Producing goods and services:* Businesses produce and sell both consumer goods and capital goods (tangibles) as also services (intangibles)
4. *Satisfying customers:* The basic purpose of business activity is meeting the needs of customers. According to P. F. Drucker, the basic purpose of business is to create a customer.
5. *Regular affair and continuous activity:* Any dealing or exchange of goods and services has to be a regular affair and a continuous activity.
6. *Profit motive:* Any business activity is conducted with the basic purpose of making profit.
7. *Uncertainty about return:* In any business there is uncertainty regarding return on capital employed. There are chances of making profits or incurring losses.
8. *Unpredictability of the magnitude of profit:* Since it is not possible to predict what is likely to happen to sales turnover and costs, there is always an element of uncertainty regarding the magnitude or rate of profit which can be earned in any business.
9. *Risk and uncertainty:* Any type of business faces two types of risks— insurable and uninsurable. Uninsurable risk is known as uncertainty. And profit is not the reward for risk-taking as such but for uncertainty-bearing.

1.5.2 Meaning and Features of Profession

A profession is a specialised activity. It involves rendering of personal services by using specialised knowledge. A person with a recognised set of skills and knowledge which qualify him to practise a certain occupation is called a professional. Usually the knowledge is gained from a lengthy process of training and is certified by examination, often conducted by a professional association. This pattern of entry into an occupation is similar to that of apprenticeship; however, the professions are usually understood to be those occupations which are located at the top of the occupational structure in terms of status, for example, doctors, architects, lawyers, etc. The professionals charge fees from their clients for rendering their services.

The basic features of a profession are the following:

1. *Organised knowledge:* A profession is based on an organised knowledge and highly specialised skill consisting of well-defined and established concepts, principles, theories and

techniques related to a particular area or field. This knowledge can be applied in practice to render personal services such as medical care and legal advice.

2. *Qualification and training:* A profession requires specialised knowledge and training in a certain specific area or particular field. To be able to do practice as a professional, one must acquire a professional qualification such as MBBS, CA or LLB, and pratical training.
3. *Professional body or association:* The existence of a recognised professional body is absolutely essential for full-fledged development of a true profession as also its regulation. Table 1.2 presents a list of some prominent professional bodies which exist in India at present.

TABLE 1.2: A List of India's Professional Bodies

Name of Profession	Name of Professional Body/Association
1. Medical	Medical Council of India
2. Legal	Bar Council of India
3. Financial accounting	The Institute of Chartered Accountants of India
4. Company secretaryship	The Institute of Company Secretaries of India
5. Cost accountancy	The Institute of Cost Accountants of India

4. *Entry restriction:* In order to become a member, one has to pass the qualifying examination conducted by a recognised institution such as the Institute of Chartered Accountants of India and undergo the required training for a specified period of time. And for a professional chartered accountant membership of the Institute is compulsory (mandatory).
5. *Ethical code:* There is well-established code of conduct which clearly and explicity specifies the norms of behaviour for the members of a profession. The code is enforced by a professional body, duly represented by its elected members.
6. *Service motive:* A professional person is guided by service motive. He (she) gives maximum priority to providing service to his (her) clients by charging a fee. The basic objective is to maintain the existing status of the profession and to upgrade its standard in the future.

1.5.3 Meaning and Features of Employment or Service

A person is said to be in employment in an enterprise when he (she) undertakes to supply his (her) services as per a written or an oral contract, for which he (she) gets wage and compensation in the form of various allowances, bonus and non-monetary benefits. The employer may be government, a public sector undertaking or a state enterprise such as the Coal India Ltd. or a private firm.

The most notable features of employment or service are the following:

(i) Employment starts as soon as one joins a service in a firm or an enterprise on wage (salary) payment. Such a firm is called an 'employer'. The employer may even be a single-owner firm or sole proprietorship concern such as the owner of a grocer's shop.

(ii) Employment involves performing paid services specified or assigned by the employer. After all, doing service means carrying out the instructions of the superior by the subordinate.

(iii) The employee is not supposed (required) to invest any capital in the enterprise where he works.

(iv) The employee gets wages/salaries and various other job-related benefits as a reward for his (her) services.

(v) An employee has to perform the job himself (herself). He (she) cannot get it done through or with the help of others. (Only managers have the second option).

(vi) An employee has to follow the rules, regulators and norms prescribed by the employer or the organisation to which he belongs.

1.6 DISTINCTION AMONG BUSINESS, PROFESSION AND EMPLOYMENT

In Table 1.3 we make a comparison among business, profession and employment.

TABLE 1.3: Business Profession and Employment

Basis of Comparison	Business	Profession	Employment
1. Method of establishment (getting started)	An entrepreneur's decision and action including completion of certain formalities, as per laws of the country/state	There is need for membership of a professional body to get full recognition and certificate to start practice. (Just paper qualification is not enough)	Appointment letter is issued by the employer or written contract is signed both by the employer and the employee
2. Nature of activity or work pursued or conducted	Purchase and sale of goods and services by using money	Personalised and specialised services, which require help of experts	Performing the job assigned and specified by the employer or the boss
3. Objective or motivation	Making profits initially (and, of course, serving society thereafter)	Rendering paid services by professionals by charging fees	Earning wages and compensation (in cash or in both cash and kind)
4. Qualifications	No need for formal qualifications (Most business leaders are born, not made)	Professional qualifications and initial (on-the-job) training are absolutely essential	There is need for acquiring general qualification or apprenticeship training in most cases
5. Initial investment (seed capital)	Need for adequate capital, the exact amount depending on the nature, form and size of business (or its scale of operation)	Little initial capital is needed for establishment of office or place of work.	No need for investing financial capital
6. Reward for effort put or return from investment	Profit, which is the incentive to and monetary reward for successful conduct of business	Professional fee	Wages and salary (compensation) as also bonus and other benefits
7. Risk of loss	High risk of loss except in routine industries such as real estate, fast food and transportation	There is always the risk of earning every little (as is found in case of unsuccessful professionals like briefless barristers	No risk of job loss unless and until the company goes into the red or becomes sick
8. Transferability of ownership/interest	Possible only after completion of necessary legal formalities	Impossible	Ruled out completely
9. Ethical code of conduct (from the behavioural point of view)	Business may join a Trade Association or a Chamber of Commerce and Industry or any pressure group and go by its rules or established norms	The professional code of conduct has to be followed by each member of a certain profession	Rules and norms of behaviour clearly specified and dictated by the employer as also the instructions given are to be followed. After all, 'service' means 'subordination' and a job involves superior-subordinate relationship

FOCUS ON TERMINOLOGY: PROFESSIONALISATION AND PROFESSION

The term 'professionalisation' refers to the introduction of professional standards into an occupation so as to bring uniformity to the credentials of its members and institute's requirement for training, as also to evaluate performance and standardise the class and qualifications of the field. A professional is a person with a recognised set of skills and knowledge which qualifies him (her) to practise a certain occupation. Usually this knowledge is gained from lengthy training and is certified by examination, often by a professional association.

Key Points

1. **Human activity:** All activities undertaken by human beings are called human activities. Such activities are two broad types — economic and non-economic.
2. **Economic activities:** Economic activities are those which are conducted for earning money, producing goods and services and spending money to satisfy human needs and desires.
3. **Non-economic activities:** All activities which are not connected with or undertaken for money earning and money spending are non-economic activities. Examples are religious, social, political and other (such as charitable) activities.
4. **Three types of economic activities:** Three types of economic activities are: (i) Business, (ii) Profession and (iii) Employment.
5. **Business:** A business is an organisation which uses resources to meet the needs of customers by providing a product or service which they demand. Business refers to producing and distributing goods and services on a regular basis for making profits and accumulating wealth. It is a broad term and includes all industrial, commercial and trading activities.
6. **Business activity:** Businesses identify the needs of consumers and other firms. Then they purchase resources — factors of production — in order to produce goods and services which satisfy these needs, usually with the aim of making profit. *Prima facie*, business activity exists to produce goods or services which meet the needs of consumers. They also produce capital goods to meet the needs of other firms.
7. **Purpose of business activity:** Business activity uses scarce resources to produce goods and services which allow the people of a country (or even of the world) to enjoy a very much higher standard of living than would be possible under self-sufficiency (involving no exchange of goods and services).
8. **The concept of adding value (added value):** A business adds value to the raw materials. It uses these to produce the good or service it sells. Added value is one of the key objectives of any business. If a customer is ready to pay a price which is higher than the cost of materials used in making or providing a good or service, then the business is said to have added value.
9. **Profession:** Provession refers to any activity requiring a recognised set of skills and knowledge such as the ones possessed by chartered accountants, doctors and lawyers.
10. **Employment:** Employment refers to working for others against receipt of wages and compensation both in cash and in kind. The employer may be a private firm, a public sector unit (or a state enterprise) or any government department such as Deptt. of Telecommunications.

KEY Terms

Business	Problem of choice
Employment	Creating customer
Human activities	Risk-bearing
Profession	Opportunity cost
Economic activities	Goods
Non-economic activities	Services
Profit motive	Added value

Assignments

SHORT ANSWER-TYPE QUESTIONS

1. Name five types of economic activities.
2. Define the term business.
3. Define a profession.
4. Mention three characteristics of a profession.
5. State the main objectives of economic activities.
6. Mention two main points of difference between economic and non-economic activities.
7. What is the main aim of human activities? [ISC 1991]
8. What is employment?
9. Give two examples of profession.
10. Give few examples of business activities.
11. What is the purpose of business activity?

ESSAY-TYPE QUESTIONS

1. Explain the nature and purpose of economic activities, giving some examples.
2. Distinguish between economic and non-economic activities.
3. What is a profession? What are its characteristics?
4. Distinguish among business, profession and employment.
5. The activities of business, profession and employment complement one another. Examine the validity of the statement.

QUESTION BANK

1. *What is the purpose of economic activities?*
2. *What is the purpose of non-economic activities?*
3. *What is the meaning of the term business?*

Ans. The term business refers to a commercial enterprise, profession or trade operated for the purpose of earning a profit by providing a product, or service. It is also called business enterprise.

4. *What is the meaning of the term profession?*

Ans. The term 'profession' refers to certain activity which requires a high level of education and standard of ethical behaviour. Professions include engineering, medicine, law, teaching, chartered, cost and management accountancy and architecture.

5. *Name three types of economic activities and discuss their nature and characteristics.*

Ans. Three main economic activities are: (i) Business (ii) Profession and (iii) Employment.

Business is a commercial activity or enterprise, profession or trade operated for making a profit by providing a useful good or service which meets the needs and wants of other people.

Profession refers to a certain activity which requires a high level of education, training and standard of ethical behaviour such as engineering, medicine and law.

Employment refers to the state of being employed or work done by a person to earn money either formally (officially) or informally (unofficially).

6. *Define each of the following terms in one sentence:*
(i) Added value, (ii) Goods, (iii) Services, (iv) Needs, (v) Wants

Ans.
(i) Added value refers to the cost of producing raw materials and the price of the finished goods sold for.
(ii) Goods are things which one can touch and use such as this book and cloth one wears.
(iii) Services are things which one person does for another such as hair-cutting, or selling of another person's goods in one's own shop.
(iv) Needs are items which we must have in order to live such as food and drink, shelter and cloth.
(v) Wants are items which we should have although we can survive without them such as a car, a computer or a holiday.

7. *Classify the following activities into Business, Profession and Employment.*
(i) Rima running her own nursing home.
(ii) Kaya working as a bank officer.
(iii) Suresh teaching commerce in a reputed school in Ranchi.
(iv) Bankim running a tea stall.
(v) Dr. Sudipta Mitra, acting as an administrator Peerless Hospital in Kolkata.
(vi) Sanjay Jhunjhunwala, Chairman of the Money Group.
(vii) Chanda Kochar, chairperson of ICICI Bank.
(viii) Virat Kohli, captain of the Indian Cricket Team.
(ix) Pawan Ruia, as Chairman of the Ruia Group.
(x) Kaushik Basu, Vice-president of the World Bank.

Ans (i) Business: (iv), (v), (ix), (vi)

(ii) Profession: (i), (v)

(iii) Employment: (ii), (iii), (vii), (viii), (x).

8. *Classify the following into economic and non-economic activities:*

(i) Teaching in St Xavier's College, Kolkata

(ii) Sanjib Kapur cooking food for his family members

(iii) Running a rose garden for exporting flower

(iv) Looking after children and elderly persons in the family

(v) Working as a domestic help in a senior citizen's house

(vi) Distributing food to flood-affected person in Assam

(vii) Rearing goats for selling meat

(viii) Taking care of cats at home

(ix) Running a share brokeage firm at home

(x) Looking after one's kitchen garden

Ans (i) Economic activities: (i), (iii), (v), (vii), (ix)

(ii) Non-economic activities: (ii), (iv), (vi), (viii), (x).

2 CLASSIFICATION OF BUSINESS ACTIVITIES

SYLLABUS

Definition and concept of business; classification of business activities.

- *Definition of business*
- *Characteristics of Business*
- *Classification of business activities:*
  - (a) *Industry: Types of industries on the basis of activity (primary and secondary) and on the basis of size (micro, small, medium and large). Role of small businesses in India.*
  - (b) *Commerce: Branches of Commerce. Commerce — its nature and functions; importance of Commerce. Branches of Commerce — trade and aids to trade. Relationship between commerce, trade and industry.*

> *Economic development is equated with industrialisation and economic progress consists of marketing at a distance.*
>
> — Alfred Marshall

LEARNING OUTCOMES

On completion of this chapter, you will be able to understand the following:

- 2.1 Levels of Economic Activity
- 2.2 Industry and its Types
- 2.3 Types of Industries
- 2.4 Putting the Three Sectors Together — Chains of Production
- 2.5 An International Comparison
- 2.6 Classification on the Basis of Size
- 2.7 The Role of Small Businesses in India
- 2.8 Commerce
- 2.9 Branches of Commerce
- 2.10 Auxiliaries (Aids) to Trade (Business and Industry)
- 2.11 Inter-relationship among Commerce, Trade and Industry
- 2.12 Economic Basis of Commerce

In chapter 1, we referred to the nature, characteristics and types of economic activities. Note that economic activity can be divided into three sectors, each one with industries of a particular type. Businesses generally operate in one of the following three sectors as shown in Fig. 2.1.

1. Primary sector businesses are those that deal with the extraction of natural resources so they include farming, forestry, fishing, oil, gas, quarrying and mining. These industries form the first stage in the chain of production.

2. Secondary sector businesses are those that manufacture products or process raw materials. They turn raw materials and components made from raw materials from the primary sector into semi-finished or finished goods. Examples include manufacture of cars, furniture, buildings and processed food.
3. Tertiary sector businesses are those that provide a service. No physical product is provided. Examples include banking, insurance, education and travel services.

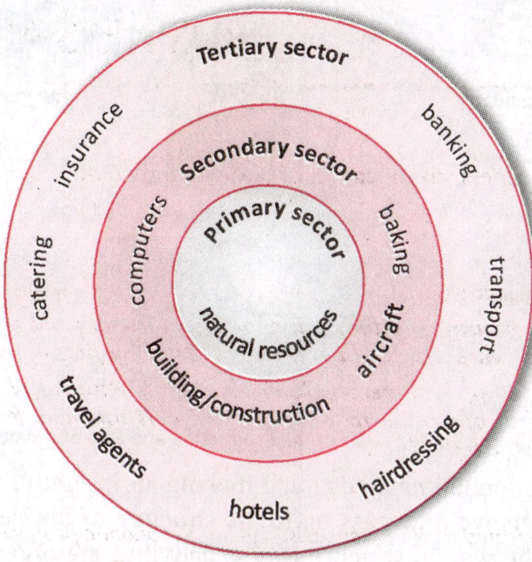

FIGURE 2.1: A Broad Overview of Three Sectors

2.1 LEVELS OF ECONOMIC ACTIVITY

Economic activity takes place at different layers. Take, for example, the case of a desk on which you sit while reading this book. Most desks are still made of wood. How many different types of businesses might have been involved in converting the wood into a finished desk ready to be sold to a final consumer? What stages of production has the wood passed through to arrive at the finished desk?

Here we see that there are three main stages from the cutting down of the timber to the sale of the completed desk. These stages are typical of nearly all production and they are called the levels of business activity.

(i) Stage 1 is called the primary stage of production. This stage involves the earth's natural resources. Activities in the primary sector of industry include farming, fishing, forestry and the extraction of natural materials, such as oil and copper ore.

(ii) Stage 2 is called the secondary stage of production. This stage involves taking the materials and resources provided by the primary sector and converting them into manufactured or processed goods. Activities in the secondary sector of industry include building and construction, aircraft making, computer assembly and baking.

(iii) Stage 3 is called the tertiary stage of production. This stage involves providing services to both consumers and other businesses. Activities in the tertiary sector of industry include transport, banking, insurance, hotels and hairdressing.

See Fig. 2.2 which lists the activities performed within each sector.

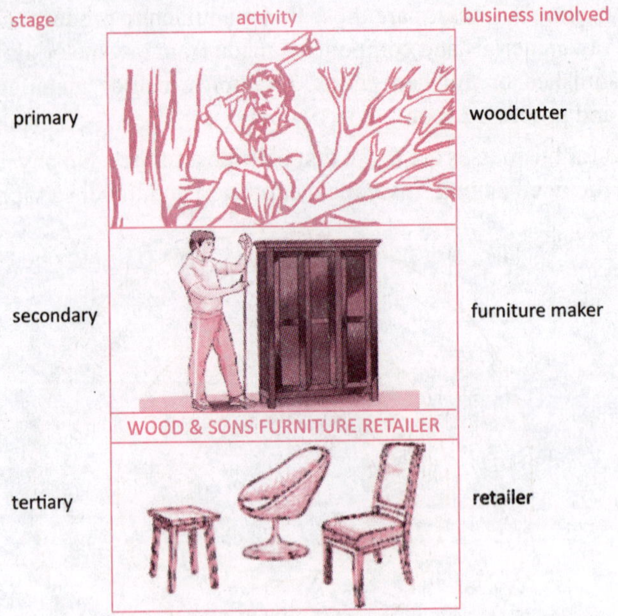

FIGURE 2.2: The Three Stages in the Production and Sale of a Wooden Desk

After gaining a background knowledge and making an insightful analysis of the nature and objectives of business firms we now pass on to the structure of business. The term 'structure of business' simply means the way in which business activities are organised or collated. In other words, it refers to certain basic and broad categories of interdependent and interrelated business activities. Two broad business activities are (1) industry, and (2) commerce. And commerce may be sub-divided into (i) trade, and (ii) auxiliaries or aids to trade (Fig. 2.3 and Fig. 2.4).

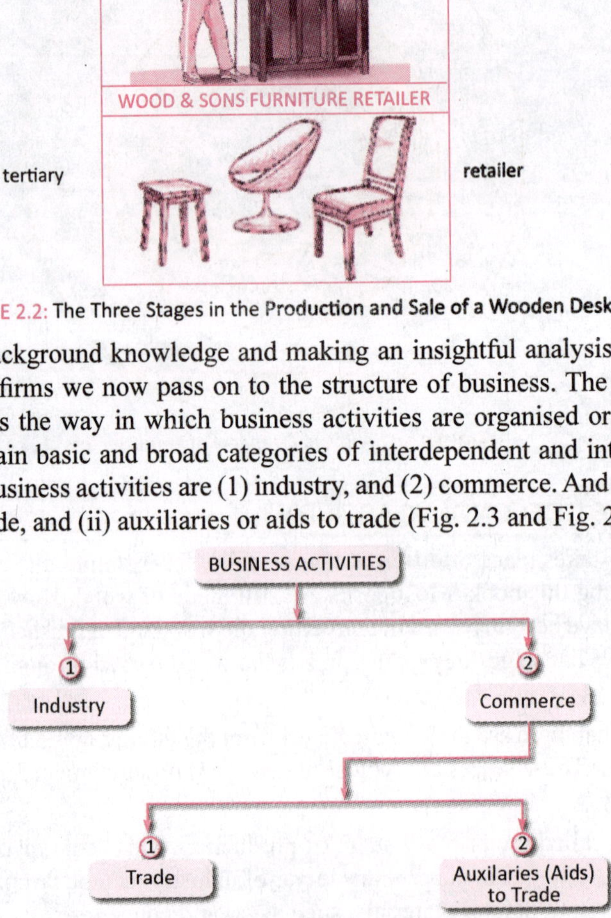

FIGURE 2.3: Two-fold Classification of Business Activities

2.2 INDUSTRY AND ITS TYPES

The term industry is used in three different senses:

(i) It is an organised activity towards a goal.

(ii) It is a sector or organisation in which labour and management work together to produce goods and render services.

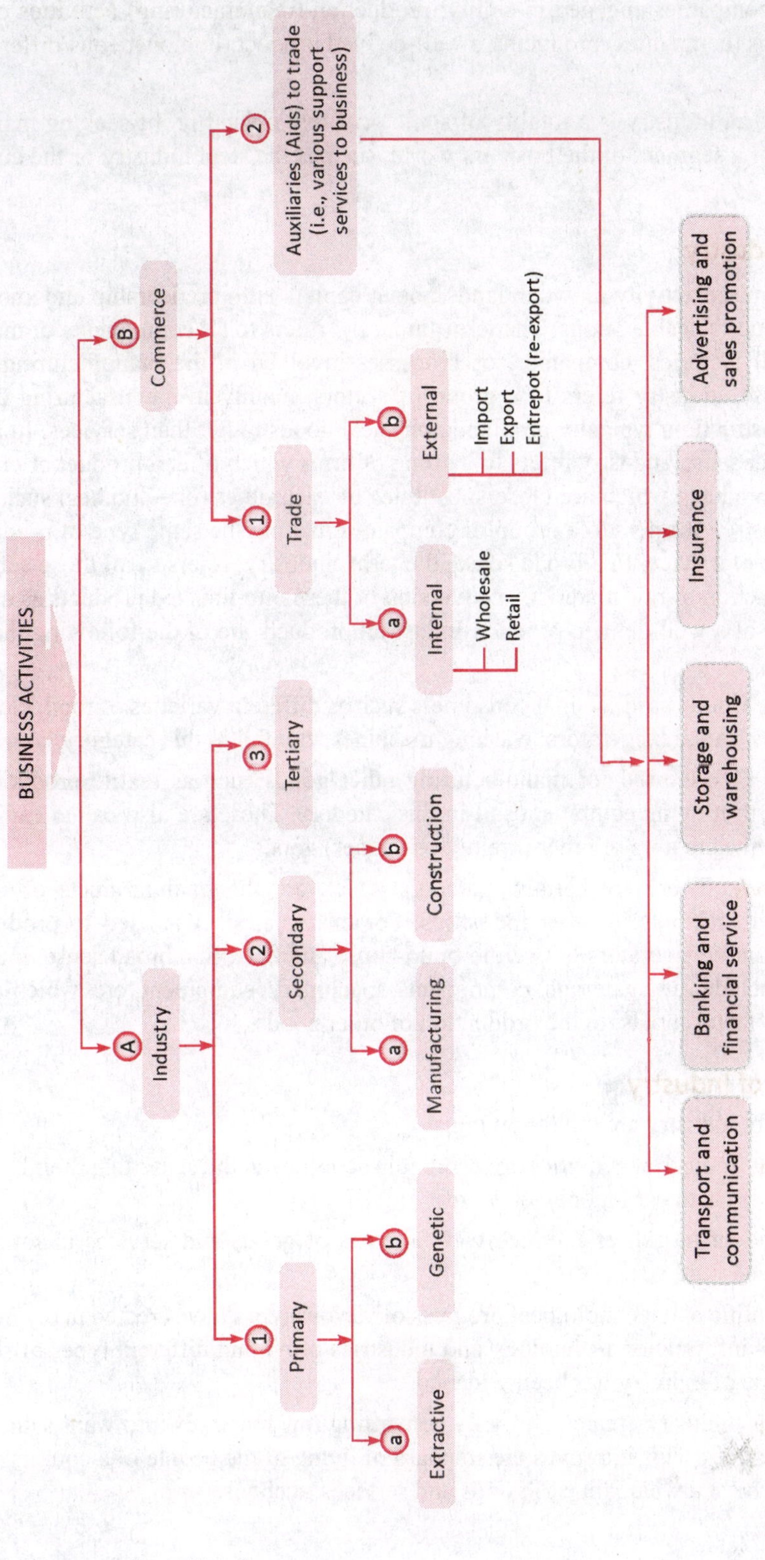

FIGURE 2.4: A Comprehensive Classification of Main Business Activities

(iii) It is a group of companies engaged in similar production (manufacturing) activities or a collection of firms (companies) producing a well-defined product (homogeneous/differentiated).

To be more specific, an industry is a totality of some privately owned profit-seeking manufacturing establishment or a segment of the business world, such as the steel industry or the automobile industry.

2.2.1 Definition of Industry

Industry refers to an organised activity in which land, labour, capital, entrepreneurship and knowledge are utilised to produce saleable goods. The term 'industry' refers to all components of manufacturing process — all factories, companies, or processes involved in the manufacturing of products. In another sense, industry refers to a group of sectors, mainly in manufacturing and construction, typically producing physical goods rather than services. In another sense, industry refers to a group of firms which offer a product or class of products which are close substitutes of each other (one another) such as steel industry or car industry. It refers to a group of companies making the same type of product or offering the same type of service. In a broad sense, the term 'industry' refers to all those activities concerned with extraction of raw materials, conversion of these into finished products as also processing or fabrication of a well-defined product. Industrial products are of the following three types:

An industry is a collection of firms producing a well-defined product.

(a) *Consumer goods:* Goods used by final consumers such as different varieties of food, cloth, televisions, radios, cars, refrigerators, washing machines, etc. fall in this category.

(b) *Producer goods:* Goods used for manufacturing other goods such as textile producing machines and earth-moving equipment fall in this category. These are also called capital goods, which are the creators of other (mainly consumer) goods.

(c) *Intermediate goods:* There are certain materials which are the final products of one industry but used as inputs in other industries. For example, steel is used to produce utensils, motor cars, refrigerators or even to build house and flats. In a broad sense, intermediate goods include raw materials, components, machinery, equipment, etc. which are used by firms as 'factor inputs' in the production of other goods.

2.2.2 Characteristics of Industry

The main characteristics of industry are the following:

(i) *Economic activity:* Industrial activities are economic activities in the sense that their basic purpose (objectives) is to earn money or profit.

(ii) *Production:* Different industries produce various types of goods and services to satisfy diverse human needs and wants.

(iii) *Wide scope:* Scientific and technological progress of various types have created many new industries such as information technology and industries providing different types of services. So the scope of industry has been widened.

(iv) *Creation of utility:* Industry creates utility by converting raw materials into want-satisfying goods and services. This improves the standard of living of the people of a country by enabling them to have a wide range of goods and services to choose from.

(v) ***Economic development:*** The economic development of a country is often equated with industrialisation. This is why the industrialised countries are called most developed countries. Industries accelerate the rate of economic growth by making efficient use of human and non-human (natural) resources. It acts as an engine of growth. And in the process it creates gainful employment opportunities, increases a country's national income and helps a country like India to earn the much needed foreign exchange.

(vi) ***Part of business:*** Industry is a major component of business. Industrial activities act as the sole driving force behind the emergence of allied business activities such as trade, commerce and aids to trade.

2.3 TYPES OF INDUSTRIES

Industrial activities are of two main types — primary and secondary, as shown in Fig. 2.5. Each type of industry has several components. A third type of industry is tertiary industry.

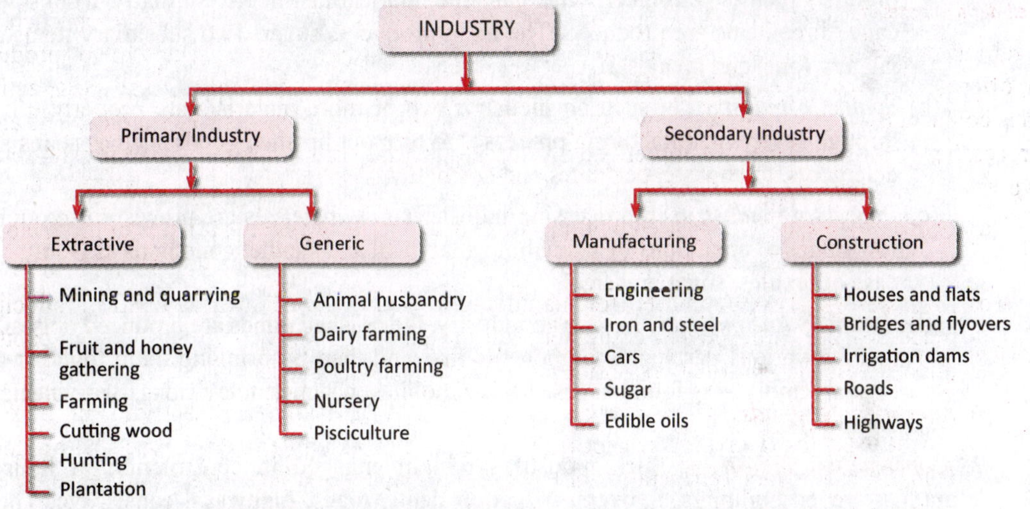

FIGURE 2.5: Two Broad Types of Industries and Their Main Components

2.3.1 Primary Industries

Primary industries remain engaged in natural resource(s)-based activities. These include all those activities which are concerned largely with the extraction, and processing of natural resources and conversion of these into saleable goods. These industries may be subdivided into the following two categories:

1. ***Extractive industries:*** These industries extract both inputs and products from the nature, i.e., from land, air, river and sea. The products of such industries are generally used by manufacturing and construction activities for producing finished goods. Some examples of such industries are mining and quarrying, lumbering, hunting, and fishing.
2. ***Generic industries:*** Generic industries are those which remain engaged in breeding plants and animals for expanded reproduction. For example, nurseries serve the purpose of plant breeding. Other examples of such industries are animal husbandry (livestock farming/growing), dairy farming, poultry farming and fish hatchery.

2.3.2 Secondary Industries

Secondary industries remain engaged in further processing of materials which have already been produced by primary industries. The mining of crude oil is primary activity, but petrol is a secondary activity. Secondary industries are of two main types: (i) manufacturing and (ii) construction.

1. *Manufacturing industries:* Such industries are engaged in the conversion or transformation of raw materials or semi-finished items into finished goods. By changing the character or the shape of things they create form utility. Examples of such industries are motor cars, textiles, finished steel, furniture, cement, sugar, edible oils, fruit juice, jam and jelly, etc. The products of extractive industries are used as raw materials of manufacturing industries. Manufacturing activities of different kinds find expression in the system of factory production. Manufacturing industries are of the following four types:
   (a) *Analytical industry:* Petroleum refining is an example of such an industry in which the basic material (crude oil) analysed is processed and transformed into a number of products such as petrol, kerosene, gasoline, lubricating oil, etc. Similarly, from sugarcane, three items are produced. The main product is sugar. Two subsidiary items are jaggery (gur) and khandsari.
   (b) *Synthetic industry:* In such an industry, two or more materials are properly mixed through severe manufacturing processes to turn out finished goods such as soaps and detergents, toothpaste, perfumes and cosmetics.
   (c) *Processing industry:* In processing industries raw materials are processed through a few stages of operations by using both analytical and synthetic methods as is found in case of textiles, sugar and steel.
   (d) *Assembly line industry:* In such an industry, the finished goods are produced only after making various parts and components first and then by bringing them together for final assembly as is found in case of automobiles, watches, televisions, two-wheelers, computers, etc.
2. *Construction industries.* Such industries remain engaged in construction of houses, multi-storeyed buildings, flyovers, irrigation dams, roads, highways, canals, etc. These industries use the products of manufacturing industries such as iron and steel, cement, lime, paints, glass, electrical goods, etc. as also the products of extractive industries such as brick, coal, stone chip, marble, etc. The products of such industries are not physically transferable. They are made or constructed at fixed locations. Although houses, flats and buildings, like roads and bridges, are immovable, their ownership can be changed or transferred.

2.3.3 Tertiary (Service) Industries

The tertiary (service) sector embraces all types of service activities which facilitate the flow of goods of primary and secondary sectors from producing to distant consuming centres. In fact, tertiary industries provide the much needed support services to primary and secondary industries as also trading (distribution) activities such as wholesaling and retailing. The industrial system of a country rides on the wheels of the tertiary sector. In turn, the railways or the road transport system get its business from the first two sectors. The tertiary sectors include transport and communication, banking and finance, insurance, storage and warehousing and advertising and sales promotion. Most of these services provide the much needed infrastructure for industry and trade and thus lend necessary support to business. These industries make the following positive contributions to business enterprises:

(i) Transportation facilitates the smooth flow of goods from a few producing areas to several (numerous) consuming centres and create place utility.

(ii) Banks provide short-term credit to industrial and trading firms to meet their working capital needs. This, in addition, provides normal banking facilities.

(iii) Insurance firms protect businesses from various kinds of measurable risks.

(iv) Warehouses provide storage facilities to producers and traders and thus create time utility.

(v) Advertising firms provide information to consumers and help to promote sale of goods.

2.4 PUTTING THE THREE SECTORS TOGETHER — CHAINS OF PRODUCTION

Making a product and supplying it to customers usually involves businesses in all three industrial sectors. Fig. 2.6 shows how business is organised in the context, take, for example, producing a loaf of bread involves:

(i) A farmer who grows the wheat (primary sector)

(ii) A miller who turns the wheat into flour (secondary sector)

(iii) A baker who makes the flour into bread (secondary sector)

(iv) A baker's shop that sells the bread (tertiary sector) to customers

(v) Transport (tertiary sector) to get the wheat from the farmer to the miller to the baker, and the bread from the baker to the bakery.

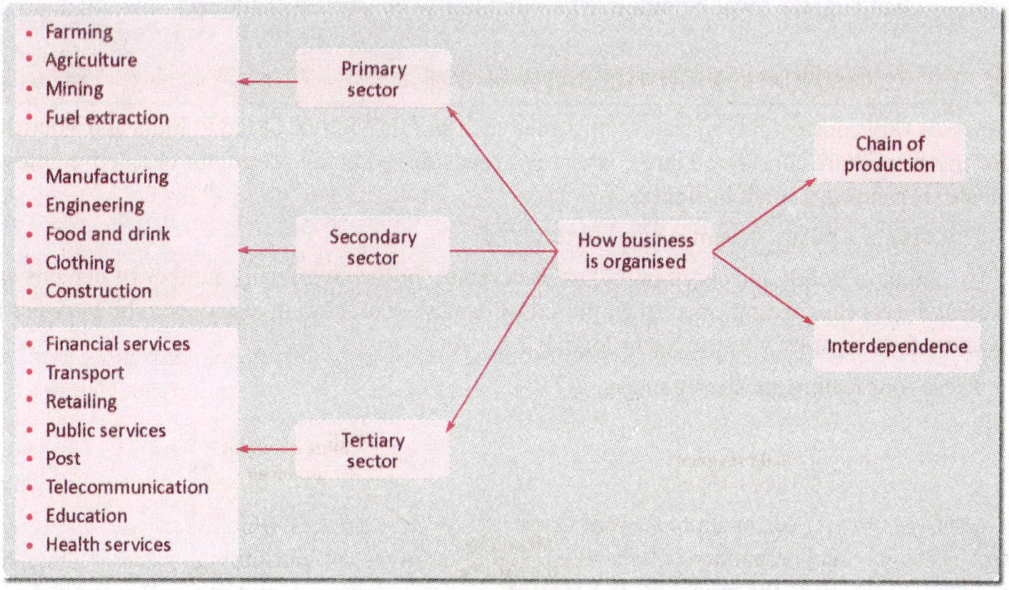

FIGURE 2.6: How Business is Organised

Each business forms part of a chain of production. The chain begins with the raw materials and ends with getting the finished products to the customer [For further illustration and clear understating of this point the student is advised to go through one of the case examples presented at the end of of the main text.]

2.5 AN INTERNATIONAL COMPARISON

What determines how countries are organised?

The mix of businesses in each sector is different in myriad countries.

- In some countries which are rich in raw materials, primary sector businesses may thrive. This is so in countries with large mineral deposits or reserves of oil, such as Zimbabwe. Qatar and the United Arab Emirates (UAE).
- In other countries, perhaps with fewer natural resources but with advanced technology, or a large labour force like China, the predominant sector might be manufacturing (secondary).
- Alternatively, countries such as Singapore have a large tertiary sector. Some countries focus on providing services to others. This might be due to limited natural resources in their country, meaning that goods can be produced more cheaply elsewhere. Usually it is because they have developed businesses or individuals want.

COMMENTARY: RELATIVE IMPORTANCE OF THREE SECTORS

Which sector of industry is most important in your country? This depends on what is meant by the term 'important'. Usually the three sectors of industry are compared by:

- The numbers of workers employed in each sector, Or
- The value of output of goods and services.

In short, as economies develop they tend to move from being focused on employment and output in the primary sector to the manufacturing sector and then to the tertiary sector.

In reality, all countries have industries in all sectors. Because factors affecting businesses are constantly changing, the 'mix' of industrial sectors is also constantly changing.

2.6 CLASSIFICATION ON THE BASIS OF SIZE

Businesses vary considerably in size. Companies such as Tata Motors, based in India and Microsoft based in America are considered large, whereas a roadside food-stall proprietor or a self-employed carpenter is running a small business.

This size of a business is measured in terms of

(i) output of goods and services, (ii) sales revenue (or turnover), (iii) number of persons employed and (iv) capital employed (the amount of capital or money) invested into the business by its owners from their own resources or loans).

These four factors are shown in Fig. 2.7.

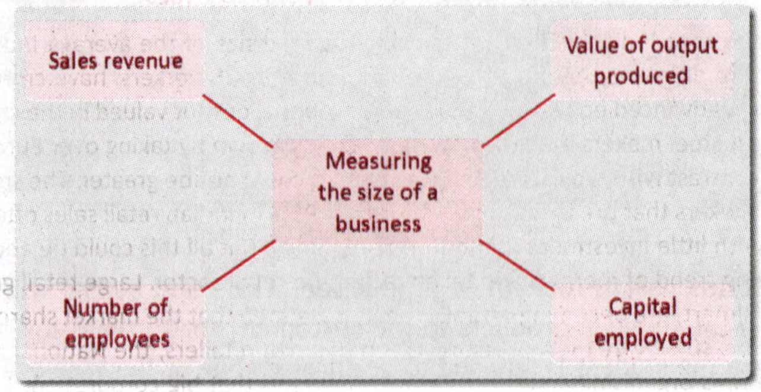

FIGURE 2.7: Measuring the Size of a Business

In general, a small business is one which is independently owned and operated, is not dominant in its field of operation, and meets certain standards of size in terms of employees or annual receipts (sales turnover).

2.6.1 Classification of Indian Industries

On the basis of size or scale of operation, industries are classified into the following four categories:

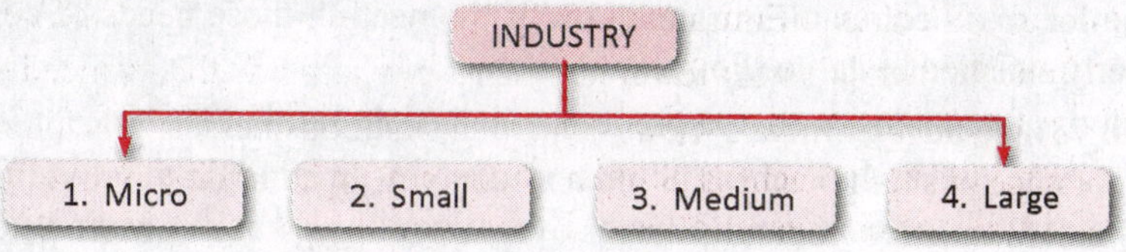

FIGURE 2.8: Four Types of Indian Industries

Small businesses hold a key position in the Indian economy. In fact, a notable feature of Indian economy since Independence has been the rapid growth of the small-scale sector. The definition of small business unit goes in terms of investment in fixed assets such as plant, equipment and machinery. Quite recently, small business has been divided into two main segments, namely, micro-enterprises and small enterprises. The asset limit in terms of investment in plant and machinery in case of manufacturing and services sectors have been specified by the Micro, Small & Medium Enterprises Development (MEMD) Act, 2006. The Act aims at facilitating the growth of small enterprises so that they can gain competitive advantage over time and ultimately emerge as medium enterprises.

As per the act, Indian industries are classified as follows:

(i) **Micro unit:** A unit in which investment in plant and machinery is upto ₹ 25 lac in case of manufacturing and upto ₹ 10 lac in case of a service organisation.

(ii) **Small unit:** A manufacturing unit in which investment in plant and machinery is more than ₹ 25 lac but less than ₹ 5 crore. In case of service organising these limits are ₹ 10 lac and ₹ 2 crore, respectively.

(iii) **Medium unit:** It is a manufacturing unit in which investment in plant and machinery is more than ₹ 5 crore but does not exceed ₹ 10 crore. In case of service enterprises, such limits are ₹ 2 crore and ₹ 5 crore, respectively.

A large unit is a manufacturing entity in which investment in plant, equipment and machinery exceeds ₹ 10 crore. In case of a service unit, the investment required is more than ₹ 5 crore.

CASE EXAMPLE: TALE OF TWO INDUSTRIES

The size of the average Indian steel plant compared to the size of the average Indian retail shop could not be more different. Steel plants employ thousands of workers, have crore of rupees of capital invested in advanced equipment and produce annual output valued in the crores too. Tata, one of the largest steel makers in the world, has recently grown by taking over European steel giant Corus. The contrast with typical Indian retail outlets could not be greater. The small shopkeepers and street hawkers that presently account for over 95% of Indian retail sales often employ just a few workers with little investment in modern technology. But all this could be about to change. There is a growing trend of mergers and takeovers in the retail sector. Large retail groups, such as Reliance and Walmart, are becoming established. It is claimed that the market share of this organised sector will be 30% by 2018. A pressure group of small retailers, the National Movement for Retail Democracy, is organising demonstrations to demand that big corporations leave the retail industry.

2.7 THE ROLE OF SMALL BUSINESSES IN INDIA

In his famous book, *Small is Beautiful*, E.F., Schemacher commented that "small does not mean inconsequential". Small scale industries are no doubt small in size but they play a big role in the economic development of a country like India and other countries at similar stages of development.

Bigger is not always better. Big businesses do not serve all the needs of the market. So there is enough scope for small companies to make profit by meeting those needs of customers which cannot be properly satisfied by large firms.

Since about 75% to 80% of India's new jobs are in small businesses, it is interesting to study the role and importance of small business in India's economy. In addition to providing employment opportunities, small firms offer other advantages over larger companies — more personal customer service and the ability to respond quickly to opportunities.

The Government of India (GOI) has assigned a very important role to the small-scale industrial units for the following reasons:

1. Balanced regional development: Large enterprises remain concentrated mainly in large metropolitan areas. So it seems that the only way to bring the benefit of industrialisation in small towns and the countryside is to encourage the setting up of small enterprises. A developing country like India can achieve industrialisation in the true sense only if it is able to penetrate into the remote corners of the country.

   A quote from R. Datt and K.P.M Sundaram is quite relevant in this context:

   "Decentralisation of industrial enterprises also helps to tap local resources — such as raw materials, idle savings and local talents — and also improves the standard of living in backward regions. Moreover, decentralisation helps to solve the problems of congestion in the few industrial towns by enlarging the area of employment."

> **BUSINESS FOCUS: PROMOTING ENTREPRENEURSHIP**
>
> Small enterprises encourage the growth of entrepreneurship which, in its turn, imparts the much needed dynamism to the economy. The growth of entrepreneurship calls for a suitable environment. In the words of Datt and Sundaram small enterprises provide that environment which encourages "a growing network of feeder and complimentary relations among plants and firms. It is in this environment that latent talents of individual entrepreneurs find self-expression in localised innovations and cost-saving measures...the latent resources of entrepreneurship can be tapped by the growth of small enterprises significantly".

2. Employment generation: Small enterprises are labour-intensive and thus create more employment per unit of capital employed. So such enterprises help to enlarge the volume of employment, mainly in rural and semi-urban areas.
3. Use of latent resources: Small enterprises are able to tap latent resources such as hoarded wealth, entrepreneural ability and untapped natural resources.
4. Alleviation of rural poverty: Development of small industries can also solve the problem of rural poverty. By providing employment opportunities to rural people, such industries generate new income. Even poor farmers can supplement their income by doing jobs in the off-season when agricultural operations come to a halt, particularly in dry areas.
5. Improved standard of life: Small industries help in improving the standard of living of the rural people. They mobilise the savings of the people, and increase their per capita income

and consumption levels. By selecting a group of villages and starting small enterprises it is possible to cater to the needs of a small area from the local centre.

6. Reducing income inequality: The income generated in a large number of small enterprises is dispersed more widely in the community than income generated in a few large firms. This means that income benefit of small enterprises is derived by a large segment of the population while large enterprises lead to more concentration of economic power. Therefore small enterprises lead to greater equality of income distribution.
7. Giving support to large industries: Small industries give necessary support to the large industries by supplying necessary raw materials and components as also in helping them in distributing their products.
8. Maintaining cultural heritage: India is known for its handicrafts and works of arts and architecture such as Kashmiri shawls or dolls of Krishnanagar (West Bengal). Small-scale units produce these items and thus sustain the cultural heritage of India.
9. Entrepreneurship development: Small businesses encourage the growth of entrepreneurship. These are a way of life for individuals who want to eke out a living independently as self-employed persons.

   The development of entrepreneurship has played a key role in the economic development of Japan in the post Second World War period. This may also happen in India if proper plans for the development of entrepreneurship are formulated and effectively implemented. Of course, it is necessary to give necessary incentives to entrepreneur.

   It is necessary to ensure that large and small industries develop simultaneously by assisting one another on a reciprocal basis. This has been the real story of the industrial economy of Japan.

COMMENTARY: HOW DO SMALL FIRMS SURVIVE?

There are several reasons why small firms continue to thrive.

1. Many people value independence. A large number of small businesses could expand but do not as their owners want to retain control. And they do not want the anxiety that being a part of a larger organisation would bring.
2. Small businesses can concentrate on the needs of smaller markets. These smaller markets may not have enough customers to sustain a large business.
3. Most large companies are not interested in producing custom-made goods. A large construction firm that specialises in building motorways or power stations will not waste resources on building an extension to your kitchen, which is the type of job ideally suited to a small builder.
4. Small firms also frequently provide an important service to large firms by producing components. This enables the larger firm to concentrate on its main tasks.
5. Small firms can be more creative. Managers and owners of small businesses are closer to their customers than top management of large firms. They may be able to identify the significance of and need for new developments more quickly.
6. In a small business, decisions are taken more quickly than in a larger business. Small businesses are often more responsive to the changing needs of their customers.

Each year a larger proportion of small business fail. Others succeed and grow, while more are established for the first time. In many countries, assistance is available to people considering starting their own businesses.

10. **Cordial labour-management relations:** Finally, as most of the small enterprises are either proprietory or partnership concerns, the relations among the workers and the employees are more cordial (harmonious) in small enterprises than in large ones.

It is high time that small-scale and large-scale industries developed simultaneously by assisting one another on a reciprocal basis, as in Japan.

2.8 COMMERCE

2.8.1 Meaning

'Commerce' is a general term used to describe processes of exchange in a trading context. Now the term is largely superseded by more specific terms such as international business and e-commerce (or e-business) in a broad sense. Commerce refers to all those activities which are connected with bringing goods from producing to consuming centres. In the language of E. Thomas, "Commercial operations deal with the buying and selling of goods, exchange of commodities and the continuation of finished products". Commerce includes not only trade but also different services such as storage and warehousing, transport and communication, packaging, insurance, banking and sales promotion which are aids to trade or incidental to it.

2.8.2 Definition of Commerce

The term 'Commerce' is used to refer three main types of business activities, viz., (i) the buying and selling of goods, (ii) the exchange of commodities and (iii) distribution of finished products. The main object of commerce is to ensure a smooth flow of goods and services from producers and traders to consumers with a view to satisfying their wants. The traders of goods and services establish links between the consumers (buyers) and producers (sellers).

Commerce is a broad term and includes all those activities which help to transfer goods and services from producers to consumers. Therefore, it includes (i) trading in goods and services, and (ii) aids (services) to trade such as transport, banking, warehousing, insurance and advertising which together facilitate the smooth movement and exchange of goods and services. Both trade as well as aids to trade help to establish indirect link between producers and consumers as shown in Fig. 2.9.

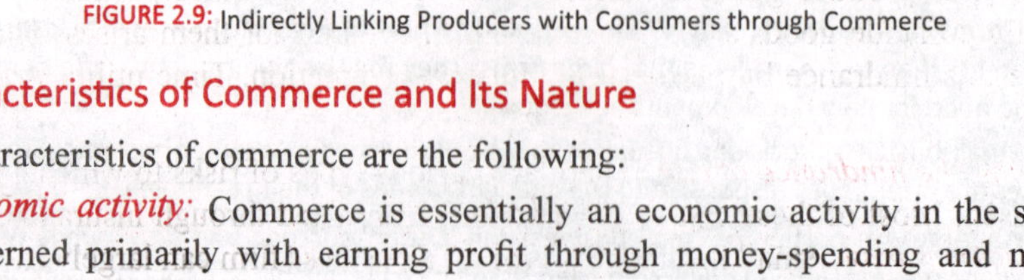

FIGURE 2.9: Indirectly Linking Producers with Consumers through Commerce

2.8.3 Characteristics of Commerce and Its Nature

The main characteristics of commerce are the following:

(i) *Economic activity:* Commerce is essentially an economic activity in the sense that it is concerned primarily with earning profit through money-spending and money-earning endeavours. A trader, for example, buys goods at low prices for selling the same at higher prices to make profit.

(ii) *Exchange of goods and services:* Commerce involves exchange and distribution of goods and services which are either purchased or produced for sale. Commerce includes both trade and auxiliaries to trade, i.e., all those economic activities which assist trade — directly or indirectly.

(iii) *Profit motive:* The main driving force behind commercial activities is profit-making. Goods distributed in charity or presented as a gift is not commerce.

(iv) *Recurring transactions:* A single and once and for all exchange or transaction is not commerce. For example, if a person sells his used car it is not commerce. Commerce refers to recurring activities.

(v) *Creation of utility:* Commerce creates two types of utility. It creates place utility by carrying goods from producing to consuming centres. It creates time utility by making goods available as and when they are demanded to satisfy human needs and wants. By creating different types of utility, commerce helps to expand the volume and value of trade.

(vi) *A component of business*: Commerce is a major segment of business. It is also an economic activity which seeks to meet people's wants and needs through various activities such as production, consumption, exchange, distribution and specialisation. [Recall that all economic activities are money-earning activities.]

2.8.4 Functions and Role of Commerce

There are various hindrances in the way of smooth flow (transfer) of goods from producers to consumers. The basic function of commerce is to remove such hindrances as that of person (through traders), that of place (through transportation), that of risk (through insurance), that of time (through storage and warehousing), that of financing (through banking), and that of knowledge (through advertising and sales promotion measures). Such hindrances arise at various stages of distribution of goods and services and the role of commerce does not end until goods and services reach the final consumers.

These functions of commerce may now be discussed one by one:

(i) *Removing the hindrance of person:* Since producers and the consumers of goods often have different localities, they are unable to establish direct contact with one another. Traders such as wholesalers, retailers, and mercantile agents operate to remove the hindrance of person by establishing an indirect link between producers and consumers.

(ii) *Removing the hindrance of place.* Goods may be produced near places of raw materials and other inputs but not near markets for saleable goods. The geographical proximity between producing and consuming centres is established by different means (modes) of transport. And place utility is created in the process.

(iii) *Removing the hindrance of storage:* The main function of a business firm or an entreprenuer is to produce goods in 'anticipation of demand'. Since production and sales do normally coincide goods are to be stored until demand for them arises. The warehouses remove this hindrance by performing the storage function. Time utility is created in the process.

(iv) *Removing the hindrance of risk:* There are various types of risks to which a business firm is exposed. Most of these can be covered and eliminated through insurance. By paying a small insurance premium a business firm can largely succeed in eliminating the various risks which it faces from time to time. And in case of an eventuality such as fire, theft and natural calamity it will get a reasonable (if not fully adequate) compensation. So it will feel safe and secured.

Risk reduction is possible through insurance.

(v) *Removing the hindrance of finance:* Both business persons and consumers need finance. Business need short-term funds to meet their working capital needs. Consumers (households) need funds for purchasing houses, flats, cars, refrigerators and other costly items. The financial needs of business and households are met by banks and other (non-bank) financial institutions which make loans for both production and consumption. And an increase in consumption expenditure boosts production.

(vi) *Removing the hindrance of information:* Often consumers are not able to take decision regarding purchase of a good unless and until they get necessary information about its quality, price, attributes (physical properties) and availability. Through advertising and various sales promotion measures, business firms make necessary and detailed information available to prospective buyers. This makes it possible for buyers to take purchase decisions.

> *Advertising gives necessary information to buyers about a product.*

2.8.5 Types of Commercial Activities

Commercial activities can be classified into two broad categories, namely, (i) trade and (ii) auxiliaries (aids) to trade as shown in Fig. 2.10.

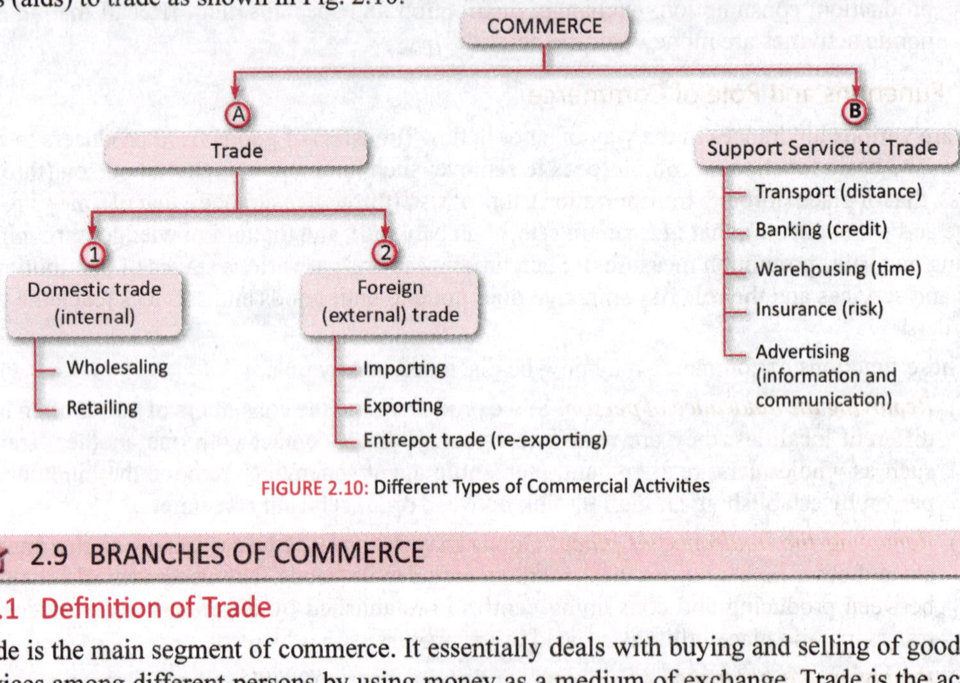

FIGURE 2.10: Different Types of Commercial Activities

2.9 BRANCHES OF COMMERCE

2.9.1 Definition of Trade

Trade is the main segment of commerce. It essentially deals with buying and selling of goods and services among different persons by using money as a medium of exchange. Trade is the activity of selling goods or services in a market in order to make profit. It is the nerve centre of commerce as all other commercial activities gravitate around trade.

Trade is a part of commerce and means of buying and selling only. It may even mean a single activity of buying or selling that is carried out. It does not include any other activity which facilitates exchange or transaction. Commerce is a broad term which includes trade as well as all those activities which facilitate trade, i.e., smooth flow of goods and services from buyers to sellers. Although the two terms 'trade' and 'commerce' are used interchangeably, there is the difference between the two. Trade is a narrow term and commerce is a broad term. In fact, the former is a sub-set of the latter. This point will become clear when we discuss more about the two terms later in this chapter.

2.9.2 Types of Trade

Trade may be classified on the basis of (i) area covered, as also (ii) volume of transactions as shown in Fig. 2.11. On area basis, trade may be classified into: (a) internal (home) trade, and (b) external (foreign) trade. On the basis of volume, trade may be classified into: (a) wholesale trade, and (b) retail trade.

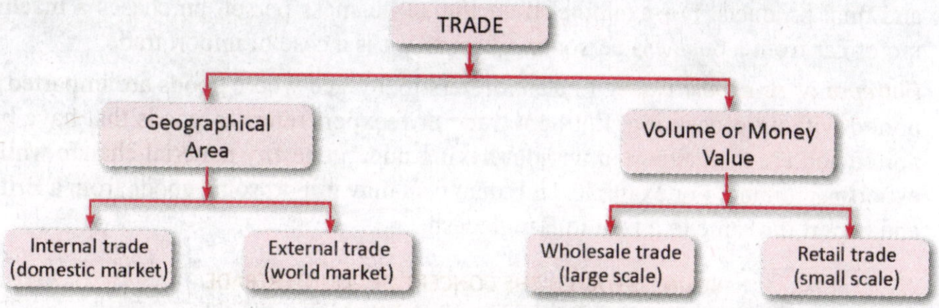

FIGURE 2.11: Types of Trade

2.9.3 Internal (Home) Trade

Internal (home) trade refers to purchase and sale of goods within the domestic territory of a country and the payments for such transactions is made in domestic (home) currency either directly or through the banks. For instance, a trader in Kolkata may purchase T-shirts from a textile (manufacture) dealer in New Delhi or a trader in Simla may sell apples to a dealer in Ranchi.

On the basis of the volume of business (or geographical area of business covered), internal trade may be further sub-classified into the following two categories:

1. *Wholesale trade (business):* Wholesale trade or wholesaling refers to business of selling goods to retailers. It relates to the business of buying goods from manufacturers and selling them in large quantities to retailers who sell in small quantities to the general public. A wholesaler is an intermediary between producer and a retailer. As a business person, he purchases goods from a manufacturer or a producer in large quantities and sells them to a retailer or a distributor in small quantities. The wholesaler serves as a link between the producers and the retailers.

   Wholesale trade describes business of selling goods to retailers.

2. *Retail trade:* Retailing refers to sale of products in small quantities by the retailer directly to the general public. It therefore, serves as a link between the wholesaler and the ultimate buyer. Retail trade can be put into three broad groups: independent traders, multiple (departmental) stores, or retail cooperatives. Retail trade is also conducted through super-bazars, self-service stores, mail order businesses, shops, vendors and peddlers.

2.9.4 External or Foreign Trade

External (foreign/international) trade involves the use of foreign currency (called foreign exchange) in making payments to foreigners and receiving payments from them. It refers to the sale (exporting) and purchase (importing) of goods and services which takes place between trading partners in different countries. External trade is subdivided into following three categories:

1. *Export trade:* Exporting refers to the sale in overseas market of a product when is produced in the firm's home market. It provides an opportunity for a firm to increase its sale potential by marketing its product in a number of foreign countries rather than relying solely on sales in its own domestic market. For example, if an Indian firm sells carpets to

a firm in Dubai, it is an example of export trade. Exports may be regarded as an important profit-seeking business activity. It provides a firm an opportunity for worldwide sales expansion and long-term profit growth.

2. *Import trade:* Importing is the sale in the home market of a product which is produced in a foreign country. Domestic firms and traders may import particular materials, components and final products. For example, if an Indian business person purchases a machine or a motor car from a business person in Germany, it is a case of import trade.
3. *Entrepot or re-export trade:* Entrepot refers to a place where goods are imported and exported without processing. Entrepot trade or reexport refers to goods that have been imported and are then exported without having undergone any material change while in the exporting country. For example, an Indian firm may import some goods from a British firm and export the same to a firm in Bangladesh.

BUSINESS FOCUS: THE CONCEPT OF COUNTERTRADE

Countertrade refers to direct or indirect exchange of certain goods for other goods in international trade, where certain foreign currencies are in short supply. It is essentially a system of trade between two parties. It takes three forms: Firstly, these may be direct exchange of goods for goods (barter). Secondly, it may involve counter purchase. Thirdly, it may take the form of buy back. Counter- purchase involves export transaction plus the commitment of the exporter to buy additional goods or services from that country. Under the buy back system the supplier of a plant or equipment is paid from the future proceeds resulting from the use of the plant.

In Table 2.1 we make a comparison of industry, commerce and trade.

TABLE 2.1: Comparison among Industry, Commerce And Trade

Basis of Comparison	Industry	Commerce	Trade
1. Meaning	Industry means production of goods and services by converting raw materials and inputs into output.	Commerce means distribution of goods and services produced and offered for sales by industry.	Trade means the process of purchase and sale of goods by using money for making profit.
2. Nature	It represents the supply side of the market.	It represents the demand side of the market.	It represents monetary exchange of goods and services.
3. Scope	It has four segments generic, extractive, manufacturing and construction.	It includes trade and various support services (called auxiliaries or aids to trade).	It includes both internal (domestic) and external (foreign / international) trade.
4. Need for initial (seed) capital	It requires a large amount of both fixed and working capital in the process of production (as also for holding of inventories of raw materials).	It requires less initial fixed capital, but large amount of working capital (for holding inventories of finished goods).	It requires little initial capital, and little working capital also if the rate of sales turnover is high, which implies, *ipso facto*, a high rate of capital turnover.
5. Type of utility created	It creates form utility by changing the form or shape of things such as conversion of a piece of wood into a writing table or an chair.	It creates both place utility and time utility through movement of goods from one place to another as also their preservation over a period of time.	It creates possession utility by transferring the title to a good from the seller to the buyer.

2.10 AUXILIARIES (AIDS) TO TRADE (BUSINESS AND INDUSTRY)

The term 'auxiliaries to business' is used to refer to the activities which provide necessary support services to business in general or industry and trade in particular. In fact, such services provide the much needed infrastructure such as transport and communication, storage and warehousing, insurance, finance and banking and so on. These are absolutely essential for the smooth conduct of business. These support services help to remove the various hindrances to trade (i.e., smooth and timely flow of goods) from producers to consumers. We may now make a broad overview of these activities:

1. **Banking and finance:** Banks provide a payment mechanism which facilitates the purchase and sale of goods. These also make it possible to carry on transaction on credit. They collect the savings of the community for making them available mainly to firms in the form of loans and advances. So they help businesses to overcome the problem of finance.
2. **Insurance:** It acts as a hedge or safety-valve against the risk of loss of goods while they are in transit or storage. We will speak more about banking and insurance in a later chapter.
3. **Transportation:** Transport helps in removing geographical barrier to trade by transferring goods from producing to different and often distant consuming centres. For example, wheat produced in Punjab and Haryana and apple produced in Kashmir are consumed in all parts of India. Transportation helps in making goods available at places where they are in demand. Modern systems of transport have virtually linked all parts of the world and thus connected different markets in an orderly fashion.
4. **Warehousing:** There is generally a time lag between the production of a good and its consumption. So there is need to store the good in warehouse. Storage, as noted earlier, creates time utility. It performs the useful function of holding a good for sometime since production and sales do not coincide. Suppose, for example, the Maruti Udyog produces 5,000 cars in the current month. But it is able to sell only 4,500 cars. This means that it is left with an unsold stock of 500 cars, which are to be stored in its warehouse for future sales. And if there is a sudden increase in demand for such cars, sales may be made from existing stock even if production lags behind demand.
5. **Communication.** Communication facilities are very important in transmitting necessary information to producers, traders and ultimately to consumers. Information is made available through postal and courier services, landline, telephone services, mobile phone services, e-mail, etc. Such services have removed the hindrance of information in the smooth conduct of business.
6. **Advertising:** Advertising informs traders and potential buyers about a product and its feature(s) or quality. It aims at pursuading or informing and the general public through TV, radio, newspapers, etc. It is used mainly for product announcements. Thus, it is essentially a communication device.
7. **Packaging:** Packaging is the means of physically protecting and selling a product. It protects product while they are in transit or are being stored, enables products to be sold in convenient retail packs in standard weights and measures, and identifies the contents of the package by means of labelling.

The attractiveness of the colour and design of the package is important in catching the eye of the buyer. In addition, the use of brand names on packaging reinforces the perceptions of the brand at the point of sale. Good packaging improves the delivery of quality products to some extent and in case of some products it even increases product life also.

2.11 INTER-RELATIONSHIP AMONG COMMERCE, TRADE AND INDUSTRY

Industry, commerce and trade are different but closely interrelated activities. The following three points are to be noted in this context:

(i) *Dependence of production on exchange:* Industry supplies goods and services for distribution through exchange which is a commercial activity. The railways, for example, get their business mainly from agriculture and industry. If there is no production, there is no need for commerce (exchange and distribution activities either). If no goods or services are produced there will be no need to carry the same from producing to distant consuming centres, scattered all over the country.

(ii) *Industrial growth and prosperity:* Industrial output will largely go waste if it is not distributed through commercial activities (such as transportation, and warehousing as also wholesale and retail trading). Commerce is the main support to industry. It keeps the wheels of industry moving by ensuring a smooth flow of goods from producers to consumers. Industry cannot survive, grow and prosper in the absence of trade and commerce. Commerce, thus, serves to ensure long-term viability of industry.

(iii) *Provision of necessary support services:* Trade provides various support services to industry which are so essential for connecting producers (sellers) with consumers (buyers). Trade lays the very foundation of auxiliary activities or aids to commerce such as transportation, warehousing, banking and insurance.

The strong interdependence among industry, commerce and trade is shown in Fig. 2.12.

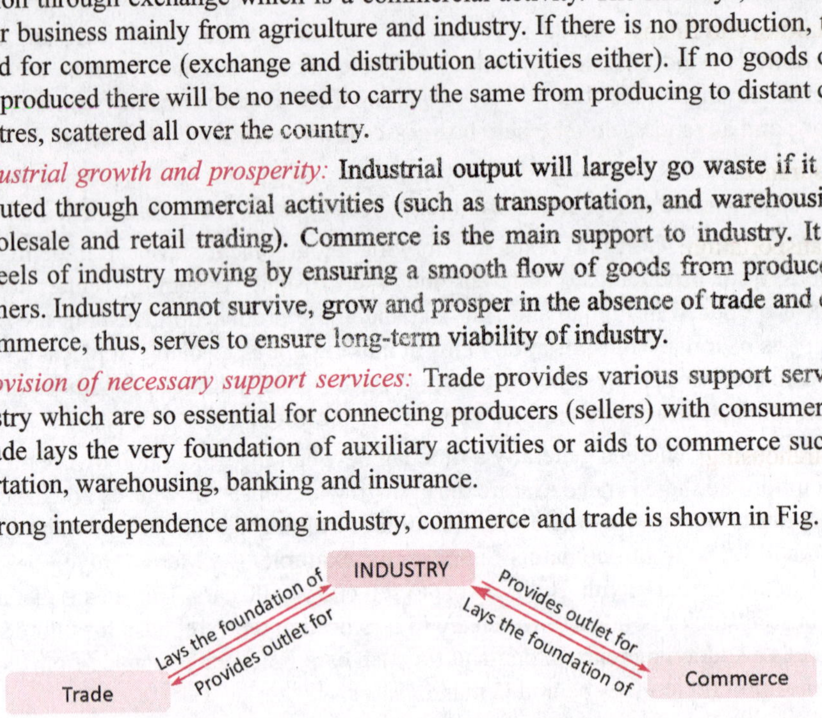

FIGURE 2.12: Links among Industry, Trade and Commerce

2.12 ECONOMIC BASIS OF COMMERCE

Economics forms the basis of most, if not all, commercial activities. Economics is concerned with the satisfaction of unlimited human wants with limited (scarce) resources. Various goods and services are produced to satisfy as many human wants as possible. And then exchange or movement of goods and services from producing to consuming centres becomes necessary to create place utility. According to Evelyn Thomas, "Economics is the study of man's behaviour in earning his living. To earn this living, men enter into a wide variety of occupations concerned with the production of goods and services that are needed by community in which they live".

While economics is concerned with the creation and distribution of wealth, commerce involves exchange of various types of goods and services. Various factors and forces conjointly add value to economic resources or factor inputs in producing wealth or economic goods which have three attributes: utility (want-satisfying power), exchangeability and scarcity. Commerce creates wealth through economic value additions (which is the difference between output value and input value). Thus, we see that economics provide the necessary background for an insightful analysis of commercial and industrial activities. Commercial intercourse which takes place in an economy is the result of the following factors:

1. *Differences in tastes and preferences:* People need various goods and services to satisfy their virtually unlimited wants but all these are not produced locally. In spite of this, human wants are satisfied through trade – domestic and foreign. Commerce makes goods and services available where they are needed and at affordable prices. Goods produced anywhere in the world are transferred to the place where consumers need them.
2. *Division of labour:* Trade is based on division of labour and its corollary specialisation. Division of labour refers to the practice of achieving greater efficiency in production by dividing tasks into smaller and smaller specialised operation. An individual usually tries to specialise in the activity in which he is relatively efficient. Like an individual a region or a country also specialises. An exchange of goods (or trade) between two individuals like a farmer and a butcher or two regions such as West Bengal and Maharashtra or two countries such as India and the USA is based on division of labour and specialisation. Each country seeks to specialise in the production of that good (or those goods) in which it has comparative advantage or relative efficiency. For example, India specialises in the production of textiles and the USA in machinery. And the theory of comparative cost (advantage) provides the basis of trade between two countries or even between two regions between the same country. Each nation (region) produces the good in which it is most efficient and buys other things (which it cannot produce efficiently or produce at all) from other countries. This is how trade between two (or more) countries arise through division of labour and specialisation. Thus, division of labour gives rise to trade as also aids to trade.
3. *Differences in factor endowments:* All countries are not equally endowed with all types of resources. Some countries are rich in oil. Others have huge parcels of arable land. Still others are having skilled labour force or modern technology. So different countries of the world cannot produce the same types of goods and at the same costs. In other words, so long as factor endowments such as stocks of natural and man-made resources vary among nations, there will always be a scope of gainful trade (exchange) in goods and services. India, for example, can dispose off its surplus output of textiles to Iran and get crude oil in exchange in which it is deficient. Therefore a region or a country can obtain those commodities which it cannot produce itself or in adequate quantities from other regions or countries. Thus, differences in geographical conditions can be an explanation (or a cause) of trade.

Thus, it is now fairly clear that commercial activities of mankind have originated from the social science called economics. The starting point of economic analysis is the existence of human wants. And commercial activities are directed towards meeting people's wants and needs.

Key Points

1. **Types of business activities**

   (a) *Industry:* The term 'industry' refers to all activities concerned with conversion of raw materials and other inputs into a well-defined product such as a motor car, T-shirt, finished steel, etc. Industries are of four types: (i) extractive, (ii) generic, (iii) manufacturing and (iv) construction.

   (b) *Commerce:* Commerce includes both trade in goods and services (i.e., buying and selling activities) as also various support services to trade such as transport and communication, warehousing and storage, banking and finance, insurance and advertising as also various sales promotion measures. All these services facilitate trade directly or indirectly. Commerce also helps to remove various hindrances to trade by using the services of traders and various agencies.

   (c) *Trade:* Trade refers to carrying on a business to buy and sell products by using money in order to make profit. It bridges the gap between producers and consumers. It is of two broad types:

   (i) *Internal (domestic) trade:* Internal trade occurs within the domestic territory of a country by using the national currency. It is conducted by wholesalers, retailers and merchantile agents.

   (ii) *External (foreign) trade:* External trade occurs between two or more countries by using foreign currencies. And various restrictions are imposed by a trading country on its exports and imports.

   (d) *Auxiliaries to trade:* There are certain activities which provide support services to trade and seek to ensure the smooth flow of goods and services from buyers to sellers. These are transport and communication, insurance, banking, warehousing, advertising and communication.

2. **Economic basis of commerce:** International trade, like domestic trade is based on two economic concepts, viz., division of labour and specialisation. Trade leads to want satisfaction of people around the world and is the result of difference in relative efficiency (comparative advantage) and factor endowments (geographical differences).

KEY Terms	
Business activities	Wholesale trade
Commerce	Retail trade
Industry	Export
Trade	Import
Auxiliaries to trade	Re-export (entrepot trade)

Assignments

SHORT ANSWER-TYPE QUESTIONS

1. Name different types of industries giving examples of each.
2. What is meant by commerce and trade? What is the relation between the two?
3. Mention different activities which come under the broad heading 'commerce'.
4. Name three important commercial activities.
5. What do you mean by auxiliaries to trade?
6. Why is transportation so important to trade?
7. What is construction industry? Give examples.
8. What is meant by the term 'commerce'?
9. What are two main functions of commerce?
10. What is trade?
11. Name some auxiliaries to trade.
12. What are the different types of industrial activities?
13. What is meant by industry?
14. How trade is classified on the basis of geographical areas covered?
15. What is business risk?
16. What are the different sources of business risks?
17. Usha Martin Black is adopting a few villages in Jharkhand for the upliftment of the poor people in the neighbourhood. Name the objective of the company.
    [**Hint:** Social objective]
18. Name the reward an entrepreneur gets for risk taking.
    [**Hint:** Profit]
19. Define industry.
20. Distinguish between genetic and extractive industries.
21. Name different types of manufacturing industries.
22. What is micro-industry?
23. What is small industry?
24. What is medium industry?
25. What do you understand by commerce? [ISC 1992]
26. Name the different branches of commerce. [ISC 1989]
27. What are 'Aids to Trade'?
28. Distinguish between industry and commerce.
29. What is trade?
30. Distinguish between the terms 'Trade' and 'Commerce'. [ISC 1987, 1990]

31. Give two reasons for commercial intercourse. [ISC 1998]
32. State two factors which give rise to the need for commerce.

ESSAY-TYPE QUESTIONS

1. "Commerce is the sum-total of those processes which are engaged in the removal of hindrances of place, person, time and exchange." In the light of this statement, discuss the hindrances that are removed by commerce. [ISC 1988]

Ans. According to James Stephenson, "Commerce embraces all those activities which help to break the barriers between producers and consumers. It is the sum-total of those processes which are engaged in the removal of hindrances of persons (trade), place (transport, packing and insurance) and time (warehousing) in the exchange (banking) of commodities".

2. Give in brief the meaning of the term 'Commerce' and discuss the factors due to which the need for commerce arises. [ISC 1987]
3. Define the term 'Commerce'. Discuss the importance of commerce in the present time. [ISC 1989]
4. 'Commerce refers to, and includes, all those activities which are necessary to bring goods and services from the place of their origin to the place of their consumption.' In the light of the above statement discuss five branches of commerce. [ISC 1990]
5. Explain the term 'industry'. What are its various types? What are their characteristics?
6. Define the terms 'industry', 'commerce' and 'trade'. Give suitable examples of each.
7. Define the term 'commerce'. Why does it play a role of great importance in the business world?
8. What are the various obstacles to free movement of goods and services from producers to consumers? How does commerce remove these hindrances to trade?
9. What do you mean by functional classification of business activities? Discuss in detail.
10. "Two main segments of business are industry and commerce.".Explain this statement.

QUESTION BANK

1. *Define the term 'Industry'.*

Ans. See text.

2. *What is Primary Industry?*

Ans. See text.

3. *What is Secondary Industry?*

Ans. See text.

4. *What is meant by industry? Explain various types of industry on the basis of activity (actvities) with suitable examples.*

Ans. See text.

5. *Mention any three characteristics of commerce.*

Ans. (i) Commerce is an activity.
(ii) Commerce involves exchange of useful goods and services.
(iii) Commerce aims at making profits.

6. *Distinguish between Industry and Commerce.*

Ans. See text.

7. *Name six hindrances which are removed by commerce.*

Ans. See text.

8. *What is commerce? Explain the nature and characteristics of commerce.*

OR

Explain fully the meaning of the term 'Commerce' in a broad sense.

Ans. See text.

9. *Explain the functions and importance of commerce.*

OR

Why does the need for commerce arise?

Ans. See text.

10. *Define the term 'Trade' and explain various types of trade.*

Ans. See text.

11. *Explain different Aids to Trade.*

OR

What do you mean by 'Aids to trade'? Explain each 'Aid to trade' in brief.

Ans. See text.

12. *"Commercial activities include trade and aids to trade." Explain.*

OR

Explain the various processes involved in commerce.

Ans. See text.

13. *Distinguish among industry, commerce and trade, explaining the main characteristics of each.*

Ans. See text.

14. *Explain the economic basis of commerce.*

Ans. See text.

15. *What is meant by direct services?*

Ans. See text.

16. *"There is close inter-relationship among industry, commerce and trade." Explain.*

Ans. See text.

17. *Mark the following statements as True or False.*
    - *(a) The sale of an used car by Mr. X is not business.*
    - *(b) Industry creates place utility.*
    - *(c) Mining is an extractive industry.*
    - *(d) Profit is not the reward for risk-taking but uncertainty bearing.*
    - *(e) Transportation removes the hindrance of place.*
    - *(f) Assembling of a TV set is a manufacturing industry.*
    - *(g) Commerce is an integral part of trade.*

Ans True: (a), (b), (c), (g)
False: (d), (e), (f).

18. *Fill in the blanks:*
    (a) *Poultry farming is a ______ industry.*
    (b) *Mining is ______ industry.*
    (c) *A steel plant is a ______ industry.*
    (d) *Underground rail of Kolkata is a ______ industry.*
    (e) *An oil refinery is a ______ industry.*
    (f) *Cloth making is a ______ industry.*
    (g) *An automobile assembly is ______ industry.*
    (h) *A fertiliser plant is ______ industry.*

Ans (a) generic (b) extractive (c) manufacturing
(d) construction (e) analytical (f) processing
(g) assembling (h) synthetic

19. *Classify the following into Primary Industry, Secondary Industry and Tertiary Industry.*
    (i) *A cattle farm*
    (ii) *A steel plant*
    (iii) *Poultry farming*
    (iv) *Constructing a shopping complex*
    (v) *Newspaper publishing*
    (vi) *Maruti car factory*
    (vii) *Pisciculture*
    (viii) *Hospital*
    (ix) *Banking*
    (x) *Teaching in a school.*

Ans Primary: (i), (iii), (vii). Secondary: (ii), (iv), (v), (vi). Tertiary: (viii), (ix), (x).

3 THE NATURE AND OBJECTIVES OF BUSINESS

SYLLABUS

Business objectives:
- *Business objectives: economic; social; human and national.*
- *Role of profit in business.*

Business can be source of progressive change.

— Jerry Greenfield
Co-founder of USA's Ben and Jerry Ice-cream (1951)

LEARNING OUTCOMES

On completion of this chapter, you will be able to understand the following:

3.1 Definition and Concept of Business
3.2 Characteristics of Business
3.3 The Necessity of Business
3.4 Business as an Economic Activity
3.5 Objectives of Business
3.6 Role of Profit in Business
3.7 Objections against Profit Maximisation
3.8 Satisficing

The term 'business' refers to any activity which seeks to provide goods and services to others while operating at a profit. The success in business is based on constantly adapting to the market.

Essentially, business is any activity carried out for profit. It includes such activities as buying, selling or producing goods and services which a person or an organisation does to make profit.

3.1 DEFINITION AND CONCEPT OF BUSINESS

Simply put, the term 'business' is used to refer to remaining 'busy', 'engaged' or 'occupied'. In the real commercial world, the term is used to the refer to the pursuit of certain economic activities by individuals such as production, distribution, trading or exchange of goods and services with a view to earning income or making profit by satisfying the needs of people.

Business refers to all those activities such as manufacturing and construction, trading (wholesaling and retailing), transport and communication, insurance, warehousing, banking and finance and so on, which are concerned with the production and/or purchase and sale of goods or services with a view to making profit.

Business is essentially an economic activity since it is concerned with money earning and money spending. Money is spent by purchasing factor inputs and raw materials and is earned by selling goods and services.

SYNOPSIS FOR LEARNING: TRUE MEANING OF BUSINESS

A business is any activity which seeks to provide goods and services to others while operating at a profit. The term 'business' is interpreted in three different senses:

(i) *Activity carried out for profit*—works such as buying, selling, or producing goods or services that a person or an organisation does to make a profit.

(ii) *Commercial organisation*—a company or other organisation which buys, sells, or produces goods or services to make a profit.

(iii) *Commercial transactions*—commercial dealings or discussions carried on between people or organisations.

3.2 CHARACTERISTICS OF BUSINESS

The common characteristics of a business activity are the following:

Business is an economic activity involving only monetary transactions.

1. Economic activity: Since business is essentially an economic activity it is carried on with a view to make a living or earning profit (which is measured in terms of money). A non-economic activity which is not connected with money making is not a business activity in the true sense.
2. Production and/or procurement of products: Business includes all those activities which are connected with production and/or procurement of goods and services for final sale, i.e. sale to customers. Production is concerned with transformation of raw materials and other inputs into useful goods and services. Procurement means collection or acquisition of goods and services for sale to households, other businesses, governments and foreigners. Industrial firms or manufacturing enterprises produce different goods and services whereas trading firms procure these from different sources for sale and resale. Thus, business is essentially an act of producing and exchanging (purchasing and selling/reselling) various types of goods and services.
3. Producing and selling goods and services: A business firm produces and sells two main types of goods and services, viz., (i) consumer goods such as food, clothes and cars, and (ii) capital goods such as machines and equipment. Services include supply of water, electricity and gas, transport and communication, insurance and banking, etc.
4. Satisfying the customers needs: Any business activity is conducted for satisfying wants of customers. Otherwise, it cannot be treated as a business activity. For example, if a person cooks food for his own consumption, it is not a business activity. But if the same person prepares food for others in his restaurant for sale to others, it is a business activity. The reason is that he earns money in the process.
5. Dealings on a regular basis: Dealings or exchange of goods and services for money have to be a regular affair or a continuous activity. A once-and-for one transaction or an isolated

exchange cannot be called business in the true sense. For instance, if a person sells his second-hand car and makes some gain, this is not a business activity. But if he is a dealer of used cars and carries on this activity regularly for earning his livelihood it is surely a business activity.

6. Profit motive: Business activities are carried on to make profits. The long-term survival of a business depends on its profit-generating capacity. Profit has to be earned to pay reward to the suppliers of capital as also for the services rendered by the entrepreneur, viz, risk-taking and uncertainty-bearing. After all, profit is the reward for and the monetary incentive to the successful conduct of business.
7. Unpredictability of return: There is uncertainty regarding the rate of return on capital employed since it cannot be predicted. In any business there is always the possibility of making profits or incurring losses. If huge losses are made, even minimum costs cannot be fully covered.
8. Risk and uncertainty: Any type of business involves risk taking and uncertainty bearing. There is always the risk of fire, theft, damage to property due to natural calamities, breakdown of machines, etc. There is uncertainty due to sudden changes in tastes and preferences of buyers, shortage or even non-availability of raw materials, transport bottlenecks or technological change which may make existing products and processes (method of production) obsolete.
9. Creation of different types of utilities: All businesses create one type of utility or another for the members of a society. *Form utility* is the value, producers add to materials through the creation of finished goods and services, such as transforming silicon into computer chips. Form utility is also created by changing the shape of things (such a chair from a piece of wood). Dell assembles computers according to customers' wishes. Form utility can exist at the retail level also. For example, a baker can make a specific type of cake from the basic ingredients. Businesses create *time utility* by adding value to products by making them available when they are needed (such as woollen garments in winter). This type of utility is created by storage of goods in warehouses or godowns. *Place utility* is created by adding value to products by making them available where people need them (such as cold drinks on the road side during summer).

3.3 THE NECESSITY OF BUSINESS

The aim of all businesses is to combine the factors of production to make products which will satisfy people's wants. Business is needed for the following reasons:

1. To alleviate poverty: Business activities are directed towards creation of want-satisfying goods and services by using scarce resources as also by improving the state of technology for raising productivity of factor inputs.
2. To generate gainful employment: Entrepreneurs such as Sam Walton (Walmart) and Bill Gates (Microsoft) not only became wealthy themselves; they also provided employment for many other people. Walmart is currently the USA's largest employer.

In today's world, most people work in one job for a daily or monthly wage. With this money, they are able to purchase a wide range of goods and services produced by many different businesses. In other words, business activity employs people as workers and pays them wages to allow them to consume products made by other people.

3. To improve the standard of living of the people: Businesses and their employees pay taxes which the central, state and local governments use to build hospitals, schools, public libraries, playgrounds, roads and other public facilities. Taxes also help to keep the environment clean, support people in need and provide police and fire protection. Thus, the wealth that businesses generate, and the taxes they pay, help everyone in their communities. A nation's businesses are part of an economic system (or society) which contributes to the standard of living and quality of life for everyone in the country. The standard of living refers to the amount of goods and services people can buy with the money they have.
4. Improving the quality of life: The quality of life refers to the general well-being of a society in terms of natural environment, clean urban environment education, health care, safety, amount of leisure and rewards and incentives which add to the satisfaction and joy which other goods and services provide. Maintaining a high quality of life requires the combined efforts of businesses, non-profit organisations and government agencies. Note that there is more to the quality of life than just making money.
5. To earn foreign exchange: A country has to import various things which it neither produce nor produce cheaply. So, it needs foreign currency. Businesses enable a country to earn foreign exchange through exports. While imports enable a country to get an assured supply of food and other essential items of consumption, exports enable the country to dispose of its surplus output after meeting domestic consumption needs. In truth, exports reduce pressure on a country's balance of payments and enable it to achieve economic self-reliance. Self-reliance means that it has sufficient foreign exchange to pay for its imports.
6. To promote social welfare: Businesses promote social welfare by discharging various social responsibilities. For example, Bill Gates and Warren Buffet spend 50% of their incomes in charity all over the world. Businesses will also promote social welfare by improving both standard of living and quality of life of people of a country.

In the words of Wheeler, "Business — like weather is with us every day. Buying and selling, hiring and firing, producing and financing, these are but a few of the many business activities which daily influence the lives of all of us directly or indirectly".

3.4 BUSINESS AS AN ECONOMIC ACTIVITY

Business is essentially an economic activity for the following reasons.

1. The main objective of a business is to sell goods and services to satisfy consumers and customers and make a profit in the process. Business is an economic activity because it is concerned with money earning and money spending.
2. Business activities involve the use of a country's scarce resources. To be more specific, businesses produce various goods and services by utilising resources which are scarce.
3. Business activities are carried out with a view to satisfying needs of people by supplying various goods and services. Business people also meet their own needs by spending their income (profit).

Thus, business is very much an economic activity. There are two reasons for this. Firstly, it is a means of generating an income. Secondly, it is a means of satisfying the wants of society.

Later in this chapter we will see that economics provided the basis of business and commerce. Any type of business or commerce has an economic root.

3.5 OBJECTIVES OF BUSINESS

3.5.1 Meaning

Business objectives refer to goals which a firm sets for itself in respect of return (profits to be earned), sales and growth of assets which, in turn, determine strategic and operational policies it adopts. Such objectives refer to targets set by the board of directors which affect decision-making throughout the organisation.

3.5.2 Types

A firm may pursue a single objective or multiple objectives. Objectives may be operationalised in terms of 'maximisation' or 'satisfactory target level'. And the time-frame in which objectives are pursued may be short-term or long term.

The primary objective of a business firm is profit maximisation.

No doubt making profit is the primary objective of a business firm (enterprise). But this is not its only or sole objective. Business objectives can be classified into two broad categories, namely, (1) economic; and (2) social, as listed in Fig. 3.1. These objectives are different no doubt, but closely interrelated and are discussed below:

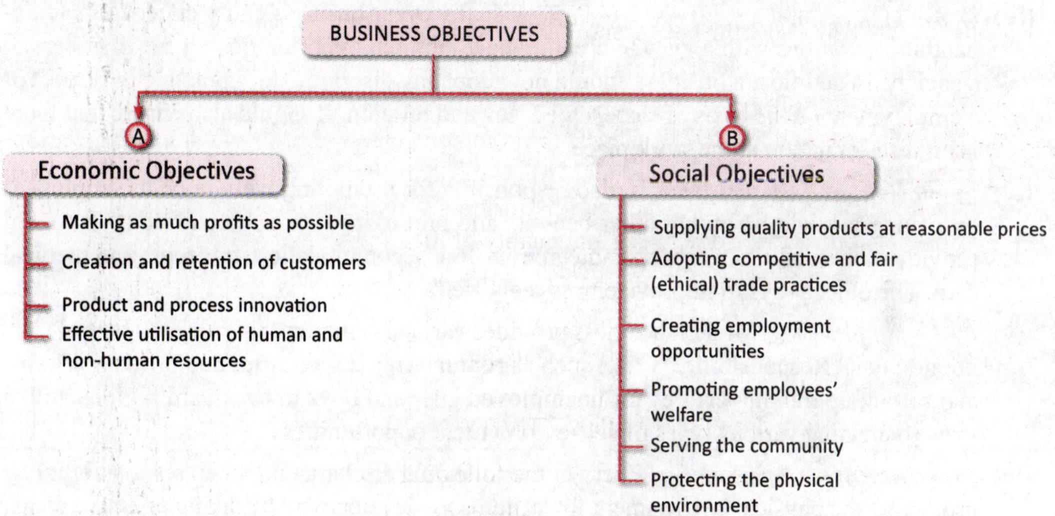

FIGURE 3.1: Multiple Objectives of Business

3.5.3 Economic Objectives of Business

The economic objectives of a business are the following:

(i) *Earning satisfactory profits:* Profits are needed to give suitable reward to entrepreneurs for putting appropriate effort, to provide internal funds for capital accumulation and to build up reserve funds.

(ii) *Satisfying customers:* The long-term survival of any business depends on its capacity to satisfy its customers. If a firm has to make profit in order to survive, it has to please the customers.

(iii) *Innovation:* Innovation means developing new and improved products as also new methods of producing existing products. A business cannot thrive without introducing new products and developing new processes (i.e., methods of production). According to Peter Drucker, business managers have only two functions, viz., innovation and marketing.

(iv) *Effective use of scarce resources:* Businesses require scarce resources such as men, machines, materials and even knowledge. Every business is supposed to make the most judicious use of these resources.

3.5.4 Social Objectives of Business

Since business firms are a part of society they have to pursue certain social goals or objectives in order to serve the society or the members of the community. The most important social objectives of a business are the following:

(i) *Supply of quality products at affordable prices:* The business has to supply quality products to satisfy the customers at reasonable prices so that most consumers can afford them. The products should be of acceptable standard, durable, reliable or genuine (not spurious) and safe.

(ii) *Adoption of fair and ethical practices:* A business firm should always follow fair business practices. It should not indulge in unethical practices such as hoarding, black marketing, charging excessive prices for its products which all go against greater public interest.

(iii) *Generation of employment opportunities:* Usually every business entity endeavours to expand its operations with a view to creating new jobs and opportunities for the members of a society. In addition, a business should not adopt any discriminatory practice in respect of a employment on the basis of caste, creed, sex and religion. It should also ensure that there is no discrimination at the work place.

(iv) *Employees' welfare:* Business is also responsible for promoting welfare of its employees by paying fair wages, giving other benefits and improving working conditions. It should provide such facilities as cheap canteen, rent-free accommodation, transport and medical care. The objective is to improve employee's welfare.

(v) *Community service:* Modern business provides various community services as part of Corporate Social Responsibility (CSR) such as running free dispensaries and primary schools and setting up training centres for unemployed girls and boys in backward regions with a view to creating various types of self-employment opportunities.

(vi) *Protection of the environment:* Every business should discharge its social responsibility by protecting the physical environment for sustainable development by taking effective measures to reduce/check air, water or noise pollution levels as much as possible. The objective is to improve the quality of life of the people. The term 'quality of life' refers to the general well-being of a society in terms of natural environment, education, health care and safety which conjointly add satisfaction and joy of the people. The more money businesses earn, the more it is potentially available to improve the quality of life for everyone.

3.5.5 Human Objectives

Any business is run by people and for serving people. Labour or the human factor is perhaps the most valuable resource of a business and one important human objective of business is promotion of labour welfare. The human objective is to help in achieving socio-economic objectives of business also by creating jobs and incomes. Businesses not only serve the people of a country but, in the process they gain by earning revenue and making profit. Thus, by helping the members of society businesses help themselves. After all, people are both producers and consumers. The human objectives of business are the following:

(i) *Labour welfare:* Businesses are supposed to give due recognition of employees by ensuring that there is dignity of labour in the workplace. Workers must also get suitable scope and appropriate (adequate) opportunities to utilise their true potential completely. Managers should be given freedom and discretionary power so that they can convert their talents into marketable skills. Keeping in view, the importance of the human factor, businesses have to make adequate provision for health, safety and welfare (social securities) of workers. This will not only impose discipline on them but also motivate them to work hard and get necessary incentive to put extra effort for getting suitable reward (monetary and non-monetary). In addition, it is the task of businesses to give workers sufficient job satisfaction so that they develop a sense of involvement in belonging to the organisation.

(ii) *Development of human skills:* If businesses are to grow and diversify, they must provide employees ample opportunities for developing new skills and attitudes towards work. Without development of human resources, growth of business is not possible in the true sense. And, economic growth is not possible without the development of the human factor which implies skill formation through employee training and education. Businesses can help self-development of workers by giving them freedom so that they become creative people with innovative zeal.

(iii) *Worker participation in management:* Workers should be invited to take part in management of an organisation (i.e., in the decision-making process) so that they develop a sense of involvement and belonging. This is likely to improve the quality of decisions since employees will provide useful (valuable) information to management freely and openly and this will usher in industrial democracy.

(iv) *Maintaining peace and harmony:* Businesses should ensure that there is peace inside the workplace. This is possible by ensuring cooperation between labour and management so that there is harmony of interests. In addition, workers should be treated as human being and honourable persons and information should be shared with them so that they can rise to the occasion in hours of crisis.

(v) *Work-life balance:* Businesses should be fair to workers so that they can maintain work-life balance. This implies that they are able to meet the demands of work and also maintain a healthy home environment. A healthy balance is likely to neutralise stress in both the places and go a long way to sustain labour/worker productivity.

3.5.6 National Objectives

Five important national objectives of business are the following:

(i) *Optimum utilisation of scarce resources:* Businesses should make efficient allocation and rational (judicious) use of a country's scarce resources as much as possibly to produce socially desirable goods and services as per national priorities and targets. They must avoid resource waste as much as possible.

(ii) *Economic self-reliance:* By developing new technology and applying the same to industry, businesses can raise exports and reduce imports (by producing import-substitute items). This will help a country to achieve economic self-reliance. This implies that it earns sufficient foreign exchange to pay for its imports so that there is no trade deficit and it is not required to incur external debt.

(iii) *Growth of small scale industries:* It is obligatory on the part of large firms to ensure that large and small firms develop on a complementary basis as is found in Japan. Small firms can be set up in large numbers as ancillaries to supply inputs to large and medium-sized firms. This will lead to generation of more and more employment opportunities in a labour surplus country like India.

(iv) *Balanced regional growth:* Businesses should also promote the development of backward areas of the country by ensuring balanced regional growth so that there is no lopsided development. In other words, some regions cannot be allowed to grow at the expense of others. To ensure the fulfilment of this objective, the Government of India earlier introduced scheme of special incentives to entrepreneurs willing to set up factories in select (notified) backward areas, called growth centres in India.

(v) *Environmental protection:* There has occurred a deterioration of the physical environment due to air, water and sound pollution. As a result, quality of life of people has gone down. So it is obligatory on the part of businesses to protect the environment by reducing their pollution levels by taking proper waste disposal measures and by reducing smoke, dirt and effluents as much as possible.

Conclusion

Objectives setting can be a complex matter. Critical factors affecting setting of objectives include who controls decision-making in the firm and various constraints — institutional, financial and environmental — impinging upon this process. A business plan will be devised to attain these set objectives. Such a plan is a report detailing the marketing strategy, production costing and financial implications of a business start-up.

3.6 ROLE OF PROFIT IN BUSINESS

Firms which are owner-controlled will tend to pursue single period or multi-period profit maximisation. Likewise, the operational goal of firm may be to maximise the value of the firm (shareholder's wealth) over the long-term. Firms which are management controlled will tend to pursue objectives such as multi-period sales revenue maximisation and asset growth maximisation.

No doubt, the most important objective of business is to make adequate profit to cover the risks of business, to give adequate reward to the suppliers of financial capital (shareholders) for risk-taking and to provide a means of livelihood to the owner and/or the entrepreneur. Undistributed profits (retained earnings) provide internal funds for modernisation and business growth through expansion and diversification. Moreover, it is necessary to earn a reasonable amount of profit for developing goodwill (market reputation) and improving public image. This is essential for ensuring long-term survival and growth of a business. These points may now be discussed one by one.

BUSINESS FOCUS: BUSINESS, ENTREPRENEURSHIP, RISK AND PROFIT

A business is any activity which seeks to provide goods and services to others while operating at a profit. An entrepreneur is a person who risks time and money to start and manage a business. Profit is the amount of money a business earns above and beyond what it spends for salaries and other expenses needed to run the operation. Risk is the chance that an entrepreneur takes of losing time and money on a business that may not prove profitable.

All enterprises do not make the same amount of profit. Those who take maximum risk may make the most profit. There is high risk, for example, in making a new kind of automobile. There is low risk in buying a few cars for starting car-rental business.

1. **Means of livelihood:** The entrepreneur engages in business with a view to earning profits which is a means of his (her) livelihood. By earning sufficient profits, he (she) can satisfy various needs and maintain a decent living standard. The term 'standard of living' refers to the amount of goods and services people can buy with the money they earn.

2. **Return to investors:** Those who invest money in a business by purchasing shares and debentures expect fair rate of return on their capital. This becomes possible if, and only if, the business makes adequate profit.

BUSINESS FOCUS: RATIONALE BEHIND POSITIVE PROFITS

Making profit is a compelled necessity, rather than a deliberate act of choice for a business for the following reasons:

(i) Earning of profits through the conduct of business activities is a way of making a living for owners and/or entrepreneurs of businesses.

(ii) It provides necessary returns to the investors, i.e., suppliers of financial capital.

(iii) It provides rewards for uncertainty bearing.

(iv) It is source of business finance. Profits provide internal funds for business growth through expansion, modernisation and diversification.

(v) A profit-making firm usually declares a high rate of dividend. And the most important determinant of the share price of a company is the last declared dividend per annum. So a firm which declares a high rate of dividend will find that its share price is rising. And people will be eager to buy the shares of this company. This will make it easy for the company to raise more external funds for achieving faster growth both through internal expansion as also through mergers and acquisitions.

(vi) High profit is a sign of thriving business and core competency of management.

(vii) A profit-earning business is an asset to the society. Such a company enjoys tremendous goodwill through reputation building.

(viii) Positive profit gives incentive for higher production.

(ix) Only efficient firms which are able to reduce costs and/or raise sales turnover make profits. Inefficient (high-cost) firms lose money and go out of business sooner or later. Thus, the profit and loss system ensures the survival of the fittest.

3. **Reward for risk-taking:** Profit is not the reward for risk-taking as such but uncertainty-bearing (taking uninsurable risks). By building up sufficient reserve funds from undistributed property businesses can try to cope with adverse situations arising from fall in demand for their products, shortage of raw materials and sudden change in government policy which goes against the private sector (such as increase in corporate tax rate.)

4. **Internal source of finance for expansion and diversification:** Profits must be earned to generate funds for reinvestment in business (through earnings ploughback). Only profit-making firms can provide adequate funds for modernisation, expansion and growth through acquisition and diversification.

5. **An indicator of efficient functioning:** If a business firm cannot make profit for a number of years consecutively, its long-term survival is threatened. And if it incurs cash loss year after year, it becomes a sick unit. Thus, profit is the true indicator of the health of a business, which gets reflected in its efficient functioning.

6. **Building reputation:** High profit, earned on a consistent basis and steady dividend payout, are regarded as index of management efficiency. This enables a firm to build its reputation in the market.

7. **Incentive for higher production:** Business people respond to monetary incentives. And profit gives the necessary incentive for higher production. So there is a constant channeling of a society's scarce resources from less profitable to more profitable enterprises. This not only ensures the survival of efficient (profit-making) firms but also effective utilisation of scarce resources having alternative uses.

3.7 OBJECTIONS AGAINST PROFIT MAXIMISATION

Making profit is no doubt of paramount importance for the long-term survival of a firm. But it is not (and should not be) the only objective of a firm. A business firm should also seek to satisfy its customers, promote welfare of its workers and other employees, and serve the interest(s) of the whole community.

In fact, the objective of profit maximisation has been criticised on the following grounds:

(i) In its pursuit of maximum profit a firm ignores the interests of customers, employees and the members of society.

(ii) A profit-seeking firm often adopts unfair means such as hoarding, cornering of essential commodities, black marketing or adulteration of food and fuel.

(iii) While striving to maximise its short-run profit, a business firm often ignores a more important objective, viz., long-term profit (or wealth) maximisation.

3.8 SATISFICING

According to H. A. Simon, instead of aiming for profit maximisation a firm might pursue a profit level just high enough to satisfy the shareholders (in terms of dividend received) and to finance its expansion plans.

BUSINESS FOCUS: SATISFICING BEHAVIOUR

Nobel Laureate economist Herbert Simon coined the term 'satisficing' which refers to the behaviour which attempts not to achieve the best possible outcome but some reasonable outcome. The key insight provided by him is that a firm does not strive to make the maximum possible profit. Instead, it postulates that firms strive to make a reasonable profit. In this sense, profit is less than objective and more a subjective constrained to which the firm must direct itself. This means that although a minimum critical level of profit must be earned by a firm initially, priority is attached to the attainment of other goals thereafter.

However, according to Peter Drucker and other management specialists, profit earning is undoubtedly an essential and desirable objective of any business, if it is to survive in the short-run and grow in the long-run. But sheer money hunting is not business in the true sense. In the words of Drucker, "The problem of any business is not the maximisation of profit, but the achievements of sufficient profits to cover the risks of economic activity and thus to avoid loss. The businessman who keep their customers , employees, investors and the society satisfied, will definitely earn good profits." Needless to say, no business or industry is run philanthropically, it has to make a profit for further growth. But this profit cannot be at the expense of labour and the community at large.

The different roles of profit are listed in Fig. 3.2.

We see that profit place 7 vital roles in business. Perhaps the most important role is that it is a reward for risk taking and uncertainty bearing.

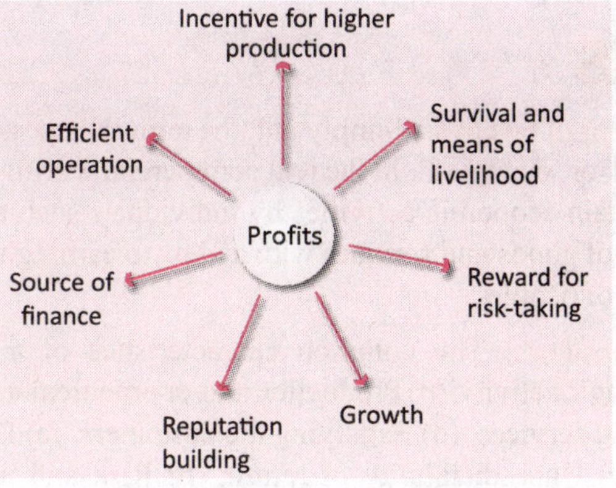

FIGURE 3.2: Seven Different Roles of Profit

COMMENTARY: MATCHING RISK WITH PROFIT

Risk is the chance an entrepreneur takes of losing time and money on a business which may not prove to be profitable. Profit is the amount of money a business earns above and beyond what it spends for salaries and other expenses needed to run the operation.

All enterprises do not succeed in making the same amount of profit. There is huge risk, for example, in making a new type of motor car which people may or may not like. It is also risky to open a business in the heart of a metropolitan city because insurance and rent are usually higher than in semi-urban areas but restricted entry and limited competition make it possible to earn large profit.

THREE CASE EXAMPLES: PHILIPS, CADBURY AND WOLSELEY

The presence of uncertainty and incomplete information in most market situations means that the goal of profit maximisation is unattainable and that in practice 'real world' firms use more pragmatic performance targets to guide their actions. For example, Philips, the electrical products company, aims to achieve a 24% return on capital employed, while other companies are concerned to enhance shareholder value:

Our aim is to "substantially outperform the support services sector as measured by shareholder return over a five year period".

In case of food and drink group Cadbury Schweppes: "Our primary objective is to grow the value of the business for our shareholders. 'Managing for Value' is the business philosophy which unites all our activities in pursuit of this objective. The objective is quantified. We have set three financial targets to measure our progress:

1. To increase our earnings per share by at least 10% every year;
2. To generate £150 million of free cash flow every year; and
3. To double the value of our shareholder's investment within four years".

Also instructive are the objectives which are set to trigger awards to company executive directors (i.e. those persons responsible for determining company objectives and policies) under Executive Stock Option Schemes. For example, Wolseley, a leading distributor of heating, plumbing and building materials, requires that the company's earnings per share growth is greater than the increase in the Retail Price Index by at least 9% over three years and the achievement also of a rate of return on capital of at least 17.5% over three years.

Key Points

1. **Definition and concept of business:** Simply put, the term 'business' is used to refer to remaining 'busy', 'engaged' or 'occupied'. In the real commercial world, the term is used to the refer to the pursuit of certain economic activities by individuals such as production, distribution, trading or exchange of goods and services with a view to earning income or making profit by satisfying the needs of people.
2. **Characteristics of business:** The common characteristics of a business activity are the following: (a) Economic activity, (b) Production and/or procurement of products, (c) Producing and selling goods and services, (d) Satisfying the customers, (e) Dealings on a regular basis, (f) Profit motive, (g) Unpredictability of return, (h) Risk and uncertainty, (i) Creation of different types of utilities.
3. **Necessity of business:** The aim of all businesses is to combine the factors of production to make products which will satisfy people's wants. Business is needed for the following reasons: (a) To alleviate poverty, (b) To generate gainful employment, (c) To improve the standard of living of the people, (d) Improving the quality of life, (e) To earn foreign exchange, (f) To promote social welfare.
4. **Role of profit in business:** Business is essentially an economic activity. There are two reason for this. Firstly, it is a means of generating an income. Secondly, it is a means of satisfying the wants of society.
5. **Objectives of business:** Business objectives refer to goals which a firm sets for itself in respect of return (profits to be earned), sales and growth of assets which, in turn, determine strategic and operational policies it adopts. Such objectives refer to targets set by the board of directors which affect decision-making throughout the organisation. Business objectives can be classified into two broad categories, namely: (a) economic and (b) social.

KEY Terms	
Economic activity	Profit maximisation
Form utility	Satisficing
Time utility	Human objectives of business
Place utility	National objectives of business
Risk and uncertainty	Sales maximisation
Social objectives of business	Economic objectives of business

Assignments

SHORT ANSWER-TYPE QUESTIONS

1. Define business.
2. Mention three essential characteristics of business.
3. What are the economic objectives of business?
4. Mention why business is necessary.
5. Give three main reasons of earning profits.

ESSAY-TYPE QUESTIONS

1. What is business? What are its essential characteristics?
2. Discuss four main objectives of business.
3. Explain the need for and functions of business.
4. Why is business treated as an economic activity? Explain.
5. What are the objections to the goal of profit maximisation? Suggest alternatives.

QUESTION BANK

1. *What is business?*

Ans. See text.

2. *Mention any three characteristics of business.*

Ans. See text.

3. *Explain why business necessary. Give four reasons.*

Ans. See text.

4. *According to P.F. Drucker, "the purpose of business is to create a customer". Do you agree?*

Ans. See text.

5. *Explain the need for and functions of Business.*

Ans. See text.

6. *Name four objectives of business.*

Ans. See text.

7. *What are business objectives? Give examples.*

Ans. Business objectives are targets set by the Board of Directors which affect decision-making throughout the organisation. Examples include: (i) to break even, (ii) to earn 20% return on net capital invested in the business, (iii) to become known as technological leaders within a market place (for example, Sony in the audio and video markets).

8. *Explain the role of profit in business. Mention six reasons.*

Ans. See text.

APPENDICES

A. Impact of Enterprise on a Country's Economy

All governments around the world are following policies that seek to encourage more people to become entrepreneurs. What are the expected benefits to the economy of business enterprise?

1. Employment creation: In setting up a new business an entrepreneur is employing not only themselves ('self-employment'), but very often, will employ other people too. If the business survives and expands, then there may be additional jobs created in the supplying businesses.
2. Economic growth: Any increase in output of goods or services from a start-up business will increase the gross domestic product of the country. This is called the economic growth, and if enough small businesses are created, it will lead to increased living standards for the people of a country.
3. Increased tax revenue: In addition, increased output and consumption will also lead to increased tax revenues for the government.
4. Firms' survival and growth: Although a high proportion of new firms fail, some survive and a few expand to become really important businesses. These will employ large numbers of workers, and add considerably to economic growth.
5. Innovation and technological change: New businesses tend to be innovative and this creativity adds dynamism to an economy. This creativity can 'rub off' on to other businesses and help to make the nation's business sector more competitive.
6. Exports: Most business start-ups tend to offer goods and services that meet the needs of local or regional markets. Some will expand their operations to the export market, however, and this will increase the value of a nation's exports and improve its international competitiveness.
7. Personal development: Starting and managing a successful business can aid in the development of useful skills and help an individual towards self-actualisation. This can set an excellent example for others to follow and can lead to further successful new enterprises that will boost the economy still further.
8. Increased social cohesion: Unemployment often creates serious social problems and this can be much reduced if there is a successful and expanding small business sector. By creating jobs and career opportunities and by setting a good example for others to follow, entrepreneurship can help to achieve social cohesion in the country.

B. Social Enterprise

Social enterprises are not charities, but they do have objectives that are often different from those of an entrepreneur who is only profit-motivated. Social enterprise is a business with mainly social objectives that reinvests most of its profits into benefiting society rather than maximising returns to owners.

In other words, a social enterprise is a proper business that makes its money in socially responsible ways and uses most of any surplus made to bring benefit society. Social entrepreneurs are not running a charity, though — they can and often do keep some of any profit made for themselves. Social enterprises compete with other businesses in the same market or industry. They use business principles to achieve social objectives. Most social enterprises have the following three common features:

1. They directly produce goods or provide services.
2. They have social aims and use ethical ways of achieving them.
3. They need to make a surplus or profit to survive as they cannot rely on donations as charities do.

Social Enterprise — Objectives

Social enterprises often have three main aims. These are:

- *Economic* — make a profit to reinvest back into the business and provide some return to owners.
- *Social* — provide jobs or support for local, often disadvantaged, communities.
- *Environmental* — to protect the environment and to manage the business in an environmentally sustainable way.

These aims are often referred to as the triple bottom line. This means that profit is not the sole objective of these enterprises. Triple bottom line refers to the three objectives of social enterprises. economic, social and environmental.

TWO CASE EXAMPLES

Example 1: **SELCO in India. This social enterprise provides sustainable energy solutions to low-income households and small businesses. In one scheme, solar-powered lighting was provided by SELCO to a silkworm farmer who depended on dangerous and polluting kerosene lamps. The farmer could not afford the upfront cost, so SELCO helped with the finance too.**

Example 2: **The KASHF Foundation in Pakistan provides micro-finance (very small loans) and social-support services to women entrepreneurs who traditionally find it very difficult to get help. This enables the women to set up their own businesses in food production, cloth making and other industries. The loans have to be repaid with interest, but the interest rates are much lower than a profit-maximising international bank would charge.**

4 INTRODUCTION TO BUSINESS ORGANISATIONS

SYLLABUS

- *Meaning and Characteristics.*
- *Types (Private sector, Public sector, Public Private Partnership (PPPs)/Joint sector).*
- *Comparison among different types of organisations.*

> *A business undertaking is a concern, company or enterprise which buys and sells, is owned by one person or a group of persons and is managed under a specific set of operating policies.* — W. Wheeler

LEARNING OUTCOMES

On completion of this chapter, you will be able to understand the following:

4.1 Meaning of Private and Public Sectors
4.2 Meaning and Definition of Business Organisation
4.3 Common Characteristics of a Business Organisation
4.4 Different Types of Business Organisations
4.5 Forms of Private Sector Organisations
4.6 Choice of the Form of Business Organisation

4.1 MEANING OF PRIVATE AND PUBLIC SECTORS

In this chapter, we make a brief review of different types (forms) of business organisations namely, viz., sole proprietorship, partnership, joint stock company, cooperatives, joint sector undertakings and public-private partnerships. All these fall under the private sector. There are also public sector enterprises or state undertakings. However, to start with, we briefly discuss the basic (common) characteristics of a business organisation.

All economies face the same three basic economic choices of what to produce, how to produce, and for whom to produce. In the Indian mixed economy, the private sector — individuals and firms — are mainly responsible for answering these basic questions. The consumer answers the "what to produce" and for whom to produce questions by casting his "rupee votes" for certain products. Firms answer the "how to produce" question by making production decisions (as discussed in Chapter 3).

A firm is an organisation that uses the factors of production (along with raw materials) to produce goods or services that consumers want. The terms "firm" and "business" can be used interchangeably. An industry is the entire group of firms that produce a similar product. For example, the Coca-Cola company is a firm. The Coca-Cola and Pepsi Cola companies are two of the dominant firms in the carbonated soft drink industry. The only time we might consider a firm and an industry to be the same is in the case of a monopoly.

Suppose you were an entrepreneur who wanted to start a business — which type of business organisation would you establish — a sole proprietorship, a partnership, a corporation, or a cooperative. Let us discuss the advantages and disadvantages of each to help you take a decision.

4.2 MEANING AND DEFINITION OF BUSINESS ORGANISATION

A business organisation is an artificial entity which is set up to produce goods and services and which remains engaged in some industrial or commercial activity. It is essentially an institutional arrangement and an organisational framework for carrying on any type of business or conducting any kind of economic activity. It may be owned, managed and controlled by a single individual or by a group of individuals who enter into a formal or informal agreement to conduct the business jointly.

Any type of business or undertaking has its own distinct identity and separate ownership. It can be distinguished from other undertakings on the basis of three criterion, viz. namely, ownership, management and control. In short, a business undertaking is an independent organisation which operates under separate ownership, management and control and carry on business activity and bears risks of different types primarily to earn profit. All business undertakings are directly or indirectly engaged in exchange of goods and services among persons and transfer of the same from place to place on a regular basis.

4.3 COMMON CHARACTERISTICS OF A BUSINESS ORGANISATION

Four basic features of a business organisation are the following:

(i) **Separate identity:** Any type of business undertaking has an identity of its own. It has a distinct name and it exists as a separate entity with its own assets and liabilities and thus separates accounts.

(ii) **Independent ownership:** A business undertaking is owned by private individuals or the government who or which make initial contribution of capital. Thus, every business firm or company has an independent ownership.

(iii) **Independent management:** Every business or undertaking has its own independent management depending on the form of organisation, legal status as also nature and size of business or scale of operation. The management of one organisation does not normally interfere with the working of other organisations except, of course, in the case of holding and its subsidiary companies. The management of each organisation takes decisions of its own concerning different aspects of business.

(iv) **Risk taking:** Any type of business undertaken involves risk. Profit is the reward for risk taking and uncertainty bearing. Some risks are no doubt covered through insurance. Others are borne by the owners. Such risks are known as uninsurable risks or uncertainties.

4.4 DIFFERENT TYPES OF BUSINESS ORGANISATIONS

Business organisations may be classified into the following three broad categories.

1. **Private sector undertakings:** These are financed, owned, operated and controlled by private persons. Their main characteristics are the following:
   (a) *Private ownership and control:* A private sector undertaking is solely owned and completely controlled by either one individual (as in the case of sole proprietorship) or a group of individuals jointly (as in the case of joint Hindu family business, partnership, joint stock company or even cooperative society).
   (b) *Profit motive:* The main driving force behind private sector undertaking is earning profit which is the reward for the risk-taking and uncertainty bearing (or successful conduct of business).
   (c) *No state participation:* There is no question of participation by the central or state governments in the ownership and control of any private sector undertaking.
   (d) *Private finance:* The seed (initial) capital of a private sector undertaking is provided by its owners, i.e. by a single person in the case of a sole proprietorship or by the partner in the case of partnership, and by making public issue of shares and debentures in the case of a joint stock company. A private sector undertaking can also raise funds by taking loans to meet its short-term (working capital) needs and its long-term (fixed capital) needs.
   (e) *Independent management:* A private sector undertaking is managed by its owners directly or indirectly, i.e. directly by the owners in the case of sole proprietorship and partnership and indirectly by the Board of Directors who appoint professional managers who are salaried people. The board members are appointed by the shareholders who, in turn, appoint or hire the managerial staff.
2. **Public sector undertakings:** These undertakings are owned either by the central or by state government. The common characteristics of such undertakings are the following:
   (a) *State ownership:* Public undertakings are fully owned by the governments or by any public authority. For example, the Coal India Limited is owned by the central government, the West Bengal State Electricity Board is owned by the Government of West Bengal.
   (b) *Government control:* The ultimate control of a public sector undertaking is exercised by the government.
   (c) *Service motive:* The basic objective of a public sector undertaking is to serve the society and promote public welfare with minimum profit. For example, the Delhi State Electricity Undertaking (DESU) provides electricity to the public at subsidised rate.
   (d) *State financing:* The government provides initial capital and funds through appropriations from its budget. The government may also extend loan to its own enterprises from the exchequer as and when needed.
   (e) *Bureaucratic management:* The management of public sector undertakings is bureaucratic in nature because their operations are governed by rules and regulations imposed mainly by the central government.

(f) *Public accountability:* Public sector undertakings are accountable to the public for their yearly performance and operational results. Their annual audit is conducted by the Comptroller and Auditor General (CAG) of India. Even their annual reports are discussed and criticised in the Parliament or even in the State Legislatures.

3. **Joint sector undertakings:** Joint sector consists of business undertakings wherein the ownership control and management is shared jointly by the central or the state governments and by the private entrepreneurs and occasionally the general public. The share capital of a joint sector undertaking (without foreign participation) is divided as follows: government 26%, private business persons 25% and the public 49%. No single individual or organisation is permitted to hold more than 25% of its paid-up capital without prior approval of the central government. For a joint sector involving foreign participation the respective shares are: government 25%, Indian entrepreneur 20%, foreign investor 20% and the investing public 35%.

   Maruti Udyog Limited, Wastinghouse Saxby Farmer, Cochin Refinery, Gujarat State Fertilisers Limited are examples of joint sector undertakings.

   Three main characteristics of joint sector enterprises are the following:

   (a) *Mixed ownership:* The government, private entrepreneurs and the investing public jointly own such enterprises.

   (b) *Joint management*: The management and control of such an enterprise lies with the nominees or representatives of the government, private investor(s) and the public.

   (c) *Sharing of capital:* The capital is shared by the government (central or state), private business persons and the general public in certain proportions as noted above. The basic idea is to pull the huge financial resources and technical know-how of the state private individuals.

4. **Public-Private partnerships:** Public-private partnerships are government services or business ventures that are funded and managed through a partnership of government and one or more private-sector companies. There are two main types of public-private partnerships (PPP):

   (a) *Government funded:* In these ventures, the government provides all or part of the funding, but the management of the organisation will be by a private business that will use private-sector methods and techniques to control it as efficiently as possible. Example: The Hope Clinic Lukuli in Kampala, Uganda, receives government funding for its malaria-prevention and HIV-testing services. These are non-profit making entities managed efficiently and successfully by the private sector. It is felt that the clinic operates the health services more efficiently than a government department would with many officials becoming involved.

   (b) *Private-sector funded:* In these ventures, which often involve large sums of capital investment, the government is relieved of the financial burden of finding taxpayers' money to pay for the project. Once the assets have been paid for, they are then managed and controlled by a government department. Example: A new London hospital has been built using private-sector finance — it is leased to the state-controlled health authority that manages and controls the hospital's health services. We will discuss more about PPP in later chapter.

Also note that for the purposes of company law and the application of many company taxes and allowances, a distinction is made between 'small and medium sized' companies and 'large' companies.

A final point to note at this stage is that with the increasing globalisation of the world economy, multinational enterprises (corporations) are becoming more prevalent in both developed and developing countries like India, Pakistan and Bangladesh.

4.5 FORMS OF PRIVATE SECTOR ORGANISATIONS

A business can take a number of 'legal' forms such as the following:

1. **Sole proprietorship:** This type of business is owned and controlled by a single person. Its owner may be the only employee, perhaps operating a small convenience store, barbershop, or speciality shop. Or, the owner may hire several employees to staff a larger business such as a restaurant, an auto service station, or a home construction enterprise. The sole proprietorship is the most common type of business.
2. **Joint Hindu family firm:** The Hindu Undivided Family (HUF) is a form of business organisation in which the family is endowed with some property through inheritance and the 'Karta', the head of the family (such as the father or a senior male member), manages its day-to-day affairs. It comes into existence due to the enactment of the Hindu Law. If the persons, who have coparcenary interest in the ancestral property of an undivided (joint) Hindu family carry on business, then the HUF comes into existence.

   Three generations next to the original property owner of the joint property in the male line with the HUF are treated as a coparcenary. The term 'coparcener' is used to refer to one of two or more coheirs of a common family property. And, in the eye of law, property inherited by a Hindu from the past three generations, viz., his father, father's father and father's grandfather is treated as 'ancestral' in the eye of the Hindu law of succession. The term 'ancestor' refers to one from whom decent is derived, especially the person back in the line starting from father. And the term 'ancestral' is used in respect of something, pertaining to, or inherited from an ancestor. A son, grandson and great grandson become joint owners of the family property simply by birth. The property is held and managed by the 'Karta', who lies at the helm of affairs of HUF.

   The membership of the Joint Hindu Family Business is governed by two alternative systems, viz, the Dayabhaga System and Mitakshara System. The former is applicable in West Bengal. Under the system, both male and female members of the family are coparceners. The Mitakshara System is applicable in all other parts of India. It allows only the male members of the family to enjoy the privilege. However, the Hindu Succession (Amendment) Bill, 2004 seeks to give women equal rights along with males as far as the division of the ancestral property is concerned.
3. **Partnership:** A partnership business is owned and controlled by two or more persons who are parties to a particular agreement. Each of them has a financial interest in the firm. The types of firms that ordinarily form into partnerships are very similar to those that become sole proprietorships. Professionals often form into partnership such as law firms and medical practices. Partnerships are also common in the skilled trade areas such as plumbing, home construction, and electronic repair services. A partnership which is set up for a spe-

cified time period or for a specific object is known as a joint venture. It is automatically terminated on the expiry of the period or on the completion of the object.

4. **Joint stock company:** A joint stock company is a business owned by a group of shareholder and its capital is divided up into a number of shares. (These can be subdivided into private limited and public limited companies). A corporation is a business that is a legal entity in itself. In a corporation, ownership of the firm (stakeholders) is separated from the operation of the firm (management). Many types of firms organise into corporations, such as manufacturing companies, financial institutions, retailers and so on. The division between owners and management occurs because a corporation sells shares of itself to many investors. These shares are also called stocks; hence stockholders are the owners of the corporation. Because there are so many stockholders, they select a Board of Directors to oversee and set goals and policies for the cooperation. The Board of Directors, in turn, hires professional management to run the company. The top official in most corporations is the chief executive officer (CEO). Beneath the CEO in the chain of command is the company President, followed by a series of Vice-Presidents — each of whom has a specific responsibility in the production, marketing or distribution functions.

5. **Cooperative society:** A cooperative is a business, owned and controlled by a group of persons called members such as workers' cooperative, weavers' cooperative, farmers' cooperative or even housing cooperative. A cooperative, or co-op is a voluntary association of people that conducts a business activity to serve its members rather than reap a profit. Members of a co-op usually belong to a group, such as producers within a certain industry, workers in a labour union, or the like. In addition, members of co-ops are usually required to pay a small fee to join the co-op. Co-ops exist all around us. For example, a food co-op allows members to shop at the co-op store, where prices for some food items are lower that those at supermarkets. Agricultural co-ops help members negotiate better prices for their output. Financial co-ops, such as credit unions, permit members to deposit and borrow money, write cheques (called share drafts), and conduct other financial transactions. You may even bump into a consumer co-op at college. Many bookstores on college campuses are organised as co-ops by members of non-teaching staff.

The nomenclatures of business organisations are presented in Fig. 4.1.

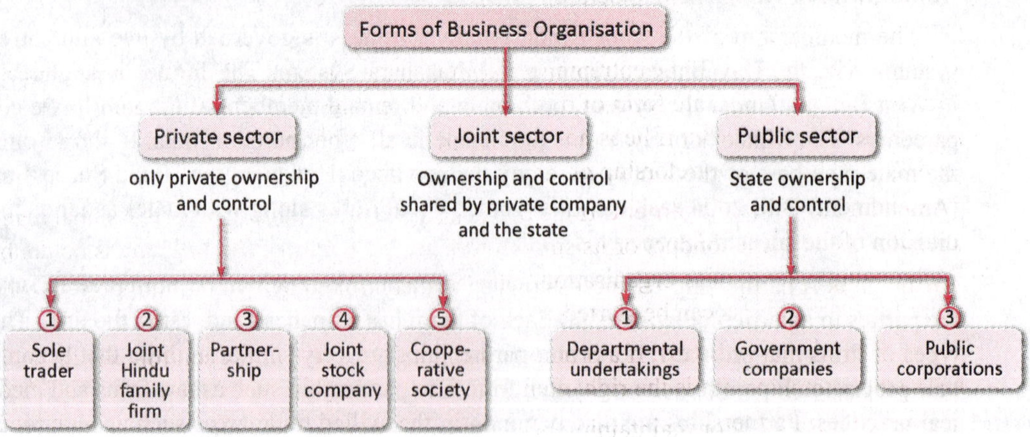

FIGURE 4.1: How Businesses are Organised

Note that simply because a business unit starts in one form of ownership, it does not have to stay in that form in perpetuity. Many companies start out in one form, then add (or drop) a partner or two and eventually become corporations, limited liabilities companies or corporations or even franchisors.

4.6 CHOICE OF THE FORM OF BUSINESS ORGANISATION

An entrepreneur has to take into account the following factors, while choosing the most appropriate legal form of business:

1. **Nature and sphere of activities:** *Prima facie*, an entrepreneur has to decide whether he wants to go for trading, manufacturing or service activity. Since a trading activity can be started on a very small scale, the sole proprietorship form of organisation is the most suitable for him (her). The same is true for rendering personal services such as that of a hair dresser, a beautician, or a masseur. But if he wants to go for manufacturing and distribution, partnership or joint stock company seems to be the most appropriate for him.
2. **Need for seed capital:** If the need for initial capital to be invested in business is small, then a sole-owned firm or a partnership firm is quite suitable. But if a huge amount of seed capital is required the corporate form of business could be appropriate.
3. **Scale of operations (size of the firm):** For carrying on business on a large scale, the joint stock company is the most suitable. But for small-scale operation, sole proprietorship or partnership form is quite appropriate.
4. **Ease of starting a business:** The formation of a joint-stock company and its registration is both a lengthy proccss and a complex exercise, compared to that of other forms of business. A prudent entrepreneur should take note of these realities before venturing out.
5. **Area of activity:** For operating at national and international levels, the joint stock company is the most appropriate form of business. But if the area of operation is narrow and restricted to a particular area or locality, then sole proprietorship or partnership is perhaps the best legal form of business.
6. **Extent of liability:** Both sole proprietorship and partnership are characterised by unlimited liability of owner, as noted earlier. But in the case of joint stock companies and cooperatives the liability of the shareholders is limited to the extent of their contribution to invested capital (i.e., the initial value of shares).
7. **Continuity of business:** If the entrepreneur desires that the business continues in perpetuity, the choice of the corporate form of business or a cooperative organisation seems to be the most appropriate one. But if he is not concerned about the duration or the life of business, he may start a sole proprietorship or a partnership firm.
8. **Professionalism in management:** If the business depends on the help of professional managers for its efficient conduct or its smooth functioning a joint stock company is no doubt the best form of business organisation. But where professional help is not required, any other form of business can be started.
9. **Types of control of business:** If a promoter wants to exercise a direct control over its business, sole proprietorship is the right choice.
10. **Secrecy of business.** For maintaining business secrecy, sole proprietorship is the best. But in a partnership, all information is shared by the partners. A single partner cannot suppress

anything about the firm. And it is extremely difficult and virtually impossible to maintain business secrecy in the case of a joint stock company since it has large number shareholders.

11. Government controls and regulations: The sole proprietorship concern or even partnership is virtually free from government control and regulation. But joint stock companies and cooperatives are subject to government controls and regulations through different types of comprehensive legislations such as the Companies Act and the Cooperative Societies Act.
12. The lure of profit: If the objective of an entrepreneur is low or a reasonable amount of profit, he should organise his business on a sole proprietorship or a partnership basis. But for making large profits a joint stock company has to be formed.

Key Points

1. Firm and Industry: All economies face the same three basic economic questions of what to produce, how to produce, and for whom to produce. In the Indian mixed economy the private sector — individuals and firms — are mainly responsible for answering these basic questions. A firm is an organisation that uses the factors of production to produce goods or services that consumers want. The terms "firm" and "business" can be used interchangeably. An industry is the entire group of firms that produce a similar product. For example, the Coca-Cola company is a firm. The Coca-Cola and Pepsi Cola companies are two of the dominant firms in the carbonated soft drink industry.
2. Meaning of business undertaking: A business organisation is an artificial entity which is set up to produce goods and services and which remains engaged in some industrial or commercial activity.
3. Characteristics: The four basic features of a business organisation are the following: (i) Separate identity, (ii) Independent ownership, (iii) Independent management, (iv) Risk taking.
4. Types: Business organisations may be classified into the following three broad categories: (i) Private sector undertakings, (ii) Public sector undertakings, (iii) Joint sector undertakings, (iv) Public-Private partnership.
5. Forms of private sector: A business can take a number of 'legal' forms such as the following: (i) Sole proprietorship, (ii) Joint Hindu family firm, (iii) Partnership, (iv) Joint stock company, (v) Cooperative society.
6. Choice of the form of organisation: Factors taken into consideration in starting a business are: (i) Business plan, (ii) Choice of the line of business, (iii) Choice of scale, (iv) Choice of the legal form of business, (v) Choice of the location of business, (vi) Financial planning, (vii) Facilities planning, (viii) Plant layout, (ix) Taking the help of business incubators, (x) Availability of required manpower, (xi) Tax planning, and (xii) Launching the enterprise.

KEY Terms

Private ownership and control	Government control
Profit motive	Cooperative society
Single owner firm	Risk bearing
Partnership	Public accountability
Joint stock company	State financing
Public sector undertakings	Bureaucratic management
State ownerships	Joint ownership
Joint sector undertakings	Share capital
Public private partnership	Independent management

Assignments

SHORT ANSWER-TYPE QUESTIONS

1. What do you mean by 'Business Undertaking'?
2. What is joint sector?
3. Name the various forms of private sector enterprises.
4. Mention three characteristics of public sector enterprises.
5. How does the nature of business affect choice of its form of ownership?
6. Name the form of business organisation owned and controlled by a single person.
7. Name the business owned and controlled by the Government.
8. Name the business organisation set up to render mutual help to its members.

ESSAY-TYPE QUESTIONS

1. Briefly explain the common characteristics of business undertakings.
2. Briefly discuss the main characteristics of private sector undertakings.
3. What is a public sector undertaking? What are its characteristics?
4. Describe the nature of joint sector undertakings. Give two examples.
5. What are the points of differences between private enterprises and public enterprises?
6. Explain various forms of business organisation in the private sector organisations.
7. Explain the various factors that should be considered while choosing the most appropriate form of business organisation.

QUESTION BANK

1. *Define the term 'Business Undertaking'.*

Ans. According to Wheeler, a business undertaking is "a concern, company or enterprise which buys and sells, is owned by one person or group of persons and is managed under a specific set of operating policies". Now see text.

2. *What do you understand by a business undertaking? Explain its characteristics.*

Ans. See text.

3. *Name three types of business undertakings.*

Ans. See text.

4. *Name three main types of business undertakings.*

Ans. Three main types of business undertakings are as follows:

(i) Private sector undertakings
(ii) Public sector undertakings
(iii) Joint sector undertakings

5. *What is meant by private sector enterprises?*

Ans. Private enterprises are those when controlled exclusively by private businessmen in the absence of government participation.

6. *Define public sector enterprises.*

Ans. Public enterprises refer to the industrial, commercial and trading undertaking which are financed, managed and controlled by central or any state government.

7. *Define joint sector enterprises.*

Ans. Joint sector enterprises are those business undertakings which are owned and controlled jointly by the Government, private enterprises and the general public.

8. *Give three examples of public sector undertakings.*

Ans. Three examples of public sector undertakings are as follows:

(i) Coal India Limited
(ii) Steel Authority of India
(iii) National Textile Corporation

9. *Give two examples of joint sector undertakings.*

Ans. Two examples of joint sector undertakings are given below:

(i) Wastinghouse Saxby Farmer
(ii) Gujarat State Fertilisers Ltd.

10. *Define the term joint sector.*

Ans. See text.

11. *Explain the main characteristics of private sector undertakings.*

Ans. See text.

12. *What is meant by Public Sector?*

Ans. The public sector refers to all those undertakings which are owned and controlled by Central and State Governments.

13. *Name the business undertakings owned and controlled by Government.*

Ans. Public sector undertakings.

14. *Explain the characteristics of public sector undertakings.*

15. *Explain the nature of joint sector enterprises with suitable examples.*

16. *Name the main forms of business organisation in private sector.*

Ans. Private sector undertakings are organised in the following forms:

(i) Sole proprietorship
(ii) Partnership
(iii) Joint stock company
(iv) Cooperative society

17. *Explain in brief the various forms of private sector undertakings.*

18. *How does the nature of business affect choice of the form of business organisation?*

19. *Explain the various factors that should be considered while choosing the most appropriate form of business organisation.*

20. *Classify the following into public sector, private sector and joint sector undertakings.*

(i) Bank of Baroda *(ii) BSNL*
(iii) IDBI *(iv) West Bengal Scooters' Limited*
(v) State Trading Corporation *(vi) Bombay Dyeing*
(vii) Reserve Bank of India *(viii) India Bulls*
(ix) Indigo Airways *(x) Air India*

Ans. 1. Public sector – (i), (v), (vii), (x)
2. Private sector – (ii), (iii), (vi), (viii), (ix)
3. Joint sector – (iv).

21. *Name the type of business enterprise reflected in the following features:*

(a) Profit maximisation *(b) Service motive*
(c) State ownership *(d) Public accountability*
(e) Bureaucratic management *(f) Joint ownership*
(g) Private-public participation in ownership.
(h) Absence of state involvement and state participation.

Ans. (a) Private sector enterprise (b) Private sector enterprise
(c) Public sector enterprise (d) Public sector enterprise
(e) Public sector enterprise (f) Public sector enterprise
(g) Joint sector enterprise (h) Joint sector enterprise

22. *Classify the following into private, public and joint sector enterprises*

(a) State Bank of India *(b) Axis Bank*
(c) Bharti Airtel *(d) Tata Motors*
(e) Wipro *(f) Palika Bazar (New Delhi)*
(g) Hindustan Machine Tools (HMT) Limited
(h) Bharat Sanchar Nigam Limited (BSNL)

(i) Wastinghouse Saxby Farmer Limited
(j) State Fertilisers

Ans (a) Public sector (b) Private sector
(c) Private sector (d) Private sector
(e) Private sector (f) Private sector
(g) Public sector (h) Public sector
(i) Joint sector (j) Joint sector

23. *Mark the following statements True/False:*
(a) Tata Consultancy Services is a private sector firm.
(b) Bank of India is a public sector firm.
(c) MMTC is a private sector undertaking.
(d) DLF is a public sector undertaking.
(e) HDFC is a public private partnership.
(f) Indian Railways is a public sector firm.
(g) Dena Bank is a private bank.
(h) ICFAI university is a private concern.
(i) Kolkata Metro is a public sector concern.
(j) Chauhan Roadways is a private sector unit.

Ans True: (a), (b), (f), (h), (i)
False: (c), (d), (e), (g), (j).

APPENDIX

A NOTE ON BUSINESS PLAN[1]

1. **Preview:** One of the major causes of small business failures is poor management. Keep in mind, though, that poor management is attributable a number of faults. It could mean poor planning, record-keeping, inventory control, promotion, or employee relations. Most likely it includes poor capitalisation.
2. **Begin with planning:** Many people are eager to start a small business. At this stage, the entrepreneur needs a business plan. A business plan is a detailed written statement that describes the nature of the business, the target market, the advantages the business will have over its competitors, and the resources and qualification(s) of the owner(s). A business plan forces potential small-business owners to be quite specific about the products or services they are willing to offer. They must analyse the nature and intensity of competition, calculate how much money they need to start business, and cover other expenses of operation. A business plan is also mandatory for talking with bankers or other investors.
3. **Writing a business plan:** A good business plan takes a long time to write, but a prospective entrepreneur gets only a few minutes, in the executive summary, to convince readers about the flexibility of his project. Since bankers receive many business plans everyday, the summary has to catch their interest quickly. There is no such thing as a perfect business plan; even the most comprehensive business plan changes as the new business evolves over time.
4. **Importance of information:** Getting the completed business plan into the right hand is almost as important as injecting the right information into the plan. Information should be as relevant as possible and complete in all respects.
5. **An important document:** A business plan is an important document setting out the business idea and showing how it is to be financed, marketed and put into practice. It is likely to be a crucial part of an attempt to raise finance from external sources such as bank.
6. **Competitive advantage:** The heart of the business plan should be, based around competitive advantage. This means identifying the features of an entrepreneur's own product or service that will make it succeed against competitors.
7. **Contents:** Every business plan should contain the following sections:
   (i) *Executive summary:* This should be short, but should contain enough information to persuade the busy banker to want to read on. It should say who the prospective entrepreneur is what the customer's 'pain' is and how will he/she 'relieve' it, why his team is ideal for the task, how much capital he needs for the start-up, and how much he is putting in him.
   (ii) *The product/service:* The entrepreneur has to explain it from the customer's point of view.
   (iii) *The market:* The entrepreneur focus has to on market trends rather than market size, such as whether the market is growing and, if so, how rapidly. Also there is a need to provide a brief analysis of key competitors.

1. Since students are supposed to do the project work on this topic, it is presented in the from of an appendix to this chapter.

(iv) *Marketing plan:* Within this section, there should be an explanation and justification for the prices the entrepreneur plans to set plus a forecast of likely sales per month for the first two to three years.

(v) *Organisational plan:* It is necessary to explain who will be in the team and how they will be managed and organised; CVs should be provided for all key managers.

(vi) *Operational plan:* It outlines how will a product or a service be produced and delivered. This could involve production in Korea in which case the entrepreneur will need to have already made contacts with willing suppliers.

(vii) *Financial plan:* The heart of this will be a cash flow forecast, that is, a prediction of monthly cash out and cash in from the start of the business until at least two years after the firm has started trading. This will give an idea of the bank balances over the start-up period, and, therefore, the financing needs.

(viii) *Conclusion:* This will include some idea of the longer-term plans for the business, including any 'exit strategy', for example, a plan to sell the business within five years.

8. **Not a factual document:** The key thing to remember is that the business plan is only as good as the information inside. As much of this will have to be estimated or guessed, it is clear that no one should treat a business plan as a factual document. It may just help steer the business in the right general direction.

9. **Developing business plans — an Evaluation:** In order to start a new business an entrepreneur needs to have a good idea of the market potential of its product(s) on the basis of a strong understanding of the customers and the nature and intensity of competition. In addition the entrepreneur needs to have the personal qualities to build effective relationships with suppliers, retailers and staff. A business plan can help to get investment from outsiders and may also help a disorganised entrepreneur to make fewer mistakes.

5 SOLE TRADER

SYLLABUS

- *Sole trader — objectives, formation, merits and demerits.*
- *Meaning and definition of sole trader; characteristics and objectives of sole trader; merits and demerits.*

> *Sole proprietorship is a business that is owned and usually managed by one person.*
>
> — W.G. Nickels and other

LEARNING OUTCOMES

On completion of this chapter, you will be able to understand the following:

5.1 Meaning and Definition of Sole Trader
5.2 Characteristics of Sole Trader
5.3 Formation of Sole Trader Business
5.4 Objectives of Sole Trading Business
5.5 Merits of Sole Proprietorship
5.6 Demerits of Sole Proprietorship
5.7 Suitability
5.8 Social Utility of Sole Proprietorship
5.9 Expansion of Sole Proprietorship
5.10 Causes of Survival of Sole Trader

Sole proprietorship or single person-owned business entity is the oldest form, the simplest and undoubtedly the most common form of business organisation. It existed in India from the ancient period.

The business of a sole trader is also known as sole proprietorship or single ownership. Such a business is established, financed, owned, managed and controlled by a single person, i.e. the proprietor or the owner. The owner bears all types of business risks and appropriates the entire profit of his (her) business and is not required to share it with any other person.

5.1 MEANING AND DEFINITION OF SOLE TRADER

5.1.1 Meaning of Sole Proprietorship

1. A sole proprietor is an individual who runs an unincorporated business on his or her own. Generally, a sole proprietor of a business is known as a sole trader and a sole proprietor of a professional practice is known as a sole practitioner.

   The Oxford Dictionary of Business, p. 467

2. Sole proprietorship is the form of business which is owned, managed and controlled by an individual. It is the simplest form of business, established with the limited resources, ability and capital of the individual known as sole trader or entrepreneur. **James Stephenson**

3. Sole proprietorship is the form of business organisation at the head of which stands an individual as one who is responsible, who directs its operations and who alone runs the risk of failure. **L.H. Haney**

5.1.2 Definition of Sole Proprietorship

Sole proprietorship is a business which is owned, and usually managed by one person.

A sole proprietor is a person who carries on a business exclusively with his own capital and takes all risks of business. He (she) provides capital, manages the business himself (herself), bears all risks and gets all profits if he succeeds in generating it. A sole proprietor is his own boss. He (she) is both the owner and the manager of his enterprise. He takes all business decisions himself (herself). This type of organisation is most suitable for small-scale business or entrepreneurship business and for providing personal and specialised services to clients or customers.

> A CASE EXAMPLE: **CAKELOVE**
>
> Warren Brown left a promising law career to create Cakelove, a bustling bakery that specialises in making pastries from scratch using natural ingredients. Brown has appeared on The Oprah Winfray Show and is regularly seen on the Food Network.

5.2 CHARACTERISTICS OF SOLE TRADER

The characteristic features of sole proprietorship are the following:

1. **Single ownership:** A single-owner concern is owned and run by only one person. It is he (she) who takes all the risk of business. He provides both financial capital and manages the business himself (herself).
2. **No separate identity:** The sole proprietor owns every asset of the business and is liable for every debt or loan. Thus, the owner is identified with the business. He has no separate legal status or entity.
3. **Seed capital:** Initial finance, called seed capital, is provided by the owner himself from his personal sources. In the case of necessity, he may also borrow money from his family members, friends and relatives to add to his own funds.
4. **Formation:** It is fairly easy to start a sole proprietary concern without undergoing any legal formalities.
5. **Risk-bearing:** The sole proprietor has to bear all the risks associated with his business.
6. **Unlimited liability:** The owner of a sole proprietor form of enterprise is personally liable for the debts incurred by his firm and this liability is unlimited. All his personal possessions are

at risk and may be seized to meet creditors' demand in the event of the business becoming insolvent. This is, in fact, one of the great disadvantages of this form of business.

7. **Management and control:** In this business, management and control are vested in one person. He takes all the decisions, procures raw materials and other inputs, employs workers and runs the business himself. He may or may not take the help of others.
8. **Continuity:** The life of a sole tradership firm depends solely upon what happens to its proprietor (owner). In the case of his death, insanity, bankruptcy or imprisonment, the firm will cease to exist. For this reason no outsider is eager to supply funds to this type of business.

The main features of a sole trader are shown in Fig. 5.1.

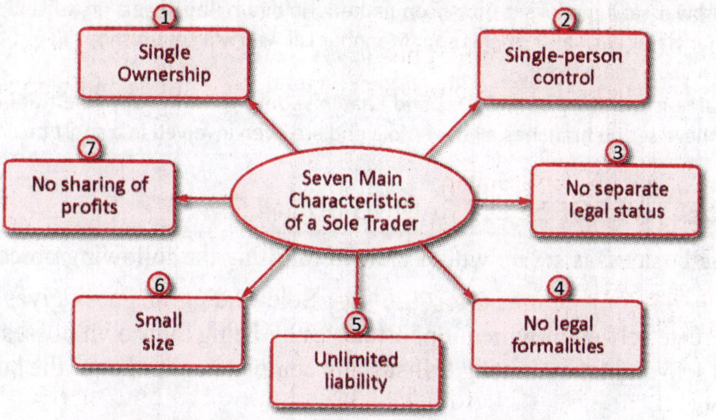

FIGURE 5.1: Distinguishing features of a sole trader

> **BUSINESS FOCUS: MIXED INCOME OF SELF-EMPLOYED PERSONS OR PROPRIETOR'S INCOME**
>
> In various small businesses such as grocer's shop or dentist's chamber, the owner himself (herself) performs all the functions. He uses its own room or building, supplies his own labour, capital, managerial ability and entrepreneurial talent and bears all the risks of business himself. So his total return includes various elements such as notional rent of his establishment, wages of labour, lost interest on his capital and profits. So his total income is a mixed one, from which the profit element cannot be found out as a separate type of income.

5.3 FORMATION OF SOLE TRADER BUSINESS

Sole trader business is started at the initiative of a single individual. He prepares the business plan or the blueprints of his prospective venture and makes arrangement for the necessary finance or seed capital. No legal formalities are to be completed for the formation of his small enterprise. Any individual can start his own business any time and where he likes. But the sole trader has to be a competent person and must have business acumen. Moreover, the business has to be carried out by as per the legal provisions. For some businesses a license from a competent authority may be needed. To start a business, the licence has to be renewed periodically to carry out business. For example, a person willing to set up a grocery store is required to obtain a licence from the local authority such as the Calcutta Municipal Corporation.

The first and foremost decision involved in the formation of a sole trading business is the selection of a proper line of business. This decision depends upon the intensity of potential demand for a product, and the adequate availability of necessary raw materials and other inputs as also the prospect of making profits. The choice of an appropriate location is another key decision which has to be based on two things, namely, (i) the requirements of actual and potential customers and (ii) the proximity to the market. The size of business or its scale of operations has also to be taken into consideration.

A sole trading business can be closed any time without any legal problem or serving any legal notice. The proprietor has just to pay the dues of its creditors fully and wind up the business.

> **CASE EXAMPLES: COCA-COLA, HALDIRAM AND OTHERS**
>
> The Coca-Cola company was formed as a corporation in 1892. But it was originally a sole trading organisation since May 8, 1886. Now it has become a global enterprise having its own trademark and brand name (under the US Patent Act).
>
> Rameshwar Lal Agarwal set up a shop named 'Haldiram Bhujiawala' in Kolkata in the memory of his father Haldiram. Later on, his son, Manohar Lal Agarwal set up shops in virtually all parts of India much like a chain store.
>
> The same is the story of K. C. Das and Khadims. Both were initially sole trading business but now they have set up branches all over India and are even involved in a sport business.

5.4 OBJECTIVES OF SOLE TRADING BUSINESS

The sole trading business is set up with a view to fulfilling the following objectives:

1. **To create self-employment opportunities:** Sole trading business gives people an opportunity to create self-employment opportunities by being their own bosses and work with dignity and self-respect by having full-say and complete control over the business as owner-entrepreneur.
2. **To fruitfully utilise surplus funds:** A person having surplus liquidity (or saving) may start sole proprietorship business to make productive use of his idle funds. This is perhaps the best possible option for a person having small funds which are not adequate to start a big business.
3. **Independent living:** Sole trading business offers ample opportunity for a person to make independent living and enjoy the psychic satisfaction and pride of ownership. Being his own master, a sole trader is at liberty to take all the decisions himself.
4. **To serve and please customer:** By operating at the grass-root level, a sole trader is involved in direct interaction with his customer. Therefore, he can understand what the customer needs and thus serves them in the best possible way because he has a real feel of the market. A sole trading business can be set up nearest to the customer so as to enable them to buy all convenient goods (daily necessities) which are available at their door steps.
5. **Equity:** Sole trading business helps to promote equity or distributive justice by ensuring fair share of income and wealth among a large number of people. It thus prevents the emergence of monopoly which creates undue concentration of wealth and economic power in a few hands.
6. **Support to large business:** Sole proprietorship units supply inputs and provide and ancillary services to big firms as is mostly found in Japan, China, Korea and India. The two sectors or segments of the industrial economy of a country grow simultaneously by assisting one another on a reciprocal basis.

Thus sole trading business has multiple objectives. And they dominate the private business sector in developing countries like India where unemployment is a perennial problem.

5.5 MERITS OF SOLE PROPRIETORSHIP

Sole proprietorships are the easiest kinds of business to start. Every city (town) has sole proprietors. Such enterprises are sources of both the joys and frustrations for the owners. Most enjoy the benefits of being their own boss and fixing their own hours of work. Other advantages include the following:

A sole proprietorship concern offers the following advantages to its owner:

1. **Ease of starting and ending the business:** The establishment of a sole tradership concern is fairly easy. All one has to do to start a sole proprietorship is to buy or lease the needed equipment (such as a saw and a hammer for a carpenter, and few chairs and tables and an oven for a road-side tea stall owner). A person with very little capital can start the business. There is no need to complete much legal formalities. Procurement of trade licence may be necessary to deal in certain products such as drugs, liquor, cooking gas, or fuel. And it is equally easy to get out of business. The owner simply stops his trading activity. There is no one to consult or discuss with others about such decisions.
2. **Being one's one boss:** Working for others does not have the same excitement as working for oneself. That is the way sole proprietors feel.
3. **Pride of ownership:** People who own and manage their own business take pride in their work. They deserve all the credit for taking the risks and supplying necessary goods and services.
4. **Leaving a legacy:** Owners can leave an ongoing business for future generations.
5. **Retention of company profit:** Owners not only keep the profits earned, but also benefit from the increasing value as the business grows.
6. **No special taxes:** All the profits of a sole proprietorship are taxed as the personal income of the owner and the owner pays the normal income tax on that company. Other taxes such as sales tax or value added tax are passed on consumers in the form of high prices of products.
7. **Flexibility of operations:** Since the proprietor is the sole decision-taker and has no need to consult colleagues when changes of policy are required, this type of organisation is extremely flexible and capable of quick and easy adjustment to changes taking place in market conditions.
8. **Maintaining secrecy:** It is easy to maintain secrecy in business. The affairs of such business are not made publicly known.
9. **Operational efficiency:** The strength of this type of organisation lies in the direct personal interest of the proprietor in the efficiency of his enterprise. Ownership and control are vested in one person who enjoys all the fruits of success and hence has a great incentive to run the firm as efficiently as possible.
10. **Self-employment:** Sole proprietorship gives self-employment opportunities to persons of modest means having necessary professional skills.
11. **Reputation building:** By being able to maintain direct (personal) contact with customers, the proprietor gets necessary feedback about their tastes, likes and dislikes. This helps in meeting the needs of customers and satisfying them as much as possible. This helps in building reputation of the firm.

12. **Economy in operations:** Since the sole trader himself performs all the functions associated with his business, he can keep business costs low, more so in view of low overheads.
13. **Freedom of enterprise:** The sole tradership firm is not excessively controlled by the government. Although sole trader has to comply with income tax, sales tax and labour and other general laws, he is not subject to any special legislation or rules and regulations. So he enjoys freedom of enterprise.
14. **Social service:** By providing employment to many people, sole tradership form of business serves a social purpose.

For all these reasons, sole proprietorship business is still far more numerous than any other type of business organisation.

5.6 DEMERITS OF SOLE PROPRIETORSHIP

Any person is not equipped to own and competent enough to manage a business. Often it is difficult to save enough money to start a business and carry it on. It is very difficult, at times, for a single person to cover the costs of inventory (raw materials), insurance, advertising, rent, computers and so on. There are other disadvantages also. These are the following:

1. **Unlimited liability — the risk of personal losses:** A single-owner firm has unlimited liability, that is, any debts or damages incurred by the business are his (her) debts and he must pay them, and, if necessary, by selling his home, car, or everything else he owns. This is a serious risk — the risk of going totally bankrupt. Complete recovery from such a situation is extremely difficult, or even virtually impossible not just due to financial loss, but due to the mental shock one receives after the event.

   Unlimited liability refers to the responsibility of business owners for all of the debts of the business.

2. **Limited financial resources:** Another disadvantage of this type of business is the strict limitation on its ability to acquire capital for expansion. Finance is restricted to the amounts which the entrepreneur is able to provide from his own sources and whatever sums he can borrow on his own security. By comparison, partnerships and corporations have a greater chance of gathering (or acquiring) much more funds needed to start and equip a business and carry it on.
3. **Management problems:** A business can be efficiently run by professional managers. They perform specialised functions such as keeping inventories, accounting and maintaining tax records. Those who are skilled sales persons are not so skilled in keeping records. Sole proprietors cannot afford to employ qualified employees at high salaries and various fringe benefits to run their businesses efficiently.
4. **Huge time commitment.** Sole proprietors have little time to do anything else in life due to less overwhelming time commitment for running the business. There is no one with him to share the work load. The owner of a grocery shop, for example, may put in 12 hours a day at least six days a week— almost twice the hours worked by a non-supervisory employee in a large company. Thus, this type of business becomes a way of life.

SYNOPSIS FOR LEARNING: HIGH TIME COMMITMENT AND CONSTANT PRESSURE

Being the sole proprietor of a company means making a major time commitment to run the business. A sole proprietor has to constantly seek out new customers and look for reliable employees when there are opportunities for growth.

5. **Few fringe benefits:** The sole owner of a firm loses the fringe benefits which often come with working for others. There is no medical benefit, no pension, no terminal benefits (such as provident fund and gratuity), no leave travel concession and no house rent allowance. So there is lack of incentive to work hard but constant pressure to save money for personal profit and security.
6. **Limited growth:** Expansion of a single-owner firm is slow and sporadic (not spontaneous). The reason is that such a firm relies on its owner for most of its creativity, business know-how and funding.
7. **Limited life span:** If the sole proprietor dies, becomes physically unfit, or retires the business ceases to exist (unless it is sold to an outsider or taken over by the heirs of the sole proprietor).
8. **Lack of specialisation:** Since the same person performs all the functions which are essential for the successful conduct of a business, the benefits of specialisation cannot be derived. Moreover, the same person may not be able to perform all the business-related functions due to incompetence and/or inefficiency as also deficiency of imagination and limited will-power.
9. **Decision-making errors:** Since the sole trader takes all business decisions without consulting others, there is, at times, excessive pressure on him. So he is likely to commit decision-making errors. And a wrong decision may, at times, become damaging for the firm. This may not only affect current and future profit prospects but because of this, the very survival of the firm may even be threatened.
10. **Loss of potential economies of large scale:** This is the age of large-scale (or mass production). However, since a sole trader operates on a small scale, he fails to derive the advantages of large-scale production in various areas of business such as making bulk purchase of raw materials, selling goods in different markets (both domestic and foreign). In short, in such a business there is loss of potential economies of scale.
11. **Uncertain future:** The future of a sole trader is uncertain. There are various reasons for this.
12. **Lack of stability:** Finally, sole proprietorship is not a stable form of business for various reasons, as noted above.

For all these reasons, many sole proprietors choose to find partners after some time to share the load. This is how a partnership business is started. In Table 5.1 we list the advantages and disadvantages of sole proprietorship business.

TABLE 5.1: Merits and Demerits of Sole Proprietorship

Merits (advantages)	Demerits (disadvantages)
1. Ease of starting and ending the business	1. Unlimited liability — the risk of personal loss
2. Being one's own boss	2. Limited financial resources
3. Pride of ownership	3. Managerial problems
4. Leaving a legacy	4. Huge time commitment
5. Retention of company profit	5. Few fringe benefits
6. No special taxes	6. Limited growth

Contd.

7. Flexibility of operations	7. Limited life span
8. Maintaining operational secrecy	8. Lack of incentive
9. Efficiency	9. Pressure to save money
10. Self-employment	10. Lack of specialisation
11. Reputation building	11. Decision-making errors
12. Economy in operations	12. Loss of (potential) economies of scale
13. Freedom of enterprise	13. Uncertain future
14. Social service	14. Lack of statbility

5.7 SUITABILITY

According to William R. Basset, "the one man control is the best in the world if that man is big enough to manage everything". But it is virtually impossible for a single person to manage and control every aspect of business.

We find one-person business prevalent in farming, retailing, real estate, repair and maintenance work, and personal services such as hairdressing. Sole tradership is most suitable in the following cases:

(a) Small business requiring very little capital and little specialisation and skill as is found in case of a grocer's shop.

(b) In those businesses where personal attention to customers is of much importance as in beauty parlours, tailoring, and professional services such as medical care and legal advice.

(c) In seasonal industries where the demand of products fluctuates sharply between off-season and peak season as in the case of woollen garments.

(d) In the production of unstandardised (differentiated) products such as embroidery, works of art and of specialised skills as in the case of Kashmiri shawls.

(e) Where an individual has a specific skill which he has inherited from his father such as carpentry or weaving cloth, so as to make out a living independently.

(f) For meeting local demand for such perishable goods such as ice-creams, cakes, pastries and convenience goods which are purchased on a regular basis, as also for laundries, retailing.

5.8 SOCIAL UTILITY OF SOLE PROPRIETORSHIP

The sole proprietorship form of business is socially desirable for the following reasons:

(i) It prevents formation of monopolies and big business and the consequent undue concentration of wealth and economic power in few private hands.

(ii) It creates ample self-employment opportunities for those who do not have enough funds to set up large and medium industries.

(iii) It generates employment for a large number of people (especially unskilled labourers) in a labour surplus country like India.

(iv) It facilitates the growth of small scale and cottage industries as also tiny units.

(v) It leads to decentralisation of the economy and diffusion of ownership.

(vi) It promotes balanced regional development of the country and thus prevents uneven or lop-sided development.

(vii) It offers people an opportunity to work with dignity and self-respect by being one's own boss.

(viii) It makes people with limited resources but strong entrepreneurial zeal efficient and self-reliant. So they do not create any pressure on the external labour market.

(ix) It encourages autonomous living for those who take pride in ownership.

(x) It gives people an opportunity to utilise their skills not only for their own benefit but also for the benefit of the whole society.

5.9 EXPANSION OF SOLE PROPRIETORSHIP

When a sole proprietorship expands, it faces the perennial problem of paucity of funds or capital starvation as also shortage of managerial skills. The sole proprietor has two options for solving this problem:

1. to appoint an assistant on a purely salary basis; or
2. to take one or more partners of his own choice to bring in more funds as well as specialised skill or expertise to manage his firm better.

Each of the options relieves the pressure of the owner and enables him to derive the benefits of division of work and specialisation.

However, both the alternatives for expansion of sole proprietorship have their own merits and drawbacks. In case the proprietor is able to arrange more capital, it is judicious on its part to employ a qualified and experienced assistant to share the huge managerial (entrepreneurial) workload. In case this is not possible, it is in the rightness of things to admit an efficient and financially strong partner who can solve both the problems.

5.10 CAUSES OF SURVIVAL OF SOLE TRADER

Small independent firms do exist is some industries even in the long run, because small firms have certain advantages over large firms. These are known as the economies of small-scale production and are discussed below:

(i) *Personal service is provided for both employees and customers:* Small firms are small enough to deal quickly and efficiently with customer enquiries.

(ii) *Decisions can be made effectively in response to any change in market conditions:* Decisions are made by one person very quickly.

(iii) Sometimes a firm has to remain small because it is restricted by its local market, e.g., small village shops will not find it worthwhile to expand because of lack of demand.

(iv) In some industries consumers demand variety and choice of products. Thus, firms remain small to be flexible and willing to adapt to any changes in demand. This applies to the fashion industry.

(v) In some industries, consumers demand a personal service. This applies to solicitors, doctors, accountants, hairdressers, etc. Consumers require a personal touch which large firms cannot provide.

(vi) *State assistance and patronage:* In developing country like India, small firms are accorded maximum priority in industrial development because they contribute to employment, rural development, decentralisation of industry and earning of foreign exchange (through exports). For these reasons, they get paternalistic care and patronage in the form of bank loans, tax concessions and assistance in marketing their products.

(vii) *Anti-monopoly device:* The free play of market forces as also economies of scale create monopolies and oligopolies. The mushroom growth of small scale units checks this trend to some extent and compete in certain areas by offering certain special things such as attachment to customers and prompt after-sale service.

In turn, small firms appear to be the best in those industries where quick decisions have to be made (e.g., advertising) or where a variety of goods produced is required (e.g., fashion) or where a personal service is needed (e.g., small retail shop selling ready-made garments).

Key Points

1. **Sole Proprietorship:** It is a form of business which is owned, managed (operated) and controlled by a single individual, who alone gets the profits as reward for risk-taking and bears the losses also.

   Features: Sole proprietorship has the following characteristics:

   (i) only one owner (who is the sole proprietor),
   (ii) common identity,
   (iii) supply of capital from personal resources (savings),
   (iv) unlimited liability,
   (v) management and control of the organisation by the same person and
   (vi) no sharing of risks, profits and losses.

   Advantages: Sole proprietorship offers the following advantages:

   (i) ease of starting and ending,
   (ii) flexibility of operation,
   (iii) prompt decision-making,
   (iv) maintaining business secrecy,
   (v) personal touch with customers (and relationship marketing),
   (vi) great motivation for hard work and seriousness,
   (vii) ability to become one's own boss,
   (viii) pride of ownership,
   (ix) low overhead costs (or fixed expenses),
   (x) retention of profits,
   (xi) minimum interference by the governments at different levels and
   (xii) no special taxes.

   Disadvantages: Sole proprietorship has the following disadvantages:

   (i) limited financial resources,
   (ii) restricted managerial ability,

(iii) unlimited liability of the owner,
(iv) uncertainty about existence (due to limited life span),
(v) non-availability of economies of scale (i.e., advantages of large-scale/mass production),
(vi) managerial inefficiency due to incompetence of the owner,
(vii) huge time commitment,
(viii) few fringe benefits and
(ix) limited growth.

KEY Terms	
Single-owner firm	Self-employment
Profits and incentives	Ease of operation
Unlimited liability	Proprietorship business
Tax concessions	Mixed income

Assignments

SHORT ANSWER-TYPE QUESTIONS

1. Define sole ownership.
2. State three characteristics of sole trader.
3. Mention the objectives of sole proprietorship.
4. Give three advantages of sole proprietorship.
5. Mention two limitations of sole trader.
6. In which situation is sole proprietorship suitable?
7. The liability under which personal property of the proprietor is also liable to pay the claims of the business is known as? [ISC 1987]
8. What is single person owning the business and having full control of it called? [ISC 1989]
9. What is the debt owned by a business to its proprietor termed as?

ESSAY-TYPE QUESTIONS

1. What is sole proprietorship? Highlight the characteristics.
2. Describe the objectives of sole proprietorship.
3. How is sole proprietorship business formed?
4. Explain the merits and demerits of sole proprietorship. [ISC 1988]
5. Explain sole proprietorship as a form of business ownership. [ISC 1992]
6. (a) What are the inherent advantages of starting a sole proprietorship business?
   (b) What are the causes of the popularity of sole proprietorship? [ISC 1990]

QUESTION BANK

1. *Define Sole Proprietorship.*

Ans) A sole proprietorship is an unincorporated business owned by a single person and not benefitting from limited liability.

2. *Mention three characteristics of sole proprietorship.*

Ans) (i) Sole proprietorship is owned and controlled by a single person.

(ii) It has no separate legal status.

(iii) The liability of a sole proprietor is unlimited.

3. *What is sole proprietorship? Explain its characteristics.*

Ans) See text.

4. *How is a sole proprietorship formed?*

Ans) See text.

5. *Explain the objectives of sole proprietorship.*

Ans) See text.

6. *Give three merits of sole proprietorship.*

Ans) (i) The sole proprietorship is the easiest type of business to form.

(ii) Another advantage to the proprietorship is one's ability to make decisions quickly. The same person is the owner and the boss. This gives him (her) the authority to make virtually all business decisions. It also gives him an enormous sense of satisfaction when the business prospers.

(iii) As the owner one is in line to reap all of the profits from the sale of the product. Profits occur when his firm's total revenues exceed its total costs. This is his reward for starting his business. As an added bonus, the tax rates for proprietors are lower than they are for corporations. This allows him to keep a larger percentage of his profit than the owners of corporations can.

7. *What is the importance of sole proprietorship from a society's point of view?*

Ans) Sole proprietorship provides gainful self-employment opportunities to persons having limited financial resources. It offers a way of making a living with dignity and self-respect by being one's own boss (the owner-entrepreneur). It also ensures fair distribution of income and wealth. Finally it leads to the development of certain hidden qualities of a person such as confidence, self-respect, initiative, energy and responsibility.

8. *Mention three limitations of sole proprietorship.*

Ans) (i) Proprietorships are not particularly easy to finance. This is because banks are hesitant to extend a loan unless one is willing to put up some collateral — most likely one's home — a guarantee that he will repay the loan. But borrowing money to cover initial expenses such as rent payments for the shop wages for one's employees, and so on is common for proprietors.

(ii) Next, the owner has unlimited liability. This means that if the business fails, the proprietor are personally responsible for all of the firm's debts. If his firm fails, he may have to sell his house, or dig into his personal savings account to pay his creditors.

(iii) Finally, one cannot be an expert in all areas of running a business. That is, as the proprietor, one will make decisions about hiring and firing workers, keeping enough office supplies on hand, monitoring inventories, attending to customers in the shop, making deliveries on schedule, involved in a serious accident that prevents him from doing his job for weeks, months, or longer. What would happen to the business? Because the success of the sole proprietorship rests mainly on the shoulders of the proprietor, proprietorships are considered the least stable type of business organisation.

9. *Explain the merits and demerits of sole proprietorship.*

OR

"The one man control is the best in the world if that man is competent enough to manage every aspect of business." Comment.

OR

Evaluate sole proprietorship as a form of business ownership.

Ans. See text.

10. *For what type of business is a sole proprietorship suitable?*

Ans. See text.

11. *In spite of the growth of his business, small firms (with single ownership) have managed to survive, grow and prosper. Explain why.*

Ans. See text.

12. *Why the liability of a sole trader is unlimited?*

Ans. The liability of a sole trader is unlimited because in the eyes of law, the sole trader and his business are one and thus, indistinguishable from each other. In addition, this business firm has no separate legal entity.

13. *Mark the following statements True or False.*
   (a) Sole trader is a one-man show.
   (b) Sole trader is the oldest form of business organisation.
   (c) There is no profit sharing in sole trading business.
   (d) The liability of a sole trader is limited.
   (e) Grocers stores are usually sole trader.
   (f) The firm of a sole trader has no separate legal status.
   (g) Sole trader business enjoys no flexibility.
   (h) Sole trader has no social utility.

Ans. True: (a), (b), (c), (d), (e), (f)
False: (g), (h).

14. *Fill in the blanks*
   (a) Risk is borne by ________ in sole tradership.
   (b) Liability of a sole trader is ________ .
   (c) There is no question of ________ sharing in sole trading.
   (d) A sole trader has no legal ________ .
   (e) The decision-making process in sole trading is ________ .
   (f) A sole trader can maintain ________ .

Ans. (a) a single individual, (b) unlimited, (c) profit sharing, (d) entity, (e) single and quick, (f) goodwill

6 PARTNERSHIP

SYLLABUS

- *Meaning and definition of partnership, features of partnership firms; types of partners and partnerships.*
- *Registration of partnership firms.*
- *Formation, meaning and contents deed; registration and consequences of non-registration.*

The partnership does not create a separate legal unit; a partnership is just a grouping of individuals.

— Peter Stimpson

LEARNING OUTCOMES

On completion of this chapter, you will be able to understand the following:

6.1 Meaning and Definition of Partnership
6.2 Features of Partnership Firms
6.3 Formation of Partnership Firm — Partnership Deed
6.4 Registration of Partnership
6.5 Types of Partnership
6.6 Types of Partners
6.7 Rights and Obligations of Partners
6.8 Merits of Partnership
6.9 Demerits of Partnership
6.10 Suitability of Partnership
6.11 Comparison between Sole Proprietorship and Partnership

The partnership form of business organisation grew mainly due to the various limitations of sole proprietorship discussed in the previous chapter. In truth, as business expands, one man finds it virtually impossible to arrange the financial resources, manage operations and bear the risks. Therefore, two or more persons join hands and pool their capital and skill to start and run a business effecting. Partnership is thus formed in order to overcome some of the drawbacks of a sole trading business unit.

In the language of Dr. P. Chandra, "A partnership firm is a business owned by one or two person. It may be viewed as an extension of sole proprietorship. The partners bear risk and rip the rewards of the business".

6.1 MEANING AND DEFINITION OF PARTNERSHIP

Partnership is an unincorporated business based on a contractual relationship between two or more people who share risks and profits. Each partner, unless a limited partner is liable for the debts and business actions of the others, to the full extent of their resources (although they are taxed as individuals). A new form of partnership, viz., limited liability partnership (LLP) was introduced in many countries of late (unlike ordinary partnerships, LLPs have to file account for public inspection).

6.1.1 Meaning of Partnership

A partnership firm is a voluntary combination of 2 to 20 persons formed for the purpose of carrying on business with a view to making profit. This type of organisation is a natural outgrowth of the one-person business. The motive, however, may not be entirely financial and partnerships are often formed in order to bring new ability, talent and enterprise into the business.

A CASE EXAMPLE: BASKINS ROBBINS (BR)

Burten Baskins and Irvine Robbins ran their ice-cream business separately for two years. Once they had succeeded independently, they became partners and were able to avoid many of the pitfalls of starting a new business from scratch. They flipped a coin to see which name would come first.

According to the Indian Partnership Act, (1932), "Partnership is the relation between (among) persons who have agreed to share the profits of a business carried on by all or any of them acting for all." The persons who form a partnership are individually known as 'partners' and collectively as a partnership 'firm'. The business is conducted by using the name of the firm. The partners usually share the task of running the business. But a partner need not play an active role. A person who joins a partnership, supplies capital and shares in the profits, but takes no part in the management of the firm is known as *sleeping* (or dormant) *partner*. Partnerships are now a common form of business organisation in such professions as law, accounting, consultancy, real estate surveying and medicine (mainly in case of nursing homes and pathological laboratories).

A partnership is a legal form of business with two or more owners.

6.1.2 Definitions of Partnership

According to Oxford Dictionary of Business , partnership is "an association formed for the purpose of carrying on a business". Other definitions of partnership go as follows:

1. Partnership may be defined as the relationship which exists between persons carrying on business in common with a view to making profit. — L.H. Haney
2. A partnership is a business owned and controlled by two or more persons who are parties to a partnership agreement. — Collins Dictionary of Business
3. A partnership is an association founded on a contract between two or more persons to combine their money, efforts, labour, or skill, or any or all of them, in lawful commerce or business, and to share the profit and bear the loss in certain proportions. — Webster's Comprehensive Dictionary

In India partnership are governed by the Indian Partnership Act, 1932. This legislature regulates the relationship (i) between the partners as well as (ii) between the partners and the part is dealing with the partnership firm.

6.2 FEATURES OF PARTNERSHIP FIRMS

Definitions reveal the notable features of a partnership firm as under:

1. Two to twenty members: At least two persons are required to form a partnership. There is no upper limit to the number of partners. But the Companies Act, 1956 specifies that any partnership consisting of more than 10 persons in the case of banking business and 20 persons in other businesses is unlawful. The same upper limit (20) has been fixed in the UK also. In India, the maximum number of partners has been fixed at 10 in the case of banking and 20 in the case of other businesses. However, partnership firms have been barred by law from going into banking business.
2. Agreement: The relation of partnership arises from agreement which is put into effect through a valid contract between (among) competent persons who are not minors, insanes, insolvents or incompetent in any way to enter into a valid contract. Any partner may enter into contract on behalf of the partnership.
3. Legal backing: A partnership business is valid, if and only if, it is associated with such business activities as production and/or distribution of goods and service, having legal backing.
4. Risk bearing and profit sharing: The risks of doing a partnership business is shared by all its partners. They share all profits (and losses) in an agreed ratio.
5. Dual role: Every partner has a dual role. He is both a proprietor and an agent of the firm. The partnership business may be carried on by all partners or any of them as the legal representative of others. Any partner can act as an agent of others.
6. Unlimited liability: Generally, partners have unlimited liability for any debts incurred by their firm. The liability of the individual partners is unlimited. In countries like the UK partnership contains one or more partners with limited liability so long as there is at least one partner with unlimited liability.
7. Restriction on share transfer. No partner can sell or transfer his share or controlling interest in the firm to either an insider or an outsider without the written consent of all other partners.
8. Shared decision-making and control: The responsibility of managing the firm on a day-to-day basis is entrusted with one or a few partners through agreement among members. But no major policy decision can be taken, without the consent of all the partners.
9. Continuity: As per the Indian Partnership Act (1932), a partnership business comes to an end as soon as any partner retires, dies or becomes insolvent. But the remaining partners can carry on business by using the firm's name, only after settling all dues of the outgoing partner.
10. Registration: Registration of partnership is not mandatory. But if the partners get the firm registered, they can avail themselves of certain benefits, to be discussed later in this chapter.

Generally, a partnership comes into existence with the execution of a partnership dead. If specifics, among other things, the capital contributions, shares, rights, duties, and obligations of the partners. It is to these issue to which we turn now.

6.3 FORMATION OF PARTNERSHIP FIRM — PARTNERSHIP DEED

Partnerships are usually governed by a partnership agreement. A partnership firm owes its origin from the signing of an agreement (either oral or written) between two or more persons who want to carry on some business for making profits. However, all the important terms and conditions of partnership agreement are to be put into writing. The written agreement is also called as the 'Partnership Deed'. It forms the legal basis of partnership.

6.3.1 Partnership Deed (Agreement)

A partnership agreement is made between (among) the partners of a partnership. A partnership agreement contains all the terms and conditions relating to partnership as also various rules and regulations governing the management of the partnership firm. It is a document which establishes a partnership, giving details of the following:

(i) Capital contributed by each partner.
(ii) Whether an individual partner's liability is limited.
(iii) The ratio in which profits will be shared among the partners.
(iv) The amount of salary and/or commission payable to the partners.
(v) Possible (necessary) procedures to be followed, for example, in the event of a partner retiring or a new partner joining.
(vi) The rights and duties of the partners relating to management of the firm.
(vii) Arbitration clause for settlement of disputes among the partners.
(viii) Mode of dissolution and settlement of business or trading accounts.

It also gives information on the following routine matters:

(i) The name and address of the partnership firm and also those of its partners.
(ii) The nature of proposed business or profession.
(iii) The proposed duration of the partnership.
(iv) Interest payable to partners on their capital or to be paid by partners on the amount drawn by them as personal loan.
(v) The exact procedure are to be followed for maintaining accounts, including the mode of operation of bank account(s).

Partnership deed is usual, although not of legal requirement, to draw up a formal deed of partnership between (among) all partners. This ensures an agreement on issues such as voting rights, the distribution of profits, the managerial role of each partner and who has authority to sign contracts.

6.4 REGISTRATION OF PARTNERSHIP

The legal registration of a partnership firm is not compulsory (mandatory). However, if the partners so desire, they can get their firm registered with the Registrar of Firms of the relevant state.

- **Procedure for Registration:** In the case of registration they will have to send to the Registrar a detailed statement in the prescribed form which furnishes the following details:

(a) the name of the firm;

(b) the main place of business (its head office);
(c) the places where the firm has opened branches;
(d) the date of joining of each partner in the firm;
(e) full names and complete addresses of the partners; and
(f) the period of the partnership agreement, specifying the proposed duration of the firm.

The statement has to be duly signed by all the partners. And it should be accompanied by the partnership deed or articles of partnership and the registration fee. If satisfied, the Registrar of Firms will enrol the name of the firm as also the names of partners on the Registrar of Firms and will issue Certificate of Registration. Any subsequent alteration in the constitution of partnership has to be officially communicated to the Registrar in writing within two weeks.

6.4.1 Advantages of Registration

The registration of a partnership firm confers the following advantages:

(i) Partners of a registered firm can take legal actions against the firm to establish their legal rights.
(ii) Partners can file suits against one another for the same reason.
(iii) The firm, in its turn, can take legal action against any of its partners, in the case of necessity.
(iv) The firm can make claim(s) against outsiders (or third parties) in a court of law.
(v) The firm, in its turn, can claim compensatory adjustment in the context of a law suit filed against it.
(vi) Third parties can collect necessary information about the firm and its partners from the Registrar of Firms before negotiating with it regarding any matter affecting them or taking any legal action against it.
(vii) A person desirous of joining as a partner can collect necessary information from the office of the Registrar.

6.4.2 Consequences of Non-Registration

An unregistered partnership firm has to face the following legal consequences:

(i) It cannot make any claims against a third party and take any legal action against him in a court of law.
(ii) It cannot ask for any adjustment for any amount exceeding ₹ 100.
(iii) It cannot take any legal action against any of the partners.
(iv) No partner of an unregistered firm can file any suit to enforce a contract which has already been signed against the firm.
(v) A partner of an unregistered firm cannot take any legal action against other partners.

6.5 TYPES OF PARTNERSHIP

On the basis of the nature of agreement among its partners, we can distinguish among the following three kinds of partnerships:

1. **Partnership at will:** A partnership-at-will is one for which no fixed term has been agreed. Any partnership may end at any time provided that notice of the intention to do so is given to all the other partners in time.

2. **Partnership for a fixed period:** Such a partnership is formed for a certain fixed time period such as 2 to 5 years. It may terminate immediately after the expiry of the specified period, if not renewed for another period.
3. **Particular partnership:** A particular partnership is established for the completion of a specific project or a certain venture such as construction of a multi-storeyed building. It comes to an end automatically as soon as project is completed.

6.5.1 General vs. Limited Partnership

The greatest disadvantage of partnership, like that of the one-person business is the fact that the liability of the partners is unlimited and they are all fully liable for the acts of the other partners. There are, however, some limited partnerships which have to be registered with the Registrar of Companies. In such firms some partners (e.g. sleeping partners) may have their liability limited to some specified sum. However, at least one of the partners must have unlimited liability.

In short, while general partners are fully liable for the debts and other acts of their companies, limited partners are liable only to the extent of their investment. The latter are not allowed to participate in management of the firm. A special partner can withdraw from the partnership any time he likes without facing any hindrance. And death, insolvency or incapacity of a special partner does not lead to the end of a partnership firm.

BUSINESS FOCUS: RESTRICTIONS ON AND THE USES OF LIMITED PARTNERSHIPS

In a limited partnership agreement several conditions are to be met:

(i) **Control:** A limited partner has no control over the day-to-day operations of the organisation since he (she) cannot take part in management.

(ii) **Liabilities:** There must be at least two partners and one or more of these general partners manage the business and are liable for both debts and financial responsibilities of the firm.

(iii) **Protection against liability:** If a limited partner becomes involved in the operation of the partnership, he (she) stands to lose protection against liability.

(iv) **Registration:** In addition, a limited partnership agreement certificate, or registration has to be filed. Such an agreement includes the names of general and limited partners, the nature of the business and the terms of the limited partnership or the date of dissolution.

(v) **Specific duration:** Since limited partnerships are often used to raise capital, there is a set term of duration for the agreement.

The most frequent use of the limited partnership agreement has been as an investment, removing the limited partner from financial liability but raising capital through his (her) investments or contributions.

Limited partnerships exist in the UK on a large scale. These are common in real estate investments and, more recently, in entertainment ventures.

6.5.2 Limited Liability Partnership (LLP)

A limited liability partnership (LLP) is a firm which consisting of both general and limited partners and some categories of business partnership can claim limited liability in a similar fashion to that enjoyed by limited companies. This type of business organisation is intended to combine the flexibility of a traditional partnership with the corporate notion of limited liability. This comparatively new form of organisation originated in India after the passing of the Limited Liability Partnership Act (2008).

LLP also combines the traditional partnership with unlimited personal liability, and governance structure of the limited liability joint stock company, based on The Companies Act (1956).

Through this refined and modified form of business, it becomes possible to ensure that professional expertise and entrepreneurial zeal, ability and initiative to join hands and carry on business operate in an efficient and flexible manner.

The notable features of an LLP are the following :

1. *Separate legal status:* An LLP is a body corporate and a legal entity separate from its partners (owners). Being an artificial person it exists only under the law.
2. *Perpetual existence.:* An LLP has an infinite life. Thus, the existence of the LLP is not threatened even if a partner dies or quits.
3. *Number of partners:* An LLP must have at least two partners. But there is no upper limit to the number of partners it can have. Suppose firm *X* has only two partners (A and B). If B quits and A carries on the business for more than six months, then A will be personally liable for the obligations of the LLP incurred during this transitional period (i.e. before any new partner is taken.)
4. *Designated partners:* Every LLP must have at least two individuals as designated partners. One of them has to be a resident of India. But in case of an LLP in which all the partners are body corporates, there is a restrictive clause: at least two individuals who are nominees of other body corporates are under the legal obligation to act as designated partners.
5. *Limited liability:* A partner is not personally liable, directly or indirectly, for any of the debts or other liabilities of the LLP or any other partner for the latter's fraudulent act.
6. *Mandatory electronic identification number for designated partners:* In India, recently Designated Partner Identification Number (DPIN) has been made mandatory. Such number is allotted to both existing and future partners. An individual is required to have a single number DPIN even if he has several such partnerships. The issue of such number after verification of the credentials of Designated Partners is essentially a precautionary measure. It serves a two-fold purpose. First, it helps the government to keep track of those who operate (manage) the LLPs. It also helps to prevent a defaulting Designated Partner from joining another LLP, by hiding his past record (such as any wrong or unlawful act).
7. *Irrelevance of the Indian Partnership Act (1932):* The provisions of the Indian Partnership Act, (1932) do not apply to an LLP. The reason is that two main characteristics of the corporate form of business, viz. separate legal status and perpetual succession are conspicuous by their absence in partnerships.
8. *Selective application of the Companies Act:* The provisions of the Companies Act relating to National Company Law Tribunal, DPIN and Registrar of Companies are all applicable to LLPs. In addition, the Central Government has been empowered to notify the provisions of the Companies Act which are applicable to any LLP, with or without modification.

6.6 TYPES OF PARTNERS

Seven different types of partners found in various diverse partnership firms, are the following:

1. **Active (working) partner:** Any person who has contributed to the business capital of a partnership and who participates in its management is an active partner. He gives sufficient working time to his partnership firm. All partners are deemed to be active partners unless otherwise agreed. Each such partner has to serve public notice of his retirement from the firm in order to make himself free from liability for any act of the firm in the post-retirement period.

2. **Sleeping (dormant) partner:** A person who has invested capital in a partnership but takes no part in its commercial activities is called a sleeping partner. He (she) has all the legal benefits and obligations of ownership and shares the profits of the partnership in accordance with the provisions laid down in the partnership agreement. He is also called a dormant partner. However, all dormant partners are liable to the third parties for all debts of their firm.
3. **Silent partner:** A silent partner is one who is inactive, though he may be known to be a partner. A person who invests money in a company but takes no active part in the management of the business is called a silent partner. Although silent partners are inactive in the operation of the business, they have legal obligations and benefits of ownership, and are, therefore, fully liable for any debts. In fact, the terms silent partner and sleeping partner are often used synonymously.
4. **Secret partner:** A secret partner is one who is a true partner in all respects, but he may like to keep this fact a secret. His name is not made publicly known. But he has unlimited liability.
5. **Nominal partner:** Nominal partners allow their name to be used for the benefit of the partnership, usually for a reward but not for a share of the profits. They are not legal partners.
6. **Partner by holding out or estoppel:** A person may represent him to the outside world orally (verbally) or through written communication that he is the partner of the firm in which case he would be liable to any outsider who granted credit to the firm on good faith (on the basis of such representation). But he is not a partner in the true sense of the term. He is treated as a partner only by the outside world.
7. **Partner-in-profit only:** A partner who has entered into an agreement with other partners that he will be entitled to a certain share of profits, without being liable for the losses, is known as 'partner in profits only'. Such a partner has no say in the management of the partnership firm. But he is liable to outsiders for any debt of the firm or any of its partners.

In Table 6.1 we present a summary view of seven different types of partners, discussed above.

TABLE 6.1: A Comparison of Seven Different Types of Partners

Nomenclature	Does he make contribution to capital?	Does he share in profits/losses?	Does he participate in management?	What is his liability for any debtor dues of the company?
1. Active Partner	Yes	Yes	Yes	Unlimited
2. Sleeping (Dormant) Partner	Yes	Yes	No	Unlimited
3. Silent Partner	Yes	Yes	No	Unlimited
4. Secret Partner	Yes	Yes	No	Unlimited
5. Nominal Partner	No	No	No	Unlimited
6. Partner by Estoppel or Holding out	No	No	No	Unlimited
7. Partner in profit only	Yes	Only profits	No	Unlimited

Minor Partner

A minor is a person who is less than 18 years old and thus, is not automatically entitled to enter into a contract. So he cannot become a partner in a firm directly but can enjoy the benefits of partnership with the consent of all other partners. The liability of the minor is limited to his share of profit (if any) in the firm. As soon as he becomes an adult after completing 18 years of age, a minor enjoys the option of becoming a full (legal) partner in the same firm. In case he is not interested in becoming a partner, he has to serve a public notice on this point within six months.

6.7 RIGHTS AND OBLIGATIONS OF PARTNERS

- RIGHTS

1. Every partner has a legal right to take part in the day-today functioning and management of the firm's business.
2. Every partners has a legal right to be consulted an expressive opinion on any matter which affect him.
3. Any partner has a legal right to gain assess to, inspect a copy any books of account, official documents and records of the firm.
4. Every partner has a legal right to get an equal share in profits of the firm, unless their are exceptional clauses in the partnership agreement.
5. Every partner has a legal right to received interest on any loan mid by him (her) to the firm

- DUTIES

1. Every partner must act honestly and diligently to discharge his duties so as to bring maximum benefit to all partners.
2. Every partner has to act within the scope of airworthy bestowed upon him.
3. Every partner has to share the losses of the firm equal with other partners unless the partnership agreement allows for any deviation from the norm.
4. Every partner has to compensate the firm fully for any loss incurred due to his negligence in connection with the normal conduct of business.
5. The liability of a partner for the debt of a firm to outsiders is unlimited.

6.8 MERITS OF PARTNERSHIP

It is often very easy to own and manage a business with one or more partners. One partner may be skilled at inventory control and accounting, while the other in selling and servicing. A partner can also provide additional money, support and expertise as well as cover (safeguard) for his other partner, when the latter is sick or on leave.

The main advantages of partnerships are the following:

1. **Ease of starting and ending the business:** No legal formalities are to be completed in starting a partnership business. An oral and written agreement is just enough to start a partnership. Even legal registration of the firm is not a must. But even if a firm wants to get itself registered, the procedure is fairly simple. The closure of a firm is equally easy, as per agreement between (among) the partners.

2. **More financial resources:** When two or more people pool their money and credit, it is easy to pay wages, rent, electricity bill and to cover other (incidental) expenses. A limited partnership is formed mainly to raise funds.
3. **Shared management and pooled (complimentary) skills and knowledge:** It is fairly easy to manage the day-to-day activities of a business if partners are carefully chosen. Partners give each other more time for business and provide different skills and ideas. Sometimes husband-and-wife teams manage hotels and restaurants, service shops and other businesses.
4. **Longer survival:** Partnerships last much longer than sole proprietorships. Since a business person is watched by his (her) partner, he (she) because more disciplined.
5. **No special taxes:** As with the sole proprietorship, all profits of partnerships are taxed as the personal income of the owners. They pay normal income tax based on their own income. They are not required to pay corporate tax.
6. **Improved decision-making:** 'Two brains are always better than one'. This proverb contains an element of truth at least in case of a partnership firm. All important decisions are taken by the collective wisdom of the partners.
7. **Sharing of risk:** The risks of doing business are shared by all partners. So each partner is exposed to less risk than in the case with a sole proprietor.
8. **Specialisation:** It is a flexible organisation which allows a greater degree of specialisation than the one-person business. Partners usually specialise in one or more aspects of the business. One may be responsible for buying, one for selling, one for production, and so on.
9. **Greater size.** Since it has greater access to capital, it can achieve greater size than the sole proprietor.
10. **Secrecy:** It is possible in a partnership to maintain secrecy of information and accounts since no public disclosure of its operational aspects is needed.
11. **Flexibility:** A partnership firm can go into any kind of business. In addition, there is no restriction on the pattern of management of the firm. Its capital structure, profit-sharing ratio and pricing policy can be changed easily and quickly, as and when required.
12. **Good effect of unlimited liability:** Unlike an incorporated company, partners are liable for the debts of the firm. However, their unlimited liability makes them extra cautious and stops them from taking drastic measures and wrong decisions so that no one suffers due to faults of others.

6.9 DEMERITS OF PARTNERSHIP

Partnerships have the following disadvantages:

1. **Unlimited liability:** Each general partner is liable for the debts of the firm, no matter who is responsible for incurring it. For instance, Mr. X is liable for his partners' mistakes as well as his own. Like sole proprietors, general partners can lose their homes, cars, and everything else they own if the business loses a law suit or goes bankrupt.
2. **Conflicts arising from profit sharing:** Sharing risk means sharing profits and that can lead to conflicts. There is a standard rule, criterion or norm for dividing profits in a partnership

and they are not always divided evenly. For example, if one partner puts in only money (called sleeping partner) and the other works for longer hours (called active partner), each may feel justified in asking for a bigger share of the profits.

3. **Disagreements among partners:** A part from division of profits, disagreements may arise over various other issues such as final authority over employees, hiring and firing employees, working hours, and purchase of expensive equipment for the firm. The solution is all terms of the partnership should be spelled out in writing to protect all parties and minimise misunderstanding.
4. **Difficulty of termination:** Since a person has committed himself to a partnership, it is difficult to get out of it. He can just quit. However, questions about who gets what and what happens next are difficult to resolve when the partnership ends.
5. **Limited resources:** Due to limited number of partners a partnership may not be able to raise as much capital as a corporate form of business. This sets a limit to its growth through expansion of its scale (size) of operation.
6. **Disorder:** Since partners differ in their skill, efficiency and, ability to manage their firm, their joint efforts may sometimes create functional disorder or even a complete mess of the whole business. This might also be a source of conflict among the partners.
7. **Delay in decision-making:** Since the consent of all the partners is required for taking all critical policy decisions, delays in decision-making is inevitable in some situations.
8. **Pitfall of agency relationship:** Because of agency relationship among the partners, the acts of a partner are binding on all other partners and thus on the firm itself. So all partners have to suffer or pay penalty for the dishonesty or incompetence of just one partner.
9. **Uncertain future:** The future of a partnership is uncertain. It may suddenly come to an end due to the death, bankruptcy or even insanity of any of the partners.
10. **Lack of public confidence:** Partnership firms do not generate much public confidence for at least two reasons. Firstly, as there is no legal provision as far their formation and dissolution are concerned. Secondly, no public disclosure of their profit and loss accounts or asset structure is made since this is not needed.
11. **Non-transferability of interest:** No partner can transfer his interest in the firm to outsiders without the unanimous consent of all other partners. This restricted clause discourages people from putting their money in partnership firms. This may create shortage of investible funds.

Thus, we see that a partnership firm can benefit from the varied experience and expertise of the partner and draw on their combined capital resources. However, its advantages and disadvantages are more or less similar or at least comparable to that of a sole proprietorship firm. The advantages and disadvantages of partnership are listed in Table 6.2, (page 93).

6.10 SUITABILITY OF PARTNERSHIP

A partnership firm is most suitable in the following situations (cases):

(i) The scale of business is small or medium.

(ii) Personal touch with the customers (clients) is absolutely essential, as in the case of most services like legal, financial, consulting, etc. It is thus convenient for professional people such as doctors, lawyers, architects, business consultant and accountants to form partnership.

(iii) It is most suitable where there is need to combine capital of one person and technical competence of another person.

TABLE 6.2: Advantages and Disadvantages of Partnership

Advantages	Disadvantages
1. Ease of starting and ending the business	1. Unlimited liability (and its bad effects)
2. More financial resources in the case of then sole traders	2. Conflicts arising from profit sharing
3. Shared management and pooled skills and knowledge	3. Disagreements among partners
4. Longer survival	4. Difficulty of termination
5. No special taxes	5. Limited resources than in the case of the stock companies
6. Improved decision-making due to collective wisdom	6. Functional disorder or complete mess
7. Risk sharing	7. Delay in decision-making
8. Specialisation and improved efficiency	8. Pitfall of agency relationship
9. Greater size	9. Uncertain future
10. Secrecy	10. Lack of public confidence
11. Flexibility	11. Non-transferability of interest and shortage of capital
12. Good effect of unlimited liability	12. Lack of stability

6.11 COMPARISON BETWEEN SOLE PROPRIETORSHIP AND PARTNERSHIP

In Table 6.3 we make a comparison between sole proprietorship and partnership.

TABLE 6.3: Difference between Partnership and Sole Proprietorship

Basis of Comparison	Sole Proprietorship	Partnership
1. Specific Act	In India, there is no separate Act for this type of business organisation	A partnership firm is governed (i.e., controlled and regulated) by Indian Partnership Act, 1932
2. Number of members	There is only one owner of the business, called the sole proprietor	In partnership, the minimum number of members is 2 and the maximum 20 in the case of non-banking businesses and 10 in the case of banking business
3. Agreement	The question of signing on agreement does not arise	A partnership business can be set up only after signing an agreement (i.e. partnership deed)
4. Maintain secrecy	Business (trade) secrecy is maintained	Business affairs are made known to every partner

Contd.

5. Financial-cum-technical base	It has weak financial-cum-technical base. The sole trader has limited ability to provide capital and necessary skills.	It has a strong foundation due to adequate capital and specialised knowledge and skills of different partners
6. Chance of survival	Its chances of survival are weak. It suddenly comes to a halt with the death of the owner	Its chances of survival are quite strong since it may continue to exist and carry on business even after the death of a partner
7. Time taken for decisions-making	Decision-making does not take much time as the proprietor makes his own independent judgment	Decision-making may be delayed as all the patners have to reach a consensus on crucial policy matters and key issues.
8. Sharing of profit	The enter profit goes to the sole proprietor	Profit is shared between (among) two or more partners as per contract

Conclusion

The survival of a partnership depends upon the continued harmonious relationship between (among) a number of people in situations which often give much scope for disagreement. Thus, where trading risks are quite high, the partnership is not a very stable form of business organisation.

Key Points

1. **Partnership.** Partnership is voluntary combination of 2 to 20 persons formed for the purpose of carrying on business with a view to making profit. It is a business owned and controlled by two or more persons who subscribe capital and share decision-taking as specified by a partnership agreement. In a partnership, two or more individuals (or partners) share equally in profits and losses. It is a form of business organisation or company in which partners are fully responsible for the partnership's liabilities. The persons who agree to join a partnership business are individually called 'partners' and collectively known as a 'firm'. Partnerships are particularly prevalent in professional services such as accounting, surveying, nursing home and legal advice.
2. **Features.** The characteristics of a partnership are the following:
   (i) two or more persons as partners and common ownership,
   (ii) agreement to carry on some gainful business activity,
   (iii) profit and loss sharing among partners,
   (iv) rights to participate in managing the business,
   (v) unlimited liability and
   (vi) restriction on transfer of share or ownership in the firm.
3. **Partnership deed:** It is a written agreement between (among) the partners of a firm, containing several clauses regarding names and addresses of partners, nature of business, capital stock and structure, profit-sharing ratio, and so on.

4. **Registration:** It is not necessary to get a partnership firm registered. But registration offers certain distinct advantages.
5. **General partnership:** In a general partnership, owners (partners) have unlimited liability and are active in managing the company.
6. **Limited partnership:** In a limited partnership, one or more persons are not involved in the management of the business and are not personally liable for the partnership's obligations. The extent to which the limited partner is liable is thus 'limited' to his (her) capital investment in the partnership. Limited partners are owners (partners) who have limited liability and are not active in the company.
7. **Partnership at will:** This type of partnership exists when partners carry on business on their own volition. It can be ended by any partner by serving notice of his intention to do so.
8. **Particular partnership:** This type of partnership is formed for a short period in order to undertake a particular project or venture. It comes to an end as soon as the project or venture is completed.
9. **Types of partners:** Six types of partners found in India are the following:
   (i) active partners,
   (ii) sleeping (dormant) partners,
   (iii) silent partners,
   (iv) partner in profits only,
   (v) nominal partner, and
   (vi) partner by holding out.
10. **Advantages of partnership**
   (i) ease of formation or starting a partnership firm as a form of business,
   (ii) more financial resources,
   (iii) shared management and pulled knowledge,
   (iv) rational decisions,
   (v) risk sharing,
   (vi) operational efficiency and flexibility,
   (vii) greater motivation to put the best possible effort due to limited liability of partners,
   (viii) maintenance of business secrecy,
   (ix) ease of ending partnership arrangement and
   (x) long-term survival.
11. **Disadvantages of partnership**
   (i) paucity of finance compared with that of a joint stock company,
   (ii) unlimited liability of each partner,
   (iii) conflict between (among) partners due to disagreements,
   (iv) slow and delayed decision-making,
   (v) division of profits,
   (vi) non-transferability of ownership,
   (vii) lack of public confidence,
   (viii) uncertainty about the future and
   (ix) difficulty of termination in some situations.

KEY Terms

Deed of partnership	Partnership at will
Limited partnership	Secret partner
Nominal partner	Dormant partner
Silent partner	Partner by holding out
Particular partnership	Minor as a partner

Assignments

SHORT ANSWER-TYPE QUESTIONS

1. Define partnership.
2. Mention any three features of partnership.
3. What is partnership deed?
4. What is limited partnership?
5. Distinguish between particular partnership and partnership as well.
6. Who is a nominal partner in a partnership?
7. What is that business unit called which, for purposes of banking business, can have a maximum of ten members as owners? **[ISC 1988]**
8. Who meets that part of a 'Firm's' liabilities which is in excess of its total assets? **[ISC 1988]**
9. Name the kind of partner who contributes capital but does not take part in the management of the firm. **[ISC 1988]**

Ans: Silent or sleeping partner.

10. Name the partnership which is formed for a particular purpose or for a fixed period and is dissolved on accomplishment of that purpose or on expiry of the fixed period. **[ISC 1989]**
11. Name the liability under which the private assets minus the private liabilities of a partner are liable to pay the liabilities of a firm. **[ISC 1990]**
12. Name the kind of partner who does not possess any contractual capacity even though he is made a partner in the partnership. **[ISC 1991]**
13. Mention the kind of partnership which is formed to carry on business for an unmentioned period. **[ISC 1991]**
14. Name the partner who is liable to persons who enter into contract with the firm in the belief that he is a partner while actually he is not a partner. **[ISC 1992]**
15. What is a written agreement signed by all the partners spelling out the terms and conditions agreed upon for setting up and conducting the business called? **[ISC 1992]**

Ans: Deed of partnership.

16. What is meant by limited liability partnership (LLP)?

Ans. Under limited liability partnership, businesses can combine the flexibility of a partnership with the protection of limited liability. Unlike ordinary partnerships, limited liability partnerships have to file accounts for public inspection.

ESSAY-TYPE QUESTIONS

1. What is partnership? Explain its features.
2. How is a partnership formed? What are the main contents of partnership deed?
3. Explain the procedure for registration of partnership firms. Also mention the consequences of non-registration.
4. Give a brief description of various types of partners in a partnership firm.
5. Highlight the merits and demerits of partnership firm of organisation.
6. Distinguish between sole proprietorship and partnership. [ISC 1988]
7. How can a partnership firm be dissolved? [ISC 1988]
8. (a) What is a Partnership Deed? What items does it usually contain? Also explain its importance.
   (b) The Indian Partnership Act 1932 has effectively ensured the registration of a firm without making it compulsory. Explain. [ISC 1991]
9. (a) Define 'Partnership' and discuss its features.
   (b) Distinguish between Partnership and Sole Tradership. [ISC 1991]
10. (a) Discuss three advantages and three disadvantages of Partnership firms.
    (b) Explain how sole tradership differs from partnership. [ISC 1992]

QUESTION BANK

1. *Define partnership.*

Ans. A partnership is an association of two or more persons for the operation of a business under existing commercial laws. Partners are generally liable for the debts of their company, unless it is a limited liability partnership where the liability is limited to the extent of the investment.

2. *What is deed of partnership?*

Ans. A deed of partnership is not a legal document yet it is usual to draw a formal deed of partnership between (among) all partners. This provides agreements on issues such as voting rights, the distribution of profits, the managerial role of each partner and who has authority to sign contracts.

3. *Suggest a simple definition of partnership.*

Ans. A partnership is a business activity formed by two or more people to carry on a business together with shared capital investment, usually shared responsibilities and, of course, shared profits.

4. *Name the partnership in which the liability of each partner is limited to the extent of investment.*

Ans. Limited Liability partnership.

5. *Mention any three features of Partnership.*

Ans. The three features of partnership are:

(i) A partnership consists of two or more persons.

(ii) The partners always sign a written or oral agreement.

(iii) A partnership is formed to carry on some business under commercial law. Profit is shared among the partners.

6. *What is partnership? Highlight its essential characteristics.*

Ans. According to Prof. Haney, "partnership is the relation between persons competent to make contract, who agree to carry on a lawful business in common with a view to private gain". Now see text.

7. *What is meant by limited liability?*

Ans. The term limited liability refers to the restriction of an owner's loss in a business to the amount of capital he has contributed (invested) in it. If a company goes into liquidation, the owners as equity shareholders can lose, at most only the share value, although director shareholders may be subject to other liabilities such as personal guarantees for bank borrowings.

8. *How is a partnership formed?*

Ans. See text.

9. *Name the document which furnishes detailed information about the terms and conditions of a partnership.*

Ans. Partnership deed.

10. *Is registration of a partnership firm compulsory?*

Ans. No.

11. *Mention any two limitations from which an unregistered partnership firm suffers.*

Ans. See text.

12. *Explain the main contents of a partnership deed.*

Ans. See text.

13. *What is the exact procedure for registration of partnership firms? Mention the consequences of non-registration?*

Ans. See text.

14. *What is Partnership at will?*

15. *What is particular Partnership?*

16. *What is limited liability partnership?*

Ans. See text.

17. *Explain different kinds of partnership.*

18. *What are the two types of partnership?*

Ans. The two types of partnership — the general partnership and the limited partnership. In a general partnership, the partners are involved in running the firm and therefore, share in the day-to-day decision-making. In a limited partnership, some of the partners run the firm while others simply invest money in it. If you were considering a partnership for your new-firm,

Coffee 4 All, a necessary first step would be to draw up a partnership contract between you and your partners. Expert legal advice is needed to specify the responsibilities of each partner, to determine how the firm's profits will be distributed, and to state how you will dissolve the firm if things just don't work out or go wrong.

19. *Who is a dormant partner?*
20. *Who is a secret partner?*
21. *What is meant by nominal partner?*
22. *What is a partner by estoppel?*
23. *Who is a partner by holding out?*
24. *Explain minor as a partner.*
25. *Explain the merits and demerits of partnership.*

Ans **Merits:** Partnerships are fairly easy to organise. Your partnership contract should also be drawn up before the business opens. It is also easier to get the start-up funding for a partnership than it is for a proprietorship. For example, you could take on one or more silent partners to supply the necessary funds. You are also more creditworthy in the eyes of the bank because the collateral that you and your partners can bring to the table is greater than that of the proprietor.

Secondly, decision-making is a more expert process in a partnership than that in a sole proprietorship. Each of your partners will, most likely, bring a special talent or skill to the firm. If a company is organised as a partnership, different partners may be skilled in customer service, accounting and payroll, maintaining inventories and supplies, and so on. And if each partner performs as you expect, all can achieve the sense of pride and accomplishment that is derived from owning a successful business.

Finally, you realise that the fruits of your labour — the firm's profits — belong to you and to your partners. Your share of the profits, and that of your partners, was carefully spelled out in the partnership contract. And your tax rates, like those of the proprietor, are lower than those faced by corporations.

Demerits: One disadvantage of partnership is that partners in a general partnership have unlimited liability for business losses. In this respect, you have the same disadvantage as the proprietor. But in a partnership you are also responsible for the business debts of your partners. In a limited partnership, your silent partners have limited liability. That is, the most they can lose in this business venture is the amount they originally contributed to it. Creditors cannot come knocking at their doors for the debts that you have created.

Another disadvantage of a partnership is that disagreements among partners can reduce the stability of their firm. Ideally, the partnership contract should specify each partner's role in the firm. But this piece of paper cannot account for your partner's personality or other character traits. Suppose one of your partners decides that is voice is more important than yours in the decision-making process, or one or more partners are slacking off? These questions concern you as you consider the best structure for your firm. Now see text for more details.

26. *Comment on partnership as a form of business organisation.*
27. *Comment on the disadvantages of partnership over sole proprietorship.*

OR

Distinguish between partnership and sole trader.

28. *Name the following:*
    (a) The partnership which is formed for a specific purpose or for a certain period.
    (b) The partnership in which the liability of every partner is unlimited.
    (c) The document which contains terms and conditions of partnership.
    (d) The partner who contributes capital but does not take part in the management of the firm.
    (e) The partner who is not a partner but becomes liable for the debts of the firm.

Ans (a) Particular partnership
(b) General partnership
(c) Partnership deed
(d) Silent partner
(e) Nominal partner

29. *Mark the following statements True/False.*
    (a) A LLP is a legal entity.
    (b) Liability of every partner in LLP is limited.
    (c) A LLP must always be registered.
    (d) The number of partners in a LLP cannot exceed twenty.
    (e) A LLP is less stable than a general partnership.
    (f) LLP is not allowed in India.
    (g) There is no limit on the number of partners in LLP.
    (h) In LLP the liability of a partner is limited.

Ans True: (a), (b), (c), (g)
False: (d), (e), (f), (h).

7 JOINT STOCK COMPANY

SYLLABUS

- *Joint Stock Company, features, merits, demerits and objectives.*

The modern corporation is the most representative and powerful form of business today. —J.K. Galbraith

LEARNING OUTCOMES

On completion of this chapter, you will be able to understand the following:

7.1 Meaning and Definition of a Company
7.2 Features of a Company
7.3 Distinction between Company and Partnership
7.4 Objectives of Joint Stock Company
7.5 Merits of a Company
7.6 Demerits of a Company
7.7 Merits and Demerits of Joint Stock Company
7.8 Causes of Popularity of a Company

One fear of owning one's own business or having a partner is the fear of losing everything the proprietor owns if someone sues the business or it makes a huge financial loss. This arises due to unlimited liability of such form of business. Many business people try to avoid this and various other disadvantages of sole proprietorships and partnerships by forming joint stock companies corporations.

The most important form of business organisation in India today is the joint stock company or the corporation. Basically, it is an association of people who contribute towards a joint stock of capital for the purpose of carrying on business with a view to making profit.

Many corporations is Tata Motors Ltd., Reliance Industries Ltd. and Hindalco Ltd. etc., are examples of corporate enterprises. A corporation is a legal entity with authority to act and have liability separate from its owners — its shareholders. Shareholders are not liable for the debts or other problems of the corporation beyond the money they invest in it by buying ownership shares, or stock, in the company. Corporate owners are not worried about losing their houses, cars, or other types of properties because of some problem faced by the business. This limited liability is perhaps the most important thing to be said in the favour of a corporation. A corporation not only limits the liability of its owners but often enables many people to share in the ownership (and profits) of a business without working there or having any other commitments to it. Corporations can choose whether to offer ownership to outside investors or remain closely held.

7.1 MEANING AND DEFINITION OF A COMPANY

7.1.1 Meaning of a Joint Stock Company

1. A joint stock company is a voluntary association of individuals for profits, having a capital divided into transferable shares, the ownership of which is the condition of membership.
   L.H. Haney
2. A company may be defined as a legal person created to engage in business, capable of owning productive assets, of entering into contracts, and of employing labour in the same way as an individual. **G.S. Stanlake**
3. A joint stock company is a form of company in which a number of people contribute funds to finance a firm in return for shares in the company. *Collins Dictionary of Business*

7.1.2 Definition of Joint Stock Company

The word 'joint stock' means capital or stock that is held jointly. A corporation or a joint stock company is an organisation in which a number of people provide financing in return for shares of stock. Anyone can become a part owner of a corporation by buying shares of the company's stock. A joint stock company is an incorporated or a registered association of persons who provide capital by purchasing shares. The capital of a company is divided into shares (or stock) of fixed amount and every person who purchases shares of the company becomes one of the owners. Thus, the shareholders are the real owners of the company, collectively though. The shares are transferable and the life of the company is not affected by the entry of new owners and exit of old owners. In short, a joint-stock company is one whose capital is divided into shares (usually transferable), some of which are held by each of the members.

7.2 FEATURES OF A COMPANY

The characteristic features of a joint stock company are the following:

1. **An artificial person:** A company is called 'an artificial person', or a 'legal person' because it is created by law. After registration, the company gets a separate legal status. This status is not related to that of its shareholders.
2. **Separate legal identity:** Once a joint stock company is formed, then it becomes a separate legal entity apart from its shareholders. It is able to enter into contracts with suppliers and customers. It can acquire and own property in its own name, enter into contracts, borrow and lend money and conduct lawful business. It can sue others and can be sued by others.
3. **Perpetual existence:** A joint stock company has no fixed life. It continues to exist in spite of exit of existing shareholders, entry of new shareholders, death, insanity or bankruptcy of its shareholders.

4. **Limited liability:** The development of joint-stock companies was given a considerable boost by the introduction of the principle of limited liability which limits the maximum loss which has a shareholder is liable for in the event of company failure. As G.S. Stanlake has put it, "The company itself is fully liable for its debts in the same way as any other person, but the liability of the shareholders is limited to the amount they have agreed to subscribe to the capital of the company. When they have fully paid for their shares they cannot be collectively called upon to meet any debts the company may incur." That is why, there is always a 'limited' word is affixed the end of a company's name, viz., Tata Motors Ltd., SAIL Ltd., etc.
5. **Formation:** A joint stock company may be formed as a **private limited** company or a **public limited** company. A private limited company can be formed with at least two (shareholder) members and a public company with at least seven (shareholder) members. A company has to get registered under the Companies Act, (1956) after submitting necessary documents to the Registrar of Companies.
6. **Transferability of shares:** Another very important feature of the joint stock company is the transferability of shares. In order to perform its function a company must have permanent source of capital. This is ensured by making shares transferable. The company can make use of the capital subscribed by the original shareholders. If these shareholders wish, they may sell their shares at any time either to other members or in the open (share) market, without affecting existence the company in any way.
7. **Separation of ownership from management:** The joint stock company enables those who cannot or do not want to take an active part in management to contribute towards business (industrial) activity by providing capital. There are peoplc who have technical and commercial expertise but do not possess the necessary financial resources to make effective use of their skills. Thus, joint stock company makes it possible for the resources owned by one group to be utilised by another group. This is known as *divorce between ownership and management*. In short, corporations are able to raise money from numerous owners (shareholders) without getting them involved in management. Figure 7.1 shows how the owners are separate from the managers and employees. The owners set out the objectives of the company and elect a board of directors. The board hire the managerial staff was in turn appoints other employees of the corporation, sets the policy guidelines and oversee the major policy issues. Thus, the owners have some say in who runs the corporation but do not control the day-to-day operations of the corporation.

Although shareholders are the owners of a joint stock company, very often it is the company's management which, in fact, controls its affairs.

8. **Separate property:** A company, being an artificial or a legal person, can own, use and dispose of property in its own name. They are separate from shareholders' properties.

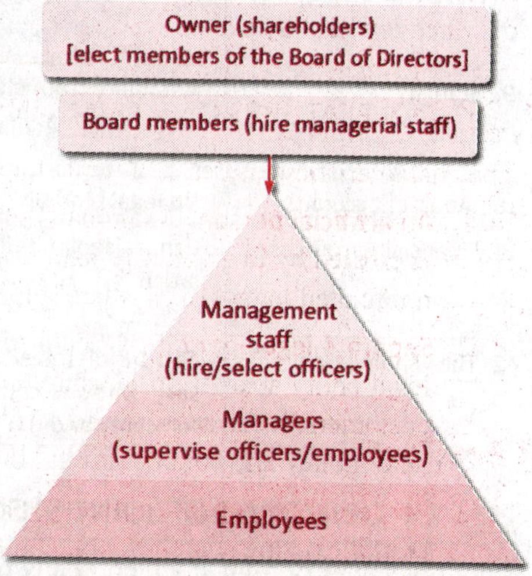

FIGURE 7.1: Owners and Managers of a Corporation

9. **Common seal:** All the activities of the company are conducted by the directors by using its common seal which is virtually its official signature. The common seal is affixed on every important document as a proof of the company's authenticity and approval.

10. **Risk-bearing:** There is diversification of risk in the case of a company. So the risk of any individual owner (shareholder) is very little. In the case of loss the liability of any shareholder is limited to the extent of the to the extent of his contribution share capital.

7.3 DISTINCTION BETWEEN COMPANY AND PARTNERSHIP

The main points of difference between *company* and *partnership* are discussed below.

Basis of Comparison	Partnership Firm	Joint Stock Company
1. Regulatory Act (legal provision)	Indian Partnership Act, 1932	Indian Companies Act, 1956
2. Number of members	Minimum 2, maximum 20 in ordinary business and 10 in banking (though not found in reality in the case of banks)	*Private Ltd. Company* (i) Minimum 2 and maximum 50 *Public Ltd. Company* (ii) Minimum 7 and maximum not specified
3. Legal status	No separate legal status from that of its partners	Separate legal status as an artificial person from that of its members
4. Liability	Unlimited	Limited
5. Management	Shared among partners	In the hands of members of the Board of Directors only
6. Transferability of shares (controlling interest)	Possible only with the full consent of all the partners	Freely transferable in the case of a Public Ltd. Company
7. Method of formation	There is no need to complete any legal formalities, and registration is optional	Only after completion of all legal formalities, incorporation is legally binding
8. Regulation(s) regarding functioning	There is no statutory regulation regarding day-to-day operations	There is need to comply with a number of statutory requirements and submit various types of returns to the Registrar of Companies
9. Stability	Instability from short life due to retirement, death or insanity of even a single partner	Long-term stability due to perpetual existence
10. Audit of accounts	No legal binding	Legally binding
11. Financial Resources	Can raise limited resources, but not much	Can raise huge financial resources by making public issue and also by borrowing on the strength of balance sheet
12. The winding-up process	Can be dissolved as and when necessary without completion of any legal formality and the process is simple	Can be wound up only as per the provisions of the Companies Act and the process is complex and time consuming

7.4 OBJECTIVES OF JOINT STOCK COMPANY

Major objectives of joint stock company or the corporate form of organisations are the following:

1. **Rapid industrialisation:** Rapid industrialisation is essential to fulfil the declared objectives

of India's Five year plans. This requires, among other things, building of an integrated infrastructure which ensures an adequate supply of power, coal, oil, steel, cement, etc. These input supplying industries are highly capital-intensive in nature and requires huge initial investment and involve high risk. Only corporate organisations can raise such vast resources which is a prerequisite for achieving rapid industrialisation.

2. **Production on a large scale:** Economic growth is not possible without a rise in productivity of resources and production of quality goods. This requires development, use and diffusion of modern sophisticated technology. Only the joint stock form of company or business organisation is capable of undertaking mass production of goods and services and distribution of the same over a wide area. Large scale operations also generate economies of scale in buying, selling, management, marketing, etc., which lead to cost reduction. This enables a joint stock company to supply goods and services at affordable prices.
3. **Efficient allocation and optimum utilisation of resources:** By using modern methods of production and distribution, a corporate organisation can make the most efficient use of a country's resources and this is of paramount importance for the smooth functioning of a modern mixed economy. A joint stock company also uses the latent resources of the country by using upgraded technology. An example of this is conversion of the garbage of cities and towns into biogas.
4. **Mobilisation of idle savings:** A public limited company can mobilise small savings of people of modest means scattered throughout the country. These pooled financial resources are channelise to industry for creating both capital goods and consumer goods. Thus, the corporate form of business organisation seeks to increase the rate of capital formation in a country which is the main source of economic growth.
5. **Economic self-reliance:** Economic self-reliance refers to a situation where a country earns sufficient foreign exchange to pay for its imports without taking any loan from the rest of the world. This requires reduction of imports and promotion of exports. To reduce imports, a country has to develop new industries which produce import substitute items such as crude oil and machinery. It is also necessary to develop new export-oriented industries to earn foreign exchange. Herein lies the role of the corporate organisations which can undertake both import substitution and export promotion at the same time.
6. **Employment generation:** Employment generation is absolutely essential for reducing poverty and inequality. Joint stock companies provide direct employment to a large number of people. They also create indirect employment opportunities by encouraging the growth of ancillary industries.
7. **Improved living standards:** Corporate organisations help to uplift the standards of living of people by supplying a wide range of quality products (both goods and services) at affordable prices. This requires huge investment on research and development (R & D) which leads to improvement in the quality of products and fall in their prices. As a result, potential buyers become actual buyers and the market for mass consumption goods widens, giving further scope for division of labour and specialisation. According to Samuelson, the present high standard of living of the people of the USA is largely attributable to the mushroom growth of the corporate form of business organisation in the post Second World War period.
8. **Growth of the social infrastructure:** One of the objectives of a joint stock company is to assist the growth of the social infrastructure which includes banking and finance, insurance, transport and communication, education and medical care.

9. **Rural development:** A corporate organisation also seeks to develop the rural economy which is still the major segment of the Indian economy. India's rural economy can be revived and rejuvenated by developing agro-based industries such as sugar, tea, cotton, jute, oilseeds, etc.

7.5 MERITS OF A COMPANY

The main advantages of the corporate form of business are the following:

1. **Limited liability:** The owners of a corporation have limited liability. This means that they are responsible for the losses of the corporation only up to the amount they invest in it. This protection for shareholders encourages many more of them to invest in such companies[1].
2. **Ability to raise more money for investment:** Joint stock companies are able to raise funds by issuing shares to large number of shareholders and thus, are able to raise more capital to finance their operations than could be a sole proprietor or even a partnership. Most large firms are joint stock companies. To raise money a corporation can sell shares of its stock to any one who is interested. There are millions of people who own parts of major companies such as Tata Steel, Mahindra and Mahindra, Larsen & Toubro, Bharti Airtel, and so on. If a company sells 10 million shares for ₹ 50 each, it will have ₹ 500 million of share capital available to build plants, buy machines, hire people, manufacture products and so on. There is no better way of raising such a huge amount of money Corporations can also borrow money (on the strength of their share capital). They borrow from individual investors by issuing bonds and debentures which are promised to redeem the instruments future with interest. Firms can also obtain loans from banks and non-banking financial institutions on both short-term and long-term basis.

   Anyone can he part owner of a corporated by buying shares of the company stock.

3. **Large size and economies of scale:** Since big corporations can raise large sums of money to work with, they can buy the latest equipment (embodying the most modern and the sophisticated technology). They can hire experts or specialists in all areas of operations. They can buy other corporations in different fields to diversify their activities and reduce risks of doing business. In short, a large corporation with huge resources can take advantage of business opportunity anywhere in the world by establishing a global network.
4. **Perpetual life:** Another advantage is the prospect of continuity. Since corporations are separate from those who own them, the death of one or more owners does not terminate the corporation. But sole proprietorships and partnerships cannot continue to exist independently of the persons who own them. The death or bankruptcy of a sole proprietor or partner or a mere unwillingness to continue will bring an unincorporated business to an end. By contrast, the existence of a joint stock company is independent of the lives and fortunes of its shareholders. If a shareholder dies his shares become the property of his heirs. If a shareholder does not like the way the company is being run he can sell his shares. But the company is in no way affected.

1 The introduction of the principle of limited liability was essential if people were to be persuaded to provide capital on the scale needed by modern industry. In the absence of limited liability enterprise becomes a very risky venture. A very modest 'investment' would put all of one's personal resources at risk.

5. **Ease of ownership change:** It is quite easy to change the owner of a corporation just by selling the shares to someone else.
6. **Ease of attracting talented employees:** Corporations can attract skilled employees by offering such benefits as stock options (the right to purchase shares of the corporation as a future date for a fixed price).
7. **Professionalism in management:** Since a company operates on a fairly large-scale and has enormous financial resources, it can afford to appoint the professional managers at high cost for efficient running of business. These experts can introduce modern management techniques such as business process reengineering and outsourcing.
8. **Risk spreading:** Since the shares of a joint stock company can be held by a large number of people, there is wide diffusion risk. So in the case of corporate collapse each shareholder does not lose much as in case of sole tradership or partnership.
9. **Huge scope for expansion:** By making public issues of shares and debentures a company can raise huge capital and thus operate on a very large-scale and derive economies in production, purchase, selling and risk bearing. All these lead to cost saving and ensure improved profitability.
10. **Public confidence:** The formation and operation of a company is governed by the provisions of the Companies Act and various other acts. These acts provide clear and specific guidelines regarding appointment and remuneration of directors, compulsory audit and publication of accounts and protection of minority shareholders. All these statutory provisions create greater confidence in the minds of the public about the short-term survival and long-term viability of joint stock companies through product and market diversification.
11. **Improved performance:** Joint stock companies are managed by the Board of Directors appointed by shareholders. The directors (i.e., the members of the Board) must report on the progress of the company to the shareholders at an annual general meeting where shareholders can, in principle, vote to remove existing directors if they are dissatisfied with their performance. So there is always a constant pressure on the directors to improve the performance of the company.

7.6 DEMERITS OF A COMPANY

The main disadvantages of corporations are the following:

1. **Initial cost:** Incorporation may cost thousands of rupees and require the services of expensive lawyers and chartered accountants.
2. **Extensive paper work:** A sole proprietor or partnership may keep rather broad accounting records. A corporation, in contrast, must keep detailed financial records, the minutes of (board and shareholders) meetings and more. They have to submit cost of such documents to the Registrar of companies periodically.
3. **Double taxation:** Corporate income is taxed twice. First, the corporation pays taxes on its income before it can distribute any, as dividends, to shareholders. Then, the dividend amount is also taxed as source. The government often taxes corporations more heavily than other enterprises, and some special taxes (such an sur tax or excess profit tax) are imposed only on corporations. Such taxes are essentially taxes on efficiency.

4. Two tax returns: An individual who incorporates must file both a corporate tax return and an individual tax return. Depending on the size of the corporation, a corporate return can be quite complex and require the assistance of a chartered accountant.
5. Size as a constraint on growth: Size can be a disadvantage as well. Large corporations sometimes become too inflexible. They get involved in red-tape[1] and fail to respond quickly to market changes. So their profitability can suffer.
6. Difficulty of termination: Once a corporation is started, it is fairly difficult to close it quickly. A very time-consuming and complicated procedure has to be followed to wind up a company.
7. Possible conflicts between shareholders and board of directors: Conflicts may arise if the Board of Directors does not serve the interests of shareholders, i.e., owners. In truth, the Board members usually try to serve their own interests.
8. Complex procedural formalities: In order to form a joint stock company, there is need to complete a large number of legal formalities. Various documents have to be drafted with utmost care and filed with the Registrar of Companies for examination and scrutiny.
9. Government controls and regulations: A company has to go by numerous provisions of various different acts or legislations. Even in internal matters such as conducting meetings, voting, auditing accounts, etc., there are statutory restrictions. The existence of so many rigidities imposed by legal constraints in running the business discourages some people to form joint stock companies or to start the corporate form of business.
10. Lack of secrecy: As per the Indian Companies Act (1956), a company is under the legal obligation to furnish detailed information about its affairs to the Registrar of Companies on a periodic basis. There is also a statutory provision relating to the publication of its quarterly results in leading regional and national newspapers.
11. Delay in decision-making: The company is managed by the Board of Directors who appoint other executives to ensure smooth and efficient functioning of the organisation. As a result, various managerial levels are created. These multiple strata leads to delay in decision-making.
12. Managerial oligarchy: The majority of shareholders (mainly small shareholders) have virtually no say in company affairs and activities. Very often directors tend to get confused. So they mislead the shareholders by submitting fabricated reports. And shareholders practically live in a world of illusion.
13. Lack of personal touch: Because of divorce of ownership and management, it is not possible to maintain personal touch with the stakeholders, viz., workers, creditors, suppliers and the community at large. The impersonal nature of management may also result in huge waste of resources and much inefficiency of operations.
14. Conflicts among shareholders. All the major corporate issues are decided by the (major) shareholders having majority of shares and thus maintaining controlling interest. These shareholders form a powerful group and are likely to ignore the interests of the minority (or small) shareholders.

1 Red-tape refers to time-consuming official rules or procedures.

15. **Fraudulent practices:** By adopting various fraudulent practices directors or promoters may use the capital raised from the public to serve their personal interests. They may also manipulate the prices of the shares in the stock exchange by showing inflated profit figures.

7.7 MERITS AND DEMERITS OF JOINT STOCK COMPANY

The merits and demerits of joint stock company form of business organisation are discussed below.

Advantages (Merits)	Disadvantages (Demerits)
1. Limited liability	1. High initial cost
2. Ability to raise more money for investment	2. Extensive paperwork
3. Large size and economies of scale	3. Double taxation of profit
4. Perpetual life	4. Two tax returns
5. Ease of ownership change	5. Size as a constraint on growth
6. Ease of attracting talented employees	6. Difficulty of termination
7. Separation of ownership from management	7. Possible conflict between shareholders and Board of Directors
8. Professionalism in management	8. Complex procedural formalities
9. Risk spreading	9. Government controls and regulations
10. Huge scope for expansion	10. Lack of secrecy
11. Public confidence	11. Bureaucracy and delay in decision-making
	12. Managerial oligarchy
	13. Lack of personal touch
	14. Conflicts among shareholders
	15. Fraudulent practices

7.8 CAUSES OF POPULARITY OF A COMPANY

A corporate form of business organisation has become very popular for the following reasons:

1. **Accumulation of huge funds:** A joint stock company can accumulate much more financial resources than any other form of business both through retention of profits and making of public issue of shares. A public limited company can have any number of member exceeding seven. Its capital is divided into a large number of shares of small denominations. Any person from any part of the world can buy such shares. Limited liability and unrestricted transferability of shares motivate people to invest in such a company by purchasing shares. The capacity to borrow and the credit standing of a company are both on the higher side.
2. **Limited liability:** Limited liability refers to the restriction of an owner's loss in business to the amount of capital which he has contributed (invested) in it. In case the company goes into liquidation, the owner as equity shareholder can lose, at most, only face value of its shares. This unique feature enables the management of a corporation to take greater risks and to operate on a large scale.

3. **Stability:** A company enjoys a continuous and unchallenged existence due to its separate legal status. This implies that there is likely to be a continuity of policy and administrative practice for years or decades. This ensures the stability of a corporate enterprise.
4. **Transferability of shares:** The shares of a public limited company are freely transferable. This means that any person can become a shareholder (owner) and is at liberty to withdraw his investment any time he likes.
5. **Spreading of risks:** The risk of loss in a company is shared by a large number of shareholders. So the risk faced by an individual shareholder is very much on the low side. Consequently, even risk-averse persons can become owners of a company.
6. **Efficient management:** A joint stock company can employ professional managers who are highly specialised persons and experts in their own areas to manage its business. This is likely to ensure efficient and effective management of an enterprise through judicious use of its resources.
7. **Expansion and growth:** Finally, a corporate form of organisation is most appropriate for large scale operation of businesses of different types. There is virtually unlimited scope for growth through expansion and diversification. The reason is that large scale production leads to emergence and realisation of economies of scale — both internal and external.

Key Points

1. **Joint Stock Company:** It is a form of company in which a number of people contribute funds to finance a firm in return for shares in the company. It is a state-chartered legal entity with authority to act and have liability separate from its owners.
2. **Features:** The notable characteristics of a company are the following:
   (i) Artificial person,
   (ii) a separate legal entity (status),
   (iii) perpetual existence,
   (iv) limited liability,
   (v) easy transferability of shares,
   (vi) separation of ownership from management,
   (vii) common seal and
   (viii) separate property (in the name of the company).
3. **Advantages of a company**
   (i) More money for investment,
   (ii) large size and economies of scale,
   (iii) limited liability,
   (iv) wider diffusion (spreading) of risk,
   (v) transferability of shares and ease of ownership change,
   (vi) perpetual life,

(vii) professionalism in management and ease of drawing talented personnel,
(viii) separation of ownership from management, and
(ix) tremendous public confidence.

4. **Disadvantages of a company**
(i) Difficulties in formation due to high initial cost and excessive paper work,
(ii) too much government control,
(iii) concentration of management in few hands and neglect of minority shareholders,
(iv) possibility of adoption of fraudulent practices by promoters/directors,
(v) slow and, at times, inordinate delay in decision-making,
(vi) size as a constraint on growth,
(vii) lack of personal touch,
(viii) difficulty of termination,
(ix) double taxation, and
(x) possible conflict of management with board of directors.

KEY Terms	
Limited liability	Separate legal status
Separation of ownership from management (control)	Incorporation
Perpetual existence	Artificial entity
Free transferability of shares	Public issue of shares
Life independent of members	Corporate governance
	Economies of scale

Assignments

SHORT ANSWER-TYPE QUESTIONS

1. Define a joint stock company. [ISC 1994]
2. State three characteristics of a company. [ISC 1997]
3. State three limitations of a company. [ISC 1996]
4. Why has joint stock company form of business become so popular? [ISC 2007]
5. What do you understand by limited liability in a joint stock company? [ISC 1997]
6. Name the feature of a company which suggests that a company is different from its members. [ISC 2002]
7. Name the feature of a company which enables it to own property in its own name? [ISC 2002]
8. Explain the characteristic of 'separate legal entity' of a joint stock company. [ISC 2004]

9. Why does a joint stock company enjoy perpetual or permanent existence? [ISC 2006]
10. What is meant by transferability of shares with respect to a joint stock company? [ISC 2003, 2007]
11. How significant is a common seal to a company? [ISC 2008]
12. Explain any two demerits of a joint stock company. [ISC 2010]
13. State two advantages of joint stock company. [ISC 2011]

ESSAY-TYPE QUESTIONS

1. "A joint stock company is an artificial person created by law, having a separate legal entity with a perpetual succession and a common seal." Explain the above statement. [ISC 2001]
2. "A joint stock company is said to be an artificial person created by law, having a separate legal entity with a perpetual succession and a common seal." Explain the above statement. [ISC 2003]
3. Discuss any five characteristics of a joint stock company. [ISC 2002, 2009]
4. Discuss the advantages and disadvantages of a joint stock company.

QUESTION BANK

1. *Define a joint stock company.*

Ans. A joint stock company or a corporation is a legal entity, operated by persons authorised to conduct a specific business to raise funds for this purpose and to acquire or sell property. It stands for an incorporated business in which investors contribute funds and receive shares in the firm.

2. *What do you understand by separate legal status of a company?*

Ans. Separate legal status of a company means that a joint stock company has a legal existence separate from its owners. It can own property, make contracts and file suits in its own name. There can be contracts between a company and its shareholders.

3. *What is perpetual existence?*

Ans. Perpetual existence means that it continues to exist as former without having any specific or limited lifespan.

4. *Mention any three features of a joint stock company.*

Ans. The three features of a joint stock company are:

(i) A company has a separate legal status.
(ii) The liability of members is generally limited to the amount of investment.
(iii) Common seal which is used in place of signatures.

5. *What is a company? Explain its characteristics.*

OR

"A joint stock company is an artificial person created by law, having a separate legal entity with a perpetual succession and a common seal." Explain.

Ans. See text.

6. *What is meant by 'going public'?*

Ans. Corporations can choose to sell stocks to the general public, or can choose to restrict the sale of stock to a small group — perhaps to the members of a family. For some, the decision is to 'go public' — to sell stocks to the general public — provides the necessary funds with which to build profitable corporations.

7. *Give three points of distinction between company and partnership.*

Ans. See text.

8. *Distinguish clearly between joint stock company and partnership.*

Ans. See text.

9. *What is meant by limited liability?*

Ans. Limited liability refers to the restriction of an owner's loss in a business to the amount of capital which has been invested in it. If a company goes into liquidation, the owner as equity shareholder can lose, at most, only the value of his share, although the director and the shareholders may be subjected to other liabilities such as perpetual guarantees for bank borrowings.

10. *What is meant by separation of ownership from control? What is its consequence?*

Ans. The separation of ownership from control refers to the feature of a joint stock company or a modern corporation in which the owners (shareholders) do not participate actively in their management. As a consequence, there is a conflict of interests between the two groups — the owners (who are the risk-takers and interested in maximum dividend) and the professional managers (who are salaried people and are interested in protecting their jobs).

11. *Why the liability of members of a joint stock company is limited?*

Ans. This is so because a company has a separate legal status different from and independent of its members.

12. *Why does a joint stock company enjoy perpetual existence?* [ISC 2012]

Ans. A joint stock company enjoys perpetual existence because it has a separate legal status independent from its shareholders. It is created by law and can be eliminated (wound up) through the process of such as the Indian Companies Act (1956), amended in 2013.

13. *Mark the following statements True/False.*

(a) A joint stock company is an incorporated body.
(b) Liability of members in a company is usually limited.
(c) A company is more stable and viable than a partnership firm.
(d) A company has perpetual succession.
(e) There is no scope for expansion in a company.
(f) A company is an artificial entity independent of its members.
(g) Every shareholder may not be a necessary member of the company.
(h) Every company is not required to have a common seal.
(i) There is no scope for conflict of interest in a corporate enterprise.

Ans. True: (a), (b), (c), (d), (f), (g)
False: (e), (h), (i).

8 TYPES OF COMPANIES

SYLLABUS

Types of companies

- *Classification of companies on the basis of mode of incorporation, liability of members, public interest ownership control and nationality.*
- *Public and private companies and their comparative studies, privileges of private companies.*

Global enterprises

- *Meaning, characteristics, merits and demerits of Global Enterprises.*

A company is known by the person who form it. — Warren Buffet

LEARNING OUTCOMES

On completion of this chapter, you will be able to understand the following:

8.1 Classification of Companies
8.2 Comparison between Private and Public Company
8.3 Privileges of a Private Company
8.4 Advantages and Disadvantages of a Private Limited Company
8.5 Advantage and disadvantages of a Public Limited Company
8.6 Government Company
8.7 Objectives and Necessity of Government Company
8.8 Advantages of Government Company
8.9 Disadvantages of Government Company
8.10 Global Enterprises: A Detailed Discussion
8.11 Characteristics of Global Enterprises
8.12 Forms of Global Enterprises
8.13 Reasons for Growth of Global Enterprises
8.14 Advantages of Global Enterprises
8.15 Disadvantages of Global Enterprises
8.16 Evaluation of the Impact on 'Host' Countries of Multinational Operations
8.17 One-Person Company (OPC)

Companies are of different types having different characteristics and nationalities. The classification of companies into different categories is made on the basis of five main criteria, viz.,

1. Mode of incorporation
2. Liability of members
3. Ownership and control
4. Public interest and
5. Nationality or jurisdiction

8.1 CLASSIFICATION OF COMPANIES

1. On the basis of mode of incorporation

On the basis of the mode of incorporation, companies are divided into the following three categories

(a) *Chartered company:* Chartered means a document issued by a government for establishing a corporate entity. Companies which are established by the Royal Charter or through a special order granted by a king or a monarch are treated as chartered companies. Such a company enjoys certain powers and privileges not shared by other companies. However, it can be set up only in a country having a system of monarchy or dictatorship. Examples of such companies are the East India Company, The Bank of England and the Hudson Bay Company. However, such companies are now a thing of the past or are corporate dinosaurs because they can not exist in democratic set-up.

(b) *Statutory company:* Statute means written law or act of a legislature, which becomes law, governing conduct within its scope. Statutes are enacted to prescribe conduct and create corporate bodies. Such a company is set up under a special act passed by the Parliament or by a State Legislature which defines the objectives and powers of such a company. So such a company does not have a Memorandum of Association and is not required to use the word 'limited' against its name. The accounts of such a company is audited through the Comptroller and the Auditor General of India. Statutory companies are autonomous bodies and they are set up to carry on business on the basis of extraordinary powers and privileges. Examples of such companies are the Life Insurance Corporation of India, the RBI, the IDBI Bank and thc Axis Bank.

There are different types of joint stock companies or corporate enterprises as shown in Fig. 8.1.

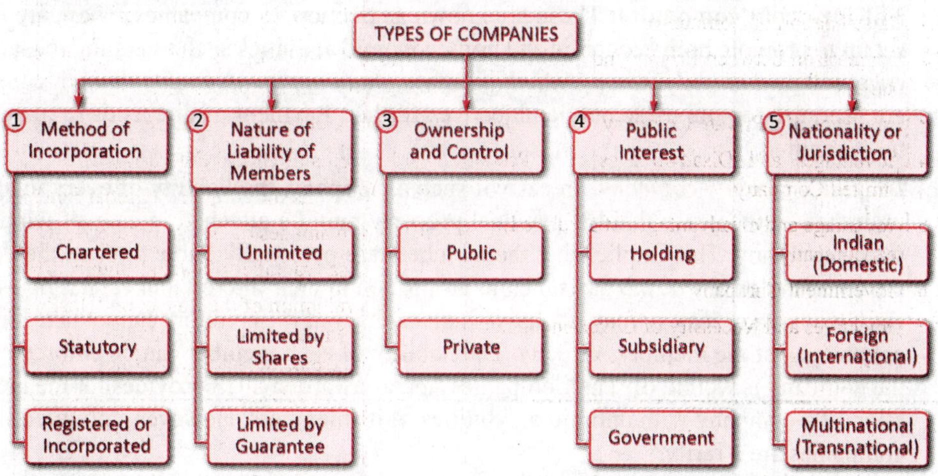

FIGURE 8.1: Different Types of Joint Stock Companies

(c) *Registered or incorporated company:* A company which is registered under the India Companies Act (1956) is called a Registered or an Incorporated company. Such companies are mostly found in India's industrial economy. There are certain special statutes governing them. Examples of such companies are the Steel Authority of India (SAIL), Maruti Udyog Ltd. and Reliance Industries Ltd. (RIL).

In India, registered companies are classified into three broad categories:

(i) company limited by shares

(ii) company limited by guarantee, and

(iii) unlimited liability company.

2. On the basis of liability of members

On the basis of liability of members, companies are divided into the following three categories.

(a) *Company limited by shares:* In case of such a company, the liability of members is limited to the face value of their shares and if a member has already paid the full face value of the shares, he owes no further liability to the company. In case of partly paid shares, the liability of members is limited to the unpaid amount (value) of their shares. In India, most joint stock companies fall in this category.

(b) *Company limited by guarantee:* In case of such a company the liability of members is limited to the amount they contribute to its assets. In case the company is wound up, this amount is called the 'guarantee' and is stated in the Memorandum of Association. The amount guaranteed by the members serves as 'reserve capital' and can be touched or utilised only at the time of extreme emergency, i.e., winding up. If such a company has any share capital, liability of its members consists of, apart from the guarantee, the unpaid amount, if any, of the shares held by them. Such a company is set up normally to promote non-business interests or to encourage non-business pursuits such as education, art, science, culture and games and sports. Examples of such companies are trade associations, chambers of commerce, stock exchanges and sports clubs. The Articles of Association of such a company has to state the number of members with which the company is to be formed and registered.

Not-for-profit companies: These are known as Section 25 companies. These are usually set up to promote both economic and non-economic activities such as commerce, arts, science, religion or philanthropy which promote public interests. Profits of such companies are used to promote these public objectives further. Payment of dividends to members is not permitted.

(c) *Unlimited liability company:* In case of such a company, the liability of every member is unlimited in the sense that his personal property may be attached in case of winding up of the company. This implies that the members are personally liable to clear the debts of the company on a *pro rata* basis, i.e., in proportion to their interest and capital investment. Such a company may or may not have share capital but the creditors cannot take any legal action against the members directly. The liability of each member can be enforced only if the company is wound of. The Companies Act, as awarded 2013 provides for the incorporation of a company with unlimited liabilities of its members. However, unlimited liability companies are a rarity.

3. On the basis of ownership and control

On the basis of ownership and control, companies are classified into the following three categories:

(i) *Holding company:* A holding company is a corporation organised for the purpose of owning stocking and managing one or more corporations. It is any company which, directly or indirectly, through the medium of another company, either holds more than half of the equity share capital of another company or controls the composition of the Board of Directors of some other company. A holding company may have one or more subsidiaries.

The Engineering Construction Company is a subsidiary of Larsen and Tubro Limited. Holding companies traditionally own many corporations in widely diverse (and often uncommitted) business areas.

Holding companies are not a different legal form of business organisation; but they are an increasingly common way for businesses to be owned. A holding company is a business organisation that owns and controls a number of separate businesses, but does not unite them into one unified company. Often the separate businesses are in different markets altogether and this would mean that the holding company had diversified interests. Keeping the businesses separate means that they are independent of each other (one another) for major decisions or policy changes. Yet there always exists the possibility of centralised control from the directors of the holding company over really crucial issues, such as major new investments.

In truth, a company may become a holding company of another company in any of the following ways:

(a) by holding more than 50% of the issued equity capital of the company.

(b) by holding more than 50% of the voting rights in the company, or

(c) by holding the legal right to appoint majority of the directors of the company.

(ii) *Subsidiary company (or simply a subsidiary):* A subsidiary is a company whose major voting stock i.e., more than 50% is owned by another firm. In such a company, a holding company (a) holds at least 51% of the total share capital or its voting right or (b) as the legal right to determine the composition of its Board of Directors solely for controlling its management; or (c) is the subsidiary of another such company.

In the language of Gerstenberg. "Any company owned or controlled by another company to the extent that it is a mere instrument to carry out the orders of the owning company is called a subsidiary company".

(iii) *Government company:* A government company is one in which at least 50% or even more of paid-up share capital is held by the central government and/or by any state government. It may be partly or wholly owned by the government at any of the two levels or both. A subsidiary of a government company is also treated as a government company. In general, public sector units which are registered under the Companies Act are also government companies. Such companies remain engaged in industrial and commercial activities. Examples of such companies are the Steel Authority of India (SAIL), the National Textile Corporation Ltd. (NTC), Bharat Heavy Electricals Ltd. (BHEL), Hindustan Machine Tools Ltd. (HMT) and State Trading Corporation of India (STC).

4. On the basis of public interest

On the basis of public interest or transferability of shares, companies are classified into the following *three* categories:

(i) *Private company:* Such a company must have a paid up share capital of ₹ 1 lac and which by its Articles of Association:

(a) restricts the right of its members to transfer shares, if any;

(b) except in case of one-person company set a limit on the number of its members to 200, excluding its employees;

(c) Prohibits any invitation to the public to subscribe to its shares and debentures.

The minimum number of members required to form a private company is 2. Such a company has to use the word 'private' in its name. It enjoys certain extra privileges and gets certain specific exemptions under the Companies Act. In general, it is a family firm (business).

(ii) *Private company:* Such a company is

(a) not a private one;

(b) has a minimum paid up capital of ₹ 5 lac; and

(c) is a private company which is a subsidiary of a public company.

In short, a public company is one which: (i) does not restrict the transfer of its shares; (ii) does not limit the number of members; (iii) can make the public issue of shares and debentures, and (iv) can accept public deposits.

A minimum of 7 persons are required to form a public company.

(iii) *Private company deemed to be public:* A private company is deemed (as per the Companies Act) to be a public company under any of the following four situations or circumstances:

(i) where a private company holds 25% or more of the paid-up share capital of a public company;

(ii) where 25% or more of the paid-up share capital of a private company is held by one or more bodies corporate;

(iii) where the average sales turnover of a private company for the last three years is more than ₹ 25 crore; or

(iv) where a private company accepts deposits from the public

Some examples of Public Companies are the following:

1. Tata Consultancy Services
2. Tata Motors
3. Fort Gloster
4. Axis Bank
5. ITC
6. Infosys Technologies
7. DLF
8. Bharti Airtel
9. Reliance Power and
10. Sheraton Hotels

After the passing of the Companies Amendment Act (2000), this category of companies has ceased to exist.

5. On the basis of nationality and jurisdiction

On the basis of nationality or jurisdiction, companies are divided into the following three categories:

(i) *Indian companies:* A company which is incorporated within the domestic territory of India is known as an Indian company. It is registered as per the provisions of the Indian Companies Act 1956. It has its registered office in India. But it is allowed to carry on business in foreign countries.

(ii) *Foreign company*: A foreign company is one which as a body corporate is incorporated outside India. It has two notable features.

(a) It has a place of business in India and conducts its business directly or through an agent, either physically or through electronic mode.

(b) It conducts any business activity in India in a different area (line).

A foreign company has to exhibit outside its office or place of doing business in India the name of the company or the country in which it is incorporated in English and in any of the regional languages. In case 51% or more of equity or paid-up share capital of a foreign company is held by one or more citizens of India and/or one or more bodies corporates incorporated in India. Such a company has to comply with the rules and regulations relating to the business carried on in India or complete necessary formalities much like an Indian company.

Every foreign company is under the legal obligation (binding) to file the following documents within 30 days of establishing its business in India:

(a) certified copies of its Memorandum and Articles of Association,

(b) complete address of its registered office,

(c) full particulars of its directors and secretary,

(d) name and address of its authorised representative in India, and

(e) complete address of its principal place of business in India.

(iii) *Multinational company:* A multinational company (MNC) is a firm in which *owns* production, sales and other revenue generating asset in a number of countries. Since it has headquarter (decision-making centre) in only one country but has production or marketing facilities in others, it is the result of previous foreign direct investment (FDI). An MNC sees itself as a global company and thus not tied to any particular country. It organises its business operations and various countries through any of the following alternatives: (a) branches, (b) franchises, (c) turnkey projects, (d) joint ventures, (e) subsidiaries, and so on Pepsi, Coca Cola, Bata, Toyota, Siemens, Nestle, Proctor and Gamble, Colgate, Unilever are all examples of multinational corporations.

8.2 COMPARISON BETWEEN PRIVATE AND PUBLIC COMPANY

1. **Number of members:** While a private company can be registered with just 2 members, a public company must have at least 7 members. And while a private company cannot have more than 50 members, a public company can have an unlimited number of members.
2. **Public issue:** A private company cannot invite the public by issuing prospectus to subscribe to its share capital. But a public company is at liberty to do this. However, there is no legal binding regarding the issue of its shares and debentures to the public.
3. **Free transferability of shares:** There is a restriction on the transfer of shares in a private limited company. Such transfer is not allowed without the consent of all the existing members of the company. But the shares of a public limited company are easily and freely transferable.
4. **Commencement of business:** A private company can start its business as soon as it is incorporated. However, a public limited company has to get the certificate of commencement of business before starting its actual operations.

5. **Articles of association:** A private limited company has to prepare and submit its own Articles of Association but a public limited company is permitted to adopt the model articles as specified in the Companies Act.
6. **Exemptions and privileges:** A private company enjoys various privileges, which are denied to a public company. It is not under the legal obligation to hold a statutory meeting or file a report. There is no restriction on it regarding the allotment of shares, appointment and remuneration of directors, rights issue, publicity of accounts,, types of shares, inter-corporate investments, loans to directors, voting by interested directors, etc. which are all applicable to public companies.
7. **Number of directors:** There has to be at least 2 directors in a private company and at least 3 in a public company.
8. **Quorum:** The presence of two members is the minimum quorum in a general meeting of a private company to be held. For holding the general meeting of a company, the presence of at least 5 members is essential for a quorum.
9. **Index of members:** A private company is not required to maintain any index of its members (apart from a general list). A public company must maintain this index in case it has more than 50 members.
10. **Minimum paid-up capital:** A private company is required to have a minimum paid-up capital of just ₹ 1 lac. In case of a public company this lower limit is ₹ 5 lac.

8.3 PRIVILEGES OF A PRIVATE COMPANY

The Companies Act has granted various privileges to the private companies. The reason is simple. Hardly any public interest is involved in these companies since they are not permitted to make public issues.

The main privileges enjoyed by a private company are listed below.

1. While a private company can be started with just 2 members, the minimum number is 7 for a public company.
2. A private company can start its business as soon as it is incorporated because it is not required to obtain the certificate of commencement of business (which is obligatory for a public company).
3. A private company is not under the legal obligation to issue or file a prospectus or statement in lieu of prospectus with the registrar of companies.
4. A private company is not legally obliged to hold statutory meeting or to submit statutory report to the Registrar of Companies.
5. A private company can allot shares directly and here is no restriction on minimum subscription.
6. A private company can have just 2 directors while a public company must have at least 3.
7. A private company is not required to issue new shares to its existing shareholders on a proportional or *pro rata* basis. It is free to issue shares with disproportionate voting rights.
8. Its directors cannot always be retired by rotation. And there is no need to take the consent of directors or to file with the registrar the decision of directors to take up the qualification shares. A private company is not required to take the permission of the government

to make loans to its directors. Directors can vote on a contract if they feel so interested. Persons can be appointed to the office of profit.

9. It is exempted from all restrictions relating to the compensation of managerial personnel, appointment of persons to office of profit, inter-corporate investment and official publication of accounts.
10. The presence of just two persons is the minimum quorum for general meeting of a private company unless there is a different provision in the Articles of Association.
11. Finally, a private company is not required to prepare an index of the official registrar of his members.

8.4 ADVANTAGES AND DISADVANTAGES OF A PRIVATE LIMITED COMPANY

A private limited company emerges when the owner of a small firm creates such a company. Such a company is a small or medium-sized business which is owned by shareholders who are often members of the same family. This company cannot sell shares to the general public, i.e., cannot make public issues of shares and debentures for raising funds to meet fixed capital needs.

The word 'limited' implies that a business has a legal form. Usually the shares will be owned by the original sole trader, relatives, friends and employees. The former sole trader often retains a controlling interest (by acquiring at least 51% of shares). New issue of shares cannot be made on the open market and the existing shareholders are permitted to sell their shares only with the consent of all other shareholders. Certain legal formalities have to be completed in setting up such a business.

The advantages and disadvantages of a private limited company are listed in Table 8.1.

TABLE 8.1: Advantages and Disadvantages of a Private Limited Company

Advantages	Disadvantages
1. Limited liabilities of shareholders	1. Legal formalities involved in establishing the business
2. Separate legal personality	2. No scope for raising capital by sale of shares to the general public
3. Continuity in the event of the death of a shareholder	3. Quite difficult for shareholders to sell shares
4. Retention of control by the owner	4. Compulsion regarding submission end-of-year accounts for public inspection (implying less secrecy over financial affairs than sole trader or partnership)
5. Ability to raise capital from sale of shares to family members friends and employees	5. Fairly difficult for shareholders to sell shares
6. Higher legal status than an unincorporated business	

8.5 ADVANTAGES AND DISADVANTAGES OF A PUBLIC LIMITED COMPANY

Recall that, a public limited company is often a larger business with the legal right to sell shares to the general public. Its share prices are quoted on the national stock exchange.

A public limited company can be recognised by the use of 'inc' after its name. It is the most common form of legal organisation for really large businesses. The reason is simple. They have access to large funds for expansion.

A public limited company has all the advantages of its private counterpart. In addition, it has the right to advertise its shares for sale (i.e., public subscription) and have then quoted on the stock exchange. This means two things at least. Firstly, a public limited company can raise huge sums by making public issue of shares. Secondly, existing shareholders may also quickly sell their shares if they so desire. This flexibility regarding buying and selling shares encourages the general public to purchase the shares in the first instance and thus invest in the business.

Another important difference between a private company and a public company relates to the 'divorce between ownership and control'. The original owners of the business are normally in a position to retain a majority of shares and continue to exercise managerial control when it gains a private company status. This is most unlikely with a public limited company due to the huge number of shares issued and involvement of numerous people and institutions as investors. These shareholders are the true owners of the company but they appoint, at the annual general meeting, a Board of Directors which controls the decision-making process and manages the organisation by appointing professional people.

The advantages and disadvantages of a public limited company are listed in Table 8.2.

TABLE 8.2: Advantages and Disadvantages of Public Limited Company

Advantages	Disadvantages
1. Limited liability	1. Legal formalities in formation
2. Separate legal identity	2. Cost of business consultants and financial advisers when creating such a company
3. Continuity	3. Share prices subject to fluctuation — sometimes for reasons beyond business control, for example, state of the economy
4. Ease of buying and selling of shares for shareholders — this encourages investment in public limited company	4. Legal requirements concerning disclosure of information to shareholders and the public, for example, annual publication of detailed report and accounts
5. Access to substantial capital sources due to the ability to issue a prospectus to the public and to offer shares for sale (called a flotation)	5. Risk of takeover due to the availability of the shares on the stock exchange
6. Higher status than an unincorporated business	6. Directors influenced by short-term objectives of major investors who hold the majority of share

This separation of ownership from control can lead to conflicts over the objectives to be set and direction to be taken by the business. The shareholders might prefer short-term profits over long-term interests. By contrast, the directors may decide to aim for long-term growth of the business, perhaps, in order to increase their own power and status. Many private limited companies convert to Inc. status for various reasons. It is possible for the directors or the original owners of a business to convert it back from a public to a private limited company's status. The reasons for doing this are likely to overcome the divorce between ownership and control. In a private limited company, it is quite usual for the senior executives to be the majority shareholders. In addition, the owner of a private limited company can take a long-term view of the business on the basis of its prospective plans and programmes. It is often alleged that the major investors of a public limited company are only interested in short-term gains. Short-termism can be damaging to the long-term investment plans of a business.

8.6 GOVERNMENT COMPANY

A government company is one in which at least 51% of the paid-up share capital is held by the central government or any state government or partly by the two types of governments. The term government company is a broad one and a subsidiary of a government company also falls in this category. It may be incorporated as a public company or a private company after being registered under the Companies Act. It may be wholly owned by the government or partly by the government and partly by private shareholders.

8.6.1 Characteristics

The most notable characteristics of a government company are the following:

1. *Incorporation:* Being incorporated or registered under the Companies Act, a government company can gain the status of a public limited company or a private limited company. Much like a private joint stock company, it is a corporate body which exists in perpetuity and has a common seal.
2. *Separate legal status:* Being a body corporate, it has a separate legal status. Like a joint stock company, it is empowered to acquire property, make contracts, sew and be sewed in its own name.
3. *Ownership:* As noted above, it is wholly or partly owned by the government. In case of partial ownership, the government is required to acquire a minimum of 51% of the total share capital.
4. *Management:* A government company is managed by a Board of Directors nominated by both the government and other shareholders. It is at liberty to formulate its own policies, rules and regulations. It is given exemption from certain provisions of the Companies Act. It is free from government control as for its day-to-day operations are concerned.
5. *Own staff:* Its employees are its own staff. Their appointment and terms and conditions of service are independently determined by a government itself. So civil service rules are not applicable to them.
6. *Autonomy in financial matter.* It can borrow freely from the open market and is totally free from financial controls applicable to government departments.
7. *Public accountability.* It is accountable to the ministry or department to which it belongs. Its annual report is placed before either the Parliament (in case of a central public sector unit) or the State Legislature (in case of a state public sector unit), and is subject to ministerial control.
8. *Emergence:* A government company emerges or is created by an executive order and its Articles of Association are drawn by the government.
9. *Exemptions:* The government enjoys the discretion of granting exemptions to a government company from the provisions of the Companies Act, subject to the approval of Parliament and adoption of necessary safeguards.

Examples: Some examples of government companies existing in India at present are the following:

1. Damodar Valley Corporation (DVC)
2. National Thermal Power Corporation (NTPC)
3. IDBI Bank
4. Hindustan Machine Tools Ltd. (HMT)
5. Steel Authority of India Ltd (SAIL) and
6. Coal India Limited (CIL).

8.7 OBJECTIVES AND NECESSITY OF GOVERNMENT COMPANY

Government companies have been set up in India with a view to fulfilling the following objectives:

1. **Promoting rapid industrialisation:** In the immediate post-independence period, India had a narrow industrial base. Very few industries of national importance existed at that time. Government companies were set up to develop basic and heavy industries to build an integrated infrastructure and supply inputs to other industries. So the stress was on development of industries such as iron and steel, oil and natural gas, petrochemicals, heavy engineering and power generation. Due to huge initial investment in such highly capital-industries, long gestation period and high risks the private sector was both unable and unwilling to develop such industries. So government companies were set up to provide necessary physical infrastructure needed to promote faster industrial growth. Since economic development was equated with industrialisation, without rapid industrialisation, economic development could not be achieved.
2. **Accelerating the rate of capital formation:** The Government of India (GOI) set up banks, insurance companies and public financial (term lending) institutions to mobilise public savings and channelise the same into various industries. In addition, profit generated by some, if not all, government companies provide revenue to the Exchequer.
3. **Employment generation:** The GOI set up a number of enterprises to provide gainful employment opportunities to a large number of persons in a labour-surplus country.
4. **Ensuring balanced regional development:** A number of government enterprises were set up in backward areas or growth centres. The objective was to ensure balanced regional development in a federal democracy or to avoid lopsided (uneven) development and the consequent regional inequality.
5. **Achieving economic self-reliance:** A few government companies have been established to reduce imports and save scarce foreign exchange as also to promote exports to earn foreign exchange. Both the measures were directed towards achieving economic self-reliance, i.e. to ensure that the country had sufficient foreign exchange to pay for its imports without depending on foreign aid or external borrowing.
6. **Moving towards a socialistic pattern of society:** The Directive Principles of State Policy declared that India was going to have a socialistic pattern of society. One way of achieving this was to hold in check undue concentration of wealth and economic power in private hands by preventing the growth of monopoly and big business. The growth of big business could be held in check by a parallel expansion of the public sector through the setting up of government companies.

7. **Promoting consumer welfare:** Government companies seek to supply essential goods and services at low prices to people of modest means, even by incurring losses or by giving subsidies. This helped to raise the standard of living of millions of Indians.

8.8 ADVANTAGES OF GOVERNMENT COMPANY

A government company offers the following advantages:

1. **Easy to form:** It can be formed easily and quickly since there is no need to pass a separate statute for the purpose. It can be created just through an executive decision of the government and registered under the Companies Act.
2. **Operational independence (autonomy):** Being a separate entity and an autonomous body, it is virtually free from bureaucratic control and political interference as for as its day-to-day operation is concerned. So it can act independently and operate on purely commercial principles (i.e., profit and loss considerations).
3. **Flexibility of operations:** Keeping in view the provisions of the Companies Act, it is possible to alter the objectives, powers and organisational set-up of a government company easily and quickly. This enables the company to take prompt decisions regarding managerial, financial or any other related matter.
4. **Managerial efficiency:** It can appoint well-paid professional managers with attractive service conditions so that there is maximum possible efficiency of management. Moreover, there is pressure on it due to parliamentary discussions on the annual reports of such companies.
5. **Collaboration:** Only through this form of organisation, the government can avail itself of managerial skill, technical knowhow and huge capital raised from both domestic and foreign sources.
6. **Public accountability:** The annual reports and functioning of government companies are discussed and debated in the Parliament. This makes such companies accountable to the public and their managers have to remain cautious (or even over-contious) all the time for avoiding public criticism and risk of job loss.
7. **Legal discipline:** The management of a government company is governed solely by the Companies Act. The disciplinary provisions of the Act help to keep the management active and productive. The Act puts pressure on the enterprise to maintain competitive parity with a private enterprise.

8.9 DISADVANTAGES OF GOVERNMENT COMPANY

A government company has the following disadvantages:

1. **Partial accountability:** A government company is not fully accountable to the Parliament or the general public for its operational performance (results). It enjoys certain special privileges (not shared by a private company) and its officers may be lured to promote their own interests by wasting public money. This is known as government failure.
2. **Undue political interference:** In reality, powerful politicians and bureaucrats interfere with the day-to-day functioning of government companies. And there is often conflict between technocrats (engineers and technically qualified personnel) and bureaucrats including

defeated politicians having no experience of managing a government company. Such interference and redtapism cause managerial slack or X-inefficiency (or internal inefficiency).

3. **Indifferent attitude of management:** Government companies are generally managed by government officers or people having political links. They have hardly any motivation to work hard and put the best possible effort to run the company on commercial principles. This is why operational efficiency is low and overhead expenses are high, more so due to top heavy administration.
4. **Board members acting as yes men:** Directors of a government company who are appointed by the government are at the mercy of the ministers and bureaucrats who are powerful and highly influential people (having not much intrinsic worth). They are very busy in buttering their political bosses and do not stand for any definite principle and can be easily swayed by their political bosses (who are just like the gods of government companies).
5. **Fear of exposure and job loss:** The annual reports of government companies are placed before the Parliament on a routine basis and brought to the notice of the general public and disclosed a to the press. At times there is excessive (undue) criticism of government companies. This develops a fear psychosis among managers and office-bearers of such enterprises. So they often feel demoralised and hesitate to take the necessary initiative to innovate and implement new ideas or methods of operation. The end result is loss of efficiency, low profit or even loss of such an enterprise year after year.

A government company is most appropriate (suitable) when the governments want: (i) to acquire or nationalise an existing enterprise in times of war or emergency, (ii) to launch an enterprise in collaboration with a private partner from a foreign company (or global enterprise) and (iii) to start an enterprise with the ultimate objective of transferring it to the private sector.

8.10 GLOBAL ENTERPRISES: A DETAILED DISCUSSION

Global enterprise refers to a multinational business organisation. Such an organisation has its headquarters in one country (called the home country) but with operating branches, factories and assembly plants in other countries (called host countries).

8.10.1 Meaning of Global Enterprises

A global enterprise or international giant has its headquarter (decision-making centre) in one country (called the home country) but it goes for worldwide sourcing. It procures raw materials, recruits labour, manufactures products and sells those in different countries of the world. The bulk of its revenue is generated by selling its products in host countries.

8.10.2 Examples of Multinational Corporations (MNCs)

As noted earlier a multinational corporation (MNC) is one which has headquarters in one country and branch offices and factories (production activities) and marketing operations in various countries. Coca Cola, for example, is originally an US enterprise but it has production centres and marketing network in most countries of the world. Other MNCs are Pepsi (USA), Ponds (USA), Brook Bond (UK), Sony (Japan), Mitsubishi (Japan), Cadbury (UK), Unilever (British-Dutch), Nestle (USA), Gillette (USA), Philips (Holland) and so on. Table 8.3 present a list of some leading MNCs operating in India.

At present most American, British and Japanese global corporations operate in India and various other countries — both developed and developing. Ford, for example, produces motor cars not only in the USA but also in Western Europe and Japan. Similarly Japanese firms procure raw materials (such as iron ore) from India, produce finished steel in Korea or Taiwan (where the wage rate is low) and sell finished steel in different countries of the world. And most Japanese firms have become processing industries and are engaged in international subcontracting business. Global enterprises such as Ford are known as multinational or transnational corporations.

BUSINESS FOCUS: WORLDWIDE SOURCING AND GLOBAL MARKETING

A multinational corporation (MNC) is one which owns production, sales and other revenue-generating assets in a number of countries. FDI by an MNC in the establishment or acquisition of overseas raw materials and components, setting up of production plants and sales subsidiaries occurs because of potentially greater cost-effectiveness and profitability in sourcing inputs and serving markets through a direct presence in a number of locations, rather than sole reliance on a single home base and imports and exports as the basis of the firm's international operations.

Global enterprises have benefited greatly from the freedoms offered by globalisation or external liberalisation. They are more than just importers and exporters. They actually produce goods and services in more than one country. The biggest multinationals have sales turnover exceeding the national income of many developing countries.

There are various Indian subsidiaries of multinationals corporations. These are listed in Table 8.3.

TABLE 8.3: Indian Subsidiaries of Multinationals

Multinationals	Indian Subsidiaries
Cadbury	Cadbury India
Procter and Gamble (USA)	P & G India
Unilever (British Dutch)	Hindusthan Unilever
Gillette	Indian Shaving Products
Ford Motor (USA)	Ford Escort
Allianz (Germany)	Bajaj Allianz
Sony	Sony India
Hewlett-Packard	HCL-HP
GEC	GEC Alsthom
Nestle (USA)	Nestle India
Suzuki (Japan)	Maruti-Suzuki Ltd.
Toyota Motor (Japan)	Toyota
Wal-Mart Stores (USA)	Wal-Mart
Samsung (South Korea)	Samsung

8.11 CHARACTERISTICS OF GLOBAL ENTERPRISES

The most notable features of MNCs are the following:

1. **Giant size:** The assets and sales turnover of MNCs run into billions of dollars. For example, the physical assets of Procter & Gamble (US) were worth 148.9 billion US dollars as on June 30, 2009. Wal-Mart Stores (US) with market capitalisation of $ 188.8 billion in 2009 and revenue of $ 405.6 billion in 2008 was one of the largest MNCs in 2009.

2. **Operations in various countries:** An MNC operates in various host countries through its huge network, i.e., branches and subsidiaries.
3. **Centralised control:** An MNC exercises control over its different branches and subsidiaries from the headquarter (which is indeed its decision-making centre). The local managers operate within the broad policy framework laid down and guidelines issued by the parent company.

BUSINESS FOCUS: COMPETITIVE ADVANTAGE OF MNCS

A global firm such as an MNC may possess various competitive advantages over rival suppliers (firm-specific advantages) in the form of patented process technology or a unique branded product, which it can better exploit and protect by establishing overseas supply facilities. Other sources of competitive advantage of MNCs are the following:

(i) *Cost reduction:* Direct investment may enable a firm to reduce its distribution costs and keep in touch more closely with local market conditions — changes in consumer tastes, competitors' actions, etc.

(ii) *Avoiding government restrictions:* Direct investment enables a firm to avoid governmental restrictions on market access such as tariffs and quotas.

(iii) *Enjoying country-specific advantages:* Direct foreign investment also enables a firm to benefit from other 'country-specific advantages' such as the avaiiability of government cash grants and subsidies on inward investment.

(iv) *Lower labour cost and superior technology:* In the case of sourcing, direct investment allows the MNC to take advantage of some countries' lower labour costs or provide access to superior technological know-how.

4. **Resource transfer:** A multinational corporation facilitates a transfer of a "package" of business resources such as technical know-how, machinery, and equipment, raw materials and of course managerial expertise and consultancy services.
5. **Modern sophisticated technology:** Most of the MNCs use modern sophisticated technology in production operations and physical distribution of their products. Such technology is capital augmenting in nature and helps to raise productivity of labour and material resources (or total factor productivity)
6. **Professionalism in management:** Multinational corporations deploy the services of trained and professionally qualified managers. They have specialised training and skills in different functional areas such as production, marketing and finance, and personnel (human resources).
7. **Access to vast international market:** Due to their enormous financial resources and superior marketing skills MNCs have wide access to vast international markets. And due to their diversified operations they are able to sell whatever they produce in different parts of the world.
8. **Oligopolistic power and market dominance:** Most MNCs do not face much competition because they operate in oligopolistic markets. Oligopoly refers to a market situation characterised by few sellers of a homogeneous or differentiated product. Due to their oligopolistic power MNCs enjoy a dominant position in the markets for various products such as soft drinks, automobiles, cell phones or even fast food such as pizza or fried chicken.

In truth, main objectives of a multinational corporation is world-wide sourcing. It goes abroad for acquiring raw materials at low prices, for employing cheap labour and for selling its products in all countries at high prices.

8.12 FORMS OF GLOBAL ENTERPRISES

Business uses different strategies to compete in global markets. The key strategies include licensing, exporting, franchising, contract manufacturing, international joint ventures and strategic alliances, as also foreign direct investment. Each provides different opportunities, along with specific commitments and risks. Figure 8.2 places the strategies on a continuum, showing the amount of commitment, control, risk, and profit potential associated with each.

1. **Licensing:** A firm (the licensor) may decide to compete in a global market by licensing the right to manufacture its products, use its trade mark to a foreign company (the licensee) for a fee (a royalty). A company, having an interest in licensing generally sends company representatives to the foreign producer to help set up operations. The licensor may also assist or work with a licensee in such areas as distribution, promotion, and consulting.

Licensing is a global strategy in which a firm (the licensor) allows a foreign company (the licensee) to produce its product in exchange for a fee (a royalty).

A CASE EXAMPLE: WARNER BROS AND HARRY POTTER BOOKS

Warner Bros. has licensed hundreds of companies all over the world to make products related to its series of hit films based on the bestselling Harry Potter books, which have been translated into more than 10 different languages. There are various other case examples like this.

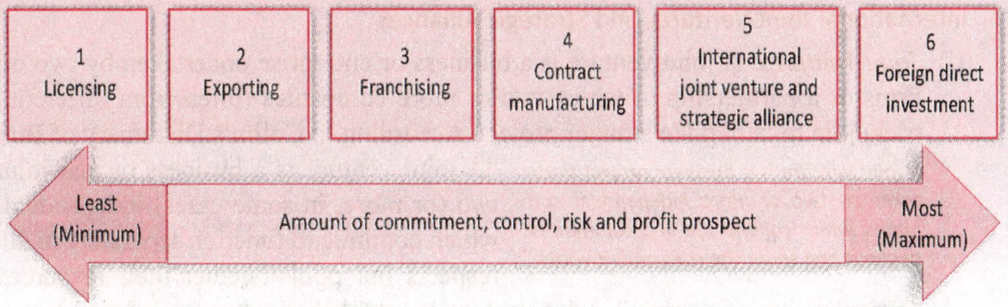

FIGURE 8.2: Strategies for Reaching Global Markets

2. **Exporting:** An export-trading company matches buyers and sellers from different countries. However, it has to deal with foreign customs offices, documentation, and even weights and measures conversions to be able to enter global markets.

BUSINESS FOCUS: INTERNATIONAL FRANCHISING

Franchising was defined and explained in an earlier chapter. International franchising means that foreign franchisees are used to operate a firm's activities abroad. This can either take the form of one foreign company being used as a franchisee for all the branches in their own country or individual franchisees are appointed to operate each outlet. McDonald's uses just one franchisee business to operate its branches in Argentina, for example. The benefits and limitations of appointing franchisees will be discussed in Chapter 16. An additional benefit is that the foreign franchisee(s) do have important local market knowledge.

3. **Franchising:** Franchising is a contractual agreement whereby someone with a good idea for a business sells others the rights to use the business name and sell a product or service in a given territory in a specified manner. Franchising is popular both domestically and internationally. For example, Dominos' serves Pizzas (with squid and sweet mayonnaise) around the globe to satisfy customers' craving. The product has appeal to different tastes.

Franchisers like Dominos' and McDonalds' know that the world is a big place with wide differences in food preferences. They also try to ensure that their products are appropriate for global markets.

4. **Branches (branch plants):** If a US company purchases more than 50% of the shares outstanding of a French firm, the former has a controlling interest and the latter becomes a foreign subsidiary. The building of a plant in Sweden by a US company is also a form of foreign direct investment (FDI). The reason is that there is both ownership and control of the new facility — a branch plant — by the US company. [FDI is discussed in the context of multinational enterprise (or corporation)]

5. **Contract Manufacturing:** In contract manufacturing a foreign company produces private-label goods to which a domestic company then attaches its own brand name or trademark. It is part of the broad category of outsourcing. Nike, for instance, has more than 700 contract factories around the world which manufacture its footwear and apparel.
Contract manufacturing enables a company to experiment in a new market without incurring high start-up costs such as building a manufacturing plant. If the brand name becomes a success, the company is said to have penetrated a new market with fairly low risk. A firm can also use contract manufacturing for a short period to meet an unexpected increase in orders.

6. **International Joint Ventures and Strategic Alliances**

   (i) *Joint Ventures:* A joint venture is a business or enterprise undertaken by two or more firms or a partnership in which two or more companies (often from different countries) join to undertake a major project. According to Collin's Dictionary of Business, "A joint venture is a business owned jointly by two (or more, in some cases) independent firms which continue to function separately in all other respects but pool together their resources in a particular line of activity". Joint venture is established when an independent firm is created by at least two other firms. Joint ventures are often mandated by the government such as that of China as a condition of doing business in their country. For example, Colgate-Palmolive entered a joint venture with one of China's largest toothpaste producers. Since then it has more than doubled its revenues in China and now exports toothpastes to 70 countries.

A joint venture is a business project undertaken by two or more independent companies which collaborate in a common endeavour and share the risks and rewards.

Reasons: Firms set up joint ventures for a number of reasons. These are the following:

1. Economies of scale and market penetration: The combining together of the resources of the two firms may facilitate the establishment of a large-scale operation, giving the joint venture access to economies of scale and increasing its penetration of the market.
2. Exploiting complementary resources: A joint venture is often particularly effective way of exploiting complementary resources and skills, with one firm, for example, contributing new technology and products and the other providing marketing expertise and distribution channels.
3. Entering unfamiliar foreign markets: In the international context, joint ventures with local partners are often used by multinational enterprises as a means of entering unfamiliar foreign markets.

Benefits: Joint ventures are usually a less expensive way of expanding a firm's business interest than undertaking full mergers and takeovers. And they allow firms to withdraw from a particular activity easily and quickly. Other benefits of international joint ventures are the following:

1. Shared technology and risk
2. Shared marketing and management expertise
3. Entry into markets where foreign companies are often not allowed unless goods are produced with inputs which are purchased locally.

Drawbacks: There are three main drawbacks of joint ventures. These are the following:

1. One partner can learn the other's technology and practices and then use what it learned to its own advantage. This is known as the penalty of taking the lead.
2. A shared technology may become too large to be as flexible as needed.
3. Perhaps the main problem with joint venture centres on the need to secure agreement between the two partners (especially if it is a 50-50 arrangement) as to how the business should be managed and developed.

CASE EXAMPLE 1: FORD TEAMS UP WITH CHINESE AUTO MAKER

A joint venture agreement has been signed between the American auto giant Ford and China's Chang' an-Automobile Group. According to the agreement, the construction of a newly launched Chang' an-Ford Motor Company will be completed in two years. Each party holds 50% of the joint venture's shares. The initial investment of the joint venture amounts to $98 million. The chang' an-Ford will manufacture and sell Ford designed cars as well as car parts and components. Ford started cooperation with its Chinese counterparts in manufacturing auto parts and components in 1978. The auto giant considers its latest move a necessary strategy to be a part of China's fast-developing auto market. The market is expected to reach 10 million cars in 2020. Chang' an-Automobile Group was established some 50 years ago and produced some 400,000 automobiles in 2004. It ranked first in China's mini-car production last year.

CASE EXAMPLE 2: NESTLE AND FRONTERRA IN DAIRY JOINT VENTURE IN TRINIDAD

A new joint venture has been announced by these companies. It creates a business that will concentrate on milk processing and the marketing of dairy products. This joint venture should strengthen the position of both companies in the Caribbean market. Nestle concentrates mainly on marketing of branded dairy products, but Fronterra is much better known as a milk-product processor. By combining forces in Trinidad and Tobago, the joint venture will gain from Fronterra's production and processing facilities and experience and Nestle's marketing expertise. The potential for success of the new joint venture, which will make and sell dairy products in Trinidad and Tobago, appears fairly strong. Much will depand, however, on milk prices and the ability of the new management team, made up of employees from both companies, to work well together.

(ii) *Strategic Alliance:* The global market is also inducing the growth of strategic alliance. Strategic alliance refers to the combining together of the resources and competence of two or more firms in a particular activity (but who continue to function separately in all other respects). A strategic alliance is a long-term partnership between two or more companies established to help each one build competitive market advantages. Unlike joint ventures, strategic alliances do not share costs, risks, management or even profits. Such alliance provides broad access to markets, capital and technological expertise. Due to their inherent flexibility, strategic alliances can establish links among firms of vasty different sizes. For example, Hewlett-Packard has strategic alliances with Hitachi and Samsung.

BUSINESS FOCUS: FOREIGN SUBSIDIARIES

A subsidiary company is one which is controlled by another company, called holding company. A subsidiary which is located in a different country is called a foreign company. An example is Hindusthan Uniliver which is a subsidiary of Uniliver, a British-cum Dutch enterprise.

7. **Foreign Direct Investment (through a Foreign Subsidiary):** Foreign direct investment (FDI) is the buying of permanent property and business in foreign nations. The most common form of FDI is a foreign subsidiary, i.e., a company owned in a foreign country by another company, called the parent company. The subsidiary operates like a domestic firm, with production, distribution, promotion, pricing, and other business functions under the control of the management of the subsidiary. The subsidiary also has to go by the laws of both the home country (where the parent firm is located) and the host country (the foreign country where the subsidiary is located).

BUSINESS FOCUS: DIRECT INVESTMENT IN SUBSIDIARIES

Empirical evidence suggests that setting up company-owned subsidiaries in foreign countries can achieve higher success rates than taking over or merging with locally-based companies.

The business cultures, organisational structures and technology differences between the company and the locally acquired businesses can often present obstacles too great to overcome. Subsidiaries can be factories set up in foreign countries, as with Toyota in the EU and South America, or retailing operations, as with Tesco in Thailand and China. They may be almost completely decentralised — where local managers take most key decisions — or organised with centralised control from head office in the home country.

The primary advantage of a subsidiary is that the parent company maintains full control over any technology or expertise it may possess. The major shortcoming is the need to block funds and combine technology within foreign boundaries. In case of strained relationships with a host country, the firm's assets could by acquired by the foreign government. US-based Nestle, for instance, has many foreign subsidiaries. It is a multinational corporation. A multinational corporation is one which produces in different countries of the world and has multinational stock ownership and management. Any large global enterprise cannot be treated as a multinational. Only firms which have manufacturing capacity or some other physical presence in different nations are to be treated as multinational.

8. **Turnkey project:** Turnkey project is a one-off major construction project such as the building of a dam, power station, etc. in another country where usually a contracted foreign firm (operating either alone or as the leader of a consortium of firms) is responsible for the design and construction of the facility.

At times the term 'turnkey contracts' is also used to refer to contracts for the provision, control and management of a wide range of services supplied as an integrated 'package' by one organisation.

A related term is 'build, operate, transfer' (BOT) project. It is a one-off major construction project such as building of a petrochemical complex in a country, in which the government is involved in contracting a foreign firm (or firms) not only to design and construct the facility, but also to finance it and run it on completion for a number of years. During this time the firm will expect to recoup its investment on the project before eventually transferring it to the government.

8.13 REASONS FOR GROWTH OF GLOBAL ENTERPRISES

Several reasons explain why businesses start to operate in countries other than their main base and grow and diversify over the years. The following four points are to be noted in this context:

(a) *Proximity to main markets:* This confers a number of advantages:

(i) lower transport costs for finished goods

(ii) better market information regarding tastes of consumer as a result of closeness to them

(iii) treatment like a local company and gaining customer loyalty as a consequence.

(b) *Lower costs of production:* Apart from lower transport costs of the completed items or finished goods, there are likely to be other cost savings:

(i) lower wages due to much lower demand for local labour compared to that in developed economies.

(ii) cheaper rent and site costs, again resulting from lower demand for commercial property — these cost savings can make the 'local' production very efficient in terms of the market in the rest of the world and can lead to substantial exports.

(iii) government grants and tax incentives designed to promote industrialisation of such countries.

(c) *Avoiding import restrictions:* By producing in the local country it is possible to avoid the payment of import duties and other import restrictions.

(d) *Accessing local natural resources:* These might not be available in the company's own country or main operating centre.

> **COMMENTARY: POTENTIAL PROBLEMS FOR MULTINATIONALS**
>
> Setting up operating plants in foreign countries is not without risks. Communication links with headquarters may be poor. Language, legal and cultural differences with local workers and government officials could lead to misunderstandings. Coordination with other plants in the multinational group will need to be carefully monitored to ensure that products that might compete with each other on world markets are not produced or that conflicting policies are not adopted. Finally, it is likely that the skill levels of the local employees will be low and this could require substantial investment in training programmes.

8.14 ADVANTAGES OF GLOBAL ENTERPRISES

MNCs have been playing an important role in developing countries like India. They bring the following benefits to the host countries:

1. Supply of financial capital: MNCs help capital-scarce developing countries by supplying the much needed financial resources and enable them to cover the domestic saving/ investment gap (i.e., the excess of investment over saving).
2. Transfer of technology: Transfer of technology refers to the transfer of techniques from countries where they are more advanced to other countries where they are less advanced (i.e., old and obsolete). Technology transfer may involve foreign direct investment, transfer of skilled personnel from more advanced countries, training of workers of developing countries, or licensing of patents. MNCs not only bring the much needed capital to developing countries but act as vehicles for the transfer of technology across national borders. Technology transfer is of great importance to India.

3. **Employment generation:** By setting up production centres and distribution networks in different parts of the world MNCs create both direct and indirect employment opportunities in the host countries.
4. **Utilisation of latent resources:** The MNCs help in the utilisation of unutilised resources of a host country by using their superior technology and thus raise the latter's income.
5. **Monopoly control:** By creating a competitive environment, MNCs indirectly help to control domestic monopolies. The inefficient firms are under pressure to improve their operational efficiency.
6. **Spread of professionalism in management:** The MNCs bring about some sort of managerial revolution in the host countries by employing professional managers who introduce the latest techniques of cost reduction, cost control and improvement of product quality.
7. **Growth of ancillary units:** Over the years, several ancillary units grow in developing countries to supply several parts and components of machines and equipment as also raw materials to MNCs. This is how MNCs often help the growth of domestic firms.
8. **Improved living standard:** By using superior technology MNCs produce and supply a wide range of quality products to consumers of developing countries. This helps to improve living standards as also the quality of life of the people.
9. **A force behind globalisation:** The MNCs lead to greater integration of an economy like that of India with the rest of the world. This is a real force behind globalisation and internationalisation of business of the host economy.

8.15 DISADVANTAGES OF GLOBAL ENTERPRISES

Multinational corporations have been criticised on the following grounds:

(i) Transfer of old and obsolete technology.
(ii) Complete neglect of national interest.
(iii) Production of only consumer goods (mainly non-essential items of consumption).
(iv) Destruction of domestic firms (or deindustrialisation of the host country).
(v) Repatriation of huge portion of profits to the home country (instead of ploughing them back in the host countries)
(vi) Not promoting national interests.
(vii) Exhaustion of non-renewable natural resources of developing countries.
(viii) Enjoyment of monopoly power by forcing numerous domestic firms to close down their operations.

Thus, MNCs have both favourable and adverse effects on developing countries like India. Thus they present a mixed picture in such countries and do not appear as an unmixed blessing.

8.16 EVALUATION OF THE IMPACT ON 'HOST' COUNTRIES OF MULTINATIONAL OPERATIONS

A. The Positive Side

The potential benefits are the following:

(i) *Inflow of foreign currency:* The investment by an MNC brings in foreign currency and, if output from the plant is exported, further foreign exchange can be earned.

(ii) *Secondary effect:* Local firms are likely to benefit from supplying services and components to the new factory and this will generate additional jobs and incomes.

(iii) *Improvement in quality and productivity:* Local firms will be forced to improve their product quality and raise resource(s) productivity to international standards either to compete with the multinational or to supply to it.

(iv) *Increase in tax revenue:* Tax revenues to the government will be boosted from any profits made by the multinational.

(v) *Improvement in management quality:* Management expertise in the community will slowly improve if and when the 'foreign' supervisors and managers are replaced by local staff, once they are suitably qualified.

(vi) *Increase in GDP:* The total output of the economy will be increased and this will raise gross domestic product (GDP).

(vii) *Employment generation:* New employment opportunities are created due to the operation of multinational corporations.

(viii) *Improved efficiency of local labour force:* Training programmes of multinational corporations are likely to improve the quality and efficiency of local people.

B. The Negative Side

The negative side of multinationals is also to be considered. The expansion of multinational corporations into a country could also generate following adverse consequences:

(i) *Exploitation:* The exploitation of the local worker workforce might take place. Due to the absence of strict labour and health and safety rules in some countries, multinationals can employ cheap labour for long hours with very few benefits that the staff in their 'host' country would demand and derive.

(ii) *Pollution from plants:* Pollution from plants might be at higher levels than permitted in other countries. The reason could be either slack rules or the fact that the 'host' government is afraid of driving the multinational away if it insists on environmentally acceptable practices. This is a sign of how powerful multinationals can be.

(iii) *Disappearance of local firms:* Local competing firms may be driven out of business due to inferior equipment and much smaller resources than the large multinational.

(iv) *Cultural degradation:* Some large Western-based businesses, such as McDonald's and Coca-Cola, have been accused of imposing 'Western' culture on other societies by the power of advertising and promotion. This could lead to a reduction in cultural identity.

(v) *Repatriation of profit:* Profits may be sent back to the country where the head office of the company is based, rather than kept for reinvestment in the host nation.

(vi) *Depletion of non-renewable natural resources:* Excessive depletion of the scarce natural resources of some countries has been caused largely by some large multinational corporations. The reason is that they have little incentive to conserve these resources, as they are able to relocate quickly to other countries once resources have run out.

Thus it is clear that multinational corporations have both merits and drawbacks. So a proper evaluation of their impact on developing countries like India is not an easy task. Much depends on existing empirical evidence and current research on foreign direct investment.

8.17 ONE-PERSON COMPANY (OPC)

The Companies Act, 2013 has, for the first time, allowed formation of a limited liability company by just one person. Such a company is described under Section 3(1)(c) as a private company. 'One-Person Company' is a one-shareholder corporate entity, where legal and financial liability is limited to the company only. In India, the J. J. Irani Expert Committee recommended the formation of one-person company (OPC).

The provisions relating to OPC are strewn all across the Companies Act, 2013. Section 2(62) of the Companies Act, 2013 defines 'One-Person Company' to mean a company with only one person as its member. Section 3(1)(c) provides that a company may be formed for any lawful purpose by one person, where the company to be formed is to be One-Person Company, that is to say, a private company by subscribing his name to a memorandum and complying with the requirements of the Act in respect of registration.

An OPC may be registered as 'limited by shares' or 'limited by guarantee'.

However, the memorandum of One-Person Company shall indicate the name of the other person, with his prior written consent in the prescribed form (Form No. INC.3), who shall, in the event of the subscriber's death or his incapacity to contract, become the member of the company and the written consent of such person shall also be filed with the Registrar at the time of the incorporation of the One-Person Company along with its memorandum and articles.

Key Points

1. **Private Sector Enterprise:** A private sector enterprise is owned, operated, managed and controlled by individuals or groups, known as entrepreneurs. Examples of such enterprises are Tata Motors, Reliance Industries, Hindalco Ltd., Larsen & Toubro Ltd. and so on. The main features of such an enterprise are the following:
   (i) It is owned by a private individual or an entrepreneur.
   (ii) It is managed either by the owners or by salaried people (paid executives)
   (iii) It is mainly guided by the profit motive.
   (iv) It is accountable to the owners for its operational performance.
2. **Public Sector Enterprise:** A public sector enterprise is owned (financed) and controlled by the government at any level (central, state, or local). Examples are the SAIL, BHEL, CIL, IOC, BPCL and HMT. Its main features are the following:
   (i) Its initial capital is provided by the government.
   (ii) It is fully controlled by the government.
   (iii) Its main objective is to promote social welfare.
   (iv) It is accountable to the Parliament as also to the general public for its financial performance.
   (v) Its management is in the hands of government officials.
3. **Joint Sector Enterprise:** In a joint sector enterprise the ownership management and control are jointly shared by the government, a private entrepreneur and the public. However, the major

percentage of shares is held by the private sector. Examples of such enterprises are the West Bengal Scooters Ltd., Cochin Refinaries, and Telerama Ltd. The features of such an enterprise are the following:

(i) Capital is jointly contributed by the government and a private entrepreneur.
(ii) Management is in the hands of a private entrepreneur.
(iii) It is accountable to both the government and the private investors.
(iv) It seeks to make profit as also to promote social welfare.

4. **Forms of Public Sector Enterprises:** There are three important organisational forms of public sector units. These are the following:
   (i) Departmental undertakings such as Posts and Telegraph, the Railways, the Telecommunication and Defence.
   (ii) Statutory corporations such as Life Insurance Corporation of India, Food Corporation of India, National Textile Corporation and Indian Airlines Corporation.
   (iii) Government companies such as Hindustan Machine Tools Ltd. (HMT), Bharat Heavy Electricals Ltd. (BHEL) and Steel Authority of India Ltd. (SAIL).

5. **Changing Role of Public Sector in India**
   (i) Development of basic and heavy industries,
   (ii) provision of public utility services,
   (iii) infrastructure building,
   (iv) ensuring (promoting) balanced regional development,
   (v) employment generation,
   (vi) reducing undue concentration of wealth and economic power in private hands.
   (vii) deriving economies of scale.
   (viii) import substitution.
   (ix) export promotion and
   (x) meeting defence needs.

6. **Global corporation:** As economies become more globalised, more and more firms start participating in foreign markets. The most common participation strategies include licensing, exporting, joint ventures and strategic alliances and direct foreign investment (through the multinational corporations). Each of these involves different levels of capital risk, and returns. A global corporation or a multinational corporation is one which operates much beyond the country in which it is incorporated. Its headquarter (decision-making centre) is located in the home country or the country of origin. But it operates in a number of foreign countries, known as host countries. For instance, Ford (the US firm) produces more cars not only in the USA but also in Western Europe and Japan. Other MNCs are Wal-Mart (USA), Volkswagen (Germany), Royal Dutch Steel (Netherlands, UK), Petrochina (China), Suzuki (Japan), Cadbury (UK), Proctor and Gamble (USA), Microsoft (USA), General Electric (USA) and so on.

   The notable features of a global corporation are the following:
   (i) Its size is gigantic and has control over huge assets in a number of countries.
   (ii) It seeks to maximise profits through worldwide sourcing, i.e., by processing raw materials and labour power at low cost and selling its products at high prices.
   (iii) Its operations are controlled from its headquarters.

(iv) It operates on a very large scale.

(v) It conducts production, distribution and research and development (R & D) activities in a number of countries.

7. **Joint Venture:** A joint venture is a commercial undertaking entered into jointly by two or more firms (enterprises). Joint ventures have a separate profit-and-loss-sharing ratio. Joint ventures often carry on their main business independently of, and at the same time as, the joint venture. Joint ventures have become a very common form of business as companies cooperate with each other in international markets, in order to share costs, exploit new technologies, or gain to access to new markets.

8. **Public-Private Partnership (PPP):** It refers to a partnership between government and the private sector for the purpose of more effectively providing service and infrastructure traditionally provided by the private sector.

9. **One-person company:** The Companies Act, 2013 has, for the first time, allowed formation of a limited liability company by just one person. Such a company is described under Section 3(1)(c) as a private company. 'One-Person Company' is a one-shareholder corporate entity.

KEY Terms	
Private sector	Exporting
Public sector	Foreign direct investment
Public-private partnership	Multinational corporation
Departmental undertaking	Licensing
Statutory corporation	Strategic alliance
Government company	Transfer of technology
Joint sector	Disinvestment of public sector units
Global enterprise	Exit policy
International joint venture	Memorandum of undertaking (MOU)
Host country	Import substitution
Worldwide sourcing	Export promotion
Franchising	Trunkey project
Home country	One-person company

Assignments

SHORT ANSWER-TYPE QUESTIONS

1. Define a government company. [ISC 2009]
2. Give two features of a private limited company. [ISC 1993]
3. Name two of the privileges enjoyed by a private limited company. [ISC 1993]
4. What is a multinational company? [ISC 1999, 2005]
5. Define a private limited company. [ISC 1995, 2000]
6. What is a government company? [ISC 1996]
7. Define public limited company. [ISC 2013]
8. Briefly describe a statutory company. [ISC 1997]
9. What is a subsidiary company? [ISC 1998]
10. Explain briefly two characteristics of a public limited company distinct from those of a private limited company. [ISC 1998]
11. Mention two characteristics under which a private company is deemed to be a public company. [ISC 2009]
12. What is a holding company? [ISC 1999]
13. Name the company which may not have share capital. [ISC 1999]
14. Distinguish between a company limited by shares and a company limited by guarantee. [ISC 2000]
15. Mention any two limitations of global enterprises. [ISC 2001]
16. When can a private company deemed to be a public company? [ISC 2002]
17. Give two privileges of a private company. [ISC 2003]
18. Give two advantages of a government company. [ISC 2004]
19. What is a multinational company? [ISC 2005]
20. Explain turnkey projects with reference to a multinational company. [ISC 2006]
21. Mention any two methods of organising the operations of a multinational corporation. [ISC 2007]
22. List any two objectives of government companies. [ISC 2007]
23. What is a company limited by guarantee? [ISC 2008]
24. Define a government company. [ISC 2009]
25. What are multinational companies? [ISC 2010]
26. Write a short note on turnkey projects. [ISC 2010]
27. Write a short note on holding company. [ISC 2011]
28. Explain joint venture in relation to multinational companies. [ISC 2013]
29. Name the following:
    (a) A company which is not allowed to issue shares to the public.

(b) A company established under a special law.

(c) A statement which a public company has to file before allotment of shares when it did not issue a prospectus.

(d) A company which carries on business without obtaining the certificate of commencement of business. [ISC 2008]

ESSAY-TYPE QUESTIONS

1. Distinguish between a public limited company and a private limited company. [ISC 2011]
2. Define a government company. Discuss the demerits of a government company. [ISC 1994]
3. Briefly discuss five privileges of a private company. [ISC 1994, 2013]
4. Discuss five advantages of a public limited company. [ISC 1995]
5. Explain four reasons for the growth of multinationals. [ISC 1995]
6. Give five differences between a private limited company and a public limited company. [ISC 1996]
7. Explain the reasons for the growth of multinational corporations in India. [ISC 1998, 2000]
8. 'Private company is a compromise between partnership and public company'. In the light of this statement, describe the merits and demerits of a private company.
9. Discuss the role of multinationals in Indian economy. [ISC 2011]
10. Explain any five privileges enjoyed by a private limited company as compared to a public limited company. [ISC 1999]
11. Define a government company and explain the merits of a government company. [ISC 2000]
12. State the merits and demerits of multinational corporations. [ISC 2002]
13. Give five differences between a private limited company and a public limited company. [ISC 2004]
14. Enumerate any five advantages of a private limited company. [ISC 2000]
15. Examine any five advantages that the host countries derive from the presence of multinational corporations. [ISC 2008]
16. Explain the terms (i) statutory company and (ii) foreign company [ISC 2009]
17. (a) Briefly explain any four merits of a government company. (b) What is a private limited company? (c) State any eight privileges enjoyed by it. [ISC 2010]
18. Explain any four advantages that host countries derive from multinational corporations. [ISC 2013]
19. What is the difference between private-sector and public-sector organisations?
20. Who (a) owns and who (b) controls a public limited company? Explain why this distinction might lead to conflict.
21. State two benefits and two risks for a business of engaging in a joint venture.
22. Why might the directors of a public limited company decide to convert the business back into a private limited company by buying a majority of the shares?
23. Explain how legal identity and continuity help businesses and companies to operate effectively.

24. Giving the examples of a sole trader business and a public limited company, explain how the relationship between ownership and control differs in these two types of organisations.
25. Using the examples of a partnership and a public limited company, explain how the legal structure of business affects its ability to raise finance.
26. List two organisations in your own country which are in the public sector.
27. What is a multinational company? What is worldwide?
28. List four examples of multinational companies operating in India.
29. Explain three possible advantages to India's economy from the existence of multinational companies.
30. (a) Briefly explain any three merits and three demerits of government companies. (b)What are the advantages of a public limited company? [ISC 2006]
31. (a) Under what circumstances is a private company deemed to be a public company?
    (b) What are the privileges of private limited companies as compared to the public limited companies? [ISC 2005]
32. (a) Explain any four advantages of a Public Limited Company over a Private Limited Company.
    (b) Briefly explain any three merits and demerits of a government company. [ISC 2012]

QUESTION BANK

1. *Name the joint stock company which cannot have more than 50 members.* [ISC 1998]

Ans. The joint stock company which cannot have more than 50 members is known as "Private Company".

2. *What is a company established under the provisions of the Indian Companies Act 1956 called?* [ISC 1989]

OR

What is a company brought into existence under the Act passed by the legislature of the country called? [ISC 1992]

Ans. A company established under the provisions of Indian Companies Act 1956 is called "Registered Company".

3. *Write the correct name of the Act which governs joint stock companies in India.* [ISC 1991]

Ans. The correct name of the Act which governs joint stock companies in India is the Companies Act, 1956.

4. *Name the company whose Profit & Loss Account and Balance Sheet are available for inspection by the general public.* [ISC 1991]

Ans. The company whose Profit & Loss Account and Balance Sheet are available for inspection by the general public is known as "Public Limited Company".

5. *What is a private company?* [ISC 1987, 1995]

OR

Define private limited company. [ISC 1997, 2000]

Ans. See text.

6. *Briefly describe a statutory company.* [ISC 19997]

Ans A statutory a company is established under a special Act passed by Parliament or by a State Legislature as the case may be. The objects and powers of such a company are defined by the Act constituting it. Therefore such a company is under the legal obligation to have a Memorandum of Association. It need not use the word 'Limited' against its name. The audit of a statutory company/corporation is conducted under the supervision and control of the Comptroller and Auditor General of India. Statutory companies generally enjoy autonomous status as they are created to carry out business requiring extraordinary powers and privileges. The Reserve Bank of India, the Life Insurance of India, the Unit Trust of India are examples of such statutory companies in operating in India.

7. *What is a subsidiary company?* [ISC 1998]
8. *What is a holding company?* [ISC 1999]
9. *Name the company which may not have any share capital.* [ISC 1999]

   OR

   What is a company limited by guarantee?
10. *What is a chartered company?* [ISC 1987]
11. *Distinguish between a company limited by shares and a company limited by guarantee.* [ISC 2000]
12. *What is a 'One-Man Company'?*
13. *Give two features of a private limited company.* [ISC 1993]
14. *Explain briefly two characteristics of a public limited company distinct from those of private limited company.* [ISC 1998]
15. *Distinguish between a public limited company and a private limited company.* [ISC 1990, 1993]

   OR

   Give five differences between a private limited company and a public limited company. [ISC 1996]
16. *Mention the circumstances under which a private company is deemed to be a public company.* [ISC 1997]

   OR

   When can a private company deemed to be a public company? [ISC 2002]
17. *Name two of the privileges enjoyed by a private limited company.* [ISC 1993]
18. *Briefly discuss the privileges of a private company.* [ISC 1994]

   OR

   Explain any five privileges enjoyed by a private limited company as compared to a public limited company. [ISC 1999]
19. *Discuss five advantages of a public limited company.* [ISC 1995]
20. *What is a government company?* [ISC 1993, 1997]
21. *Define a government company and explain the merits of a government company.* [ISC 2000]
22. *Define a government company. Discuss the merits of a government company.* [ISC 1999]

23. *What is a multinational company?* [ISC 1994, 1999]

Ans. A multinational company refers to a corporation which operates, i.e., owns and controls production and service facilities in two or more countries. It is also called international corporation, multinational enterprise and transnational corporation. It usually operates in a number of countries. Since it is headquartered in only one country but has production or marketing facilities in others, it is a result of pressures of foreign direct investment (FDI). According to United Nations, a multinational corporation is "an enterprise which owns or controls production or service facilities outside the country of its origin." In the language of W. H. Moreland, "multinational corporations or companies are those enterprises whose management, ownership and controls are spread in more than one foreign country". Coca-Cola, Pepsi, Bata, Philips, Nestle, etc. are examples of multinational companies.

24. *Explain four reasons for growth of multinationals/global enterprises.* [ISC 1996]

OR

Explain the reasons for the growth of multinational corporations in India. [ISC 1998]

OR

Explain the reasons for the growth of multinational companies in India. [ISC 2000]

25. *Discuss that benefits of multinational corporations for a 'host' country like India.*

26. *Mention limitations of a multinational corporation/global enterprise.* [ISC 2000]

27. *Briefly state the various forms in which multinational corporations operate.*

Ans. Multinational corporations operate in the following forms:

(a) Franchises
(b) Branches
(c) Subsidiaries
(d) Joint ventures
(e) Contract manufacturing and
(f) Turnkey projects

28. *Classify the following into Public Company, Government Company and Global Enterprise. (i) Idea Cellular, (ii) Damodar Valley Corporation, (iii) Hindustan Machine Tools (HMT), (iv) Apollo Pharmaceuticals, (v) Unilever and (vi) Mitsubishi.*

Ans. (i) Public company
(ii) Government company
(iii) Government company
(iv) Public company
(v) Global enterprise
(vi) Global enterprise

29. *What is joint venture? What are the reasons for joint venture?*

30. *What is licensing? What is its advantage and what are its limitation?*

APPENDIX

Longest MNCs in the World

An MNC is one which manufacture and markets products in many different countries and has multinational stock ownership and management. Multinational corporations are typically extremely large corporations like Nestle, but not all large global businesses are multinationals. For example, a corporation could export everything it produces, deriving 100 percent of its sales and profits globally, and still not be a multinational corporation. Only firms that have *manufacturing capacity* or some other physical presence in different nations can truly be called multinational. Table A.1 lists the 10 largest multinational corporations in the world.

TABLE A.1: The Largest Multinational Corporations in the World, 2013-2014

Company	Country
1. Royal Dutch Shell	Netherlands
2. Wal-Mart Stores	United States
3. Exxon Mobil	United States
4. Sinopec Group	China
5. China National Petroleum	China
6. BP	Britain
7. State Grid	China
8. Toyota Motor	Japan
9. Japan Post Holdings	Japan
10. Chevron	United States

CASE STUDY 1

MULTINATIONAL CHALLENGES AND OPPORTUNITIES IN INDIA FOR COMPANIES LIKE WIPRO

Challenges faced by some companies can be create opportunities for others. In the late 1970s. IBM was selling obsolete and outdated machines in India. The Indian Government told the company to shift to newer equipment or it would have to quite IBM left, creating opportunities for Indian companies such as Wipro which was a very small company in the late 1970s. But by 2006, the company grew to be a $2 billion firm by providing information technology, business process operations, and R&D facilities, serving customers all over the world.

Wipro, under Azim H. Premji, took advantage of the emerging outsourcing trend Developed counties started manufacturing outsourcing to China, while India, with a well-educated English-speaking workforce began outsourcing services. Wipro and other Indian companies provided services such as call centers, payroll software for foreign companies, interactive training systems, and portfolio management for insurance companies. Today, India is considered to be the low-cost quality IT services provider.

These high-tech companies, such as Wipro, can draw students from highly respected institutes such as the Indian Institute of Technology, Kanpur, and the Indian Institute for Management Ahmedabad. Wipro, which began as a peanut oil producing company, is now growing rapidly in the innovative business with sophisticated R&D capabilities.

CASE STUDY 2

LEADING THE WAY TO COST-EFFECTIVE CARS IN THE GLOBAL MARKET

With high fuel prices and saturated markets in developed countries, automakers focus now on emerging markets. These markets measure cost-effective cars and manufacturers are responding. However, cars should not only be cost-effective; they must also be strong, durable and reliable quickly (safe). Carlos Ghosn, Penault-Nissan's CEO, in the past focused on large, expensive cars. Renault plans are to build a $3,000 car with Bajaj Auto Ltd., an Indian motorbikes maker, Ranault has been fairly successful with its Logan model that sold in India for about $ 7,500 — a car that was suited for the middle class. Renault moved to the low-cost car, produced in Romania. While Logan has failed to any inroad in Western Durope, it is now produced in seven countries including Columbia and Russia.

Chryster together with China's Chery Automobile Co. is planning to sell cars in Europe under the Dodge brand name. General Motors plans operations in Argentina and Brazil and opening engineering centers in India, Korea, and Brazil.

Traditionally, customers in developing countries bought used European and Japanese cars. Now, African customers look for cost-effective cars. New cars form China are replacing used cars from developing countries. Chinese companies such as Great Wall, Chery Automobile Co., and Geely Group Ltd, are making inroads in Africa. India's TATA Motors is offering a car for less than $2,500. Western manufacturers such as France's Renault and Japan's Nissan Motors Co. are working together with India's Mahindra & Mahindra Ltd. to develop a $ 3,000 car.

Emerging countries demand cost-effective cars and global carmakers are responding to these needs using global strategies. International demand for cost-effective cars can help unify countries.

9 FORMATION OF COMPANIES

SYLLABUS

- *Stages of Formation of a Company.*
- *Promotion, meaning, role and types of promoters.*
- *Incorporation of a company — Meaning and steps of incorporation (including filing of documents), certificate of incorporation.*
- *Memorandum of Association and Articles of Association (excluding alterations) and distinction between the two documents.*
- *Meaning and contents of MOA and AOA. Distinction between the MOA and AOA.*
- *Commencement of business, Steps, Certificate of Commencement.*
- *Prospectus and statement in lieu of prospectus — meaning and contents only.*

> *The memorandum of Association sets out the constitution of the company. It is, so to speak, the charter of the company and provides the foundation on which the structure of the company is built. It enables persons who deal with the company to know its permitted range of activities.* — Lord Macmillan

LEARNING OUTCOMES

On completion of this chapter, you will be able to understand the following:

9.1 Meaning of Promotion
9.2 Stages in Promotion
9.3 Promoters
9.4 Incorporation of a Company
9.5 Commencement of Business
9.6 Documents Used in the Formation of a Company
9.7 Memorandum of Association (MOA)
9.8 Articles of Association (AOA)
9.9 Difference between MOA and AOA
9.10 Prospectus
9.11 Statement in Lieu of Prospectus
9.12 Minimum Subscription
9.13 Judging the Soundness of a Company from the Prospectus

In order to ensure the existence of a joint stock company, it is necessary to complete several legal formalities and take various procedural decisions. Company formation calls for two things at least: planned actions and conscious efforts. To be more specific, the following stages are involved in the formation of a company:

1. promotion
2. incorporation
3. flotation or Capital Subscription, and
4. commencement of business.

A private limited company has to complete the first two stages. But a public limited company has to complete all the four stages. The stages in formation of a company are presented in the chart below.

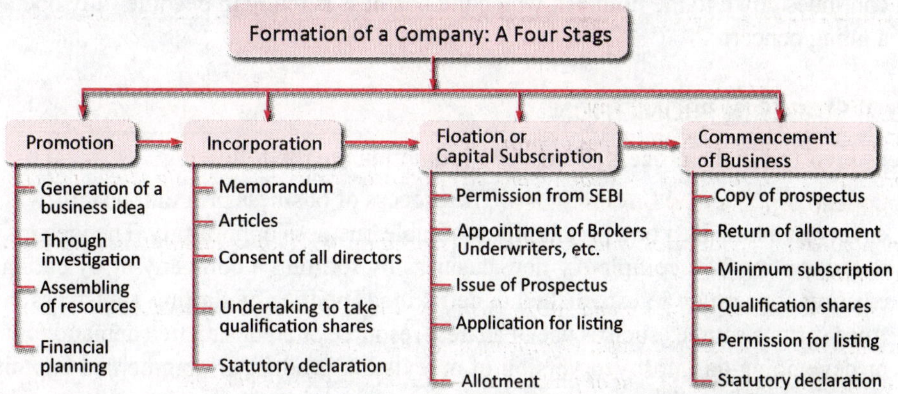

9.1 MEANING OF PROMOTION

In truth, 'promotion' is the first stage in company formation. In the language of C.W. Gerstenberg, "Promotion is the discovery of business opportunities, and the subsequent organisation of funds, properties and managerial ability into a business concern for the purpose of making profits therefrom."

Promotion involves the discovery of a business idea, its investigation and combining all necessary resources to set up a business as a profit-making enterprise. According to Prof. Haney, "Promotion is the process of organising and planning the finances of a business enterprise under the corporate form".

The process of promotion begins with the conception of an idea from which the business is to be evolved and ends with the launching of the enterprise as a going concern. Persons who perform the task of promotion are known as promoters or entrepreneurs. A promoter conceives of the idea of a business enterprise, analyses its prospects, works out a tentative scheme of organisation, brings together the necessary resources of money, materials, machinery, people and managerial ability, and floats an enterprise.

A joint stock company may be promoted in any of the following two ways:

(i) by converting an existing partnership or proprietorship firm into a joint stock company; or
(ii) by setting up a new company altogether to take up a new line of business.

The process of business promotion starts when someone conceives an idea regarding some business which can be profitably undertaken by setting up a company. It encompasses preliminary and detailed survey-cum-investigation of the technical and economic feasibility of the idea, collating various elements of a business enterprise and making adequate provision of finance necessary to start a profit-seeking enterprise as a running concern.

Four Definitions of Promotion:

1. Promotion is the process of organisation and planning the finances of a business under the corporate structure of an enterprise
2. It is the process of creating a specific business enterprise through aggregation of activities pursued (conducted) by all those who participate in building the enterprise.
3. Promotion involves four steps: discovery, investigation, assembling and financing.
4. Promotion starts with the discovery of an idea from which a business is to be evolved and continues down to the points at which the business is ready to become fully operational as a going concern.

9.2 STAGES IN PROMOTION

Four steps involved in the process of business promotion are the following:

1. **Conception of a new business idea:** The process of business promotion starts with the discovery of a new idea or a potentially profitable business opportunity. The idea may related to the starting of a completely new business by forming a company or by taking over an existing concern or an established undertaking. The idea of starting a business may come from various sources such as use of a latent resource or an unsatisfied demand for a product or developing an improved version of an existing product or commercial exploitation of an innovative idea. The person who conceives a new idea or develops the new idea of any other person is known as the promoter. At the very preliminary stage an insightful analysis is also made embracing all the different aspects of the business. Many new companies fail even at the very early (nascent) stage because they were originally based on wrong ideas or faulty concepts.
2. **Details investigation-cum-verification:** Before putting the idea of establishing a business into practice it is necessary to thoroughly investigate the utility, practicability and economic feasibility (profitability) of the idea. Such investigation is necessary to establish the soundness of the business proposition in terms of is technical (engineering) feasibility and commercial viability (i.e., whether it will be profitable or not). Detailed investigation involves an in-depth study or a survey of market demand for the product(s) of the firm under consideration, cost and availability of raw materials, machinery and other factors of production, degree and intensity of actual and potential competition, likely selling price(s) of its product(s) and its profit prospects and so on. Such investigation may be conducted with the contributions of professional people — such as engineers, values, financial analysts and so on.

   After the completion of investigation the major findings are listed and summarised in the form of a report called project or feasibility report. The report enables the persons(s) concerned to assess whether the new business proposition is likely to yield a fair return on investment and is justified in terms of various risks to be undertaken. The report containts necessary information and data collected, estimates of cost and revenue, opinions of experts as also their recommendations. It is judicious on the part of the promoter to verify the report through independent appraisal for the purpose of cross checking and before giving the proposal final approval.

3. **Assembling:** In the next step the promoter starts assembling various business elements with a view to giving the idea a concrete shape. This step involves a number of sub-steps such as making contracts for purchase of materials, machines tools and equipment, etc. In addition it is necessary to take decisions regarding the site (plant) location, layout, etc. of the business. Plans are to be prepared for the recruitment of various types of workers and executives required by the firm.
4. **Financing:** In the final stage financial plans are prepared with respect to capitalisation (or degree of leverage), capital structure (i.e., the proportion of debt and equity in total funds to be raised), timing and method of capital issue (i.e., floatation of shares, etc. The business proposition is made publicly known through a 'prospectus' in order to persuade the general public to buy shares of the company (in case of a new unit). At this stage agreements are also made with underwriters, stock-brokers, etc. The process of promotion comes to an end with the actual issue of shares and debentures.

9.3 PROMOTERS

The term 'promoter' has not been defined in the Companies Act because it has just commercial and not any legal implication. Simple put, a 'promoter' is a person who discovers a new business opportunity, collates the necessary human and non-human resources, gets the enterprise officially registered and sets it in motion as a running concern. The promoter ventures out to form a business enterprise from a scratch and makes its operational after taking all necessary steps (i.e., from conception to action). The task of a promoter is performed by an entrepreneur. In this context we may cite the examples of a few pioneering promoters in India such as J.N. Tata, G.D. Birla, R.N. Mukherjee, G.M. Modi and Dhirubhai Ambani.

9.3.1 Meaning and Definition of a Promoter

A 'promoter' is essentially a person conscious of the possibility of transforming an idea or a concrete proposal into a business venture which has strong prospects of making profit, who brings together the various persons concerned and who finally superintends the various steps necessary to bring the new business into existence.

Alternatively stated, a promoter is one who acts as a pioneer to form a company so that a new business idea is put into effect and set it going and to take the necessary steps to accomplish that purpose.

The promoter is an enterprising person having or showing the ability to think of new projects or new ways of doing things and make them successful. He combines a number of business operations by which a company is brought into existence. He activates that machinery which enables a business organisation to get incorporated as an artificial and legal entity.

There are various definitions of the term 'promoter'. According to *the Oxford Dictionary of Business*, "A promoter is a person involved in setting up and funding a new company, including preparation of its articles of its association and memorandum of association, registering the company, finding directors and raising subscriptions." The pioneering promoters in India were J.N. Tata, G.D. Birla, R.N. Mukherjee, G.M. Modi and D. Ambani. Some leading U.S. promoters include G.D. Rockefeller, Henry Ford and, of course, Bill Gates.

To quote *the Oxford Dictionary of Business* once again, "The promoter is in a position of trust with regard to the new company and may not make any undisclosed profit or benefit at its expense.

A promoter may be personally liable for the fulfillment of a contract entered into by, or on behalf of, the new company before it has been formed."

9.3.2 Types of Promoters

A promoter may be an individual, a firm, a financial or a even non-financial institution or even the government (Central or State). See chart below. We now make a brief review of at least types of promoters.

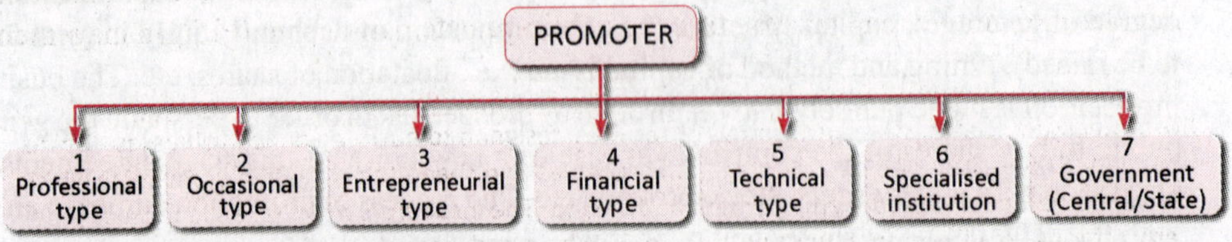

1. *Professional promoters:* Professional promoters refer to those specialised agencies whose whole-time occupation is business promotion. As specialised in new venture creation these professionals promote business enterprises and hand over such enterprises to their owners for management and control.
2. *Promoters by chance:* Such promoters are not specialised persons in the formation of companies since promotion is not their full-time (or only) job. They promote their own firms without taking any external help and own and manage their own enterprises, though not necessarily or always in a professional way (manner).
3. *Entrepreneurial promoters:* An entrepreneur is a person who discovers a new business opportunity or conceives a new business idea, does the necessary groundwork to establish a business unit and then proceeds one step ahead to promote a new company and then to run the unit. He (she) is someone who makes a business idea fructify, either through his own effort or by organising others to do the work. Such an entrepreneur is also called a promoter because he takes necessary risk and plays the leadership role in promoting a new company.

BUSINESS FOCUS: THE ROLE OF THE ENTREPRENEUR

An entrepreneur is someone who takes the financial risk of starting and managing a new venture. Most entrepreneurs see the opportunities which others see, but they also have the courage and initiative to act quickly.

New business ventures started by entrepreneurs can be based on a totally new idea or a new way of offering a service. They can also be a new location of an existing business or an attempt to adopt a good or a service in ways which no one else has tried before.

4. *Financial promoters:* Financial (investment) promoters float new enterprises when the stock market is in good state and the overall business environment is favourable. They specialise in marketing shares of newly floated companies at high prices with a view to earning a good profit margin.
5. *Technical promoters:* Some technically qualified people often promote new ventures on the basis of their specialised knowledge and training in certain specific areas.
6. *Specialised institutions:* Some specialised financial and non-financial institutions such as Industrial Development Bank of India and National Industrial Development Corporation provide managerial and technical assistance for the promotion of new enterprises apart

from supplying initial finance (or seed capital). These institutions collaborate with entrepreneurs in new venture creation. Many of them provide a wide range of services for launching new enterprise.

7. *Government as promoter:* In the Post-Independence period the Government of India emerged as a major promoter of industrial and commercial undertakings. It has promoted enterprises in various diverse fields. State governments have also acted as business promoters by setting up commercial corporations or by joining hands with the private sector under the joint venture scheme or even public-private partnership (PPP) management.

BUSINESS FOCUS: INCUBATORS

A business incubator is an organisation of services designed to nurture young businesses. It aims to reduce the failure rate of early stage of companies and speed the growth of companies which have the potential to create employment and wealth. The incubators could take the form of properly offering small workshop units with secretarial help and managerial services.

9.3.3 Role of Promoters

The functions (roles) of promoters are the following:

1. *Conceiving a business idea:* The promoter first conceives the idea for starting a business and then tries to search out or identify the area of potentially profitable investment and then on the basis of his knowledge, foresight, prudence and past experience of business start-ups and failures he undertakes preliminary risk analysis and makes an estimate of seed (initial) capital required.
2. *Undertaking feasibility study:* The promoter makes detailed investigation to ascertain whether his planned business venture has any genuine profit prospect or not, often in consultation with engineers and accountants, market researchers and so on. Such investigation is known as feasibility study. It seeks to determine which of the range of decisions is likely to give a satisfactory return in a financial appraisal or an economic appraisal of the alternatives.

   The promoters have to conduct the following kinds of feasibility studies:

   (a) *Economic appraisal:* The economic appraisal of the project is a method of capital budgeting or long-term investment decision which makes use of discounted cash flow-techniques to determine a preferred investment. The technique discounts over the project's life the expected annual economic costs and economic benefits.

   (b) *Financial appraisal:* Financial appraisal is the use of financial evaluation techniques such as ratio analysis, profitability index, or risk analysis to determine which of the range of possible alternatives is preferred. These techniques are used to assess a business problem in financial terms. These two types of appraisal are to be supported by technical feasibility study.

   (c) *Technical appraisal:* It is also necessary to check and ensure that a business idea is technically feasible. A project is technically feasible if appropriate technology or necessary raw materials and other inputs are domestically available or can be imported.
3. *Acquisition of resources and gathering them.* After the successful completion of the feasibility study, the promoter takes steps to give his embryonic idea a practical shape. This involves a number of steps such as making contracts for the purchase of materials, land, machinery, tools and implements. Decisions have to be taken on key issues such as the

size, location and layout of the enterprise as also its plants. Plans are prepared for the recruitment and selection of required manpower (e.g., managers, supervisors and workers.)

4. *Preparation of documents:* The promoters are the people who prepare the two most important legal documents, viz., the memorandum of association and the articles of association.

   The memorandum of association is an official document which gives details of a company's existence. It must be signed by the first subscribers and must contain the following information: (i) the company's name; (ii) a statement that the company is a public company; (iii) the full address of its registered office; (iv) the objectives of the company; (v) a statement of limited liability; (vi) the amount of the guarantee; and (vii) the amount of authorised share capital and its division.

   Articles of association are the documents which govern the running of a company. It sets out voting rights of shareholders, conduct of shareholders' and directors' meetings, power of the management, etc. The articles are submitted with the memorandum of association when application is made for incorporation. The articles constitute a contract between the company and its members. However, this applies only to the rights of the shareholders in their capacity as members.

   After incorporation promoters have to prepare a prospectus or an authentic statement in lieu of prospectus for raising capital from the market as also for obtaining the certificate for starting business operations.

   A prospectus is a document which gives necessary details about new issue of shares and invites the public to buy shares or debentures in the company. A copy has to be filed with the Registrar of the Companies. The prospectus must conform to the provisions of the Companies Act (1956), describe its aims, capital structure and any past history of the venture and may contain future profit forecasts.

5. *Motivating signatories to the memorandum of association:* To make their effort really fruit-bearing the promoters induce and motivate renowned business persons and famous executives to be the signatories (or founder members) to the memorandum of association. While for a public company a minimum number of seven signatories is required, in case of a private company the minimum number is two. The promoters also find out some competent people to act as directors for the first time.

6. *Making initial contracts:* The promoters make initial contracts with respective parties for the purchase of property such as land, buildings and factory sheds, machinery which require huge initial investment. They also enter into arrangements with the suppliers of materials and distributors of the company's products such as wholesalers and retailers.

7. *Appointment of bankers and recruitment of agents:* The promoters appoint merchant bankers, underwriters and solicitors for managing initial public offering (IPO), i.e., issue of new capital.

8. *Getting business licence:* The promoters also take steps to get licence from the Government. Of course, this is necessary only if the product to be manufactured by the company is covered by the industrial licencing policy of the government, as per the Industries (Development and Regulation) Act, 1951.

SYNOPSIS FOR LEARNING: FUNCTIONS (ROLES) OF PROMOTERS

1. Conceiving a business idea
2. Undertaking feasibility study
3. Acquisition of resources and gathering them
4. Preparation of legal documents
5. Motivating signatories to the memorandum of association
6. Making initial contracts
7. Appointment of bankers and agents
8. Getting business licence

9.3.4 Legal Status of a Promoter

Even if a promoter performs all functions necessary to start a company he is not an agent of it . The reason is that a non-existent principal (i.e., an association which is yet to be incorporated) does not have the legal right to appoint an agent. So the promoters themselves remain personally liable for the initial contracts made before incorporation if, of course, they are neither ratified nor adopted by the company after its incorporation.

A promoter is not a trustee of the company either. However, he must show honesty and integrity in its dealing. if he makes some personal gain by taking advantage of his position, he will have to account for such gains and take necessary remedial measures. For instance, if the promoter gets some commission from the supplier of machinery and equipment he has to surrender the same to the company.

A promoter is to be held liable if he fails to discharges the following obligations:

1. He does not surrender secret personal gains out of the dealings made on behalf of the company during its promotion stage.
2. He does not deposit all the payments received on behalf of the company in the latter's bank account(s).
3. He has to be careful and hard working during the promotional stage.

9.4 INCORPORATION OF A COMPANY

Incorporation is the act of forming a company by carrying out (or completing) the necessary legal formalities. This is obligatory because a company is a legal person separate and distinct from the people who own it, usually with a limited liability.

Company formation refers to the whole process of forming a joint stock company, which involves a number of steps (stages) such as (a) drawing up a memorandum of association; (b) preparation of articles of association; (c) application to the Registrar of Companies for a certificate of incorporation; (d) issuing share capital; and (e) commencing business. Incorporation essentially refers to the registration of a joint stock company as a body corporate under the Indian Companies Act, 1956. The Act is a body of legislation providing for the regulation of joint stock companies. India's company law encouraged the development of joint stock companies by establishing the principle of limited liability and it now provides for the protection of shareholders' interest by controlling the formation and financing of companies. It is accomplished by the Registrar of Companies after completion of the promotional work. The Company Registrar is the officer of a joint stock company who is responsible for maintaining an up-to-date share register and for issuing new share certificate and cancelling old ones as shares are bought and sold on the stock market.

Immediately after receiving 'The Certificate of Incorporation/Registration' a private company as a profit-seeking entity may commence business (i.e., production and/or trading). But the provisions regarding a public company having share capital is different. It has also to obtain 'The Certificate of Commencement of Business' after it has secured 'The Certificate of Incorporation'.

9.4.1 Steps in Incorporation of a Company

As per statutory provisions the following steps are to be followed in incorporating or registering a company:

1. *Submission of applications:* An application for the registration of the company is to be submitted to the Registrar of Companies of the state/region in which the registered office of the company is to be located.
2. *Approval of the name of the company:* It is necessary, in the next step, to get the proposed name of the company approved by the Company Registrar.
3. *Submission of documents:* In the next step the following documents are to be submitted or filed with the Registrar:
   (a) *Memorandum of Association (MOA):* It is perhaps the most important document of the company or its constitution, so the say. It defines the objectives of the company and establishes its relationship with the external world. Simply put, memorandum its a written record or document within a business. It is a legal document, officially registering an Indian firm within her domestic territory, as also an official company document, registered with the Registrar of Companies. A memorandum of association sets out (specifies) company name, status, address of the registered office, objectives of the company, statement of limited liability, amount of guarantee and the amount of authorised share capital. The contents of the MOA are discussed in detail under the heading 'Main Documents of the Company' later in this chapter.
   (b) *Articles of Association (AOA):* AOA set out the by-laws of the company as far as its internal management is concerned.

BUSINESS FOCUS: ARTICLES OF INCORPORATION

Articles of incorporation (AOS) refer to the legal document needed for creating a corporation in India.,i.e., a document which creates a joint stock company and set forth its purpose and structure according to the laws of the country in which it is established. AOS are also known as corporate charter.

   (c) *Notice:* Legal notice regarding the physical location of the office of the company has to be served. This is a statutory requirement as per sections 146 of the Companies Act.
   (d) *Agreements:* As per the provisions of the Companies Act (Section 33) it is legally obligatory on the part of a company to submit (file) copies of the agreements, if any, of a company with any individual, firm, or any other company.
   (e) *List of directors:* It is obligatory on the part of the company to submit the list of directors with their names, addresses, and other details to the Registrar of Companies.
   (f) *Written consent of the directors:* Those persons whose names are proposed as directors must send their written consent, clearly stating that they have no objection in accepting the post they are offered and thus act as the director of the company. It is also necessary for directors to subscribe for or acquire necessary qualifying shares.

(g) *Statutory declaration:* It is also necessary to file a declaration to the effect that all legal formalities regarding incorporation have been completed. This declaration may be signed by an advocate of a High Court or Supreme Court or by a chartered accountant or by a proposed director or even the proposed secretary of the company.

4. *Payment of fees:* While filing the above documents it is necessary to pay the prescribed filing and registration fees as also stamp duty to the Registrar. The amount of registration fees payable varies with the amount of authorised capital of the company. If the company is not planning to issue share capital, then the amount of fees payable will depend on the number of its members.
5. *Registration:* The Registrar of Companies will have to scrutinise all the necessary documents meticulously and if he is fully satisfied with due and full compliance of legal formalities regarding registration, then only he enters the name of the company in his register.
6. *Certificates of registration/Incorporation:* Soon after registration the Registrar of Companies will issue this certificate, duly signed by him in which he specifies its date of issue. The certificate of incorporation is a legal registration document of a company. It is written statement by the Registrar of Companies confirming that a new company has fulfilled the necessary legal requirements for incorporation and is now legally constituted. The certificate of incorporation is one which is issued by the Registrar of Companies to a new joint stock company whose MOA and AOA are acceptable to him. A company's legal existence starts from the date of its incorporation and thereafter it is able to enter into contracts in its own name. [Note that a contract is a legally enforceable agreement between two or more parties generally relating to a transaction for the purchase or sale of inputs, goods and services.] From the date of issues of the certificate, the company acquires a separate legal status and becomes an artificial person with perpetual existence and common seal.

9.5 COMMENCEMENT OF BUSINESS

In order to obtain 'the certificate of commencement of business' without which any business operation cannot be legally started, a public company has to file an application before the Registrar along with valid documents and necessary proofs that it has accomplished the following tasks:

1. If the company while making public offer for sale of its shares has issued a 'prospectus', then it has to submit a copy of the same to the Registrar. A prospectus is a document prepared by a joint stock company as an invitation to the public to subscribe for shares in the company. The prospectus gives details of the company's past trading record, current capital structure and borrowings. Prospectuses are published as the first stage of an offer for sale of shares. Alternatively a company has to file a legal (official) 'statement in lieu of prospectus'.
2. In case a prospectus has already been issued the company has to give a valid proof of the fact that it has received a minimum subscription, as specified in prospectus, in cash.
3. The proof that company directors have made full payment for acquiring qualifying shares on a pro rata basis, i.e., in the same proportion as other shareholders have paid.
4. A legal declaration either by the directors or the secretory in support of the fact that all the above formalities have been duly completed.

5. If, after thoroughly scrutinising all the above documents and papers the registrar feels totally satisfied or convinced then only he issues 'the certificate of commencement of business,' through which he gives the formal permission to the company to start its business operation.

9.6 DOCUMENTS USED IN THE FORMATION OF A COMPANY

All joint stock companies are obliged to file certain documents to give necessary information for public inspection and to circulate accounts to their shareholders. The information is transmitted through a few documents. Two main documents are the Memorandum of Association (MOA) and Articles of Association (AOA).

1. **MOA:** The MOA is the document which forms the basis of registration of a company, (i) listing the subscribers to the capital, (ii) the number of shares, (iii) the name and address of the company and (iv) where appropriate, its powers and objects, (v) The memorandum also states that the liability of its members (shareholders) is limited.
2. **AOA:** The AOA set out the rules by which the company will be administered, e.g., the voting of the directors and the calling of meetings.

Two other documents which are to be prepared and filed are:

3. **Prospectus:** A prospectus serves the following six purposes:
   (i) It is an invitation to the general public to subscribe to the shares and debentures of the company.
   (ii) It makes the public aware of the company and encourages people to invest money in the company.
   (iii) It provides an authentic (or a genuine) record of the terms and conditions on which shares and debentures have been issued.
   (iv) It identifies the persons who can be held responsible in case any untrue or incorrect statements is made in it.
   (v) It reflects the business policies and programmes of the company.
   (vi) It helps the investors to take proper investment decisions.
4. **Statement in lieu of prospectus:** A public company having share capital is not legally constrained to not file and publish a prospectus if it wants to raise its capital privately without public disclosure. In such a case, it has to file a 'statement in lieu of prospectus' with the Registrar of Companies at least three days before the allotment of shares. It must be duly signed by all the directors. It has to be dated and should indicate when it was submitted to the Registrar.

   Statement in lieu prospectus is supposed to be in the form set out in Part 1 of Schedule III of the Companies Act, 2013. The contents of this statement are almost similar to the those of a prospectus. The statement must not contain any untrue or false statements. A private company is not required to either file a prospectus or a statement in lieu of prospectus with the Registrar of Companies. All the provisions of the Companies Act which are applicable to prospectus in respect of registration, alteration, liability for untrue statements, etc., are equally applicable to a statement in lieu of prospectus as well.

These documents are now discussed in detail.

9.7 MEMORANDUM OF ASSOCIATION (MOA)

The Memorandum of Association is the most important document of a joint stock company. It defines the objects and specifies the power of a company. It also spells out the company's relationship with the external world.

9.7.1 Meaning of Memorandum

In the language of Lord Cains, "The Memorandum of Association of a company is its charter and defines the limitations of the powers of company. It contains the fundamental conditions upon which alone the company is allowed to be incorporated". Memorandum thus lays the foundation stone from which the superstructure of a company is built. The Memorandum of Association (MOA) is a legal document which must be filed with the registrar of companies before a joint stock company can be incorporated. In addition, the MOA is perhaps the most basic (key) legal document on the basis of which a company can be incorporated. Thus it is the foundation on which the structure of a company is laid. Being the charter (constitution) of the company, it spells out the objects, sphere of activities as well as the scope of its operations. It is alterable only in exceptional cases as per the provisions of the Companies Act and which governs the external relationship between the company and outsiders (third parties).

The MOA sets out the purpose of formation of a company

In essence, the memorandum of association sets out the purpose for which the company concerned has been formed and the amount and different classes of share capital. The memorandum is drawn up on the formation of a company together with the articles of association which represent a contract between the company and its shareholders and set out the powers of directors and provide the legal framework of the company.

Purpose: The purpose of the memorandum is to enable the shareholders, creditors and other stakeholders to know what is its line of business. A company cannot go for any such operation or undertake any such activity for which there is no reference (mention) in the memorandum.

9.7.2 Significance of Memorandum

The Memorandum of Association is the most important document of a company. The reasons are the following:

1. *The basis of incorporation:* The MOA forms the basis of incorporation in the sense that a company cannot be registered without it.
2. *Fixing boundaries:* It fixes boundaries of a company's activities. Any activity undertaken or performed outside the scope of the MOA is treated as *Ultraviars* and is thus void. The word ultraviars implies 'beyond the powers'. The term denotes the act of an official or corporation for which there is no authority in law or MOA.
3. *Public disclosure:* It brings to the notice of public an important information, viz., the purposes for which money will be utilised by the company.
4. *Limits of liability:* The shareholders are made clear about the extent of their liability through the MOA.
5. *Corporate objectives:* It explicitly specifies the objectives of the company.
6. *Official transaction(s):* It makes it possible for outsiders to know whether the company is authorised to enter into any type of transaction.

7. *Names of promoters:* It furnishes details about the names and addresses of the promoters of the company.

9.7.3 Contents of Memorandum

The memorandum must contain certain compulsory clauses stating:

(a) the name of the company,
(b) the objectives of the company,
(c) the country in which the company is situated,
(d) whether it is limited by shares or other means,
(e) the amount and division of share capital and
(f) the signatures of the subscribers forming the company, each of whom must take at least one share.

1. *The name clause:* Under this clause, the name of the company is stated, subject to the following specifications:
   (a) The word "Limited" or "Private Limited" has to appear as the last word in case of every public or private company (limited by shares).
   (b) Due care has to be taken to ensure that the proposed name is not almost identical or resembles closely the name of another existing company or a firm.
   (c) The proposed name should not carry any impression that it is related to any government department or local authority in any way, i.e., either directly or indirectly. The name of the company has to be printed inside the common seal of the company and put on all important documents, particularly those relating to any dealings of the company with outsiders (third parties).
2. *The registered office clause:* The address of the Registered Office along with name of the State in which the company's registered office is situated are to be mentioned in the memorandum.
3. *The objects clause:* This is indeed the focal point of the Memorandum of Association. It puts on record the objects of the company or its line of business. The company cannot do any business other than the one specified in the Memorandum.
4. *The liability clause:* This clause states that the liability of members is limited to the amount, if any which still remains unpaid on the shares allotted to them. In case of 'companies limited by guarantee', this clause specifies the amount which every member has to contribute to the assets of the company in case it decides to wind up (i.e., close down its business)
5. *The capital clause:* Every limited company is under the legal obligation to state the amount of its share capital such as ₹ 5 lacs registered and the division of its shares of fixed denomination (such as 5,000 shares of ₹ 100 each.)
6. *The association or subscription clause:* Under this clause, the signatories to the memorandum have to get their signatures duly attested by a witness. These signatures are a legal proof that the signatories are desirous of forming a company and agree to purchase qualifying shares, if any. Each subscriber has to take at least 1 share. While for a public company there must be at least 7 signatories, for a private company the minimum number is 2. This provision does not apply in case of other companies.

SYNOPSIS FOR LEARNING: SIX CLAUSES OF MEMORANDUM OF ASSOCIATION

1. The Name Clause
2. The Registered Office Clause
3. The Objects Clause
4. The Liability Clause
5. The Capital Clause
6. The Association or Subscription Clause

9.8 ARTICLES OF ASSOCIATION (AOA)

The articles of association governs the internal relationship between a company and its shareholders

The articles of association may be treated as the legal constitution of a joint stock company which governs the internal relationship between the company and its members or shareholders. The articles govern the rights and duties of the members as also various aspects of administration of the company. They will contain, for instance, the powers of the directors, the conduct of meetings, the dividend and voting rights assigned to separate classes of shareholders, and other miscellaneous rules and regulations.

In essence, articles of association represent a contract between a company and its shareholders and set out the powers of the directors and lay down the legal framework of the company. The articles of association are drawn upon the formation of a company together with the company's MOA which sets out the purpose for which the company has been formed and the amount and different classes (types) of share capital. The Article are essentially a set of rules relating to the internal management of a company. The articles clearly define and specify the duties, the rights and the powers of the members of Board of Directors, and its modus operandi, i.e., mode of operation. It also specifies how the internal regulations of the company may be changed from time to time depending on changing situations or circumstances.

A public limited company is permitted by law to adopt Table A (i.e., the model set of 99 articles given in Schedule I of the Companies Act). Any other company is under the legal obligation to file its articles of association along with the memorandum at the time of its registration. The Articles of Association should be printed, divided into separate paragraphs and numbered in chronological order (i.e., arranged with the earlier provisions preceding the later ones), and signed by at least seven persons (who have already signed on memorandum) in the presence of at least one witness, who has to attest the same to give it a full legal status.

9.8.1 Contents of Articles of Association

The Articles of Association contain necessary and detailed provisions relating to the following:

1. total amount of share capital as also different classes of shares,
2. legal rights of each type of shareholder,
3. lien on shares, forfeiture of shares for non-payment of calls and share transfer,
4. procedures for conduct of meeting as also for voting, quorum, and proxy,
5. appointment, remuneration and removal of directors as also their powers, rights and responsibilities,
6. procedures for change in the volume and composition of share capital,
7. matters relating to distribution of dividend,
8. provisions for keeping statutory books and
9. legal procedure for winding up of the company.

9.9 DIFFERENCE BETWEEN MOA AND AOA

The main points of differences between the Memorandum and Articles of Association are presented in Table below.

Basis of Comparison	Memorandum of Association	Articles of Association
1. Purpose	To furnish necessary details (documents) about the charter or the constitution of the company.	To put on record all the rules and regulations for the smooth day-to-day operation and management of the company.
2. Scope	It specifies objects and spheres of operation of the company.	It specifies ways and means to achieve the objective mentioned in the Memorandum.
3. Legal status	It is the main document of the company under the Companies Act.	It is an additional document and lends necessary support to the Memorandum.
4. Relationship of the company and with outsiders and insiders	The external relations between the company and outsiders (the stakeholders) are controlled and regulated by it.	The internal relationship between the company and its members (shareholders) are governed by it.
5. Filling with the Registrar of Companies	There is compulsion in the matter. Filling this document with the Registrar of Companies before incorporation of a company is mandatory.	Filing of Articles is not the legal obligation of company which is always at liberty to adopt the model articles listed under Table 'A' of the companies Act.
6. Legal implication	Any act committed beyond the Memorandum is treated as void and has no legal implication for the company.	Any acts committed by going beyond the Articles can be ratified by the shareholders, as and when necessary.
7. Possibility of alteration	It is extremely difficult, if not virtually impossible to alter this document.	The articles can be amended, if necessary, easily and quickly without an extension of endeavour.

9.10 PROSPECTUS

A prospectus is a document prepared by a joint stock company as an invitation to the public to subscribe for shares in the company. The prospectus gives details of the company's past trading record, current capital structure and borrowing. A prospectus is published as the first stage of an offer for sale of shares. A prospectus is a statement of a company's or an organisation's present strength and future prospects, published as part of a quest for support or investment, normally when a company goes public, i.e., offers its shares for sale. A prospectus is prepared with the help of an issuing house, lawyers and reporting accountants.

Three common elements of a prospectus are the following:

(i) There must be an invitation to the general public.

(ii) The invitation has to be made "by or on behalf of the company".

(iii) The invitation has to be "to subscribe or purchase its shares or debentures or any such long-term financial instrument".

The prospectus of a company serves the following purposes:

(i) The prospectus is essentially a summary report of the company's past performance and present operations.

(ii) It also highlights the future plans, programmes of the company and indicates its near-term and long-term prospects.

(iii) It gives an open invitation to the public to subscribe to its shares and debentures.

(iv) It serves as a legal document by clearly putting on record (or spelling out) the terms and conditions on the basis of which the company shares have been allotted and debentures have been issued.

(v) It clearly identifies the persons who can be held responsible in case of any wrong statement made in it gets detected.

9.10.1 Importance of Prospectus

A prospectus serves the following purposes:

(i) *Invitation to the public:* *Prima facie*, it is an invitation to the public to subscribe to the shares and debentures of the company.

(ii) *Inducement to invest:* It informs the public about the company and encourages (induces) the general public to invest money in the company.

(iii) *Any official document:* It serves as an official record of the terms and conditions relating to any issues of shares and debentures.

(iv) *Identification of miscrient(s):* It identifies the person who has done anything wrong and can be held responsible for any incorrect or false statements made in it.

(v) *Disclosure of business policies:* It brings into focus the business policies and programmes of the company and the relevant details to the notice of the public.

(vi) *Rational investment:* It enables the investors to take rational investment decisions.

9.10.2 Contents of the Prospectus

Only through the prospectus potential investors can judge the real strength of the company.

A prospectus has to furnish the following details:

(i) The name of the company and full address of its registered office,

(ii) The main objective (mission) of the company (i.e., its scope of operation or its sphere of activities),

(iii) the number and classes of shares and the nature and extent of the interest of shareholders in the company's tangible assets and share of profits of the company.

(iv) Certain particulars about the redeemable preference shares intended (planned) to be issued, and, if so, the date and method of redemption,

(v) qualifying shares of directors,

(vi) any provision in the articles relating to the remuneration of the directors and the managing director,

(vii) full names, addresses and occupations of the directors, the managing director or any manager,

(viii) the 'minimum subscription', i.e., the minimum subscribed capital which has to be raised by issuing shares as determined by the directors,

(ix) the date and timing of both opening and closing of the subscription list,

(x) the application money and the pattern of allotment of each type of shares,

(xi) rights and privileges associated with each type of shares as also the restrictions imposed on it, and

(xii) the place and the time at which copies of audited balance sheets and income statements or profit and loss accounts may be inspected by any concerned person.

The prospectus has to disclose all the required information fully. It should not suppress any information. Any omission concealment, suppression or misstatement of truth in the prospectus may falsify it since it will mislead prospective investors. Those who had applied for shares on the basis of a false prospectus may repeal (annul) the allotment of shares. They can also claim damages from the directors and other office bearers of the company who are found guilty of issuing a false or a misleading prospectus. These persons are likely to be held liable for damages, if any, and may be legally penalised. Any prospectus has to be dated and signed by each director of the company making public issue. A copy of the prospectus has to be filed with the Registrar of Companies and can be issued to the public after getting approval from the Registrar.

Shelf prospectus: It is a prospectus in respect of which securities or class of securities included therein are issued for public subscription. Such prospectus is valid for one or more issues over a certain specified period of time. There is no need to issue a further prospectus during this period.

Herring prospectus: Such a prospectus does not contain full details of the price or the number of securities to be issued on the basis of it. It is issued only by those companies which raise capital through the book building process.

FOCUS ON TERMINOLOGY: BOOK AND BOOK BUILDING

Book refers to the record of a trader's investments and amounts owed — a statement of all the holding of a trader and the amount he (she) is due to pay or has borrowed.
Book building refers to gathering information to determine offering price through research done about potential institutional investors. The objective is to determine the optimum offering price for a new issue of stock.

9.11 STATEMENT IN LIEU OF PROSPECTUS

A public company may decide not to go for the issue of necessary capital if it succeeds in acquiring the required capital without going public (without making public issues). In such a situation it will have to file a 'Statement in lieu of Prospectus' with the Registrar of Companies.

Such a statement is drafted in line with the specifications given in " Schedule III" of the Indian Companies Act (1956). It contains virtually the same information as is given in a prospectus. It has to be signed by all directors and the copy of the same has to be filed with the registrar at least three days before any share allotment is made. However, a private company is outside the provisions of 'prospectus' or a 'statement in lieu of the prospectus'.

A statement in lieu of prospectus is issued only when a company decides to raise capital from private sources, i.e., when a private company is converted into a public company.

9.12 MINIMUM SUBSCRIPTION

A joint stock company making any public or rights issue of shares or debentures can make full allotment of shares or debentures only after receiving a minimum subscription against the proposed issue of securities. The term 'minimum' refers to the nominal amount of shares applied for. As per the guidelines issued by the SEBI 90% subscription against an issue must be received before making the public allotment of shares. In case the minimum subscription is not received within 120 days of the issue of prospectus, the amount received from applicants has to be refunded within the next 10 days. The clause serves a definite purpose. It ensures that a public limited company can start its business operations even without acquiring the minimum amount of money required to meet its initial expenses and working capital needs.

The amount of minimum subscription is determined by the directors of a company. It needs to meet the following requirements:

(a) initial expenses,

(b) commission of underwriters,

(c) working capital,

(d) the cost of any property – purchased (acquired) or likely to be purchased,

(e) repayment of any loan made for the above purpose, and

(f) any other legitimate business expense.

Initial or preliminary expenses are associated with the formation of a company. These are treated as notional (fictitious) assets which are written off over a certain specific time period. Such expenses are incurred to cover the following costs:

(i) cost of preparing and printing the MOA and AOA;

(ii) cost of preparing, printing and circulating the prospectus;

(iii) cost of registering the company (filing of documents, payment of stamp duty and fees, etc.);

(iv) cost of preliminary agreements;

(v) cost of preparing and printing application forms, letters of allotment and share certificates; and

(vi) fees charged by valuers for reports, certificates, etc.

9.13 JUDGING THE SOUNDNESS OF A COMPANY FROM THE PROSPECTUS

Investors should pay special attention to the following aspects (or key indicators) of a prospectus to ascertain the soundness of the proposed issue of shares/debentures such as:

1. **The nature of business.** The prospective investor should examine carefully the condition of the industry, demand and supple conditions, availability of raw materials and non-material inputs, the nature and intensity of competition, export and import activities and prospects and, of course, government policy towards the industry to which the company belongs. In case of an existing company, it may be necessary to analyse its past profits, the present value of its assets and of course, the scope for expansion.

2. **Objective(s) of the company.** The current success and future prospect of a company depend on its objectives or goals. It is, therefore, necessary to examine whether the objectives are

pragmatic (achievable) in the light of present conditions and constraints as also under the prevailing environment — internal and external.

3. Competence and reputation of promoters and directors: The competence credibility and reputation of the promoters and directors have to be judged properly. The professional qualifications, work experience, honesty and integrity of directors and top executives of the company are also to be assessed.
4. Capital structure: There is need to make an insightful analysis of the adequacy or the otherwise of a proposed issue, the amount of minimum subscription, the proportion between (among) different types of securities and rights of various classes of shareholders. It is also necessary to be sure of the fact that the burden of fixed payments is not unduly high (excessive).
5. Past record: Finally, in case a private limited company has been converted into a public limited one, it is necessary to take into consideration the past profit, as also assets and liabilities of the company. It is also necessary to know why the conversion was made.

Key Points

1. Formation of a company: In order to ensure the existence of a joint stock company, it is necessary to complete several legal formalities and take various procedural decisions. Company formation calls for two things at least: planned actions and conscious efforts.
2. Promotion: Promotion begins when a budding entrepreneur first conceives a business idea or project (venture) which appears to be potentially profitable. It includes feasibility study, acquiring of resources and making provision for raising funds necessary to start an enterprise and transform it into a going concern. Persons who take the lead in these matters are known as promoters. These are the people who take the primary responsibility for starting a business. The functions of a promoter are the following:
   (i) generation of new business idea,
   (ii) an in-depth analysis of the project,
   (iii) making adequate arrangement for necessary resources such as machinery, materials and manpower,
   (iv) entering into written contacts and signing agreements with commercial banks and underwriters (merchant banks and issue houses) and
   (v) preparation of legal documents for submission to the registrar of companies for approval of projects.
3. Stages in formation of a company: A company comes into existence only after passing through a series of stages which are both time consuming and cost raising.
   Four broad stages are the following: (i) promotion, (ii) incorporation (registration), (iii) floatation or capital subscription, and (iv) commencement of business. While a public company has to pass through all the stages, a private company can commence business after completing the first two stages.
4. Certificate of incorporation: When a company completes all the formalities related to registration, the Registrar of companies issues it a certificate of incorporation which gives it a separate legal status.

5. **Certificate of commencement of business:** The registrar issues this certificate to a public company after it has successfully raised the necessary paid-up capital and completed the legal formalities. This certificate entitles the company to start functioning.

6. **Documents required in company formation:** Three documents are required in company formation: (i) Memorandum of Association, (ii) Articles of Association, and (iii) Prospectus.
   If a public company does not want to raise any capital by making any public issue of shares and debentures, it is required to file a statement in lieu of prospectus with the registrar of companies.

7. **Memorandum of Association:** This principal document lays down all the conditions which a company has to fulfill for being incorporated. It enables the shareholders, creditors and all stakeholders to know what is its area of operation (or business activities).
   The memorandum of Association contains the following six clauses: 1. Nameclause, 2. registered office clause, 3. objects clause, 4. liability clause, 5. capital clause, and 6. subscription clause

8. **Articles of Association:** It is essentially a consolidated list of the rules relating to internal management of a company. the articles also define and specify explicitly (i.e., in clear terms) the rights, duties, responsibilities and powers of the board members, i.e., members of the Board of Directors.
   Articles of association contain detailed information on the following:
   1. amount of share capital and different classes of shares,
   2. procedure for share allotment,
   3. procedure for issuing share certificates,
   4. procedure for share transfer, and
   5. procedure for forfeiture of shares in exceptional circumstances.

9. **Prospectus:** It is a broad term and means any notice, circular, advertisement or any other document inviting the general public to subscribe to a company's shares and/or debentures. It is an open invitation or an offer to public subscription to a company's paid-up or (authorised) capital.

10. **Statement in lieu of prospectus:** A public company may decide not to go for the issue of necessary capital if it succeeds in acquiring the required capital without going public (without making public issues). In such a situation it will have to file a 'Statement in lieu of Prospectus' with the Registrar of Companies.

11. **Minimum subscription:** A joint stock company making any public or rights issue of shares or debentures can make full allotment of shares or debentures only after receiving a minimum subscription against the proposed issue of securities. The term 'minimum' refers to the nominal amount of shares applied for.

12. **Judging the soundness of a company from the prospectus:** Investors should pay special attention of a prospectus to ascertain the soundness of the proposed issue of shares/debentures such as: (i) the nature of business, (ii) objective(s) of the company, (iii) competence and reputation of promoters and directors, (iv) capital structure and (v) past record.

KEY Terms	
Formation of a company	Prospectus
Promotion of a company	Memorandum of association
Minimum subscription	Statement in lieu of prospectus
Articles of association	Promoters

Assignments

SHORT ANSWER-TYPE QUESTIONS

1. Define company promotion. [ISC 2006]
2. Who is a promoter? [ISC 2006]
3. What is certificate of incorporation? [ISC 1999]
4. What is a 'Prospectus'? [ISC 2005]
5. What is statement in lieu of prospectus? [ISC 2000, 2004]
6. What is the significance of 'The Subscription or Association Clause' of the Memorandum of Association? [ISC 1993, 2013]
7. State two differences between the Memorandum of Association and the Articles of Association. [ISC 1993]
8. Give two objectives of a Prospectus. [ISC 1995]
9. What is 'minimum subscription'? [ISC 1993, 2002]
10. When is a 'Statement in lieu of Prospectus' filed? [ISC 2000]
11. Give the purpose of Memorandum of Association. [ISC 1994]
12. What is a prospectus? [ISC 1995]
13. State any two conditions which are essential for grant of the certificate to commence business. [ISC 1995]
14. What is the Articles of Association? [ISC 1995]
15. What is the significance of the object clause of the Memorandum of Association? [ISC 2005]
16. What are the two ways in which a company can be promoted? [ISC 2012]
17. What is the significance of the object clause of Memorandum of Association? [ISC 2005]
18. What are the two ways in which a company can be promoted? [ISC 2012]
19. When can a private limited company commence its business? [ISC 1996]
20. What does the capital clause of Memorandum of Association contain? [ISC 1996]
21. What are the main contents of the prospectus of a company? [ISC 1998]
22. What are the additional requirements of a public limited company, after incorporation, to obtain a certificate of commencement? [ISC 1998]

23. State two essential qualities of a successful promoter. [ISC 1999]
24. Describe briefly a Certificate of Commencement of Business. [ISC 1999, 2013]
25. Define the term 'promoter'. [ISC 2000]
26. What is the option available to a public limited company with regard to the articles? [ISC 2001]
27. What is 'association clause' in a memorandum? [ISC 2003]
28. Mention two ways in which a joint stock company may be promoted. [ISC 2003]
29. State two objectives of issuing a prospectus. [ISC 2003]
30. What is the significance of the 'object clause' in a Memorandum of Association? [ISC 2005, 2010]
31. What is the role of Table A in company formation? [ISC 2008]
32. Under what circumstances can a public limited company file a statement in lieu of a prospectus? [ISC 2008]
33. Write briefly on minimum subscription. [ISC 2008]
34. What is a certificate of incorporation? [ISC 2009]
35. Mention the steps necessary for the incorporation of a joint stock company. [ISC 2011]
36. Write two objectives of a prospectus of a company. [ISC 2011]
37. What does the capital clause of Memorandum of Association contain? [ISC 2012]

ESSAY-TYPE QUESTIONS

1. What is Memorandum of Association? Give the contents of the Memorandum of Association? [ISC 1993, 1999]
2. Explain the different documents which are required to be submitted for the registration of a company. [ISC 1993]
3. Outline the difference between Memorandum of Association and Articles of Association. [ISC 1994]
4. What are the important contents of a Prospectus? [ISC 1994]
5. Who is a promoter? Identify four functions of a promoter. [ISC 1995]
6. Explain the contents of the Articles of Association. [ISC 1995]
7. What is Memorandum of Association? Briefly explain its clauses. [ISC 1996]
8. What is 'certificate of incorporation'? Discuss different documents, in brief, that are required to be submitted to the Registrar of Companies for incorporation of a public limited company. [ISC 1996]
9. Who is a promoter? What is his role in the promotion of a company? [ISC 1997]
10. Explain the various stages of promotion of a company. [ISC 1997]
11. Explain the main contents of the Articles of Association of a joint stock company. [ISC 1997]
12. Distinguish between 'Memorandum of Association' and 'Articles of Association' of a company. [ISC 1997]
13. Describe the steps necessary for the incorporation of a joint stock company. [ISC 1998]
14. How can a prospective investor judge from the prospectus whether the company is a sound one or not? [ISC 1998]

15. What is meant by Prospectus of a Company? Is it compulsory to issue a prospectus?
16. Explain four functions performed by a promoter of a company. [ISC 1999]
17. Enumerate and explain the documents to be submitted to the Registrar for the incorporation of a company. [ISC 2000]
18. Explain all clauses of a memorandum of association. Compare this document with the articles of association on the basis of two features. [ISC 2001]
19. Differentiate Memorandum from Articles. [ISC 2003]
20. Write a note on stages in the incorporation of a private limited company. [ISC 2006]
21. Explain the steps involved in the promotion of a company. [ISC 2007]
22. Differentiate between Memorandum of Association and Articles of Association of a company. [ISC 2009, 2010]
23. The Memorandum is considered as the prime document in company formation. Give three reasons to justify this statement. [ISC 2011]
24. What is the significance of Articles of Association for a joint stock company? Give any three contents of the Articles of Association. [ISC 2013]
25. (a) What are the additional requirements that a public limited company has to fulfil after its incorporation in order to obtain a certificate of commencement?
    (b) Enumerate the functions of a promoter. [ISC 2012]
26. (a) State and explain any four key documents to be filed with the Registrar for incorporation of a public limited company.
    (b) Mention any four contents of a prospectus. Explain how a prospective investor can judge the soundness of a company. [ISC 2008]

QUESTION BANK

1. *What are the two ways in which a company can be promoted?* [ISC 2012]

OR

Name two ways in which a company can be promoted. [ISC 1999]

OR

Mention two ways in which a joint stock company may be promoted. [ISC 2003]

Ans. A joint stock company can be promoted either by
(i) by converting a partnership firm into a company or, by
(ii) by incorporating a new company.

2. *Explain the various stages of promotion of a company.* [ISC 1997]

Ans. See text.

3. *Briefly describe the steps involved in the formation of a public limited company.* [ISC 1988]

Ans. Formation of a public limited company involves, in addition to promotion, the following stages:
(a) incorporation or registration.
(b) capital subscription or floatation, and
(c) commencement of business.
For details see text.

4. *Who is a promoter?* [ISC 1994]

OR

Define the term "Promoter". [ISC 2000]

Ans. A promoter is an entrepreneur or business person who gives birth to a business unit. According to S. Francis Palmer, "Promoter means a person who originates the scheme of promotion of the company, has the Memorandum and Articles prepared, executed and registered and finds the first directors, settles the terms of preliminary contracts and prospectus (if any) and makes arrangement for advertising and circulating the prospectus and raising capital".

5. *What are the persons who discover business opportunity and organise funds, property and managerial ability into a business company called?* [ISC 1990]

Ans. The persons who discover business opportunity and organise funds, property and managerial ability into a business company are called "Promoters".

6. *State two essential qualities of a successful promoter.* [ISC 1999]

Ans. Two essential qualities of a successful promoter are the following:

(i) perfect foresight and strong initiative as also

(ii) courage, confidence and resourcefulness.

7. *Who is a promoter? Identify four functions of a promoter.* [ISC 1995]

OR

Who is a promoter? What is his role in the promotion of a company? [ISC 1997]

OR

Explain four functions performed by a promoter of a company. [ISC 1999]

Ans. See text.

8. *What is a certificate of incorporation?* [ISC 1994, 1995, 1999]

Ans. See text.

9. *Explain the different documents which are required to be submitted for the registration of a company.* [ISC 1993]

OR

Discuss different documents, in brief, that are required to be submitted to Registrar of Companies for incorporation of a public limited company. [ISC 1996]

OR

Enumerate and explain the documents to be submitted to the Registrar for the incorporation of a company. [ISC 2000]

Ans. See text.

10. *Describe the steps necessary for the incorporation of a joint stock company.* [ISC 1998]

Ans. See text.

11. *When is a company born?* [ISC 1988]

Ans. A company is born on the date mentioned in the certificate of incorporation issued by the Registrar of Companies.

12. *When can a private limited company commence its business?* [ISC 1996]

Ans. A private limited company can commence its business as soon as it succeeds in obtaining the certificate of incorporation.

13. *State any two conditions which are essential for the grant of the certificate to commence business.* [ISC 1995]

Ans (i) The shares payable in cash have been allotted and that cash has actually been received from allotted shares. The number has to be equal to and not less than the minimum subscription.

(ii) The company is not liable to refund any money to the applicants by reason of failure to apply for or to obtain permission for shares or debentures to be traded in any recognised stock exchange.

14. *Describe briefly as certificate of commencement of business.* [ISC 1999]

Ans See text.

15. *What are the additional requirements of a public limited company, after incorporation, to obtain a certificate of commencement of business?* [ISC 1998, 2012]

Ans While a private company can commence business immediately after incorporation, a public limited company must obtain the certificate of commencement of business. For this purpose it is required to file the following documents with the Registrar of Companies:

(i) A copy of the prospectus or statement in lieu of prospectus.

(ii) A declaration that the directors have fully paid for the qualification shares they have acquired in cash. This amount has to be equal to what is payable by other subscribers on application and allotment.

(iii) A declaration that the shares payable in cash have been allotted and that cash has actually been received from allotted shares. The number has to be equal to and not less than the minimum subscription.

(iv) A declaration that the company has applied for or obtained permission for the shares to be traded on any of India's 22 recognised stock exchanges.

(v) A statutory declaration signed by a director or secretary of the company stating that necessary official formalities have been completed.

The Registrar will scrutinise the above documents and if he is satisfied that the documents are in proper, order, then only he will issue a Certificate of Commencement of Business. A company can start its business from the very date mentioned in the certificate. In truth, the certificate serves as a concrete proof of the fact that the company has completed all the legal formalities and is thus legally (officially) permitted to commence its business operations.

16. *Name the fundamental document which determines the scope of activities of the company and defines its relationship with the outside world.* [ISC 1989]

Ans The word 'fundamental document' which determines the scope of activities of a company and defines its relationship with the external world is known as "Memorandum of Association".

17. *Name the clause in a company's Memorandum of Association which defines and specifies the scope of a company.* [ISC 1990]

OR

Name the clause in the Memorandum of Association that restricts the scope of activities within which the managerial personnel can act in the name of the company. [ISC 1992]

Ans The clause in a company's Memorandum of Association which defines and specifies the scope (boundary) of activities of a company is called the "object clause".

18. *What is the significance of 'The Subscription' or 'Association Clause' of the Memorandum of Association'?* [ISC 1993]

OR

What is 'Association Clause' in a memorandum? [ISC 2003]

The subscription or Association Clause in a memorandum of association contains the full names, occupations and addresses of subscribers who make a declaration under their signatures duly attested by witnesses that they are desirous of forming a company and agree to take qualification shares, if any. There has to be a minimum of 7 signatories in case of a public company and at least 2 in case of a private company. The importance of this clause lies in the fact that it brings into notice of the public the promoters of the company.

19. *Give the purpose of Memorandum of Association.*

The government of India insists that certain legal stages are completed before a company may be established in order to protect investors and creditors. To start with, a MOA must be completed. It states the name of the company, the address of the head office through which it can be contacted, the maximum share capital for which the company seeks authorisation and the declared aims of the business.

The last two points in this definition are of much interest to shareholders. Knowing the maximum share capital implies that the relative importance of any one share can be determined. Being aware of the company's aims means that shareholders can avoid businesses which may operate in markets and products — such as liquor — that they may not want to be associated with.

20. *What is the significance of the objects clause of the Memorandum of Association?*

The Objects Clause is to be treated as the core of the MOA in the sense that it defines the power of the company and explicitly specifies the scope of its activities. This clause enables shareholders and creditors to ascertain the very purpose for which their money will be utilised. For this reason, the object clause is of considerable importance to both the companies as also those who deal with it. A company can make alterations in the Objects Clause only if it gets the approval of the central government and after completing all legal formalities.

The Companies Act specifies that the Objects Clause has to be divided into (a) the main objects of the company and its subsidiary ones, i.e. objects incidental or ancilliary to the attainment of the main objects and (b) any other object of the company. Keeping in view the relative importance of different objects a company should state the objects as clearly and precisely as possible.

21. *What do you mean by Articles of Association (AOA)?*

The document called AOA covers the internal workings and the control of a business — for example, the names of directors and the detailed procedures to be followed at the meetings.

22. *What does the capital clause of Memorandum of Association contain?* [ISC 1996]

The Capital Clause of the MOA figures out the total amount of the authorised share capital with which a company is registered. It also gives information about the division of authorised capital into shares of a fixed denomination and the number and types of shares to be allotted or invested. Every company limited by shares is under the legal obligation to include this clause in the MOA.

23. ***Name different clauses of Memorandum of Association.*** [ISC 1987]

Ans. The Memorandum of Association contains the following six clauses:

(i) Name Clause (ii) Situation Clause
(iii) Objects Clause (iv) Liability Clause
(v) Capital Clause (vi) Subscription Clause

24. ***Briefly explain the contents of the Memorandum of Association of a joint stock company.*** [ISC 1999]

OR

What is the Memorandum of Association? Give the contents of the Memorandum of Association. [ISC 1993]

OR

What is Memorandum of Association? Briefly explain its clauses. [ISC 1996]

OR

What is a Memorandum of Association? Explain its important clauses. [ISC 1999]

OR

Explain all the causes in a Memorandum of Association.

Ans. See text.

25. ***Name the document containing the rules and regulations for conducting the internal affairs of a company.*** [ISC 1988]

Ans. See text.

26. ***What is the Articles of Association?*** [ISC 1995]

Ans. See text.

27. ***What is the option available to a public limited company with regard to the articles?*** [ISC 2001]

Ans. A public company limited by shares has two options: (i) It may file its own articles of association. (ii) Alternatively it may adopt Table A Schedule I of the Companies Act which contains the model set of articles. By comparison, a company limited by guarantee without having share capital may file its own articles or adopt Table A. A company limited by guarantee but having share capital may adopt Table D. Finally, an unlimited company may adopt Table E.

28. ***State two differences between the Memorandum of Association and the Articles of Association.*** [ISC 1999]

OR

Compare Memorandum of Association with the Articles of Association on the basis of any two features. [ISC 2001]

Ans. See text.

29. ***Outline the differences between Memorandum of Association and Articles of Association.*** [ISC 1994]

OR

Distinguish between Memorandum of Association of a company. [ISC 1990, 1997]

OR

Differentiate memorandum from articles. [ISC 2003]

Ans. See text.

30. *Explain the contents of the Articles of Association.* **[ISC 1995]**

OR

Explain the main contents of the Articles of Association of a joint stock company. **[ISC 1997]**

Ans. See text.

31. *What is a prospectus?* **[ISC 1995]**

Ans. See text.

32. *Give two objectives of a prospectus.* **[ISC 1993, 2002]**

OR

State two objectives of issuing a prospectus. **[ISC 2003]**

Ans. The two main objectives of a prospectus are the following:

(a) To inform the public about the new company; and thereby encourage them to invest in the shares and debentures of the company;

(b) To provide an authentic record of the terms and conditions on which the public has been invited to subscribe to the company's shares and debentures.

33. *What are the important contents of a prospectus of a company?* **[ISC 1994, 1998]**

Ans. See text.

34. *Name the statement a public company has to file before allotment of shares if it had not issued a prospectus.* **[ISC 1987]**

Ans. If a public company does not issue a prospectus, it has to file "statement in lieu of prospectus" before allotment of shares.

35. *When is a 'Statement in Lieu of prospectus' filed?* **[ISC 1994, 2000]**

Ans. See text.

36. *What is the least amount for which shares of a company must be subscribed, within 120 days of the date of issue of prospectus called?* **[ISC 1990]**

Ans. The least amount for which shares of a company must be subscribed within 120 days of the date of issue of a prospectus is called "Minimum Subscription". This amount constitutes 90% of the amount offered for subscription.

37. *What is 'minimum subscription'?* **[ISC 1988, 1993]**

Ans. A company cannot proceed for allotment of shares and debentures unless it receives a minimum of 90% subscription to the issue. This percentage is called minimum subscription and it refers to the nominal amount of shares applied for. If the minimum subscription is not received within 120 days of the date of issue of prospectus, the amount received on application be refunded to the applicants within 10 days after the expiry of 120 days of issue of prospectus.

38. *What is the purpose of minimum subscription?*

Ans. The purpose of minimum subscription is to hold in check the formation of those companies which are not in a position to raise sufficient capital to meet their minimum financial needs so as to be able to cover initial expenses as also to make provision for working capital.

39. *How can a prospective investor judge from the prospectus whether the company is a sound one or not?* **[ISC 1998]**

Ans. See text.

40. *Under what circumstances can a public limited company file a statement in lieu of a prospectus?* [ISC 2008]

Ans. A public limited company can file a statement in lieu of prospectus in the following two circumstances:

(a) When it raises capital without inviting the public to subscribe to its shares or debentures.

(b) When it issues a prospectus, it is not in a position to make allotment of shares or debentures to receive minimum subscription.

41. *What does the capital clause of memorandum of association contain?* [ISC 2012]

Ans. The capital clause of memorandum of association specifies the sources of Authorised Capitals of the company, its division into shares and the face value per share.

42. *Mark the following statements True/False.*

(a) A private company does not need a certificate of incorporation.

(b) A public company is legally obliged to issue a prospectus.

(c) The Memorandum of Association is needed only by a public limited company.

(d) Every company has to prepare its own Articles of Association.

(e) A certificate of commencement of business is needed by a public company.

(f) A private company can be formed by two members.

(g) A private company cannot raise capital from the public.

(h) A single person cannot form a jont stock company.

Ans. False: (a), (b), (c), (d)

True: (e), (f), (g), (h).

43. *What does each of the following imply?*

(i) The process of formation of a joint stock company.

(ii) The person/organisation who/which sets up an enterprise.

(iii) The document which gives the birth certificate of a company.

(iv) The document which defines the objects and powers of a company.

(v) The document which contains rules and regulations for managing internal affairs of a company.

(vi) The document which gives permission to a company to commence its operation as a business unit.

(vii) The document which invites the public to subscribe to the shares and debentures of a public limited company.

(viii) Doing research on potential institutional investors to determine the optimum offering price for a new issue of stock.

(ix) The minimum amount which must be raised before making share allotment.

(x) Prospectus issued while raising capital through book building.

Ans.

(i) Promotion (ii) Promoter

(iii) Certificate of Incorporation (iv) Memorandum of Association

(v) Articles of Association (vi) Certificate of commencement of business

(vii) Prospectus (viii) Book-building

(ix) Subscription (x) Red-herring prospectus

10 PUBLIC ENTERPRISES AND PUBLIC-PRIVATE PARTNERSHIPS

SYLLABUS

- *Public Sector Undertakings — meaning; characteristics, objectives, role and criticisms. Forms of Public Sector Undertakings (Departmental undertakings, Public Corporations and Government companies — definitions, features, merits and demerits).*
- *Public Private Partnerships*
- *Meaning and features of PPPs.*

Private ownership of industries is now a retreat throughout the world as governments privatise

— Alan Griffins and Stuart Wall

LEARNING OUTCOMES

On completion of this chapter, you will be able to understand the following:

10.1 Meaning and Characteristics of Public Enterprises
10.2 Objectives of Public Enterprises
10.3 Role and Rationale of Public Enterprises
10.4 Criticisms of Public Enterprises
10.5 Growth of Public Enterprises in India
10.6 Forms of Organisation in Public Sector
10.7 Departmental Undertakings
10.8 Public Corporations
10.9 Government Companies
10.10 Problems of Public Enterprises
10.11 Suggestions for Improvement
10.12 Public Utilities
10.13 Public-Private Partnerships (PPP)

The term 'public sector' refers to those parts of the economy which are not controlled by individuals, voluntary organisations, or privately owned companies. The public sector thus, includes, *inter-alia*, government owned firms.

In every country, there exists some enterprises which are owned by the state – usually central or state government. Since these organisations are in the public sector, they are referred to as public corporations or public enterprise.

Public (state) ownership of industry in India has mainly been through public corporations. These enterprises are quite separate from the government itself. They run their businesses without close supervision but within the constraints imposed by government policy. These constraints include limits to the amount they can borrow and, therefore, invest and may also include limits to the wages and salaries they can offer.

Public sector organisations do not often have profit as a major objective. In many countries the publicly owned TV channels have as their main priority the quality of public-service programmes. State-owned airlines have safety as a priority.

The First Industrial Policy of the Government of India (GOI), announced in 1948, established in India a mixed economic system. And in India both private sector and public sector exist side by side in trade, commerce and industry and take decisions. In this chapter we shall study the nature of private and public sector enterprises and also various forms of public sector enterprises (units).

10.1 MEANING AND CHARACTERISTICS OF PUBLIC ENTERPRISES

10.1.1 Meaning of Public Enterprises

The term 'public sector' is used to refer to business organisations financed (owned) and controlled by the government of a country.

According to A. H. Hanson, "Public enterprise means state ownership and operation of industrial, agricultural, financial and commercial undertakings". In the words of S. S. Khera, "By state undertakings is meant the industrial, commercial and economic activities carried on by the Central Government or by a state government, and in each case, either solely or in association with private enterprise, so long as it is managed by a self-contained team or group". According to the Encyclopaedia Britannica, a public enterprise is "an undertaking that is owned by a national, State or local government, supplies services or goods at prices, and is operated on a more or less self-supporting basis".

A public sector enterprise in India is financed and controlled by either central government, a state government or a local authority. Normally the central government owns and operates a business. Examples of such enterprises are Life Insurance Corporation of India (LICI), Hindustan Machine Tools Ltd. (HMT), Indian Oil Corporation (IOC), Food Corporation of India (FCI), State Trading Corporation of India (STC), the Bharat Sanchar Nigam Ltd. (BSNL), the Steel Authority of India Ltd. (SAIL), the Coal India Ltd. (CIL), the National Textile Corporation (NTC), Oil and Natural Gas Corporation (ONGC), etc.

10.1.2 Characteristics of Public Sector Enterprise

1. *Legal status:* A public corporation (or a nationalised firm) has a separate legal identity like a company.
2. *Ownership:* The government owns the capital. There are no private shareholders.
3. *Control:* The government appoints the members of the controlling Board. They have functions very similar to directors. But they are answerable to the government and not to shareholders.
4. *Policy:* In general, the policy to be pursued by a public corporation is determined by the government and a Minister is usually given the responsibility for seeing that the corporation is acting within the broad policy requirements laid down by the Parliament.

10.1.3 Distinction between Private Enterprises and Public Enterprises

In comparing a private company with a public enterprise the following points are to be noted:

1. *Control:* The joint stock company is controlled by a board of directors elected by the shareholders. But the public corporation is controlled by a board appointed by the government.
2. *Ownership:* A joint stock company is owned by the shareholders. But there are no shareholders in the public corporation which is owned by the state.
3. *Finance:* A company raises its capital by the issue of shares to the general public. But the public corporation obtains most of its needed capital directly from the Exchequer.
4. *Motives:* The company exists primarily for the purpose of making profits. But the aim of the public corporation is to act in the public interest and to cover its costs.

In Table 10.1 we make a comparison between the two sectors.

TABLE 10.1: A Comparison between the Private Sector and the Public Sector

Basis of Comparison	Private Sector Enterprise	Public Sector Enterprise
1. Ownership	It is owned by individuals (the shareholders)	It is owned by either by the Central or any State Government.
2. Primary objective (motivation)	Its main objective is to earn as much profits as possible.	Its primary purpose is to promote maximum social welfare.
3. Social (non-profit) objectives	Social objectives are of secondary importance even through some firms discharge their social responsibilities quite well on their own volition like the Tata Foundation.	Social objectives such development of notified backward area, employment generation and equitable distribution of wealth are of primary and paramount importance.
4. Operational efficiency	It is likely to operate efficiently since the process of decision-making does not take much time.	Due to slow decision-making redtapism and bureaucratic control there is loss of operational efficiency.
5. Financial control	It is free from any type of financial control by the Government.	It is subject to all types of rigid and stringent financial control by the Government.
6. Day-to-day management of operations	It is managed by professionally qualified persons.	It is managed mostly by retired Government officials and defeated politicians.
7. Accountability to the public	It is accountable only to its owners (the shareholders) and not to the public.	It is accountable to the public through the Parliament for its actual performance and operational results.

10.2 OBJECTIVES OF PUBLIC ENTERPRISES

In India, public enterprises have been assigned the all important task of realising the objectives laid down in the Directive Principles of State Policy. The public sector as a whole seeks: (a) to reach the commanding heights of the economy and compete closely with the private sector in producing a wide range of goods and services, (b) to promote faster economic development in terms of social gain or improvement in the physical quality of life of people rather than on consideration of profit, and (c) to generate commercial surplus with a view to providing necessary financing of various developmental activities.

The main objectives of public enterprises in India are as follows:

1. **Implementation of the industrial policy:** The expansion of the public sector takes place in accordance with the provisions of the Government's Industrial Policy of 1948, 1956 and 1980 and 1991. The policy of 1956 had placed a great responsibility upon the Central Government to set up and develop heavy and basic industries. Accordingly, the Government has set up a large number of industrial enterprises such as several steel plants, heavy electrical factories, petrochemical units heavy machine manufacturing firms, engineering and electronics units. The industrial policy of 1980 also has placed a great responsibility upon the government in the sphere of not only capital goods but also mass consumption goods.
2. **Balanced regional development:** The expansion of public sector has become necessary to strengthen the industrial infrastructure by setting up several capital goods industries in underdeveloped and backward region so as to reduce regional imbalance or disparity in development.
3. **State control over basic industries:** The expansion of public sector has become necessary to gain control over the commanding heights of the economy. To achieve this objective the public sector is being expanded to bring and keep under state control strategic industries such as iron and steel, petro-chemicals, heavy engineering, oil refineries, vital drugs, ship-building and so on. This enables the government to make these industries free from monopoly control of the private sector.
4. **Building up a socialistic pattern of society:** Public sector is being expanded to build up a socialistic pattern of society in which the means of production and the essential enterprises (such as banking, insurance, transport, coal mining, etc.) gradually come under State ownership and management.
5. **Prevention of private monopolies:** The expansion of the public sector has become necessary preventing further growth of monopolies in the private sector. The presence of such monopolies is not desirable in a socialistic pattern of society. The growth of public enterprises can check these trends and thus reduce the unequal distribution of income and wealth in private hands.
6. **Promotion of social welfare:** Public enterprises are organised for increasing welfare of the people. In private industries the main objective is profit maximisation — even by ignoring public interest almost completely. But the basic objective of public enterprises is maximisation of social welfare.
7. **Capital investment for basic and heavy industries:** There are many industries where private investment is not sufficient, e.g., in the heavy and capital goods industries, as it takes long time to get adequate returns from such industries. They have long gestation periods. The expansion of the public sector is absolutely essential to increase investment in those industries for strengthening the economic infrastructure the country.
8. **Removal of the abuses of private enterprises:** The expansion of public enterprises is also necessary to remove the limitations and abuses of private enterprises, such as high prices, profiteering, cornering of essential commodities, misuse, misallocation and wastage of scarce resources.

9. **Fund for economic development and capital formation:** Public enterprises have been providing commercial surplus for economic development. Thus they help to accelerate the rate of capital formation and enable the economy to achieve faster economic growth.
10. **Takeover of sick units:** Another reason for the expansion of the expansion of the public sector is the takeover of a large number of sick industrial units (such as Indian Iron and Steel Works, Braithwaite, a numbers of textile mills, jute mill and tea gardens) by the Government. The basic objective is to nurse such units back to health and protect jobs and income of the employees.

10.3 ROLE AND RATIONALE OF PUBLIC ENTERPRISES

The Second Industrial Policy announced by the GOI in 1956 emphasised the importance of expansion of the public sector in India's mixed economy for achieving faster industrial growth and rapid industrilaisation. The rationale behind this policy will be clear from the following points:

1. **Development of basic and heavy industries:** Only the government can establish basic or heavy industries such as iron and steel, coal mining, heavy engineering, power generation, etc. which are of strategic importance to the nation. There are basically input supplying industries and at the same time highly capital-intensive in nature. Such industries require huge initial investment which is beyond the capacity of the private sector.
2. **Provision of public utility services:** The Government alone can set up public utility concerns for supplying water, electricity, cooking gas, transportation, etc. for promoting social welfare.
3. **Infrastructure building:** Only public enterprises can build strong and integrated infrastructure which is composed of a railway network, roads and highways, communication system, generation and distribution of power, production and distribution of fertilisers, as also the setting up of financial infrastructure in the form of commercial and development banks.
4. **Promoting balanced regional development:** One of the objectives of the GOI's industrial policy is to ensure balanced regional development. This is why public enterprises were set up in industrially backward states such as Bihar, Orissa, Madhya Pradesh, etc. By developing public enterprises in all parts of the country it would be possible to avoid lopsided (uneven) development of the economy.
5. **Employment generation:** One of the economic roles of a welfare state is to generate gainful employment opportunities. This is why stress was laid on setting up public enterprises in all the regions of the country.
6. **Reducing undue concentration of economic power:** Public enterprises are also established to hold in check undue concentration of wealth and economic power in private hands so that the inequality in the distribution of income and wealth does not increase over time. It was felt that large public sector enterprises would act as a counteracting force against the emergence of private monopolies and big businesses as also the adoption of restrictive trade practices by them.
7. **Deriving economies of scale:** The economies of scale (or advantages of large-scale or mass production) could be derived only by setting up of large enterprises (with huge initial investment) in such areas as steel, power, coal, oil, textile and telecommunication. But it is not possible to derive such advantages in small enterprises such as min-steel plants or in the handloom sector of the textile industry.

8. **Import substitution and export promotion:** A number of public sector units have been set up to produce import-substitute items, i.e, goods which were imported earlier. The objective has been to save foreign exchange by reducing the country's dependence on imports as also to enable the country to achieve rapid industrialisation and economic development. For example, HMT has produced watches and other import-substitution items. Some public enterprises have also been set up to earn foreign exchange for the country by exporting their products. For example, five integrated steel plants have been set up under the SAIL not only to meet domestic demand but also to export steel.
9. **Meeting defence needs:** A few public sector units have been set up for the production of defence items which were so important for protecting the country from foreign aggression and ensuring external security. And, as Adam Smith put it long ago, " Defence is more important than opulence."

SYNOPSIS FOR LEARNING: MULTIPLE ROLES OF PUBLIC ENTERPRISE

1. Development of basic and heavy industries.
2. Provision of public utility services.
3. Infrastructure building.
4. Promoting balanced regional development.
5. Employment generation in a labour-surplus country.
6. Reducing undue concentration of wealth and economic power in private hands.
7. Deriving economies of scale, i.e., advantages of large-scale production.
8. Import substitution and export promotion.
9. Meeting defence needs.

10.3.1 The Role of the Public Sector in India since 1991

With the announcement of the New Industrial Policy 1991, the role of the public sector in India has got diluted. The public sector which achieved steady and quite rapid expansion from 1950-51 to 1990-91 suddenly received a serious jolt. The reform period (starting from July 1991) saw a contraction of the public sector due to the adoption of the policy of economic liberalisation, privatisation and globalisation (LPG) by the GOI. The following trends and tendencies will bring into focus the changing role of the public sector in India since the early 1990s:

1. *Selective thrust:* The number of industries exclusively reserved for the public sector has been reduced from 17 to 8 initially and to 3 thereafter. The GOI has also permitted private enterprises to compete closely in selected areas even with the enterprises falling within the reserve list. As a result the private sector has got involved in infrastructure building or power supply, subject to regulations. Public sector has now to concentrate its activities only in selected priority and strategic areas such as defence, high-tech and basic infrastructure.
2. *Spread of professionalism in management:* The Boards of Directors of public sector enterprises have been reconstituted by appointing professional managers. They have been granted greater autonomy so that they can show better performance (by wiping out losses and generating profits). They can therefore improve the operational efficiency of their units.
3. *Improvement of performance through MOU:* Public sector enterprises had to sign memorandum of undertaking (MOU) to improve their performance. Through such memorandum the Government has fixed the performance targets of the managers of public sector

enterprises. And because of this it is now possible to hold the managers accountable for the results of their respective enterprises.

4. *Partial privatisation of selected units:* Partial privatisation of a few select public sector units has been done through an act of disinvestment. For instance, the Government has sold 25% of the shares of Videsh Sanchar Nigam Ltd (VSNL) to the Tata Group. The shares of a few other such units (including NTPC and ONGC) have also been offered for sale to private enterprises, mutual funds, employees and even general public in the open market.
5. *Revival of sick units:* Guidelines have been issued for revival of sick public sector units mainly to give job protection in India's labour-surplus economy. The GOI has declared that the interest of the workers are to be considered first before taking a decision on the exit of a sick unit.
6. *National Renewal Fund:* In 1992 the GOI set up the National Renewal Fund (NRF) for retaining and reabsorption of employees if some units are closed down or some employees become redundant.
7. *Raising financial resources:* In order to raise financial resources and gain a wider public participation a portion of the stocks and shares of public sector enterprises has been offered to mutual funds, public financial institutions, the general public and the workers. The Government has sold its stake in public sector units in a phased manner in order to reduce its fiscal deficit (since public sector units always required budgetary support and were a permanent burden on the Exchequer).

SYNOPSIS FOR LEARNING: PUBLIC SECTOR REFORMS UNDER NEW INDUSTRIAL POLICY, 1991

In the post-liberalisation period (i.e., since July 24,1991) the GOI has adopted the following reform measures in the public sector:

(a) Reducing government equity in all nonstrategic public sector enterprises to 26% or even less, depending on the needs of a situation.

(b) Restructuring and reviving weak (or sick) but potentially viable public sector units.

(c) Closing down those sick public units which stand no chance of survival (as part of its 'exit policy'.)

(d) Protecting the interests of workers of the public sector units through retraining, relocation and reabsorption.

10.3.2 Disinvestment of Shares

The main thrust of public sector reforms in India has been the disinvestment of a select public sector units. The primary objective behind this move is to give necessary budgetary support and bring fiscal deficit of the GOI to 3% of GDP. The second objective was to improve the operational efficiency of such enterprises. The programme commenced in 1991-92 and till 2012-13 the Government had raised a sum of ₹ 113,140 crores.

The Central Government constituted the Disinvestment Commission in August 1996 to give it necessary advice on its various disinvestment programmes. In order to ensure transparency in the disinvestment programme, sealed tenders are invited for the sale of shares of select public sector units and shares are offered to the highest bidder, i.e., those who are ready to pay the highest price. In fact, the industrial policy of 1991 declared that the GOI decided to adopt the policy of disinvestment of the PSUs. The Government could either sell its enterprises completely to the private sector or disinvest a part of the equity held by it either to the private companies or offer a portion of its equity in the open market for absorption by the public or institutional investors — domestic and foreign. In this context we may note the difference between disinvestment and privatisation.

10.4 CRITICISMS OF PUBLIC ENTERPRISES [ARGUMENTS AGAINST PUBLIC ENTERPRISES]

No doubt public enterprises (PEs) have made notable contribution to India's economic growth through new investment or by raising the country's overall rate of capital formation. This became evident from the fact that a sudden fall in public investment from the mid-1960s to mid-1970s as also during the late 1990s led to considerable slowdown in industrial growth. However, while some PEs made positive contribution to India's economic growth, most of them had incurred losses in the first four decades of planning (1951-91). The trend countries till date.

- **Causes of Poor Performance**

We may now discuss briefly the cause of poor performance of PEs. These are the following:

1. *Lack of profit and loss consideration:* Initially the profitability criterion was not given due importance as far as the working of PEs were concerned. Instead the stress was given on the social obligations of such enterprises. It is only in recent years that the profitability aspect of their operations has been given some importance.
2. *Wrong location:* One of the causes of low profitability of PEs is the location of such enterprises at wrong places. The main reason is that most such units were set up here and there mainly on political considerations. The location decision was not based any rational economic canon.
3. *Underutilisation of installed capacity:* Low capacity utilisation has been one of the main reasons for the poor performance of several PEs. Huge initial production capacity has been created by taking foreign loans and using foreign technical know-how on easy terms (i.e., at low rates of interest and long repayment period). But most PEs failed to make full utilisation of their installed production capacity. This problem has arisen for a number of reasons such as overestimation of demand, administrative delays, choice of wrong production techniques, lack of proper work environment and culture, labour trouble, breakdown of machines due to lack of maintenance, reluctance to install balancing equipment and indifferent attitude of management toward up-gradation of technology mainly due to lack of incentives.[1]
4. *Lack of proper feasibility studies:* Most PEs were set up without making proper feasibility studies which would take into consideration such factors as the production process to be used, the availability of essential raw materials such as fuel as also inputs such as power, skilled manpower, cheap credit, transport and communication facilities. These factors were not taken into consideration while launching projects. Hardly any calculation was made of the demand for the product of an enterprise and its production potential. It is also surprising to note that in case of number of units such as the Trombay Fertiliser Project, Hindustan Insecticides and Indian Telephone Industries, tenders were invited even though no project report was prepared.
5. *Delay in completion of project:* Hardly any consideration was given to the time schedule within which a public sector project had to be completed. Most projects were commissioned much later than the scheduled date. Consequently the cost of construction

1. Managers of PEs get a fixed compensation. So like private monopolist they lead a quiet life without being bothered about improving production technology.

increased unnecessarily. For instance, the Trombay Fertiliser Project was supposed to be completed within 3 years. But it took 6-7 years to complete the project. So there was a huge cost overrun (escalation).

6. *Lack of professionalism in management:* There occurred no spread of professionalism in PEs. The members of the boards were appointed politically. There was domination of IAS officers most of whom had no professional background or managerial competence. This accounted for inefficient functioning of many such enterprises.

   Most PEs were characterised by top heavy administrative structure in which there existed a disproportionate number of managers and board members. These people put extra burden on PEs due to high cost (on account of deputation pay, leave-salary, PF and pension contribution) and low efficiency.

7. *Defective recruitment procedure and faulty manpower planning:* Due to faulty manpower planning there was overstaffing in most organisations. More persons were recruited than needed to perform a particular task or sub-task. Most PEs did not undertake proper human development programmes. Moreover the method of recruiting was wrong in most cases. In truth, defeated politicians and retired officials were damped into PEs without assessing their true potential, ability and competence. This is why purely bureaucratic approach was followed in the administration of these undertakings.

8. *Absence of rational pricing policy:* Most PEs did not adopt a rational pricing policy for their products. This is why they failed to achieve an optimal utilisation of resources and improve their profitability.

9. *Unnecessary political interference:* Undue political pressure has forced the management of several PEs to abandon sound commercial principles (based on profit-and-loss considertions) while taking investment, production, and pricing decisions.

Comments

Inadequate trading surpluses generated by PEs are attributable to their long gestation period, shortage of trained and expert personnel, at least in the initial stage, faulty planning, wrong pricing policies and monopolistic nature of several PEs. All these led to organisational slack or X-inefficiency (by making managerial staff lethargic). The PEs make inefficient use of resources and productivity of resources is low in most cases due to lack of proper accountability. There is no doubt that there may be losses in the initial stage but PEs should not be perennial loser and thus a permanent burden on the Exchequer.

10.5 GROWTH OF PUBLIC ENTERPRISES IN INDIA

At the time of independence, public sector in India was confined mainly to railways, communications, defence production and public utility services. Since then the growth of public enterprises has been fairly rapid and virtually spectacular. At present the major segment of the public sector are public utilities (e.g., railways, post and telegraph, etc), manufacturing concerns (e.g., BHEL, SAIL, etc.), trading organisations (e.g., STC, MMTC, etc.) and service organisations (e.g., NIDC, SBI, LIC, etc.).

However, the strategic role of the public sector has become diluted to some extent by the latest Industrial Policy (announced in July 1991). And the trend has been toward the privatisation of loss-making public sector enterprises on the one hand and disinvestment of a number of such units including profit-making ones.

As a result the contribution of the public sector to India's GDP and employment generation has fallen steadily in the last two and half decades. In spite of this we cannot deny the importance of the public sector in India's mixed (and, at present, market-based) economy.

Table 10.2 provides an overview of the growth of public sector in India.

TABLE 10.2: Growth of Central Government Enterprises*

	2012-13	2011-12	2010-11	1999-00
Running enterprises (No.)	229	225	220	232
		₹ crs		
Capital employed	1,510,373	1,387,821	1,153,947	302,947
Turnover	1,945,777	1,822,049	1,498,018	389.199
PBIT**	190,271	196,671	159,298	42,270
Less: Interest	37,789	35,911	26,521	20,233
Profit before tax	166,308	147,231	136,951	22,037
Profit after tax (PAT)	115,298	89,246	136,951	14,331
PAT to turnover (%)	5.9	6.7	5.4	3.7
PAT to capital employed (%)	9.1	9.2	8.7	4.7

* Excluding banks, insurance companies and financial institutions
** Profit before interest and tax.

10.5.1 The Pattern of Investment

More than 20% public sector investment has been made by the Central Government on basic infrastructural industries such as power, coal, petroleum as also heavy (high capital-intensive) industries such as steel, fertiliser and heavy engineering (21%) in 2004-05. However, the maximum investment (22.4%) has been made in financial services (mainly in commercial banking and insurance companies). By contrast, only 5.5% of total investment was made in textiles and 1.2% in consumer goods.

A related point may be noted in this context. A number of sick units belonging mainly to textiles and consumer goods were taken by the Central Government from the private sector, mainly for the purpose of protecting jobs.

Also that recall since July 1991 the Government of India has been disinvesting in public enterprises under the policy of economic liberalisation and privatisation as part of its economic reforms programme.

10.6 FORMS OF ORGANISATION IN PUBLIC SECTOR

Public sector enterprises are owned, operated and managed by the Government. However, they are controlled by the Parliament. As shown in Fig. 10.1 three main types of public enterprises operating in India at present are the following:

1. **Departmental undertaking:** It is the oldest type of public enterprise in India. It is financed and controlled by a department of the Government such as the Deptt. of Telecommunication, Railway deptt., Deptt. of Broadcasting, etc.

2. **Statutory corporation:** It is an autonomous body corporate, created by a special Act passed by the Central or State Legislature to undertake business activities and responsibilities entrusted to it. Some examples are Life Insurance Corporation of India (LICI), National Textile Corporation, Damodar Valley Corporation, and Indian Airlines Corporation.
3. **Government company:** It is a company which is formed and registered under the Companies Act (1956) and in which majority of paid-up (share) capital (51% or more) is held by the Government. Some examples of such companies are Bharat Heavy Electricals Ltd. (BHEL), the Hindusthan Machine Tools Ltd. (HMT), and the Steel Authority of India Ltd. (SAIL).

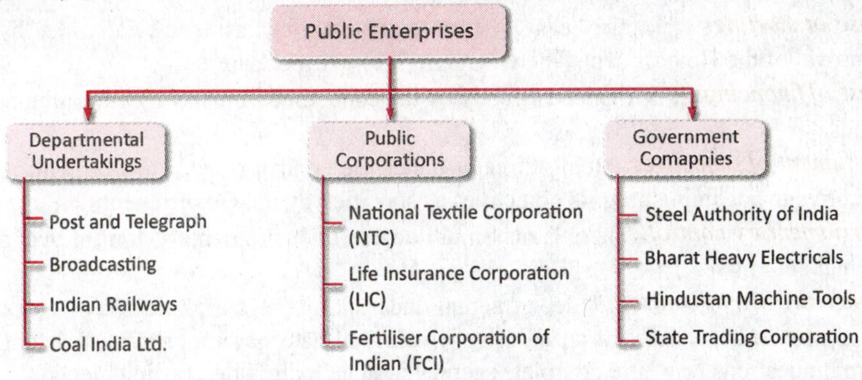

FIGURE 10.1: Three Types of Public Sector Enterprises

10.7 DEPARTMENTAL UNDERTAKINGS

10.7.1 Meaning of Departmental Undertaking

A departmental undertaking is organised, financed and controlled just like as any other Government department under a particular Ministry. However, may be run either by the Central Government or by a State Government. Some other such enterprises (apart from those mentioned above) are: (1) the Chittaranjan Locomotive Works, Chittaranjan, (2) the Integral Coach Factory, Perambur, (3) the Diesel Locomotive Works, Varanasi, (4) the National Instrumental Factory, Kolkata; (5) Coal India Ltd., Dhanbad.

10.7.2 Features of a Departmental Undertaking

The main features of departmental undertaking are the following:

1. *Just an extension of government department:* It is an inherent or integral part of department under a particular Ministry of either the Central or a State Government. For instance, railways are attached to the Railway Ministry.
2. *Financing:* It is financed by the Treasury from its annual appropriations and its revenues go straight into the Treasury. Its annual budget is to be passed either by the Parliament or any State Legislature.
3. *Management and control:* A departmental undertaking such as Indian Railways is managed by the Government department which is under direct control of the same Ministry, viz., Railway Ministry.
4. *Accounting and budgeting:* All budgetary, accounting and audit controls to which Government departments are subject are also applicable to any departmental undertaking.

5. *Staffing:* All the terms and conditions relating to selection, recruitment, appointment and service of permanent staff are almost (if not exactly) the same as those of other civil servants.
6. *Sovereign status:* It enjoys the sovereign status of the Government. It can be sued by following the same procedure, which applies in case of Government at the central or state level.

10.7.3 Merits of a Departmental Undertaking

A departmental enterprise offers the following merits:

1. *Ease of starting:* It is fairly easy to form and start a departmental enterprise by getting approval of the Government. There is no need to get it registered.
2. *Ease of financing:* It is financed directly by the concerned ministry by allocating necessary funds.
3. *Fulfilment of objectives:* Being directly under the control of the Government, it is quite effective in accomplishing its objectives as specified by the Government.
4. *Parliamentary control:* There is maximum degree of Parliamentary control over a departmental enterprise.
5. *Concentration of control:* A departmental undertaking has a high degree of concentration of control. It is suitable for an industry which is of national importance such as Deptt. of communications or where complete secrecy is to be maintained (as in defence).
6. *Judicious use of funds:* There is very little scope of misuse of public money due to strict budgetary control, accounting and auditing.

10.7.4 Demerits of a Departmental Undertaking

A departmental enterprise has the following demerits:

1. *Long Delay in decision-making:* Due to strict control by the Parliament and the Government, a departmental undertaking does not have much flexibility in taking decisions. So delay in decision making is almost inevitable. Unnecessary and, at times, excessive political interference leads to inordinate delay in decision-making.
2. *Lack of competitive spirit:* Due to complete absence of competition and lack of profit motive, a departmental undertaking is not at all responsive to the needs of the consumers in particular and the society in general.
3. *Delays and redtapism:* There is excessive and undue centralisation of control in a departmental undertaking. This results in redtapism and loss of initiative and enterprise. This is one of the major causes of inefficiency of such an enterprise.
4. *Lack of autonomy:* Being completely dependent upon budgetary allocation by the Government, a departmental undertaking cannot take any type of long-term financial decision.
5. *Political interference:* Too much political interference in the day-to-day operation of the undertaking leads to loss of freedom of the managers. Therefore they cannot discharge their functions efficiently.
6. *Traditional-bound approach:* Managers of departmental undertakings have conservative (non-experimental and static) outlook. They are essentially risk-averse people. They have hardly any incentive to go for a new and potentially profitable venture. So they cannot explore and exploit new opportunities which arise from time to time due to changing economic environment.

10.7.5 Suitability of a Departmental Undertaking

A departmental undertaking is most suitable in the following cases:

(a) Where secrecy is of strategic importance as in defence industries.

(b) Where the Government desires to maintain its own controlling power in strategic areas (sectors) such as defence, broadcasting and railways.

(c) Where price control-cum-rationing is essential to ensure that the poor and weaker sectors of society get a minimum amount of certain essential commodities at fair prices.

(d) Where more and more revenue has to be generated for extending a particular service through further investment, as in the case of railways.

10.7.6 Departmental Undertakings at a Glance

Merits	Demerits
1. Ease of starting	1. Long Delay in decision-making
2. Ease of financing	2. Lack of competitive spirit
3. Fulfilment of objectives	3. Delays and redtapism
4. Parliamentary control	4. Lack of autonomy
5. Concentration of control	5. Political interference
6. Judicious use of funds	6. Traditional-bound approach

10.8 PUBLIC CORPORATIONS

10.8.1 Meaning of Public Corporation

A public corporation is a business enterprise owned and controlled by the state and is also known as a nationalised enterprise. A public (statutory) corporation is a body corporate created through a special act passed by the Central or State Legislature. Its objects, powers and functions are all defined by the statute. In the words of the late USA President Roosevelt "a public corporation is an organisation that is clothed with the powers of the Government, but is possessed of the flexibility and initiative of private enterprise".

Public corporations are most suitable for providing transport services, supplying water and electricity as also for providing public utility services such as insurance and banking. Some examples of such enterprises are the Food Corporation of India, the Employees' State Insurance Corporation, the Central Warehousing Corporation and 18 State Financial Corporations.

A public corporation is thus a combination of public ownership, public accountability and business management for subserving public ends. The Life Insurance Corporation of India, the Reserve Bank of India, the Employees State Insurance Corporation and the Small Industries Development Bank of India are all examples of public corporations. Note that an enterprise does not become necessarily a public corporation just by using the word 'corporation' in its name. For example, the Damodar Valley Corporation is a Government company and is not a public corporation. Public limited companies are in the private sector of industry — but public corporations are not.

This statement may initially appear to be puzzling, though not paradoxical. But the truth is that pubic limited companies and public corporations are not exactly identical. They differ each other in more ways than one.

10.8.2 Features of a Public Corporation

The most notable features of a statutory corporation are the following:

1. *Governed by an Act of Parliament:* The powers, duties, responsibilities as also the functions of a statutory corporation are laid down by the statute, passed either by the Parliament or a State Legislature.
2. *Separate legal status:* Being a body corporate it has a separate legal status. So it can sue and can be sued. It can sign contracts and buy, own and hold property in its own name. In addition, it has a perpetual existence and a common seal, like a public limited company.
3. *Ownership:* Since it is wholly owned by the Government its entire equity capital is with the Government.
4. *Management:* The corporation is managed by the Board of Directors and the members of the Board are appointed by the Government. Each member of the Board enjoys full autonomy in his (her) day-to-day functioning. There does not exist any type of government interference as far as the day-to-day operation of the corporation is concerned.
5. *Financial autonomy:* The corporation enjoys autonomy in financial matters. It can raise funds by borrowing from the public (by selling bonds or long-term securities) as also from the Government.
6. *Freedom from budgeting and accounting controls:* In most normal circumstances it is not subject to the strict budgetary and related controls to which a Government department is subject.
7. *Accountability:* A public corporation is fully accountable to the Parliament or State Legislature for its operational results. It has to submit its annual report to the Parliament or State Legislature every year as a matter of routine, so to say.

10.8.3 Merits of a Public Corporation

A public corporation enjoys following merits

1. *Operational flexibility:* Even though it enjoys the power of the Government, it is free from all the rigidities and delayed actions observable in departmental undertakings. In other words, it enjoys the flexibility of a private enterprise.
2. *Stability:* A public corporation can take long-term policy decisions subject to the powers enjoyed by it under the law. It is not affected by ministerial changes or changes even in the ruling party.
3. *Financial freedom:* It can finance any expansion or diversification programme easily and quickly by using its own resources or, if necessary, by borrowing from the public by selling long-term credit instruments.
4. *Accountability:* It is accountable to the Parliament which exercises direct control over it. So it cannot take any decision which goes against public interest.
5. *Rational pricing policy:* The pricing policy of a public corporation is based on profit-and-loss considerations, like that of a private corporation. However, this is accompanied by the service motive, so that the consumers are protected and the interests of society are promoted.

6. *Independence in staffing function:* The corporation enjoys full autonomy in appointing its required managers and staff personnel. In addition, it can take the help of or hire the services of professionals or experts for performing highly specialised functions.

10.8.4 Demerits of a Statutory Corporation

Statutory corporations have the following demerits:

1. *Illusory autonomy:* In reality government officials and political leaders often interfere with the day-to-day functioning and management of the corporation. So the autonomy and flexibility enjoyed by a corporation is highly illusory.
2. *Appointment of incompetent directors:* In most cases the members of the Board of Directors of a corporation who are appointed by the Government do not have the required qualifications, experience, training as also skills and ability needed to manage the corporation professionally.
3. *Inefficiency:* Public corporations are often treated as models of inefficiency. Since they do not face much competition and are not guided by the profit motive, there is no pressure on them to improve their operational efficiency and show improved performance year after year.
4. *Monopoly pricing:* Most loss-making public corporations charge higher prices for their products to eliminate their losses. Since they enjoy monopoly power, consumers are totally powerless or helpless. Take, for example, the case of some electric supply corporations which are still publicly owned and operated.
5. *Rigidity of charter:* The charter of a statutory corporation is inherently rigid. It is so rigid that incorporation of any new objective is extremely difficult, if not virtually impossible. The statute has to be amended only by going through a highly complicated and time-consuming process.

10.8.5 Public Corporation at a Glance

Merits	Demerits
1. Operational flexibility	1. Illusory autonomy
2. Stability	2. Appointment of incompetent directors
3. Financial freedom	3. Inefficiency
4. Accountability	4. Monopoly pricing
5. Rational Pricing Policy	5. Rigidity of charter
6. Independence in Staffing function	

10.9 GOVERNMENT COMPANIES

10.9.1 Meaning of Government Company

A government company is one in which the major portion of the paid-up share capital (at least 51%) is held by either the Central Government or by one or more State Governments. The remaining portion of the paid-up capital can be subscribed by individuals and/or institutional investors.

A government company is formed and registered under the Companies Act, (1956). The Act has certain special provisions for such a company. Some of the government companies are:

Hindustan Steel Ltd., Hindustan Insecticides Ltd., Bharat Aluminium Ltd., Hindustan Antibiotics Ltd., Hindustan Cables Ltd., Hindustan Shipyard Ltd., and Sindri Fertilizers Ltd.

10.9.2 Features of a Government Company

The main characteristics of a public company are the following:

1. *Ownership:* The major portion of the paid-up capital of such a company is held by the Government. The rest may be contributed by private firms or financial institutions, insurance companies, etc., as noted above.
2. *Separate legal status:* Like a joint stock company a government company also enjoys a separate legal status. It has perpetual existence and it uses a common seal. It can sue any person or a company and be sued either by an insider or an outsider, enter into contracts, and buy, acquire and hold any tangible property in its own name.
3. *Professional management:* Like a joint stock company a government company is managed by a Board of Directors. The Board members are appointed by the Government and other shareholders. The former are professional managers who often introduce modern management techniques for cutting costs and raising profits.
4. *Nonapplicability of standard accounting procedures:* Since government companies are to go by the provisions of the Companies Act and other relevant Acts, they are not subject to all the accounting and audit laws and procedures which are applicable to different Government agencies.
5. *Accountability:* A government company is under the legal obligation to present its annual report on its working and progress either to the Parliament or any State Legislature, depending on the case.

10.9.3 Merits of a Government Company

A government company enjoys the following merits:

1. *Ease of starting:* It is fairly easy to form and start a government company on the basis of the executive and exclusive decision of the Government. There is no need to pass any special act for the purpose.
2. *Operational independence:* Since a government company has a separate legal status and is an autonomous body it enjoys operational (managerial) independence. There is no direct parliamentary and ministerial control over its functioning. It also enjoys independence in financial and personnel matters (such as appointment of different staff members).
3. *Operation on the basis of commercial principles:* Since a government company enjoys complete independence in respect of its functioning, it can operate on purely commercial (i.e., profit-and-loss) considerations.
4. *Deployment of skilled and knowledgable personnel:* The Government company can harness the talent, managerial skill, specialised knowledge, technical competence and expertise of the private sector. In fact, only this type of company employs what P.F. Drucker calls 'knowledge workers' who are more efficient than others.
5. *Accountability.* Autonomy in day-to-day functioning does not rule out accountability. Managers of government companies are accountable to the Parliament or the State Legislature. So they have to be cautious in their approach and show operational efficiency which gets

reflected in the annual report of their company. In fact, managers of such enterprises have to be efficient just to avoid public criticism and protect their own jobs.

6. *Competitive outlook.* Since a government company has to follow sound policies (compete closely with its private counterpart), and make every possible attempt to raise productivity and reduce cost in order to survive and generate operational surplus. After all market competition ensures the survival of the fittest.

10.9.4 Demerits of a Government Company

A government company has the following demerits:

1. *Absence of professionalism:* The members of the Board of Directors of a government company often consist of defeated politicians and retired civil servants with no managerial experience. This may prevent the spread of professionalism in such enterprises and adoption of modern managerial principles and techniques.
2. *Illusory autonomy:* A government company is autonomous only on paper. The smooth and efficient functioning of such an enterprise is often hampered by excessive and undue interference and involvement of government officials, ministers, political parties and leaders.
3. *Avoidance of constitutional provisions:* Since the accounts of a government company are not audited by the Comptroller and Auditor General of India, a government company is able to evade an important constitutional responsibility which is discharged by other types of public enterprises.
4. *Dilution of the Companies Act:* With the formation of government companies the Companies Act gets diluted because the Government has the supreme power to specify the relaxations which can be given to such companies from the main provisions of the Companies Act.

10.9.5 Government Company at a Glance

Merits	Demerits
1. Ease of starting	1. Absence of professionalism
2. Operational independence	2. Illusory autonomy
3. Operation on the basis of commercial principles	3. Avoidance of constitutional provisions
4. Deployment of skilled and knowledgeable personnel	4. Dilution of the Companies Act
5. Accountability	
6. Competitive outlook	

10.9.6 Suitability of a Government Company

A government company is quite suitable in the following cases:

(i) Where the government seeks to exercise full control over a company in the private sector, without outright state take-over or nationalisation.

(ii) Where the government is desirous of collaborating with a private enterprise for a common endeavour.

(iii) Where a giant project requires both government planning and financing of investment.

10.10 PROBLEMS OF PUBLIC ENTERPRISES (PEs)

We may now discuss briefly the problems of PEs. These are the following:

1. **Lack of profit and loss consideration:** Initially the profitability criteria was not given due importance as far as the working of PEs were concerned. Instead the stress was given on the social obligations of such enterprises. It is only in recent years that the profitability aspect of their operations has been given some importance.
2. **Wrong location:** One of the causes of low profitability of PEs is the location of such enterprises at wrong places. The main reason is that most such units were set up here and there mainly on political consideration. The location decision was not based any rational economic cannon.
3. **Underutilisation of installed capacity:** Low capacity utilisation has been one of the main reasons for the poor performance of several PEs. Huge initial production capacity has been created by taking foreign loans and using foreign technical know-how on easy terms (i.e., at low rates of interest and long repayment period). But most PEs failed to make full utilisation of their installed production capacity.
4. **Lack of proper feasibility studies:** Most PEs were set up without making proper feasibility studies which would take into consideration such factors as the production process to be used, the availability of essential raw materials such as fuel as also inputs such as power, skilled manpower, cheap credit, transport and communication facilities. These factors were not taken into consideration while launching projects. Hardly any calculation was made of the demand for the product of an enterprise and its production potential.

   It is also surprising to note that in case of number of units such as Trombay Fertiliser Project, Hindustan Insecticides and Indian Telephone Industries, tenders were invited even though no project report was prepared.
5. **Delay in completion of project:** Hardly any consideration was given to the time schedule within which a public sector project had to be completed. Most projects were commissioned much later than the scheduled date. Consequently the cost of construction increased unnecessarily. For instance, Trombay Fertilizer Project was supposed to be completed within 3 years. But it took 6-7 years to complete the project. So there was a huge cost overrun (escalation).
6. **Lack of professionalism in management:** There occurred no spread of professionalism in PEs. The members of the boards were appointed politically. There was domination of IAS officers most of whom had no professional background or managerial competence. This accounted for inefficient functioning of many such enterprises.[1]
7. **Defective recruitment procedure and faulty manpower planning:** Due to faulty manpower planing there was overstaffing in most organisations. More persons were recruited than needed to perform a particular task or sub-task. Most PEs did not undertake proper human development programmes. Moreover the method of recruiting was wrong in most cases.
8. **Absence of rational pricing policy:** Most PEs failed to adopt a rational pricing policy for their products. This is why they failed to achieve an optimal utilisation of resources and improve their profitability.

1 Managers of PEs get a fixed compensation. So like private monopolies they lead a quiet life without being borthered about improving production technology.

9. **Unnecessary political interference:** Undue politcal pressure has forced the management of several PEs to abandon sound commercial principles (based on profit-and-loss consideration) while taking in vestment, production, and pricing decisions.

10.11 SUGGESTIONS FOR IMPROVEMENT

Certain suggestions may be put forward for improving the working of PEs and making them more efficient:

(i) Firstly, it is necessary to prepare detailed construction plans and feasibility reports so as to avoid delays and cost escalations in such enterprises.

(ii) Secondly, there should be a change in the price policy of PEs. Some enterprises should be permitted to operate on the basis of commercial (i.e., profit-and-loss, considerations. The reason is that profit is the most important index of business efficiency.

(iii) Thirdly, some top positions in some PEs should be opened to its employees so as to provide necessary incentives to them. Moreover, there is need to train professional and technical personnel into management.

(iv) Fourthly, it is necessary on the part of the government to improve labour management relations in PEs.

(v) Fifthly, it is vitally important to provide greater functional autonomy to the management of PEs.

(vi) Finally, it is necessary, on the part of the government, to shift to professional management in PEs.

10.12 PUBLIC UTILITIES

Public utility is an enterprise which provides a certain essential good or service like water, electricity, gas, transport and postal service for promoting social welfare rather than making maximum profit. In developed countries such as the UK and the USA, most of these goods and services are provided by privately owned (but publicly regulated) companies. In developing countries like India, Pakistan, Sri Lanka and Bangladesh, most of these items are produced by publicly owned Corporations.

10.12.1 Definition of Public Utility

A public utility is a company which maintains the infrastructure for a public service, and often provides the service using that infrastructure. Since public utility concerns offer indispensable services to consumers, they are normally state-owned and regulated. These are natural monopolies which arise due to absolute cost advantages. Such monopolies lead to saving of a society's scarce resources through efficient (economical) operation. Let us take a simple example. If the Post and Telegraph Department is privatised, three postmen will go to the same village to deliver one parcel each. So there will be unnecessary duplication or multiplication of the same service which can avoided if the service be rendered by a single person.

Since consumers have no alternatives to certain essential services, the natural monopolies, in effect, perform a public function — promotion of social welfare by providing some absolute necessities and emergency services such as protection from fire or supply of water in times of scarcity. In order to prevent these firms from exploiting their monopoly positions, the government substitutes public regulations for competition. Even if the public utility concerns incur losses by supplying certain services at less than cost-prices, they cannot be allowed to reduce production capacity since they provide an essential service to consumers. So it is not desirable on the part of the government to reduce suppliers of such services, if these are provided at a loss.

In most countries, laws prohibit the formation of monopolies in the market for public utilities which sell natural gas, water and electric power. These companies' prices and profits are usually controlled by public authorities in order to protect the interests of buyers. In recent years we find a trend towards deregulation of natural monopolies or public utility concerns, increased competition among utility companies and, ultimately, lower prices for consumers.

Public utility concerns are different from public enterprises. Such concerns are wholly owned by the government and enjoy monopoly power. Examples are the Calcutta Municipal Corporation, Calcutta Road Transport Corporation, Delhi State Electricity Undertaking (DSEU). Another example is the fire brigade.

10.12.2 Public Utility Entry

The entry of a new enterprise in the public utility arena is controlled by a regulatory commission. Ordinarily a firm entering such a regulated industry must first obtain approval from the commission in the form of a certificate of public convenience and necessity. By restricting entry, it is thought that destructive competition may be avoided so that public utilities have financial stability and are able to provide continued service.

10.13 PUBLIC-PRIVATE PARTNERSHIP (PPP)

Economic development requires proper infrastructure in the form schools, hospitals, roads, airports, dams, electricity grids (power plants), telecommunication networks and water supply and sanitation. Such infrastructures are financed by governments — or by foreign aid when countries are less developed — and by private money as countries grow richer and develop sophisticated financial markets.

An example of a government-sponsored infrastructure scheme is the Trans-European Networks Programme launched by the European Union (EU) in 1994 in the fields of transport, energy and telecommunications. It was funded by European governments, the EU and the European Investment Bank (the Regional Development Bank) and involves public-private partnerships.

10.13.1 Definition of Public-Private Partnership

Public-private partnerships are projects which are funded and operated through a partnership between the government and one or several private companies. In other words, these are government services or business ventures which are funded and managed through a partnership of government and one or more private-sector companies.

Public-private partnership refers to private-sector involvement in a traditionally public-sector service — a partnership between the government and the private sector for the purpose of more effectively providing services and infrastructure traditionally provided by the public sector. The abbreviation as *PPP*, *P*3 or P^3 is also used for this arrangement.

10.13.2 Importance in Mixed Economies

Mixed economies like India, Pakistan and Sri Lanka are emphasising public-private partnership (PPP) mode of operations to improve and strengthen their infrastructure with a view to promoting faster economic growth.

The PPP (or P3) is essentially a legal agreement between government and private sector for the creation of assets and the delivery of community services. Such contracts lead to division of responsibilities and sharing of risks among various partners involved in the agreement. Under such an arrangement, the government or the public sector remains actively involved in the project althrough. And the private sector is made responsible for commercial functions such as project design, construction, financing and day-to-day operations.

In the PPP, the ownership of the asset may remain with the government and the responsibility and risk of delivery and project funding are shared by both the government and the private sector.

Forms: PPP can take various forms such as Service Contract, Management Contract, Lease, Concession, Build-Own-Operate (BOO), Build-Operate-Transfer (BOT) and Build-Own-Operate-Transfer (BOOT) and divesture. Divesture means being stripped off assets.

Indian Examples: To extend the efforts of the public sector, the Eleventh Five Year Plan (2007-12) laid stress on the participation of the private sector, especially in the form of PPP, in the build-up of both physical and human capital as also technological upgradation and diffusion. Accordingly, both the central and state governments have promoted PPPs in such sectors as power, ports, highways, airports, tourism and urban infrastructure. Two dozens of projects which have already been completed and are listed in Table 10.3.

TABLE 10.3: Some illustrative PPP Projects in Infrastructure

Sl.No.	Projects	Sl.No.	Projects
1	Bangalore International Airport, Karnataka	13	Colaba Bandra Metro Corridor Line-III, Mumabi
2	Rajiv Gandhi International Airport, Hyderabad	14	Jhajjar Power Transmission Project, Haryana
3	Indira Gandhi International Airport, New Delhi	15	Mundra Port, Gujarat
4	Chhatrapati Shivaji International Airport, Mumbai	16	Pipavav Port, Gujarat
5	6 Laning of Jaipur-Kishangarh National Highway	17	Gangavaram Port, Andhra Pradesh
6	8/6 Lanin of Delhi-Gurgaon Expressway	18	Krishnapuram Port, Andhra Pradesh
7	Hyderabad-Vijaywada National Highway	19	Vadodara-Bharuch State Highway Gujarat
8	Offshore Container Berths, Mumbai Harbour	20	Indore-Edelabad State Highway, Madhya Pradesh
9	Deep Draft Iron Ore Berth, Paradip Port	21	Yedshi-Latur-Nanded State Highway, Maharastra
10	Mega Conainer Teminal, Chennai	22	Jaipur-Bhilwara State Highway, Rajasthan
11	Multi-purpose Cargo Berths, Kandla	23	Delhi Western Peripheral Expressway (KMP Expressway), Haryana
12	Hyderabad Metro Rail-Project, Hyderabad	24	Bridge across River Godavari between Yanam-Edurulanka, Andhra Pradesh

10.13.3 Features of Public-Private Partnership

The characteristic features of public-private partnership are the following:

(i) The PPP seeks to develop or promote partnership arrangement between government and the private sector.

(ii) This arrangement is made to embark on a project of strategic importance to a nation (such as construction of national highways, flyovers and bridges.)

(iii) The project fund is largely provided by the private enterprise, with the government making just a marginal contribution or the government may just supply the initial infrastructure without which a project cannot take-off.

(iv) It is most appropriate for big projects having a long gestation period such as metro railway or a long bridge above a river, such as the Third Hooghly Bridge of Kolkata.

(v) Revenue is shared between the government and the private enterprise on a contractual basis (i.e., at a predetermined ratio)

The concept of PPP was introduced in India in 1992 in the form of private finance initiative (PFI) for such projects as highways, hospitals, electrical power, sea-ports, airports and telecommunication. PPP seeks to provide quality infrastructure as quickly as possible. The Central Government has set up Public-Private Partnership Appraisal Committee (PPPAC) for approving the proposed PPP projects. A few States in India have made similar arrangement to promote PPP.

10.13.4 Merits of Public-Private Partnership

The merits of PPP are the following:

1. *Reduction of financial burden:* By bringing in benefit to all parties involved, the PPP creates a win-win situation. Private investment and involvement reduces the financial burden of the government.
2. *Efficient management of resources:* Private sector is also found to be more efficient in managing both physical and financial resources.
3. *Use of modern technology and cost reduction:* Since the private sector remains more equipped with most modern production technology, its involvement reduces cost and improves production (operational) efficiency.
4. *Shorter gestation period:* As responsibilities are shared and each party is accountable to the extent of its responsibility, PPP projects are likely to be implemented without delay or time lag.
5. *Risk sharing:* In the PPP, along with rewards, risks also get shared through diversification.
6. *Long-term return:* The partners from the private sectors are likely to benefit from such arrangements as they get a long-term investment opportunity and a steady and dependable stream of revenue from the assets.
7. *Learning:* The private sector also gets the opportunity to learn from the experience of handling of the projects which would otherwise, would be exclusively undertaken in the public sector.
8. *Expansion of business:* From such experiences acquired from handling projects the private sector is in a position to expand its business in other areas and gain access to wider markets.

10.13.5 Socio-economic Benefits of Public-Private Partnership

The public-private partnership (PPP) arrangement offers the following benefits:

1. *Attraction of private investment in infrastructure:* PPP attracts private sector investment in infrastructural projects such as highways, ports, etc. without which economic development is likely to lopsided (or uneven) or is likely to occur slowly.

2. *Social gain:* Finally, the society as a whole benefit from the availability of improved infrastructure and uninterrupted supply of services at concessional rates. Its promotes social welfare.
3. *Employment generation:* It creates gainful employment opportunities both directly and indirectly, i.e., by helping the growth of industry, trade and commerce.

Conclusion

It is anyone's guess that the development of an economy and the creation of an enabling environment for business require an integrated infrastructure consisting of roads, railway network, air and water transport, generation and distribution of power, telecommunication, water supply, irrigation and storage. Keeping in view the huge investment required for creating infrastructure, the PPP arrangements are increasingly being made for creation, operation and maintenance of physical infrastructure both in developed and developing countries.

Key Points

1. **Public Sector Enterprise:** A public sector enterprise is owned (financed) and controlled by the government at any level (central, state, or local). Examples are the SAIL, BHEL, CIL, IOC, BPCL and HMT. Its main features are the following:
   (i) Its initial capital is provided by the government.
   (ii) It is fully controlled by the government.
   (iii) Its main objective is to promote social welfare.
   (iv) It is accountable to the Parliament as also to the general public for its financial performance.
   (v) Its management is in the hands of government officials.
2. **Forms of Public Sector Enterprises:** There are three important organisational forms of public sector units. These are the following:
   (i) Departmental undertakings such as Posts and Telegraph, the Railways, the Telecommunication and Defence.
   (ii) Statutory corporations such as Life Insurance Corporation of India, Food Corporation of India, National Textile Corporation and Indian Airlines Corporation.
   (iii) Government companies such as Hindustan Machine Tools Ltd. (HMT), Bharat Heavy Electricals Ltd. (BHEL) and Steel Authority of India Ltd. (SAIL).
3. **Changing Role of Public Sector in India**
   (i) Development of basic and heavy industries,
   (ii) provision of public utility services,

(iii) infrastructure building,
(iv) ensuring (CBSE promoting) balanced regional development,
(v) employment generation,
(vi) reducing undue concentration of wealth and economic power in private hands.
(vii) deriving economies of scale.
(viii) import substitution.
(ix) export promotion and
(x) meeting defence needs.

4. **Public utility:** Public utility refers to an industry or enterprise providing basic services to the public, such as energy, water, postal services, telephones which are owned by the state. However, even in case of private ownership (as is the case in the UK and the USA) it is subject to public regulation. Since these industries or enterprises are natural monopolies (at least in a local area) a special policy towards them is essential if the public is not to be exploited. Regulatory authorities pay close attention to the prices charged, safety standards and of course, the quality of service they provide.

5. **Public-Private Partnership (PPP):** It refers to a partnership between government and the private sector for the purpose of more effectively providing service and infrastructure traditionally provided by the private sector.

KEY Terms	
Departmental undertaking	Statutory corporation
Public sector	Government company
Public utility	Public-Private partnership

Assignments

SHORT ANSWER-TYPE QUESTIONS

1. Define public enterprises.
2. Mention three objectives of public enterprises.
3. What is the main role of public enterprises in a mixed economy?
4. Account for or mention the causes of the growth of public enterprises in India.
5. Name the three types of public enterprise in the Indian context.
6. What is departmental undertaking?
7. Define a public corporation.
8. Define a government company.

9. Mention three main problems faced by public enterprises in India.
10. What are public utilities?
11. Give two examples of public corporations operating in India.
12. Name two government companies.
13. Name the following:
    (a) A corporation established through a special Act of Parliament. [ISC 1990]
    (b) Industrial and commercial undertakings owned and managed by the government. [ISC 1992]
    (c) A joint-stock company wholly owned by the government.
    (d) Undertakings which enjoy monopoly, supplying essential public services under government ownership and control.
    (e) What is Public-Private Partnership (PPP)?

ESSAY-TYPE QUESTIONS

1. Public ownership can also take the form of direct state ownership in private sector companies. Explain.
2. (a) What is the rationale of Public Enterprises in underdeveloped countries like India?
   (b) Explain the shortcomings of Public Enterprises in India. [ISC 1989]
3. (a) What is a Public Corporation? Explain its characteristics.
   (b) Discuss the advantages of a Public Corporation. [ISC 1990]
4. (a) Define the term 'Public Utility'. Explain the important economic characteristics of public utilities.
   (b) What are the certain exclusive privileges enjoyed by the public utilities which are not available to other business enterprises? [ISC 1991]
5. Briefly explain the main economic characteristics of public utilities that differentiate them from other business enterprises. [ISC 1992]
6. (a) What is a Public Corporation? Point out its chief characteristics.
   (b) Discuss two chief merits and two chief demerits of a Public Corporation.

QUESTION BANK

1. *What do you understand by Public Enterprises?*

Ans. See text.

2. *Give any three objectives of public enterprises.*

Ans. Three main objectives of public enterprises are:
   (i) to accelerate industrialisation in the country, and
   (ii) to ensure balanced regional development of the country,
   (iii) to generate employment opportunities in a labour-surplus country.

3. *What, according to the Industrial Policy Resolution 1956, is the role of public sector in India?*

Ans. The role of public sector was stated in the Industrial Policy Resolution 1956 as under: "The need for planned and rapid development requires that all industries of basic and strategic importance or in the nature of public utility services should be in the public sector. Other industries which are essential and require investment on a scale which only the state, in the present circumstances, could provide have also to be in the public sector. The state, has, therefore, to assume direct responsibility for the future development of industries over a wide area".

4. *Explain the distinguishing characteristics of public enterprises.*

Ans. See text.

5. *Distinguish between Public Enterprise and Private Enterprise.*

Ans. See text.

6. *Discuss the rationale for the establishment of public enterprises in a developing country like India.*

Ans. See text.

7. *Explain the role of public enterprises in India.*

Ans. See text.

8. *List the advantages and disadvantages of public sector enterprises.*

Ans. TABLE : Advantages and Disadvantages of Public Sector Enterprises

Advantages	*Disadvantages*
1. A public enterprise is managed with social objectives than solely with the profit motive.	1. A public enterprise is an model of the inefficiency due to lack of strict profit targets.
2. Loss-making services might still be kept operating if their social benefit is large enough.	2. Government subsidies add to inefficiencies.
3. Finances are raised mainly from the government (the public exchequer).	3. Government may interfere with business decisions for political reasons, for example, by opening a new branch in a certain area to gain popularity (even if it is not economically viable).

9. *Highlight the main shortcomings of public enterprises.*

Ans. See text.

10. *What the three main forms of public enterprises.*

Ans. The three main forms of public enterprises are:

(i) departmental undertakings.

(ii) public corporations, and

(iii) government companies

11. *What is a departmental undertaking?*

Ans. See text.

12. *Explain the features, merits and demerits of departmental undertakings.*

Ans. See text.

13. *What is a Public (Statutory) Corporation?*

Ans. See text.

14. *What is Public-Private Partnership (PPP)?*

Ans. In a broad sense, PPP is one of a range of cooperative ventures between government and the private sector, including joint ventures, outsourcing and the sale of equity stakes in state-owned businesses. The goals of PPPs is to extend the perceived qualities of private management to the delivery of public services.

15. *What is a government company?*

Ans. See text.

16. *Explain the features, merits and demerits of Government company form of public enterprises.*

Ans. See text.

17. *Make a comparative study of three different forms of public enterprises.*

Ans. See text.

18. *Define the term 'Public Utilities'.*

Ans. See text.

19. *Explain the essential characteristics of public utilities.*

Ans. See text.

20. *What is Public-Private Partnerships (PPP)?*

Ans. See text.

21. *Name three public enterprises owned and managed by local self-government.*

Ans. Local self-government or municipal authorities own and manage the following public enterprises: (i) public transport of the city, (ii) electricity and (iii) milk supply.

11 COOPERATIVE ORGANISATION

SYLLABUS

- *Cooperative organisations — meaning; characteristics, advantages and disadvantages; Types of co-operative organisations, distinction between joint stock companies and cooperative organisations.*

> *Cooperative is a business owned and controlled by the people — producers, consumers or workers with similar needs — who pull their resources for mutual gain.*
>
> — W.G. Nickels and others

LEARNING OUTCOMES

On completion of this chapter, you will be able to understand the following:

11.1 Meaning and Definition of a Cooperative Organisation
11.2 Characteristics of Cooperative Organisation
11.3 Distinction between a Cooperative Organisation and a Joint Stock Company
11.4 Formation of a Cooperative Society
11.5 Different Types of Cooperative Societies
11.6 Advantages of Cooperative Organisation
11.7 Disadvantages of Cooperative Organisation
11.8 Suitability of Cooperatives

Some people do not like the notion of owners, managers, workers, and buyers. They are separate individuals with separate goals. So they have formed cooperatives, a different kind of organisation to meet their needs for electricity, child care, housing, health care, food, and financial services. A cooperative is owned and controlled by the people who use it — producers, consumers, or workers with similar needs who pool their resources for mutual gain. Electric cooperatives serve 42 million U.S. consumer-members in 47 states — or 12 percent of the population.

Members democratically control these businesses by electing a board of directors that hires professional management. Some cooperatives ask members/customers to work for a number of hours a month as part of their membership duties.

Another kind of cooperative is formed to give members more economic power as a group than they have as individuals. The best example is a farm (or an agricultural) cooperative. The goal at first was for farmers to join together to get better prices for their food products. Eventually the idea expanded, and farm cooperatives now buy and sell fertiliser, farm equipment, seed, and other products at concessional prices for distribution among men members. Cooperatives have an advantage in the marketplace because they don't pay the same kind of taxes corporations pay.

In many countries — both developed and developing — cooperatives are still a major force in agriculture and other industries today. It is against this back that the study cooperative society.

In truth, till the beginning of the 19th century, the most common forms of business organisation were individual proprietorships and partnerships. The joint-stock company was coming into existence in large enterprises. But all the enterprises had one thing in common: they aimed at maximum profit for the owners. Many a time these concerns used even unfair methods to get profits for their owners. On the one hand, the consumers were charged very high prices, and, on the other, the workers were forced to work for long hours. In order to overcome these difficulties a new form of business organisation came into existence, viz., the cooperative society.

A cooperative is a different kind of organisation set up to meet the diverse needs for its members such as housing, food and financial services (loans). A cooperative is owned and controlled by the people who form it — producers, consumers, or workers with similar needs to pool their resources for mutual gain. Cooperative organisations are owned by people with a common objective, i.e. sharing the risks and the profits.

There are two main types of cooperatives. The first is the producer, or worker cooperative. This is owned by the people who work in the firm.

The second is the consumer or retail cooperative. A consumer cooperative is owned by the customers who purchase shares. The benefits go to the owners (called members) in the form of a fixed dividend on shares and to customers in the form of lower prices.

11.1 MEANING AND DEFINITION OF A COOPERATIVE ORGANISATION

A cooperative society is a form of organisation wherein persons voluntarily join hands as human beings on the basis of the principle of equality for the promotion of the economic interests of its members. It is essentially a joint enterprise of those who are not financially strong, and, therefore, come together not with a view to get profits but to overcome disability arising out of the lack of adequate financial resources.

FOCUS ON TERMINOLOGY: COOPERATIVE SOCIETY

1. Cooperative organisation is a society which has as its objective the promotion of economic interest of its members in accordance with cooperative principles.
   The Indian Cooperative Societies Act (1912)
2. Cooperative society is a form of business organisation in which customers and employees are joint partners and share the profits. *Bloomsbury Pocket Dictionary of Business*

A cooperative society is a voluntary organisation of individuals who join hands to promote their common interests. It is a business organisation which is jointly owned by the people who operate it, with all profits shared equally. The basic objective of a cooperative organisation is to serve the interest of its members. It is generally formed and registered under the Indian Cooperative Societies Act (1912). Today we find different types of cooperative societies, in such areas as credit, retailing, housing and marketing. In some countries not only consumers' cooperatives and producers' cooperatives but also workers' cooperatives are found.

11.2 CHARACTERISTICS OF COOPERATIVE ORGANISATION

The notable features of a cooperative form of business organisation are the following:

1. **Voluntary association:** A cooperative organisation is essentially a voluntary association of a homogeneous group of people such as consumers or producers or workers or farmers. People form and join a cooperative for improving their economic conditions and promoting their own interests through collective effort. In other words, members want to achieve collective self-reliance.
2. **Unrestricted membership:** Any person can join a cooperative society, irrespective of caste, creed, religion or sex.
3. **Separate legal status:** A cooperative society has to get itself registered with the Registrar of Cooperative Societies as per the Cooperative Societies Act (1912). As soon as registration is complete it becomes a body corporate much like a joint stock company and enjoys a separate legal status. It can acquire property in its own name, can enter into contracts with others, can sue others and can also be sued by any outsider. Moreover, it exists in perpetuity in spite of exit of old members and joining of new members.
4. **Limited liability:** The liability of the members of a cooperative society is limited to the extent of their contribution to share capital.
5. **Service motive:** A cooperative organisation is not guided solely by profit motive alone. It is established primarily to serve the interest(s) of its members and at times those of the society.
6. **Self management and control:** A cooperative society is democratic in nature since each member has one vote. And equal voting right ensures effective and efficient management and control of such a society. Only the elected members of the managing committee or the board of directors look after the day-to-day operations of the society. No outsider or professional manager is appointed for the purpose.
7. **Utilisation of surplus:** The operating surplus of a cooperative organisation is not distributed among the members in the form of dividend. A certain fixed proportion of profits is transferred to the Statutory Reserve Fund and then from the residue a reasonable rate of interest is paid on the capital contributed by the members.
8. **Equality of rights:** The members of such organisation enjoy voting rights irrespective of the number of shares held by them. This instills cooperation, unity and equality of rights among members.
9. **Protection from bad debt:** Transactions take place on cash basis. Due to inadequate capital, goods cannot be supplied on credit. This practice saves the cooperative from any danger of bad debt. And the liability of each member remains limited.
10. **Non-transferability of shares:** A minimum of ten adult persons is required for the formation of a cooperative society and get it registered under the Indian Cooperative Societies Act (1912) or the relevant State Act, as applicable. Since membership is open there is no upper limit to the number of members that can be admitted in a particular society. However, there

is a limit on the number of shares an individual member can hold. Such holding cannot exceed 10% of the total share capital of a cooperative and may even be less than a maximum of ₹ 1,000. The shares are not transferable as in the case of other forms of business.

11. **Security:** Cooperative organisations in India are subject to State control. They are required to be registered under the Act of 1912. Thus, they too enjoy a corporate status due to such things as common seal, perpetual succession, limited liability and legal entity. This no doubt ensures a sense of security among the members.
12. **Social status:** Finally, owing to its social status, a cooperative society also enjoys certain advantages. It is granted various exemptions or concessions relating to stamp duty, registration fees, payment of income tax and interest payable on bank loans.

BUSINESS FOCUS: COOPERATIVE MOVEMENT

A cooperative form of business is the result of organised effort to share profits from joint business which is the out growth of cooperative movement. Such a movement aims to share profits and benefits from jointly owned commercial enterprises among members. The movement began in Rochdale, Lancashire, England, in 1844 by 28 weavers and developed to include manufacturing and wholesale businesses as well as insurance and financial services. The Coop in the UK and the Mondragon Cooperative in Spain are two of the best-known examples of premier cooperative societies.

Over the years numerous cooperative societies have been set up in developing countries like India where they have gained strong foodhold mainly in rural and semi-urban areas. Cooperative societies are now found even in urban areas, mainly in the housing and banking sectors.

The main characteristics of a cooperative organisation are listed in Fig. 11.1.

FIGURE 11.1: The Main Characteristics of a Cooperative Organisation

11.3 DISTINCTION BETWEEN A COOPERATIVE ORGANISATION AND A JOINT STOCK COMPANY

The main points of difference between the cooperative form of business organisation and the joint stock company are listed in Table 11.1.

TABLE 11.1: Distinction between Cooperative Organisation and Joint Stock Company

Basis of Comparison	Cooperative Organisation	Joint Stock Company
1. Basic objective	Service motive is of primary importance. Profit making is a secondary objective.	Profit motive (except for public or nationalised enterprise) is of paramount importance. Service motive comes thereafter.
2. Legal provision	The Central Cooperative Societies Act, 1912 or any State Cooperative Societies Act.	The Companies Act, 1956.
3. Number of members	Minimum: 10 Maximum: Not specified by law	*Minimum* (i) Private Company: 2 (ii) Public Company: 7 *Maximum* (i) 50 in case of a private company (ii) Not specified in case of public company
4. Liability of members	Generally limited but the society may opt for unlimited liability if considered appropriate for giving full protection to all its members.	Limited to the amount of capital contributed by a shareholder.
5. Transferability of shares	The shares are not transferable.	The shares are freely transferable in case of a public company.
6. Limits on individual-share-holding	At all times limits are placed on individual share holding.	There is no upper limit in case of a public company.
7. Issue of fresh share capital	This method is adopted to admit new members in order to strengthen the financial base of the organisation and make it viable in the long run.	New share has to be offered first to existing shareholders.
8. Exemptions	Exempted from paying stamp duty and registration fees.	No such exemption is given.
9. Utilisation of surplus	Disbursement of dividend at fixed rate on capital contributed by members plus bonus (in same cases) on a *pro rata* basis, i.e., in proportion to purchases made by members from the Consumers' Cooperative Store.	Dividend as declared at the Annual General Meeting (AGM) of the company.

11.4 FORMATION OF A COOPERATIVE SOCIETY

For registration of a cooperative society certain legal formalities have to be completed. To start with an application in the prescribed form has to be submitted to the Registrar of Cooperative Societies of the State in which the society's registered office is to be located. At least 10 persons above the age of 18 years and having common interests have to submit a joint application for forming a cooperative society of their own. The application should contain the following information:

(i) The name and address of the society.

(ii) The aims and objects for which the society is being formed.

(iii) The names, addresses and occupations of the members.

(iv) Total share capital and its division among members.

(v) The formalities to be completed for the admission of new members, and

(vi) Two copies of the bylaws (rules and regulations) of the society.

A cooperative has two options. It can adopt the model bylaws given in the Cooperative Societies Act. Alternatively it can frame its own bylaws.

On receiving the application of registration along with the copies of bylaws from intending members, the registrar of cooperative societies carefully scrutinises them in order to check and verify that they quite accord with the provisions and spirit of the Cooperative Societies Act. If he is fully satisfied, he will enter the name of the society in the register and will issue a certificate of registration soon. After receiving the certificate of registration, the society gains the status of a body corporate having a separate legal status with perpetual succession and limited liability of its members.

A cooperative society can be registered only if it satisfies certain prescribed norms and conditions. Five of these are presented below:

1. There must be at least 10 adult members.
2. The members should be bound together by some common interests, e.g., they may belong to the same occupation, locality or employer.
3. They have to submit a joint application to the Registrar of Cooperative Societies.
4. Each member has to give an undertaking to buy at least one share.
5. A copy of bylaws has to be submitted to the Registrar.

A managing committee is entrusted with the task of running managing a cooperative society. Members of this committee are elected by all members of the society at its annual general meeting. A managing committee consists of 7 or more members who elect among themselves the following office bearers:

1. President
2. Vice-president(s)
3. Secretary
4. Joint Secretary, if any, and
5. Treasurer

If someone suddenly resigns, a coopted member is taken in for a part of the year (i.e., until the next election is held).

The general body of shareholders frames (formulates) the broad objectives and policies of a cooperative society. However, its detailed programmes and procedures are determined by the managing committee. The committee also gets progress reports from its office bearers (who work in an honorary capacity) and it is accountable to all members at the annual general meeting. It is obligatory on the part of a cooperative society to audit its annual accounts and submit its annual report to the Registrar of Cooperative Societies.

11.5 DIFFERENT TYPES OF COOPERATIVE SOCIETIES

Cooperative societies are classified into different categories according to the nature of the services which they render. The main types of cooperatives are the following:

1. **Consumer (retail) cooperative:** A consumer (retail) cooperative is an organisation which is owned by its consumers. This form of organisation provides an alternative mechanism for a firm to identify consumer wants: interacting directly with consumers to replace market forces. In many cases all consumers do not contribute share capital. In spite of this, they receive a small annual dividend based on profits or sales revenue. This type of cooperative was launched in 1844 by 28 Rechdale Weavers who combined to establish retail outlets. The members enjoyed the benefits of good-quality products at fair prices as also a share of the profits (as dividend) based on the amount of each member's purchases.
2. **Producer cooperative:** Such societies are formed by small producers of a particular area or locality to help the members with capital, materials and equipment to utilise their skills and turn out useful products. Such a society also helps the members to sell their products either directly or by establishing links with marketing cooperatives.
3. **Credit cooperative:** Cooperative credit societies are set up to make loans to their members both in rural and urban areas. Members' contributions are pooled to give financial assistance to needy members at concessional rates of interest with long repayment periods. The objective is to protect the members from the greedy moneylenders who exploit them by charging very high rates of interest. Cooperative credit societies also encourage the members to save more. Thus cooperatives help to mobilise small saving for the purpose of investment. In the absence of such cooperatives some potential saving would go waste by being diverted to consumption spending.

FOCUS ON TERMINOLOGY: TWO MAIN TYPES OF COOPERATIVE

A cooperative is an organisation carrying on any of the various economic activities for the mutual benefit of its members. The members work together for a common purpose. A consumers' cooperative, such as a cooperative store, buying and selling even at less than market prices, distributes the savings over cost of operation to its members in proportion to their patronage. A producers' cooperative conducts marketing operations by the pooling the output that of primary producers, usually farmers. This is found in most European countries.

4. **Marketing cooperative:** Marketing cooperatives, located in both rural and urban areas, help the farmers and artisans to sell their products at remunerative prices. Such a cooperative collects the output of its members throughout the year and sells the same at reasonable prices in goods times. The profits are distributed among members on a pro rata basis. Marketing cooperatives eliminate middlemen and ensure fair trading as regards weights and measures as also through proper accounting practices.
5. **Workers' cooperative:** This is an organisation which is owned and controlled by those who work for it. To be fully accepted as a workers' cooperative, such an organisation must adhere to the general principles of the International Cooperative Alliance, including the requirement that each member has an equal vote at general meetings. Voting should not be proportional to share capital. In some industries workers have formed cooperatives in order to protect their jobs. The overall management of such cooperatives is usually vested in a committee of the employee-owners.
6. **Farmers' cooperative:** A cooperative society is a type of business organisation common in labour-intensive activities, such as agriculture (and are often found in communist countries). Agricultural cooperatives are encouraged in the developing countries, where individual farmers are too poor to take advantage of costly capital goods (such as plant, equip-

ment and machinery) and large-scale (mass) production. In this case several farmers pool resources to jointly purchase and use agricultural machinery. Cooperative farming seeks to promote modern mechanised farming by supplying improved seeds, and chemical fertilisers and providing irrigation facilities. The objective is to raise productivity, i.e., yield per hectare so that the economic conditions of farmers gradually improve.

7. **Housing cooperatives:** Housing cooperative societies are formed mainly in urban areas by those people who want to have their own houses or flats. The basic objective is to provide low-cost housing facility to people of modest means (such as low- and- medium-income groups). Different types of housing cooperatives are found in India. These societies are allotted land by the appropriate authority at concessional prices. They give the purchased plots to their members who take the initiative in constructing their own houses. Such societies can also arrange for housing loans for their members at low rates of interest with long repayment period from public financial institutions or housing development corporations such as HDFC and HUDCO. Other societies acquire land, construct houses and allot the same to the members who make payments in instalments. The allotments of flats or apartments is done on the basis of the lottery system.

11.6 ADVANTAGES OF COOPERATIVE ORGANISATION

The cooperative form of organisation has been gaining popularity over the year mainly because it offers a number of advantages. These are the following:

1. **Ease of formation:** A cooperative society can be formed with a minimum of 10 members who can get the society registered by following a very simple and standard procedure.
2. **Equal voting rights:** The voting rights are related to membership and has no relation to the number of shares purchased by the members. Each person has only vote, irrespective of his contribution to the society's investment capital.
3. **Democratic style of management:** Management of a cooperative is democratic in nature mainly due to equitable voting system. No one can act as a leader and no one has to be a follower either.
4. **Limited liability:** The liability of the members in a cooperative organisation is limited as mentioned earlier. This is ensured by the fact that the by-laws of a cooperative are properly checked by the registrar at the time of registration.
5. **Perpetual existence:** A cooperative society exists in perpetuity as noted earlier. Its life is not affected by the death, insolvency or conviction of any member.
6. **Government assistance:** Since cooperatives are not guided solely by the profit motive various types of grants, loans and financial assistance are offered to them to ensure their smooth and efficient functioning. This is more so in view of the fact that one of the objectives of the governments at State levels is to promote such organisations which serve certain social purposes such as employment generation and helping the weaker sections of society.
7. **Cost-effective operation:** Since cooperatives are formed for achieving collective self-reliance, each member strives to do the best for his own organisation. And since everyone develops a sense of involvement and belonging, every possible effort is made by each member to reduce costs of doing business. So operational efficiency can be improved the

costs of operations can be reduced and more profits can be made equitable for distribution among the members. After all, people respond to incentives.

8. **Steady supply of goods and services at fair prices:** Consumer cooperatives ensure a steady and regular supply of certain essential goods at fair prices. This becomes possible due to the elimination of middlemen who add a large profit margin over costs while fixing product prices.
9. **Ethical business practices:** Cooperatives adopt fair and ethical business practices. They do not get involved in hoarding, speculation and black marketing of consumer goods.
10. **Judicious use of surplus:** Only a portion of trading surplus of a cooperation is transferred to the reserve fund and the residual is distributed among members in the form of bonus on the basis of their purchases. This leads to a judicious use of surplus. In addition, the surplus is equitably distributed among the members.
11. **Tax benefit:** Cooperatives have an advantage in the market place because they do not pay the same kind of taxes which corporations have to pay.

BUSINESS FOCUS: MANAGING A COOPERATIVE

A critical issue which is faced by cooperatives is how to organise the management function: should all members of a cooperative be actively involved in management or should managerial functions be delegated to specialist managers? There is the obvious danger with the former that decision-making could be slowed down, that responsibility will be unclear and that many of those involved in management will not be sufficiency competent. But if the specialists are employed, some of the democratic characters of the cooperative will be lost.

11.7 DISADVANTAGES OF COOPERATIVE ORGANISATION

The cooperative form of business has the following disadvantages:

1. **Inadequacy of investible funds:** Cooperative societies cannot mobilise adequate capital from the public for expanding their operations since the rate of dividend is very low. In addition since each member has only one vote no member has an incentive to contribute more capital.
2. **Managerial inefficiency:** The assured market for the goods and services offered by a cooperative makes managers complacent. They lead a quiet life without taking any business risk. In addition, a cooperative does not take the help of professional managers. Since incompetent members normally manage cooperatives, inefficiency is bound to arise sooner or later.
3. **Excessive government control and regulation:** The cooperatives are closely scrutinised and excessively controlled and regulated by state governments.
4. **Lack of secrecy:** Since the cooperatives are required to make full disclosure of their mode of operation as also operational results to their members, secrecy cannot be maintained. This often creates conflicts among the members and frustrates the very purpose of the organisation—helping members to help themselves.
5. **Lack of motivation:** Since very nominal dividend (i.e., 6.25%) is paid to members, the managers suffer from incentive problem. They do not get motivated to do the best of their ability for the society.

6. Rift among members: Due to difference of opinions among members in many cases, management is unable to perform even its routine functions smoothly and efficiently.
7. Misuse of funds: The basic business principles are avoided by most cooperatives. And this leads to their collapse. A simple example will make the point clear. The misuse of funds for personal gains may lead to recurring losses, and thus may act as a threat to the survival of the cooperative society. And in the past many cooperative credit societies have disappeared due to the fact that they made loans to the members without adequate collateral security.

The main advantages and disadvantages of cooperative are listed in the Table 11.2.

TABLE 11.2: Advantage and Disadvantages of Cooperative Organisation

Merits (Advantages)	Demerits (Disadvantages)
1. Ease of formation	1. Shortfall of investible funds
2. Equal voting rights	2. Managerial (operational) inefficiency
3. Democratic style of management	3. Excessive government controls and regulations.
4. Limited liability of each member	4. Lack of secrecy
5. Perceptual existence	5. Lack of motivation
6. Different types of government assistance	6. Possibility of rift among members, leading to conflicts
7. Cost-effective operations.	7. Misuse and misappropriation of members' funds
8. Uninterrupted flow of goods and services to members at fair (reasonable) prices	
9. Ethical business practices	
10. Judicious use of surplus	

A CASE EXAMPLE: COOPERATIVES IN SPAIN

Many believe that cooperatives are not a sustainable alternative to conventional business organisations. However, the Mondragon area of North Spain proves that cooperatives are quite sustainable. In this area 20,000 workers are employed in a large number of cooperatives in all sectors of the local economy. Their success is attributable to cooperation among cooperatives, facilitating the sharing of skills and resources, and the existence of a strong support structure, including a bank, providing finance and business skills. In spite of various problems (such as farmers' debt and merger of firms), cooperatives are still a major force in agriculture and other industries today.

11.8 SUITABILITY OF COOPERATIVES

From a study of the characteristics of cooperative society, it seems that these organisations nicely fit into the framework of small or medium-sized enterprises and that too on a regional basis. To some extent it can play an effective role in substituting the state enterprises due to harmony of interests among the members. However, such substitution is possible only at the grassroot level, i.e., for distribution of rural credit or essential commodities. The complete absence of profit motive makes such organisations totally unsuitable for replacing joint stock companies. It is because corporate entities strive to maximise the return on capital employed and thus go for optimum capitalisation.

It is important to note that, unlike cooperatives, joint stock companies encourage speculative activities for the personal gains of investors, thereby alluring even poor people to invest in risky stocks and shares. Voluntary and open membership also renders such organisations unsuitable for the spread of professionalism. In areas which call for technical and professional expertise of high order, cooperatives do not appear to be quite suitable. The reasons is simple. Membership cannot be made open for all and democratic principles cannot be followed (applied) at the expense of professional skill and decision-making ability. Moreover, cooperatives cater to a concentrated group of members. It is not possible to satisfy numerous consumers, scattered all over the country through cooperatives. Moreover, due to low demand for the products of cooperatives, it is not possible to achieve operational efficiency either. In case of state enterprises, too, where public fund is involved, the government may not find cooperatives suitable to take up the responsibility. This is because the actions of and internal rivalries among the members may ruin the very objective of promoting common interest. Moreover, non-professional bodies or persons without expertise are not competent enough to operate on a large base or wider sacle. Therefore, cooperatives should be encouraged at the grassroot and block levels and utilised as an effective instrument for distributing certain essential commodities at fair prices. This can also help in elimination of artificial scarcity of such commodities and the consequent exploitation of the poor. Cooperatives can also play an important role in supplementing various distribution networks of state enterprises.

In India, with the setting up of rural cooperative banks and also various consumer cooperatives, some success has been achieved in protecting the farmers as also the consumers. Thus, cooperatives can play an effective role in optimum allocation of the country's limited resources. But lack of professional attitude makes cooperative societies unsuitable for effective and productive utilisation of resources and thus, for promoting faster economic growth.

Key Points

1. **Cooperatives:** These are a very common form of organisation in some countries, especially in agriculture and retailing. It is common to differentiate between producer or worker cooperatives that are involved with making goods and consumer (or retail) cooperatives that sell goods and services.
2. **Features:** Certain features are common to all the cooperatives these are the following:
   (i) All members can contribute to the running of the business, sharing the workload, responsibilities and decision-making, although in larger cooperatives some delegation to professional managers takes place.
   (ii) All members have one vote at important meetings.
   (iii) Profits are shared equally among members.

In agricultural cooperatives, the members arrange for the purchase of seeds and materials in bulk so that they may benefit from economies of scale. The cooperative often buys the produce of the members and then sells it collectively in order to obtain a better price.

3. Advantages: The advantages of such business units are the following:
   (i) Buying in bulk
   (ii) Working together to solve problems and take decisions
   (iii) Good motivation of all members to work hard as they benefit from shared profits.
4. Disadvantages: The potential drawbacks can include:
   (i) Poor management skills, unless professional managers are employed.
   (ii) Capital shortages because no sale of shares to the non-member general public is allowed
   (iii) Slow decision-making if all members are to be consulted on important issues.

KEY Terms

Cooperative organisation	Statutory reserve fund
Consumer (retail) cooperative	Limited liability
Producer cooperative	Perpetual existence
Credit cooperative	Government assistance
Marketing cooperative	Cost-effective operation
Workers' cooperative	Cooperative movement
Farmers' cooperative	Ethical business practices
Housing cooperative	Tax benefit
Voluntary organisation	Judicious use of surplus
Separative legal status	Equal voting rights
Service motive	Ease of formation

Assignments

SHORT ANSWER-TYPE QUESTIONS

1. Define cooperative organisations.
2. State three characteristics of cooperative organisation.
3. How is a cooperative society formed?
4. Mention three points of distinction between a cooperative society and a joint stock company.
5. "The main object of cooperative organisation is to serve its members." Comment.
6. Name an association of persons who join together for the purpose of obtaining economic and social benefits for themselves on an equal footing. [ISC 1992]

ESSAY-TYPE QUESTIONS

1. What is cooperative organisation? What are its characteristics?
2. Discuss the advantages and disadvantages of cooperative organisation.
3. Explain the procedure for the formation of a cooperative society.

QUESTION BANK

1. *Define a cooperative society.*

Ans. The International Labour Organisation (I.L.O.) has defined a cooperative society as "an association of persons usually of limited means, who have voluntarily joined together to achieve a common economic end through the formation of a democratically controlled organisation, making equitable contributions to the capital required and accepting a fair share of risks and benefits of the undertaking".

2. *Mention any three characteristics of cooperative organisation.*

Ans. See text.

3. *Explain the main characteristics of cooperative organisation.*

Ans. See text.

4. *How many members are required to form a cooperative society?*

Ans. At least 10 members are required to form a cooperative society.

5. *How is a cooperative society formed? Explain.*

Ans. See text.

6. *Mention any three advantages of cooperative organisation.*

Ans. Three advantages of cooperatives are the following:

(a) Buying in bulk
(b) Working together to solve problems and take decisions
(c) Good motivation of all members to work hard as they will benefit from shared profits.

7. *What are cooperatives? Mention three common features of cooperatives.*

Ans. Cooperatives are non-profit seeking organisations formed by people belonging to the same profession or activity for furthering the interests of their members and enjoying tax benefits from the government. These are a very common form of organisation in some countries, especially in agriculture and retailing. We usually differentiate between producer or worker cooperatives that are involved in making goods and consumer (or retail) cooperatives that sell goods and services. Three main features of cooperative are the following:

(i) All members can contribute to the running of the business, sharing the workload, responsibilities and decision-making, although in larger cooperatives some delegation to professional managers takes place.
(ii) All members have one vote at important meetings.
(iii) Profits are shared equally among members.

8. *What are the functions of agricultural cooperatives?*

Ans In agricultural cooperatives the members arrange for the purchase of seeds, fertilisers and materials in bulk so that they may benefit from economies of scale. The cooperative often buys the produce of the members and then sells it collectively in order to obtain a better price.

9. *State any three disadvantages of cooperative organisation.*

Ans The three disadvantages of cooperatives are the following:

(a) Poor management skills, unless professional managers are employed

(b) Capital shortages because no sale of shares to the non-member general public is allowed

(c) Slow-making if all members are to be consulted on important issues.

10. *Explain the advantages and disadvantages of a cooperative society.*

Ans See text.

11. *Under what circumstances cooperative society is an appropriate form of business organisation?*

Ans See 11.8.

12. *Mark the following statements True or False.*

(a) A cooperative society is essentially a voluntary organisation.

(b) A cooperative society has an independent legal status.

(c) Registration of a cooperative society is mandatory.

(d) In a cooperative society every member can cast only one vote.

(e) The main motive of a cooperative society is to serve its members.

(f) NAFED is a housing cooperative.

(g) AMUL brand milk and chocolate are the products of a cooperative society.

(h) IFFCO is a cooperative society which produces and sells chemical fertilisers.

Ans True: (a), (b), (c), (d), (e), (g), (h)

False: (f).

13. *Fill in the blanks:*

(a) Registration of a cooperative society ________ compulsory.

(b) Three has to be at least ________ persons to form a cooperative society.

(c) Liability of a member or a cooperative society is ________ .

(d) A cooperative society enjoys ________ existence.

(e) The main purpose (objective) of a cooperative society is ________ .

(f) Every member of a cooperative society has ________ vote(s).

(g) A cooperative ________ subject to statutory control by the government.

Ans (a) is, (b) ten, (c) limited, (d) perpetual, (e) service, (f) one, (g) is.

12

SOCIAL RESPONSIBILITY OF BUSINESS AND BUSINESS ETHICS

SYLLABUS

Concept and need for social responsibility.

- *Responsibility towards owners, investors, consumers, employees, government and community.*
- *Responsibility of business towards protection of environment; Meaning and importance of business ethics.*

Social responsibility refers to fashionable concern for non-monetary and societal issues by corporations, as expressed in annual statements detailing financial contributions to social causes, health projects, charities and educational scholarships as well as community involvement designed to boost corporate image. It is also termed social responsiveness. — G.T. Kurian

LEARNING OUTCOMES

On completion of this chapter, you will be able to understand the following:

12.1 Concept of Social Responsibility
12.2 Need for Social Responsibility
12.3 Responsibilities towards Different Interest Groups
12.4 Business and Environmental Protection
12.5 Meaning and Importance of Business Ethics
12.6 Elements of Business Ethics
12.7 Social Audit

A business does not operate in a vacuum. It is an integral part of society. So it must follow the ethical norms of the society. Just as an individual has to be a good citizen, contributing what he can to society, a corporation needs to be a good citizen as well. This simply means that it should be guided by the principles and practices which are considered 'right' by the society or the community at large. A business enterprise or a firm has to interact with owners, workers, customers, suppliers, other businesses and, of course, governments at different levels. It has to discharge its obligations towards each of these stakeholders as also the whole community. In this chapter, we will discuss the concept of corporate responsibility, i.e., responsibility of business firms towards different groups and communities as also ethical aspects of business operations. Ethics and social responsibility are closely related. Social responsibility is the conscious effort to operate in a manner which benefits all stakeholders. Ethical behaviour is often socially responsible and vice versa.

Business ethics refers to the moral value which governs business behaviour, and restrains companies from pursuing the interests of shareholders at the expense of all other interests. Most firms pursue the goal of maximisation of profits, but in practice there are other values which appear to matter to companies. However, not all decisions can actively be seen as profit-maximising such as donating to charity, for example. Some people attempt to defend the idea of profit-maximisation by saying that in the long-term, firms do maximise profit by behaving as good citizens. There is every reason to believe that firms, which are run by human beings after all, are subject to conflicting pressures of selfishness and social behaviour. Towards the end of the 1990s, when protests against multinational companies became strong, a fashion towards corporate social responsibility emerged, with companies forcing themselves to demonstrate their ethical credentials. This partly appeared to be a response to protesters, partly a genuine attempt by companies to use their influence for the social good, and partly as an informal and fashionable means of attaching attractive values and positive attributes to brands. It is against this backdrop an informal and fashionable that we study two related issues, corporate social responsibility and business (corporate) ethics.

12.1 CONCEPT OF SOCIAL RESPONSIBILITY

12.1.1 Definition and Meaning of Corporate Social Responsibility

Corporate social responsibility (CSR) is the expectation that a business or an individual will strive to improve the welfare of society. From a business perspective, this translates into the public expecting businesses to take active steps to make society better by virtue of the business being in existence. According to the World Business Council for Sustainable Development, CSR is "the continuing commitment by business to behave ethically and contribute to economic development while improving the quality of life of the work force and their families as well as of the local community and society at large." More succinctly, as Mallen Baker says, "it is about how companies manage the business process to produce an overall positive impact on society".

Corporate responsibility refers to the whole dimension of social responsibility which includes everything from hiring minority workers to making safe products.

FOCUS ON TERMINOLOGY:
SOCIAL OBLIGATION, SOCIAL RESPONSIVENESS AND SOCIAL RESPONSIBILITY

The concept of corporate social responsibility (CSR) of business has been defined/described in different ways. It has been called 'profit-making only', 'going beyond profit making', 'any discretionary corporate activity intended to further social welfare, and 'improving social or environmental conditions'. The concept of CSR, becomes fairly clear if we compare it with other two similar concepts, viz., social obligation and social responsiveness. Here we refer to the view of S.P. Robbins and M. Coulter. In their view, social obligation refers to "a firm's engaging in social actions because of its obligation to meet certain economic and legal responsibilities." Social responsiveness refers to "a firm's engaging in social actions in response to some popular social need." Social responsibility refers to a business's intention, beyond its legal and economic obligations, to do the right things and act in ways that are good for scoiety." Ethics and social responsibility are closely related. Social responsibility is the concious effort to operate in a manner which benefits all stakeholders. Ethical behaviour is often socially responsible and vice versa.

In other words, CSR is a business philosophy which stresses the need for firms to behave as good corporate citizens, not merely obeying the law but conducting their production and marketing activities in socially desirable ways. This means that they should behave in a manner which avoids causing environmental pollution or exhausting finite (non-renewable) natural resources.

During the early 1990s the public was very much concerned with the quality of the environment. Many firms responded by engaging in recycling and striving to lower quantities of waste as much as possible.

Some businesses behave in a more socially responsible manner voluntarily and spontaneously because the managers want to do so. Other businesses do so because of fear of environmentalists and consumer pressure groups and the media, and (deep) concern for their public image.

It is argued that socially responsible behaviour can pay off in the long run, even if it may involve some short-term sacrifice of profits. This is why today many businesses are becoming more concerned about social issues and their obligation to return to society some of their profits. It is important for business to be ethical as well as generous. For example, TISCO has made a notable contribution in such areas as community development, social welfare, tribal development and rural industrialisation. Timerland is a company with a long-standing commitment to community service. The company's "path of service" program(me) offers employees 40 hours of pay time off each year to serve the community.

CSR is the concern businesses have for the welfare of society, not just for their owners. CSR goes well beyond being ethical. It is based on a commitment to integrity, fairness and respect.

In short, CSR is a broad term and includes everything from hiring minority workers to making reliable and safe products, minimising pollution, using energy wisely, and providing a safe work environment— essentially everything which has to do with acting responsibly within society.

In Fig. 12.1 we see that total CSR can be subdivided into four primary criteria : economic, legal ethical, and discretionary responsibilities. These four criteria fit together to form a monolithic entity—the whole of a company's social responsibilities.

BUSINESS FOCUS: ORGANISATIONAL AGENDA

All organisations cause environmental problems and disasters as a direct result of their activities. organisations have also responsibilities. Four responsibilities are outlined in Fig. 12.1.

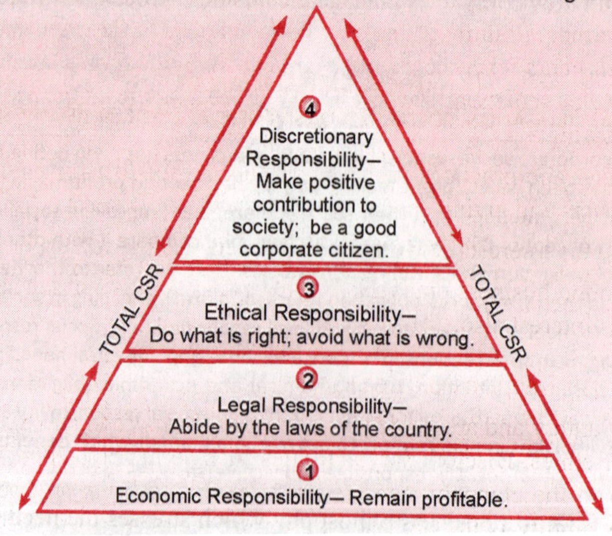

FIGURE: 12.1: Four Layers of Corporate Social Performance

12.1.2 Economic Responsibilities

A business is any entity that seeks to provide goods and services to others while operating at a profit. So it must fulfil its following economic responsibilities:

(i) Promoting the interests of investors (shareholders) by earning a fair rate of return on capital employed.

(ii) Using human, natural and man-made resources efficiently.

(iii) Growing through earnings ploughback or reinvestment of undistributed profits.

Economic responsibility of business consists of operating a corporate on a profit-oriented basis. So its sole mission is to increase profits as long as it stays within the rules of the game.

12.1.3 Legal Responsibilities

Legal responsibility defines what society considers as important with repect to appropriate corporate behaviour. This means that businesses are expected to fulfill their economic goals within the framework of legal requirements by different regulatory agencies at central, state and local levels. Examples of illegal acts by corporations are fraud, deliberately selling defective products, performing unnecesary repairs, deliberately misleading consumers and billing clients for work not done. Organisations which conciously break these laws are poor performers in this category.

A company's legal obligations include the following:

(i) To obey the various economic, labour and other laws of the country.

(ii) To pay taxes and clear other government dues (such as annual licence fee) in time.

(iii) To extend the best possible cooperation to the government so that planned socio-economic objectives are fulfilled.

12.1.4 Ethical Responsibilities

Ethical responsibility includes behaviours which are not necessarily codified into law and are unlikely to serve the corporation's direct economic interests. To be ethical, organisation's decision-makers should act with equity, fairness, and impartiality, respect the rights of individuals, and provide different treatment of individuals, only when relevant to the organisation's goals and tasks. Unethical behaviour occurs when decisions enable an individual or a company to gain at the expense of other people or society as a whole. To be more specific, ethical responsibilities are concerned with the following:

(i) To adopt fair trade practices such as charging reasonable prices of products, supplying quality products and giving adequate publicity to give necessary information to buyers.

(ii) To safeguard the interests of workers, consumers and the society or the whole community.

(iii) To follow sound business practices for promoting interests of the society, and, in the process, its own interest also.

12.1.5 Discretionary Responsibilities

These are purely voluntary and are guided by a company's desire to make social contributions not mandated by law or ethics. Discretionary activities include generous philanthropic contributions that offer no return to the company and are not expected to bring any benefit to the company. Discretionary responsibility is the highest criterion of social responsibility because it goes well beyond societal expectations to contribute to the welfare of the community. These obligations are in addition to those mentioned above. businesses can exert their own discretion to discharge the following responsibilities:

(i) To promote the welfare of the local community.

(ii) To help those who are weak and marginalised.

(iii) To help educate workers and the public at large.

(iv) To create gainful employment opportunities for the local people.

BUSINESS FOCUS : EXAMPLES OF CORPORATE SOCIAL RESPONSIBILITY

Some renowned companies have been engaged in discharging their social responsibilities. We present a short list below:

1. TISCO set up Tata Steel Rural Development Society (TSRDS). It has launched community development project in more than 600 villages located in Bihar, Orissa and M.P.
2. Usha Martin Black Ltd. of the Jhawar Group set up Krishi Gram Vikas Kendra in Ranchi (Jharkhand) to reduce the disparity in living standards between their workers and outsiders.
3. Hindustan Ciba-Geigy launched an ambitious project in 1990 for banishing leprosy completly from Goa.
4. The pharmaceuticals firm Lupin Laboratories launched 'Lite for Life' programme in 1993 to ensure that tuberculosis is eliminated from India sooner or later.
5. Finolex Industries started the Hope Foundation in 1979 for the diagnosis and treatment of cancer.
6. The Bill and Melinda Gates Foundation pledged to spend $29 billion on health, education and overcoming poverty.
7. Warren Buffett also channeled $31 billion to the Gates Foundation to help in finding cures for the most fatal diseases.
8. Green Mountain Coffee Roasters calls itself "a force for good in the world," and claims: "We celebrate and support the power of business and individuals to bring about position changes, locally and globally." The company sets aside 5% of pretax earnings each year for good causes and publishes an annual report on corporate social responsibility .

At present, Google practices philanthropy. It made a pledge to investors when it went public to reserve 1% of its profits and equity to benefit diverse groups in society ranging from those fighting disease to those developing a commercial-plug-in electricity-powered car.

12.2 NEED FOR SOCIAL RESPONSIBILITY

We have already noted that CSR is the obligation of the management of an organisation to make decisions and take actions which will enhance the welfare and interest of society as well as the organisation. In old days, social responsibility was hardly thought. A company's most important goal was to earn money in any way it could. Today profit-seeking enterprises generally make a point of 'putting something back' into society as well as taking something out. See Fig. 12.2.

However, everyone does not agree with these new priorities. There are two exactly opposite view points.

Supporters of CSR believe that businesses owe their existence to the societies they serve and cannot survive and succeed in their ventures, if they fail to discharge their social obligations. Firms have access to society's natural and human resources (manpower), in which every member of society has a stake. Supporters of CSR acknowledge that businesses have deep obligations to investors.

However, they also argue that the proper discharging of CSR enables a firm to make more money (profit) for investors in the long run. Studies show that companies with good ethical reputation attract and retain better employees, draw more customers, and enjoy greater employee loyalty.

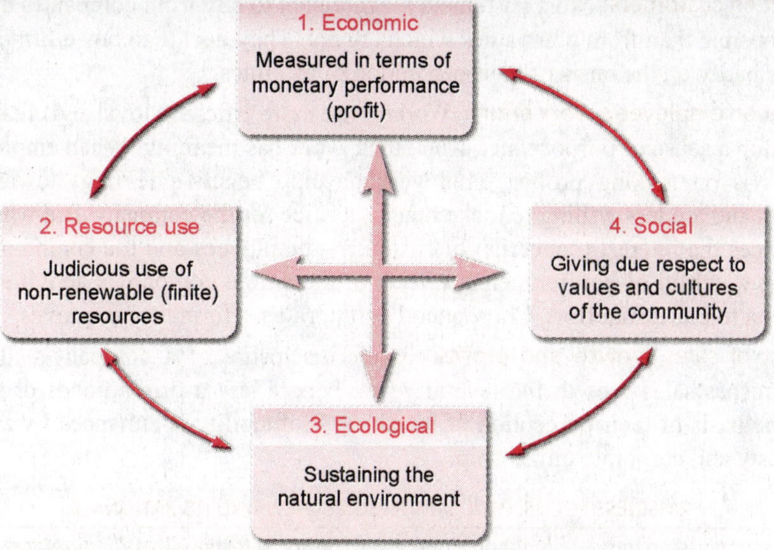

FIGURE: 12.2: Four Major Responsibilities of Business

The arguments in favour of corporate social responsibility are the following:

1. Public support: Public opinion supports companies which pursue, along with the profit maximisation objective, social goals.
2. More profits in the long run: By sacrificing some profit in the short-run, socially responsible companies stand a strong chance of making more profits in the long-run. (The maximisation of long-term profit is known as wealth maximisation which is the much desired goal of every modern organisation.)
3. Public image: Being socially responsible gives business a favourable public image that can help government regulation.
4. Improved community environment: Active involvment of business can help solve various social problems such as unemployment, poverty and price inflation.
5. Avoiding further regulation and control: By behaving in a socially responsible manner businesses can avoid further government controls and regulations.
6. Striking a balance between power and responsibility: Businesses have considerable power and, at the same time, they have a large amount of responsibility to discharge in order to balance that power.
7. Interest of shareholders: If a firm discharges its social responsibility the price of its share is likely to increase in the long-run. By contrast, investments in unethical firms earn abnormally negative returns for long periods of time.
8. Resource endowments: Businesses have the resources to support public and charitable projects which need financial support.

9. **Prevention is better than cure:** Businesses should prepare themselves for the war in peace time and not in war time. This means that they should address social problems before they become serious and not only difficult but costly to correct also.
10. **Effect on customers:** Most customers are more opt to buy from companies that are socially responsible than from companies which are not. They decide to buy a firm's goods or services partly on the basis of their perception of its ethics.
11. **Effect on employee's work effort:** Workers are more efficient, loyal and creative when they develop a sense of purpose, i.e., when their work has meaning. When employer's primary focus is on making profits, employees develop negative feelings toward the organisation and are less willing to make much sacrifice for the company. But when managment balances the interest (concerns) of customers, employees and the community, apart from being watchful of environmental effects of the whole company's activities, workers are willing to put extra effort. Consequently corporate performance improves.
12. **Effect of sales growth and profits:** Public disclosure of a company's illegal activities diminishes sales growth for several years. People buy a firm's goods or services partly on the basis of their perception of its ethics. Profitability is enhanced by a reputation for honesty and corporate citizenship.

BUSINESS FOCUS: PAUL SAMUELSON'S VIEW AND ITS RATIONALE

"A large corporation those days not only may engage in social responsibility", said Nobel Laureate Paul Samuelson, "it had damned well better to try to do so". That is, a company must be concerned for society's welfare as well as its own profits. Beyond the fact of ethical obligation, the rationale for this view is that since businesses create problems such as environmental pollution, they should help solve them. In addition, they often have the resources to solve problems in ways which a non-profit enterprise does not.

Not everyone thinks that CSR is a good thing. Some critics of CSR believe that a manager's sole role is to compete and win in the market place. Even Milton Friedman made the famous statement that the only social responsibility of business is to make money for shareholders. He thought doing anything else was moving dangerously toward socialism. Other critics of CSR believe that managers who pursue CSR are doing so with other people's money—which they invested to make that money, not to improve society. In this view spending money on CSR activities virtually amounts to stealing from investors.

12.3 RESPONSIBILITIES TOWARDS DIFFERENT INTEREST GROUPS

Stakeholders are groups or individuals who have a stake in , or an expectation of, the organisation's performance. It includes owners (shareholders), employees, customers, suppliers, government and society as shown in Fig. 12.3. The environmental stance of an organisation is influenced by the perceptions of its stakeholders and the relative power which each possesses. And it is widely believed that 'good ethics' and consideration of wider stakeholder interests will pay in the long-run.

Modern management experts have identified three main categories of stakeholders:

(i) those internal to the enterprise, such as employees/management and shareholders;
(ii) those immediately external to the enterprise, for example, suppliers and customers; and
(iii) other external stakeholders, such as the community and pressure groups (such as activist groups, unions, political groups and the media.)

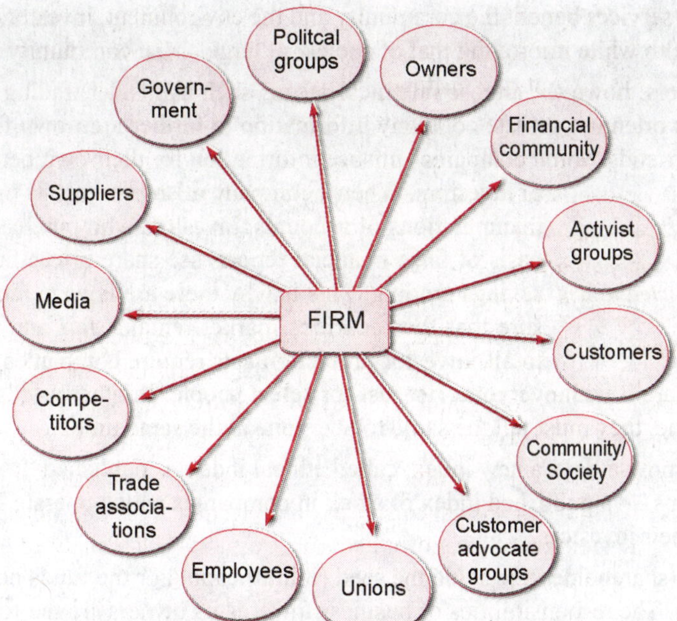

FIGURE: 12.3: Stakeholders involved with a Firm

A business is responsible to all these stakeholders. We now discuss the concept of CSR from the point of different stakeholders. Companies have a responsibility to create a win-win situation for stakeholders. For customers, the company must provide safe products and services with real value. For society the company should improve the quality of life by using improved (clean/non-polluting) technology or at least not destroy the environment. The company should not engage in unfair competition with rivals and restrictive trade practices such as tie-in sales (full-line forcing) and destructive price wars. The company should develop new ways of increasing customer value through product and process innovations. The company should work with suppliers in a cooperative manner. It must go by the rules and regulations of governments at different levels. The company must provide shareholders with a reasonable profit. It must provide employees with safe places to work and satisfactory working conditions with adequate pay and benefits.

COMMENTARY: DOES IT PAY TO BE SOCIALLY RESPONSIBLE?

Is there any relationship between social responsibility and financial performance? Researchers have not yet found consistent results on this crucial issue. But one thing is clear at least. Although there is no clear link between social responsibility and profits, it is certainty true that social responsibility does not hurt performance, but scandals do hurt corporate reputations, which can hurt sales. Social responsibility does benefit many stakeholders in many different ways. In fact, recruiters are seeking candidates committed to corporate social responsibility.

12.3.1 Responsibility towards Owners and Investors

Some people believe that a business person must make money before he (she) can do good. Others believe that only by doing good, he can also perform well.

Many investors believe that it makes financial as well as moral sense to invest in companies which plan ahead to create a better environment. By choosing to put their money into companies whose goods and services benefit the community and the environment, investors can improve their own financial health while improving that of society at large or the community as a whole.

Some investors, however, choose unethical means such as insider trading to make gain. For example, insiders often use private company information to further their own fortunes or those of their family and friends. Some companies misuse information for their own benefit at the expense of investors. When a company misrepresents its profitability through manipulations of accounts, investors who purchase its shares on the basis of false financial reports see share prices falling and their life savings eroding. This is why there are laws in most countries to ensure that the securities market remains fair and equally accessible to all. Investor protection acts require companies which release any information to share it with everyone, not just for select people. In other words, if companies tell anything to anyone, they must tell the same to everyone at the same time.

Insider trading refers to an unethical activity in which insiders use private company information to further their own interests and build their own fortunes or those of their family and friends.

This is why, now-a-days a new index, called ethical index, is published. It is a list of stocks in conscientious firms — a published index of stock in companies which operate by moral standards approved of by their investors.

The owners (shareholders) provide the seed (initial) capital or the funds needed to set up and carry on business. The responsibilities of business towards its owners are the following:

(a) To ensure a fair and a steady return on investment to its shareholders in the form of dividends.

(b) To ensure adequate safety of funds invested by shareholders.

(c) To improve the profitability of the company so as to increase the market value of the company and to ensure capital appreciation.

(d) To keep the owners well-informed about current financial status of the company as also its progress from time to time.

(e) To conserve both the financial and physical assets of the company.

(f) To protect the interest of all investors so that there is no erosion of their personal wealth.

12.3.2 Responsibility towards Employees

Perhaps the best social programme in the world is a job. Businesses have a responsibility to create jobs if they want to grow. It is also necessary to ensure that hard work, seriousness and talent are suitably and fairly rewarded. Employees need realistic hope of a better future, which comes only through a chance of promotion. In truth, what most influences a company's effectiveness and financial performance is responsible human resource management.

If a company treats employees with respect, those employees will respect the company as well. Mutual respect can make a huge difference in a company's bottom line.

One way a company can demonstrate commitment and caring is to give employees salaries and benefit packages which help them reach their personal goals. In addition, increased benefits reduce employee turnover. This means that employees are unlikely to leave the company.

12.3.3 Responsibility towards Customers

Four basic rights of customers are (1) the right to safety, (2) the right to be informed, (3) the right to choose, and (4) the right to be heard. These rights will be achieved only if businesses and consumers recognise them and take necessary action in the market place.

Every business firm has to realise the importance of pleasing customers by offering them real value. Since half of new businesses fail, this responsibility is not very easy to meet. Many companies fail due to dishonesty and failure to please customers. The pay-off for socially conscious behaviour, however, can be new customers who admire the company's social efforts — a powerful competitive edge. All other things being the same, a socially conscious company is likely to be viewed more favourably than others.

No doubt customers' satisfaction has been the ultimate source of all business success in the past. Therefore businesses have to discharge the following responsibilities to customers:

(a) to produce those goods which meet the needs of all consumers having different tastes and preferences and different purchasing power (buying capacity);
(b) to supply certain essential consumers' goods at fair prices;
(c) to ensure prompt delivery of good and quick after-sales services to customers;
(d) to listen to customer complains, and redress grievances quickly to their full satisfaction;
(e) to ensure a steady flow of products (goods and services) to customers as and when they need them;
(f) to make sure that advertisements and other sales promotion materials published by a business to make its products marketable give correct information to buyers and can be taken at face value;
(g) to adopt ethical (fair) trade practices; and
(h) to develop cordial (friendly) relations with customers (the most valuable asset of a company);

It is not enough for companies to brag about (or take pride in) their social responsibility efforts; they must line up to the expectations they raise or face the consequence. As W.G. Nickels and others put it, "customers prefer to do business with companies they trust and, even more important, don't want to do business with those they don't trust. Companies earn customers' trust by demonstrating credibility over time; they can lose it at any point."

12.3.4 Responsibility towards Suppliers

A business firm has to discharge the following responsibilities towards its suppliers:

(a) to ensure regular payments to suppliers and maintaining time schedule of such payments;
(b) to give opportunities to small-scale suppliers to do business by giving them orders on a regular basis;
(c) not to exploit the suppliers through proper and fair dealings with them;
(d) to give necessary encouragement to the suppliers to improve the quality of their products so as to be able to meet or match competition, and
(e) to keep the suppliers well informed about the firm's future plans well in advance so that the suppliers can respond to changing demands for their goods by producting and offering new and improved products.

12.3.5 Responsibility towards Government

The major responsibilities of business toward government are the following:

(a) to go by the laws of the country as also the policies issued by governments at different levels (central, state and local);

(b) to make timely payment of taxes and to avoid tax evasion and avoidance;
(c) to avoid bribing government employees for getting favour;
(d) to hold in check undue concentration of wealth and economic power and formation of monopolies in the forms of cartels and business combines;
(e) to adopt fair trade practices and set examples for others; and
(f) to avoid illegal (faked) transactions in foreign trade such as under invoicing and overinvoicing of exports and imports.

12.3.6 Responsibility towards the Community

Businesses are also partly responsible for promoting social justice. Many companies feel that they have a role in building communities which goes well beyond simply 'giving back'. To them, charity is not enough. Their social contributions include cleaning up the environment, building community toilets, providing computer lessons, caring for the elderly and supporting children from low-income families. Certain specific responsibilties of a business towards the larger community and society are the following:

(a) to take some positive measures for the improvement of the place where its plant or factory is located;
(b) to promote the welfare of the local community by setting up health care centre and dispensaries as also primary schools;
(c) to ensure safety of local surroundings;
(d) not to engage in those activities which create air, water and sound pollution;
(e) to use clean (non-polluting) technology;
(f) to ensure judicious use of scarce natural resources;
(g) to create gainful employment opportunities mainly for the local people;
(h) to supply quality products to customers;
(i) to improve the physical quality of life of the workers in particular and the community in general and
(j) to give due respect to socio-cultural values.

In Table 12.1 overleaf we summarise the different types of obligations of businesses towards various stakeholders.

So what conclusion can we draw about social involvement and economic performance? Research work suggests that a company's actions do not hurt its economic performance.

BUSINESS FOCUS: SOCIAL RESPONSIVENESS OF TIMES OF INDIA GROUP

In their endeavour to be socially responsible, many organisations donate money to philanthropic and charitable causes. In addition, many organisations ask their employees to make individual donations to these causes. For many companies, their social actions are being viewed as being society responsive than socially responsible. However, such actions are still beneficial for society. For example, Times of India started an initiative to tackle the problems of mass illiteracy.

Educated readers of the paper were urged to donate two hours of their time for children who needed help and guidance for reading and writing. The group advertised its publications reading "Teach India: Let's learn to teach" and "WE 'VE JUST IDENTIFIED THE PERFECT SOLUTION TO ILLETERACY—YOU."

TABLE 12.1: Obligation of Business towards stakeholders

Types of Stakeholders	Business Obligation
1. Owners (shareholders)	Fair return on capital invested, safety of personal wealth, or appreciation of wealth, disclosure of information about current operation of business and its future plans and programmes.
2. Consumers	An assured supply of quality products (both goods and services) at fair prices, adoption of unrestrictive trade practices, developing cordial relationships with customers and providing prompt after-sales services.
3. Employees	Fair wages and job security, healthy and safe work environment, staff welfare measures and job satisfaction
4. Suppliers of inputs	Fair dealing, timely payment and constructive suggestions for improvement of quality of inputs and maintenance of delivery schedules.
5. Government	No tax evasion and avoidance, compliance with various laws and adherence to government policies
6. Society at large (or the whole community)	(i) Adoption of no unfair and socially harmful business (trade) practices, (ii) generation of no pollution, (iii) promotion of community welfare and (iv) implementation of adequate safety measures against hazardous practices.

12.4 BUSINESS AND ENVIRONMENTAL PROTECTION

Business activity is essentially the conversion of the resources of nature into goods and services to satisfy the needs, wants, and desires of human beings.

Human beings are constantly striving to both make the best of the limited resources that we have, as well as constantly trying to discover untapped resources, or improve the efficiency of how we use these limited resources. If it is the case that we as human beings constantly want to improve our standard of living we will need faster economic growth to increase the amount and range of goods and services available to us for consumption and enjoyment. But what happens if in the pursuit of such economic growth we are both exhausting the finite resources at our disposal as well as generating negative externalities in the form of pollution and other types of environmental damage?

Business plays a pivotal role in this generation of economic growth but also is responsible for the creation of environmental problems. As producers they are the direct generators of a large proportion of negative externalities. Industries such as steel, cement, oil, power generation, chemicals, and transport are heavy polluters in various ways.

So businesses have an important role to play in protecting the environment. Indeed business itself can play a vital role in developing 'environment-friendly' technologies — given the right incentives. It is against this backdrop that we study the role of business in protecting the environment.

Perhaps pollution is the most serious environmental problem today. For that reason, in India and almost all countries of the world, concern about environmental pollution has grown considerably in recent years. Pollution can be defined as unwanted or detrimental changes in a natural system. The term pollution refers to the occurrence of an unwanted change in the environment caused by the introduction of harmful materials or production of harmful conditions (i.e., cold, dust, smoke, heat, sand, etc.). Examples of pollution include smoke and noise from vehicles, aeroplanes and factories, creating air pollution and discomfort; nuclear tests, polluting the environment and exposing human life to radioactive discomfort. Often the emission of asbestos dust by a plant or factory endangers the health of not only the employees but also local residents. The factory may also discharge its waste into a river and cause water pollution and adversely affect the livelihood of both washer-men and fishermen who are dependent on the supply of clean water from the river. Excessive discharges of waste materials into the oceans reduce the capacity to provide habitat for fish stocks. Thus, it is essential, for the business firms to take measures for the protection of the physical (external) environment in its own interest.

BUSINESS FOCUS: THE BHOPAL DISASTER

A tragic event occurred in Bhopal in 1984. The release of methyl isocyanate, a poisonous gas from the Union Carbide's Plant caused 2,600 deaths and many long-term consequences for the surrounding community such as blindness and disablement. Many people became completely unfit for work during the rest of their lives.

No doubt, efforts to protect the environment may increase a company's costs, but they also allow the company to charge higher prices, increase market shares, or both. Corporate managers should take note of this reality.

12.4.1 Causes of Environmental Pollution

Pollution is associated with ecological degradation, caused by environmental stresses originating from natural phenomenon or from human activities. Examples of large-scale pollution in India include the discharge of sewage into the surrounding seas, discharge of effluents from factories into rivers, air pollution from motor vehicles and factories and noise pollution from motor vehicles and aircrafts.

The pollution problem also arises because the ability of the environment to absorb waste is finite. For example, the natural breakdown of effluents in the seas and the river will not give rise to serious pollution as long as discharges are below some minimum level. But above these levels discharges will give rise to rapid increases in pollution.

In general, we rely on science and technology to improve our quality of life. However, technological progress often offers short-term solutions to our problems but can create new forms of pollution. We may now give a brief description of different types of pollution.

The development of the steam engine allowed machines to replace human labour but increased the amount of smoke and other pollutants in the air and increased the need for fuel. The modern chemical industry has produced many extremely valuable synthetic materials such as plastics, pesticides and medicines but has also produced toxic pollutants.

Pollution is caused by the discharge of harmful elements into the environment which get mixed into air, water and land. There are different types of pollution as shown in Fig. 12.4 their causes are the following:

1. *Air Pollution:* Two main types of air pollution are — air pollution and water pollution. Air pollution is primarily a by-product of energy consumption. Impurities in fuels lead to emissions of sulphur and particulate matter. Burning carbon-based fuels leads to emission of carbon dioxide, which is a major pollutant.

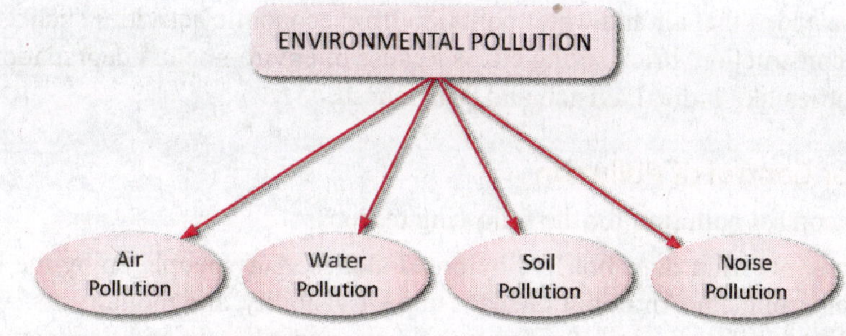

FIGURE 12.4: Types of Environmental Pollution

Air pollutants are at their worse in urban areas due to undue concentrations of people, both as sources of pollution (directly and indirectly) and as victims of pollution. Air pollution can lead to health problems, including sickness as well as irritation, reduced human performance due to loss of energy and growing tiredness. Smoke from chimneys or factories and fumes from internal combustion engines lead to air pollution and causes both lung and eye problems. It is the responsibility of businesses to check the use of hazardous chemicals and to control air pollution by adopting various corrective measures, including the installation of pollution control equipment.

2. *Water Pollution:* Water pollution occurs mainly due to depositon of organic material in waterways or lakes. Another really serious problem is pollution of ground water, caused by leaking of storage facilities on the surface and the leaking of pesticides and fertilisers into the ground water. Such pollution occurs due to emission of noxious gas and water from factories, and piles of wastes from urban households. Water pollution leads to destruction of marine resources (which are one of the major items of exports of India at present). It also pose a threat to human life by causing several diseases. The presence of toxic metals in drinking water like arsenic is a pollutant. This leads to contamination of water and creates human health problems such as skin disease. Thus it is high time that every industrial unit took steps to check water pollution.

BUSINESS FOCUS: TWO CASE EXAMPLES

Industrial waste from production process can enter the sea and so impact on commercial fisheries. The gradual pollution of Japan's inland sea, between Honshu and Shikoku, in the 1950s and 1960s severely damaged fish stocks. A similar situation can be seen in the North Sea and in many of Europe's rivers.

3. *Soil Pollution:* Excessive application of chemical fertilisers causes soil pollution. This leads to soil erosion, making it unfit for farming. In order to check this it is necessary for industrial enterprises to use necessary solid waste disposal methods.

4. *Noise Pollution:* Noise pollution is unwanted sound. This is not just an 'annoyance', but a serious health hazard as well. Continuous exposure to noise can cause loss of hearing, cardio-vascular problems, impatience, violent behaviour and, worse still, even mental disorder. Thus, it is in the rightness of things for industrial units to install proper sound proof equipment so as to keep the level of noise down.

In short, pollution is generated as a by-product of producing goods. A large economy like that of India generates more pollution than a small economy like Singapore, all other things being equal.

It may be added that air and water pollution from economic activities such as manufacturing and construction, brick laying etc. is a cause of environmental degradation in developing countries like India, Pakistan and Bangladesh.

12.4.2 Need for Control of Pollution

There is need to control pollution for the following reasons:

1. *Aesthetic look:* Man does not live by bread alone. Many people enjoy the beauty of the natural environment. Air pollution leads to poor visibility, and monuments become discoloured. Water pollution spoils the beauty of rivers and lakes. In addition, contaminated water and impure air create odour pollution. Thus, the need to protect the natural environment by improving the quality of air and water need not be overemphasised.
2. *Reduction of nuisance:* Noise is the worst form of pollution. So it is absolutely essential to reduce the level of noise so that people can live quiet and peaceful life and can communicate smoothly.
3. *Reduction of health hazards:* The incidence of non-communicable diseases such as cancer, heart attack and lung problems is on the rise year after year. The proximate cause of these ailments can be brought under control to a large extent by controlling pollutants in the physical environment. Water pollution has to be avoided at any cost not just to avoid diseases but also to conserve fish and other marine resources. This is why the Ganga Action Plan was taken in the early 1990s.
4. *Ensuring traffic safety:* Air pollution generates smog in winter. This often creates safety problems for all modes of transport — air, road and rail. Poor visibility often causes major accidents. So it is of paramount importance to check air pollution as much as possible.
5. *Reducing economic losses:* Pollution control can reduce economic losses suffered by the community at large. For instance, air pollution leads to soiling of clothes which means higher laundry charges. In addition, due to dumping of hazardous chemicals and other unwanted industrial wastes on land, society has to suffer in terms of damage to vegetation and loss of soil fertility. Thus it goes without saying that pollution control is really the need of the hour.

The successful conduct of business depends on the well-being of people who are the customers of the goods and services supplied by business firms and producing units. This, in its turn, depends, to a large extent, on the preservation and protection of physical environment. So we now briefly discusss the role of business in environmental protection.

12.4.3 Approaches to Pollution Control

Business gains its legitimacy and states by meeting the needs of society, and over the years society has been expressing a clear need for more environmentally-sustainable practices. One way for business to demonstrate its commitment to greater responsibility for protecting the environment is by changing its *modus operandi* (i.e., method a technique of operation) from the so-called 'traditional methods' to more responsible approaches to addressing environmental issues.

Various approaches can be adopted to check environmental pollution. The most commonly used approaches are given below:

1. *Environmental evaluation (or impact assessment):* Any type of industrial activity should be permitted after a comprehensive assessment of its impact on the physical environment.

For example, all government agencies in India are under the legal obligation to submit The Environmental Impact Statement for their prospective projects. The objective is to examine all likely effects of an industrial project before it is cleared or given final approval. There is also need for an environmental audit for preventing undue pollution of the environment.

BUSINESS FOCUS: GREEN (ENVIRONMENTAL) AUDIT

Green or environmental audit is an examination of an organisation's production, distribution and marketing activities which concentrate upon the environmental impact of these activities. Green audits can assist an organisation in identifying sources of environmental pollution or excessive resource usage so that it can then seek to improve its performance.

2. *Setting pollution control standards:* Certain specific standards have been fixed to set an upper limit on permissible level of specific pollutants. For example, the Government of India has fixed Euro 11 Emission norms for small cars manufactured domestically to keep air pollution low.
3. *Regulations:* In India water pollution is brought under control through regulations. This is why industrial licensing procedures have been so framed as to regulate industrial and municipal discharge into rivers, canals and other water bodies (such as lakes and irrigation dams). Certain types of wastes and pollutants (effluents) can be discharged only after treating them by using appropriate and prescribed technology. The Government of India has also passed The Environment Protection Act in 1986 to control all types of pollution. The Act defines pollution as the presence of any pollutant such as solid, liquid or gaseous substances which cause considerable damage to the physical environment.
4. *Ban:* A widely used approach now is to either ban or restrict use of unsafe or hazardous substances. For example, some Indian States have totally banned smoking in public places and use of polythene bags.

It is felt that legislative control over toxic substances is absolutely essential to check environmental pollution. This is why the Government of India enacted new and more stringent rules and regulation immediately after the Bhupal Tragedy of 1984.

BUSINESS FOCUS: TOWARDS A PRECAUTIONARY APPROACH TO ENVIRONMENTAL PROTECTION

It is felt that a really cost-effective way to prevent environmental damage is to take early action in order to ensure that irreversible environmental damage does not occur. It is judicious on the part of companies to consider the following:

1. *Prevention rather than cure.* While it is true that preventing environmental damage entails both opportunity cost and implementation cost, remediating environmental harm after it has occurred can cost much more, e.g., for treatment costs, or in terms of corporate image.
2. Investing in sustainable operations. Investing in production methods that are not sustainable, i.e., that deplete resources and degrade the environment has a lower, long-term return than investing in sustainable operations. In turn, improving environmental performance means less financial risk. This is an important consideration for insurers.
3. Research and development. Research and development related to more environmentally-friendly products can have significant long-term benefits.

12.4.4 The Role of Business in Environmental Protection

It is the social responsibility of every business to hold all types of pollution in check and adopt positive measures to protect the natural (physical) environment. Businesses can do the number of things to protect the environment. The following measures may be suggested in this context:

(i) Eco-friendly (clean) and low-waste technology can be used in industrial plants and factories.

(ii) Renewable energy — electricity generated by wind, solar and geothermal power and hydro-power — should also be used to the maximum possible extent.

(iii) The rate of recycling of industrial wastes should be increased. old computers and other electronic equipment can be recycled or donated.

(iv) There should be scientific treatment of all waste materials before their release into the physical environment.

(v) Modern plants and equipment should be used to minimise the level of pollution.

(vi) Business houses should abide by the norms set by pollution control board(s).

(vii) By investing in alternative energy technology business can save a lot of energy.

(viii) Positive steps should be taken to plant trees, clean rivers, lakes and ponds, and protect wildlife.

(ix) Business should replace several incandescent bulbs by fewer compact flurecent bulbs (CLFs) to produce and generate fewer emissions.

(x) Business firms should encourage employees and customers to save (store) documents digitally and not print out millions of paper copies. By doing this firms can reduce waste and thus their operating cost.

(xi) Business houses should seriously try to develop eco-friendly products. The government has already launched a new scheme under which products are labelled ECOMARK. This implies that they are environment friendly, according to certain prescribed rules.

In this context we refer to green management. Green management refers to a form of management in which managers consider the impact of their organisation on the natural environment.

BUSINESS FOCUS: GREENING THE ENVIRONMENT

Environment protection now-a-days goes by the name 'greening the environment'. A number of environmental disasters brought a new spirit of environmentalism. over the years managers have started considering the impact of their organisations on the natural environment. This is known as green management. How do organisations go green and save the natural environment? Managers and organisations can do many things to protect and preserve the natural environment. Stores such as Fab India and Colour Plus only give paper bags. Many shops encourage people to bring their own bags. The solar stream cooking system has been set up at Tirupati's Tirumala Devasthanam. Many remote villages have been electrified through solar energy. Many companies have changed their products and production processes. MRF has recently launched a new tubeless, eco-friendly rubber tyre which reduces rolling resistance and saves fuel. Bajaj Auto has installed wind power generation units to conserve energy as also to save power. Subway, a leading sandwich chain, has reduced its use of paper by serving fast food with less wrapping and using baskets made party of recycled material to hold food. It has also switched to 100% recycled paper napkins, which is likely to save 1.5 lakh trees every year.

Conclusion

Environmental quality is a public good; that is, everyone gets to enjoy it irrespective of who pays for it. The challenge for companies is to find the public goods which will appeal to their customers. Many corporations are publishing reports which put on record their net social contribution. To do that, a company must measure its positive social contributions and subtract its negative social impacts. This is done through a technique, called social audit. A social audit is a systematic evaluation of an organisation's progress toward implementing socially responsible and responsive programmes. It measures work place issues, the environment, product safety, community relations, global operations, human rights and, of course, respect for the rights of local people.

No doubt, social audits force organisations to consider their social responsibility beyond the level of just feeling good or managing public relations. In addition to social audits conducted by companies, four types of groups closely watch and monitor how well companies discharge their ethical and social responsibilities:

(i) *Socially conscious investors:* They insist that a company extends its own high standards to its supplies of goods and services.

(ii) *Environmentalists:* They put pressure by naming companies which do not go by certain environmental standards.

(iii) *Union officials:* They control or avoid violations and force companies to comply to avoid negative publicity.

(iv) *Customers:* They make buying decisions based on their social conscience.

BUSINESS FOCUS: IMPORTANCE OF SELF-REGULATION AND ENVIRONMENTAL AUDIT

Business should always adopt voluntary self-regulatory measures (schemes). This is likely to have considerable impact on the environment. Self-regulation schemes require organisations to go by the norms and follow the practices which involve making information available to the public, mainly through an environmental policy statement, together with clear targets and objectives needed to meet the policy. In such schemes, considerable stress has to be placed on plans to achieve continual improvements and of integrating environmental issues without those matters and issues of concern of general management. Environmental audits as also detailed statements on the progress made in respect of environmental objectives are of paramount importance from the point of view of protection and preservation of the natural environment. The concept of environmental audit, in particular, requires organisations to monitor and collect detailed informations in order to judge whether the desired improvement has been achieved.

It is not enough for a company to be right in respect of ethics and social responsbility. It has also to convince its customers and society that it is right. To summarise, it is evident that there are many non-legally binding reasons why organisations need to be aware of their impact on the natural environment and, perhaps, to take action to improve the situation. The sort of environmental agenda which an organisation adopts will be influenced by both environmental context and the extent of stakeholders' power and interest.

The protection of the physical environment is of paramount importance today due to its deterioration day by day for a number of reasons. While human beings are generally responsible for environmental decay and loss of environmental quality, business persons are no less responsible for pollution, and deterioration of the quality of life. This is why an environmental accounting system has been introduced and made a part of the national accounting system of a country.

CASE EXAMPLE: VIRGIN'S GREEN IDEA LOSES ITS PULLING POWER

Virgin Atlantic airline sold its new environmental policies to airline passengers as a bold, green initiative that would save thousands of tonnes of carbon dioxide from their flights. But Virgin Atlantic has quietly abandoned its plans to tow the Boeing 747 jumbo to the end of runways instead of powering up the jet engines to do this. It was found that pulling these giant planes a long way weakened the structure of the landing gear. Other green initiatives by Virgin — part of a claim to make it the most environment-friendly airline in the world — are not having much impact either. It offered free train tickets to business-class passengers in place of large chauffer-driven cars to take them to the airport — but only 1% accepted. And only 5% of the total fuel used on a normal flight had been replaced by biofuel on a recent test flight which Virgin claimed made it 'the first airline in the world to fly on renewable fuel'. Jeff Gazard, a member of the USA's Aviation Environment Federation, said, 'Virgin is using bogus green initiatives in an attempt to make passengers feel less guilty about flying and persuade governments to allow the airline industry to continue to grow at its present unsustainable rate'. So, some observers see this type of corporate 'socially responsible' move as just a 'greenwash' or 'window dressing'.

12.5 MEANING AND IMPORTANCE OF BUSINESS ETHICS

In Europe, CSR is 'business ethics', which is more about keeping one's nose clean and upholding moral standards. By comparison, in developing countries like India CRS is straight charity or philanthropy.

It is anybody's guess that every business is supposed to carry its operations in an ethical manner. In a general sense, ethics is the code of moral principles and values which govern the behaviour of a person or a group with respect to what is right or wrong.

12.5.1 Meaning of Business Ethics

Ethical behaviour includes an unfailing demand for honesty and an insistence that everyone in the company gets treated fairly. Many business people have made the news by giving away huge sums to charity, thus setting a model of social concern for their employees and others.

Ethics may be defined as society's accepted standards of moral behaviour, that is, behaviours accepted by society as right than wrong. Integrity, respect for human life, self-control, honesty, courage, and self-sacrifice are right. Cheating, cowardice, and cruelty are wrong. Business ethics are the applications of ethical standards to commercial enterprises. These are moral guidelines for the conduct of business based on notions of what is right, wrong and fair.

It is easy to criticise business people for moral and ethical shortcomings. But employees also frequently violate safety standards and goof off several hours a week.

In recent years many firms and industries have attempted to develop codes of conduct which can be used to guide managers when making decisions.

Organisational ethics begins at the top, and the leadership by example of efficient and successful managers can help uplift corporate values in employees.

Trust and cooperation between workers and managers must be based on fairness, hoensty, opinion and moral integrity. According to W.G. Nickels and others. "A business should be managed ethically for many reasons—to maintain a good reputation; to keep existing customers and attract new ones; to avoid law suits; to reduce employee turnover; to avoid government intervention in the form of new laws and regulations controlling business activities; to please customers, employees and society; and simply to do the right thing.

BUSINESS FOCUS: SOME UNETHICAL BUSINESS PRACTICES

There are often reports from cell phone service representatives who actually lie to get customers extend their contracts—or even extend their contracts without the customers' knowledge. Some phone representatives hang up on callers to prevent them from cancelling their contracts. They resort to such unethical tactics. The reason is that poorly designed incentive systems reward them for wrong doing. Overambitious goals and incentives can create an environment in which unethical actions like this can take place.

1. Adulteration of food articles, e.g., mixing of small stones with rice, wheat and pulses.
2. Sale of spurious drugs, home-made soft drink with levels of reputed companies.
3. Use of colours not permitted by law.
4. Putting water in injections.
5. Sale of Korean watches by giving the emboss of Japanese firms such as Seiko or Citizen.
6. Sale of harmful drugs which lead to addiction.
7. False advertisement which implies giving incorrect information to buyers.
8. Using the environment as a sink for disposing of waste materials and contaminated water.
9. Not paying fair wages to workers or forcing them to work beyond normal hours.
10. Insider trading—the illegal trading of a company's stocks by people using confidential company information.

Examples of Business Ethics

Every business is supposed to conduct its operations in an ethical manner or in a socially desirable way. The following are some examples of ethical business practices:

(i) To charge fair prices for their products.
(ii) To use correct weights for measuring merchandise.
(iii) To comply with tax laws of the country.
(iv) To make reasonable profits from business/trading and not to remain engaged in profiteering.
(v) To supply genuine and safe products to customers.
(vi) To give fair treatment to all employees (i.e, avoid discrimination at work place).

BUSINESS FOCUS: THE POSITION OF THE CONSUMER

Environmental issues are becoming increasingly important in consumers' buying decisions. Many consumers are ready to reward companies by buying products of an organisation which shows ethical behaviour. They may be prepared to pay a higher price or actively seek out those companies which they believe to be ethical. Consumer power is gradually becoming influential in respect of products made by using child labour.

Amazon.com has a reputation for being an ethical company and its employees are expected to always act ethically, and in the best interest of the company. By contrast, Indians' trust in corporations has been strained because of unethical behaviour of executives in a number of firms and banks. The loss of public trust threatens the integrity of business. It is in this context that we refer to the importance and significance of ethical behaviour in business.

12.6 ELEMENTS OF BUSINESS ETHICS

Making ethical decisions in business is not a simple process. For example, it is enough to say that ethical business decisions are those which are simply within the law. Suppose a corporation acquires the right (by legal purchase) to a large tract of land where rain forests are located. It would certainly not be in the public's interest, or ethical to clear-cut these natural resources in order to make a profit. It would be legal no doubt, but it would be ethically inappropriate behavour. In addition, the laws in place may not provide proper guidelines to prevent decisions detrimental to society.

12.6.1 Setting Corporate Ethical Standards

In recent years more and more companies have adopted written codes of ethics. Compliance-based ethics codes lay stress on preventing unlawful behaviour by increasing control and penalising those who do wrong. Integrity-based ethics codes define the organisation's guiding values to create an environment which supports ethically sound behaviour, and stress shared accountability.

The following six steps are likely to improve business ethics:

1. *Top management support:* Top management must adopt and unconditionally support an explicit corporate code of conduct.
2. *Employee understanding:* Employees must understand that expectations for ethical behaviour begin at the top and that senior management expects all employees to act accordingly.

BUSINESS FOCUS: THE ETHIC OF SUSTAINABILITY

In the context of globalisation corporations around the world are embracing a new idea called sustainability. Sustainability refers to "economic development which generates wealth and meets the needs of the current generation while saving the environment so that future generations can meet their needs as well." With a philosophy of sustainability, managers incorporate environmental and social concerns into every strategic decisions, revise policies and procedures to support unsustainable efforts and measure their progress toward sustainability goals. ABN AMRO is the first company to float a fund which invests in sustainable development. The AMRO Sustainable Development Fund invests in companies with high disclosure policies on environmental, social and corporate governance yardsticks. In helping Indians to invest in socially responsible firms, CRISIL launched a 50-scrip ESG (environment, social and governance) Index which tracks the top Indian companies on the basis of three parameters — corporate governance, ethics and social responsibility. The top 10 companies by weight in the Index are Infosys, ITC, Aditya Birla Nuvo, Dr. Reddy Labs, Wipro, Jubilant organosys, Axis Bank, GTL, RIL and HUL.

3. *Management training:* Managers and others must be trained to consider the ethical implications of all business decisions.
4. *Setting up an ethics office:* An ethics office must be set up with which employees can communicate anonymously. Whistle-blowers (insiders who report illegal or unethical behaviour) must be protected from retaliation.
5. *Public disclosure:* Outsiders such as suppliers, contractors, distributors, and customers must be told about the ethics programme. The reason is that the pressure to put aside ethical considerations often comes from outside (external) sources. And it helps employees resist such pressure when everyone knows what the ethical standards are.
6. *Timely action:* The ethics code has to be enforced with timely action if any rules are broken. This is the most effective way to communicate to all employees that the code is serious.

The last step seems to be most critical. Irrespective of how well intended a company's ethics code is it is worthless if not enforced.

Perhaps the most important factor in enforcing an ethics code is selecting an ethics officer. The most effective ethics officer set a positive tone, communicate effectively and establish cordial relations with all employers. They are equally comfortable as counsellors and investigators and can be trusted to maintain confidentiality, conduct objective investigations, and ensure fairness. Thus they can clearly demonstrate to stakeholders that ethics are important in any (or every) aspect of business activity.

12.7 SOCIAL AUDIT

Social audit is essentially an examination of an organisation's employment performance, its responsiveness to customers, its environmental impact (pollution); and its impact upon the community. Social audits can assist an organisation in identifying deficiencies in its performance in the above respects so that the organisation can develop policies to improve its performance in all directions, keeping in view the overall interest of society (or community). In India the Tata Group has taken the first initiative in this direction.

CASE EXAMPLE: MEASURING CORPORATE SOCIAL RESPONSIBILITY

There could not be a much bigger contrast between the USA's Exxon Mobil and the Soft Touch Community Arts Cooperative.

Exxon has an estimated sales turnover of $45 million per hour — but Soft Touch has an annual turnover of $700,000 — yet they both produce annual social audits (called corporate citizenship reports in the USA). Social auditing is a system of reviewing a company's operations, to examine its social impacts and to compare social performance with any social objectives the organisation might have. This makes the process very useful for social enterprises — such as Soft Touch — and businesses keen to correct a poor reputation — the Exxon Valdiz oil tanker disaster in 1989 is the worst the world has ever seen.

Exxon's social audit contains a huge quantity of evidence concerning the company's social impact. For example, it gives details of the amount of oil the company split into the environment in one year, employee facilities, percentage of all employees who are women, sponsorship of ethnic minority councils and the financial support for a large teacher training programme in the USA. The directors of Exxon are determined to match the best social performance in the oil industry.

Soft Touch depends for its funding from many state bodies. It needs to convince them of the social value of its work. This can only be done by gaining feedback from the young, disadvantaged people it helps. Many local councils were so impressed by the content of the social audit which showed that they increased their funding.

Alan Kay, social audit adviser, admits that the labour and finance resource commitment required in compiling a detailed social audit can be great. Kay says that, on a cost-benefit basis, social auditing is most likely to produce gains for big companies and charities. 'I am not sure that this is of benefit to businesses of perhaps ten staff. Which stakeholders are going to read the social audit of a small local shop?'

Key Points

1. **Social responsibility of business:** In one sense, the concept of corporate social responsibility (CSR), like business ethics, means distinguishing rights from wrongs and doing rights. It means being a good corporate citizen. CSR can be defined as management's obligation to make choices and take actions which will contribute to the welfare and interest of society as well as the organisation. CSR refers to the notion that corporations are expected to go above and beyond following the law and making a profit.

2. **Arguments in favour of social responsibility:** Six arguments in favour of corporate social responsibility are the following:
   (i) Business is created by members of society and it makes use of society's resources. So business has to discharge certain obligations to the society and its various stakeholders with which it has constant interaction.
   (ii) In the long-run self-interested behaviour of the business (i.e., profit maximisation) induces it to assume various social responsibilities.
   (iii) If businesses follow socially responsible policies, there will be need for less government control and regulation of business.
   (iv) Businesses have always to discharge moral obligations which are beyond the scope of law.
   (v) By fulfilling its social obligations a business firm can improve its public image considerably. This is likely to pay rich dividends in the long-run.
   (vi) Now consumers have also become much conscious of their rights. Various consumer organisations can force businesses to behave in a socially desirable way.
3. **The top of the pyramid:** The responsibilities of an organisaton in today's corporate world should take the following priorities:
   (i) Be a good corporate citizen (philanthropic responsibility)
   (ii) Be ethical in its practices (ethical responsibility)
   (iii) Obey the law (legal responsibility)
   (iv) Make a profit (economic responsibility)
4. **Responsibility towards different stakeholders:** A corporation has the following responsibilities to its stakeholders:
   (i) *Owners and inventory:* Fair return on capital invested, safety of funds, capital appreciation, disclosure of information about current operation of business and its future plans and programmes.
   (ii) *Employees:* Fair wages and compensation package, job-related benefits, job, security, healthy and safe working conditions (environment), staff welfare measures, and job satisfaction.
   (iii) *Consumers:* Supply of quality products at reasonable (fair) prices, adoption of unrestricted trade practices, and courteous services.
   (iv) *Government:* No tax evasion and avoidance, compliance with various laws and adherence to government policies.
   (v) *The community:* Avoidance of unfair and socially harmful business (trade) practices, generation of no pollution, promotion of community's welfare, and adoption of adequate safety measures against risky operation and hazardous practices (operations).
5. **Business and environmental protection:** Industrial enterprises are largely responsible for environmental pollution. They pollute the environment by injection of harmful substances in the atmosphere. Four main types of pollution are:
   (i) air pollution, (ii) water pollution
   (iii) noise (sound) pollution and (iv) land (soil) pollution.

   It is the responsibility of business to protect its external environment, by checking water, air, noise and soil pollution.

6. **Social audit:** A social audit is a measure of a firm's social behaviour. Many large and progressive organisations set social objectives and try to measure whether they have met the objectives. Many large corporations like Tata Steel include a social audit in their annual report. All socially responsive firms conduct regular social audits.
7. **Business ethics:** Ethics are the standards of right and wrong that influence behaviour. Right behaviour is considered ethical, and wrong behaviour is treated as unethical. Ethics go beyond legal requirements. Every firm is expected to carry on business in an ethical manner. For instance, widely adopted business practices such as adulteration of food items, hoarding and black marketing of essential commodities are undesirable from the society's point of view and so are, therefore, treated as unethical. However, it is not always possible to draw a line between ethical and unethical behaviour, such as accepting a gift (ethical) versus accepting a bribe (unethical).
8. **Elements of business ethics:** Business ethics has the following key elements:
   (i) Top management commitment and support.
   (ii) Development of a code of ethics, i.e., a formal statement of the company's values concerning ethics and social issues.
   (iii) Serving the community beyond what is specified by law.
   (iv) Permitting employee's involvement and participation in management.
   (v) Periodic evaluation and monitoring of ethical programmes.
9. **Ethics of sustainability:** A big challenge for manufacturing companies is sustainability — meeting the needs of the present without compromising the ability of future generations to meet their own needs.

KEY Terms	
Business ethics	Soil pollution
Corporate social responsibility	Green management
Stakeholders	Accountability
Ethics of sustainability	Social responsiveness
Air pollution	Social audit
Water pollution	Environmental audit

Assignments

SHORT ANSWER-TYPE QUESTIONS

1. What is meant by 'social responsibility of business'?
2. Present three arguments in favour of corporate social responsibility.
3. Mention the responsibilities of business towards consumers.
4. Define 'business ethics'.
5. What are the key elements of business ethics?

ESSAY-TYPE QUESTIONS

1. What do you understand by corporate social responsibility? Explain the case for social responsibility.
2. State and explain the social responsibility of business towards different interest groups.
3. What is business ethics? Explain its elements.
4. (a) Why should businesses assume social responsibilities? Give any four reasons in support of your answer.
   (b) Discuss any six responsibilities of a business towards the customers. [ISC 2013]

QUESTION BANK

1. *Define the term 'social responsibility'.*

   OR

   Explain the concept of social responsibility.

   OR

   What is meant by social responsibility?

Ans. See text.

2. *Why should business assume social responsibility?*

Ans. See text.

3. *Explain the concept of social responsibility of business. What are the arguments to justify why business should assume social responsibilities?*

Ans. See text.

4. *Present any three arguments against social responsibility of business.*

Ans. Three arguments against social responsibility of business are the following:

(i) An involvement of business in social activities is likely to dilute its main objective (i.e., profit maximisation).

(ii) The discharge of social responsibility is likely to make domestic industries less competitive in the global market.

(iii) Business people are not much aware of social issues and social needs. So they may not feel comfortable in social matters.

5. *Explain the case against social responsibility of business.*

Ans. See text.

6. *What are the responsibilities of business towards its owners/investors?*

Ans. See text.

7. *What are the responsibilities of business towards its employees?*

Ans. See text.

8. *What are the responsibilities of business towards the consumers?*

Ans. See text.

9. *What are the responsibilities of business towards the government?*

Ans. See text.

10. *What are the responsibilities of business towards the community at large or the general public?*

Ans. See text.

11. *Explain the social responsibilities of business towards different interest groups.*

Ans. See text.

12. *What is meant by environmental pollution?*

Ans. See text.

13. *What are the causes of environmental pollution in India?*

Ans. The causes of various types of pollution in India given below:

(i) Air pollution (ii) Water pollution
(iii) Land pollution (iv) Noise pollution

14. *Explain the need for pollution control.*

Ans. Environmental pollution poses a serious threat to human health and the quality of life. Pollution makes air harmful to breathe, water unsafe to drink and land unfit to grow healthy food. Controlling environmental pollution is absolutely essential for the following reasons:

(i) To reduce health hazards (ii) To reduce safety hazards
(iii) To reduce economic loss (iv) To reduce inconvenience
(v) To improve the quality of life

15. *Explain alternative approaches to pollution control.*

Ans. See text.

16. *Explain the role of business in the protection of the physical environment.*

Ans. See text.

17. *Define business ethics.*

Ans. Business ethics refer to the moral principles concerning acceptable and unacceptable behaviour by business people. Executives are supposed to maintain a high sense of values and conduct honest and fair practices with the public.

18. *What is Business Ethics? What are its elements?*

Ans. See text.

19. *Should businesses accept their social responsibilities?*

Ans. See text.

20. *(a) Explain the responsibilities a business operating a large chain of supermarkets has to its stakeholders.*

(b) Discuss how this business might overcome the problems resulting from a conflict of stakeholder objectives (interest).

21. *Mark the following statements True or False.*

(a) In the ultimate analysis corporate social responsibility serves the interest of business itself.

(b) The principle of trusteeship was popularised by Mahatma Gandhi.

(c) Business has no responsibility for protecting the environment. It is the responsibility of governments at all levels.

(d) There is no role of ethics in business behaviour since it militates against profit-making.

(e) Business is responsible to all sections of a society.

(f) Code of ethics lies at the heart of honest and truthful business practices.

Ans True: (a), (b), (e), (f)

False: (c), (d).

22. *Fill in the blanks:*

(a) Corporate social responsibility is justified on ______ grounds.

(b) All sections of society are called ______ .

(c) Business is a creation of ______ .

(d) Pollution control is supposed to be the joint responsibility of both ______ and government.

(e) Pollution control ______ economic benefits.

(f) The passing of an environmental protection act alone is not ______ to control pollution.

(g) Top management commitment is ______ essential for ethical conduct of business activities.

(h) Constant monitoring is ______ to ensure ethical behaviour in business.

(i) Corporate social responsibility is also known as ______ .

Ans (a) moral, (b) stakeholders, (c) society, (d) business, (e) generates, (f) enough, (g) absolutely, (h) indispensable and (or absolutely essential), (i) corporate social responsiveness.

13 E-BUSINESS AND OUTSOURCING

SYLLABUS

- *E-business—Scope and benefits. Resources required for successful e-business implementation, on-line transactions, payment mechanisms, security and safety of business transactions.*
- *Outsourcing—Concept, need and scope of BPO and KPO.*
- *Smart cards—Meaning and utility.*

Consumers no longer go shopping, they always are shopping.

— Chuck Martin
US CEO of Mobile Future Institute

LEARNING OUTCOMES

On completion of this chapter, you will be able to understand the following:

13.1 Preview
13.2 Meaning of E-business
13.3 Online Transactions and Payment Mechanisms
13.4 The Scope of E-Business
13.5 The Benefits of E-Business
13.6 The Limitations of E-Business
13.7 Resources Required for Successful Implementation (conduct) of E-Business
13.8 Security and Safety of Transactions in E-Business
13.9 The Concept and Nature of Outsourcing
13.10 The Need for and Benefits of Outsourcing
13.11 Scope of Outsourcing
13.12 Knowledge Process Outsourcing (KPO)
13.13 Smart Card

13.1 PREVIEW

In truth the internet has sprouted a world of small web-based businesses selling everything from staplers to refrigerator magnets to wedding dresses. Web-based businesses have to offer more than the same merchandise customers can buy at stores. They must offer unique products or services.

One of the simplest ways to start a web-based business is through *affiliate marketing*. It is an online marketing strategy in which a business rewards individuals or other businesses. Each visitor or customer affiliates itself to the website.

Commerce can be defined as the performance of business transactions (e-business) through electronic, primarily Web-based means. It is the exchange of electronic transactions (i.e., commerce) between autonomous organisations, consumers, and/or vendors.

Traditionally, commerce involves material sourcing, distribution systems, manufacturing, wholesaling, retailing and ultimately reaching the customer. Each of these steps required the transfer of information, usually in the form of printed documents.

However, the late 1990s saw the emergence of electronic business (e-business, in short). The movement to e-business attempted to speed up the vendor-to-customer cycle time while simultaneously reducing the costs of these activities and financial transactions.

Initially this involved electronic data transfer system like electronic data interchange (EDI) or electronic funds transfer (EFT), or the use of fax machines to send order documents.

More recently e-business has affected all areas of business, including share market transactions, banking as also video rental and delivery. Food, household goods, and even cleaning services can be acquired through paperless means. For example, traditional bookstores compete with services like Amazon. com which can be accessed through the Web.

Note that e-business is also based on e-mail. There is, in addition, e-mall, where people can do their shopping on-line and make purchases and payments directly over the Internet. Another form of e-business is the enterprise resource planning (ERP) which integrates an entire organisation through an internet environment.

Electronic business or, in short e-business refers to such activities as the buying, selling, and trading of goods, and services as also information over the Internet by means of the World Wide Web (www). E-business has risen dramatically since the commercialisation of the Internet in the mid-1990s. The convenience, availability, speed and global reach of the Internet has been exploited by such companies as Amazon.com, the book sellers and American Management Systems, an IT consulting firm, located in Virginia. IBM relies on both intranets and extranets for carrying on E-business also includes provision of both goods and services over the Internet by application service providers (ASP). Thus, E-business also includes e-services and can be conducted through Dell Computers' Website.

13.2 MEANING OF E-BUSINESS

Since term e-business refers to the use of computers and the internet to link both the internal operations of a business (that is, transactions and communications between the various departments/divisions of the business) and its external dealings and relationships with its suppliers and customers. There are two interpretations of the term 'e-business'. In a broad sense, it refers to the conduct of business on the Internet, including the electronic purchasing and selling of goods and services, serving customers, and communications with business partners. It refers to a company which engages in E-business. In a narrow (restricted sense), it refers to a company which conducts the main part of its business on the Internet.

E-business refers to business conducted electronically, especially via Internet.

DEFINITIONS OF E-BUSINESS

1. E-business refers to the business of a company that engages in e-commerce.
   Oxford Dictionary of Business and Management
2. E-business is the use of computers and the Internet to link both the internet operations of a business and its external dealings and relationships with its suppliers and customers.
   Collins Dictionary of Business

13.2.1 Concept of E-Business

Simply put, E-business refers to the exchange of goods, information products, or even services via an electronic medium such as the Internet. Originally limited to buying and selling, it now includes such functions as customer services, marketing, and advertising. At present it refers to the method of buying and selling goods and services over the Internet. It is a form of direct selling/marketing which enables a supplier to sell direct to the final customers without the need for traditional 'middlemen' — wholesalers and store retailers. In other words, it is a technique of elimination of inter intermediaries in the whole chain of distribution.

FOCUS ON TERMINOLOGY: E-BUSINESS PROCESSES

E-business processes refer to various stages of trading over Internet. These are the flow of information through planning, design, manufacture, sales, order processing, distribution and quality in an e-business. It can include retailing over Internet (known as e-tailing), business-to-business (B2B) commerce, business-to-customer (B2C) dealings, intranets and extranets, online marketing, and online presence of any technique (method) that is used for some type of commercial relations (for example, customer loyalty programmes, relationship marketing and customer services).

In a narrow sense, it includes only those transactions ordered and paid online. However, in a broad sense it includes all online sales transactions which are conducted largely or substantially on-line, and which also includes a critical non-Internet component.

FOCUS ON TERMINOLOGY: E-PROCUREMENT

E-procurement is an aspect of e-business. In a narrow sense, it refers to purchasing of products over Internet. In a broad sense, it refers to the business-to-business sale and purchase of goods and services over an electronic network such as the Internet.

13.2.2 Difference between E-Business and E-Commerce

The term 'E-business' is used in a broad sense and includes buying and selling of goods and services and also serving the customers in various ways and collaborating with the business partners by using electronic device(s). By contrast, the term 'E-commerce' is used in a narrow sense. It refers to using the Internet to order and pay for products or services. Thus e-commerce can be treated as best as a subset of e-business. See Fig. 13.1.

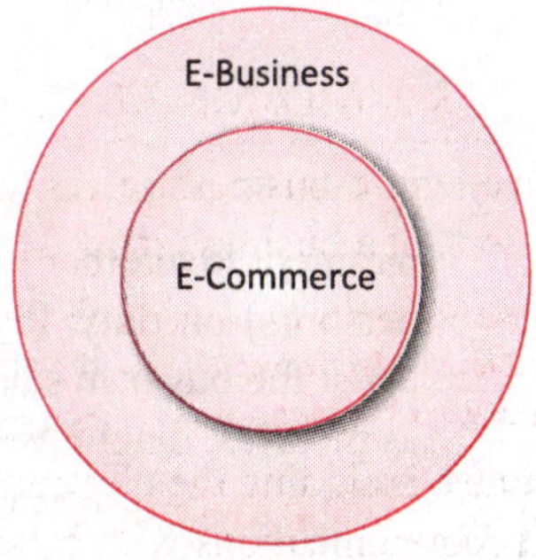

FIGURE 13.1
Commerce as a Sub-set of e-Business

In short, while e-commerce refers to paying for goods and services, e-business covers the whole range of business transactions which takes place via electronic media such as e-mail or the Web.

Any e-commerce transaction normally occurs when a consumer buys a ticket online or bus something from a departmental store or a shopping mall and pays for it after receiving the product directly online while ordering it. It also takes place when a firm pays another firm for buying inputs or obtaining supplies of finished goods via its website. But e-business includes (i) buying and selling of goods and services, (ii) serving the customers and (iii) having dealings with the business partners.

13.3 ONLINE TRANSACTIONS AND PAYMENT MECHANISMS

Needless to say, e-business technique is universally applicable. It can be used in any phase or type of a business transaction such as routine/repeat transactions as also off and on transactions in which payments may be through cash or credit. See Fig. 13.2. There can also be one-time or just a single transaction through cash payment only. In each case, the following standard procedure is followed:

1. **Search for seller's website:** It involves the intending buyer searching out and identifying the right type of seller, as is done by any consumer for purchasing a shopping good. An online buyer succeeds in finding the seller's website by going through the following procedure: (i) He first selects a menu item from the screen. (ii) He then relies on a search engine and follows a random-walk procedure to find the website of the appropriate seller. (iii) He may not make a transition from one website to the desired seller's website. (iv) Finally he may select the desired seller's website from newspaper advertisement or on recommendation of a neighbour.

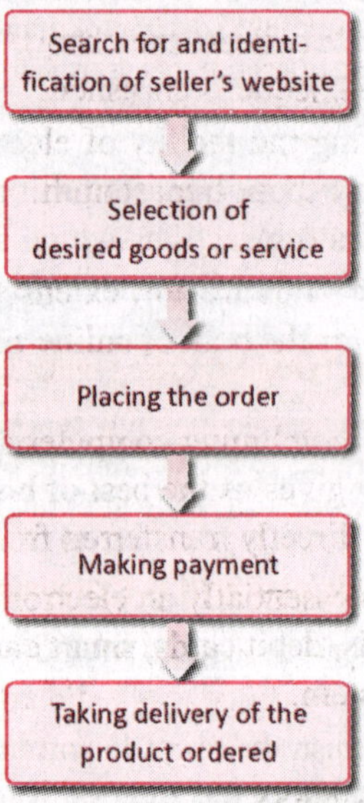

FIGURE 13.2: Steps in an Online Transaction

2. **Selection of desired good/service:** In a departmental store, the buyer moves from one department to another to find one desired product/service. He may take the help of the sales person(s) on duty. In the same way, in an 'e-shop', there is a search engine or index to assist the buyer in selecting the desired product/service, through visual presentations such as pictures, diagrams or even verbal descriptions.
3. **Placing the order:** While looking through various articles in the online store, the customer can pick and put the selected items in the shopping cart or the box supplied. This is virtually an online record of what the customer wants to buy. This technique may be followed

while buying books and stationery items from Flipkart. This virtually amounts to placing an order with the seller.

4. **Making payment:** Usually payment for an online purchase is made through credit/debt card. A buyer may also pay by cheque or by cash in case of home delivery.
5. **Delivery:** In e-business, electronic products such as software information or even music can be delivered online through downloading. For other goods the seller has to maintain a suitable distribution network such as post or courier service, taking into account the nature of the goods, cost of delivery, and, of course, expectation of buyers. For perishable goods such as foodstuffs, home delivery from a local agent is perhaps the best method. At times the customer is required to collect the goods personally from the seller's local distribution centre. For certain items such as air tickets, which are brought and paid for on time, there is no need for delivery. This is why an air ticket is called e-ticket.
6. **Post-sale activity:** After getting delivery of the product ordered, the buyer is likely to need some service associated with the product purchased.

13.3.1 Modes (Methods) of Payment for Online Transactions

The following methods may be used for making payments for online transactions:

1. *Cash-on delivery (COD):* The payment for the goods ordered becomes due and in online may be made in cash as soon as goods are delivered.
2. *Cheque:* The online seller first collects the cheque from the customer. And then only he delivers goods as soon as the cheque is encashed.
3. *Net-banking transfer:* By using the facility of electronic transfer of funds over the net a customer may transfer a specified amount from his account to that of the seller. This saws both time and cost of transaction.
4. *Credit and debit cards:* These cards are now extensively used for making online payments. In fact, payment from banks for the bulk of online consumer orders are made through such cards.
5. *Digital cash or e-money:* By combining computerised convenience with security and privacy digital cash or e-money gives us the best of both worlds. In an electronic cash transaction, the specified value is directly transferred from customer's chip to that of the seller.

It is to be noted that e-money is essentially an electronic medium for making payments. It is a broad term and includes credit cards, debit cards, smart cards, electronic funds transfer and even automated clearing house (ACH) system.

13.4 THE SCOPE OF E-BUSINESS

Note that e-business can include retailing over the Internet (known as e-tailing), business-to-business commerce (B2B), business to consumer (B2C), intranets and extranets, online marketing and online presence of any form that may be used for some dealing type of commercial relations such as customer loyalty programmes and customer services. Fig. 13.3 shows the applications of e-commerce for four types of business. These are discussed below:

1. **Business-to-Business (B2B) Applications:** The term B2B (business-to-business) refers to an enter-prise which sells products or provides services to other firms (businesses). For example, an aerospace engine company such as Rolls-Royce or GE sells aircraft engines to the world's leading airline carriers, or a management consultancy firm selling strategic

The business-to-business (B2B) marketing consists of individuals and organisations that sell goods and services to other businesses. A manufacturer, for instance, buys its parts and supplies in the B2B market.

advice to major banks or industrial manufacturers. Likewise, Intel is a business-to-business company which sells semi-conductor components for information machines and systems. At the same time it is quite successful in managing a visible brand. Several Indian firms such as Maruti Udyog Ltd., Telco, Bajaj Auto, Kinetic Honda and Thermax are also actively involved in B2B commerce.

2. **Business to Customer (B2C) Applications:** Under this system a business firm sells products or provides services to end-use consumers or audiences. Examples are food retailers, movie theaters, domestic appliance retailers, or firms providing life insurance to individuals. For example, Amul.com sells its branded products online under the marketing system.

3. **Customer-to-business (C2B) Applications:** It refers to online practice where the consumer offers, for example, a service, product, or product idea to a company. It refers to online exchanges in which consumers search out sellers, learn about their offers, initiate purchases and sometimes even fix terms of transactions. This is just the reverse of the conventional marketing practice and is facilitated by the Internet.

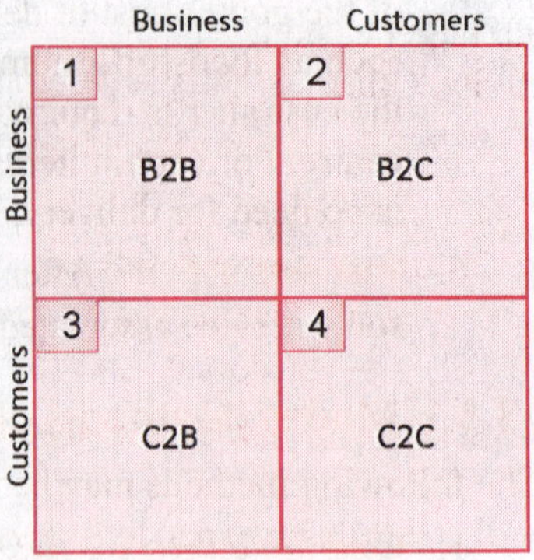

FIGURE 13.3
Four Types of On-line Transactions

BUSINESS FOCUS: TWO MAIN MARKETS

There are two major markets in the real world of business: the consumer market and the business-to-business market. The consumer market consists of all individuals or households that want goods and services for personal consumption or use and have the resources to buy them. The business-to-business (B2B) market consists of all the individuals and organisations that want goods and services to use in producing other goods and services to sell, rent, or supply goods to others. Oil-drilling, cash registers, display cases, office desks, public accounting audits, and business software are B2B goods and services.

The buyer's reason for buying — that is, the end use of the product — determines whether a product is a consumer good or a B2B product. A cup of yogurt that a student buys for breakfast is a consumer product. However, when Haldiram's Pure Food purchases the same cup for sale to its customers, it is treated as a B2B product.

4. **Customer-to-customer (C2C) Applications:** It refers to the online practice, where one customer carries on a transaction with another customer, usually through a third party who will charge a fee, as in e-Bay.com. In other words, it refers to online exchanges of goods and information between (among) final consumers.

The volume and value of transactions conducted via computer and associated networks has grown rapidly from the late 1990s and it is predicted that in future a large proportion of business transactions will be conducted through electronic commerce.

The modern view is that an e-business transaction is one step among many in building a lasting relationship with the buyer. This approach requires a long-term, holistic view of the e-business purchasing experience, so that buyers are influenced not by convenience but by some unique attraction to an e-business website. Since customers can very easily switch to buying from a competing Web site, customer loyalty is the most precious asset for an e-business site. Traditional businesses must deal with competition from B2B and B2C firms, and *vice-versa.*

13.5 THE BENEFITS OF E-BUSINESS

The World Wide Web (www) and the Internet brought many benefits to business by extending their marketing and communication techniques. The Internet has enabled marketing, previously dominated by the technique of 'pushing messages' and products to become much more interactive with target customers. The reason is that the Internet provides instantaneous and high-speed inter-activity. Other advantages offered by the Internet are the following:

1. **Wider customer choice:** Customers have wider choice and greater control over how they engage and interact with sellers and merchants.
2. **Customisation:** Internet enables marketers to customise products, messages, and services to small audiences of common interest, and, normally, with the complicity and permission of the customer.
3. **Help to low-cost marketing channel:** The Internet also enables a much lower-cost marketing channel to sell directly to customers. This often makes it possible to completely eliminate expensive channels.
4. **Benefit to small enterprises:** Small enterprises get enormous benefit, because the Internet gives them global reach and wide search facilities at much lower cost than traditional channels of international marketing.
5. **Initiating instant dialogue:** Marketers can have instant dialogue with each other (one another) and their customers.

In addition e-business provides several other advantages over offline business. These are the following:

(i) *Tapping mass markets:* E-business provides sellers with a means of tapping into a mass market.

(ii) *Shopping from home:* A major attraction of e-business for customers is the convenience of being able to 'shop' from home. There is no need to visit a retail outlet.

(iii) *Convenience:* It is more convenient for both the buyer and the seller, as there is no need for face-to-face interaction. In addition, Web-based stores remain open for 24 hours a day.

(iv) *Sales promotion:* It can be used as a very effective tool of sales promotion. Catalogues and other sales-related information (like launching of a new product) can be transmitted to traders (both wholesalers and retailers) and potential buyers through the internet.

(v) *Launching of new products:* In fact, it is fairly easy to launch a new product through the Internet by providing complete information about it to the dealers and the customers.

(vi) *Cost reduction:* E-commerce is a technique of reducing the costs of acquiring a customer and completing a sale. In addition, since a single computer operator can handle all operations from the receipt of business enquiry to the execution of order, the need for costly manpower is substantially reduced.

(vii) *Economy of operations:* Through paperless exchange of information, it is possible to make considerable saving of time, money and effort associated with receiving orders and executing the same under the conventional way of doing business.

(viii) *Quick delivery:* E-business purchasing decisions can be made fairly quickly, since a vendor can present all relevant information immediately to the buyer.

(ix) *Low inventory cost:* Since a business firm can get necessary supplies from the vendors quickly, there is no need to maintain large inventories of raw materials and intermediate goods. In addition, since less working capital remains blocked in inventories, the interest cost of holding inventories is also low.

(x) *Quick payments:* Payments between business firms and customers and also between business firms can also be expedited (i.e., made as quickly as possible).

(xi) *Reducing entry barriers:* E-business reduces barriers to entry. So even small firms can offer their products alongside companies having big names in the market and wide reputation.

(xii) *Conferring competitive advantage:* By eliminating the 'middlemen' selling costs and prices can be lowered. This gives competitive advantage to firms.

13.6 THE LIMITATIONS OF E-BUSINESS

There are several limitations of e-business. These are the following:

1. **Lack of personal touch:** The main problem with e-business is lack of personal touch between buyers and sellers. So this mode of business goes against relationship marketing, i.e., marketing which is based on interpersonal relationship. That is why this type of business is not suitable for those firms or enterprises in which personal attention and personalised service are the keys — such as made-to-order dress or interior decoration.
2. **Realisation problems:** Customers often lose confidence in e-commerce largely due to its inability to deliver during busy seasons. Realisation problems also arise due to shipping delays, mix-up of goods, and website crashes due to network congestion.
3. **High installation costs:** Various types of costs are involved with the initiation of e-commerce. They are the following :
   (a) *Connection:* The establishment of direct link with the Internet involves high connection cost.
   (b) *Hardware/Software:* Costs of sophisticated computer, modem, routers, etc. are also quite high.
   (c) *Set-up:* This includes employee labour (person) hours associated with designing and installing a suitable website.
   (d) *Maintenance:* Since organisations require trained staff to initiate, update and maintain the Internet facilities and Web pages, there are also costs of employee training. Of course some of the functions and services can be outsourced to reduce workload and, at the same time, get round the clock Internet facility (or support service).
4. **High risk:** There are high risks associated with the successful conduct of business by dot. com organisations. The rate of failure is quite high.
5. **Security:** The security problem for online business is a genuine one. Most people are very reluctant to disclose their credit card numbers via Internet in order to protect themselves against cyber-crime. Recent years have witnessed a wave of credit fraud. So building the confidence of customers about the integrity of the process is a precondition for the success of e-business.

6. **Consumer resistance:** The costs associated with the return or the exchange of an unsuitable merchandise is high, more so in case of bulky items such as furnitures. Moreover in case of certain items coming from distant places, prompt delivery is not possible. Apart from these, customers want to test a costly item before actually buying it. In case of a car, for instance trial run (or test driving) is more a rule, rather than an exception. For this reason, consumers resist e-commerce dealings (transactions).
7. **Corporate vulnerability:** The easy and speedy availability of product details, catalogues, and other relevant information about a business through its Website poses a serious threat, viz., to the accessibilities by its rivals. Extracting necessary information from the competitors' web pages is a serious problem and is known as Web farming.
8. **High costs:** The disadvantages of e-procurement are largely felt by suppliers and include the high costs associated with sophisticated information systems and modern technology; downward pressure on prices; and the ease with which customers can compare and switch suppliers. Both suppliers and buyers may welcome or regret the decreased personal contact of sales visits, telephone calls, and face-to-face competitive tendering.
9. **System and data integrity:** Data protection and integrity of the system which handles the data often cause serious concern. Computer viruses are a genuine and perennial problem. Viruses cause unnecessary delays, file backups, and storage problems which are all wasteful. The danger of hackers accessing files and corrupting accounts just adds to stress associated with the existing operations which are inherently wasteful.

13.7 RESOURCES REQUIRED FOR SUCCESSFUL IMPLEMENTATION (CONDUCT) OF E-BUSINESS

In truth, e-business has tremendous potential for progressive and forward-looking business enterprises. Successful conduct of such business requires the following resources:

1. **Hardware:** The first essential pre-requisite for the implementation of e-commerce is the availability of adequate computer hardware, i.e., the electrical circuits and electromechanical devices which make up a computer system, including CPU (central processing unit), disk drives, keyboard and VDU (visual display unit). A business computer must have adequate speed, memory and nodes so that it can handle a business firm's current as also expected future volume of transactions.
2. **Telecommunication facilities:** To be able to do e-business an organisation or enterprise must have access to effective telecommunication system, supplied by any Internet Service Provider (ISP) such as Mahanagar Telephone Nigam Ltd. (MTNL) or Bharat Sanchar Nigam Ltd. (BSNL) simply through a modem and telephone line.
3. **Company's own website:** To be able to carry out e-business, a company must develop its own comprehensive website, which will facilitate its communication with customers, other firms and even different government departments. The information should furnish such details as past record of the business and its product offering along with pictures, graphs and other visual displays or presentations. Detailed catalogues and available price lists of different products should also be accessed from the website.
4. **Qualified and trained personnel:** A business firm should have technically qualified and properly (adequately) trained personnel who can use computer networks and the Internet

for smooth conduct of e-business. Only properly trained people can handle trade enquiries, obtain and process customer orders and maintain prompt and timely delivery schedules.

5. **Efficient system of payment:** For the successful conduct of e-commerce, a business enterprise has to develop an efficient system of receiving payments for goods supplied. This is facilitated by electronic transfer of money from the customers. Likewise, the business enterprise has to make necessary arrangements with commercial banks and credit card agencies for electronic transfer of any refund to customers.

13.8 SECURITY AND SAFETY OF TRANSACTIONS IN E-BUSINESS (E-BUSINESS RISKS)

"Secure" information may be at risk from hackers who break into companies' networks; from employees who steal it; or from companies' own incompetence, poor gate-keeping, or sloppy procedures. Computer security is more complicated today than ever before. The reason is that computers are accessible not only in areas within the company but also in all areas of other companies with which the company carries on its business.

13.8.1 Security Problems Related to e-Commerce

From its very inception e-commerce has been facing various problems which pose a threat to safety and security of business transactions. The most serious problems are the following:

1. **Risks of dealings:** Three common risks associated with online transactions are the following:
   (a) *Default on order:* A seller may flatly deny that the customer ever placed any order with him (her).
   (b) *Default on delivery:* At times, goods may be delivered at a wrong address or wrong items, i.e., goods other than those ordered may be delivered to the buyer.
   (c) *Default on payment:* The seller may not always be able to realise the payment for the goods already supplied even though the customer claims that he has already made the payments. To solve such problems the seller has to confirm that the customer has entered the correct information from the cookies. Cookies are pieces of information, such as registration data or user preferences 'sent by a website over the Internet to a Web browser that the browser software is expected to save and send back to the server whenever the user returns to that website'. Customers can also protect themselves by shopping only from well-established or reputed websites.
2. **Risk of theft (fraud):** Credit cards may be stolen and used for purchasing goods by thieves who may represent themselves as genuine cardholders. The cardholder has to be extra cautious in order to prevent such fraudulent practices.
3. **Identity theft:** The legitimate collection of personal customer information also opens up the door to identity theft. Identity theft refers to obtaining an individual's information such as credit card number(s) for illegal purposes.
4. **Fraudulent practice:** A business person may operate a fake website (which does not exist) to deceive and to cheat customers. After collecting advance payments from the customers against their orders he may just run away. He may also go to the extent of misusing confidential information about customers, which is unlawful.

5. **Pure risk:** The risk that most concerns business people is pure risk. It threatens the very existence of some firms. Hackers and viruses are an increasing threat to computers, and identity theft is common. Theft and fraud can destroy a small business completely.

BUSINESS FOCUS: TWO TYPES OF STORAGE RISK

Risk is the chance of loss, the degree of probability of loss, and the amount of possible loss. There are two different kinds of risks:

(i) Speculative risk can result in either profit or loss.

(ii) Pure risk is the threat of loss with no chance for profit, such as the threat of fire, accident, or theft.

6. **Data storage and transmission:** If due to hacking an information goes into wrong hands it could be misused. For this, cryptography should be used as a safeguard. It is a method restricting who can access website. It is a powerful means of restricting access to part or all of a website, whereby only a user with an assigned 'key' can read the information on request.
7. **Brand-hijacking:** Internet makes it possible to create powerful brands fairly quickly. By contrast brand identity created through radio, T.V., press and other media is both time-consuming and cost-raising. An internet brand may even destroy same existing brands causing huge loss to their owners. For instance, Amazon emerged as a leading bookseller very quickly and it had thrown tough challenge to well-established brands such as Barnes and Nobel. Universal Serial Bus (USB) storage devices (flash drives and memory cards) have become hijackers' latest targets. It is high time that every company established its brands in cyber space so that things do not go out of hand.
8. **Viruses:** An ongoing security threat is the spread of computer viruses over the Internet. A virus is a piece of programming code inserted into other programming which usually lies dormant until triggered to cause some unexpected and, for the victim, usually undesirable event. Users pick up viruses by unknowingly downloading infected programming over the Internet or sharing an infected USB storage device. Often the source of the infected file is unaware of the viruses. Some viruses can be quite harmful, erasing data completely.

FOCUS ON TERMINOLOGY: HACKING AND VIRUSES

Hacking: Hacking means entry of an unauthorised person into one's website. A hacker is an individual with a good understanding of the structure and operations of computer networks. He may deliberately break into confidential systems. In many cases there is no bad intention. But hackers can cause damage by inadvertently introducing viruses or commands which disrupt the proper working of the system. Hackers who set out to destroy computer systems deliberately can do even greater damage than accidental intrusions. Those who have really malign intentions are known as crackers.

Viruses: Different types of viruses can enter a system through e-mail or disc drive floppies or affected websites and can erase all the information stored in a computer. Until the viruses are removed through proper cleaning all business operations come to a grinding halt. In such a situation, a loss of potential revenue is inevitable.

9. **Phishing.** Phishing is another type of online security threat. It refers to the flaudulent use of e-mail and fake websites to obtain financial information such as credit card numbers, password, and bank account information.

13.8.2 Methods to Ensure Security and Safety of e-Business Transactions

In e-business, security problems arise through the Internet as also through hacking and viruses. And in order to ensure security and safety of e-commerce, the following precautions are to be taken:

(i) *Clear identification:* The sender of a document has to be clearly identified.

(ii) *Confidentiality:* The contents of a message should be such that these cannot be scanned by unauthorised persons.

(iii) *Integrity:* It is necessary to ensure that changes in messages cannot be made without giving (making) remarks.

(iv) *Non-repudiation:* The sender of a message has to be directly connected to the contents of the message so that the recipient is not in a position to flatly deny that he has not received the message.

(v) *Avoiding phishing scam:* Finally, the best way to avoid a phishing scam is never to access a website through a link in an e-mail message. Instead, it is better to open a new window and go to the home page of the company's website directly.

13.8.2.1 Encryption

Encryption is an aspect of e-business. It refers to putting information in code for transmission over Internet. To be more specific, it is a means of encoding information, especially financial data, so that it can be transmitted over the Internet without being read by unauthorised persons.

Within an Internet security system, a secure server uses encryption when transferring or receiving data from the web. Credit card information, for example, that could be targeted by a hacker, is encrypted by the server, turning it into special code that will then be decrypted only when it is kept safely within the server environment. Once the information has been acted upon, it is either deleted or stored in encrypted form.

13.8.2.2 Digital Signature

A digital signature is simply an authentication code to verify the source of a document.

The authentication of a digital signature requires a digital ID, or a digital certificate, which is issued by an appropriate authority. The digital ID is sent with the message with a view to verifying the identity of the sender. Digital signatures are to be encrypted as soon as they are delivered from the certification authority as also when they are used in the message.

13.8.2.3 Cyber Crime Cell

Computer hacker Gary McKinnon has perpetrated the biggest hacking of military computers ever detected, when he temporarily disabled US national security systems while searching the Internet for information on UFOs. There are various other instances of computer hacking. This is why the governments of some countries have set up Cyber Crime Cells to inquire into the cases of hacking and other crimes and arrest the criminals and take necessary legal action against these who are found really guilty.

13.8.2.4 Protection from Cyber Attack

Often we see articles in newspapers about a company being hacked by some outside (or even inside) individuals or groups which steal our private information, such as credit card numbers, addresses and so on. Cyber risk insurance can help a business prepare for the worst. For example, it will cover a company if its employees or customers decide to file against them in case their information is leaked or divulged.

BUSINES FOCUS: E-COMMERCE TO M-COMMERCE

E-commerce is gradually becoming M-Commerce. The process of transition is outlined in Figure 13.4.

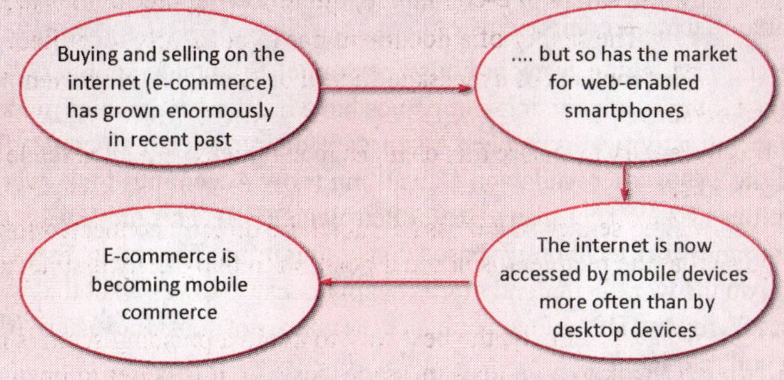

FIGURE 13.4: Transition from E-Commerce to M-Commerce

The term E-commerce (electronic commerce) refers to all buying and selling carried out on the internet. M-commerce (mobile commerce) specifically involves transactions which are done through a mobile telecommunications network. These transactions can range from the small, such as eBay purchase, to the potentially huge such as trading stocks and shares. M-commerce works in a similar way to E-commerce, with websites and apps adapted or originated from mobile and hand-held devices. It can also include direct carrier billing when purchases can be added to a mobile cell phone. Another function is tap-to-pay, where a customer makes payment using a mobile device which has already been installed with credit card information *via* a programming such as Google Wallet, on Paytm Wallet.

The customer holds the device against a payment enabled with a technology called near-filled communication. This establishes a radio connection between the two devices to complete a transaction.

It may finally be noted that a web-based business is not always a fast road to success. It can, at times, be a short cut to failure. Hundreds of high flying .coms crashed after promising to revolutionise the way we shop.

13.9 THE CONCEPT AND NATURE OF OUTSOURCING

Staying competitive may call for outsourcing. Outsourcing means contracting with other companies (often in other countries) to do some or all the functions of a firm, like its production or accounting tasks. However, outsourcing involves loss of jobs to overseas competitors.

The other side of the outsourcing is insourcing. Many foreign companies are setting up design and production facilities in India. For example, Korea-based Hyundai operates design and engineering in some parts of India and produces cars. Two leading Japanese auto-makers, viz., Honda and Toyota have been producing cars and two-wheelers in India for years. Insourcing creates many new jobs in India and helps offset those being outsourced.

13.9.1 Meaning of Outsourcing

Outsourcing refers to buying of components, finished products and services from outside the firm rather than self-supply from within a firm.

Outsourcing is farming out a particular function, perhaps an entire process, to a third party. If, for instance, a company's maintenance manager pays someone to come in and water the plants in the reception area of the office, that is outsourcing. Outsourcing means the buying of components, sub-assemblies, finished products, and services from outside suppliers rather than by supplying them internally. A firm may decide to buy in rather than supply internally because it lacks the technical expertise, physical capital, or space required to do so. It may also be able to buy in more cheaply or more quickly than manufacturing in-house. In some situations, even computer, legal and personnel services have been outsourced as well as the more traditional manufactured components.

Outsoursing (i.e., switching from in-house personnel to outside supplier) has been around for ever in that, for example, advertising companies have handled companies marketing for years, while certain financial activities have been taken care of by specialist people. But the concept really took off in the 1990s after Anderson Consulting (now Accenture) took over the day-to-day accounting operations of the oil company Bharat Petroleum (BP). This move was quickly followed by other companies and other technology-based consulting firms. The rationale was that firms such as Anderson could do the work better and more cheaply because it was what they specialised in (or concentrated on), leaving the BP to focus on its core (main, not subsidiary) activities of exploring for oil, drilling it and refining it.

Outsourcing, or contracting out, is often introduced wth the goal of increasing efficiency and reducing costs, or to enable the organisation to develop greater flexibility or to concentrate on core business activities. The term 'subcontracting' is sometimes used to refer to outsourcing.

Outsourcing is of two types: business process outsourcing (BPO) and Knowledge process out sourcing (KPO). BPO means contracting out of a company's in-house function to an external agency. For example, a company like TCS mav outsource its pay-roll accounting from S.R. Batlibouy and Co.

13.9.2 Business Process Outsourcing (BPO)

IT outsourcing (ITO) is a subset of business process outsourcing (BPO). Business process outsourcing (BPO) is a form of outsourcing which uses a third party to take responsibility for certain business function such as human resources (HR) and finance. The concept is a wide one and includes processes like billing, purchasing and finance. Indian contractors call these 'non-voice' work. Following a separate (independent) path, it spreads to customer relations management and technical support via call centres which were often located in other countries.

Some management experts call BPO as 'offshoring'. However, the truth is that the word BPO means 'relocating part of one's business abroad, not surrendering ownership'. Paying a call centre in Kolkata to deal with one's customers is merely offshore outsourcing. This is different from domestic outsourcing which implies loss of jobs.

13.9.3 Scope of BPO

Business firms may outsource the following processes to highly specialised BPO firms:

(i) customer support services,

(ii) telemarketing services,

(iii) administrative support services such as data entry, document conversion, form precessing and scanning,

(iv) customer relations management (CRM),

(v) accounting service, and

(vi) human resource management (HRM).

Some of the leading BPO companies in India are Genpact, IBM Daksh, Wipro BPO, TCS BPO, Infosys BPO, Aegis, etc. Every year some new firms are joining the business.

13.9.4 The Nature and Features of Outsourcing

The most common features of outsourcing are the following:

1. *Contracting out:* Outsourcing involves giving some work to other firms. In 2003, Procter & Gamble outsourced its IT functions to Hewlett-Packard, its human resources department to IBM and its facilities management to Jones Lang LaSalle. It reasoned that specialists in each process would be able to improve operational efficiency and quality of service. And the scale of the improvement was quite substantial (dramatic) — much beyond expectations. So far, the exercise has been a classic example of why management reaches for outsourcing.
2. *Non-core activities:* In general only non-core activities are outsourced. This point has already been discussed. In case of a school, book store and canteen are treated as non-core activities. So they are outsourced to outsiders.
3. *Involvement of a third party:* A business process is generally outsourced to a third party to minimise the company's risk. A large company having several plants may set up a separate unit to perform certain common functions or provide certain services such as recruitment, selection, training, payroll accounting and customer support services. Alternatively, such services may be outsourced to an external agency (or to a third party) which specialises in providing such services on a fully contractual basis.
4. *Fees:* The outsources charge a fee for performing any activity on a purely contractual basis.

At present outsourcing is popularly associated with IT Enabled Services (ITES). It is also known as business process outsourcing (BPO). For example, call centres provide services to their clients on the basis of direct communication. 'Customer Care' accounts for most of call centre activities with handling of inbound (customer queries and grievances) and outbound activities (market surveys, payment rewinds up, and telemarketing for 24 hours and 7 days a week).

13.10 THE NEED FOR AND BENEFITS OF OUTSOURCING

Outsourcing is usually done because it is more cost-effective to use outside suppliers or because outside suppliers are more technically competent or can supply a wider range of items. To be more specific, the need for outsourcing arises for the following reasons:

1. **Performance on the basis of specialisation:** Outsourcing enables a firm to get various tasks performed with maximum possible efficiency through specialised agencies.
2. **Concentration on core activities:** By outsourcing certain services, a business firm can fully concentrate on its core activities.
3. **Search for excellence:** Outsourcing enables a company to search for and succeed in achieving excellence in both core activities and non-core activities.
4. **Achieving economy:** Outsourcing some activities is cost effective. That is why, letters, mails and correspondences are outsourced to courier agencies by most firms. Much cost-saving is achieved by large firms through this device.
5. **Achieving smooth conduct of routine activities:** Outsourcing of routine business activities to large firm activities enables a firm to perform its day-to-day functions such as delivering mail, maintaining plant, machines and product facilities fairly smoothly.

6. **Business growth:** Less-strategic tasks can be outsourced globally so that companies can focus on areas in which they can excel and grow.
7. **Global economic growth:** Consumers benefit from lower prices generated by effective use of global resources and developing nations like India and Korea achieve export-led growth, thus fueling global economic growth.
8. **Job creation:** Outsourced work allows companies to operate efficiently. This enables them to hire more workers.

13.11 SCOPE OF OUTSOURCING

Business has two segments: core and non-core. The business which a firm treats as central to its survival and long-term strategy is called core business. Any other business, called non-core business may be viewed as peripheral to the firm's purpose and are therefore outsourced.

The following services are usually outsourced:

1. **Financial services:** Any type of business firm requires different types of financial services in such areas as pay-roll accounting services, merchant-banking, underwriting, etc. Small and medium-sized manufacturing and commercial enterprises find it really convenient and economical to depend upon external financial agencies for such services. For example, Tata Steel may outsource financial services from the City Bank for issuing ADRs/GDRs in global capital markets. There is tremendous scope for outsourcing in such areas as lease financing, credit rating, raising venture capital, factoring, housing loan, mutual funds and credit cards.
2. **Advertising:** Large business firms normally depend upon reputed advertising agencies for copyrighting, designing, developing and releasing (transmitting) advertisement materials for their products — both goods and services. Some big advertisers such as Colgate, Hindustan Unilever, Nestle an other signed agreements (contracts) with leading ad agencies. Under the system, an advertising agency undertakes to provide all services connected with advertising such as copy designing, film production, media planning, etc. on payment.
3. **Courier service:** Large business firms have to send hundreds or even thousands of letters, parcels, etc. everyday or week and they use the services of such firms as Blue Dart, DTH, Overnight Express and DTDC. These firms collect all articles from the offices of their clients and dispatch them to their destinations much faster than post offices can do.
4. **Customer support service:** Companies offer various types of services to customers to support the purchase and use of products such as prompt after-sales service, customer care, opportunity to exchange an unsuitable product and loan from banks as in the case of houses, cars and two-wheelers. Companies are becoming aware of the fact that customer service is very much effective and fruit-bearing type of non-price method of gaining sustainable competitive advantage in a highly competitive market. Most customers now-a-days need home delivery of goods, maintenance service for durable goods and, information about new brands with added features. Businesses gain from connecting fully on the sales function and by outsourcing all types of customer support services. For example, KB Capital and other companies have set up call centres in major metropolitan cities of India to provide and extend support services to their customers all over the world.

13.11.1 Outsourcing: An Overall Evaluation

The global trend towards outsourcing will continue as firms seek further ways of improving operational effectiveness, more so as new opportunities arise due to globalisation. The process is not without its risks, however. Before any substantial business-process outsourcing of complete functions is undertaken or before any stage of the production process is outsourced, the company must undertake a substantial cost-benefit analysis of the decision. Having closed or run down a whole department to outsource its functions, it would be both time-consuming and cost-raising to reopen and reestablish it if it was found that the outsourcing had failed.

One of the key factors in any business decision on outsourcing is to decide what is a truly core activity that must be kept within the direct control of the business. Of course, these core activities vary from business to business.

CASE STUDY: WORLD'S AIRLINES INCREASE OUTSOURCING

There is one area where major national airlines and their cut-price competitors agree – aircraft maintenance is a lot cheaper when it's performed by low-paid mechanics working for outsourcing companies. Jet Blue, Southwest, Qantas, America West and United are among the big airlines which outsource all major maintenance of their aircraft to contractors in other countries. Jet Blue's A320 Airbus planes are sent to El Salvador for maintenance, for example. US Airways recently cut 2,000 skilled mechanics' jobs as it outsourced most of its maintenance and repair work.

It wasn't long ago that all global airlines employed their own teams of highly qualified and highly paid aircraft engineers. They were all licensed by their own country's civil aviation authority and could earn at least $60 an hour. Mechanics working for outsourcers do not have to be licensed – only their supervisors must be fully qualified. In El Salvador, the mechanics earn between $10 and $20 an hour.

Most airlines have also outsourced consumer-enquiry call centres, baggage handling and in-flight catering and merchandising. Malaysia Airlines recently denied rumours that it was about to outsource its in-flight retail operation called Golden Boutique. The airline has made clear its desire to 'mutually separate' non-core operations. The company described its in-flight business as 'non-core but good value'. So it may want to remain in complete control of this with its own employees.

13.12 KNOWLEDGE PROCESS OUTSOURCING (KPO)

Meaning of KPO: BPO is largely concerned with carrying out routine processes. Some outsourcing providers handle employees' expense claims over the Internet. The so-called 'knowledge process outsourcing' (KPO) farms out brain power, in the shape of research, analysis and technical skills. It generates the following benefits

Benefits

1. *Sale of assets:* The primary benefit which companies expect from KPO is sale of assets and payroll cuts.
2. *Cost reduction:* Outsourcing lowers cost because the provider enjoys stronger economies of scale or, if the outsourced work goes offshore, through lower labour costs. Other compelling motives may include getting work done more efficiently and effectively and tighter budgetary control through more predictable costs.

3. *Quality of information:* Outsourcing helps maintaining quality and security of information. These are perennial concerns for many companies.
4. *Greater discipline:* Finally, the most useful contribution of outsourcing to the practice of management is that it is embedding a discipline of looking at absolutely everything in the business.

13.12.1 Scope of KPO

KPO encompasses the following services:

(i) Business research,
(ii) Investment analysis (such as equity research),
(iii) Data analysis
(iv) Market research and consumer survey
(v) Valuation of corporate assets
(vi) Routine business operations, support services, and management of strategic issues
(vii) Legal research and
(viii) Patent research.

13.12.2 KPO vs. BPO

Although KPO is just a continuation of BPO, the former is a more complex endeavour than the latter. KPO focuses on knowledge-intensive business processes which require highly specialised personnel.

KPO focuses mainly on technical professionalism. The people who are hired to serve in KPO service companies are more diverse and technically competent with MBA degrees as also medical, engineering, design and various specialist business skills. KPO delivers much higher value to organisations than BPO. The reason is that it provides business expertise rather than business process expertise. So KPO involves making a transition or a paradigm shift — from standardised processes to advanced analytical thinking, highly technical skills and decision-making ability are based largely on past experience and current trends.

13.12.3 The Need for and Benefits of KPO

The need for KPO is felt by large companies because it offers the following advantages:

(i) KPO firms solve the problems of their clients in a comprehensive manner because they specialise in certain specific service areas.
(ii) They provide services to their clients at low costs. Even small clients are often beneficiaries.
(iii) KPO increases both the efficiency and effectiveness of the client(s) in the conduct of the outsourced activity.
(iv) KPO facilitates the client companies in concentrating on their own core activities.

Both KPO and BPO are complex but useful endeavours. Both help modern businesses in more ways than one. There is much greater scope for KPO than BPO as emerging modes of doing business in a knowledge-intensive world.

The main services covered under BPO and KPO are listed in Table 13.1.

TABLE 13.1: Major Services covered under BPO & KPO

Under KPO	Under BPO
1. Business and technical analyses	1. Merchant banking
2. Marketing research	2. Factoring service
3. Industrial research and development (R&D)	3. Advertising service
4. Writing and editing of advertisement materials and content development	4. Courier service
5. Animation and design	5. Processing of transaction
6. Legal services	6. Technical support
7. Employee Training and managing consultancy	7. Various types of customer support services
8. Data analysis	8. Sale of different type of insurance polices
9. Network management	

13.13 SMART CARD

13.13.1 Meaning of Smart Card

A smart card is a plastic card containing a built-in micro chip (micro processor) which stores and updates information, typically used in carrying out financial transactions.

It can store and process transactions and maintain a bank balance, thus providing a secure, portable medium for electronic money. Financial details and personal data stored on the card can be updated each time the card is used. A smart card is normally used in carrying out financial transactions. Unlike an ordinary debit card or cash card, a smart card memorises all transactions in which the card is used. Other uses include storing one's medical records. Smart card was first introduced by the USA's Motorola company in 1977.

13.13.2 Utility of Smart Card

Invented in France, where they called *cartes a memoire*, a smart card is a portable card containing microprocessor and memory. As an electronic funds transfer tool, a smart cards comprises a credit card, debit card, phone card and drivers' licence card. A smart card replaces the typical magnetic strip on a credit or debit card with a microprocessor. The card can then store various types of information including the holder's bank balance. Traders can use this information to check the card's validity, spending limits as also transactions can debit up to that amount on the card. It can be used as plastic or e-money, a credit facility being drawn down as it is used and recharged by the bank or store or may be used as automatic teller machine (ATM) cards.

Smart cards can carry identification information for the individual and can be used for electronic payment systems. Unlike an ordinary debit card or credit card, a smart card memorises all transactions in which the card is used. Other uses include storing a person's medical records.

Key Points

1. E-business. E-business refers to the use of computers and the Internet to link both the internal operations of a business and its external dealings and relationships with its suppliers and customers. e-business essentially refers to the business of a company which engages in e-commerce.

2 E- commerce. Electronic commerce (e-commerce) refers to the use of the Internet to buy and sell goods and services. For this, a company is supposed to have a website which provides details of products and contracts. It is essentially a method of direct selling/marketing which enables a supplier to sell direct to the final customer without the need for traditional 'middlemen'— wholesalers and store retailers. It facilitates commercial transactions through new ways of transferring and processing of information. It implies paperless exchange of business information using electronic data interchange (EDI), e-mail, and other modes of network-based technology.

3. Scope of e-business. There are two major types of e-commerce transactions: business-to-consumer (B2C) and business-to-business (B2B).

   Internet has become very important in the B2B market, where businesses sell goods and services to one another, such as IBM selling consulting services to a commercial bank. Websites have become the new stores.

4. Benefits of e-business: Six main benefits of e-business are the following:
   (i) Global reach and unlimited market,
   (ii) direct link of a business with both its customers and business partners,
   (iii) prompt response and quick delivery,
   (iv) new product launch,
   (v) economy, and
   (vi) instant payments.

5. Resources required for e-business: To be able to use e-commerce facilities, a business firm should have the following IT infrastructure: (i) a computer with a browser, (ii) a telephone connection, (iii) an internet connection with Internet Service Provider (ISP), (iv) trained and qualified personnel (knowledge workers in P.F. Drucker's terminology) and (v) necessary support services. Internet makes two important services available to business, namely, (a) World Wide Web (www), and (b) e-mail. These services conduce to e-business.

6. Outsourcing: The term 'outsourcing' refers to switching from in-house personnel to outside supplier for obtaining goods and services from outside suppliers, i.e., the use of external suppliers as a source of finished products, components, or even services It is the process whereby one firm contracts with other companies, often in other countries, to perform some or all of its functions like its production or accounting tasks. It implies transfer of the provision of services previously performed by in-house personnel to an external organisation, usually under a contract with agreed standards, cost and conditions. Areas traditionally outsourced include legal services, transport, catering and security. An increasing variety of activities, including IT services, training, and public relations are now being outsourced.

7. **Types of services to be outsourced:** Business firms offer various types of services to their customers or clients. The most important services which can be outsourced are the following:
   (a) financial services such as accounting, underwriting of shares and securities, registration of share certificates as also their transfers,
   (b) advertising,
   (c) courier service and
   (d) various support services to customers.
8. **BPO and KPO:** Business process outsourcing (BPO) and knowledge process outsourcing (KPO) are new trend setters and pathfinders in business due to the advances of Information Technology (IT) in various directions.
9. **Logistics:** Logistics is the planning, implementing and controlling of the physical flow of materials, final goods and related information from points of origin to points of consumption to meet customer requirements at a profit. moving goods from one place to another is a major part of logistics.
10. **Web farming:** Extracting necessary information from the competitors' webpages is a serious problem and is known as Web farming.
11. **Asynchronism:** Lack of synchronism, or coincidence in time.
12. **Cookies:** Cookies are pieces of information, such as registration data or user preferences 'sent by a Website over the Internet to a Web browser that the browser software is expected to save and send back to the server whenever the user returns to that Website'.
13. **Hacking:** Hacking means entry of an unauthorised person into one's website. A hacker is an individual with a good understanding of the structure and operations of computer networks.
14. **Viruses:** Different types of viruses can enter a system through e-mail or disc drive floppies or affected websites and can erase all the information stored in a computer. Until the viruses are removed through proper cleaning all business operations come to a grinding halt. In such a situation, a loss of potential revenue is inevitable.

KEY Terms

Virus	B2B transaction
Hacking	B2C transaction
E-money	Credit card
E-business	Debit card
E-commerce	Smart card
M-commerce	Identity theft
Automated clearing house (ACH)	Business process outsourcing (BPO)
Internet	Knowledge process outsourcing (KPO)
Extranet	Brand-hijacking
Outsourcing	Phishing
Encryption	Cyber crime

Assignments

SHORT ANSWER-TYPE QUESTIONS

1. Define e-business.
2. Name the activity which involves not employing staff directly but using an outside (external) agency or organisation to carry out some business functions.
3. Define outsourcing.

Ans. Outsourcing refers to the performance outside a firm or plant of a production activity which was previously done inside or manufacture of inputs to a production process, or a part of a process, in another location, especially in another country.

4. What is the full form of the terms BPO and KPO?
5. Give three examples of e-business.
6. Distinguish between B2B and B2C types of e-business.

Ans. Business-to-business (B2B) e-business refers to the businesses using online marketing to reach new business customers, serve current customers more effectively and gain buying efficiency and obtain better prices. By comparison, business-to-customer (B2C) e-business refers to businesses selling goods and services online to final consumers (households).

7. Mention any three requirements for successful implementation of e-business.
8. What are smart cards?

ESSAY-TYPE QUESTIONS

1. Explain the basic concept of e-commerce. What benefits can be driven by a firm from it?
2. Discuss the meaning of e-commerce.
3. Mention the areas where the concept of e-commerce can be applied.
4. What, according to you, is the future prospect of e-commerce?
5. What type of resources are needed by a firm for successful implementation of e-commerce? Explain.
6. Discuss the essential pre-requisites for successful conduct of e-commerce.
7. Comment on the security and the safety needs of business transactions.
8. What is meant by an outsourcing of services? Comment on its importance.
9. Highlight the different types of services that could be outsourced.
10. Briefly discuss the nature and importance of outsourcing of business activities.
11. What do you mean by BPO? Explain any two types of outsourced services, with which you are familiar.

QUESTION BANK

1. *Define e-business.*

Ans E-business is simply the process of carrying out business transactions over the internet.

2. *What is the scope of e-business? Describe briefly.*

Ans See text.

3. *Explain modus operandi of online transactions.*

Ans See text.

4. *Discuss the advantages of e-business.*

Ans See text.

5. *Discuss the limitations of e-business.*

Ans See text.

6. *Explain the resources required for successful conduct of e-business.*

Ans See text.

7. *Discuss the possible threats to e-business transactions.*

Ans See text.

8. *Explain or highlight the security and safety needs of e-commerce transactions.*

Ans See text.

9. *Explain the concept of BPO.*

Ans See text.

10. *Discuss the need for outsourcing.*

OR

What is outsourcing? What are its benefits?

Ans Outsourcing refers to the process of using external organisations to provide a firm the necessary services it requires and that it previously supplied from within, e.g., maintenance, cleaning, catering, computer support and telecommunication services.

The benefits of outsourcing are as follows:

(i) It reduces costs and improve service levels as well.

(ii) It frees up resources to enable the firm to focus on its core business and its most profitable areas of activity.

11. *What is B2B marketing?*

Ans Business-to-business marketing refers to marketing activity where the focus is inter-business buying and selling, e.g., providing management consultancy services to a bank. B2B marketing lays stress on the importance of relationship-building, key account management, face-to-face meetings, commercial negotiation and the establishment of business networks and alliance. In truth, B2B transactions occur on a much large-scale than consumer transactions. So they demand a more involved approach. While most B2B transactions are complex, some are simple or straight e.g., the reordering of photocopy paper or a replacement of printer cartridge.

12. *What is B2C marketing?*

Ans) Business-to-consumer (B2C) marketing refers to marketing activity where the focus is on final consumers, e.g., purchasing of laundry detergent and confectionery by a household. Since there are a large number of consumers mass marketing techniques have to be employed such as advertising and promotion of brands. However, due to advances in technology, many organisations involved in B2C marketing are now laying stress on customer-relationship management.

13. *What is outsourcing? What is BPO? Discuss the reasons for outsourcing in recent years.*

Ans) Outsourcing refers to using another business (a 'third party') to undertake a part of the production process rather than doing it within the business using the firm's own employees.

Business process outsourcing is a form of outsourcing that uses a third party to take responsibility for certain business functions, such as human resource HR and finance. The growth of outsourcing in recent years by many businesses is not just driven by shortage of capacity. There are other major reasons for outsourcing such as the following:

(a) *Reduction and control of operating costs.* Instead of employing expensive specialists that might not be fully used at all times by the business, it could be cheaper to 'buy in' specialist services as and when needed. These specialist services offered by other firms may be cheaper because the latter benefit from economies of scale, as they often provide similar services to a large number of businesses. Much outsourcing involves offshoring — buying in services, components or completed products from low-wage economies.

(b) *Increased flexibility.* By removing departments from the staff payroll and buying in services when needed, fixed costs are converted into variable costs. Additional capacity can be obtained from outsourcing only when needed and contracts can be cancelled if demand falls, much more quickly than closing down whole factories owned by the business.

(c) *Improved focus on core business.* By outsourcing 'peripheral' activities, the management of a business can concentrate on the main aims and tasks of the business. These are called the 'core' parts of the business. So a small hotel might use management time to improve customer service and outsource the accounting function completely.

(d) *Access to quality service or resources that are not available internally.* Many outsourcing firms employ quality specialists that small and medium-sized businesses can not afford to employ directly.

(e) *Free-up internal resources for use in other areas.* If the human resources department of an insurance company is closed and the functions bought in, then the office space and computer facilities can be made available to improve customer service.

14. *What is core business?*

Ans) Core business is the business in which the firm sees as the central to its survival and long-term strategy. Other businesses may be viewed as peripheral to the firm's purpose and are therefore, sold or closed.

15. *Briefly discuss four potential drawbacks of outsourcing.*

Ans) Four potential drawbacks to outsourcing are the following:

(a) *Loss of jobs within the business.* Jobless caused by outsourcing have a negative impact on staff motivation. Workers who remain directly employed by the organisation may develop fear psychosies as they suffer from a loss of job security. Bad publicity may result from redundancies too, especially if the business is accused of employing very low-wage employees in other countries in place of jobs lost. This could lead to the firm's ethical standards being questioned.

(b) *Quality issues.* Internal processes will be monitored by the firm's own quality-assurance system. This will not be easy when outside contractors are performing important functions. A clear contract with minimum service-level agreements will be needed. The company contracting out the functions may have to send quality-assurance staff out to the business undertaking the tasks the objective is to ensure that product quality and customer-service standards are being met.

(c) *Customer resistance.* Outsourcing can create customer resistance. And it can take various forms. Overseas telephone call centres have led to criticism about inability to understand foreign operators. Customers may object to dealing with overseas outsourced operations. Bought-in components and functions may raise doubts in the customers' minds over quality and reliability.

(d) *Security.* Using outside businesses to perform important IT functions may be a security risk. If important data were lost by the business, who would take responsibility for this. This is not clearly specified.

16. *Distinguish between BPO and KPO.*

Ans. See text.

17. *Explain the meaning and utility of smart cards.*

Ans. See text.

18. *Outline one way in which the problem of capacity shortage might be overcome by a manufacturing business.*

Ans. See text.

19. *Apart from production, list four business functions or processes that can be outsourced.*

Ans. See text.

20. *Would you advise an airline to outsource recruitment and training of airline cabin crew? Explain your answer.*

Ans. See text.

21. *Explain two benefits to an insurance company of outsourcing its customer-service telephone answering system to an overseas call centre.*

Ans. See text.

22. *Are there some functions that you believe a large international hotel business should not consider outsourcing? Explain your answer.*

Ans. See text.

23. *Recent trends in labour recruitment have been towards employing more part-time staff on temporary contract and outsourcing more often. Explain the reason.*

Ans. See text.

14 STOCK EXCHANGE

SYLLABUS

- *Meaning and importance.*
- *Functions and services.*
- *Major Stock Exchanges in India (BSE, NSE, DSE, ASE) — types and locations.*
- *Types of operators — Brokers, Jobbers, Bulls and Bears.*
- *Terms Used in Stock Exchange — ex-dividend, cum-dividend, spot delivery, forward delivery.*
- *SEBI — functions and objectives.*

Self-explanatory

> *The stock exchange is people's capitalism in which everyone can take part in the purchase and sale of a society's financial capital.*
>
> — P.A. Samuelson

LEARNING OUTCOMES

On completion of this chapter, you will be able to understand the following:

14.1 Meaning of Stock Exchange

14.2 Features of Stock Exchange

14.3 Functions of Stock Exchange

14.4 Services of Stock Exchange

14.5 Major Stock Exchanges in India

14.6 Types of Operators

14.7 Terms Used in Stock Exchange

14.8 SEBI — Objectives and Functions

Finance is life-blood of industry and of course, trade and commerce. And different types of companies have different financial requirements and sources.

Join stock companies can raise long-term capital (called investment finance) by issuing shares. People and institutions are encouraged to buy these shares in the knowledge that there is a well-established market where they can sell these shares. This is the stock exchange. It is a market in existing securities, that is, shares and debentures issued by companies and securities issued by the government.

Various types of organised markets have been established in India and other countries to facilitate buying and selling of financial assets such as shares and securities of both private corporations and public enterprises. The stock market is an organised market, such as a stock exchange or an over-the-counter market where stocks and bonds (debentures) are actively traded.

The stock exchange is a market in which securities are bought and sold. There are stock exchanges in most capital cities, as well as in the larger provincial cities in many countries. The New York Stock Exchange (NYSE), London Stock Exchange (LSE) and Tokyo Stock Exchange (TSE) are the largest in terms of market capitalisation and turnover, although London lists the securities of more companies, particularly overseas companies, than either the TSE or NYSE.

Continental European exchanges are often referred to as bourses in French. Stock exchanges facilitate savings and investment by making it possible for investors to dispose off securities quickly if they wish to do so (in the secondary market) and for companies, governments and other organisations to raise new capital in the primary market (or the new issue market). Ready marketability requires that:

(a) new issues should be made and backed up by reputable borrowers or institutions;
(b) information should be available on existing securities;
(c) competition should exist among market makers, and
(d) there should be adequate liquidity.

There should be both a legal framework and market rules to prevent fraud and unlawful practice such as insider trading regulation. There are various trading systems on stock exchanges (such as order driven and quote driven), but most trading floors have given way to automated screen trading and telephone markets. These new technologies and deregulation have permitted the development of new systems for trading securities outside the stock exchanges.

14.1 MEANING OF STOCK EXCHANGE

The stock exchange is an organisation where members can buy and sell (exchange) securities such as shares, debentures and bonds on behalf of companies and individual investors. Only those securities which are listed in the official book of stock exchanges can be traded. The Securities Contracts (Regulation) Act 1956 has suggested the most comprehensive definition of the stock exchange. According to the Act a stock exchange is "an association, organisation or body of individuals, whether incorporated or not, established for the purpose of assisting, regulating and controlling business in buying, selling and dealing in securities".

The stock exchange is also known as the stock market or the securities market. It deals in such securities as equity and preference shares, debenture or bonds issued by both joint stock companies and public corporations. A stock exchange is organised by an association of its members which include both jobbers and brokers.

14.2 FEATURES OF STOCK EXCHANGE

The main features of the stock exchange are the following:

(i) A company which has obtained permission to have its shares traded on the stock exchange will find it much easier to raise new capital by making an issue of shares. The stock exchange, therefore, is an essential part of the capital market i.e., the market for long-term funds.

(ii) A stock exchange is a market for transactions in approved securities issued by companies, governments and local authorities.

(iii) A stock exchange is run by an association of its own members.

(iv) Its geographical jurisdiction or area of operation is clearly specified by a regulatory agency

(v) The basic purpose of a stock exchange is to assist, to regulate and to control buying and selling in securities.

(vi) It operates as per the rules formulated and guidelines issued by the Securities and Exchange Board of India (SEBI).

14.3 FUNCTIONS OF STOCK EXCHANGE

When an individual buys a share in the stock exchange, the person who has sold the security receives money in exchange for the share but the corporation which initially issues that share acquires no new funds. A corporation acquires new funds only when its securities are sold in the primary market for the first time. In spite of this secondary (share) market performs the following important functions:

1. **Ensuring liquidity:** Secondary markets make it easier to sell second-hand financial instruments to raise cash, that is, they make the financial instruments more liquid. A stock exchange provides a market where holders of shares and long-term securities can always sell them. This means that companies and governments can use the funds for a long period, but the providers of these funds can always convert their securities back into cash, any time they like. The increased liquidity of these instruments then makes them more attractive and thus easier for the issuing firm to sell new shares in the primary market.

   Investors can convert their money into securities and vice-versa easily and quickly. This makes shares as liquid as money and induces people with surplus funds to buy securities even for a short period of time.

2. **Price determination:** The secondary market determines the price of each class of security which an issuing firm sells in the primary market for the first time. Investors who buy securities in the primary market will pay the issuing corporation no more than the price they think the secondary market will set (quote) for this security. The higher the price of the security in the secondary market, the higher will be the price that the issuing firm will receive for a new security in the primary market and hence the larger the volume of financial capital it can raise. Conditions in the secondary market are, therefore, the most relevant to corporations issuing securities.

3. **Information transmission:** The stock market is a highly competitive market in which the price of a share is determined by the free play of market forces, i.e., the forces of demand and supply. The prices at which transactions take place become known to the general public. This enables investors to decide which shares to buy.

4. **Long-term funding:** Stock markets assist business firms in finding long-term funding to finance their capital needs, such as expanding the scale of operation, developing new products and processes (or method of production). After all we cannot over-emphasise the importance of long-term funding. Given a choice, businesses normally prefer to meet their long-term financial needs by using retained earnings or borrowing from a lending institution (such as a bank or an insurance company). However, if long-term funds are not available from retained earning or a lender, a company may be able to raise funds by issuing

corporate stocks or debentures. Recall from Ch. 9 [Formation of a Company] that selling stock by a corporation is known as equity financing and issuing corporate debentures is a form of debt financing.

5. **Building people's financial future:** Stock markets provide private investors a place to buy and sell securities that can help them build their financial future, that is, to accumulate wealth. This encourages people to save more.
6. **Ready market:** People will be prepared to purchase shares, bonds, and debentures much more readily when an institution such as the stock exchange provides a ready market where they can buy securities and, if they so wish, sell their securities.
7. **Mobilisation of savings:** Stock exchanges not only mobilise existing savings but also induce the people of a country to save more to get higher return through investment in various types of securities.
8. **Raising capital:** Stock exchanges help in mobilising saving of individuals and surplus funds of business firms for investment in securities and thus for productive capital formation. In order to finance long-term projects, both joint stock companies and the governments need to borrow money for long periods of time. Company shares represent permanent loans — there is no provision for repayment. Many government securities and corporate debentures are not redeemable for many years after the date of issue. Thus, the raising of capital by private industries and governments is greatly facilitated.

   According to Keynes, stock markets offer one single advantage: they are the best way to bring people with money to invest together with people who can put that investment to productive use.

9. **Safety of transactions:** The shares of listed companics arc publishcd in thc stock exchange yearbook. This protects the public against fraud. In addition, stock exchange transactions ensure fair dealing by controlling such activities as overtrading, insider trading, speculation and manipulation of share prices by spreading false rumours.

   Stock exchanges protect the interest of shareholders by providing adequate safeguard.

10. **Barometer of economic progress:** Stock exchanges act as a barometer of an economy's progress. In other words, it indicates the health of the economy or the state of the economy such as prosperity and recession. Booms or depressions get reflected in stock exchange indices such as the Sensex, the NIFTY and the Junior NIFTY. The stock market provides a daily 'barometer of industrial and commercial efficiency' to the extent that movements in share prices reflect commercial success.
11. **Efficient allocation of capital:** It follows as a corollary that price movements in the stock market tend to direct funds to those industries where share prices are rising. The reason is simple. Rising of share prices indicate that relevant companies are using capital more profitably than other companies. People normally buy the share of those companies which are performing well. And their performance gets reflected in the dividends declared. Since the share prices of profit-making companies rise, they are actively traded. Such companies, called blue chip companies can easily raise fresh capital through new issues. The new issues of such companies are often oversubscribed and sold at a premium. By comparison, new issues by loss-making companies do not generate much public response and are to be underwritten by merchant banks. Thus, stock market ensures an efficient allocation of investors' funds or a society's financial capital.

12. **Control of corporate sector:** Every company which wants to make new issues in the stock exchange has to follow the guidelines issued by the stock exchange regulatory authorities from time to time. This enables the stock exchange to control the functioning of joint stock companies in the public interest.
13. **Acting as a source of business information:** By listing the securities of most public limited companies a stock exchange acts as a business intelligence center. By disseminating information on the external environment and business trends stock exchanges exert indirect influence on corporate decision-making.
14. **Valuing wealth:** Share prices provide a means of valuing wealth held in the form of securities. This is important for assessment of taxes on capital and wealth.
15. **Assessment of compensation payments:** Market prices of shares are also used for correct assessment of the compensation system when firms are nationalised or there is need for proper valuation of the firm in case of a takeover bid.

To sum up our discussion in the words of as expert, viz., C. D. Deshmukh, "the economic services which a well-constituted and efficiently-run securities market can render to a country with a large private sector, operating under the normal incentives and impulses of private enterprise are considerable. In the first place, it is only an organised securities market which can provide sufficient marketability and price continuity for shares so necessary for the needs of investors. Secondly, it is only such a market that can provide a reasonable measure of safety and fair dealing in the buying and selling of securities. Thirdly, through the interplay of demand for and supply of securities, a properly organised stock exchange assists in a reasonably correct evaluation of securities in terms of their real worth. Lastly, through such evaluation of securities, the stock exchange helps in the orderly flow of savings as between different types of competitive investments".

14.4 SERVICES OF STOCK EXCHANGE

Stock exchange renders valuable services to companies, investors — private and institutional and the community at large. These are discussed below:

14.4.1 Services to the Corporate Sector

(i) *Wide market:* Although the stock exchange is a market for existing (old) securities, it indirectly serves as a sales counter for new securities. A new company can easily make new issues if its shares are listed on its stock exchange. Since a huge amount of securities is purchased and sold on a stock exchange, it is a wide market having domestic and international dimensions (more so due to financial globalisation). Therefore a company can raise a huge amount of capital from various types of investors.

(ii) *Status:* Since stock exchange makes a close scrutiny of a company before listing its securities, investors have great faith and much confidence in such a company. Listing enhances the goodwill and credit-standing of a company.

(iii) *High share prices:* Since listed securities are in high demand their market value is fairly high. High share prices raise the market value of a company in times of mergers, acquisitions or take-over bids.

(iv) *Price stability:* Stock exchanges help to minimise undue fluctuations in share prices through the impersonal market forces, i.e., the forces of demand and supply. It provides scope for long-term investment and short-term speculation in company shares and securities.

14.4.2 Services to Investors

(i) *Liquidity of investment:* An efficient functioning of the stock market makes shares liquid since these can be easily and quickly converted into cash. Easy marketability makes investment in securities attractive.

(ii) *Safety:* By advertising share prices, stock exchange protects the public against fraud. It also ensures safety and security of investors through fair dealings. This is. So because transactions are carried out under certain prescribed rules and regulations and under strict supervision and control of dealers by the management of a stock exchange.

(iii) *Collateral:* The securities traded in a stock exchange can be used as a collateral security for taking loans or raising funds.

(iv) *Publicity:* Price quotations on a stock exchange are published in newspapers so investors are able to find out the market value of their securities. Moreover, price trends enable an investor to make rational choice of securities. He is enabled to decide when to sell his securities or to buy new ones with his idle saving or unused money.

(v) *Silent guide:* Investors can decide about purchase and sale of securities on the basis of quoted prices of shares. A stock exchange, therefore, serves as silent guide to investors.

(vi) *Better bargains:* By taking the advice and help of professionals, even a layperson can make gainful investment.

(vii) *Risk reduction:* A stock exchange lists security only when it is satisfied about its true worth or market value. This very fact raises the confidence level of investors. Thus the risk associated with trading in listed securities is reduced.

14.4.3 Services to the Community at Large

(i) *Financing:* Stock exchanges help to develop the habit of saving and financial investment among people. They help to mobilise public savings which may otherwise remain unused or deposited in banks at low interest. They help in financing industries and thereby conduce to the process of economic development of a country like India which suffers from shortage of capital. In fact, financial capital raised through the stock market is converted into real capital such as plant, equipment, machinery and structure without which industrial development in particular and economic development, in general, are not possible.

(ii) *Channel for profitable investment:* A continuous assessment and market valuation of securities help investors in deciding which securities to buy and which ones to sell. This, in its turn, leads to a rational allocation of invertible funds among different projects. A country's financial resources are automatically channelised into more profitable ventures.

(iii) *Financing government projects:* The governments of developing countries like India require a large amount of fund for undertaking various schemes of economic development. Government agencies can sell bonds through stock exchanges for developmental purposes.

(iv) *Barometer of the economy:* Stock exchanges are treated as the barometer of the economy. This is so because every major change in social, political and economic conditions has an effect on share prices. In fact, when most share prices are rising, the economy is found to be in its expansionary phase or the upsaving of the business cydo. And a fall in most share prices indicates a depressionary situation or downsaving. In fact, the Great World Trade Depression of October 1929 occurred due to collapse of the New York Stock Exchange or the Wall Street Crash.

14.5 MAJOR STOCK EXCHANGES IN INDIA

A stock exchange is organised either as a public limited company or as a society of its members. Every stock exchange is managed by a Board of Directors or an Executive Committee Governing Board. The members of this Board are elected from among its members. The executive members elect from among themselves the President and the Vice-President. The Board formulates and implements policies, rules and regulations. These rules and regulations are in quite conformity with the laws governing stock exchanges.

As per the Securities Contracts (Regulation) Act 1956 only those exchanges which have got official recognition by the Central Government can function. In addition, each of the stock exchanges has its own specific jurisdiction. At present, there are 21 stock exchanges and are located at the following cities:

Mumbai, Kolkata, Chennai, Delhi, Ahmedabad, Hyderabad, Indore, Bengaluru, Kochi, Kanpur, Pune, Guwahati, Gangtok, Jaipur, Mangalore, Patna, Bhubaneshwar, Rajkot, Vadodara, Coimbatore and Meerut.

The Bombay Stock Exchange is known as Dalal Street and the Calcutta Stock Exchange as Lyons Range.

In Table 14.1 we present a list of four major stock exchanges of India.

TABLE 14.1: Four Major Stock Exchanges in India

Name and Location of India's Four Major Stock Exchanges	Year of Establishment	Type of Organisation
1. Bombay Stock Exchange (BSE) Phiroze Jeejeebhoy Towers, 25th Floor, Dalal Street Mumbai 400001	1875	Voluntary Association
2. National Stock Exchange (NSE) Mahindra Towers I Floor, A wing R.B.O., Worli Mumbai 400018	1992	Public limited company
3. Delhi Stock Exchange (DSE) Asaf Ali Road, New Delhi 110002	1947	Company limited by shares
4. Ahmedabad Stock Exchange (ASE) Manok Chowk, Ahmedabad 380001	1894	Voluntary Association

14.6 TYPES OF OPERATORS

The following four types of operations are now found in India's stock markets:

1. **Broker:** A broker is an agent of investors who matches buyers with sellers of securities. In other words, a broker is a commission agent who carries out security transactions on behalf of his clients who are not members of any stock exchange. He acts for or on behalf of a large number of clients and charges a nominal commission for the service(s) offered (i.e., purchases and sales of shares and securities). He provides an immensely useful service to the ordinary investor who does not have either the required skill or the expertise in security trading.
2. **Jobber:** A jobber is a dealer in stocks and shares. He has no contact with the investing public except through a stock broker. He deals with the brokers who act on behalf of the

investors. Thus, the jobber buys securities from and sell the same to members of stock exchanges who function as brokers. While a broker works on commission basis, the jobber operates with a profit motive. The reason is that the broker is not a speculator but just a commission agent. By contrast, a jobber buys and sells shares on his own behalf for making capital gains.

3. **Market-maker:** In recent years, the jobber has been replaced by the market maker — an intermediary who creates a market for financial obligation. He is a dealer in securities who undertakes to buy and sell securities as the principal and is, therefore, obliged to announce buying and selling prices for a particular security at particular times.
4. **Tarawaniwala:** The tarawaniwala plays a dual role in the stock market. *Prima facie*, he acts on his own account just as a jobber. At times, he also acts as a commissioning agent or a broker. A tarawaniwala provides both a ready and a wide market for securities, but his dealing may lead to speculative pressures and manipulation of share prices, artificially though. And their own transactions may hurt the interests of their clients.

14.7 TERMS USED IN STOCK EXCHANGE

- **Ex-Dividend**

Ex-dividend means without dividend. The purchaser of a security quoted ex-dividend does not have the right to the next dividend when due. This belongs to the seller. The prefix ex means 'excluding'.

Suppose, for example, *A* sells (ex-dividend) 100 shares of *XYZ* Limited to *B* at ₹ 100 per share on 31.03.2017. On 30.04.2017 the company declares a dividend of ₹ 2,500 on these shares. *A* is entitled to receive this dividend since the seller of shares has the claim to dividends immediately after the sale.

- **Cum-Dividend**

Cum-dividend means with dividend. The purchaser of a security quoted cum-dividend is entitled to receive the next dividend when due. The term 'cum' is used in a similar sense as in the care of bonus issues or rights issues. Suppose *A* sells 100 shares of a company cum-dividend to *B* at ₹ 100 per share on 31.03.2017. On 30.04.2017, the company declares a dividend of ₹ 2,500 on these shares. B is entitled to receive this amount as dividend even if his name does not appear in the book of accounts of the company. This means that in case of cum-dividend, the buyer has the right to claim the dividends declared immediately after the sale of shares.

- **Spot Delivery**

Spot means on the spot market — a market for exchange (purchase or sell) of securities in the present (as opposed to a forward or futures market in which the exchange takes place in the future). In the spot market, shares and securities are delivered at spot price, i.e. the present value of an asset as opposed to future or forward prices. In case of dealings in securities, it is the same as actual price(s).

- **Forward Delivery**

The term 'forward' means that a prospective amount of a share/security is obtained by a contract between a buyer and a seller. Under this the seller (the broker) undertakes to provide the client with a fixed number of shares on a fixed future date at a fixed price (price fixed now irrespective of whether actual price goes up or down i.e., above or below this agreed price). The forward price refers to a price of a share on a forward market in which delivery of shares is made at a future (pre-fixed) date.

- **Stock**

The term 'stock' refers to ownership of a corporation represented by shares that are a claim on the corporation's earnings and assets. Stock is a particular type of security, usually quoted in units of ₹ 100 value rather than in units or proportion of total capital, as in shares. Stock (or stocks) and shares have now become synonymous and the original distinction between stocks and shares is no longer valid.

- **Blue Chip**

The term 'blue chip' refers to first class equity shares which run hardly any risk of capital loss even in times of recession or depression. Companies selling such shares are known as blue chip companies.

- **Stock Market Index**

A stock market index is the weighted average of the values of a select list of shares. The composite value of the shares gets reflected in the index. The list keeps on changing with the passage of time. The two most important indices of India are the SENSEX and the NIFTY.

- **SENSEX**

The Bombay Stock Exchange sensitive index (SENSEX) is a market capitalisation weighted index of the shares of 30 select companies. The index has been prepared by taking those companies which are the most representative sample of large, well-established and financially sound enterprises, also known as blue chip companies. The Sensex extensively appears in newspapers and television. It is extensively used to measure the day-to-day performance of India's stock markets.

The BSE index is taken as a benchmark index of India's capital market. It is treated as the barometer of the Indian Stock Markets since it indicates the state (health) of these markets. The year 1979 is taken as the base and its base value has been fixed at 100 points. It was first computed in 1986. The Sensex serves the following purposes:

(i) *To measure movements in the stock market:* The Sensex reflects movements (ups and downs) in the Indian stock markets. It is widely used to judge the health of the markets.

(ii) *Benchmark for funds:* Since the Sensex consists of only blue chip companies, it gives a balanced representation of India's industrial economy. This makes it possible for fund managers to use it as the benchmark to assess the performance of their mutual funds.

In truth, small investors institutional investors and money managers extensively use this index for their own specific purposes since it answers their needs.

The Sensex is reconstituted (revised) from time to time in order to represent the changing profile of the Indian economy. The companies included in this index and their weights are revised at periodic intervals.

- **NIFTY**

The Nifty is the stock index of 50 large companies on the national stock exchange. It is treated as the flagship index of the National Stock Exchange (NSE). It is calculated by taking a weighted average of 50 constituent scrips. It represents (captures) over 50 different sectors of the Indian economy.

Nifty is useful for various reasons. These are the following:

The Nifty helps investors and laypersons to judge the state of the stock market and the Indian economy. The rise in Nifty gives a signal that Indian companies are performing well and the economy is in the upswing (i.e., recovery/prosperity phase) of the business cycle.

Individual and institutional investors can use the Nifty to keep a track on market movements. This makes it possible to compare the performance of a specific company in the context of the overall movement of the market.

Shareholders can assess the performance of management of their company. Jobbers and brokers in the stock exchange can judge market sentiments to assess whether there is any irrational exuberance. Like the Sensex, Nifty is also reconstituted from time to time.

14.8 SEBI — OBJECTIVES AND FUNCTIONS

The number of investors in the securities market in India increased steadily during the 1980s. At the same time, various unfair practices on the part of companies, brokers, merchant bankers and investment advisers were detected by the Government. In order to give investor protection, the Government of India established the Securities and Exchange Board of India (SEBI) in April 1988 under the administrative control of the Finance Ministry. Subsequently, it became a statutory body having perpetual existence and common seal under the Securities and Exchange Board of India Act, 1992.

Companies trading on the National Stock Exchange (NSE) must register with the Securities and Exchange Board of India (SEBI) and provide it with annual updates. The SEBI also established specific guidelines which companies must follow when issuing financial securities such as equity shares, debentures or bonds. For example, before issuing either equity shares or debentures for sale to the public, a company must file a detailed registration statement with the SEBI which includes extensive economic and financial information. The condensed version of that registration document — called a prospectus — must be sent to all prospective investors, i.e., those who are desirous of buying shares and securities. A company must file a prospectus with the SEBI before being able to issue stock.

Companies trading on the National Stock Exchange must register with the SEBI and provide it with annual updates.

The SEBI is the central agency that has the responsibility for regulating various stock exchanges in India. It plays both a supervisory and a regulatory role over the functioning of stock exchanges spread throughout the country. It has been set up as a statutory body with a view:

(i) to help investors by requiring full disclosure of financial information by firms selling stocks;

(ii) to regulate and improve the functioning of the stock markets in India and

(iii) to promote the overall development of India's capital market.

14.8.1 The Five Objectives of the SEBI

Five main objectives of the SEBI are the following:

(i) to regulate the functioning of all the stock exchanges in India,

(ii) to protect the rights and promote the interests of investors,

(iii) to educate the investors,

(iv) to prevent unfair trading practices and thus to ensure fair dealing in stock exchanges, and

(v) to evolve and enforce a code of conduct and establish fair prices for intermediaries such as brokers, merchant bankers, underwriters and bankers to the issue.

> **SYNOPSIS FOR LEARNING: THE ULTIMATE OBJECTIVE OF SEBI**
>
> The ultimate objective of SEBI is to protect the investors from unfair trading practices, to regulate the working of the securities market and to promote the development of India's capital market.

14.8.2 The Functions of SEBI

The functions of SEBI can be classified into three broad categories: (i) investor protection, (ii) security market regulations and (iii) development of the capital market. These are now discussed in details:

1. **Investor protection:** SEBI gives protection to investors by taking the following major steps:

   (i) *Prohibiting price rigging:* The SEBI seeks to ensure that there is no scope for price rigging. Price rigging refers to an attempt to make a profit on a security market by overriding the normal market forces. This often involves taking a long position or a short position in the market which is quite substantial to influence share prices and then supporting or depressing the market by further purchases or sales. The SEBI holds price rigging in the securities market in check by prohibiting all types of unfair practices. It keeps a close watch on operators so that there is no price rigging.

   (ii) *Checking fraudulent practices:* The SEBI holds fraudulent practices by corporate enterprises in check making new issues of securities. For instance it takes strong actions against the directors of a company if it finds that the prospectus contains wrong information which induces investors to purchase securities.

   (iii) *Prohibiting insider trading:* The SEBI prohibits insider trading. It has established guidelines to prevent insiders within the company from taking advantages of privileged information they may have. Insider trading refers to usage of knowledge or information which individuals gain through their position which allows them to benefit unfairly from fluctuations in share prices. Insiders within a firm are permitted to buy and sell shares in the company they work for on the basis of information about shares not available to the investing public.

   Insider trading occurs when employees of an organisation buy its shares by taking unfair advantage of information not available to the investing public.

   (iv) *Educating investors:* The SEBI has adopted several steps such as issue of small brochures and training of investors. The objective is to educate investors in share trading.

2 **Regulation:** The SEBI performs the following functions in its role of a regulator:

   (i) *Conducting security transaction:* The SEBI regulates the conduct of security transaction by enforcing various rules and regulations.

   (ii) *Controlling different players:* The SEBI controls and regulates the functions of those who are directly or indirectly associated with the securities market. In this context, mention may be made of stock brokers, sub-brokers, share transfer agents, bankers to an issue, trustees of various trust deeds, registrars to issue, merchant bankers, underwriters, portfolio managers, and investment advisors or consultants. It also gets the activities of relevant persons registered.

(iii) *Controlling investment scheme:* The SEBI regulates the working of collective investment schemes including those of mutual funds. Prior SEBI registration is required by the relevant financial institutions before commencing business.

(iv) *Self-regulation:* The SEBI promotes and regulates self-regulatory organisations.

(v) *Controlling insider trading:* The SEBI holds insider trading in check and controls takeover bids. It can take penal measures against hostile take-overs or mergers. Recall that insider trading involves buying or selling a stock on the basis of company information not available to the investing public. [It is sometimes difficult to identify insider trading.]

(vi) *Share acquisition:* The SEBI regulates the acquisition of a major portion of shares (51% or more) of a company.

(viii) *Checking unfair trading practises:* The SEBI takes necessary steps to check fraudulent and unfair trade practices in the securities market.

(viii) *Inspection and enquiry:* Through direct inspection, holding of enquiry and audit of the stock exchanges and intermediaries the SEBI exercises direct and indirect control of the securities market.

3. **Development of the capital market:** The SEBI performs the following functions as per as the development of India's capital market is concerned.

   (i) *Trading of intermediaries:* The SEBI undertakes various programmes for the training of intermediaries such as jobbers and brokers.

   (ii) *Provision of information:* The SEBI provides necessary information to investors about the working of the securities market. The basic objective is to educate the investors.

   (iii) *Promoting on-line trading:* The SEBI promotes on-line trading through the registered stock brokers.

   (iv) *Conducting equity research:* Finally, the SEBI conducts equity research and publishes useful information on the basis of it for the benefit of investors, traders and other intermediaries.

14.8.3 The Role of SEBI

The SEBI has been making ceaseless efforts since its very inception for ensuring smooth functioning and steady growth of India's capital market. It has also been playing a key role in protecting investors. Over the years, it has taken the following steps to accomplish its objectives:

(i) Registration of all brokers and sub-brokers at different stock exchanges.

(ii) Registration and control of merchant bankers which make initial public issues.

(iii) Control and regulation of mutual funds.

(iv) Holding insider trading in check.

(v) Issue of regulations for portfolio managers.

(vi) Issue of broad and clear guidelines for disclosure and investor protection.

(vii) Issue of guidelines for the Governing Boards of stock exchanges.

(viii) Formation of advisory committees for both segments of capital markets (primary and secondary).

(ix) Launching of Stock Invest Scheme to stop delayed refunds.

(x) To hold misuse of promoters' quota in check.
(xi) Issue of clear guidelines for preventing arbitrary and uncontrolled pricing of initial public issues.
(xii) Fixing rules for active participation of foreign institutional investors in the securities market.
(xiii) Issuing clear guidelines for floatation of public sectors bonds.
(xiv) Launching of demat trading in shares and securities .
(xv) Formulation of code for mergers (acquisitions) and (hostile) takeovers.

In short, the SEBI has made quite some progress and achieved success in fulfilling its declared objectives. It has emerged as the leader, supervisor, advisor and controller of India's financial market and financial system.

Key Points

1. **Stock exchange.** The stock exchange is an organisation where members can buy and sell (exchange) securities such as shares, debentures and bonds on behalf of companies and individual investors. Only those securities which are listed in the official book of stock exchanges can be traded. The Securities Contracts (Regulation) Act 1956 has the most comprehensive definition of the stock exchange. According to the Act a stock exchange is "an association, organisation or body of individuals, whether incorporated or not, established for the purpose of assisting, regulating and controlling business in buying, selling and dealing in securities". The stock exchange is also known as the stock market or the securities market. It deals in such securities as equity and preference shares, debentures or bonds issued by both joint stock companies and public corporations. A stock exchange is organised by an association of its members which includes both jobbers and brokers.

2. **Functions and importance of stock exchange**
   (i) Ensuring liquidity
   (ii) Price determination
   (iii) Information transmission
   (iv) Long-term funding
   (v) Building people's financial future
   (vi) Ready market
   (vii) Mobilisation of savings
   (viii) Raising capital
   (ix) Safety of transactions
   (x) Barometer of economic progress
   (xi) Efficient allocation of capital
   (xii) Control of corporate sector
   (xiii) Acting as a source of business information

(xiv) Valuing wealth

(xv) Assessment of compensation payments.

3. **The National Stock Exchange of India (NSEI):** The National Stock Exchange of India was set up by public financial (term-lending) institutions and nationalised commercial banks in November, 1992. It became operational from July 1, 1994 with a view to providing country-wide screen-based and on-line trading facilities to numerous investors scattered all over the country through an electronic clearing-cum-settlement system.

4. **Over the Counter Exchange of India (OTCEI):** All securities are not traded on registered stock exchanges. The over-the-counter (OTC) market provides companies and investors with means to trade stocks not listed on national security exchanges (such as the NSEI). The OTC market is a network of several thousand brokers who maintain connection (contacts) with one another and buy and sell securities through a nationwide electronic system. Trading is conducted between two parties directly, instead of through an exchange.

5. **The Securities and Exchange Board of India (SEBI):** The SEBI is the central agency that has responsibility for regulating various stock exchanges in India. It plays both a supervisory and a regulatory role over the functioning of stock exchanges spread throughout the country. Companies trading on the National Stock Exchange must register with the SEBI and provide it with annual updates. The SEBI has been set up a statutory body with a view:

   (i) to help investors by requiring full disclosure of financial information by firms selling stocks;

   (ii) to regulate and improve the function of the securities markets; and

   (iii) to promote the development of India's capital market.

KEY Terms	
Brokers	Secondary market
Jobbers	Blue chirps
Bulls	Barometer of economic progress
Bears	Ex-dividend
Cum-dividend	Stock market index
Spot delivery	SENSEX
Forward delivery	NIFTY
Insider trading	SEBI
Share acquisition	NSE
Equity research	Educating investors
On-line trading	Price rigging

Assignments

SHORT ANSWER-TYPE QUESTIONS

1. Define a stock exchange. Why is it called people's capitalism?
2. State any two functions of a stock exchange.
3. Mention the names of four main stock exchanges in India.
4. What is a Bull?
5. What is a Bear?
6. What is a Stag?
7. What is the full form of the following terms?
   SENSEX, NIFTY, SEBI

ESSAY-TYPE QUESTIONS

1. What is stock exchange? Briefly discuss its functions.
2. Explain the services rendered by a stock exchange to the investors and to the traders.
3. Explain the following terms:
   (i) Ex-dividend (ii) Cum-dividend
   (iii) Spot delivery (iv) Forward delivery.
4. Distinguish between the following pairs of words which represent two sides of the same coin:
   (i) Broker and jobber (ii) Bull and bear
   (iii) Ex-dividend and cum-dividend (iv) Spot delivery and forward delivery.
5. What are objectives of SEBI?
6. Discuss the functions of SEBI.

QUESTION BANK

1. *Define a stock exchange.*

Ans. See text.

2. *What is a stock exchange?*

Ans. A stock exchange, according to the Securities Contracts Regulation Act, 1956, "is an association, organisation or body of individuals whether incorporated or not, established for the purpose of assisting, regulating and controlling business in buying, selling and dealing in securities".

3. *State the essential features of a stock exchange.*

Ans. See text.

4. *State any two functions of a stock exchange.*

Ans. See text.

5. *Why is stock exchange called the barometer of an economic?*

Ans. See text.

6. *Explain the importance of stock exchange.*

Ans. See text.

7. *Explain the functions of a stock exchange.*

Ans. See text.

8. *Explain the services rendered by stock exchanges to the members of society.*

Ans. See text.

9. *List the recognised stock exchanges in India.*

Ans. There are 21 recognised stock exchanges in India, located in:
Mumbai, Kolkata, Delhi, Chennai, Ahmedabad, Hyderabad, Bangalore, Pune, Cochin, Guwahati, Indore, Jaipur, Kanpur, Ludhiana, Bhubaneshwar, Coimbatore, Mangalore, Patna, Rajkot, Vadodara. In addition there is National Stock Exchange (NSE), Mumbai.

10. *Who is a broker?*

Ans. A broker is an intermediary between a buyer and a seller in a stock market who works receives commission by purchasing and selling shares on behalf of clients.

11. *Who is a jobber?*

Ans. A jobber is a dealer in securities who always buys and sells specific securities at all times in his own account and is a market maker (or even a speculator). Normally, a jobber is permitted to deal only with brokers and not with the general public.

12. *Who is a bull on the stock exchange?*

Ans. See text.

13. *What is meant by a bear on the stock exchange?*

Ans. A bear is a speculator who sells security in expectation of a fall in prices. Bears who sell securities which they do not possess are described as having 'sold short'.

14. *What is listing?*

Ans. The term 'listing' comes from the published list issued by the stock exchange authorities.

15. *What is listed security?*

Ans. A listed security is one which has been officially accepted for trading and quotation on a recognised stock exchange.

16. *What is meant by spot delivery?*

Ans. See text.

17. *Who is a stag on a stock exchange?*

Ans. A stag is a speculator who subscribes to new issues, in the expectation that they will rise to the premium over issue prices and who sells the allotment of securities at a profit when dealings in them begin.

18. *Discuss the objectives of SEBI.*

Ans. See text.

19. *Explain the functions of SEBI.*

Ans. See text.

20. *What is future trading? How does it differ from forward trading (contract)?*

Ans. The term 'futures' is used to refer to a vehicle for the purchase and sell of financial instruments at some future date. Futures take the form of a fixed and binding contract for a fixed number of shares to be sold at a fixed price at a fixed future date.

Future is a negotiable instrument. It differs from a forward contract since futures contracts are in fixed numbers of shares intended to be traded, whereas forward contracts are once-only transactions.

21. *What do the following abbreviations stand for: (a) BSE, (b) NSE.*

Ans. (a) BSE: Bombay Stock Exchange

(b) NSE: National Stock Exchange

22. *Expand the following assignment acronyms: (a) DSE, (b) ASE*

Ans. (a) DSE: Delhi Stock Exchange

(b) ASE: Ahmedabad Stock Exchange

APPENDICES

COMPANIES INCLUDED IN SENSEX

- ITC
- HDFC
- Tata Consultancy Services
- ONGC
- Axis Bank
- Bharti Airtel
- Maruti Suzuki
- NTPC
- Dr. Reddya Laboratory
- BHEL
- Reliance ind.
- L & T
- HDFC Bank
- SBI
- Sun Pharmaceuticals
- Hind. Unilever
- Wipro
- Bajaj Auto
- Coal India
- Cipla
- Tata Power
- Infosys Tech
- ICICI Bank
- Tata Motors
- M & M
- Tata Steel
- Sesa Goa
- Hero Honda
- Gail India
- Hindalco

COMPANIES INCLUDED IN NIFTY

- ITC
- HDFC
- ICICI Bank
- HDFC
- SBI
- Sun Pharmaceuticals
- Bharti Airtel
- Tata Steel
- Reddy's Laboratory
- Bajaj Auto
- Hindalco
- United Spirits
- Coal India
- Cipla
- Tata Power
- BPCL
- ACC
- Reliance Industries
- L & T
- HDFC Bank
- Tata Motors
- Hind. Unliver
- M & M
- Sesa Sterlit
- Kotak Mahindra Bank
- Tech Mahindra
- UltraTech Cement
- Lupin
- Hero MotoCorp
- Cairn
- Grasim Inds.
- IDFC
- Bank of Baroda
- NMDC
- DLP
- Infosys Tech
- Infosys
- ONGC
- Axis Bank
- HCL Techno
- Wipro
- Maruti Suzuk
- NTPC
- Asian Paints
- Power Grid
- Induslnd Bank
- GAIL (I)
- BHEL
- Ambuja Cement
- Punjab National Bank
- Jindal Steel

Note: The lists keep on changing from time to time. For the latest position, contact the concerned stock exchanges.

THE NOMENCLATURE OF STOCK EXCHANGE (THE TERMS USED IN STOCK EXCHANGE)

1. Blue chip. The term blue chip refers to the equity shares of highly large and reputed companies. Such companies normally have high market capitalisation and a liquid market for their shares.
2. Trading floor (ring). This refers to the area in a financial market set aside for face-to-face dealing between (among) floor traders. Only members and their authorised agents can enter the trading floor or the ring of the stock exchange. With the use of automated screen trading, floor trading has become much less frequent of late.
3. Stock. A stock is a financial security (an ordinary share) issued by a joint stock company as a means of raising long-term capital. Stockholders are equivalent of shareholders and are the owners of the company.
4. Shares. A share is one of number of titles of ownership in a company. A share confers on its owner a legal right to a part of the company's profit (usually by payment of a dividend) and to any voting right attaching to that share.
5. Share capital. Share capital refers to the money employed in a joint stock company which has been subscribed by its shareholders in the form of ordinary shares and which will remain as a permanent source of finance as long as the company remains in existence.
6. Share certificate. A share certificate provides evidence of ownership of shares in a company. It states the name of the company, the number and class of shares owned, and the serial number of the shares. It is stamped by the common seal of the company and usually signed by at least one director and the company secretary. It is not a negotiable instrument.
7. Scrip. A scrip refers to the certificates that show ownership of shares or debentures (i.e., the capital raised by subscription.)
8. Dividends. This is part of a firm's profits that a firm may (but is not required to) distribute to stockholders as either cash payments or additional shares of stock. Dividends are declared by a corporation's board of directors and are generally paid annually (and sometimes twice a year, called interim dividends).
9. Stag. A person who applies for shares in a new issue with the expectation that the price when trading begins will be higher than the issue price. Often measures are taken by the issues to prevent excessive stagging. Issues often scale down share applications to prevent such quick profit-taking.
10. New issue. Any new security, but especially a share being offered on a stock exchange for the first time. [See 'Floatation in the text'.]
11. Kerb market. Any informal financial market such as one for dealing in securities not listed on a stock exchange.
12. Issue price. The price at which a new issue of shares is sold to the public.
13. Issuing house. A financial institution, usually a merchant bank or an investment bank, which specialises in the flotation of private companies on a stock exchange.
14. Issue by tender. A type of offer for sale in which an issuing house asks investors to tender for a new issue of shares of other securities, which are then allocated to the highest bidder. Normally, the tender document states the lowest price acceptable.

15. Offer for sale. An invitation to the general public to purchase the stock of a company through an intermediary, such as a merchant bank or an issuing house. This method of floating of shares is of two types: a public issue and an issue by tender.
16. Underwriter. A financial institution, usually a merchant bank, which guarantees to buy a proportion of any unsold shares, bonds, etc. when a new issue is offered to the investing public.
17. Private placing. The selling of shares in a company to a selected group of individual or institutions either as a means of floatation or to raise additional capital for a listed company.
18. Introduction. A method of issuing new shares in which a broker or an issuing house takes small quantities of a company's shares and issues them to clients at opportune moments. It is also used by existing public companies which wish to issue additional shares.
19. Long position. A position held in securities such that a rise in the market increases the value of the position.
20. Stock split. In a stock split, the par value per share is reduced and the number of shares is increased proportionately. This has been done by Bharti Airtel recently.
21. Share buybacks. A share buyback means that a company repurchases its own shares from the market. This has been done by Reliance Industries a few years ago. This has been done since management believe that the stock of the company was undervalued.
22. Initial public offering (IPO): It refers to the process by which a private firm sells shares of stock to the public for the first time in the new issue market mainly through a merchant bank.
23. Jobber: Traditionally jobber has been treated as a wholesale stock dealer who bought and sold shares in his (her) own account. Now this function is being performed by market makers.
24. Broker: An agent who buys and sell securities on a stock exchange on behalf of clients and receives remuneration for this service in the form of commission.
25. Market maker: An intermediary who creates a market for a financial obligation — a dealer in securities on the stock exchange who undertakes to buy and sell securities as a principal and is, therefore, obliged to announce buying and selling prices for a particular security at a particular time.
26. Bull and bear: If the actual prices of shares are higher than their expected or normal levels a bullish tendency is supposed to exist in the stock exchange. This is observed during economic upturn or prosperity. By contrast when actual share prices fall below their expected levels a bearish tendency is supposed to exist in the stock exchange. This is observed if there is economic downturn such as a brief recession or even a mild depression.

15

WHOLESALE TRADE (WHOLESALERS)

SYLLABUS

- *Wholesales.*
- *Meaning and services of wholesaler to retailer, customer and producer.*

> *Wholesaling is the function of by-products in relatively large quantities from manufacturers and 'breaking bulk', and on-selling these products in smaller quantities to retailers.*— Collins Dictionary of Business

LEARNING OUTCOMES

On completion of this chapter, you will be able to understand the following:

15.1 Meaning and Definition of Wholesale Trade
15.2 Characteristics of a Wholesaler
15.3 Necessity or Functions of a Wholesaler
15.4 Services of a Wholesaler
15.5 Types of Wholesalers
15.6 Survival or Elimination of Wholesalers

In this and the next chapters, we will be concerned with channels of distribution, i.e., the route used in the physical distribution of a product from its manufacturer to the ultimate buyer of that product. Functionally, a typical distribution channel consists of three basic interrelated operations:

(a) manufacturing (making the product);
(b) wholesaling (the holding of large stocks and 'breaking-bulk' into retail packs); and
(c) retailing (the sale of the product to the final buyer).

In truth, depending upon the trade practice, the nature of the product and the characteristics of the market being served, and the relative costs and marketing effectiveness of using different channel intermediaries, a number of distributive channels configurations may be identified as Figure 15.1 illustrates. Line 1 shows a conventional channel structure with the products through independent intermediaries at each separate stage. Alternatively (Line 2), a retailer such as a super-

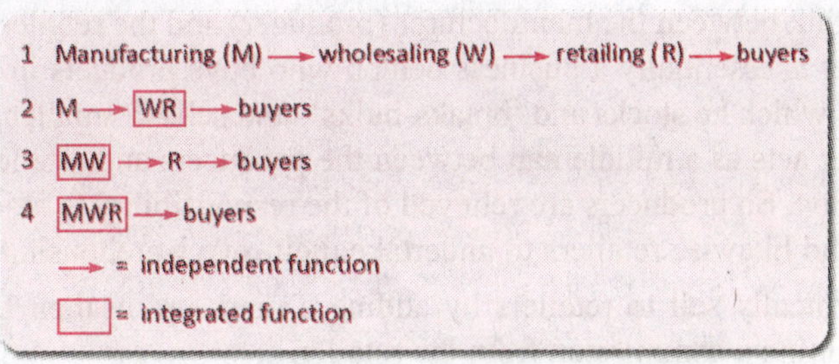

FIGURE 15.1: Examples of Typical Channels of Distribution

market chain may buy in bulk directly from manufacturers and undertake the wholesaling function itself as an integrated wholesaling-retailing operation; a manufacturer may combine the production and wholesaling functions (line 3), on-selling to independent retailers, or, alternatively, combine all three operations (line 4), selling direct to final buyers.

Additionally, at some stage in a channel, Sales Agents, whose primary function is to generate new business contacts, may be employed. They may be employed by a manufacturer to obtain new wholesale customers or a wholesaler seeking new retail accounts. In Fig. 15.2 we illustrate distribution network (chain) of Kitchenware (UK)

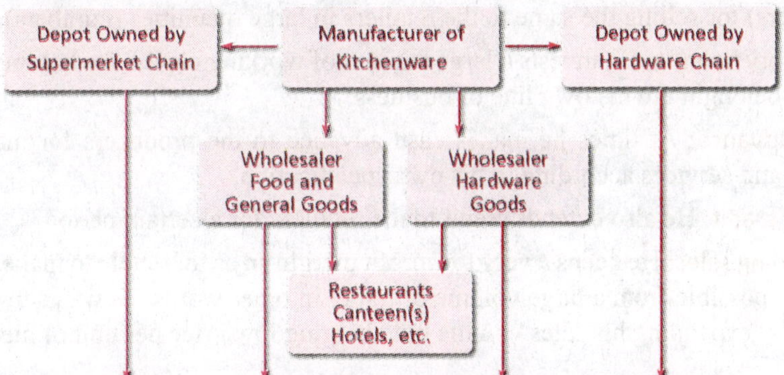

FIGURE 15.2: Some Distribution Channels for Kitchenware

15.1 MEANING AND DEFINITION OF WHOLESALE TRADE

The term 'wholesale trade' or simply 'wholesaling' refers to the function of buying products in relatively large quantities from manufacturers and 'breaking bulk', and selling these products in small quantities to retailers. Now we pass on to a detailed discussion of wholesale trade.

15.1.1 Meaning of Wholesale Trade (Wholesaler)

The wholesaler is the middleman between producers and retailers.

A wholesaler is a marketing intermediary who purchases goods (merchandise) in large quantities for sale to other organisations such as retailers, manufacturers, and hospitals. A wholesaler is part of B2B system, discussed in an earlier chapter.

He is an important link between the manufacturer (producer) and the retailer in the chain of distribution. A wholesaler is essentially a business person who buys products in fairly large quantities from manufacturers which he stocks and 'breaks-bulks', and sells in smaller quantities to retailers. Thus, the wholesaler acts as a middleman between the producers and retailers of a product in the channel of distribution. So producers are relieved of the responsibility to stock and distribute their goods to retailers, and likewise retailers to undertake their own warehousing.

Wholesalers typically sell to retailers by adding a mark-up on their buying-in prices from suppliers or by obtaining a commission from the retailer.

15.2 CHARACTERISTICS OF A WHOLESALER

The main characteristic features of a wholesaler are the following:

1. **Linking producers and retailers:** The wholesaler is an essential link between the producers and the retailers.
2. **Specialised purchase and sale:** The wholesaler usually specialises in the purchase and sale of certain items belonging to a specific (particular) product line, such as say paper, food articles (like rice, sugar, salt, cloth, tea, coffee, pulses, atta etc.)
3. **Bulk purchase:** He purchases goods in bulk quantities (numbers) from producers (manufacturers) for selling the same to the retailers in large quantities (numbers).
4. **Inventory holding:** He invests a large amount of working capital for holding inventories of goods belonging to his own line of business.
5. **Cash advance:** At times he makes cash advance to the producers for manufacturing of goods and services according to his own specification.
6. **Giving credit:** He also extends credit to the retailers for a certain period.
7. **Expanding sales:** He keeps a very low profit margin so as to be able to make as much (total) gain as possible from a large volume of trade. In other words, he wants to earn maximum profit by expanding his sales volume but charging low price per unit of merchandise sold.

15.3 NECESSITY OR FUNCTIONS OF A WHOLESALER

The above functions conjointly lead to smooth flow of goods (merchandise) from producers to consumers as shown in Table 15.1.

TABLE 15.1: Functions of a Full-Time Wholesaler

A full-service wholesaler will	The wholesaler may perform the following services for customers
1. Provide a sales force for selling the goods to retailers and other buyers.	1. Buy goods the market for final goods need and make them available to customers.
2. Communicate manufacturer's advertising deals and plans.	2. Hold inventory, thus reducing customers' costs.
3. Maintain inventory, thus reducing the amount of the inventory suppliers have to hold.	3. Send goods to customers as quickly as possible.

contd.

4. Arrange transportation facilities.	4. Provide market information and business consultancy services.
5. Supply capital by paying cash or ensuring quick payments for goods.	5. Provide financing through granting credit, which is especially critical to small retailers.
6. Provide suppliers with market information they cannot afford to collect or cannot gather themselves.	6. Order goods in the types and quantities as desired (specified) by customers.
7. Undertake credit risk by granting credit to customers, and absorbing any bad debts, thus relieving the supplier of this burden.	7. Undertake market research to know the changing needs of customers
8. Assume product-related risk by taking title.	

15.4 SERVICES OF A WHOLESALER

The wholesalers render the following services to manufacturers, retailers and customers:

15.4.1 Services to Producers or Manufacturers

1. *Facilitating mass production:* The wholesaler facilitates mass production of goods by enabling the manufacturer produce on a large scale and thus derive to the advantage of large scale associated with it. The manufacturer expands his scale of production only if there is an assured market for his product (which is created by the wholesaler)
2. *Burden sharing:* The wholesaler enables the manufacturer to specialise fully in manufacturing, by being relieved of the burden of distributing his product (as also and, at the same time, by being free from the risks associated with it.)
3. *Transmitting market information:* Due to their links with retailers who, in their turn, are in direct touch with customers or the actual (final) buyers of goods (merchandise), the wholesaler transmits important information about changes in tastes and preferences, fashions and needs of consumers to producers (manufacturer).
4. *Production focus:* The wholesaler purchases the goods immediately after production and store them until demand for them appears in the market. This enables the manufacturer to concentrate fully on production.
5. *Risk-taking:* The wholesaler takes risks associated with dealing in the goods produced by different manufacturers, more so in case of perishable goods which cannot be returned if they remain unsold.
6. *Financial assistance:* The wholesaler makes advance to the manufacturer against the goods to be purchased.
7. *Storage and transportation:* Wholesalers set up distribution warehouses which store goods until they are needed. Many organisations exchange tangible goods which require storage while they are waiting to be sold, largely due to time lag between production and sale (consumption). For example, books, dry fruits and even clothing require some degree of storage between the time they leave the manufacturer and when they need delivery to customers. Wholesalers provide the necessary storage service. They who provide transportation facilities by giving free delivery to retailers and sometimes to customers (in case of direct sales).

15.4.2 Services to Retailers

The wholesaler offers the following services to retailers:

1. *Ready supply of goods:* For supplying a large variety of goods to the consumers, the retailer has to depend upon the wholesalers. By doing this the retailers are relieved of the trouble of searching out and identifying goods from different manufacturers located at different places.
2. *Advantages of small purchase:* By being able to purchase different varieties of goods in small quantities from the wholesalers, the retailers can manage their operation with a small amount of working capital and minimise the cost of holding finished goods inventories.
3. *Credit facility:* The wholesalers make sale of goods to the retailers on credit. And retailers are enabled to make payments to the wholesalers after realising their sales revenue.
4. *Costless transmission of information:* The wholesalers give information to retailers on the arrival of new types of products in the markets (as also their prices, features and uses) from time to time.
5. *Assumption of risk:* The wholesalers save the retailers from various types of risks of storing the goods such as spoilage, pilferage, loss of weight, etc.
6. *Provision of transport facilities:* The wholesaler makes free delivery of goods to retailers by providing transport facilities. So retailers are able to save not only money (transport cost) but time also.
7. *Facilitation of sale:* The wholesaler often assists the retailers in selling products on the basis of advertising and other sales promotional measures taken by the former.

15.4.3 Services to Customers

1. *Assured supply:* Wholesalers maintain ready stocks so as to enable customers to buy goods from retailers as and when they like.
2. *Low price:* Wholesalers are the main force behind large scale (mass) production. This, in its turn, keeps prices of merchandise low. Prices get adjusted through the operation of the impersonal market forces, i.e., demand and supply.
3. *Information:* Wholesalers furnish detailed information about types, quality and uses of new and improved products as and when they appear in the market.
4. *Matching the needs of customers:* Wholesalers make a large variety of goods available to match the needs and wants of customers. Customers have a wide choice to match their tastes and preferences.
5. *Market research:* Big wholesalers conduct market research to improve product quality and to help producers know the changes in tastes and preferences of buyers. Consumers indirectly gain from such research.

In Fig. 15.3 we list the various services offered by wholesalers to manufacturers, retailers and consumers.

Thus wholesalers render various services directly to manufacturers, retailers and indirectly to customers or the final buyers of products. These functions are no doubt very important form the point of view of the smooth functioning of a country's trading system. The whole process of trading virtually starts with the wholesalers and is completed at the retail stage.

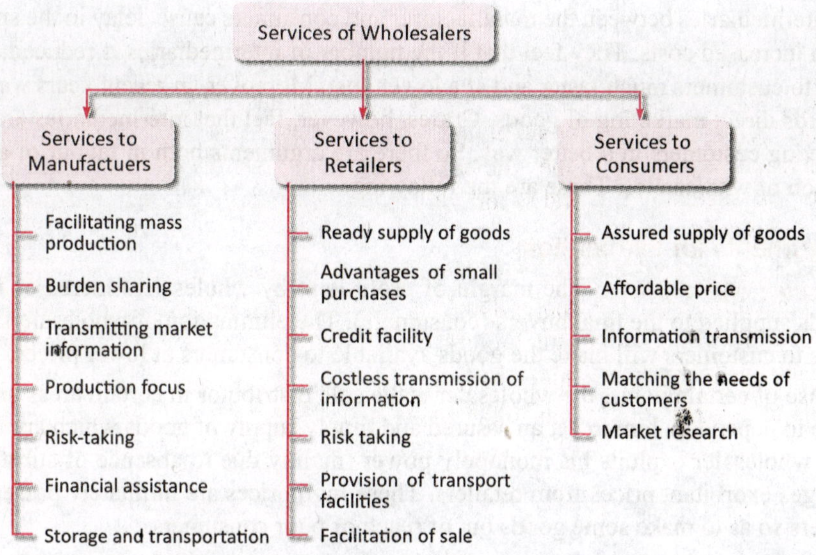

FIGURE 15.3: Multiple Service Provided by Wholesalers

15.5 TYPES OF WHOLESALERS

Wholesalers are of the following four types:

1. Merchant wholesalers: They are independently owned firms which take title to the goods they handle. Such independent wholesalers may operate a single warehouse or a chain of warehouses giving wider regional coverage and in many cases national distribution.
2. Rack jobbers: They are wholesalers who furnish racks or shelves full of merchandise to retailers. They deal in such items as music, toy, hosiery, and health and beauty aids to retailers. They display the products and sell them on consignment. This means that they keep title to the goods until they are sold and they share the profits with the retailer.
3. Cash-and-carry wholesalers: They serve mostly small retailers with a limited assortment of products. According to Collins Dictionary of Business, " Cash and carry is a form of wholesaling which requires customers (mainly retailers) to pay cash for products bought and to collect these products themselves from a warehouse. By eliminating the costs involved in offering credit terms and a delivery service, such wholesalers are able to offer products at highly-competitive prices. In general, retailers go to such wholesalers, pay cash, and carry the goods back to their stores. An example of such a wholesaler is Kolkata Metro (located in Eastern Metropolitan bypass).
4. Drop shippers: They take orders from retailers and other wholesalers and get the goods shipped directly from a producer to a buyer. They own the goods but do not handle, stock, or deliver any good. This is done by the producers. Drop shippers tend to handle bulky products such as coal, lumber and chemicals.

15.6 SURVIVAL OR ELIMINATION OF WHOLESALERS

There is hardly any doubt that wholesalers render very useful services connected with internal trade. However, some people are sceptical about the need for wholesalers. They feel that a large number of intermediaries between the manufacturer and consumers cause delay in the smooth flow of goods and increased costs. They feel that if the number of intermediaries is reduced, goods can be delivered to customers much faster and at a lower cost. Moreover, in recent years we have seen a trend towards direct marketing of goods. Critics, however, feel that intermediaries are indispensable for serving customers in a better way. So there are arguments both in favour of and against the elimination of wholesalers. These are the following:

15.6.1 Arguments for Elimination

1. *Charging higher prices:* The margin of profit kept by wholesalers increases the cost of goods supplied to the final buyers (consumers). The elimination of wholesalers and direct sales to customers will make the goods available to consumers at lower prices.

   In case of certain items, the wholesaler is the sole distributor in certain areas and retailers have to depend on him to get an assured and timely supply of goods which are in demand. The wholesaler exploits his monopoly power (mainly due to absence of substitutes) and charges exorbitant prices from retailers. These high prices are ultimately passed on to the buyers so as to make some goods out of reach of poor consumers.
2. *Creating artificial shortage:* By hoarding goods and thus restricting the free flow of goods from manufacturers to consumers, wholesalers create artificial shortage. They do this with the expectation of selling the same at higher prices later.
3. *Adulteration:* Some wholesalers even go to the extent of indulging in adulteration of goods. The objective is to make more profit than what is possible through normal trading practice.
4. *Direct marketing:* Wholesalers have no role to play in case of products which are sold directly by manufacturers, for example, Bombay Dyeing, Titan, Raymond's, Tanishq, etc.
5. *Large retailers:* In case of certain products, large and well-established retailers can afford to buy their requirements in bulk directly from the producers or manufacturers. This makes the services of wholesalers useless or the wholesalers totally redundant.
6. *Speculation:* Many wholesalers engage in unethical trade practices such as speculation to make quick profits by exploiting the consumers.

15.6.2 Arguments against Elimination

1. *Key link:* Wholesalers form a key link in the channel of distribution. By performing various functions they render valuable services to customers. How? By ensuring smooth flow of goods from producers to consumers.
2. *Specialisation:* Since wholesalers have specialised knowledge of goods, they are able to operate on a large scale. And in the process they relieve the manufacturers of diverse functions which are expensive and difficult for them to perform. Because of wholesalers, manufacturers can concentrate on production fully.
3. *Country-wide distribution:* Most goods are produced by numerous small units or enterprises. Retailers are usually small and remain scattered here and there. So wholesalers are indispensable for transferring goods from producing to distant consuming centres all over the country.
4. *Warehousing and stock-holding (storage):* Due to the presence of wholesalers, both manufacturers and retailers are relieved of the burden of maintaining huge stocks of goods in their warehouse (which most of them do not have) and bearing the costs of holding inventories.

Conclusion

On balance it appears that is not easy to eliminate the wholesalers from the channel of distribution. However, because of high distribution costs, some companies such as Woodland and Wal-Mart have been trying to eliminate independent wholesalers from their systems and do the job themselves. This means that they provide their own warehouses and have their own trucks (See Table 15.1). As things stand today, it is not possible to eliminate the wholesaler. His services are indispensable and invariable because no manufacturer or retailer can offer these services so efficiently like the wholesaler. And as long as the wholesaler performs marketing functions more efficiently and at lower costs than other intermediaries, the survival of the wholesaler will not be threatened. The presence of wholesalers and their active participation in the channel of distribution enable both manufacturers and retailers to perform their own specialised functions. However, what is of paramount importance is that the wholesalers render their functions satisfactorily and to the best advantage of manufacturers, retailers and consumers.

Key Points

1. **Wholesaler:** A wholesaler is essentially a merchant or a trader who sells large quantities for retail purposes only and does not sell directly to the general public. He collects goods from manufacturers and sells the same in different quantities to different types of retailers. Three main types of wholesalers are the following:
   (a) Pure wholesalers, who concentrates fully on bulk buying and selling in large quantities.
   (b) Manufacturer wholesaler, who nicely combincs thc functions of manufacturing and product distribution with different types of retailers .
   (c) Retailers wholesaler, who sells goods to both retailers and consumers through his own retail outlets.
2. **Functions of wholesalers:** By performing various types of functions, the wholesaler gives various types of service to manufacturers, retailers and consumers. Thus he forms an important link between producers and retailers from one side and retailers and consumers from another side. The function of wholesalers are: (i) buying and assembling, (ii) storage and warehousing, (iii) transportation, (iv) grading and packaging, (v) financing, (vi) risk-taking, (vii) information transmission, (viii) promotion, (ix) market research.
3. **Elimination of wholesalers:** There are arguments both in favour of and against elimination of wholesalers. Since they perform a number of very important and useful functions they cannot be (or should not be) eliminated easily and quickly.

KEY Terms	
Braking bulk	Elimination of the wholesalers
Channel of distribution	Wholesale trade
Buying and assembling	Sales agents
Storage and warehousing	Grading and packing
Provision of transport facilities	Risk taking
Financial assistance	Market research

Assignments

SHORT ANSWER-TYPE QUESTIONS

1. Give two arguments in favour of survival of wholesalers. [ISC 1988]
2. List two services of a wholesaler to a retailer. [ISC 1990]
3. Mention two characteristics of wholesale trade. [ISC 1992]
4. Give two reasons for the elimination of wholesalers. [ISC 1992]

ESSAY-TYPE QUESTIONS

1. Explain the meaning and describe the characteristics of wholesale trade.
2. Briefly discuss the functions of a wholesaler.
3. (a) Discuss five services rendered by wholesalers and large-scale retailers. [ISC 1991]
   (b) Elaborate briefly the causes which have led to the decline in the importance of wholesalers.
   (c) Briefly discuss four important documents that pass between a wholesaler and a retailer. [ISC 1992]
4. (a) Discuss briefly the chief functions of a wholesaler.
   (b) Describe five similarities between wholesalers and large-scale retailers.
5. (a) Discuss the essential characteristics of wholesale trade.
   (b) What role does a wholesaler play in the marketing of goods? [ISC 1990]
6. Explain the main types of wholesalers.

QUESTION BANK

1. *Define a wholesaler.*

Ans. See text.

2. *Explain the functions of a wholesaler.*

Ans. text.

3. *Discuss the services rendered by wholesalers to producers and retailers.*

Ans. See text.

4. *Explain different types of wholesalers.*

Ans. See text.

5. *Is the wholesaler necessary? Do you think he should be eliminated? Give reasons for your answer.*

Ans. See text.

6. *Give arguments for and against the elimination of wholesaler.*

Ans. See text.

16

RETAIL TRADE (RETAILERS)

SYLLABUS

- *Retail trade — meaning, characteristics of retail trade. Distinction between wholesale and retail trade.*
- *Types of retail trade — Itinerant and small-scale fixed shops; departmental store, chain store, mail order houses, teleshopping, franchise, consumer cooperative stores, hypermarkets and automatic vending machines.*
- *Meaning, features, merits and demerits to be covered.*

> *Retailers operate at the final end of a distribution channel for a product or products which also includes manufacturers and wholesalers.*
>
> — Collins Dictionary of Business

LEARNING OUTCOMES

On completion of this chapter, you will be able to understand the following:

16.1 Meaning of Retail Trade
16.2 Characteristics of Retail Trade
16.3 Distinction between Wholesaler and Retailer
16.4 Necessity or Functions of a Retailer
16.5 Services of Retailers
16.6 Types of Retail Trade
16.7 Departmental Store
16.8 Chain Stores or Multiple Shops
16.9 Distinction between Departmental Stores and Chain Stores
16.10 Mail Order Business Houses
16.11 Consumers' Cooperative Stores
16.12 Supermarkets and Hypermarkets
16.13 Franchise
16.14 Teleshopping
16.15 Automatic Vending Machine

Retailers are those traders who remain engaged in the retail trade (business). A retailer forms the last link in the channel of distribution of goods. He acts as an intermediary between the wholesaler and the final buyer (consumer). He purchases goods from the wholesaler and sells the same in very small quantities to ultimate users through what is called bulk breaking. His activities remain concentrated to his own locality or the place in which his shop exists. Examples of retailers are departmental stores, superbazars, hypermarkets hawkers and, of course, small grocers (shopkeepers).

16.1 MEANING OF RETAIL TRADE

Simply put, retailing refers to the activities involved in selling directly to the ultimate consumer for personal and non-business use. It embraces direct-to-customer sales activities of the producer, whether through his own stores or by house-to-house canvassing or by mail order business.

A retailer is an individual or an organisation who (which) sells to ultimate consumers (people like you and me). Retailing includes all activities directly related to the sale of products to ultimate consumer for personal use. Retailers differ from wholesalers, who distribute the product to business, not ultimate consumers. For every successful large retailers like ASDA ; Wal-Mart, Marks and Spencer, or Tesco plc. there are thousands of small retailers. They have two common features:

(i) They link producers and end customers.

(ii) They provide a very useful (perhaps invaluable) service to both.

Retailing refers to a business which stocks a particular type of product (such as a shoe shop) or an extensive range of products (such as a department store) for sale to consumers. Retailers operate at the final end of a distribution channel for a product or products, which also involves manufacturers and wholesalers.

No doubt, some retailers (such as butchers) are involved in the preparation and packaging of products before their final sale and provide personal service. However, most retailers are engaged in selling prepackaged complete items on a self-service basis.

16.2 CHARACTERISTICS OF RETAIL TRADE

Retailer are of different types. Their scale of operation also varies. In spite of this, we find the following common characteristics of retailers:

(i) Retailers form the last and final link in the channels of distribution. They purchase mainly from wholesalers and, at times, from manufacturers even, for selling to final buyers.

(ii) Retailers sell goods in small quantities.

(iii) Retailers operate in local markets mainly due to limited size of the market for their products.

(iv) Retailers sell a wide variety of goods.

(v) Retailers normally operate near the residential areas; but at times they have their shops inside certain main markets or near some big factories.

BUSINESS FOCUS: RETAIL OUTLET

Retail outlet refers to business premises or facilities for selling products to consumers. A retail outlet takes the form of a shop or store which buyers visit to make purchases, or it could be automatic vending machine or Kiosk located in a hotel or restaurant. Apart from 'point of sale' geographically located with easy reach of prospective customers, retail sales can be made by direct delivery or through the post to a buyer's home as, for example, in mail order selling.

(vi) Very little investment is required in retailing.

(vii) Retailers usually get involved in non-price competition and provide some benefits to their customers such as short-term credit (for a month) and free home delivery.

(viii) Window dressing at the retail store is absolutely essential for attracting customers.

It refers to any practice which attempts to make a situation look better than it really is.

16.3 DISTINCTION BETWEEN WHOLESALER AND RETAILER

It is necessary for a student of commerce to know the distinction between wholesaling and retailing clearly. The distinction between the two can be understood by defining the functions of each. Some producers deal only with wholesalers and do not sell directly to retailers or to end users (consumers). Some producers deal with both wholesalers and retailers but offer much higher discount to wholesalers. In turn, some wholesalers sell to both retailers and consumers.

The difference between wholesaling and retailing is this : A retail sale refers to the sale of goods and services to consumers for their own (personal) use. A wholesale transaction is the sale of goods and services to businesses and institutions such as schools or hospitals for final use, or to wholesalers or retailers for resale.

Wholesalers make business-to-business (B2B) sales. Most of them offer a number of useful services. Traditionally, wholesalers have been providing their retail customers with credit facilities and a delivery service but in recent years cash and carry wholesaling has become a prominent feature of distribution system almost everywhere. In addition, with the emergence of large chain store retailers (for example supermarkets). The wholesaling function of stocking and breaking-bulk has itself become increasingly integrated with the retailing operation, with retailers taking particular advantage of the price discounts associated with bulk buying directly from manufacturers.

16.4 NECESSITY OR FUNCTIONS OF A RETAILER

Retailers normally perform the following functions :

(i) They collect and assemble goods from different producers (manufacturers).

(ii) They sell goods in small quantities to the customers, according to their needs and convenience.

(iii) They arrange for transporting goods from wholesalers, if the latter do not provide transport facilities.

(iv) They store goods before actual sale.

(v) At times they provide credit facilities to customers.

(vi) Some retailers even provide free home delivery to customers.

(vii) They take a portion of risk associated with any business.

(viii) Since they are in direct touch with ultimate buyers (final consumers) of goods and services, the retailers get necessary feedback from the former. The retailers then pass on the market information to wholesalers and manufacturers who derive a lot of benefit from such information.

FOCUS ON TERMINOLOGY: RETAIL OUTLET AND RETAIL MIX.

Retail outlet refers to the physical location of retail operations where goods are sold directly to consumers. Retail mix refers to the mix of variables, including locations, merchandising communications, pricing, services, physical attributes, and personnel, which form the overall strategic marketing components of retailing.

Retailers also use their bulk-buying power to obtain substantial price discounts from manufacturers and thus exert strong discretionary (market) power in the use of price as a competitive weapon. In addition, the large retailer groups have established an extensive own-label brand business in direct competition to manufacturers' brands. This has also increased their marketing opportunities by enabling them to compete closely with their rival retailers.

The functions of a retailer are listed in Fig. 16.1.

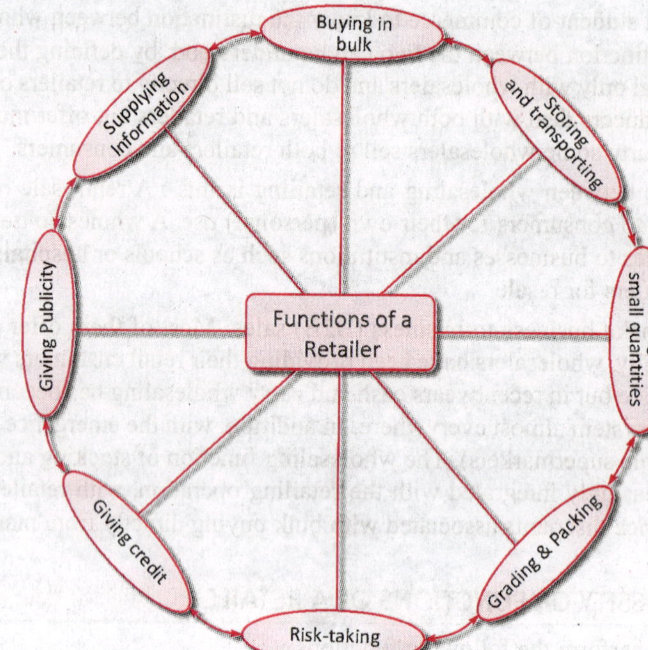

FIGURE 16.1: Functions of retailer are listed in figure

16.5 SERVICES OF RETAILERS

The retailers provide a number of useful services to both manufacturers and wholesalers and help them in selling their products to consumers. They also provide various type of services to consumers. These are discussed below.

16.5.1 Services to Manufacturers and Wholesalers

The services provided by retailers to manufacturers and wholesalers are the following:

1. *Distribution of goods:* By acting as the last link in the chain (channel) of physical distribution of goods, the retailers connect the wholesalers with the consumers.
2. *Ascertaining customers' needs:* By virtue of their direct contact with the customers, the retailers help both the manufacturers and the wholesalers in ascertaining the actual and potential needs of customers.
3. *Supplying information:* On the basis of latest and primary information about the tastes and preferences of buyers, retailers advise the wholesalers and the manufacturers on the need to effect improvements of existing products or place altogether new products on the market.
4. *Burden sharing:* Retailers relieve the wholesalers of the complex and time-consuming task of dealing with numerous customers having different requirements, diverse temperament and wide variations in purchasing power.

5. *Risk sharing:* Retailers share risks with both manufacturers and wholesalers by carrying stock of their products for future sales. Such stockholding of finished products is essential because production and sale do not always coincide.

16.5.2 Services to Consumers

The services provided by retailers to consumers are the following:

1. *Steady flow of goods:* Retailers make necessary goods available to the customers in small quantities. And since the consumers are assured of continuous supply of a goods they are not required to spend money unnecessarily to buy goods beyond their current needs. They know that they can buy any quantity of a goods they need any time they like.
2. *Wider choice.* A retailer keeps a large variety of goods produced by various different companies. So consumers get a wide variety of goods to choose from.
3. *Free advice to customers.* A retailer not only offers afters sales service but free-sales service to customers in the form of advice. This helps them to make proper choice (of a particular product) in order to satisfy their needs. He then advises them about the method of use and usefulness of different products.
4. *Personalised services.* Retailers maintain personal contacts with this customers for satisfying them in case of any complaint regarding product quality and usage.
5. *Credit facility.* Retailers offer credit to their customers for a short period. Owners of most groceries follow this practice. Most retailers such as Subway, Spencers and Pantaloons accept credit cards. The repair of TV sets virtually amounts to giving credit to customers, indirectly though. However, such service is usually provided by the manufacturers as per arrangement with retailers.
6. *Free home delivery.* Some retailers such as suppliers of fast food make free home delivery to the customers.
7. *After-sale service.* Big retailers provide after-sales service, if needed within the guarantee period (usually one year).
8. *Creation of place utility.* Being situated near residential areas, retailers supply their merchandise exactly where they are needed. This is how they create place utility.

16.6 TYPES OF RETAIL TRADE

As shown in Fig. 16.2 the retailers or retail organisations are of two main types, namely,

1. Itinerant or mobile traders, and
2. Fixed shop traders.

16.6.1 Itinerant or Mobile Retailers

In their incessant (constant) research for customers mobile vendors move from place to place to make their merchandise available everywhere. They are just like footloose industries which are capable of being located anywhere. In another sense, they are just like offshore banks which do not have any fixed location. Since they are petty traders and keep very low stocks. they are required to invest a very small amount of money to be able to carry on their business smoothly and effectively. In other words, their capital requirement is low due to high stock turnover. Hawkers, peddlers, market traders, roadside shops, etc. are all examples of itinerant vendors.

The salient features of itinerant traders are the following:

(i) In a desperate attempt to make a living somehow they move from here and there and also in public transport to reach the customers.

(ii) They usually sell low-value items of daily use such as peanuts, vegetables, fruits, toys, or even used books.

(iii) They mostly sell ordinary products manufactured locally.

(iv) They do not quote fixed prices for their products. Instead the prices are ultimately settled through haggling, negotiation or bargaining between the sellers (hawkers) and the buyers (customers).

In fact, mobile retailers operate mainly in the buyers' market, in which the sellers do not have much market power. Fig. 16.2 presents the nomenclature of retail trade.

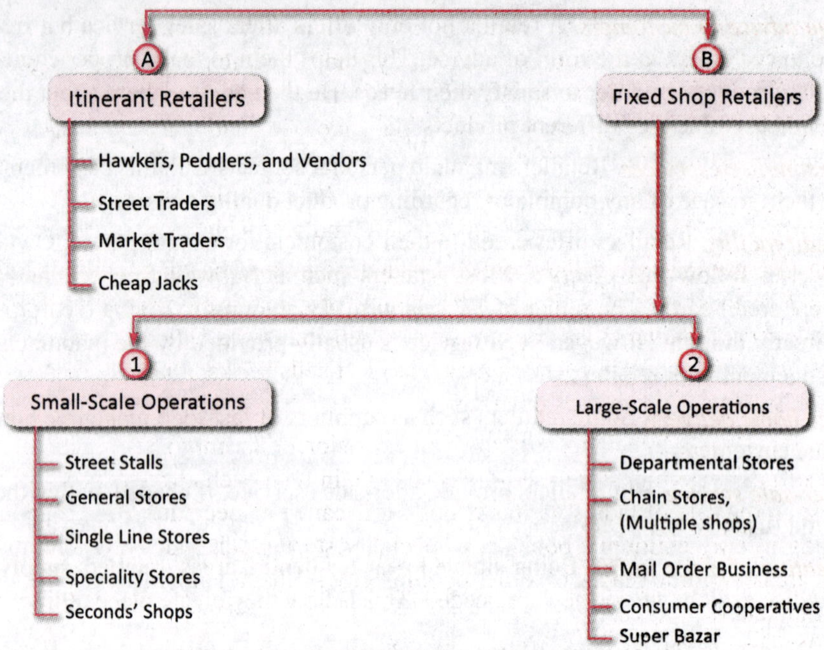

FIGURE 16.2: Different Types of Retail Organisation: A Broad Overview

16.6.2 Fixed Shops (Small Scale Retail Shops)

Fixed shop vendors are those who have permanent business centres and, therefore, are able to operate in sellers' market. This means that the customers who look for the retailers to satisfy their diverse needs. Fixed shop traders can move anywhere in search of customers. Their investment is as large as they have to keep sufficient stock of each item they want to sell everyday.

The characteristics of fixed shop retailers are the following:

(i) Having large resources, they are able to operate on large scale — much larger than that of internet traders.

(ii) They deal in a wide range and variety of products including standard domestic items or convenience goods and at times, even consumer durables or shopping goods.

(iii) They provide various useful services to their customers such as free home delivery, consumer credits, repair and maintenance of domestic appliances such as washing machines, air conditioners, etc.

Six main types of fixed shop retailers are the following:

1. *Street Stalls:* Such stalls are found mainly at street crossings or in the main streets which remain congested throughout the day. A stall is an improvised structure — a table or a temporary platform on which the goods are put for display. The stall-holders usually sell cheap products such as newspapers, magazines, toys, pens or even hosieries.
2. *General Stores:* General stores are located in residential areas to sell most items of daily use by households. The owner-cum-manager of such a store is a sole proprietor who is in constant personal touch with his customers. A general store may be a single-line store or a multi-line store.
3. *Single-lens Stores:* It may be noted that a single-lens store specialises in the sale of a specific line of goods such as books, stationary, shoes, medicine, readymade goods such as small bags, purses, exercise books, etc. For instance, medical stores such as Appollo Pharmacy or Frank Ross deals only in medicine. Likewise, stationary shops deal only in stationary goods of different qualities, variety of sizes and designs to meet the requirements of school and college standards as also offices. An example of such a store is the Office Link which has branches in all shopping malls and prime places in any metropolitan city.
4. *Multi-line stores:* A multi-line store comes under the broad heading 'multiple retailing' and deals in various types of products. It has no line of specialisation in the true sense. Emami, Starmark or Crossword is an example of multi-line store which offer a wide range of goods. It has a branch in every shopping mall. It sells books, musical items, CDs, writing pens, chocolates and various other items.
5. *Speciality Stores:* Speciality stores are an extension or an improved version of single-line stores. If a single-line store selling only one main item such as readymade garments specialise in the sale of ladies garments only, it is called a speciality shop. Similarly, a shop dealing in only children's books is a speciality store. Such shops are normally found in posh areas in prime places of a metropolitan city so that a large number of customers can be attracted.
6. *Seconds' Shops:* These stores deal in second-hand (used) goods such as books, clothes, furnitures, or even TV sets. Such goods are meant for low-income groups who cannot afford to buy new goods at original (often high) prices.

16.6.3 Large-Scale Retail Organisations

Large-scale retailing has assumed considerable importance of late. Large retail stores buy directly from manufacturers for direct sale to customers. Several large retail stores exist in every metropolitan city of India. Such stores are of the following types:

1. Departmental Store
2. Chain Stores or Multiple Shops
3. Mail Order House
4. Consumers' Cooperative Store
5. Super Bazar

We now discuss the features as also the advantages and disadvantages of such stores one by one.

16.7 DEPARTMENTAL STORE

The departmental store originated in France. The first departmental store *Bon Murche* was started functioning in Paris from 1852. Departmental stores have become very popular in most countries today — both developed and developing. Examples are Spencers, Robinson, Pantaloons, Wachel Mollah and Samabayika of Kolkata and Mustafa of Singapore. A departmental store is a retailer which sells a wide variety of products. According to the Oxford Dictionary of Business and Management a departmental store is "a retail organisaton that carries a wide variety of products — typically clothing, home furnishing and household goods; each department is managed by specialist buyers or merchandisers". In the words of Philip Kotler, "A department store carries several product lines, typically clothing, home furnishing, and household goods, where each line is operated as a separate department managed by specialised buyers or merchandisers".

A departmental store is a large- scale retail organisation, having many departments, each dealing in a separate line of product under one roof having centralised location.

The term 'departmental' denotes the fact that a typical store will be divided up into a large number of sections each offering a particular kind of merchandise: the food department, the footwear department, the toys and games department, the video game department, etc. Departmental stores may be under single-shop ownership or run as a multiple chain store business.

Chain stores compete mainly by offering customers convenience 'everything under the same roof', personal service and good quality products rather than on the basis of self-service and cut prices. The larger department stores are able to raise their profit margins by getting volume discounts from manufacturers as well as by promoting their own 'label brands'.

16.7.1 Features of Departmental Store

The notable features of a departmental store are the following:

1. *Product variety and large size:* Since it deals in a large variety of products, such as garments, musical systems, DVD players, televisions, watches and even fruits, vegetables, fish and meat, its size is fairly much larger than other retail stores (houses).
2. *Central location:* It is generally located at a central place so that people from different parts of the city may easily visit it for purchasing both convenience goods (such as food articles) and shopping goods (such as televisions).
3. *Centralised purchasing:* Although such a store makes a centralised purchasing, at times the task is assigned to the persons in charge of different departments, having specialised product knowledge.
4. *Departmental organisation:* From the operational side, it is departmentalised. The product offered for sale are classified into several categories or subcategories and each department specialises in one or more related lines.
5. *Decentralised operations:* Although all the departments are under centralised control system, in case of selling we find decentralised operation. However, since various departments operate under the same roof, it is possible to satisfy all expected human wants at one place. In spite of decentralised sales, there is unified control in a departmental organisation.

   Management control and sales are centralised. Purchases are decentralised.
6. *Services:* There is a nice and adequate arrangement for providing certain services to the customers like entertainment such as TV programmes, restaurants or fast-food centres inside the stores as also free home delivery and prompt after sales service.

7. *Division of labour and specialisation:* This is an age of super-specialisation. And modern departmental stores rely on the principles of division of labour and specialisation by assigning different tasks/sub-tasks to different persons so that each one can use his (her) specialised knowledge in serving the customers in the best possible way.
8. *Efficient management:* A departmental store appoints trained, qualified and efficient managers who can apply modern techniques of sales management and thus attracts a large number of customers. The customers feel satisfied and happy by getting the services of qualified and knowledegeable sales force, who can explain the characteristics (attributes) of products to buyers.
9. *Large-scale advertising:* Through extensive advertising a departmental store is able to attract customers from all parts of a city. By making special offers (such as discount sales) they are able to attract an abnormally large crowd even on Sundays (when other shops usually remain closed).
10. *Attractive look:* Since a large departmental store is located in a well furnished and nicely decorated building, it has a very attractive look. So it may act as a crowd-puller.

16.7.2 Advantages of Departmental Stores

Departmental stores offer the following advantages:

1. *Centralised location:* A departmental store is usually located in the central place of a city so that people from different parts of the city or surrounding localities, may have easy access to it.
2. *Customer convenience:* By being able to purchase most of the goods, they require from a single store, customers are able to save time and effort. They can also buy goods of their own choice, i.e., both quality products and branded items.
3. *Auxiliary services:* By providing a number of services to their customers such as free home delivery and short-term credit, they are able to attract a large number of customers.
4. *Economies of size:* A departmental store is able to derive various advantages of large scale operations. There is spreading of overheads over a number of departments. As a result such a store can keep prices of its free of cost products competitive and offer additional services to the customers.
5. *Advertising:* A departmental store can go for aggressive advertising to push its products. It can also go for attractive window display which acts as a very effective tool of self-advertising.
6. *Professionalism in management:* Due to their strong financial position, departmental stores can afford to employ skilled and professionally qualified personnel. Because of centralised purchase a departmental store can employee professional buyers having adequate product knowledge. This serves a two-fold purpose (i) efficiency of operations and (ii) maximum consumer satisfaction.

16.7.3 Disadvantages of Departmental Stores

The drawbacks of a departmental store are the following:

1. *Huge investment:* The establishment of a departmental store involves huge investment of initial (seed) capital. The cost of running the business is also quite high. And the ultimate

burden of high cost operations is to be borne by the customers in the form of higher product prices.

2. *Higher prices:* Since big departmental stores provide recreational facilities and various other benefits they have high overheads, which are ultimately covered by charging high prices of the goods they sell. So consumers suffer.
3. *Locational disadvantage:* Departmental stores may be located at faraway places, which are beyond the reach of most people — the people of modest means. In addition, the overall in-charge of such a store often finds it quite difficult to supervise and manage several departments, staffed by numerous sales persons who often vie with one another for winning customers. It is very difficult to control and supervise these people. So visiting departmental stores is not just a time-consuming but also cost-raising affair for them. Thus, locational disadvantages shies away many potential customers.
4. *Additional expenses:* Window dressing and interior decoration make huge addition to overhead cost and thus reduce net earnings of such stores.
5. *Lack of personal touch:* Many people have misgiving about departmental stores mainly due to lack of personalised attention and artificial behaviour of the sales persons, who do not often give due recognition and weightage to their valued customers.
6. *Supervisory problem:* The overall incharge of a departmental store often finds it quite difficult to supervise and manage several departments, staffed by numerous sales persons who often vie with one another for winning customers. It is very difficult to control and supervise these people.

16.8 CHAIN STORES OR MULTIPLE SHOPS

16.8.1 Meaning of Chain Stores

A chain store is a multi-branched retail business. According to Oxford Dictionary of Business and Management chain stores or multiple shops refer to " a large chain of shops (usually ten or more) owned by the same retailer. Compared with independent retailers, they benefit from economies of scale and so can charge lower prices to consumers. Multiple shops have therefore become dominant in many areas of retailing such as packaged groceries".

All types of retailers, ranging from specialist shops to supermarkets can be organised to take advantage of the growth and competitive opportunities offered by large-scale operations. Unlike single-shop concerns, chain stores operate a whole network of stores each located in strategic points serving large populations. So they are in a position to expand their sales potential. Furthermore, by selling the same general range of products in all of their stores and utilising a centralised buying system, chain stores are able to secure volume discounts from manufacturers (i.e., price discounts for large purchases). In addition, the larger chain stores have found it advantageous to establish their 'own label' brands as a means of maximising the sales potential of the whole group.

The chain stores display all goods in the same way and sell only standardised items. Some examples of chain stores are Bata, Tanishq, Apollo Pharmacy and Raymond shops. However unlike departmental stores, chain stores have a limited variety and range of product offerings. For instance, Khadim stores offer only footwear and related items for retail sales.

16.8.2 Features of Chain Stores

The salient features of chain stores are the following:

1. *Complete specialisaton:* Chain stores specialise in a single product. All Khadim shops, for example, sell footwear and other related items like socks, and shoe polish.
2. *Elimination of intermediaries:* When organised by manufacturers, multiple shops go without the services of both wholesalers and retailers. And when organised by wholesalers, they seek to go without depending on retailers.
3. *Centralised purchasing and decentralised selling:* While chain stores make purchase through the central office, selling is totally decentralised.
4. *Adherence to uniform standard:* Chain stores follow uniform standards as far as shops, floor layout and product display are concerned.
5. *Uniform prices:* Chain stores charge uniform price for their products from all counters. This helps in building reputation.
6. *Cash sales:* Chain stores, unlike departmental stores, do not extend any credit to their buyers. In other words, they carry on business on purely cash and credit basis.

16.8.3 Advantages of Chain Stores

Chain stores offer the following advantages:

1. *Large scale production:* Chain stores enable manufacturers to carry on production on a large-scale and sell directly to the consumers through various retail outlets so as ensure full control over product distribution.
2. *Sale of standardised items:* The goods offered for sale by chain stores are of good and assured quality. So buyers can buy such goods with full faith and complete quality assurance.
3. *Benefits of centralised advertising:* Although products are advertised through the head office, the benefits of advertisement are spread over all the shops scattered in different parts of a metropolitan city.
4. *Distinct identity:* All branches of a multiple shop follow almost the same style and adopt the same design and have a distinct look. People can easily identify each of them as belonging to a particular business house such as Pantaloons, Haldiram, etc. Chain stores succeed in attracting more customers through window display and centralised advertising than their competitors. Since they are located at different parts of a city customers can buy from any branch of their choice which is either close to their residence or their offices.
5. *Risk reduction:* By transferring unsold goods from one store to another it is possible to clear stocks. Thus, risk reduction is achieved through spatial diversification, i.e., conduct of sales operations at different branches.
6. *Operational flexibility:* In addition, it is fairly easy to shift a store from one place to another. Thus, there is enough flexibility in operation.
7. *Contact at the grass root level:* The manufacturer can have first-hand information about the likes and dislikes of customers since a chain store has contacts at the grassroot level due to direct sales to customers.
8. *Low competitive prices:* Since chain stores establish a direct link between the manufacturer and the consumers, the cost of distribution is low. So products can be sold at low prices.

16.8.4 Disadvantages of Chain Stores

Chain stores have the following disadvantages also:

1. *Limited range of products:* Each store offers a narrow range or a limited variety of products simply because it keeps the product of only outsiders.
2. *Lack of attractive services:* Many chain stores do not offer free home delivery to customers and provision of customer credit facility is not then usual business practice. So common people are not usually attracted to chain stores.
3. *Lack of product variety:* Chain stores offer only a few standardised products which often lack variety. So consumers do not have wide choice. These products do not often meet the need of rich customers. The reason is simple. Afterall people derive extra satisfaction from product variety.
4. *Lack of personal touch:* All chain stores are managed by paid (salaried) persons who do not have much personal interest in each and every customer. They have hardly any incentive to convince and persuade customers to make purchase from such store.
5. *Loss of specialisation (competitive advantage):* A manufacturer doing retail trading through chain store may not be able to perform both production and distribution functions with equal efficiency. Being a jack of both trades, it is master of none — it is neither a specialised producer, nor an efficient distributor.
6. *Operational inflexibility:* The manager of a retail store has hardly any discretionary power. He has to sell only the fixed basket of goods supplied by the main (head) office. In addition, all the terms and conditions of sale are laid down by the central office. So the manager of chain stores do not enjoy operational flexibility.

16.9 DISTINCTION BETWEEN DEPARTMENTAL STORES AND CHAIN STORES

In Table 16.1 we make a comparison between Departmental Store and Chain Store. This will enable us to clearly understand their similarities and differences.

TABLE 16.1: Comparison between Departmental Store and Chain Store

Basis of Comparison	Departmental Store	Chain Stores or Multiple Shops
1. Nature of store or shop	There is one store under the same roof with many separate and different departments.	There are several shops which remain scattered over different areas, through not always far away from one another.
2. Variety of products offered for sale	It deals in a wide range of goods. In addition, different varieties of the same goods are also available in most cases.	They deal in one specialised item such as ready-made garments.
3. The main objective	It provides all types of goods to meet most of needs of an average customer (not, of course, special ones).	They meet the need of customers only partly.
4. Physical location	It is centrally located in a metropolitan city like Kolkata or Chennai.	The chain stores remain scattered in many parts of any metropolitan city.
5. Types of customers	Its customers are the top brass of society with high income and taste for only branded items.	The customers are high and middle income groups with diversified tastes.

Contd.

Basis of Comparison	Departmental Store	Chain Stores or Multiple Shops
6. The level of advertising effort put	Advertisement effort is put only at the local level.	Advertisement is made over a wide area or even a whole region as in the case of Apollo pharmacy.
7. Type of window display	Each store is unique in its artistic style of decoration	All shops look identical due to the same type of window display
8. Provision of consumer credit	Credit is offered to only reputed and credit- worthy customers.	Only cash sale is made
9. Diffusion of risk	There is concentration of all risks in a single shop.	Risk spreading through dispersed locations.
10. Provision of extra facilities	Various allied facilities are provided to customers like restaurant, bars and entertainment (through TV channels)	No extra facility is provided to customers, as soon as deals are closed.

16.10 MAIL ORDER BUSINESS HOUSES

Mail order is a direct marketing technique. It is the means of retailing products to consumers through the post. Mail order firms supply catalogues to prospective customers who either themselves or through agents make purchases for delivery to their homes. Mail order concerns typically combine wholesaling (stock large quantities of products and breaking bulk) and retailing functions, supplying customers from a central warehouse. Such firms compete mainly by offering customers convenience (i.e., home shopping) and by the provision of instalment credit facilities on purchases. Mail order methods may also be used to sell industrial goods.

According to Oxford Dictionary of Business, "The mail-order house is a firm which specialises in selling goods direct to customers by post. Orders are obtained from all illustrated catalogues supplied by the firm or by agents, who introduce the catalogue. The low costs of selling, especially in the absence of retail premises, enable the mail order houses to offer goods at competitive prices."

SYNOPSIS FOR LEARNING : MAIL ORDER SELLING

Mail order means supplying goods in response to orders received by post. It is essentially concerned with selling against orders received through the post directly from the consumers/purchasers or agents. The order may be in response to advertisements. Alternatively, the orders may be made from catalogues.

Mail order houses maintain detailed list of potential customers and send their product literature by post on the basis of it. They also mail reply paid cards to potential buyers to ensure quick response from them. After receiving orders they will procure the goods and despatch the same to customers by value payable by post (VPP). Occasionally goods are sent by railway parcel in which case the railway receipt(s) are forwarded to the customer through VPP. Now-a-days many mail order houses such as Flipkart or Amazon also execute their orders through couriers to ensure quick delivery or to avoid loss of goods in transit.

Mail order business is most suitable in the following cases:

(i) products of standardised quality which are identified by brand name;

(ii) goods which are very popular to masses who are located in widely diverse areas.

(iii) convenience goods which do not require demonstration or whose handling and/or use does not require any special skills such as washing machines or computers; and

(iv) durable goods which are not destroyed or spoiled in transit such as books, cameras, drugs and medicines, sports goods, cosmetics and beauty aids, and domestic appliances of small value (such as water purifier, micro-oven etc.).

The growth of mail order business is attributable due to the following factors:

(i) expansion of postal facilities mainly in rural areas;

(ii) development of railway network and other means of transportation due to construction of metal roads in rural areas and new roads/high ways/flyovers in urban areas which have helped in establishing link between rural and urban areas;

(iii) rapid increase in circulation of newspapers, magazines, and journals; and

(iv) an increase in the desire of people to have wider choice from large variety of goods as also the quality products (due to the so-called revolution of rising expectations).

Quite recently some Indian business houses have advertised their products through T.V. to generate public interest in their products. They also booked orders over both phone and website. This new type of trading is called teleshopping.

16.10.1 Features of Mail Order Business

The main features of mail order business are the following:

1. *No personal contact:* Goods are ordered through post and received through post. There is no personal contact between buyers and sellers.
2. *Payment at the time of arrival of goods:* No cash advance is made in most cases while placing order. Goods are usually delivered to customers by VPP. The postmen will deliver the goods after receiving full payments from customers. Thus, the post office acts as the collection agent of the mail order house.
3. *Importance of brand name:* In mail order business, the customer does not get the opportunity to see the goods before buying them. So brand name is very important here. This is why customers send the orders by mentioning the brand name and, at times, the code number of the products he orders.
4. *Key role of advertising:* Advertisement is the main marketing weapon of mail order business. Information about availability of various products as also their attributes (such as safety, reliability, durability and guarantee/warranty) and product quality is transmitted to the prospective buyers through such media advertising as newspapers, trade journals and various types of magazines.
5. *Small capital requirement:* Mail order businesses can be started with very little initial capital. The reason is that there is no need to keep large stocks of saleable products. Goods can be produced by manufacturers according to buyers' specification after receiving orders. Another reason for low capital requirement is that it is not necessary to set up such business in a central location. Since business activities can be conducted even from the residence of its proprietor, there is considerable cost saving. (After all no rent has to be paid).

16.10.2 Advantages of Mail Order Business

The advantages enjoyed by both sellers and buyers from mail order businesses are the following:

1. *Convenience of buyers:* The buyer is not required to go to the retail store to take delivery of the goods. He can get them near his residence. He is also given money-back guarantee in case of dissatisfaction with the product. He also gets an opportunity to return an unsuitable product within a certain period.
2. *Economical (low-cost) operation:* The mail order business can be located at any place. So the cost of operation is low. The reason is simple. There is no need to pay high rent or to maintain a large sales force or to have showrooms for product display.
3. *Need for small investment:* Since goods can be procured after receiving orders from customers, there is not much lock-in effect, i.e., locking of capital of a person or a trader. So a person with very little initial capital can operate such business.
4. *Direct contact:* The mail order business gives the sellers an opportunity to establish direct touch with his customers. So the sellers will know the reaction of customers and satisfy them fully if there is any grievance or any dissatisfaction.
5. *Wide reach:* Mail order business is most suitable for those companies whose potential customers remain widely dispersed.
6. *No bad debt:* Since the post office acts as both the carrier of goods and the collector of sale proceeds, there is no chance of any bad debt. The postal network enables a business person to meet the needs of numerous customers scattered all over the country.

16.10.3 Disadvantages of Mail Order Business

Mail order business has the following disadvantages also:

1. *Lack of personal touch:* Since there is no personal touch or contact between the sellers and buyers, the latter has no scope for seeing and examining the goods before buying them. If goods are sold on a purely sale or return basis, there will be wastage of money on account of postage, transport cost and/or incidental expenses, if buyers return unsuitable goods.
2. *Additional expenses:* Mailing goods by post is a costly affair from the customers' point of view because they have to bear the postage also.
3. *Unsuitability for differentiated products:* Mail order business is not at all suitable for those products (including certain agricultural products) which are not of uniform standard and/or quality. Hence this cannot be sent through post.
4. *No provision of auxiliary services:* Customers do not get any credit facility nor any after sale service from the seller.
5. *Delays:* There may be a delay in sending the goods to the customers due to the postal delays and misplacement of goods in post offices.
6. *Limited variety of product offerings:* Mail order retailing is largely meant for selling a limited variety of goods. Such business is not suitable for selling perishable goods and items which require demonstration or display before sale.
7. *Limited scope:* Mail order houses have quite some appeal to those customers who can read and write. But in developing countries where many people are illiterate (particularly in rural areas where there is maximum concentration of people) mail order retailing does not have much scope.

16.11 CONSUMERS' COOPERATIVE STORES

16.11.1 Meaning of Consumers' Cooperative Stores

Consumers' cooperative store is a purely voluntary organisation of consumers. In India, it is organised as per the guidelines of and registered under the Cooperative Societies' Act. It is owned and run by its members, i.e., consumers who supply the initial capital. This means that the customers themselves are the shareholders. The store is guided solely by service motive. It seeks to serve its members in the best possible way. By eliminating the wholesalers and retailers, cooperative stores are able to sell their products to their members at low prices. They buy large quantities of goods directly from the producers (manufacturers) at low prices and are able to sell them to their members at less than market prices. This is how cooperatives serve their consumer members.

16.11.2 Features of Consumers' Cooperative Stores

The main features of consumers' cooperative are the following:

1. *Purely voluntary association:* A consumers' cooperative store is a purely voluntary association of consumers who are members-cum-shareholders. It must have at least ten members to start with.
2. *Open membership:* Any one can become a member of a cooperative by buying the required number of shares. A member is totally free to withdraw from the society any time. This decision is completely voluntary.
3. *Share capital:* The capital of a cooperative society is divided into shares of equal value. Each member has to purchase a minimum number of shares of certain value.
4. *Democratic nature:* Since each member has only one vote, no one can exert much influence on the functioning of store in any way. So such a store is democratic in its setup and nature.
5. *Interest and bonus:* Each member gets a small sum as interest on his share capital. In case the society is able to make some profit, a bonus is also given to each member on a pro rata basis (i.e., on the basis of the value of items purchased in an accounting year.)
6. *Spirit of cooperation:* The main driving force behind the formation of a cooperative store is the spirit of cooperation so that win-win situation is created, by saving members from the middleman who charge high prices for even highly essential items of consumption.
7. *Only cash sales:* Since sales are made only on cash basis, there is no possibility of incurring loss arising out of bad debt.

16.11.3 Advantages of Consumers' Cooperative Stores

The consumers' cooperative stores offer the following advantages to its members:

1. *Ease of formation:* It is fairly easy to form a cooperative society. Not much legal formalities and rigidities are involved in the process.
2. *Large membership:* Since the value of shares is low, and benefits are attractive at least to people of modest means, many people voluntarily join a cooperative. So membership is large.
3. *Limited liability:* The liability of each member of a cooperative store is limited to the value of their shares, as is found in case of joint stock companies.

4. *Participative management:* Cooperative societies are managed in a friendly manner because all members have equal voting power and each member has the right to take part in its management just like any other member.
5. *Government patronage:* Most state governments extend their support, cooperation and patronage to such societies.
6. *Very low operating cost:* Cooperative stores are not required to spent money on advertisement and on window display. So their operating costs are very low.
7. *Low product prices:* Since a cooperative store purchases goods directly from manufacturers for distributing of the same to its members, it can keep the prices of the goods low.

16.11.4 Disadvantages of Consumers' Cooperative Stores

Consumers' cooperative stores have not become much popular because they have various disadvantages. These are the following:

1. *Narrow financial base:* Such stores are generally formed by people having low income who cannot contribute much to share capital. So the financial base of a cooperative store is weak. This restricts the scale of operation (or the volume of business) of such a store.
2. *Lack of initiatives:* Due to limited (and at times negligible) benefits offered by cooperative societies, there is hardly any initiative among consumers to form such societies.
3. *Managerial inefficiency:* Managerial inefficiency is a common problem of cooperative stores. The reason is that consumers do not have the competence or the qualities of professional managers.
4. *Lack of incentive:* Due to the absence of suitable reward for appropriate effort, consumers lack the incentive for improving the operation of cooperative stores. In other words, the motivation to work hard and manage the stores well is totally lacking.

16.12 SUPERMARKETS AND HYPERMARKETS

16.12.1 Meaning of Supermarket

A supermarket is either a medium-sized or a large self-service store which carries a wide variety of food, household products and other goods and sells these goods in large volumes at relatively low prices. Such a store sells mainly groceries and packaged goods, usually in urban areas. A related concept is a super store — a large store which sells almost everything from groceries to packaged goods to clothing, usually outside the metropolitan cities.

A supermarket is organised much like a departmental store so as to enable a customer to buy various types of goods under one roof. However, unlike a departmental store there are no sales persons to interact with customers and help them in taking buying decisions. The customers can freely buy different types of goods according to their own choice without being advised or influenced by others. In addition, a super market does not offer any auxiliary service like a departmental store. Sales are made on cash basis. And there is no provision of giving free home delivery of goods.

16.12.2 Features of Supermarkets

The notable features of a supermarket are the following:

1 *Wide variety of goods:* A supermarket normally offers a wide range of groceries and food

articles for sale. It also offers other convenience goods such as drugs, cosmetics and many items of daily use by households.

2. *Convenience of shopping:* Much like a departmental store, a super market gives the consumer an opportunity to buy all goods according to the requirements of the customer belonging from the same roof.
3. *Self-service:* Since it is run on the basis of 'help yourself', it is also known as self-service store.
4. *Low cost entity:* A supermarket is a low cost retail market much like one-pound shop of the U.K. and two-dollar shop of Singapore.
5. *Central location:* Keeping in view the convenience of buyers, supermarkets are normally set up at central locations.

16.12.3 Advantages of Supermarkets

A supermarket offers following advantages:

1. *Large-scale operations:* Being a large retailing store, a supermarket enjoys all the benefits of large scale such as bulk purchase of goods and large volume of sales.
2. *Customer sovereignty:* Customers take necessary time to make their purchases and are at full liberty to compare different brands of a product and select goods according to their own judgement and choice without being influenced by sales person. So the customers are the sovereign or the king.
3. *Convenience of the buyers:* The customers enjoy the convenience of purchasing all the items they need.
4. *Low overheads and low product prices:* Due to low administrative as also sales and distribution, overheads cost per unit of a product is low. This gets reflected in low prices charged from customers.
5. *No bad debt:* Due to cash sales there is no chance of bad debt.
6. *Large sales turnover:* The total turnover of a supermarket is usually high for at least three reasons: (a) central location, (b) supply of better quality products and (c) unusually low price.
7. *Low price:* Due to huge turnover, its operational expenses are low. So it can sell goods at low prices. A supermarket can sell goods at low prices for another reason — direct purchase from producers and thus the elimination of middlemen (or intermediaries) takes place.

16.12.4 Disadvantages of Supermarkets

Supermarkets have the following limitations:

1. *Lack of personal touch:* Due to lack of personal attention some people do not go to the supermarket. There is lack of personal touch due to absence of sales persons.
2. *Restricted operations:* Supermarkets cannot offer those products which require guidance and advice by the sales persons who have sufficient product knowledge. This automatically restricts the scope of operations of supermarkets.

3. *Mishandling of goods:* Since there is the opportunity to inspect the goods before buying them, potential customers often cause damage to goods by handling them carelessly. And super market find it not only difficult but virtually impossible to sale such damaged goods.
4. *High overheads:* In reality, most super markets are unable to offer their products at low prices more so because of high overheads.
5. *Lack of suitability for small towns:* Setting up, managing, and operating a supermarket requires huge investment (both initial and recurring). So its turnover has to be high in order to keep overhead expenses low. Therefore we cannot think of taking up a high cost project like establishing a supermarket in a small town where not much turnover is expected at least in the initial few years.

A hypermarket combines the feature of the supermarket and discount shopping in a single location. It is really a big retailed establishment. In India any retail store occupying a space of at least 5,000 sq. feet is treated as a hypermarket and it is normally situated within metro and city limits while in western cities such as Orlando and New Jersey, hypermarkets are located outside metropolitan city limits. A hypermarket offers a wide range of goods (mainly household items of daily use such as clothes, food, drinks as also durable goods such as television, furniture, etc.). There is display of goods on a large scale and self-service. On certain specific items, discount is offered. Hypermarkets are found mainly in Europe and South America and more than 50,000 types of products are offered for sale in a standard hypermarket.

A hypermarket is larger than a supermarket. About half of the space is usually earmarked for grocery items. The rest of the space is occupied by general merchandise including clothes, shoes, hardwares, televisions, washing machines, children's toys, cameras, refrigerators, jewellery, furniture, etc. Some hypermarkets also lease space to banks, bars and restaurants.

16.12.5 Advantages of Hypermarkets

(i) A hypermarket offers wide choice since everything is available under the same umbrella.
(ii) It offers attractive deals on bulk purchase so that consumers feel that they are getting their money's worth.
(iii) It offers wide range of every product or various differentiated products.
(iv) It is well-organised.
(v) It offers quality products.
(vi) The ambience is good and attractive.
(vii) It operates efficiently.

Due to large scale and locational advantages, consumers in India now prefer the hypermarket idea. A hypermarket offers a combination of affordable prices and convenient locations. Examples of hypermarkets in India are Star India Bazar, Spencer's Hyper, Big Bazar, D'Mart, Reliance Mart, Bharti Easy, Day Hyper and Hyper City, Mani Square, Quest, etc.

16.12.6 Disadvantages of Hypermarkets

The setting up of a hypermarket outlet is a very costly affair. It requires a minimum investment of ₹ 5-6 crores. The gestation period is fairly long. It takes about 3-5 years for a hypermarket to cover all costs and reach the break-even point (at which there is neither profit nor loss).

16.13 FRANCHISE

A special form of business ownership is franchise. Franchise are mostly found in retail trade. A franchise agreement is an arrangement whereby someone with a good idea for a business (the franchisor) sells the right to use the business name and sell a product or service (the franchise) to others (the franchisees) in a certain region or territory. Those people, who are not comfortable with the idea of starting their own business from scratch, would rather join a business with a proven track record through a franchise agreement. This type of business is most suitable for those who want to start from an established platform rather than starting from a scratch and build their own house brick by brick. A franchise can be formed as a sole proprietorship, a partnership or a corporation. Some of the best-known franchises are McDonald's, Subway, 7-Eleven, Weight Watchers Body Shop and Holiday Inn.

16.13.1 Meaning of Franchise

Franchise is a business that uses the name, logo and trading systems of an existing successful business. A franchise is not really a form of legal structure for a business; rather it is a legal contract between two firms.

BUSINESS FOCUS: FIVE DIFFERENT MEANINGS OF FRANCHISE

1. A licence granted by a company (the franchisor) to an individual or firm (the franchisee) to operate a retail, food, or drug outlet where the franchisee agrees to use the franchisor's name; products; services; promotions; selling; distribution; and display methods; and other types of company support. McDonald's and Midas Holiday Inn are examples of franchise operations.
2. Right to market a company's goods or services in a specific territory, which right has been granted by the company to an individual, group of individuals, marketing group, retailer, or wholesaler.
3. Specific territory or outlet involved in such a right.
4. Right of an advertiser to exercise an option to sponsor a television or radio show, as well as the granting of such a right by the broadcast medium (as "to exercise a franchise" or "to grant a franchise").
5. Right granted by a local or state government to a cable television operator to offer cable television service in a community.

This contract allows one of them, the franchisee, to use the name, logo and marketing methods of the other, the franchiser. The franchisee can, separately, then decide which form of legal structure to adopt. Franchises are a rapidly expanding form of business operation. They have allowed certain multinational businesses, which are now household names, to expand much more rapidly than they could otherwise have done.

- **Examples:** The most popular businesses for franchising are restaurants (fast food and full service) and petrol pumps with convenience stores such as the Subway. McDonald's, the largest restaurant chain in the United States in terms of sales, is often considered the gold standard of franchising. Retail stores, financial services, health clubs, hotels and motels and automotive parts and service centres are also popular franchised business.

16.13.2 Advantages of Franchise

Franchising has penetrated every aspect of business life by offering products and services that are reliable, convenient, and competitively priced. The main advantages of franchises are the following:

1. *Management and marketing assistance:* Compared with someone who starts a business from scratch, a franchisee usually has a much greater chance of succeeding because he or she has well-established product or branded item to sell, gets help in choosing a location, and is assisted in all the phases of promotion and operation. It is like having one's own store but with full-time consultants when one needs them. Franchisors usually provide intensive training. Some franchisors help their franchisees with local marketing efforts. Franchises also have a network of fellow franchises facing similar problems who can share their experiences with the software programme that helps them to build customer databases along with quick and personal one-on-one phone and e-mail support.
2. *Personal ownership:* A franchise operation is still one's own business, and the franchisee enjoys as much of the incentives and profits as any sole proprietor would. He is still his own boss, although he must follow more rules, regulations, and procedures than with his own privately owned business.
3. *Nationally recognised name:* With an established franchise, one gets instant recognition and support from a product group with established markets and customers around the world.
4. *Financial advice and assistance:* Two major problems for small business owners are arranging financing and learning to keep good records. Franchisees often get valuable assistance and periodic advice from people with expertise in these areas. In fact, some franchisors provide financing to potential franchisees as valuable parts of the franchise system.
5. *Lower failure rate:* The failure rate for franchises is usually much lower than that of other business ventures[1].

16.13.3 Disadvantages of Franchise

There are, however, some potential drawbacks of franchising. These are the following:

1. *Large start-up costs:* Most franchises demand a high fee for the rights to the franchise. And start-up costs are, therefore, quite high.
2. *Profit sharing:* The franchisor often demands either a large share of the profits in addition to the start-up fees or a percentage commission based on sales, not profit. This share is called royalty.
3. *Management regulation:* Management "assistance" often becomes managerial orders and directives. Franchisees feeling burdened or even overburdened by the company's rules and regulations may lose the drive to run their own business. Often franchisees will collude or join hands to resolve their grievances against franchisors rather than fighting their battles individually alone.
4. *Coattail effects:* What happens to one's franchise if fellow franchisees fail? The actions of other franchises have an impact on ones future growth and profitability. Due to this coattail effect, a franchisee could be forced out of business even if his particular franchise has been profitable. McDonald's and Subway franchisees complain that due to the company's relentless growth, some new stores have taken business away from existing locations, squeezing franchise's profits per outlet.

1 However, franchising has grown so rapidly that many weak franchises have entered the field.

5. *Restrictions on selling:* Unlike owners of private businesses, who can sell their companies to anyone of their choice and on their own terms and conditions, many franchisees face restrictions on the resale of their franchises. To control quality, franchisors often insist on approving the new owner, who must meet their specifications and match their standards.
6. *Fraudulent franchisors:* Most franchisors are not large systems like KFC and Subway. Many are small and obscure companies about which prospective franchises know very little. And most of the time they do not keep their promise.

Table 16.2 lists the advantages and disadvantage of franchising.

TABLE 16.2: The Advantages and Disadvantages of Franchising

Advantages of a Franchised Business	Disadvantages (Possible Limitation)
1. Fewer chances of new business failing as an established brand and product are being used.	1. A share of profits or sales revenue has to be paid to franchiser each year.
2. Advice and training offered by the franchiser.	2. The initial franchise licence fee can be expensive.
3. National advertising paid for by franchiser.	3. Local promotions may still have to be paid for by franchise
4. Supplies obtained from established and quality-checked suppliers.	4. No choice of supplies or suppliers is allowed.
5. Franchiser agrees not to open another branch in the local area.	5. Strict rules over pricing and layout of the outlet reduce owner's control over his/her own business.

Diversity in Franchising

A lingering issue in franchising is the number of women who own franchises. Because women in general are collaborative and want to create win-win relationships they make wonderful franchisors. Women are not just franchises any more; they are becoming franchisors as well. Those women, who are finding it difficult to get financing for growing their business are now turning to franchises to help cover their expansion costs.

Home-Based Franchises

Home-based businesses offer many obvious advantages, including relief from the stress of commuting, extra time for family activities, and low overhead expenses. One disadvantage is the feeling of isolation. Compared to home-based entrepreneurs other business people (engaged in franchisee business) feel less isolated. Experienced franchisors often share their knowledge of building a profitable enterprise with other franchisees.

E-Commerce in Franchising

The Internet has changed franchising in many ways. Most brick-and-mortar franchises have expanded their businesses online and created virtual storefronts to deliver increased value to customers. Many franchisors, however, prohibit franchisee-sponsored websites because conflicts can erupt if the franchisor creates its own website. Sometimes franchisors send "reverse royalties" to franchisees who believe that their sales were hurt by the franchisor's online sales.

Using Technology in Franchising

Franchisors often use technology, including social media, to extend their brands, to meet the needs of both their customers and their franchisees, and even to expand their businesses.

Franchising in Global Markets (or International Franchising)

Franchising today is truly a global effort. What makes franchising successful in global market is its quality, convenience and a predictable level of service. No doubt global franchising creates great opportunities. At the same time adapting products and brand names to different countries create cultures challenges due to diversity of tastes and preferences.

16.14 TELESHOPPING

Teleshopping is the sale of goods and services over the telephone. Quite extensive growth of this type of retailing is attributable to rapid developments in computer assisted and television shopping networks. Teleshopping is the sale of goods and services by telephones. Many companies use it to supplement or replace in-store selling and complement online selling. Many send a catalogue to customers so that they can order by calling a toll-free number. Many electronics retailers provide a help feature online that performs the same function or serves the same purpose.

Teleshopping (or telephone selling) is a form of direct marketing in which a seller of a product contacts customers by telephone in order to establish an initial contact with them. Interested customers may then be visited by a sales representative of the firm with a view to completing the deal.

16.14.1 Advantages of Teleshopping

The main advantage offered by teleshopping is the convenience enjoyed by the customers. The customer can purchase a product without visiting the seller. This saves time, money and effort which are all scarce. Customers can make payment very easily through credit cards. In India, companies such as Naaptol, Shop 18, etc. offer teleshopping facilities, thanks to computer systems which made it easier to do shopping by playing recorded messages and then recording the information given by customers. In the language of P. Kotler, "properly designed and targeted telemarketing provides many benefits including purchasing convenience and increased product and service information".

16.14.2 Disadvantages of Teleshopping

Teleshopping, however, has three main drawbacks. Firstly, it does not offer the opportunity to examine a product before buying it. Secondly, computerised systems used in teleshopping are expensive. Finally, illiterate and quarter-educated people do not rely much on teleshopping.

In spite of all these, teleshopping is gradually becoming more and more popular in India, mainly in urban areas.

16.15 AUTOMATIC VENDING MACHINE

16.15.1 Meaning of Automatic Vending Machine

Automatic vending refers to using machines rather than relying on human labour for selling different types of goods. Vending machines supply mainly convenience goods when customers deposit the required amount of money. These machines provide the benefit of location. They are found in airports, office buildings, schools, petrol pumps (service stations) and other areas where people want convenience goods. We have already discussed about such machines in an earlier chapter.

FOCUS ON TERMINOLOGY: CONVENIENCE GOODS

Convenience goods refer to those goods which consumers usually buy quite frequently, immediately, and with the minimum of comparison and buying effort. Alternatively they are fairly inexpensive items which consumers choose frequently with a minimum of thought and effort.

Vending machines are operated by inserting coins. These are used for selling such items as milk, soft drinks, chocolate, and even platform tickets. Automatic vending is a form of non-manual retailing since products are sold through a machine. So there is no face-to-face contact between the buyer and the seller. Automatic vending machine is very useful for selling standardised products such as cosmetics, tea, coffee, cigarettes etc. For example, Mother Diary sells a particular variety of milk through such machines. Once sold, the goods cannot be returned or exchanged by inserting them in such machines.

16.15.2 Usefulness of Automatic Vending Machine

Vending machines are suitable in the following cases:

(i) For selling highly standardised products which are of uniform size, standard and weight.
(ii) For selling packed and low value branded items.
(iii) For mass consumption and first moving items, i.e., products having high turnover.
(iv) Where the consumer has full product knowledge and does not require any purchase advice.

16.15.3 Advantages of Automatic Vending Machine

The advantages of using the vending machines are the following:

(i) It is fairly convenient to buy goods from such machines instantly (without loss of time).
(ii) Vending machines provide prompt and at times instant service to buyers.
(iii) Vending machines enable consumers to help themselves.
(iv) Goods can be purchased any time since such machines offer 24-hour service.
(v) Very small space is required for installing such a machine.

16.15.4 Disadvantages of Automatic Vending Machine

The disadvantages of vending machines are the following:

(i) Customers cannot inspect or check any items before buying. So they may get goods which are not of standard or acceptable quality.
(ii) Only non-durable consumer goods such candies, chocolates, cigarettes, soft drinks, tea, coffee, etc. are sold through such machines.
(iii) Special packs are to be developed by manufacturers to suit the size and storing capacity of the machine.
(iv) Constant watch is necessary to replenish the stock of items in the machines.
(v) The purchase price and installation cost of a vending machine is very high.
(vi) There is need for frequent servicing and repair for keeping the machines operational. So the maintenance cost is also high.

Key Points

1. **Retailing:** Retailing is the function of selling products to its ultimate buyers. It refers to sales activities involved in selling goods and services directly to final consumers for their personal use. Retailers purchase goods mainly from wholesalers and at times, directly from producers and sale directly to the end customers.

2. **Retailer:** A retailer is a distributor who sells goods and services to customer. Consumer goods are largely sold through retailers and intermediaries rather than directly. Retail shops are normally located near residential areas. Some retail shops provide free home delivery. Others extend credit facility to selected customers. Six most notable features of retailers are the following:
   (i) Retailers purchase saleable goods from producers or wholesalers and supply the same to final buyers (mainly consumers)
   (ii) Retailing forms the last link in an elaborate chain/channel of distribution.
   (iii) Retailers do bulk breaking and sell in small quantities only in local areas and markets.
   (iv) Most retailers offer a large variety and a wide range of goods for sale.
   (v) Retailers also provide after-sales service to customers, including free home delivery in case of such goods as groceries, medicines, books and fast food.
   (vi) Retailers help the customers in choosing the right types of products so that they get their money's worth and feel satisfied.

3. **Main functions of retailers:** Eight most important functions performed by the retailers are the following:
   (i) Assembly of goods,
   (ii) bulk breaking of goods,
   (iii) selling to consumers in small quantities,
   (iv) storage of goods for future sale,
   (v) risk taking,
   (vi) getting feedback from buyers and passing on the information to the wholesalers and producers,
   (vii) free home delivery of certain goods to customers,
   (viii) extending credit facilities to buyers,

4. **Services to manufacturers and wholesalers:** Retailers extend the following services to producer (manufacturers) and wholesalers:
   (i) physical distribution of goods,
   (ii) finding out the true needs of customers through direct interaction(s) with them.
   (iii) giving relevant information and appraising them of the favourable and adverse reactions of buyers.
   (iv) sparing them from the tedious and time-consuming job of selling to buyers in small quantities all the time.
   (v) sharing risk with wholesalers/producers (as is usually found in case of purchase of groceries).

5. **Services to consumers:** Retailers provide the following services to consumers:
   (i) ensuring smooth and continuous flow of goods and services,
   (ii) supplying a wide range and a large variety of goods,
   (iii) giving advice to customers on the basis of experience and contact with people at the grass-root level,
   (iv) supplying cost-free services,
   (v) giving free home delivery to customers,
   (vi) credit facility,
   (vii) supplying convenience goods at convenient locations, and
   (viii) providing prompt after-sales service either directly or through agents of manufacturers.
6. **Two types of retailers:** Two main types of retailers are (1) mobile or itinerant traders (vendors) consisting of (a) peddlars and hawkers, (b) street traders, (c) market traders, (d) cheap jacks; and (2) fixed shop traders. The latter are sub-divided into two main categories. They are mainly small scale operators and large scale operators. The former consists of (a) street stalls, (b) general stores, (c) speciality store, (d) second-hand goods shop. The latter consists of (a) departmental store, (b) multiple shops, (c) mail-order house, (d) consumers cooperative stores, (e) supermarkets.
7. **Departmental store:** A departmental store such as Marks & Spencers or Pantaloons is essentially retail outlet which handles a wide range and different varieties of goods which are grouped into various separate departments for the purpose of sales promotion, giving customer service, performing accounting function and exercising control. Each department is, at times, treated as a separate profit centre. A departmental store is an outlet, organised on a large scale, and having a number of departments under the same umbrella so that buyers are not required to move from here to there to acquire their needed merchandise. The activity of each departments remain confined to only one specialised area of business. These departments are centrally organised, managed and controlled to ensure that they belong to a single establishment and thus are a monolithic entity. In spite of all these, the stock of each department is maintained and handled separately.
8. **Chain stores and multiple shops:** The term 'chain stores' or 'multiple shops' is used to refer to a large chain of shops (usually 10 or more) owned by the same retailer, such as the Apollo Pharmacy, or Haldiram's Food Chain. Thus, a chain store is essentially a multibranch retail business. All types of retailers, ranging from specialist shops to super markets can be organised to take advantage of the growth and competitive opportunities offered by large-scale operations. Unlike single-shop concerns and independent retailer, chain stores benefit from economies of scale and so can charge lower prices to consumers. Chain stores have, therefore, become dominant in many areas of retailing such as packaged groceries.
9. **Mail order house:** Mail order is a direct marketing means of retailing products to consumers through the post. This is why mail order business is also known as 'selling through post' for the retailer. From the customers' point of view it is 'shopping by post'. Mail order firms supply catalogues to prospective customers who (either themselves or through agents) make purchase for delivery to their homes. Mail order concerns combine wholesaling (i.e., stocking large quantities of products and breaking bulk) and retailing functions, (i.e., supplying customers from a central warehouse). Such firms compete mainly by offering customers'

convenience (i.e., home shopping) and by the provision of instalment credit facilities on purchases. Mail order methods may also be used to sell industrial products..

10. **Franchisee:** A franchise agreement is an arrangement is an arrangement whereby somone with a good idea for a business (the franchisor) sells the right to use the business name and sell a product or service (the franchise) to others (the franchisees) in a certain region or territory. This type of business is most suitable for those who want to start from an established platform rather than starting from a scratch and build their own house brick by brick.

11. **Teleshopping:** Teleshopping is the sale of goods and services by telephones. Theleshopping (or telephone selling) is a form of direct marketing in which a seller of a product contacts customers by telephone in order to establish an initial contact with them. Interested customers may then be visited by a sales representative of the firm with a view to completing the deal.

12. **Automatic vending machine:** Automatic vending is a means of retailing products to consumers via vending machines. It is also known as non-store retailing. Vending machines augment conventional point-of-sale retailing (shops and stores). Such machines also provide a comparatively inexpensive and convenient way of making products available. These machines have been extensively employed in selling, for instance, food and beverages, chocolates, cigarettes and other convenience goods

KEY Terms	
Mobile traders	Speciality store
Telemarketing	Second-hand goods shop
Paddlers and hawkers	Departmental store
Street traders	Multiple shop
Market traders	Mail order house
Cheap jacks	Consumer cooperative store
Fixed shop traders	Supermarkets and hypermarkets
Street stalls	Automatic vending machine
General store	Franchise
Risk-sharing with wholesalers	Chain store

Assignments

SHORT ANSWER-TYPE QUESTIONS

1. State two services of a retailer to consumers. [ISC 1987]
2. What are Automatic Vending Machines?
3. List two disadvantages of the Mail Order Business. [ISC 1987]

4. Mention two characteristics of Chain Stores. [ISC 1989]
5. Define a Mail Order Business. [ISC 1989]
6. List two merits of Departmental Stores. [ISC 1989]
7. Give two differences between a Wholesaler and a Retailer. [ISC 1989]
8. Mention two reasons for the survival of Small Scale Retail Shops. [ISC 1992]
9. Mention two forms of Large Scale Retail Business. [ISC 1990]
10. Mention two services rendered by the retailers to the wholesalers. [ISC 1991]
11. State two reasons for the unpopularity of the Departmental Stores. [ISC 1991]
12. Enlist two essential conditions for the success of the Mail Order Business. [ISC 1991]
13. Give one advantage and one disadvantage of Large Retailers over Small Retailers. [ISC 1991]
14. Mention two factors to be considered before establishing a retail outlet. [ISC 1992]
15. Mention two advantages of Mail Order Business. [ISC 1992]
16. What are Hypermarkets? [ISC 1992]
17. What is Teleshopping?
18. What is Franchising?

ESSAY-TYPE QUESTIONS

1. What conditions must be present in goods in order to qualify for mail order business? [ISC 1990]
2. Describe the services rendered by the retailers to the manufacturers and the consumers while performing their functions.
3. Discuss the important factors to be considered in establishing a retail business. [ISC 1989]
4. (a) Discuss five special features of Retail Trade and distinguish it from Wholesale Trade. [ISC 1989]

   (b) Explain what is meant by Mail Order Business. Discuss its merits and demerits. [ISC 1988]
5. (a) What is retailing? How are retailers useful to consumers?

   (b) What are chain stores? Discuss the special features of chain stores. [ISC 1990]
6. (a) Discuss five advantages which a large retailer enjoys over a small retailer.

   (b) Explain five differences between Multiple Shops and Departmental Stores. [ISC 1992]

QUESTION BANK

1. *Define Retail Trade.*

Ans. See text.

2. *State the characteristics of Retail Trade.*

Ans. See text.

3. *Distinguish between Wholesaler and Retailer.*

Ans. See text.

4. *Give any three functions of a Retailer.*

Ans (i) A retailer buys different types of goods keeping in view the requirements of consumers.
(ii) He keeps a ready stock of goods.
(iii) He sells goods to ultimate consumers.

5. *Explain the functions of a retailer.*

Ans See text.

6. *Discuss the services rendered by retailers to consumers and wholesalers.*

Ans See text.

7. *What is telemarketing?*

Ans Telemarketing involves using the telephone to sell directly to consumers and business customers. In general, telephone marketing is directed towards consumers but, B2B marketers also use telemarketing extensively. Marketers use *outbound* telephone marketing and to sell directly to customers and businesses. They also use inbound toll free numbers to receive orders from television and print ads, direct mail or catalogues.

8. *Explain the term 'Itinerants'.*

Ans See text.

9. *Distinguish between hawkers and pedlars.*

Ans See text.

10. *What do you mean by cheap jacks?*

Ans See text.

11. *Who is an independent retailer?*

Ans See text.

12. *How does large scale retailing pose a threat to the small scale retailers? Explain why.*

Ans See text.

13. *Account for the survival of small scale retail shops in the face of stiff competition from large scale retailers.*

Ans See text.

14. *What is Hire Purchase System? How does it differs from Deferred Payment System?*

Ans Hire purchases system is a system of retailing under which a customer purchases consumer durables (e.g., refrigerator, television, washing machine, car, etc.) on an instalment basis. The payment is made over a few years through EMIs. The higher purchasers gets possession of the article without delay but he does not become the true owner until he has cleared his dues fully after paying the last instalment. If the buyer defaults in making payments, the seller may confiscate the article as per contract.

Under the defferred payment system, the buyer becomes the owner of the article just by paying the first instalment. He pays the balance amount in instalments as soon as he get the article in his hand. If he fails to pay instalments, the seller cannot confiscate the article. The seller can just see for recovery of his dues.

15. *Explain the advantages and disadvantages of hire purchase system for consumers and traders.*

Ans See text.

16. *What is a Departmental Store? Explain its advantages and disadvantages.*

Ans. See text.

17. *What is a multiple shop system? State its merits and demerits.*

Ans. See text.

18. *Distinguish between departmental stores and chain stores.*

Ans. See text.

19. *What are consumer cooperative stores? Discuss their advantages and disadvantages.*

Ans. See text.

20. *What is a Supermarket? State its merits and demerits.*

Ans. See text.

17 PROCEDURE AND DOCUMENTS USED IN HOME TRADE

SYLLABUS

Documents used in home trade

- *Documents and procedure in home trade — inquiry; quotation; catalogues; order; invoice; debit note; credit note.*
- *Price quotations — cash discount and trade discount.*

The procedure followed in home trade and documents used are much simpler than those of foreign trade.

— E. Thomas

LEARNING OUTCOMES

On completion of this chapter, you will be able to understand the following:

17.1 The Procedure of Home Trade
17.2 Differences between Invoice and Proforma Invoice
17.3 Price Quotations
17.4 Trade Discount
17.5 Cash Discount
17.6 Statement of Account

Home trade means trade within the domestic territory of a country. The buyer and seller finalise the terms and conditions through mutual negotiation and bargaining. The terms and conditions of trade or transactions relate to price, quantity, quality, discount structure, mode of delivery of goods and system of payments. In this chapter the discuss various issues related home trade. Firstly, we discuss the related detailed procedure of home trade. Then we discussed various documents used in such trade.

17.1 THE PROCEDURE OF HOME TRADE

Any transaction in home trade involves the following steps.

1. **Enquiry:** To start with, the seller receives an enquiry from the intending buyer. Enquiries are made as soon as a seller brings his goods to the notice of buyers through advertisement

and other sales promotion measures. Enquiries will be received through post or telephone or through a proper representative of the buyer.

In general, the prospective buyer makes enquiry from a number of suppliers to get the best bargain, i.e., to buy goods from the cheapest source and with longest credit.

Through an enquiry, a prospective buyer makes a request to the seller to furnish the following information:

(i) Quality, size, design, quantity and other specifications of goods to be purchased
(ii) Price per unit
(iii) Terms of delivery
(iv) Terms of payment
(v) The last date of validity of the offer.

The intending buyer must give in the enquiry full description of the goods to be purchased. An enquiry should be made in clear and simple language with as precise a specification as possible. It must be complete in all respects.

We present below a simple specimen of an enquiry.

Specimen of an Enquiry

AHUJA BOOK STORE

62D, Lajpat Nagar, Delhi 110007 • Telephone No: 4264141, 4365151

Enquiry No. 16/07/2016

Date: 16 August, 2016

The Sales Manager
S. SARKAR & CO. LTD
61, Basant Bihar, New Delhi 110025

Dear Sir,
Please furnish details about the availability, price, terms of delivery, terms of payment, discount and other trade terms, the date up to which the offer is valid for the following books:

Code No.	Trader Terms	No. of Copies
05314	ISC Commerce for Class XI	400
05315	ISC Commerce for Class XII	500
05316	ISC Economics for Class XI	700
05317	ISC Economics for Class XII	700

Yours faithfully
For Ahuja Book Store
Kamal Ahuja
Partner

2. **Quotation:** In response to an enquiry made by the buyer, the seller sends price quotations which appear in catalogue. A quotation is basically a written reply to an enquiry sent by a seller to a prospective buyer. Through a quotation and price list, the seller makes an offer to the buyer to supply certain goods at a particular price. Of course, certain terms and conditions apply. Through a quotation, the seller tries to convert enquires into orders. The following information is furnished through a quotation:

(i) Quality, size, design and other specifications of goods available for sale.
(ii) Quantity of goods available.
(iii) Price per unit.
(iv) Terms and mode of delivery.
(v) Terms as also conditions as also mode of payment.
(vi) The last date of validity of the offer.

Specimen of an Quotation

S. SARKAR & CO. LTD
61, Basant Bihar, New Delhi 110025
Telephone No. 23875705, 23898012

Date: 20 August, 2016

To,
The Partner
Ahuja Book Store
62D, Lajpat Nagar, Delhi 11007

Dear Sir,
Thank you for you enquiry No. 16/07/2017 dated 16 August, 2016. The required information is given below:

Code No.	Trader Terms	No. of Copies Available	Price ₹	Delivery
05314	ISC Commerce for Class XI	700	240	Ready
05315	ISC Commerce for Class XII	700	275	10 days from order
05316	ISC Economics for Class XI	900	300	Ready
05317	ISC Economics for Class XII	700	325	10 days from order

Terms of payment: 60 days credit
Trade Discount: Upto 500 copies 25% above 500 copies 30%
Cash Discount: 5% for payment in 10 days
3% for payment in 20 days
2% for payment in 30 days

Offer is valid till August 31, 2016

Yours faithfully
For S. Sarkar & Co. Ltd
S.K. Seth
Dy. General Manager, Marketing

And on the basis of quotation the buyer places an order with the seller. We present below a specimen of quotation.

3. **Catalogue:** If the intending buyer wants further information, the seller may send a catalogue to him. A catalogue is a printed handbook which gives information about the goods available for sale, their prices as also other terms and conditions. It furnishes details about the quantity, price, quality, size, code number, etc. of goods as also the mode of delivery

and the terms of payment. On the basis of this information, the prospective buyer is in a position to place orders.

4. **Order:** After receiving quotations from various suppliers the buyer makes a close scrutiny of each, compares them and selects the supplier who offers the most favourable terms and conditions. If satisfied in all respects, the buyer sends an order for the purchase of goods. An order is a formal acceptance by the buyer of the offer made by the seller through quotation, catalogue and price list. An order furnishes information about the following:
   (i) Number of order for future reference.
   (ii) Name and address of the buyer.
   (iii) Quantity and quality of goods required.
   (iv) Price to be paid.
   (v) Time, mode and place of delivery.
   (vi) Terms as to credit, discount, packing, etc.
   (vii) Special instructions, if applicable.

   An order is generally prepared in triplicate. One copy is sent to the seller, the second one to the godown and the third one is kept for official records.

   A specimen of the order is given below.

Specimen of an Order

BHATIA BOOK STORE

62D, Lajpat Nagar, Delhi 110007
Telephone No: 3962142, 39245171

Enquiry No. 16/07/2017

Date: 16 August, 2016

The Sales Manager
S. Sarkar & Co. Ltd.
61, Basant Bihar, New Delhi 110025

Dear Sir,
Please supply the following books:

Code No.	Trade Terms	No. of Copies
05314	ISC Commerce for Class XI	580
05315	ISC Commerce for Class XII	580
05316	ISC Economics for Class XI	750
05317	ISC Economics for Class XII	750

Yours faithfully
For Ahuja Book Store
Kamal Ahuja
Partner

5. **Acknowledgement:** After receiving the order the supplier sends an acknowledgement. The objective is to inform the buyer about the receipt and acceptance of the order. A stamp is put on the order with the date of receipt; a serial number is given; and this is officially recorded in the order receipt book for future reference.

6. **Execution of order:** It is in the rightness of things for the supplier to carefully scrutinise the contents of the order. After this he makes necessary arrangements for procurement of the goods from different sources such as his factory or godown or from the market. The goods are then checked carefully and compared (tallied) with the order. After this the goods are properly packed, labelled and marked as per the specification and instruction of the buyer. Then the goods are despatched by road or rail transport. The mode of transport to be used depends on the nature of the goods, distance to be covered, cost of transportation and, of course, the instructions given by the buyer. However, before despatching the goods, little ground preparation is necessary. To be more specific, the supplier has to be sure that the goods are properly placed on the carrier and are adequately insured against theft or damage.

7. **Advice note:** In the next stage, the seller sends an advice note to the buyer and informs him about the dispatch of goods and requests him to take delivery of the same. Two things are sent along with the advice note, namely, viz., invoice and documents of title. An advice note serves the following three purposes:

   (i) It enables the buyer to take delivery of the goods by following necessary steps.

   (ii) It enables the buyer to identify the goods and check whether it is according to his own specification.

   (iii) Finally, it informs the buyer about the exact time of arrival of goods at his own place.

   While despatching the goods by his own vehicle, the seller sends a Delivery Note to the buyer. In this note details of the goods are given. This enables the buyer to check the goods before returning the note duly signed. Delivery notes contain three types of information: (i) name and address of the buyer, (ii) name and address of the seller and (iii) necessary details about the goods despatched.

8. **Invoice:** An invoice is essentially a document summarising goods supplied, together with prices. To be more 'specific', an invoice is a document sent by a supplier to a customer that itemises the products supplied to the customer, their prices, and the total amount of money owed by the customer for these products. An invoice is usually sent after the products have been shipped with their associated delivery note and serves to inform the customer that payment is required. Differently put, a sales invoice is a document sent by the seller of goods or services to the buyer, detailing the amounts due, discounts available, payment dates, as also the account numbers and credit limits.

   An invoice is a written statement sent by the seller to the buyer giving full description of the goods. This document enables the buyer to know about the goods sent by the seller. Normally it is prepared in triplicate — two copies are kept by the seller and one copy is sent to the buyer. Out of two copies kept by the seller — one copy is sent to the Accounts Department and one copy is kept in office records.

   A sales invoice contains the following details:

   (i) The seller's name and place of origin;

(ii) The date of despatch of goods;

(iii) Order number;

(iv) The name and address of the buyer (i.e., the ultimate destination of goods);

(v) Invoice number, date as also the order number;

(vi) Quantities of goods supplied as also a broad description of goods;

(vii) Any incidental expenses incurred by the seller on behalf of the buyer (for the purpose of reimbursement);

(viii) Trade discount or price concession if any offered to the buyer;

(ix) Price per unit and net amount which is to be paid by the buyer;

(x) Terms of payment;

(xi) The date and mode of despatching goods (i.e., whether by road transport or by railways);

(xii) The mode of sending railway receipts (RR);

(xiii) Marks on packages to clearly indicate whether the consignment is complete in all respects or not and other incidental matters, if any.

(xiv) Errors and omission expected (E & OE);

(xv) Signature of the seller.

The main functions of invoice are the following:

(a) It is a written document of the transaction. On the basis of this document, buyers and sellers make entries in their respective books of accounts.

(b) It helps the buyer to compare it with the order placed and with goods received.

(c) It informs the buyer about the price per unit, discount received and net amount payable.

(d) It helps the buyer to determine the cost of goods and estimate the selling price.

A specific sample of an invoice is presented in the next page.

Different Types of Invoice

There are various types of invoice. A brief description of some of them is given below:

- *Inland invoice:* When the seller and buyer reside in the same country and the invoice is sent by seller to buyer, it is known as inland invoice.
- *Foreign invoice:* When the seller and buyer are not residing in the same country and invoice is sent by the seller to the foreign buyer, it is known as foreign invoice. It can also be called as export invoice from the side of exporter and import invoice from the side of importer.
- *Outward invoice:* When an invoice is sent by the seller to its buyer it is called outward invoice as it goes out of the office of the seller.
- *Inward invoice:* When an invoice is sent by the seller to the buyer it is called outward invoice to him but it virtually becomes an inward invoice to the buyer.
- *Proforma invoice:* It may be used by the seller to the buyer as soon as the transaction is complete. [Details of such invoice are given below.]

INVOICE

A. BOSE & CO. LTD.

72A, C. R. Avenue, Kolkata 700073

Phone No. 033 2477834 Date: 5th March, 2016

Fax No. 0330247899

Invoice No. 92/3/13

Order No. 4/53

R. Singh & Co. Ltd.

20B/1 Dayal Marg, Ranchi, Jharkhand

Sl. No.	Description	Quantity	Rate	Amount	Remarks
1.	Jute bags	450	150.00	67,500	
2.	Jute-make fancy goods	150	50.00	7,500	
3.	Jute calenders	200	120.00	24,000	
4.	Jute carpets	120	1000.00	1,20,000	
	Total			2,19,000	
	Less: Trade discount @ 10%			21,900	
				1,97,100	
	Add: CST @ 2%			3,942	
				2,01,042	
	Less: Octroi @ 1%			2,010	
				1,99,032	
	Add: Railway freight			2,000	
				2,01,032	

(Rupees Two lakhs one thousand and thirty two only)

Despatched per goods train

Terms: 3% for two months

E & OE

for A. Bose & Co. Ltd.

Samir Bose

Deputy General Manager

9. **Proforma Invoice:** An invoice is sent by the seller to the buyer when the transaction is complete. But proforma invoice, which is prepared in the same form, is sent before the transaction is complete. That means that proforma invoice is sent before the real sale just to inform the prospective customer that if he chooses any particular good about the exact amount he would be required to pay. When the goods are sent on 'sale or return basis' or in 'consignment' business proforma invoice is used. Such invoice is sent in the following cases:
   (i) If goods are sent to the consignee for sale.
   (ii) If goods are sent on sale or return basis for prospective customer.
   (iii) If the goods are sent to a foreign country, a copy of the invoice has to be submitted to Customs Authorities for the purpose of calculation of customs duty.

17.2 DIFFERENCES BETWEEN INVOICE AND PROFORMA INVOICE

Four differences between invoice and proforma invoice are the following:

1. While invoice is a genuine or real statement about the cost of goods sold, proforma invoice is a notional (or imaginary) invoice or just a quotation presented in the form of an invoice.
2. While an invoice is sent by the seller to the buyer after dispatch of goods, proforma invoice is sent before it.
3. While invoice is used in all types of contracts of sale — domestic and foreign, proforma invoice is used mainly in foreign trade and at times in contingent sale.
4. Finally, while invoice forms the basis for making entries in the book of account, proforma invoice offers no such basis.

The main points of difference between an invoice and a proforma invoice are shown in Table 17.1.

TABLE 17.1: Difference between Invoice and Proforma Invoice

Invoice	Proforma Invoice
1. It is sent by the seller to the buyer.	1. It is sent by the seller to the prospective buyer.
2. It is sent by the seller to the buyer after the sale or when the transaction is complete.	2. It is sent by the seller before the sale transaction is complete
3. It is written document of sale and on the basis of this the seller and the buyer make entries in the book of accounts.	3. It is not a legal document in the true sense.
4. It is used in all types of sale — inland and foreign.	4. It is used in consignment sale, sale on approval and foreign trade.

5. **Delivery of goods:** When the goods reach the destination, the buyer takes delivery and possession of the same with the help of Railway Receipt and other supporting documents to title. If the goods meet the specification given in the order, the buyer makes arrangement for their storage. Otherwise he will return the good to the seller along with a complaint note.
6. **Payments:** The buyer may send the payment for goods purchased in cash or by money order, cheque or bank draft. He may also make use of credit instruments such as promissory note or bill of exchange and the seller will honour the same if it is sent on or before the due date.

It is also possible to meet payment in the form of cash on delivery (COD), Documents against Acceptance (D/A) and Documents against Payment (D/P).

After selling goods on credit, the seller sends a statement of account to the buyer. It is just a reminder to the buyer for timely payment of the balance amount.

Debit Note

The document which is issued at the time of debiting an account for any reason is called 'debit note'. A debit note is a document issued by a supplier to a customer charging the customer for any additional products supplied to the customer for which payment has not been received. Goods may be returned for various reasons such as manufacturing defects, supply of goods not ordered, charging more than the actual/quoted/price of a good. This document is issued at the time of returning goods and it is to be attached with the goods returned. It may be issued by the buyer to seller or by the seller to the buyer. In the debit note, the names of buyer and seller, quantity of goods, unit price, total value, etc. are all mentioned. On the basis of counterfoil of debit note, the Purchase Return Book is written (prepared). The format of debit note is similar to an invoice.

As mentioned, a debit note is normally issued by the buyer to the seller but sometimes it is sent by the seller to buyer also.

In the following cases, the buyer may send a debit note to the seller:

(i) when the goods are returned by the buyer to the seller;
(ii) when the seller has charged more than the actual unit price;
(iii) when allowance is made for supplying defective goods to the buyer;
(iv) when through mistake an extra amount has been charged by the seller; and
(v) when by mistake the seller has sent a good which was not mentioned in invoice;

In the following cases seller may send debit note to the buyer:

(i) when the seller forgot to record few legitimate expenses in the invoice;
(ii) when by mistake the seller has sent that goods not mentioned in invoice;
(iii) when the buyer has failed to return the container within the due date and the price of the container has not been recorded in the invoice; and
(iv) when by mistake the seller has been charged lower than the price quoted in the invoice.

The following is the specimen of a debit note:

Debit Note: 20

RATAN ELECTRIC STORES
25A, M.G. Road, Siliguri, Jalpaiguri

Date: 5th March, 2016

To,
Khaitan Electricals Ltd.
1B, BBD Bag
Kolkata 700001

We have debited your account as follows:

Date	Invoice No.	Particulars	Amount
08.04.17	125/4/2017	100 pieces Bulbs @ ₹ 8	800.00
		50 pieces switch @ ₹ 12	600.00
			1400.00
		Less: Trade discount @ 10%	140.00
			1260.00

E & OE

for Ratan Electric Stores
Mr. Samir Dutta
Proprietor

Credit Note

The document which is sent at the time of crediting an account for any reason is called 'credit note'. A credit note is issued by a supplier to a customer giving the customer credit for any products return by the customer for which payment has already been received. When the goods are returned for some reason by the buyer a credit note is prepared by the seller and sent it to the buyer to inform him that his account has been credited. In the credit note, the names of buyer and seller, quantity of goods returned, price etc. are written. The credit note can also be issued to any other person if some thing is credited to his account for any other reason. The format of credit note is similar to invoice. From the counterfoil of credit note the Sales Return Book is prepared.

The following is the specimen of a credit note:

Debit Note: 20

KHAITAN ELECTRIC STORES

1B, BBD Bag, Kolkata 700001

Date: 16 April, 2016

To,
Ratan Electric Stores
25A, M.G. Road,
Siliguri, Jalpaiguri

We have credited your account as follows:

Date	Invoice No.	Particulars	Amount
08.04.17	125/4/2017	100 pieces Bulbs @ ₹ 8	800.00
		50 pieces switch @ ₹ 12	600.00
			1400.00
		Less: Trade discount @ 10%	140.00
			1260.00

E & OE

for Ratan Electric Stores
Mr. M.B. Khaitan
Sales Manager

A credit note is a document which is issued either by the seller to the buyer or by the buyer to the seller.

A seller may send a credit note to the buyer in the following cases:

(i) When the buyer has returned the goods due to damage in transit or inferior quality.

(ii) When the containers are returned by the buyer.

(iii) When the extra amount charged or price per unit is more than the actual discrepancy found in the invoice.

(iv) When goods actually received by the buyer is lower than its invoice value.

(v) When only few goods are damaged in transits but the buyer readily agrees to take the goods at lower than their invoice price.

A buyer may send a credit note to the seller in the following cases:

(i) When by mistake the seller has sent more goods than shown in the invoice.

(ii) When the unit price charged by the seller is lower by discrepancy found, in the invoice.

(iii) When the seller has sent few more goods by mistake.

(iv) When the buyer has failed to return the containers within the due date since price of the containers have not been charged in the invoice.

17.3 PRICE QUOTATIONS

Five different ways in which price may be quoted are the following:

1. **Loco Price:** It refers to the price of goods quoted when they lie at the place and time of sale. The buyer has to incur all other expenses associated with carrying the goods from the sellers' godown.
2. **F.O.R. (Free on Rail):** This refers to the cost of carrying the goods to the railway station by the seller. It includes all expenses till the goods are loaded into the train. This means that the railway freight and all other expenses thereafter, are to be borne by the buyer.
3. **C. & F. (Cost and Freight):** This price quotation includes both the cost of goods and all incidental expenses incurred for transferring the goods to the port of destination. Such a quotation must mention the name of the port of destination at which the delivery will take place, as for example, C & F Kolkata.
4. **C.I.F. (Cost Insurance and Freight):** The term *cif* is used to denote the respective contractual obligations of sellers and buyers of a good which is exported. Thc term CIF is used to refer to the price of a traded good including transport cost. It stands for '*Cost, Insurance and Freight*'. But is used only as these initials (usually lower case: *cif*). It means that a price includes the various cost, such as transportation and insurance needed to transfer (move) a good from one country to another.

   Under a *cif* contract, the seller pays the cost of transporting the goods to the port of shipment, the loading charges and the freight charges to the port of destination, plus all insurance cover up to this point from then on the buyer bears that cost of unloading, transporting, and insuring the good to its final destination.
5. **Franco:** It includes all expenses borne by the seller till the goods reach the buyer's place of delivery. This means that the buyer is required to pay only the price of goods.

17.4 TRADE DISCOUNT

Generally the manufacturers or big traders sell their products at the same prices all over the country. The price of a particular product is mentioned in the catalogue. As they want to sell their products at the same prices everywhere they allow some let off amount on the catalogue price to the retailer. Otherwise, if the maximum retail price (MRP) is printed on the packing, the manufacturers are bound to sell their products by the same prices everywhere. For example, in these cases manufacturers allow some let-off amount to wholesalers and retailers. This let-off amount is called 'trade discount'. Cigarettes, chocolates, etc. are sold everywhere at same prices. The advantages of allowing trade discount are the following:

(i) The goods can be sold everywhere at the same price,

(ii) The same catalogue can be used in any part of the country.

(iii) The business person can increase his/her sales turnover by increasing the rate of trade discount.

(iv) The business person can meet or match competition by changing the rate of trade discount.

17.5 CASH DISCOUNT

Normally manufacturers and big traders sell their goods on credit mainly for increasing their sales turnover. In this way the amount of debt amount increases but a large amount of working capital gets blocked. However, by giving huge discount a business may face liquidity crisis. And just to be able to recover the money the trader may request the debtor to clear the dues before the due date of payment. But the debtors may tell the businessmen that if the dues are paid before the stipulated date, they need some rebate. Alternatively the businessmen can declare if the dues are cleared before due date some rebate will be given. In general business persons allow this type of rebate or discount for quick recovery of dues (which are often very large). This type of rebate is called 'Cash Discount'. In Table 17.2 we show the main points of difference between the two types of discounts.

Distinction between Trade Discount and Cash Discount

The main points of difference between trade discount and cash discount are presented in Table 17.2.

TABLE 17.2: Distinction between Trade Discount and Cash Discount

Trade Discount	Cash Discount
1. It is given to increase the sales turnover.	1. It is given to encourage the debtor, to clear his dues before the stipulated due date.
2. It is allowed at the time of purchase of goods.	2. It is allowed at the time of payment.
3. It is calculated on catalogue price.	3. It is calculated on net sales after allowing trade discount.
4. It is not taken into the book of accounts and is not officially recorded.	4. It is taken into the book of accounts and officially recorded.
5. It is allowed as a custom of trade.	5. It is allowed for prompt payment in case of credit sale.

17.6 STATEMENT OF ACCOUNT

The statement of account is a periodic statement sent to a customer by a supplier which sets out both the money value of products supplied to the customer over a monthly or other period, and any amount still owned by the customer for these products. A statement of account is sent by a supplier some time after an invoice has been sent.

A statement of account is a consolidated statement which a seller sends to his buyers from time to time. Simply put, it is a summary for customers of the transaction which occurred over the proceeding month (or any other period). It is just a reminder to the buyer about the amount due from him.

Key Points

1. **Home trade:** Home trade means trade within the domestic territory of a country. The buyer and seller finalise the terms and conditions through mutual negotiation and bargaining. The terms and conditions of trade or transactions relate to price, quantity, quality, discount structure, mode of delivery of goods and system of payments.
2. **Steps involved in home trade:** (i) Enquiry, (ii) Quotation, (iii) Catalogue, (iv) Order, (v) Acknowledgement, (vi) Execution of order, (vii) Advice note, (viii) Invoice, (ix) Delivery of goods, (x) Payments.
3. **Debit note:** The document which is issued at the time of debiting an account for any reason is called 'debit note'.
4. **Credit note:** The document which is sent at the time of crediting an account for any reason is called 'credit note'.
5. **Price quotations:** (i) Loco price, (ii) Free on Rail [F.O.R.], (iii) Cost and Freight [C & F], (iv) Cost Insurance and Freight [C.I.F.], (v) Franco.
6. **Trade discount:** Manufacturers allow some let-off amount to wholesalers and retailers. The let-off amount is called 'trade discount'.
7. **Cash discount:** In general business persons allow this type of rebate or discount for quick recovery of dues (which are often very large). This type of rebate is called 'Cash Discount'.
8. **Statement of account:** A statement of account is a consolidated statement which a seller sends to his buyers from time to time. Simply put, it is a summary for customers of the transaction which occurred over the proceeding month (or any other period).

KEY Terms	
Enquiry	Credit note
Catalogue	Trade discount
Invoice	Cash discount
Proforma	Quotation
Invoice	Statement of account
Debit note	Advice note
Execution of order	Delivery note
Order	Consignment note

Assignments

SHORT ANSWER-TYPE QUESTIONS

1. What is meant by an enquiry? [ISC 1989]
2. What is catalogue? [ISC 1987]
3. What do you understand by invoice? [ISC 1988]
4. What is a debit note? [ISC 1987, 1989]
5. Give two reasons of preparing a statement of account. [ISC 1988]
6. What is meant by cash discount? [ISC 1989]
7. List two methods of preparing orders. [ISC 1989]
8. Give one purpose of preparing an invoice. [ISC 1990]
9. What is the role of debit and credit notes? [ISC 1991]
10. Distinguish between cash discount and trade discount. [ISC 1992]
11. Give one advantage of cash discount. [ISC 1992]
12. Give one distinguishing factor between a debit note and a credit note. [ISC 1990]
13. What do you understand by a quotation? [ISC 1990]

ESSAY-TYPE QUESTIONS

1. How is trade order executed? [ISC 1987]
2. What is an invoice? Discuss its importance to the buyer. [ISC 1988]
3. Distinguish between:
   (i) Trade Discount and Cash Discount
   (ii) Debit Note and Credit Note
   (iii) Deferred payment System and Hire Purchase System
   (iv) Invoice and Proforma Invoice. [ISC 1992]
   [**Hint:** Ans. to (iii) is given in a different chapter.]
4. (a) Define an order and discuss the essentials of an order.
   (b) Explain four important methods of procuring orders. [ISC 1990]
5. (a) (i) Distinguish between Invoice and Proforma Invoice.
   (ii) Explain the objectives of preparing a Statement of Account.
   (b) What is the meaning and object of a Quotation? [ISC 1989]

QUESTION BANK

1. *When is an invoice prepared by a trader? State the information it contains.*

Ans. See text.

2. *What is Proforma Invoice? When is it used?*

Ans. See text.

3. *When are debit note and credit note issued?*

Ans. See text.

4. *What documents are used in connection with the despatch and delivery of goods? What purposes do they serve?*

Ans. See textThe following documents are used in connection with the despatch and delivery of goods:
   (a) Advice note.
   (b) Delivery note.
   (c) Consignment note.
   [For details see text.]

5. *What is a 'Statement of Account'. Explain its basic purpose.*

Ans. See text.

6. *Distinguish between cash discount and trade discount.*

Ans. See text.

7. *Distinguish between Invoice and Proforma Invoice.*

Ans. See text.

8. *Distinguish between debit note and credit note*.

Ans. See text.

18 CHAMBER OF COMMERCE AND INDUSTRY

SYLLABUS

- *Role of Chambers of Commerce and Industry and Trade Associations.*
- *Meaning and functions of Chambers of Commerce and Trade Associations.*

> ***The chamber of commerce has taught me to tap into the power of collaboration to use referrals to develop genuine relationships, and to share advice with fellow entrepreneurs.***
>
> — Amy Chase Founder, Crompton Collective

LEARNING OUTCOMES

On completion of this chapter, you will be able to understand the following:

18.1 Meaning of Chamber of Commerce
18.2 Trade Association versus Chamber of Commerce
18.3 Objectives of Chamber of Commerce
18.4 Functions of Chamber of Commerce
18.5 Role of Chamber of Commerce
18.6 Types of Chamber of Commerce
18.7 Chambers of Commerce in India

Chambers of commerce and trade associations are a normal feature of commerce and industry for many decades. A chamber of commerce and industry is the premier representative body formed by the business community for the benefit of the community and the socio-economic environment as a whole.

18.1 MEANING OF CHAMBER OF COMMERCE

A chamber of commerce may be defined as a *voluntary association* of business firms engaged in manufacturing, trading, etc. of a particular locality, region or a country. Chambers of commerce are non-profit making organisations, serving the interests of business entities, in particular, and society, in general, through multifarious activities. Distinct from other business or trade associations, the composition of membership of a chamber of commerce in all-embracing, as it is open to entrepreneurs, enterprises, industry and trade associations, as well as professionals covering all sectors of economy.

The origin of chamber of commerce and industry could be traced back to the year 1599, when the term 'Chamber of Commerce' was coined in Marseilles, France. The Marseille Province Chamber of Commerce was set up as the world's earliest chamber of the commerce by the local business community. Since then, chambers of commerce have been formed in scores of countries across the globe, though the organisation of such chambers differs from country to country. In our country, chambers of commerce are registered as societies or Sec 25 companies and function as voluntary organisations.

18.2 TRADE ASSOCIATION VERSUS CHAMBER OF COMMERCE

A trade association is a voluntary organisation of business entities engaged in the same area of activities. For instance, Indian Sugar Mills Association has members all of which are sugar manufacturers. Similarly, we have chemical manufacturers, paper manufacturers associations, etc. Although both chambers of commerce and trade associations are non-profit making voluntary associations of business enterprises, they differ on three main counts:

1. **Scope and Nature:** As mentioned earlier, members of trade associations are engaged in the same trade, whereas membership of a chamber of commerce is open to all enterprises. Obviously then, whereas members of a trade association are essentially competitors, members of a chamber are not, as they represent diverse sectors of an economy.
2. **Name:** Further, trade associations are known by the trade or industry it represents. Indian Sugar Mills Association, Indian Paper Mills Association, etc. In contrast, a chamber of commerce is generally known by the name of the region or country it represents like Bengal Chamber of Commerce and Industry, London Chamber of Commerce and Industry, Indian Chamber of Commerce, etc.
3. **Representation:** A trade association represents the interests of the particular business enterprises, say paper, sugar and chemicals, etc., whereas chamber of commerce and industry functions to promote and protect the interests of business community in general of a locality or region or a country.

18.3 OBJECTIVES OF CHAMBER OF COMMERCE

The objectives of chamber of commerce are the following:

1. To promote and protect interests of member organisations engaged in trade, commerce, manufacturing, etc., in various ways.
2. To act as a catalyst for developing commerce and industry in a locality, region or country as a whole, as the scope of the organisation may be.
3. To deal suitably with the legislative and other measures (like taxation) affecting the business and industry.
4. To communicate with government and other public authorities, and with similar associations in other places on various matters of mercantile and industrial interest.

5. To collect and circulate (among members) information and statistics on various matters of general, commercial and industrial interest, and also exchange relevant information with any other association with similar objectives.

18.4 FUNCTIONS OF CHAMBER OF COMMERCE

In line with those broad objectives chambers of commerce perform multifarious activities. They act as a forum or platform for business organisations to discuss matters of mutual interest and provide a wide range of services to their members (including owners of small businesses), information on business opportunities locally and nationally, expert advisory services, export intelligence and arrange visits and participation in overseas trade fairs and also issue of certificate of origin. Some of these functions are the following:

(i) *Providing information to members:* Chambers of commerce collect information on export prospects, trade channels, potential markets in India and abroad and transmit such information, collected from all possible sources through survey and research through their members. They have separate statistical departments for the purpose. They also publish books, magazines of business interests.

(ii) *Advice:* They provide various types of advice to their members in such critical matters as improvement in product quality, protection of physical environment and promotion of export-import trade.

(iii) *Representation:* They make representation on behalf of members to the government on proposed legislations concerning state take-over on nationalisation of an industry or any existing legislation which is hampering smooth conduct of business and commercial activities such as fringe benefit tax or minimum alternate tax (MAT) and pricing-cum-distribution control, etc.

(iv) *Advising government:* They advise governments — local as well as federal (i.e., central) — in matters concerning developments of trade/and industry in the region or country — in particular, and economic development, in general. They, in the process, exert pressure on the government in adopting business conducive policy measures.

(v) *Inter-state activities:* Chambers of commerce seek to promote inter-state activities such as registration of vehicles, framing surface transport policies and, of course, construction of state roads and national highways.

(vi) *Harmonisation of indirect tax rates:* Earlier chambers used to interact with their respective state governments to harmonise sales tax rates and evolve a rational and uniform sales tax structure in all states. Since the appointment of Jha Committee in 1975, Chambers fought for the introduction of value added tax and have succeeded in their effort. They have taken up the case for goods and services tax (GST) on the pattern of its counterpart in Singapore.

(vii) *Obtaining concession regarding excise duty:* The chambers interact with the government to create pressure for lowering excise duties, so that the product prices could be lowered and more profits could be made through an increase in sales turnover.

(viii) *Provision of training:* In recent years, a particular concern of many chambers of commerce has been the provision of training facilities and centres, run either independently or in conjunction with various government organisations. At the national level this movement is represented by FICCI (New Delhi).

(ix) *Setting ethical norms:* They set ethical business standards and trade norms to be followed by their members and prescribe codes of conduct for them also.

(x) *Forum for interaction:* They act as a forum for enabling the members to discuss different issues and to exchange their views on matters affecting them by conducting meetings and organising conferences and seminars at local, state and national levels.

(xi) *Trade fairs and exhibitions:* They participate in overseas trade fairs and exhibitions to provide information to their members about existing and emerging business opportunities abroad.

(xii) *Arbitration:* Chambers of commerce also act as arbitrators for solving problems and disputes among member business organisations.

(xiii) *Developing public awareness:* Chambers make the public aware of various issues which affect them directly and indirectly. They publish information on consumers' rights and their protection, introduction of new products and services, and social responsibility discharged by their members through such measures as village adoption and setting up health centres in rural areas either on a temporary or on a permanent basis.

18.5 ROLE OF CHAMBER OF COMMERCE

Objectives and functions reveal that the chambers of commerce play a crucial role in promotion of commerce and industry by rendering multifarious valuable services to both business firms and the government. For the business firms:

(i) It provides a platform to discuss common problems and exchange views;

(ii) It helps in creating and/or expanding market for the products of their member organisations (by organising trade fairs/exhibitions in India and abroad);

(iii) Disseminate information (free of charge) and organises seminars,

(iv) Resolves differences among business entities, etc.

Government also (valuable inputs or suggestions of business community from one place which are vital in the formulation of economic (both monetary and fiscal) policies, rules and regulations, preparation of budgets, and also receives assistance in tackling various socio-economic problems in the areas of literacy, sanitation, employment, pollution, etc.

18.6 TYPES OF CHAMBER OF COMMERCE

Chambers of commerce may be formed at local (regional), national and international levels.

1. **Local/Regional Chamber of Commerce:** A local/regional of commerce deals with problems of local/regional trade and industry. Businessmen operating in a particular region or state form these chambers of commerce to protect and promote commerce and industry in a particular region or state.
2. **National Chamber of Commerce:** A national chamber of commerce consists of businessmen operating in different parts of the country as its members and seeks to protect and promote commerce and industry in the entire country.
3. **International Chamber of Commerce:** It consists of members from many countries of the world. India is a member of this chamber of commerce. Its headquarters is located in Paris

(France). It aims at improving the conditions of business and business relations among nations and to encourage better international understanding.

18.7 CHAMBERS OF COMMERCE IN INDIA

In India, chambers of commerce and industry have been functioning at both state/regional and national level. The following is an illustrative list:

1. State/Regional Chambers
   (a) Bengal Chamber of Commerce and Industry
   (b) Goa Chamber of Commerce (Goa)
   (c) Indian merchants Chamber (Mumbai)
   (d) Madras Chamber of Commerce
   (e) Punjab, Haryana and Delhi (PHD) Chamber of Commerce and Industry
2. National Level Chambers
   (a) Federation of Indian Chambers of Commerce and Industry (FICCI)
   (b) Associated Chambers of Commerce and Industry (ASSOCHAM)
   (c) Confederation of Indian Industry (CII)

These three national level chambers actually act as apex organisations — members of which are local regional chambers of commerce and various trade associations. We now discuss below these three entities briefly.

FICCI

It was set up in New Delhi as early as in 1927 as an apex chamber of commerce. Founded by late G. D. Birla and Purushottam Thakur on the advice of Mahatma Gandhi, its history is closely interwoven with India's struggle for independence, its industrialisation, and its emergence as one of the rapidly growing global countries. Having both individual and corporate members, FICCI's membership consists of more than 500 chambers and trade associations, 20 overseas chambers and 1500 associate members (like individuals, firms and companies). As a premier organisation, representing the interests of traders and industrialists all over the country, FICCI is backed by nation-wide network of local, state-level and regional chambers, trade associations, etc.

A non-government, not-for-profit organisation, FICCI is the voice of India's business and industry. From influencing policy to encouraging debate, engaging with policy makers and civil society, FICCI articulates the views and concerns of commerce and industry. It provides a platform for networking and consensus building within and across sectors. Through its (nearly) 400 professionals, FICCI is active in 88 sectors of the economy. It works closely with the government on policy issues, enhancing efficiency, competitiveness and expanding business opportunities for industry through a range of specialized services and global linkages.

CII

The origin of CII can be traced back to 1895 when five engineering companies joined hands to form the Engineering and Iron Trade Association (EITA). Subsequently, its name was changed to Indian Engineering Association in 1912. This Association represented primarily the big British firms and, therefore, another association called Engineering Association of India (EAI) was formed in 1942. EAI represented small and medium engineering firms mostly owned and promoted by Indians and had different origins and management styles from the IEA. In 1974, these two associations merged and formed the Association of Indian Engineering Industry. (AIEI) keeping in view the greater interests of the engineering industry in the country. The merger meant a stronger association capable of harnessing larger resources and providing a wider range of services.

In 1986, its name was changed to Confederation of Indian Industry (CEI), reflecting the growth and expansion of the organisation since 1974. With effect from January 1, 1992, the name was changed to Confederation of Indian Industry (CII) as it was felt that in the post-liberalisation era there would be inter-sectoral integration through a process of diversification and expansion, where the engineering firms would diversify into non-engineering areas (like L&T promoted L & T Infotech) and vice-versa. CII is the apex organisation for industry in India with membership consisting of over thousands of companies renging from public to private sectors. It operates through a federal structure comprising the national council, regional councils and state — zonal councils. It has also set up nearly 60 offices in India and overseas.

CII, like FICCI, also acts as a catalyst for promotion and development of Indian industry, by continuous dialogue with the policy makers, planners, and helping them in policy formulation, by providing the business firms a platform for discussion and exchange of views on matters of common interest, by conducting relevant research, data collection or compilation and dissemination of information among member firms and associations, by organising trade fairs etc. and through cooperation with counterpart organisations. It thus plays a proactive role to create and sustain an environment conducive to growth of industry in India and help in enhancing their efficiency, competitiveness and expanding business opportunities.

ASSOCHAM

Associated Chambers of Commerce and Industry of India (ASSOCHAM) was promoted in 1920 by 5 promoter chambers — Bombay Chamber of Commerce and Industry (Mumbai), Cochin Chamber of Commerce and Industry (Cochin), Indian Merchants Chamber (Mumbai), the Madras Chamber of Commerce and Industry (Madras) and PHD Chamber of Commerce and Industry. Headquartered in New Delhi, ASSOCHAM is also an apex chamber like FICCI and CII, having under its fold more than 400 chambers and trade associations and serving thousands of members all over India.

ASSOCHAM has 59 Expert Committees that provide the necessary platform to its members of interaction and aid formulating policy recommendations to facilitate economic, industrial and social growth. The organisation represents the interests of industry and commerce and acts as an interface between industry, government and other relevant stakeholders on policy issues and initiatives. It plays a special role in promoting international trade and interacts with counterpart international organisations to resolve bilateral economic issues.

Key Points

1. **Chamber of commerce:** It is a non-profit making voluntary organisation of business entities engaged in trading, manufacturing, etc., in a locality/region/state/country. A chamber of commerce represents business entities engaged in diverse sectors, viz., steel, paper, sugar, etc.
2. **Trade association:** A trade association, like chamber of commerce is also a voluntary organisation. But unlike chamber of commerce, here all business entities are engaged is same area of activity. For example, all members of Indian Sugar Mills Association are engaged in sugar manufacturing.
3. **Role of chamber of commerce:** Chambers play a crucial role in the promotion of commerce and industry by rendering a variety of services to both business firms and the government. Indeed, it works as an interface between the two.
4. **Types of chambers:** Chambers of commerce are of three types, viz., local/regional, national and international. In India, we have both local/state level chamber of commerce, viz., Bombay Chamber of Commerce, Goa Chamber of Commerce at the state level, and FICCI, CII, ASSOCHAM at the national level.

KEY Terms	
Trade association	Regional chamber of commerce
Apex chamber of commerce	CII
Non-profit making organisation	National chamber of commerce
FICCI	ASSOCHAM

Assignments

SHORT ANSWER-TYPE QUESTIONS

1. Define a chamber of commerce.
2. Give two main reasons for the establishment of chambers of commerce.
3. Enumerate the points of distinction between chambers of commerce and trade associations.
4. Name any three national level chambers of commerce in India.
5. Mention two functions of a chamber of commerce.
6. How do chambers of commerce try to secure political decision in favour of businessmen?

ESSAY-TYPE QUESTIONS

1. What is a chamber of commerce? How does it differ from a trade association?

2. Explain the important functions of chambers of commerce.
3. Discuss the role of any two famous chambers of commerce in India.
4. Explain the advantages of chamber of commerce.
5. How do chambers of commerce protect and promote the business interests of their members?

QUESTION BANK

1. *What is a chamber of commerce?*

Ans. See text.

2. *What is a Trade Association?*

Ans. See text.

3. *What is the similarity between Chamber of Commerce and Trade Associations?*

Ans. Both chambers of commerce and Trade Associations are voluntary and non-profit organisations of businessmen. They perform by large and similar functions.

4. *Distinguish between Trade Associations and Chambers of Commerce.*

Ans. See text.

5. *Give any three functions of a chamber of commerce.*

Ans. The three functions of a chamber of commerce are the following:
   (i) Collecting and publishing information useful to business community.
   (ii) Influencing public opinion and legislation in favour of businessmen.
   (iii) Organising trade fairs and exhibitions for promoting business interests.

6. *Explain the functions of chamber of commerce.*

Ans. See text.

7. *Give names of three Chambers of Commerce in India.*

Ans. The names of three chambers of commerce in India are the following:
   (i) Punjab, Haryana and Delhi (PHD) Chamber of Commerce.
   (ii) Bengal Chamber of Commerce.
   (iii) Indian Merchants Chamber

8. *State the names of three trade associations in India.*

Ans. The three trade associations in India are the following:
   (i) Indian Sugar Mills Association
   (ii) India Jute Mills Association
   (iii) All India Foodgrain Dealers' Association.

9. *What does the following terms stand for? (a) FICCI, (b) CII*

Ans. (i) FICCI = Federation of Indian Chambers of Commerce and Industry. (ii) CII = Confederation of Indian Industry.

10. *What are the objectives of a chamber of commerce?*

Ans. See text.

11. *Mark the following statements True or False.*
    (a) *A trade association represents the interests of one trade or industry.*
    (b) *A chamber of commerce is a regional body.*
    (c) *FICCI is an apex body.*
    (d) *CII is an apex body.*
    (e) *ASSOCHAM is an apex body.*
    (f) *AIOE is an association of employees.*
    (g) *PHD Chamber of Commerce is a body of firms in Delhi, Haryana and Punjab.*
    (h) *Trade Associations and Chambers of commerce are non-profit making organisations.*

Ans. All are true.

12. *Match the items under Column A with those under Column B.*

Column A	Column B
(i) FICCI, ASSOCHAM	(i) Trade Association
(ii) PHD Chamber of Commerce	(ii) Trade Association
(iii) Indian Sugar Mills Association	(iii) Apex Chamber of Commerce
(iv) Indian Cotton Mills Association	(iv) Local chamber of commerce
(v) Indian Paper Mills Association	(v) Trade Association
(vi) Trade Association	(vi) Members doing similar businesses
(vii) Chamber of Commerce	(vii) Members doing different businesses

Ans. A. (i) (ii) (iii) (iv) (v) (vi) (vii)
B. (iii) (iv) (i) (ii) (v) (vi) (vii).

19 THE NATURE AND SCOPE OF FOREIGN TRADE

SYLLABUS

- *Meaning, difference between internal trade and external trade.*
- *Meaning and characteristics of international trade; problems of international trade; advantages and disadvantages of international trade.*

> *Everyone knows that some international trade is beneficial. Many people are skeptical, however, about the benefits of trading for goods that a country could provide for itself.*
>
> — Paul. R. Krugman (Nobel Laureate, 2005)

LEARNING OUTCOMES

On completion of this chapter, you will be able to understand the following:

19.1 Meaning of International Trade
19.2 Characteristics of International Trade
19.3 Difference between Internal Trade and External Trade
19.4 The Basis of Foreign Trade
19.5 Difficulties or Problems of International Trade
19.6 Importance and Advantages of International Trade
19.7 Disadvantages of International Trade
19.8 Documents used in International Trade
19.9 The Balance of Payments (B/P)
19.10 Types of Price Quotations used in Foreign Trade

No country in the world is self-sufficient today. Almost every country is having trading relation with the rest of the world. And all countries, to a greater or lesser degree, engage in international trade with other countries. This is true no matter which economic system is in place — capitalist, socialist or mixed. The growth of world trade in recent years has been very rapid. In addition, the huge expansion in trade between certain countries, for example China with the USA and the EU, has had a great impact on their economic development.

When people say that 'the world is getting smaller every day,' they are referring not only to the increased speed and ease of transportation and communication but also to the increased use of international markets to buy and sell goods, services and financial assets.

Signs of international transactions are all around us. The clothes we wear come from various countries. The oil we consume comes from Venezuela, Iran, Iraq and other countries. The same can be said of the shoes we wear, the appliances we use, and many different services we consume. Furthermore, many products are manufactured in India by using important parts produced in other countries. At the same time, many Indian imports are manufactured with important components made in India.

The increased internationalisation of economic life is made even more complicated by foreign-owned assets. More and more companies in many countries are owned partially or totally by foreigners. In addition, foreigners purchase shares of Indian companies.

International trade is an integral point of the economic activities of a nation. The reason is that in today's world no country is totally self-sufficient. It cannot produce all the goods it needs for consumption or accumulation (investment) with its own resources (factor endowments). And even if it can produce everything it requires, it cannot produce most of the items efficiently (i.e., at low cost). So it produces certain items in which it has relative efficiency, consumes a certain portion of it and sells its surplus output to other countries. Selling goods to other countries is known as exporting. Through exports, a country like India earns foreign exchange. And this is utilised to buy other goods which India needs but cannot itself produce or produce cheaply (i.e., at low cost) with its own resources and by using its existing technology. Buying goods from other countries is known as importing. Imports enable the people of a country to consume those goods which they need to satisfy their wants (at low costs) and desires but which they cannot produce in adequate quantities or cannot produce at all. Thus, international trade enables a country to increase its consumption possibilities.

International (foreign) trade consists of both exporting and importing activities. The use of the currencies of different countries (called foreign exchange) is involved in receiving payment for export as also for making payment for imports of goods and services. In this chapter, we will study the meaning, nature and importance of international trade as also the various procedures related to exports and imports of goods (called merchandise or visible items).

19.1 MEANING OF INTERNATIONAL TRADE

19.1.1 Definition of International Trade

International trade means buying and selling of goods by one country from and to other countries or from the rest of the world. It consists of the exchange of goods and services between (among) the people of different countries.

International trade is of the following six types:

(i) *Import trade:* It involves purchase of goods from foreign markets for consumption and production in the home country.

(ii) *Export trade:* It involves supply of domestic goods to foreigners.

(iii) *Entrepot or re-export Trade:* It involves the import of foreign goods for re-exporting them for making profit. For example, an Indian trader imports goods from China and exports the same to Africa.

(iv) *Outsourcing:* We have already discussed the issue of outsourcing in an earlier chapter. Outsourcing refers to "locating services or production process abroad. Prominent examples are telemarketing, medical diagnosis, publishing, web development and engineering. These differ from the more conventional international trade in goods because today, with rapid and low-cost communication, such processes can be economically located where costs are lower. Low-cost communication makes it possible to have Indian architects work on designs for New York firms today."[1]

(v) *Counter trade (Trading):* Counter trading is a complex form of business in which several countries are involved. And each one trades goods or services for those of others' counter trading is a complex form of business in which several countries are involved. And each one trades goods or services for these of others. It refers to the direct or indirect exchange of goods for other goods in international trade. Such trade is generally resorted to when there is shortage of particular foreign currencies or when countries apply foreign exchange controls. Such trade is often based on barter in which part or all of payments is made in a form other than hard currency (such as dollar, pound or Euro) — that is, in goods or services.

(vi) *Intra-industry trade:* Now-a-days we also find extensive intra-industry trade. India both exports and imports computers and related equipment. Likewise, Intel produces high-end semi-conductors. It has facilities in the USA, as well as in China, Malayasia and the Philippines, and the company often ships products manufactured in one country to be assembled and tested in another country. Similar patterns of intra-industry specialisation and trade are found in case of cars, textiles, finished steel and various other items.

19.2 CHARACTERISTICS OF INTERNATIONAL TRADE

Just as internal trade is trade among the people of India international trade is trade among Indians and foreigners. The common features of international trade are the following:

1. **Exchange of goods:** International trade involves purchase of goods from other countries and sale of goods to them in exchange. Importing is buying products from another country. Exporting is selling products to another country. However, nowadays we find another type of trade, known as entrepot trade. Such trade occurs when goods are imported from a country with the objective of exporting them to some other country (or countries).
2. **Parties involved in external trade:** The parties usually involved in international trade may be either individuals and business firms or even governments of two or more countries. For example, certain items one imported in India through a government agency called the State Trading Corporation of India (STCI).
3. **Use of foreign currencies:** In any export or import activity currencies of different countries are involved. For example, India pays for its imports in foreign currency. The conversion of a foreign currency into rupee or vice versa is controlled and regulated by an exchange control authority such as the Reserve Bank of India.
4. **Restrictions:** There are various restrictions on the free movement of goods across national borders. The Government of India now imposes tariffs on imports called customs duties.

1 P.A. Samuelson and W.D. Nordhaus: *Economics* (TMH; 19th edn. 2011), p. 430

For exports and imports of certain goods there is requirement for licensing. In some countries, import quotes (physical limits) are imposed. There is also state trading in case of certain goods, called canalised items.

5. **Risk:** Various types of risks are associated with international trade such as exchange rate fluctuations, perils of sea and spoilage of goods due to delayed arrival of ships. And marine insurance is necessary to protect traders from such risks.
6. **Lengthy process:** Due to geographical distance and physical barriers, shipment of goods to other countries is a difficult and time consuming process. In general, there is a time lag between export of the goods by a country and the receipt of the same by the importer of another country.
7. **Language problem:** Due to differences in languages between two countries, entering into import and export transactions involves problems. For example, trading with China is difficult to some extent because most Chinese people cannot communicate in English.

19.3 DIFFERENCE BETWEEN INTERNAL TRADE AND EXTERNAL TRADE

The main points of difference between internal trade and external trade are listed in Table 19.1.

TABLE 19.1: Difference between Internal Trade vs. External Trade

Basis	Internal Trade	External Trade
1. Meaning	Internal trade refers to the trade between different people within the domestic territory of a country.	External trade refers to the trade among the people of two or more countries (nations).
2. Government restrictions	Internal trade is free from most, if not all, government restrictions.	There are various types of restrictions on international trade, e.g., licensing, quotas, tariffs, foreign exchange control and specification of quality of goods which are imported and exported.
3. Mode of transport	Since road or rail transport is used, the cost of transport is low.	Mainly sea or air transport is used for long distances. So transport cost is high.
4. Degree of risk(s)	Not much risk is involved in transit.	It involves various types of risks in transit. Sea transport involves much more risk than surface transport.
5. Language(s)	There is not much language problem within the same country as there is a national language.	The use of different languages in different countries hinders the free flow of trade by creating various barriers to communication.
6. Method of making payment	Since payment can be made either in cash or through cheque, the collection of payments is simple and easy.	Since payments are made through banks, the collection procedure is both time-consuming and costly.
7. Currency	A single currency such as the rupee is used throughout India in all types of transactions.	Currencies of two or more countries are involved. So exporters and importers have to agree on a particular rate of exchange between the two before getting involved in trading.
8. Laws, rules and regulations	Internal trade is governed by national laws, rules and regulations.	International trade is governed by the law of different trading nations, international laws and, of course, customs formalities.

19.4 THE BASIS OF FOREIGN TRADE

International trade refers to trade between (among) two (or more) countries in goods or merchandise. It is based on differences between countries in their competitive advantages (or 'comparative advantages'). So they to supply different products on the basis of international division of labour and specialisation. This generates flow of exports and imports between (among) countries.

Inter-country variations in comparative advantage are reflected both in terms of their differential cost structures (i.e., price competitiveness) and different skill levels (i.e., product differentiation competitiveness). These, in turn, are determined in large measure by the country's basic factor endowments (natural resources, labour and capital) and degree of economic maturity (level of per capita income, general cost and price levels, scientific and technical skills, etc.). Resource availability and skills indicate the product range which a country is technically capable of supplying, while *relative* cost, price and product differentiation factors dictate which of these products it is economically appropriate for the country to produce, i.e., those products in which it has a comparative advantage or relative efficiency over other countries.

In fact, there are various causes of international trade or, in other words, there are different sources of international trade arising from differences in productivity of labour and capital and factor endowments. In fact, international trade arises from differences in comparative advantage or relative efficiency of two or more countries in the production of two or more commodities. For example, if with the same quantity of labour, India can produce more cloth and less machinery than the USA, India will export cloth to the USA and import machinery from the USA. This is the essence of David Ricardo's age-old theory of comparative advantage which suggests that international trade is based on differences in relative efficiency of two countries in the production of the same two commodities. If two countries are not equally efficient in the production of the same two goods by using the same amount of resources (measured in standard labour hours) a basis of trade between them will always exist from the supply side.

The modern view of comparative cost is that a labour-abundant (capital-scarce) country like India produce and export labour-intensive goods like textiles. And a capital-abundant (or labour-scarce) country like the USA will export a capital-intensive good such as machinery.

The optimisation of benefits of international trade is best achieved by conditions of free trade, (i.e., the absence of restrictions on trade such as tariffs and quotas). This view was given operational validity by the international community through the establishment of the World Trade Organisation (WTO) and the formation of various regional free trade blocs.

19.5 DIFFICULTIES OR PROBLEMS OF INTERNATIONAL TRADE

There are various problems associated with the smooth conduct of international trade. Some of these problems are really complex. In addition, there are various hindrances (barriers) to such trade. The most common problems which restrict the flow of international trade are the following:

1. **Use of different currencies:** Each trading nation has its own currency and the currency of one country is not normally accepted in another country. Only the US dollar is accepted as an international medium of exchange (because it a fully convertible currency, i.e., convertible on both the current and the capital account). Hence, foreign trade involves conversion of one currency into another at the current rate of exchange.

2. **Tariff and non-tariff barriers:** There are various restrictions on exports and imports. Different countries impose different types of restrictions mainly on imports such as import tariffs, import quotas, foreign exchange controls, etc. Such restrictions reduce the volume of trade.
3. **Risk associated with movement of goods:** Due to lack of geographical proximity and various physical barriers, movement of goods from one country to another is costly, time-consuming and often a hazardous process. Goods are also exposed to a high degree of risk during transit.
4. **Time lag:** In general, there is a time lag between the shipment of the goods by the exporter and the receipt of the same by the importer. Some extra time is needed to receive payment from importers.
5. **Language and script:** Each country has its own language and its own script as well. This creates genuine communication problem among the traders of different countries. The problem becomes really serious in those countries such as China and Cambodia where most people do not speak English.
6. **Lack of direct contact:** Due to the absence of direct contact between the seller and the buyer, the former finds it really difficult to assess the creditworthiness of the latter and for the latter to ascertain the reliability of the former. Thus, international trade implies getting involved with strangers or with people in unknown territories.

Local Content Requirement or Rule of Origin

A major drawback of international trade is the existence of local content rule. This refers to the stipulation by a country that for a product to qualify as an authentic (genuine) domestically manufactured product (that is originating in the country) the product has to be manufactured mainly from locally supplied as opposed to imported components (which may be cheaper and of better quality). Local content rules are used by governments mainly to prevent the operation of the so-called 'screw driver' plants (plants producing only final products from mainly imported components). Such plants are established to circumvent tariffs, quotas and anti-dumping duties imposed on imported final products.

Dumping

Dumping refers to the sale of a product by a firm in an export market at a price below that charged in its own domestic market. This is done to increase the firm's market share in export markets in the long-run. However, such unfair trade practice goes against the rule of the WTO (to be discussed in Ch. 22).

Voluntary Export Restraint (VER)

A new form of import restriction is in operation now. This is known as voluntary export restraint (VER). It is essentially a restriction on a country's import which is achieved by negotiating with a foreign exporting country for inducing it to restrict its export. For example, Italy can restrict imports of shoes from Indonesia. If it wants to protect its domestic market from Indonesian competition, it must discourage import of shoes as a whole. This might induce a number of countries to adopt retaliatory measures against Italy. However, if Italy can persuade Indonesia to voluntarily limit its export, this potential problem is solved. A bilateral agreement on the export side allows

Italy to discriminate against Indonesian imports alone without formally breaking WTO principles such as reciprocity and non-discrimination.

Trade War

The benefits of international trade may be offset by trade war. It refers to the use by a number of countries of trade restrictions through tariffs and quotas to reduce imports and subsidies and tax concessions to raise exports. These actions are usually self-defeating, leading to lower trade and incomes for all. It refers to a period in which each of any two trading nations alternate in further restricting trade from the other — more specifically, the process of imposing prohibitive tariff (to stop imports) and retaliation. Retaliation refers to the process of one country raising its tariff to secure some advantage, to which another country responds by raising its tariff, the first raises its tariff still further and the process goes on and on.

19.6 IMPORTANCE AND ADVANTAGES OF INTERNATIONAL TRADE

No country in the world is totally self-sufficient today, i.e., it is not capable of producing everything to meet the consumption needs of its people. And even if a country can produce most, if not all the items, it cannot produce them more efficiently (i.e., at low cost). Two countries can trade to their mutual benefit even when one of them is more efficient than the other at producing everything and when producers in the less efficient country can compete only by paying lower wages. As P. Krugman has put it, " trade provides benefits by allowing countries to export goods whose production makes relatively heavy use of resources that are locally abundant while importing goods whose production makes heavy use of resources that are locally scarce". Thus, through exports and imports, a country can derive the advantages of (international) division of labour and specialisation. This is due to the differences in factor endowments among nations, i.e., stocks of natural resources and levels of skill among workers and, of course, differences in technology. Foreign trade enables every country to specialise in the production of those goods which require the use of abundant factors (such as land, capital and labour force).

Through trade, nations can improve their available consumption. If no trade takes place, every nation has to remain satisfied with its own production. Free trade (or even restricted trade) expands consumption options of nations.

Uncommon Sense

It is a common sense that countries will produce and export goods for which they are uniquely qualified. However, the uncommon sense is that each country will benefit if it specialises in the production and export of those goods which it can produce at relatively low cost. Conversely, each country will benefit if it imports those goods which it produces at relatively high cost. International trade increases a country's consumption possibilities and makes its people better off. A country is able to get those goods which it needs but cannot itself produce. Similarly, it can get certain things at lower prices through imports. To be more specific, workers in India can obtain a larger quantity of consumer goods for the same amount of work when they specialise in their areas of relative efficiency. Thus, it improves the standard of living of the people of the trading nation. International trade also acts as an engine of economic growth. By importing capital goods such as machines and strategic raw materials such as crude oil, a country can achieve faster economic growth.

The advantages (benefits) of international trade are the following:

1. *Efficient allocation and optimal use of resources:* Free trade enables countries to shift production in their own areas of relative efficiency (or comparative advantage). Foreign trade leads to international division of labour and specialisation and thus the use of the scarce resources of a country becomes efficient.
2. *Improving standard of living:* Foreign trade increases the standards of living of the people of a country by supplying those goods and services which it cannot produce efficiently or produce at all. For example, India is able to consume more petrol than it is able to produce domestically. Similarly, Iran is able to consume tea which it cannot produce.

BUSINESS FOCUS: COMMON MISCONCEPTION ABOUT TRADE

To quote Nobel Laureate Paul Krugman, "It is a common misconception that trade is harmful if there are large disparities between countries in productivity or wages. On one side, business people in less technologically advanced countries, such as India, often worry that opening their economies to international trade will lead to disaster because their industries won't be able to compete. On the other side, people in technologically advanced nations where workers earn high wages, often fear that trading with less advanced, lower wage countries will drag their standard of living down".

3. *Acting as an engine of growth:* By specialising in the production of those which a country such as India has comparative advantage (relative efficiency), it can increase its value of production due to an increase in labour productivity. As a result, it can generate a surplus even after meeting its consumption needs. And this surplus (or a major portion on it) can be exported to other countries to earn foreign currencies which can be utilised to import other goods (i.e., goods which a country cannot produce at low cost or cannot produce at all). By enabling a developing country like India to utilise its latent resources, trade acts as a growth-promoting factor (or a growth-driver).

BUSINESS FOCUS: MASS PRODUCTION AND COMPETITIVE ADVANTAGE

No doubt, the most important reason for international trade is the differences among countries in production costs. This is partly attributable to differences in labour costs, but largely to economies of scale. Some companies or countries enjoy economies of scale. This means that they tend to have lower average costs as their volumes of production continue to increase. So when a particular country succeeds in developing a product, it can become the high-volume, low-cost producer. The economies of scale (size) give it a significant cost and technological advantage over other countries, which find it cheaper to buy from the low-cost producer than to make the product itself. Large-scale production is an important advantage in industries with major research-and-development expenses. As the market leader, Boeing can spread the enormous cost of designing, developing, and testing a new plane over a large sales volume. This means that it sells aircraft (planes) at a lower price than its competitors such as Airbus.

4. *Stabilisation of commodity prices:* Foreign trade promotes competition among nations. And the forces of competition lead to equalisation of the prices of commodities throughout the world.
5. *Employment generation.* Foreign trade helps to create new employment opportunities by promoting export-oriented industries.

6. *Economies of size (scale):* International trade also allows countries to specialise in producing narrower range of goods, giving them greater efficiencies of large-scale mass production.

7. *Cordial relations among nations:* International trade promotes friendly rather than hostile relations among nations since there is a harmony of interests. So wars and strained international relations can be avoided.

8. *Other benefits of trade:* The benefits of international trade are not restricted to trade in goods (merchandise). International migration and international borrowing and lending are also forms of mutually beneficial trade — the first a trade of labour for goods and services and the second a trade of current goods for the promise of future goods. Finally, international exchanges of risky assets such as stocks and bonds can benefit all countries by allowing each country to diversify its wealth portfolio and reduce the variability of its income. These invisible forms of trade yield gains which are real (or genuine).

In recent years, there have been moves to reduce restrictions on international trade. These measures have been a major force behind the 'globalisation' process. Globalisation refers to the increasing freedom of movement of goods, capital and people around the world. This shrinking of the world is now having a major impact on business activity, especially from multinational corporation or international giants. The free-trade movement and the increasing use of the Internet are narrowing the differences that existed in the past between national markets, reducing the importance of national borders and making it easier for firms to trade with and locate in many countries. This is forcing firms, which were once protected by national governments, to become internationally competitive. The recent moves towards free trade have been driven by:

1. **The World Trade Organisation (WTO):** This is made up of countries committed to the principle of freeing world trade from various restrictions. It holds regular meetings to discuss reductions in tariffs and quotas and these have to be agreed by all members. Recently, China joined the WTO and other countries are concerned about the effect of such a major producer of goods — with very low labour and other costs — competing freely with them. [See Chapter 22 for a detailed discussion of WTO.]

2. **Free-trade Blocs:** These are groups of countries, often geographically integrated to one another, that have arranged to trade with one another without restrictions. The best examples are NAFTA (USA, Canada, Mexico in the North American Free Trade Association) and ASEAN (Association of South East Asian Nations). The members of the European Union (EU) also trade freely among themselves, but the EU is more free than a free-trade bloc. The danger with these blocs is that they may agree to impose trade barriers on other groups of countries in order to gain competitive advantage against imports from these other groups or non-member countries.

19.7 DISADVANTAGES OF INTERNATIONAL TRADE

International trade is not an unmixed blessing. It has the following disadvantages or drawbacks:

1. **Dependence on imports:** Dependence on foreign goods may create a crisis in times of war or emergency. For example, in times of Gulf War, American exporters refused to sell their products to enemies, i.e., the Gulf countries.

2. **Decline of domestic industries:** Unrestricted imports may lead to decline of a developing country's infant industries. There may be uneven or inadequate development of the economy due to excessive dependence on imports.
3. **Job loss:** International trade can adversely affect the owners of resources which are 'specific' to industries which compete with imports, that is, cannot find employment in other industries.
4. **Distribution of income:** While nations generally gain from international trade, such trade may hurt workers and benefit the owners of capital within nations.
5. **Limits to growth:** Exports of non-renewable natural resources such as minerals, ores, coal, etc. may set limits to the growth of domestic industries by creating shortage of raw materials.
6. **Unfair competition:** Foreign trade allows the developed countries to get involved in unfair competition with the developing countries which have no bargaining power in international commodity markets. This may create rivalry between (among) different countries and may even result in trade war. The present trade war between the USA and Japan illustrates this point. The advantages and disadvantage of free trade are listed in table 19.2.

TABLE 19.2: The Advantages and Disadvantages of Free Trade

Advantages	Disadvantages
1. The global market contains more than 7 billion potential customers for goods and services.	1. Domestic workers (particularly in manufacturing-based jobs) can lose their jobs due to increased imports or production shifts to low-wage global markets.
2. Productivity grows when countries produce goods and services in which they have a comparative advantage.	2. Workers may be forced to accept pay cuts from employers who can threaten to move their jobs to lower-cost global markets.
3. Global competition and less-costly imports keep prices down; so inflation does not curtail economic growth.	3. Moving operations overseas because of intense competitive pressure often means the loss of service jobs and growing numbers of white-collar (i.e., desk) jobs.
4. Free trade inspires innovation for new products and keeps firms competitively challenged.	4. Domestic companies can lose their comparative advantage when competitors use advanced (and low-cost) production techniques in low-wage countries.
5. Uninterrupted flow of capital gives countries access to foreign investment, which help keep interest rates low.	5. Domestic industries may be destroyed due to dumping i.e., sale of foreign goods in domestic market at less-than-cost prices.

In practice however, the benefits of international trade are often unequally divided between (among) countries. This inevitably tends to create situations in which national self-interest is put before international obligations and extensions of international cooperation.

19.8 DOCUMENTS USED IN INTERNATIONAL TRADE

The following documents are used in foreign trade:

1. Indent
2. Letter of Credit
3. Bill of Entry
4. Bill of Sight

5. Dock Challan
6. Bill of Lading
7. Mate's Receipt
8. Shipping Order
9. Shipping Bill
10. Insurance Policy
11. Consular Invoice
12. Certificate of Origin
13. Advice Note
14. Dock Warrant
15. Port Trust Dues Receipt
16. Documentary Bill of Exchange – D/A or D/P

These documents will be defined and explained in the next two chapters.

19.9 THE BALANCE OF PAYMENTS (B/P)

The balance of payments of a country is a statement of a country's trade and financial transactions with the rest of the world over a particular time period, usually one year. The account is divided into two main parts: (a) Current account, and (b) Capital and financial account.

The current account shows India's profit or loss in day-to-day dealings. It is made up (compiled) under two headings. The 'visible' trade balance (or the balance of trade) indicates the difference between the value of merchandise Exports and Imports of goods (raw materials, foodstuffs, oil and fuel, semi-processed and finished manufacturers). 'Visibles' are so called because they consist of tangible goods that can be seen directly and recorded by the country's customs and excise authorities as they move into or out of the country. The second group of transactions make up the 'invisible' trade balance. These transactions include earnings from, and payments for, such services as banking, insurance, transport and tourism. It also includes interest, dividends and profits on investments and loans, and government receipts and payments relating to defence, maintenance of embassies, etc.

'Invisibles' are so called because basically they represent transactions that cannot be seen directly. These can be compiled only indirectly from company returns, governments accounts, foreign currency purchases and sales data from banks.

In addition to current account transactions, there are also currency flows into and out of the country related to capital items. The capital and financial account is made up of a number of elements including: receipts and payments related to foreign direct investment (money spent by companies on setting up or acquiring overseas manufacturing plants, sales office, etc.); receipts and payments related to portfolio investment (monies spent by mainly financial institutions in purchasing overseas stocks and shares, government bonds, etc.); and receipts and payments related to interbank transfers (for example, foreign currency deposits with Indian commercial banks taking advantage of higher Indian interest rates compared to those in other financial centres).

19.10 TYPES OF PRICE QUOTATIONS USED IN FOREIGN TRADE

Terms of sale, or trade terms, differ somewhat in international trade from those used in domestic trade. In India's domestic trade, it is customary to use FOB (free on board, meaning that the price is established at the door of the factory), freight collect, prepaid, or COD (cash, or collect on delivery). International trade terms often sound similar to those used in domestic trade but generally have different meaning. International terms indicate new buyers and sellers are dividing risk and obligation and, therefore, the cost of specific kinds of international trade transactions.

In addition to the cost of acquiring foreign goods, the importer has also to bear other costs such as freight, insurance, etc. involved in shipment of goods from the exporter's place to that of the importer. The price to be actually paid by the importer is determined by the type of price quoted by the exporter. In international trade, the following types of price quotations are often used:

1. **Cost and Freight (C & F):** To a named overseas port of import. It refers to an export contract in which the seller pays the cost of shipping the good, to the port of destination, i.e., the cost of goods and all incidental expenses incurred for taking the goods to the port. Such a quotation must include the name of the port at which delivery of an exported item will take place, e.g., C & F Kolkata.
2. **Cost, Insurance and Freight (CIF):** If the seller (exporter) also pays the cost of marine insurance it is known as cost, insurance and freight (CIF).

   Thus, CIF = C & F + marine insurance charges.

   A CIF quote is more meaningful to the overseas buyer because it includes the costs of goods, insurance, and all transportation and miscellaneous charges to the named place of debarkation.
3. **F.A.S.:** The price includes cost of the goods and charges for delivery of the goods along side the shipping vessel. The buyer (importer) is responsible for the cost of loading onto the vessel, transportation and insurance.

SYNOPSIS FOR LEARNING: FOUR PRICE QUOTATIONS IN EXTERNAL TRADE

C & F = F.O.B. + Freight

C.I.F. = C & F + Marine insurance charges

F.A.S. = Cost of goods + packing charges + transport to port + export duty + dock charges.

F.O.B. = F.A.S. + loading charges.

4. **Free on Board (F.O.B.):** At a named inland point of origin, at a named port of exportation, or at a named vessel and port of export. The price includes the cost of the goods and delivery to the place named.

- **Loco Price:** It includes the unit cost of producing goods as also a normal profit margin. The buyer has to bear the expenses of lifting and transferring the goods from the factory or warehouse as also other incidental expenses. It is also known as ex-factory price.
- **In Bond Price:** This price includes all the expenses associated with carrying goods to bonded warehouse located at or near the port of destination. The importer can take delivery of the goods from the warehouse after customs clearance i.e. after completion of customs formalities and payment of customs duties.
- **Landed Price:** It covers all expenses till the goods are discharged at the port of destination. It is payable by the exporter.
- **Duty Paid Price:** It refers to in-bond price inclusive of import duties.
- **Franco or Rendu:** It refers to price which includes all charges and expenses for carrying the importer's goods to the warehouse or shop of the importer.

Key Points

1. **International trade:** International ('foreign' or 'external') trade refers to the exchange of goods and services between one country such as India and another such as the USA (called bilateral trade) or one country and the rest of the world (called multilateral trade).

2 **Types of international trade:** Three main types of international trade are:
   (a) *Import trade:* It involves purchase of goods from foreign markets for consumption and production in the home country.
   (b) *Export trade:* It involves supply of domestic goods to foreigners.
   (c) *Entrepot or re-export Trade:* It involves the import of foreign goods for re-exporting them for making profit. For example, an Indian trader imports goods from China and exports the same to Africa.

3. **The basis of foreign trade:** There are various causes of international trade or, in other words, there are different sources of international trade arising from differences in productivity of labour and capital and factor endowments. In fact, international trade arises from differences in comparative advantage or relative efficiency of two or more countries in the production of two or more commodities.

4. **The advantages (benefits) of international trade:** Six main benefits of international trade are the following:
   (i) Efficient allocation and optimum use of resources,
   (ii) Improvement on standard of living,
   (iii) Acting as an engine of growth,
   (iv) Stabilisation of commodity prices,
   (v) Employment generation and
   (vi) Generation of economies of scale (size).

5. **Difficulties or problems of international trade:** There are various problems associated with the smooth conduct of international trade. Some of these problems are really complex. The most common problems which restrict the flow of international trade are the following: (i) Use of different currencies, (ii) Tariff and non-tariff barriers, (iii) Risk associated with movement of goods, (iv) Time lag, (v) Language and script, (vi) lack of direct contact.

KEY Terms

Local content requirement	Comparative advantage
Foreign trade	Dumping
Import trade	International division of labour
Export trade	Balance of trade
Entry pot trade	Balance of payment
Trade as an engine of growth	Current account of BOP
Advantages of international trade	Capital account of BOP
Disadvantages of international trade	Tariffs and quotas

Assignments

SHORT ANSWER-TYPE QUESTIONS

1. Define foreign trade.
2. Name two types of International Trade. [ISC 1988]
3. Give two characteristics of Foreign Trade. [ISC 1992]
4. Mention three advantages of Foreign Trade.
5. State two differences between Domestic and International Trade.
6. Give two disadvantages of Foreign Trade.
7. What is Balance of Payments?
8. Give two demerits of International Trade. [ISC 1990]

ESSAY-TYPE QUESTIONS

1. Discuss the advantages (importance) of International Trade.
2. Discuss five differences between Home Trade and International Trade. [ISC 1987]
3. Explain the chief characteristics of International Trade.
4. Discuss the advantages of International Trade.
5. In what respects does home trade differ from foreign trade? [ISC 1990]
6. What is meant by international trade? Discuss its chief characteristics. [ISC 1988]
7. Discuss the advantages and disadvantages of international trade. [ISC 1989]

QUESTION BANK

1. *Define international trade.*

Ans. International trade refers to exchange of goods and services between one country and another country (bilateral trade) or between one country and many other countries (called multilateral trade). It involves export trade (direct and indirect), import trade (direct and indirect), entrepot trade and counter-trade.

2. *Why is there any need for foreign trade?*

Ans. There is need for foreign trade because no country is self-sufficient in the production of all goods and services which it needs. So it has to buy those things from other countries which it cannot produce or produce cheaply. It arises due to differences in factor endowments such as natural resources, labour and capital, technology, tastes and preferences as also productivity of resources which gets reflected in costs and prices.

3. *Mention any three characteristics of foreign trade.*

Ans. See text.

4. *Distinguish between domestic and international trade.*

Ans. See text.

5. *What are the benefits of free trade between (among) nations?*

Ans. Seven main benefits of free trade among nations are the following:

(a) *Wider choice:* By buying products from other nations (importing), consumers are offered a much wider choice of goods and services. Many of these would not have been available to them at all without international trade because the farming or production facilities might not have existed in their own country, for example bananas in Europe or deep-sea fish in Botswana.

(b) *Import of much needed raw materials:* The same principle applies to raw materials — for example, the UK steel industry depends entirely on imports of foreign iron ore.

(c) *Industrialisation:* Imports of capital goods can allow a developing economy to increase its pace of industrialisation.

(d) *Growing competition:* Importing products create additional competition for domestic industries and this should encourage them to keep costs and prices down and make their goods as well designed and of as high quality as possible. In truth, imports often pose threat to domestic monopolies.

(e) *Gains from specialisation:* Countries can specialise in their own areas of comparative advantage (relative efficiency) and import those products they are best at making and import those that they are less efficient in producing compared to other countries. This is called comparative advantage.

(f) *Specialisation based on division of labour:* It can generate economies of scale or widen the scale of operations and markets for saleable products and provide further (secondary) benefits to consumers due to fall in costs and prices.

(g) *Improvement in living standards:* Multilateral trade improves the living standards of all consumers all over the world by enabling them to buy products more cheaply than those which were produced just within their narrow domestic territories. This becomes possible due to an efficient allocation of the world's limited resources.

6. *What are the drawbacks of international trade?*

OR

What are the risks associated with international trade?

Ans. By engaging in trade, countries can build up improved political and social links and this can help to resolve differences among them. Trading internationally can also have drawbacks. The potential risks include the following:

(a) *Output loss:* There may be loss of output and jobs from those domestic firms that cannot compete effectively with imported goods.

(b) *Decline of domestic industries:* There may be a decline, due to imports, of domestic industries that produce very important 'strategic' goods, for example coal and foodstuffs; this could put the country at risk if there were a conflict between countries or due to any other factor leading to a loss of imports.

(c) *Transitional dislocation:* The switch from making goods that cannot compete with imports to those in which the country has a comparative advantage may take a long time. This again, will cause job losses and factory closures before other types of industries are set up and displaced workers are reabsorbed.

(d) *Threat to infant industries:* Newly established businesses may find it almost impossible to survive against strong competition from existing (well-established) importers. This will prevent infant industries, which are in nascent stage, from growing and gaining maturity.

(e) *Dumping:* Some importers may dump goods at below cost price in order to eliminate competition from domestic markets. 'Dumping' means selling a good at low price for destroying certain high-cost and initially inefficient industries.

(f) *Loss of foreign exchange:* If the value of imports exceeds the value of exports (products sold abroad) for a number of years then this could lead to huge loss of foreign exchange. This is why many countries (particularly those in Africa) are unable to finance purchases of essential food articles to feed their growing population.

7. *Mention three advantages of international trade.*

Ans. International trade can bring both consumption and production gains to a country, serving to raise its living standards and improve its productive efficiency. International trade enables countries to consume some goods and services more cheaply by importing them, and also to obtain some resources and products from other countries which would otherwise be totally unavailable because domestic producers are unable to supply them (for example, a scarce raw material or high-technology product). International trade promotes productive efficiency by encouraging a reallocation of resources away from areas of the economy best served by imports into industries where the country itself has a comparative advantage over its trade partners.

20 EXPORT TRADE

SYLLABUS

- *Export trade — Meaning, objectives and procedure of export trade*

> *Export should be encouraged because they bring prosperity to a nation through inflows of precious metals.*
>
> — Josiah Child (A promient mercantilist)

LEARNING OUTCOMES

On completion of this chapter, you will be able to understand the following:

20.1 Meaning and Types of Export Trade
20.2 Need for Export
20.3 Export Promotion Measures
20.4 Objectives of Export Trade
20.5 Export Trade Procedure
20.6 Documents used in Export Trade
20.7 Charter Party

20.1 MEANING AND TYPES OF EXPORT TRADE

Exporting is the sale in an overseas market of a product which is produced in the firm's home market.

Exports may be viewed by the firm as merely an extension of home sales, serving to provide extra business as a means of allowing the firm to operate its productive capacity to the full. More generally, exports may be regarded as an important profit centre in their own right, providing the firm with opportunities for worldwide sales expansion and long-term profit growth.

Exporting may be undertaken indirectly or directly. Indirect exporting involves the contracting of independent agents to establish wholesale and retail sales contacts, and importers/distributors to handle the physical distribution of the product. Often, however, independent agents/distributors lack the commitment or resources required to maximise the firm's overseas sales potential. For this reason, direct exporting may be preferred, requiring the appointment of the company's own overseas sales personnel and the establishment of overseas sales offices, depots and sales subsidiaries to handle local distribution and marketing. Exporting may be conducted on a 'standalone' basis or, as in the case of multinational enterprises as part of a more complex foreign market servicing strategy involving also licensing and overseas production

The physical act of transporting goods to export markets may be done by the supplier's own distribution division or by using the services of independent howlers, fleet operators and freight forwarders. Documentation required in connection with export consignments includes a bill of lading, certificate of origin, weight note, insurance and (where appropriate) an export licence. Exporting may be undertaken according to a free on board (f.o.b.) contract, a cost, insurance and freight (c.i.f.) contract, or a cost and freight (c & f) contract.

Export finance is provided by the commercial banks in the form of short-term credits (often underpinned by letters of credit) and backed in India by the government's export credit and guarantee corporation (ECGC).

20.2 NEED FOR EXPORT

No country in the world is completely self-sufficient. It has to import various items to meet the needs of its people such as food and oil as also machinery and also other capital goods for promoting industrialisation. The reason is that it cannot produce these items at all or produce them cheaply (i.e. at low cost). However, there is need for foreign exchange, to import any type of goods or services. And these have to be earned by exporting other goods which the country can produce cheaply or efficiently (i.e. at low cost). And foreign exchange is earned in the process. So exports normally (largely) pay for imports. Thus, exporting is necessary not only for the normal functioning of the economy (and thus, meeting the needs of the people) but also for accelerating the process of growth (through import of capital goods such as machinery and equipment).

20.3 EXPORT PROMOTION MEASURES

Realising the importance of exports, the Government of India (GoI) has adopted various export promotion measures. It has given fiscal concessions to exporters such as exemption from or refund of excise duty paid to produce export items loan at low (concessional) rates of interest, cash subsidy and supply of raw materials at low prices.

Trade delegations are sent abroad several times a year to explore export possibilities of certain goods to new areas and regions. Bilateral trade agreements are signed with a few countries to promote exports and get preferential treatment from them. Trade fairs and exhibitions are also been organised on a regular basis. The GoI has also set up various institutions for promoting exports.

These are the following:

(i) Export Promotion Councils (such as Engineering Export Promotion Council).

(ii) Export Inspection Council.

(iii) Commodity Boards (such as the Tea Board and the Coffee Board).

(iv) The Board of Trade.

(v) Indians Trade Promotion Organisation.

(vi) Indian Institute of Foreign Trade (IIFT).

(vii) The Federation of Indian Export Organisations (FIEO).

(viii) Directorate of Exhibitions and Commercial Publicity.

(ix) Export Credit and Guarantee Corporation (ECGC).

(x) Trade Development Authority (TDA).

(xi) State Trading Corporation (STC).

(xii) Minerals and Metals Trading Corporation (MMTC).

These are all organisational measures for promoting export.

In addition, Export-Import (EXIM) Bank of India was set up as a specialised financial institution to promote exports. The main objective of the Bank is to coordinate the activities of various institutions connected with (or involved in) financing foreign trade.

The main functions of the EXIM Bank are as follows:

(i) It provides medium term and long-term credit to Indian exporters.

(ii) It provides finance for export of consultancy and allied services.

(iii) It assists in setting up joint ventures in other countries as also for export oriented units in India.

(iv) It offers merchant banking services to exporters and importers.

(v) It undertakes surveys of foreign markets and explore such markets for boosting exports.

Such nationalised commercial banks also provide financial assistance to the exporters as pre-shipment and post-shipment credit. Pre-shipment credit is given to exporters to purchase raw materials, process them and produce finished goods for exporting them. Such credit is given on the basis of export orders and letters of credit possessed by exporters. Post-shipment credit is extended in the form of advances against bills of exchange and shipping documents drawn under letters of credit.

20.4 OBJECTIVES OF EXPORT TRADE

Exporting of goods and services is undertaken for the following reasons:

1. **To find out an outlet for surplus output:** If a country can produce more output than it requires to meet its own needs, it will seek an outlet for disposing of the surplus output. Export is the excess of domestic production over domestic consumption. This excess output is called export surplus. And a country which is able to generate such surplus can sell it in foreign countries to earn foreign exchange.

2. **To make full utilisation of its resources:** Export trade expands a country's market for goods. It is no longer required to operate in the narrow domestic market. The market is virtually the entire world. In fact, export acts as a vent for surplus. It means that a country — specially a developing one — may be able to gain by exporting the products of factors which would not be employed at all without trade.

3. **To earn foreign exchange:** By exporting goods, a country earns valuable foreign exchange (currencies) which is scarce in developing countries like India. These are used to import food, oil and other goods (called maintenance imports) as also to import machinery and

other capital goods (called developmental imports). Imports of capital goods which are in short supply in India is important for stepping up her developmental efforts.

4. **To create jobs and incomes:** Exports help to generate employment in a labour surplus country like India. Since many new people are recruited in export-oriented industries, as a result national income goes up. Consequently, the standard of living of its people is likely to improve with it.
5. **To generate tax revenue:** Production activities associated with export trade generate revenue for the government of a country in the form of excise duty. This extra revenue enables the government to spend more money on public welfare.
6. **To promote international cooperation:** Finally, multilateral trade promotes cooperation among nations and improves their relations in the political arena. This helps to avoid retaliation and trade war.

20.5 EXPORT TRADE PROCEDURE

Export trade procedure differs from country to country and from period to period depending upon the export-import policy of the country under consideration. The procedure of exporting goods from India is governed by the rules and regulations spelt out by the GoI from time to time. The general procedure for exports from India is described below.

The GOI officially announces the rules and regulations for the export of goods at periodic intervals. In general, the following steps are involved in an export transaction:

1. **Making trade enquiry and obtaining quotation:** The process of export trade is initiated with the receipt of an enquiry by the exporter from the importer regarding price, quantity and quality of goods which latter plans to buy from the former. The importer gives reply in the form of price quotation which specifies price as also the trade terms. Both enquiry and quotation should contain such details as the goods required, their broad description, catalogue number, sizes, rates or other relevant features, the number or quantity, time and method of delivery as also method of packing.
2. **Securing export order or indent:** After accepting the quotation, the importer will place an order with the exporter either directly or through a specialised agency appointed for the purpose. It is known as the Indent House. In the order (indent), the importer gives necessary instructions and precise specifications regarding the goods to be shipped by the exporter. It furnishes necessary details regarding the size and quality of the goods as also their shipment required. It also specifies the price the importer is ready to pay for a good on the basis of the price quoted by the exporter.

BUSINESS FOCUS: LETTER OF CREDIT

A letter of credit is a non-negotiable order from a domestic bank to a bank abroad, authorising payment to a named person a particular sum of money or up to a limited sum. A letter of credit is usually received by an exporter who wishes to have proof that it will be paid before he ships goods or who wishes to minimise delay in payment for the goods. A letter of credit is to be confirmed as soon as it is recognised by the paying bank. A letter of credit may be irrevocable or revocable, depending on whether or not it can be cancelled at any time.

3. **Receiving letter of credit:** After accepting the order from the importer, the exporter will try to find out the former's creditworthiness. At this stage, the exporter asks the importer to

send him a letter of credit. Now the importer has to open an account with his own banker and get a letter of credit in favour of the exporter or his banker, who agrees to accept the bill of exchange drawn by the exporter up to a certain limit, i.e., amount specified in the bill.

4. **Obtaining export licence:** If the goods to be exported are on the negative list prior export licence is needed before shipping them abroad. For this an application has to be made well in advance to the Director General of Foreign Trade (DGFT) by paying the necessary licence fee. If the application is cleared, the appropriate authority will issue an export licence giving details of goods. It will also fix the time limit, specifying the date before which the export order has to be executed.
5. **Exchange rate fixation:** In order to avoid any dispute in future, it is necessary for both the parties to agree to a certain rate of exchange (i.e., the price of one currency, such as the Indian rupee in terms of another currency such as the US dollar). This is absolutely essential since exchange rates fluctuate every now and then. And undue exchange rate fluctuations create uncertainty or increase the risk of trade and reduce the volume of trade.
6. **Production (procurement) of exportable items:** The exporters will either produce the goods or procure the goods from other sources as per the importer's order and go through a process of quality control. If he is able to meet the quality standards, the Export Inspection Certificate will be issued to him. Then he will proceed to make necessary arrangements for shipment of the goods to the importer's point.
7. **Packaging and marking:** For ensuring safe despatch of goods proper packaging may be done by the exporter either directly or through some agent as per the standards specified by both the shipping company and the customs authorities. Each package should be distinctly marked and it should clearly indicate the port of destination as also the name of the importer. It should also clearly mention the gross weight, the weight of the container, and the net weight in order to facilitate proper location and storage of goods as soon as the goods arrive at the port of destination.
8. **Insurance cover:** Before despatching the goods, they are to be adequately insured against perils of sea. A copy of the policy is to be sent to the importer along with the bill of lading. Otherwise, the shipping company may refuse to carry the goods and the commercial bank may also refuse to discount the documentary bills of exchange.
9. **Completion of necessary shipping formalities:** The exporter enters into an agreement with a shipping company for booking space in a ship for delivering goods to the port of importer. The shipping company, in its turn, will issue a 'Shipping Order' which gives instructions to the captain of the ship to receive, on board certain goods from the exporter.
10. **Completion of all customs formalities:** The exporter has to prepare a Shipping Bill and submit an application to export. A shipping bill is a form used by the customs department before goods can be exported from India. It is also required when removing goods from a bonded warehouse. It contains information regarding: (a) ports of loading and discharge, (b) particulars of exporters, (c) name of ship, (d) broad description of goods as also, (e) the estimated value of goods. The exporter will have to get "Mate's Receipt" on delivery of the goods on board the vessel.

    After presenting the Mate's Receipt at the office of the shipping company, the exporter will obtain a document called 'Bill of Lading'. It may be noted that a bill of lading is a document acknowledging the shipment of a consignor's goods for carriage by sea. Each consignor receives a bill issued (normally by the captain of the ship) on behalf of either the shipowner or a charterer under a charter-party. The bill gives details of the goods. The exporter will have to pay the port charges before bringing the goods in the shipment shed for thorough inspection. Now a customs officer will do the needed inspection of the goods on the basis of declaration given in the Shipping Bill. If he is satisfied, then only he will give permission to load the goods on the ship.

BUSINESS FOCUS: MATE'S RECEIPT

The mate is a subordinate to the captain of a ship. Before the captain issues a final bill of lading, the mate issues a provisional receipt, known as the mate's receipt. This is just to acknowledge the receipt of the good on board the ship. It may be noted that the mate's receipt is not a document of title to the goods like a bill of lading.

11. **Obtaining mate's receipt and bill of lading:** On delivery of goods to the dock, the Dock Receipt is issued to the exporter. In case the goods are directly handed over to the Captain (Master) of the ship or his immediate subordinate called the 'Mate', the exporter will get a Mate's Receipt. The Captain will now receive the goods on the basis of shipping order issued by the shipping company. The exporter will carry the Mate's Receipt to the company for paying the freight. After making payment the Bill of Lading will be issued in his name.
12. **Preparation of trading invoice:** The exporter will have to prepare three copies of invoice containing information on the quantity, quality, description as also the prices of goods. An invoice is a document sent by an exporter to an importer which itemises the products supplied to the customer, their prices, and the total amount of money owed by the customer for these products. An invoice is normally sent after the products have been shipped with their associated delivery note, and serves to inform the customer that payment is required. The exporter will send two copies of it to the importer and retain the third copy for his own record. The exporter will also send the Consular Invoice issued by the Trade Consul of the importing country located in the exporting country to the importer. This invoice is useful when the goods are subject to *ad-valorem* customs (import) duty, i.e., duty as a certain proportion (percentage) of the value of the goods to be shipped.
13. **Sending of shipping documents:** The exporter will draw a bill of exchange on the importer of the value quoted in the invoice. He will send this bill along with the shipping documents to the importer through his bank in order to obtain payment for the goods. Shipping documents usually consist of the following:
    (i) a commercial invoice,
    (ii) bill of lading,
    (iii) insurance policy or certificate,
    (iv) weight note,
    (v) quality certificate, and, if required,
    (vi) a certificate of origin,
    (vii) consular invoice and
    (viii) export licence.

All these documents are attached with the bill of exchange. This is why the bill is also called documentary bill. These documents contained in the bill enable the importer to release the goods from the concerned authorities at the port of destination.

14. **Getting payment:** The exporter's bank will place the bill as also the supplementary documents to the importer's bank. In case it is a document against presentation (D/P) bill, the importer's bank will make immediate payment. But if it is just a document acceptance (D/A) bill, the importer's bank will accept the bill and collect all the relevant documents first. Then only it will make the payment against the bill on the due date.

FOCUS ON TERMINOLOGY: DOCUMENTS AGAINST ACCEPTANCE (D/A) AND DOCUMENTS AGAINST PRESENTATION (D/P)

The term 'documents against acceptance' (D/A) refers to a method of payment for goods which have been exported in which the exporter sends the title and shipping document with a bill of exchange to a bank at the port of destination. The bank releases the goods when the bill has been accepted by the consignee. If the documents are in order, there is an obligation to pay for them, even if the goods have been lost in transit. In such a situation, the buyer has to hold the insurance policy to provide recompense for the lost goods.

By comparison, the term 'cash against documents' is used to refer to the terms of payment for exported goods in which the shipping documents are sent to a bank in the country to which the goods are being shipped, and the importer then collects the documents by paying the invoice amount in cash to the bank. Having the shipping documents, it enables the importer to take delivery of the goods on their arrival at the port of destination. This is known as 'documents against presentation' (D/P).

20.6 DOCUMENTS USED IN EXPORT TRADE

Due to its complex nature international trading activities (i.e., exporting and importing) require the use of several documents such as commercial invoice, consular invoice, bill of lading, insurance policy, and bill of exchange. Proper documentation is a must for smooth conduct of foreign trade. These documents serve to protect the interests of both importers and exporters. Through these documents, the importer gets the goods he orders and the exporter receives payments for the sale of goods outside his country. Apart from these documents, there is need for bill of entry in some countries. It is a statement about imports or exports for customs authorities — a statement of the nature and value of goods to be imported or exported. It is prepared by the shipper and presented to a customs house.

20.6.1 Set of Shipping Documents

A complete set of shipping documents contains the following:

(i) invoice,

(ii) bill of lading,

(iii) insurance policy,

(iv) freight receipt,

(v) customs clearance certificate,

(vi) consular invoice, and

(vii) certificate of origin.

20.6.2 Export Documents

Each export shipment involves many documents to satisfy government regulations and controls of export business as well as to meet requirements for international commercial transactions. The most frequently required documents are export declarations, consular invoices or certificates of origin, bills of lading, commercial invoices, and insurance certificates. Some additional documents are also necessary. These are import licence, export licence, packing list, and inspection certificates for agricultural products (in case of some countries such as the USA and Germany).

Export documents are meant to ensure smooth and timely movement (flow) of goods from one country to another. Two broad categories of documents used in export trade are the following:

1. Main documents and 2. Supplementary documents.

The various components of these two sets of documents are presented in Table 20.1.

TABLE 20.1: Two Broad Categories of Export Documents

Main Export Documents	Supplementary Export Documents
1. Commercial invoice	1. Proforma invoice
2. Packing list	2. Intimation for inspection
3. Bill of lading	3. Shipping instructions
4. Certificate of inspection	4. Insurance declaration
5. Insurance policy	5. Shipping order
6. Certificate of origin	6. Mate's receipt
7. Bill of exchange	7. Application for certificate of origin

20.6.3 Main Export Documents

These documents serve two main purposes: (a) transfer of goods from the exporter to the importer and (b) realisation of payment by the exporter from the importer. We now give a broad description of those documents:

1. *Commercial invoice:* It is prepared by the exporter and sent to the importer in order to serve as a document of contents as also as a bill of the value of the goods at the same time. So it serves a dual purpose. *Prima facie* it contains a broad description of goods, number of packages, weight and volume of packages and other details. It also contains name and address of the importer, export order number, unit price of each exported item, total value of imports as also the terms and conditions of payment.
2. *Packing list:* It contains various details regarding the date of packing of export goods, detailed specification and list of exported goods, invoice number, order, number and date, details of shipping and bill of lading number.
3. *Bill of lading:* A bill of lading is a document used to ship internationally traded goods which gives the holder (the consignee) the right to take possession of the goods. It gives details of the goods shipped, the identification marks and number of crates, etc., the name of the ship, ports of embarkation and destination, rate of freight, etc. Bills of lading are drawn up by shipowners, the original being sent to the consignee with copies being retained by the captain of the ship and the freight forwarder.
4. *Certificate of inspection:* It is an official document in support of the fact that the export consignment has been duly and fully inspected as per the official guidelines and is issued

by the Export Inspection Agency of a specific zone from where the goods are to be exported.

5. *Insurance policy:* In order to got adequate protection of the export items from various risks of loss or damage during shipment from one country to another, the exporter is required to get the goods insured and get an insurance policy. It is a document which sets out the terms and conditions of an insurance contract. The insurance policy has to be despatched to the importer along with the bill of lading.
6. *Certificate of origin:* It is a document used to authenticate the country of origin of internationally traded goods. Most trading nations accept such certificates issued by government departments of their trade partners or their appointees. In general, a certificate of origin is a document declaring origin of imported goods — a document showing where imported goods come from or from where goods were imported.
7. *Bill of exchange:* It is a financial document (security) which is used to extend business credit usually for three months. The lender draws up a bill of exchange for a specified sum of money payable at a certain future date, and the borrower agrees to pay the amount involved by signing (i.e., accepting) the bill. A foreign bill is drawn by the exporter (called drawer) instructing the importer (called drawee) to make payment now or at some future date, as specified in the bill. In case payment from the importer falls due immediately on presentation of the bill, it is called a sight bill. The words 'usance' is used in a foreign bill of exchange to indicate that the period of the bill should commence from the date on which the drawee is presented with it for acceptance, i.e., has sight of it. And if payment is to be made at a certain future date, it is called a usance bill. Once a usance bill is accepted by the importer, the exporter can discount it with commercial bank and realise payment.

Foreign bills of exchange are of the following two types:

(i) *Clean bill:* This is an ordinary bill of exchange and is drawn by the exporter when he is fully confident about the creditworthiness of the importer. No condition is attached to it as far as the delivery of documents is concerned.

(ii) *Documentary bill:* It is a bill of exchange which is attached to the shipping documents of a consignment of goods. These include the bill of lading, insurance policy, dock warrant and invoice.

20.6.4 Auxiliary (supplementary) Export Documents

Certain documents are required for the preparation of the main (or principal) export documents. The supplementary documents, in fact, lend necessary support to the main documents and are now briefly discussed below.

1. *Proforma invoice:* The term 'proforma' refers to prescribing a set form or procedure. For instance, a proforma invoice may be sent to a customer in advance of a transaction to facilitate paperwork. This document is sent at the most critical stage of exporting. Since it contains an offer made by the exporter to the importer, it gives a prior intimation about the willingness of the exporter to supply a good of a specified quality at the quoted price as also the trade terms and payment conditions, i.e., timing of payments.
2. *Intimation for inspection:* Through this document, the exporter can inform the Export Inspection Agency that the exportable items can now be inspected by the Agency.

3. *Shipping instructions:* This document is used by the exporter to pass necessary instructions to the shipping agent regarding exportable items.
4. *Insurance declaration:* It contains the exporter's declaration regarding the quality, quantity, and price of exportable goods so that he can obtain an insurance policy.
5. *Shipping order:* The exporter has to sign an agreement with a shipping company or its agent for booking the required space in a ship for transferring the good to the port of destination (where the importer is located). The shipping company will issue a shipping order which gives necessary instructions to the captain of the ship for receiving the specified quantity of goods from the exporter whose name appears in the order.
6. *Getting mate's receipt:* Once the goods are loaded on the ship the immediate subordinate to the captain will issue the Mate's Receipt to the exporter or the forwarding agent. This receipt gives details of the quantity of goods, number of packages and condition of packing. (We have already discussed about this receipt earlier in this chapter.)
7. *Application for certificate of origin:* This form is to be filled in by the exporter and he has to furnish necessary details about the goods and their place of production (manufacturing) or assembling. It has to be submitted to the trade consul or a recognised (reputed) chamber of commerce. The purpose is to get a certificate of origin (which has to be sent to the importer).

BUSINESS FOCUS: PACKING AND MARKETING

In addition to completing all documentation, special packing and marking requirements must be considered for shipments destined to be transported over water-subject to excessive handling, or destined for those countries or regions having extremes of weather or unprotected outdoor storage (warehousing) facilities. Packing which is adequate for domestic shipments often falls short for goods subject to diverse conditions. Protection against rough handling, moisture, extreme climates (high and low temperature), and pilferage may require heavy crating, which increases total packing costs as well as freight because of increased weight and size.

20.7 CHARTER PARTY

The term 'charter party' is derived from the word 'charter' which refers to the hiring of all or part of the cargo or passenger-capacity of a ship, aircraft etc. for a particular purpose for a particular period of time.

The term charter party refers to formal (written) agreement between the ship owner and the exporter under which the whole ship or a substantial part of it is hired to carry goods for a specified voyage or for a certain time period. Being a contract of affreightment, it contains all the terms and conditions of the contract such as the following:

1. Name of the ship
2. Place of loading
3. Port of destination
4. Name of the exporter (consignor)
5. Name of the importer (consignee)
6. Amount of freight.

A charter party is of two main types:

Voyage Charter: In case ship is hired for a specified journey (voyage), it is known as voyage charter. For example, a ship may be hired to carry goods from Kolkata to Singapore. In such case, the time taken by the ship to complete the journey is not taken into consideration.

Time Charter: In a time charter, the ship is hired for a specified time period, e.g., from January 1, 2016 to March 31, 2016. During this period the ship may be used to undertake any voyage or voyages.

Key Points

1. **Steps involved in export trade.** At least 14 different steps are involved in export trade. These are the following:
   (i) *Making trade enquiry and obtaining quotation:* The process of export trade is initiated with the receipt of an enquiry by the exporter from the importer regarding price, quantity and quality of goods which the latter plans to buy from the former.
   (ii) *Securing export order or indent:* After accepting the quotation, the importer will place an order with the exporter either directly or through a specialised agency appointed for the purpose. It is known as the Indent House.
   (iii) *Receiving letter of credit:* After accepting the order from the importer, the exporter will try to find out the former's creditworthiness. At this stage, the exporter asks the importer to send him a letter of credit.
   (iv) *Obtaining export licence:* If the goods to be exported are on the negative (or banned) list prior export licence is needed before shipping them abroad.
   (v) *Exchange rate fixation:* In order to avoid any dispute in future, it is necessary for both the parties to agree to a certain rate of exchange.
   (vi) *Production (procurement) of exportable items:* The exporters will either produce the goods or procure the goods from other sources as per the importer's order and go through a process of quality control.
   (vii) *Packaging and marking:* For ensuring safe despatch of goods proper packaging may be done by the exporter either directly or through some agent as per the standards specified by both the shipping company and the customs authorities.
   (viii) *Insurance cover:* Before despatching the goods, they are to be adequately insured against perils of sea.
   (ix) *Completion of necessary shipping formalities*: The exporter enters into an agreement with a shipping company for booking space in a ship for delivering goods to the port of importer. The shipping company, in its turn, will issue a 'Shipping Order' which gives instructions to the captain of the ship to receive, on board the ship certain goods from the exporter.

(x) *Completion of customs formalities:* The exporter has to prepare a Shipping Bill and submit an application to export and complement customary formalities.

(xi) *Obtaining mate's receipt and bill of lading:* On delivery of goods to the dock, the Dock Receipt is issued to the exporter.

(xii) *Preparation of trading invoice:* The exporter will have to prepare three copies of invoice containing information on the quantity, quality, description as also the price of goods.

(xiii) *Sending of shipping documents:* The exporter will draw a bill of exchange on the importer of the value quoted in the invoice. He will send this bill along with the shipping documents to the importer through his bank in order to obtain payment for the goods.

(xiv) *Getting payment.* The exporter's bank will place the bill as also the supplementary documents to the importer's bank the importer's bank will accept the bill and collect all the relevant documents first. Then only it will make the payment against the bill on the due date.

KEY Terms	
Charter party	Bill of lading
Voyage charter	Consular invoice
Time charter	Forwarding agent
Indent	Merchandise
Dog challenge	Order from
Mets receipts	Later of credit
Certificate of origin	Indent houses

Assignments

SHORT ANSWER-TYPE QUESTIONS

1. What is an indent? [ISC 1988]
2. What do you understand by Dock Challan? [ISC 1992]
3. What is Mate's Receipt?
4. Define Bill of Lading.
5. What is meant by Certificate of Origin?
6. What is Consular Invoice?
7. Name any five documents used in the exporting of goods.
8. State two functions of a Bill of Lading.
9. Is bill of Lading a negotiable instrument?

10. Mention two kinds of a charter party. [ISC 1987]
11. Mention two characteristics of Bill of Lading. [ISC 1988]
12. Define a charter party. [ISC 1990]
13. Name the corporation which insures against the risk, furnishes guarantee and provides supplementary finance in export trade. [ISC 1991]

ESSAY-TYPE QUESTIONS

1. Give a brief outline of the procedure for exports of goods. Mention the important documents involved therein?
2. Describe in brief the various steps involved in exporting goods.
3. What is meant by Bill of Lading? Discuss the importance of Bill of Lading in foreign trade. [ISC 1987]
4. Define a forwarding Agent. Explain the formalities performed by forwarding agents in the exporting of goods. [ISC 1987]
5. Explain briefly the procedure for exporting cotton to England by a Delhi merchant. [ISC 1989]
6. Explain the purpose and types of Bill of Lading. [ISC 1989]
7. Define Bill of lading and discuss its importance. [ISC 1990]

QUESTION BANK

1. *What is Documentary Bill of Exchange?*

Ans. See Text.

2. *Distinguish between D/A and D/P bills.* [ISC 1991]

Ans. Documents against Acceptance (D/A) and Documents against Presentation (D/P)

The term 'documents against acceptance' (D/A) refers to a method of payment for goods which have been exported. In this case the exporter sends the title and shipping document with a bill of exchange to a bank at the port of destination. The bank releases the goods when the bill has been accepted by the consignee. If the documents are in order, there is an obligation to pay for them, even if the goods have been lost in transit. In such a situation the buyer has to hold the insurance policy to provide recompense for the lost goods.

By comparison, the term 'cash against documents' is used to refer to terms of payment for exported goods in which the shipping documents are sent to a bank in the country to which the goods are being shipped, and the importer then collects the documents by paying the invoice amount in cash to the bank. Having the shipping documents enables the importer to take delivery of the goods on their arrival at the port of destination. This is known as 'documents against presentation' (D/P).

3. *What are the objectives of exporting goods or merchandise?*

Ans. See text.

4. *Briefly discuss the procedure involved in export trade.*

Ans. See text.

5. *What is an Indent? Explain its purpose.*

Ans. Indent refers to ordering of goods using a special order form.

6. *Describe the role of the following in International Trade.*
(i) Forwarding and Clearing agents (ii) Indent Houses [ISC 1991]

Ans. See text.

7. *Distinguish between a Bill of Lading and a Charter Party.* [ISC 1992]

Ans. Bill of lading refers to the receipts given by a transportation company to an exporter when the former accepts goods for transport. It includes the contract specifying what transport service will be provided and the limits of liability.

The term charter party refers to a party or a group which hires a whole ship or aircraft for a specified period or for a specified voyage or flight.

8. *Discuss briefly the documents which are usually used in the exporting of goods.*

Ans. See text.

9. *What is a Bill of Lading? What purpose(s) does it serve?*

Ans. See text.

10. *What is Letter of Credit?*

Ans. See text.

11. *What is Consular Invoice?*

Ans. See text.

12. *What is certificate of origin?*

Ans. See text.

13. *What are Indent houses?*

Ans. See text.

14. *Mark the following statements True or False.*
   (a) *The order placed by an importer is called is called Indent.*
   (b) *The certificate of origin is sent by an exporter to an importer.*
   (c) *Consular invoice is sent by an importer to an exporter.*
   (d) *Bill of Lading is a negotiable instrument.*
   (e) *Shipping order is the same as the shipping bill.*
   (f) *Letter of credit is sent by an importer to an exporter.*

Ans. True: (a), (b), (d), (f)

False: (c), (e).

15. *Fill in the blanks:*
   (a) *Indent is prepared by ______.*
   (b) *A letter of credit is sent by ______ to ______.*
   (c) *Mate's receipt is issued by the ______ captain of the ship.*
   (d) *Certificate of origin helps to reduce ______.*
   (e) *Consular invoice is issued by the consul of the ______ country in the ______.*
   (f) *Charter party is an agreement between ______ and ______.*

Ans. (a) importers, (b) importer, exporter, (c) assistant to the, (d) custom duty, (e) importing, exporting, (f) shipowner, exporter.

21 IMPORT TRADE

SYLLABUS

- *Import trade.*
- *Meaning and functions of import trade: objectives, purpose and procedure.*

> *Exports pay for imports. This is the essence of price-specie-flow mechanism.* — David Hume

LEARNING OUTCOMES

On completion of this chapter, you will be able to understand the following:

21.1 Meaning of Import Trade
21.2 Objectives, Purpose and Functions of Import Trade
21.3 Import Trade Procedure
21.4 Documents used in Import Trade

We have already discussed the pros and cons of international trade in Ch. 19 and have noted that its involves both export trade and import trade. We have discussed export trade in the last chapter. In this chapter we discussed the various aspects of import trade.

21.1 MEANING OF IMPORT TRADE

Import trade involves purchasing goods from other countries either directly or indirectly, i.e., through certain agents. In India and other developing countries the government regulates and controls import trade to ensure judicious use of foreign exchange, restrict imports of non-essential items (mainly luxury goods) and promote the development of domestic industries which have strong potential of growth.

Importing is meant for the sale in the home market of a product which is produced in a foreign country. Domestic producers may import particular materials, components and final products either because they are unobtainable from domestic sources or because foreign producers can supply an input more cheaply or supply an alternative version of the final product. Similarly, importing may be undertaken (indirectly or directly) by foreign-based firms as an adjunct to their exporting operations. In some cases, locally based agents may be contracted by overseas producers to develop sales outlets and importers/distributors may be appointed to handle physical distribution. In other cases, in order to build up a stronger position in the market, foreign producers may prefer instead to establish their own sales offices and subsidiary companies to handle local distribution sales and marketing.

21.2 OBJECTIVES, PURPOSE AND FUNCTIONS OF IMPORT TRADE

No country in the world is completely self-sufficient today since it cannot produce everything to meet its diverse needs. Therefore, a country like India has to import certain other goods from other countries. According to the theory of comparative cost, a country should import those commodities in the production of which it is relatively inefficient, i.e., which it cannot produce at lower costs than other countries. Developing countries like India import capital goods such as machinery, equipment, etc. as also raw materials and crude oil which are required for promoting faster economic growth and for accelerating the pace of economic development. Similarly, essential commodities are imported to bridge the domestic supply-demand gap. In fact, imports of India and other developing countries are of two types, namely, maintenance imports and developmental imports. Maintenance imports refer to purchase of food and other items of domestic consumption. Imports enable such countries to cover the excess of domestic consumption over domestic production. By contrast, developmental imports are necessary to promote industrialisation. Such imports consist of mainly capital goods fertiliser and fuel.

In truth, the main objectives of the import trade are the following:

1. **To accelerate the pace of industrialisation:** Developing countries input scarce raw materials, capital goods and modern sophisticated technology required for achieving faster industrial growth.
2. **To bridge domestic demand-supply gap:** A country imports those goods which are in demand but not available in the country in sufficient quantities or not at all. For example, India imports crude oil to bridge the domestic supply demand gap.
3. **To improve living standards:** Imports enable Indian consumers to enjoy a wide variety of products of high quality. Consequently, their standard of living is likely to improve.
4. **To overcome food crisis:** In times of crop failure (due to drought or flood), a country faces a critical food situation. So it becomes necessary to import food articles to prevent starvation and avoid famine like conditions.
5. **To meet defence needs:** Developing countries like India, China and Brazil also import various types of defence equipment for their army, air force and navy. Such imports enable them to defend their national territories from foreign aggression. And long ago Adam Smith rightly commented that "Defence is more important than opulence".

21.3 IMPORT TRADE PROCEDURE

Different procedures are laid down and followed in different countries for importing goods. For any particular country this depends on two things, viz., (i) the legal requirements and (ii) trade procedures and practices which remain in force in the country. In India, importing involves the following steps:

1. **Making trade enquiry and receiving quotation:** To start with an Indian importer has to make trade enquiries from different exporters, by giving detailed specifications of the

products required by him, such as its quality, design and size. He will send a letter of enquiry to each potential exporter to collect information regarding the availability of goods, their prices as also the terms and conditions relating to delivery of goods and the method of obtaining payment on time (i.e., on the due date).

The importer will receive a quotation (or proforma invoice) from the exporter in response to his enquiry. The quotation gives such specification (or details) as ready availability of the good, its quality, size, colour and the supply price as also the terms and conditions of sale.

2. **Obtaining licence:** If the importable item is on the restricted list of permissible imports (not a banned item) there is need to obtain an import licence. So the intending importer has to submit an application in a prescribed form to the DGFT. The importer is also required to furnish details as per the requirement of the form. The form, duly filled in is to be submitted to the licensing authority (i.e., DGTD) after paying the licence fee.

   If, after scrutinising the application, DGTD is fully satisfied, it will issue an import licence which specifies the terms and conditions of import. It may also issue the 'Quota Certificate' which sets the upper limit on the volume and money value of goods which could be imported. The import licence is issued in duplicate. The first is "For Customs Purposes" and is to be presented by the importer to the customs authorities at the time of clearance of goods. The second is "For Exchange Control Purposes" and is required for getting necessary foreign exchange from an authorised dealer or a commercial bank such as the SBI.

3. **Arrangement of foreign currency:** In India, both inflows and outflows of any foreign currency are controlled by its central bank, i.e., the Reserve Bank of India. For getting foreign exchange, the importer has to apply to the Exchange Control Department of the R.B.I. If, after proper scrutiny of the application, the R.B.I. is satisfied, it will sanction the release of necessary foreign exchange for the importer. Then the importer will get foreign exchange from an authorised dealer by depositing the required amount of rupees.

4. **Placing the order or indent:** On the basis of different trade directories the importer will contact the potential exporter (or the foreign supplier) who will send a Pro forma Invoice which gives details of price and terms and conditions of contract. On the basis of the invoice, the importer may place an order with the exporter which is also called an indent. Such an indent gives details about the quantity, quality and other specifications of goods as also shipping instructions.

FOCUS ON TERMINOLOGY: PROFORMA INVOICE

Proforma invoice is a sales invoice sent by an exporter to an importer, usually before some of the invoice details are known. For example, in import trading a proform a invoice may be sent to the importer at the port of shipment, based on a notional weight although the contract specifies that the buyer will pay for the weight ascertained on landing the goods at the port of destination. When the actual (landed) weight is known, a final invoice is sent.

An indent may be placed either directly with the exporter or through a specialised firm or intermediary or agency house called 'Indent House' which helps to establish link between exporters and importers through their offices located in different countries. On a commission basis however the importer has to first enter into an agreement with the indent house before placing an order.

5. **Sending letter of credit:** In the next step a letter of credit (LOC) is issued by the importer's bank in favour of the exporter. It is essentially an undertaking to honour the bill of exchange drawn by the exporter on the importer up to the agreed limit. It is a proof of the credit-worthiness of the importer.

   A letter of credit is issued by the importer's bank against the amount deposited by the importer with it. The importer will send the letter of credit to the exporter who will make arrangements for the shipment of goods on receipt of the letter.

6. **Receiving shipping documents:** The exporter will send prior intimation of shipment of goods by him to the importer, indicating the likely date of arrival of the ship at the port of destination. The exporter will also draw a bill of exchange on the importer for the value of the goods payable to the former and attach to it all necessary shipping documents such as invoice, insurance policy, bill of lading, consular invoice and, of course, the certificate of origin. All these documents are to be presented together (i.e., at a time) for getting the goods released from the shipping company.

   Since the bill of exchange is supported by all necessary documents, it is also called 'documentary bill'. It is a bill of exchange attached to the shipping documents of a consignment of goods. These documents include the bill of lading, insurance policy, dock warrant and invoice. Such a bill may be either D/P bill or D/A bill. In case of D/P bill, the exporter gives instructions to his banker to hand over the documents to the importer or his bank only after receiving a full payment of amount quoted in the bill. By comparison, in case of D/A bill the documents will be handed over to the importer or his banker on acceptance of the bill of exchange by the importer. Such a bill is payable after a certain agreed period of time which normally varies between one month to six months.

7. **Appointment of clearing agent:** As soon as the ship arrives at the port of destination, the importer has to make necessary and timely arrangement for the clearance of goods from the customs authorities either directly or through some authorised 'clearing agent'. Since the clearance of goods from the dock takes some time and involves the completion of several legal formalities, most of the importers appoint clearing agents as and when necessary on a purely commission basis.

8. **Clearance of goods:** Customs clearance is mandatory for taking delivery of goods from the dock. The following steps have to be followed for getting such clearance:

   (a) *Delivery order:* To start with the importer has to get the 'delivery order' on the back of the bill of lading from the shipping company. This will enable him to take delivery of the goods from the customs authorities.

   (b) *Port Trust Dues Receipt:* The importer will have to fill in a form, known as 'Application to Import' in duplicate and submit it either to the 'Port Trust Office' or to the 'Landing and Shipping Dues Office', which collects a fee on all goods entering India's domestic territory. When the importer pays the charge, one copy of Applications to Import (called Port Trust Dues Receipt) is returned to him.

   (c) *Bill of entry:* A bill of entry is supplied by the customs office and contains details of the licence, types of goods and the shipping company as also customs duty payable. It has to be filled in triplicate by the importer and submitted to the customs office along with the 'Port Trust Dues Receipt'.

(d) *Payment of import duty:* On the basis of Bill of Entry, the customs office will calculate the amount of customs duty payable by the importer. It will also examine the import licence. After payment of customs duty, the importer will get a 'release order', which will entitle him to take delivery of the imported goods either from the customs office or from the bonded warehouse.

9. **Taking delivery of goods:** After getting due clearance from the customs department the importer or his clearing agent will have to submit the delivery order and release order from the customs authorities to the dock authorities. The concerned dock official will issue a 'gate pass' so that the importer or his agent can take the goods out of the dock to the importer's godown or factory either through railways or road transport.

10. **Making payment:** The whole import procedure is completed as soon as payment is made to the exporter. If no advance payment is made to the exporter the importer will make full payment on the due date as soon as the Bill of Exchange (i.e., D/A Bill) is presented to him.

21.4 DOCUMENTS USED IN IMPORT TRADE

The importer has to get customs clearance before taking delivery of the goods from the dock. Before taking delivery, three main documents are to be submitted to the customs authority. These are the following:

1. **Delivery order:** The importer has to obtain the 'delivery order' or get the order endorsed on the back side of the bill of lading from the shipping company, so as to become eligible (entitled) to take delivery of the goods.
2. **Port Trust dues receipt.** The importer has to fill in a form, known as the 'Application to Import' or the 'Port Trust Dues Receipt' in duplicate. And he is required to submit it to the 'Port Trust Office' or 'Landing and Shipping Dues Office'. All imported goods are chargeable. This charge is imposed by the office to cover the cost of services provided by the dock authorities in connection with the arrival of imports. As soon as the importer pays the charge, one copy of the Application to Import is returned to him.
3. **Bill of entry.** It is a detailed statement of the nature and value of a consignment of goods prepared by the shipper of the consignment for paying customs duty and customs clearance. The importer or his agent has to fill in this form, obtainable from the customs office in triplicate. It has to be submitted to the customs office along with the 'Port Trust Dues Receipt'. A bill of entry gives the following details:
   (i) name and address of the importer,
   (ii) import licence number,
   (iii) port of destination,
   (iv) name of the country from where goods have been imported,
   (v) name of ship, its nationality and number,
   (vi) packages, numbers and marks,
   (vii) description of goods (quantity and money value of imported items) and, of course,
   (viii) customs duty payable (both the rate and the amount).

4. Dock challan: As soon as the importer completes all the customs formalities he has to fill in a form in duplicate. The form is known as 'Dock Challan'. An importer can either do it himself or appoint an agent to do this. This is needed for paying dock charges. It is possible to take delivery of imported goods only after clearance of dock dues.

21.4.1 Indent

An indent is an order of goods placed by the importer to the exporter. It gives the following details:

(i) quantity of (physical volume) goods to be imported,
(ii) quantity, design and size of goods,
(iii) method of packing and marking,
(iv) instructions on shipment and insurance,
(v) mode (method) of payment, and
(vi) period (time) of delivery.

21.4.2 Letter of Credit

As mentioned earlier letter of credit is a document used to effect payment for internationally traded goods, usually as part of a contract for the sale of goods. It ensures that the supplier receives prompt and guaranteed payment. At the same time the purchaser gets a short-term line of credit. To be more specific, under this facility, a purchaser in country A of goods supplied by a firm in country B can arrange a letter of credit from his bank (i.e., the bank issuing credit), authorising it to make payment to the supplier either through a branch of the bank in country B or through a bank (i.e., the negotiating bank) holding the supplier's account. Under a contract of sale of goods this is done as soon as the documents stipulated in the letter of credit, such as the bill of lading, insurance policy and certificate of origin are presented to the negotiating bank.

21.4.3 Consular Invoice

It is an export invoice which has been certified in the exporting country by the consul of the importing country. This document is required by the customs authorities to charge the correct import duties. In some countries a certificate of origin is also required along with the invoice.

21.4.4 Bill of Lading

It is a document acknowledging the shipment of a consignor's goods for carriage by sea. A consignor receives a bill issued (normally by the master of a ship) on behalf of either the shipowner or a charterer under a charter-party. The bill performs three functions: (i) it is a receipt for the goods; (ii) it summarises the terms of the contract for carriage; and (iii) it serves as a valid document of title to the goods. (Note that it is not a negotiable instrument.)

The bills of lading are of two types:

(i) *Clean bill:* The bill of lading gives details of the goods; if the packages are in good condition and proper order a clear bill is issued. If they are not, the bill will say so.

(ii) *Dirty bill:* A dirty (foul or claused) bill of lading carries a clause or endorsement by the master or mate of the ship on which goods are carried to the effect that the goods (or their packing) arrived for loading are in a damaged condition.

21.4.5 Chartering

Chartering means hiring the whole of a ship or an aircraft. The hirer is called the charterer and the document setting out the terms and conditions of the contract is called the charter-party. It is of two types:

(a) *Time charter:* In a time charter the ship or aircraft is hired for a specified period and for a specified number of voyages. Usually the owner operates it and the charterer pays fuel and storage cost.

(b) *Voyage charter:* In a voyage charter, the ship or aircraft is hired for a single voyage between stated ports to carry a stated cargo or for a fixed number of voyages rather than for a fixed period.

21.4.6 Air Waybill (Air Consignment Note)

An air waybill is a document made out by a consignor of goods by air freight to facilitate swift delivery of the goods to the consignee. It gives the name of the consignor and the loading airport, the consignee and the airport of destination, a description of the goods, and the marks, numbers and dimensions of the packages.

Key Points

1. **Procedure involved in import trade:** The following ten steps are involved in import trade:
   - (i) Making trade enquiry and receiving quotation
   - (ii) Obtaining licence
   - (iii) Arrangement of foreign currency
   - (iv) Placing the order or indent
   - (v) Sending letter of credit
   - (vi) Receiving shipping documents
   - (vii) Appointment of clearing agent
   - (viii) Clearance of goods
   - (ix) Taking delivery of goods
   - (x) Making payment.
2. **Documents used in import trader**
   - (i) *Quota certificate:* A quota certificate states the volume or the quantity and value of goods which can be imported by a trader. It is issued along with the import licence.
   - (ii) *Letter of credit:* A letter of credit is a non-negotiable order from a bank to a bank abroad, authorising payment to a named person a particular sum of money or up to a limited sum.
   - (iii) *Indent:* An indent is an order of goods placed by the importer to the exporter.
   - (iv) *Port trust dues receipt:* The importer has to fill in a form, known as 'Application to

Import' in duplicate. And he is required to submit it to the 'Port Trust Office' or 'Landing and Shipping Dues Office'.

(v) *Bill of entry:* It is a detailed statement of the nature and value of a consignment of goods prepared by the shipper of the consignment for customs duty.

(vi) *Dock challan:* As soon as the importer completes all the customs formalities he has to fill in a form in duplicate, called dock challan.

(vii) *Mate's receipt:* The mate is a subordinate to the captain of a ship. Before the captain issues a final bill of lading, the mate issues a provisional receipt, known as the mate's receipt.

(viii) *Bill of Lading:* It is a document acknowledging the shipment of a consignor's goods for carriage by sea.

The bills of lading are of two types: (a) Clean bill, (b) Dirty bill.

3. **Chartering.** It means hiring the whole of a ship or an aircraft. The hirer is called the charterer and the document setting out the terms and conditions of the contract is called the charter-party. Chartering is of two types: (i) Time charter, (ii) Voyage charter.

KEY Terms	
Letter of credit	Bill of lading
Quota certificate	Bill of entry
Indent	Dock challan
Clearing agent	Chartering
Mate's receipt	Port trust

Assignments

SHORT ANSWER-TYPE QUESTIONS

1. What is import trade?
2. Outline the steps involved in import trade.
3. Mention the documents used in import trade.
4. What is a Bill of Entry? **[ISC 1988]**

ESSAY-TYPE QUESTIONS

1. Give a brief account of the documents used in import trade.
2. Describe the steps (procedures) involved in import trade.
3. Write short notes on: (a) Clearing Agent, (b) Bill of Entry, (c) Bill of Lading and (d) Chartering.
4. Discuss the steps necessary for importing goods from a foreign country. **[ISC 1987]**

5. Distinguish between excise duty and customs duty. [ISC 1989]

Ans. Excise duty is an indirect tax imposed by the government on a good (at the production or manufacturing stage) mainly on tobacco, petrol and alcoholic drinks, the demand for which is highly price-inelastic. Governments use excise duties both as a means of raising revenue and as an instrument of fiscal policy.

By comparison, a custom duty is a form of consumption tax which is levied by the government on foreign products imported into the home country. Custom duties are used mainly to raise revenues for the government, although they can serve, to reduce domestic spending on imports and thus to the save foreign exchange.

QUESTION BANK

1. ***What purpose does import trade serve?***

Ans. See text.

2. ***Explain the procedure for importing goods into India and mention the documents to be used in the process.***

Ans. See text.

3. ***Name the main documents used in import trade.***

Ans. The main documents used in import trade are as follows:

(i) Import licence
(ii) Indent
(iii) Letter of credit
(iv) Documentary Bill of Exchange
(v) Bill of Entry
(vi) Bill of Sight
(vii) Port Trust Dues Receipt
(viii) Application to Import
(ix) Advice Note
(x) Bill of Lading.

4. ***What is Documentary Bill Of Exchange?***

Ans. See text.

5. ***Mark the following statements True or False.***

(a) OGL represents Government list.

(b) Bill of entry is prepared for assessing the duty payable on imported items.

(c) D/A stands for 'Documents against Acceptance'.

(d) D/P stands for 'Documents against Payment'.

Ans. True: (b), (c)

False: (a), (d).

6. ***Fill in the blanks in each of the following statement:***

(a) No separate (individual) licence is needed for importing goods under the ——— list.

(b) Any trade-related advice is sent by ——— to ———.

(c) The document which is prepared to calculate import duty is known as ———.

(d) A ——— is prepared when the importer has not much information.

(e) Port Trust Dues Receipt is issued only after payment of all ——— charges.

Ans. (a) OGL, (b) exporter, importer, (c) the Bill of entry, (d) Bill of sight, (e) dock.

22 WORLD TRADE ORGANISATION (WTO)

SYLLABUS

- *WTO — Meaning and objectives.*

> *The position of developing countries in the WTO is a subject of concern. In the past, their interests have been taken into account by means of escape clause. However, many are now 'graduating' to developed status; and transition periods are running out.*
>
> — Dermot. McAleese

LEARNING OUTCOMES

On completion of this chapter, you will be able to understand the following:

22.1 Backdrop
22.2 Organisation structure
22.3 Objectives of WTO
22.4 Principles of WTO
22.5 Functions of WTO
22.6 Major WTO Agreements
22.7 Successes and Failures of WTO
22.8 Impact of the WTO on Indian Economy

There are a number of ways of looking at World Trade Organisation (WTO). Essentially, the WTO is a place where member countries try to sort out the (complex) problems related to international trade they face with each other, and ensure a level playing field for all, thus, contributing to economic growth and development.

22.1 BACKDROP

Founded in 1995 after the 8-year "Uruguay Round" of talks, WTO succeeded the General Agreement on Tariffs and Trade (GATT). For nearly seven decades, WTO and GATT have helped to create a strong and prosperous international trading system, thereby contributing to global economic growth. GATT was established after the World War II (in 1948) in the wake of other multilateral institutions viz. World Bank and IMF (International Monetary Fund) — dedicated to international economic cooperation and growth by lowering tariff barriers to international trade.

Eight rounds of negotiations took place under GATT. The eighth or "Uruguay Round" was launched in September 1986 to renegotiate trade agreements and extend the trading system into several new areas, notably trade in services and intellectual property and to reform trade in sensitive sectors of agriculture and textiles. After 8 years of discussion, the Final Act concluding the Uruguay Round and officially establishing the WTO regime was signed on 15th April 1994 by 123 nations during the ministerial meeting at Marrakesh, Morocco (and hence known as the Marrakesh Agreement), replacing the GATT. Established in 1995, WTO has a wider scope than GATT, which includes services, agriculture, and intellectual property, not just trade in goods. Most of the issues which WTO focusses are derived from previous trade negotiations, especially from the Uruguay Round.

22.2 ORGANISATION STRUCTURE

With its headquarters in Geneva, WTO has, at present, 164 members — Afghanistan became the 164th member on 29th July 2016 — and 20 observer governments. In addition to nations, European Union is also a member. The WTO describes itself as "a rule-based, member-driven organisation — all decisions are made by member governments, and the rules are the outcome of negotiations among members". The highest decision-making body of the WTO is the ministerial conference which meets roughly every two years. Decisions are generally taken by consensus of the entire membership. A General Council conducts the organisation's business in the intervals between Ministerial Conferences. Specialised subsidiary bodies, also comprising all members, administer and monitor the implementation by members of the various WTO agreements. The Secretariat of WTO employs over 600 staff, and its experts — buyers, economists, statisticians and communication experts — assist WTO members on a daily basis to ensure inter alia, that negotiations progress smoothly, and that the rules of international trade are correctly applied and enforced.

22.3 OBJECTIVES OF WTO

WTO's main purpose is to help trade flow as freely as possible, because this is important for economic development and well-being of all the member nations. The major objectives of WTO are thus:

(i) To make optimum use of world's resources;

(ii) To ensure full employment;

(iii) To expand production;

(iv) To raise the standards of living;

(v) To expand trade in goods and services; and

(vi) To achieve sustainable development through protection of environment.

22.4 PRINCIPLES OF WTO

The WTO establishes a framework for trade policies; it does not define or specify outcomes. At its heart are the WTO agreements, negotiated and signed by the bulk of member nations. Although these agreements are lengthy and complex, five simple, fundamental principles run throughout all of these agreements. These principles (specified below) are the foundations of the multilateral trading system.

1. **Non-discrimination:** A country shall not discriminate between its trading partners and also it will not discriminate between its own and foreign products, services and nations. It implies two things. One, a country granting Most Favoured Nation (MFN) treatment to some trading partner(s) must grant the same to all other WTO members. Second, imported goods shall not be treated less favourably than domestically produced goods. This was introduced to tackle various non-tariff barriers to trade.
2. **Reciprocity:** Nations shall try to provide similar concessions for each other.
3. **Transparency:** Negotiations and process must be fair and open with the same set of rules for all. The members are required to publish their trade regulations, to respond to requests for information by other members, and to notify changes in trade policy to WTO. The WTO system also tries to improve predictability and stability, discouraging the use of trade barriers arbitrarily, to encourage investment, job creation, etc.
4. **Special and differential treatment:** Over three-fourths of WTO members being developing countries and countries in transition to market economies, the WTO agreements give them transition periods to adjust to the more unfamiliar, perhaps, difficult WTO provisions.
5. **Safety values:** In specific circumstances, WTO members are able to restrict trade. The WTO agreements permit members to take measures to protect not only the environment but also public health, animal health and plant health. However, these measures must be applied in the same way to both national and international businesses.

22.5 FUNCTIONS OF WTO

Given its objectives, the main functions of WTO are:

(i) WTO acts as a forum for all multilateral trade negotiations among members. These include: individual countries commitments to lower customs tariff, and other trade barriers, keep open service markets, and agreeing on rules governing the conduct of international trade (e.g. anti-dumping, subsidies, product standards, etc.).

(ii) WTO facilitates settlement of disputes among members regarding the interpretation and application of the agreements thereby ensuring trade flows smoothly.

(iii) WTO administers and implements the application of the WTO's agreed rules for trade in goods, services and intellectual property rights.

(iv) WTO monitors and reviews the trade policies of members, and also ensures transparency of regional and bilateral trade agreements.

(v) WTO organises hundreds of technical cooperation commissions to build capacity of developing countries' governments officials in international trade matters.

(vi) WTO cooperates with other multilateral institutions such as the IMF and the World Bank involved in global policy making.

(vii) WTO maintains regular dialogue with NGOs, parliamentarians, other international organisations, the media and the general public on various aspects of the WTO with the aim of enhancing cooperation and increasing awareness of WTOs missions and activities.

While (i) and (ii) are the main functions, other five are additional functions of WTO. Key functions of the WTO are shown in Fig. 22.1.

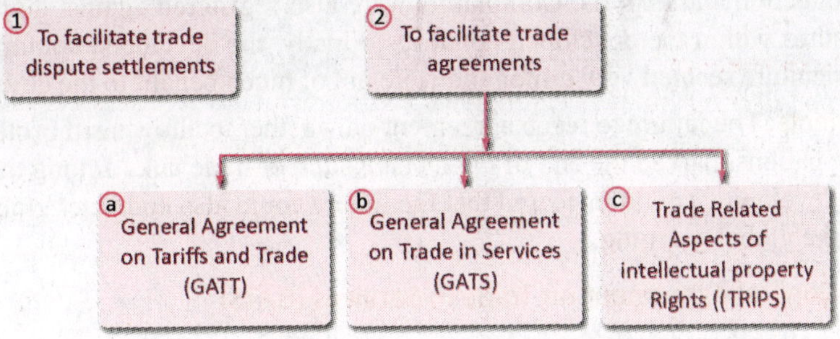

FIGURE 22.1: Key Functions of the WTO

22.6 MAJOR WTO AGREEMENTS

The WTO was born out of negotiations and everything WTO does is the result of negotiations. The bulk of WTO's current work comes from the 1988-94 negotiations under GATT. In recent rounds, WTO members have tried to solve non-tariff problems and other current issues, such as trade in agriculture and services, transfer of technology, and non-monetary barriers put up by countries to discourage free trade. The Doha Development Round which began in November, 2001, is a trade round, focussing on integrating the developing countries in the world economy, and on opening market access between these countries and the developed world. The WTO oversees about 60 different agreements. The four major agreements are as follows:

1. Agreement on Agriculture (AOA)

An important area for reform is agricultural trade barriers. Developing countries like India claim that agricultural protectionism by developed countries (such as the USA, Canada and the members of the European Union) has made it very difficult for them to sell their agricultural products to the most developed nations. Thus, their primary avenue for income growth has been closed. At the Doha trade round, both developed and developing nations made promises to improve market access for agricultural and other products via reduction in export subsidies, quotas and tariffs. The agreement on agriculture includes three aspects: market access, domestic support and export subsidies. Market access refers to the ability of firms from one country to sell in another. The market access provision includes tariffication of the non-tariff barriers (i.e. conversion of non-tariff barriers such as quotas into tariffs) and gradual reduction of such tariffs by 36% in the case of developed countries over a six-year period, and by 24% in the case of developing countries over a ten-year period.

The Agreement on Agriculture (AOA) seeks to evolve an equitable reforms programme on trade in farm products (mainly food and industrial raw materials) among the member countries. It provides for liberalisation of such trade by gradual reduction of tariff and non-tariff barriers so as to give member countries free access to one another's markets, while at the same time giving due consideration to the issue of food security in low-income countries. The WTO has well recognised that only through rapid development of agriculture it would be possible to ensure food security and achieve poverty alleviation in developing countries. However, in 2003 meeting of trade ministers in Cancun, Mexico, disagreements were very prominent on agriculture, and particularly in developed country export subsidies (especially on cotton textiles). Developing countries pushed hard developed countries to remove these subsidies, because those subsidies undercut developing countries' production and exports. Complaints were also registered against domestic agricultural support measures within the developed countries. Finally, the developed countries' changes with respect to agriculture seemed very minor and were not of much benefit to the developing countries.

- **Comments:** The failure to reach agreement on whether to allow tariff protection for farmers in developing nations marked the end of the Doha Round of trade talks among the members of the WTO. Some developing countries feared that the failure could also endanger global agreements on other issues like global warming.

2. The General Agreement on Trade in Services (GATS)

The General Agreement on Trade in Services (GATS) is the first and the only set of multilateral rules governing international trade in services. The inclusion of services in trade negotiations was primarily due to the increase in the importance of the services sector in the developed world, and also due to the greater potential for trade in services brought about by the advances in communication technology over the past few decades.

- **Coverage:** All services are covered under GATS, and the Most Favoured Nation (MFN) treatment applies to all services as well. GATS identified four ways of trading services:

(i) *Cross-border supply:* Services supplied from one country to another.

(ii) *Consumption abroad:* Consumers or firms making use of a service in another country (i.e. tourism).

(iii) *Commercial presence:* A foreign country setting up a branch or subsidiary in another country and

(iv) *Presence of natural reasons:* Individuals travelling to another country to supply services.

These definitions are necessary because the trade in services, is a much more diverse area than the trade in manufactured goods. The GATS calls for 'rational treatment' in services, meaning that any country is to treat foreign services providers in the same fashion as domestic service providers. New procedures were also adopted for the settlement of disputes.

3. Trade-Related Intellectual Property Rights (TRIPS)

Inconsistent treatment of intellectual property rights (through patents, trademarks and copyrights) across countries can distort international trade flows. Keeping this in view, in the Uruguay Round of trade negotiations completed in 1994, agreement was reached on harmonisation of such practices, commonly known as the Trade-Related Aspects of Intellectual Property (TRIPS).

The reason is that advanced countries have experienced a shift from depending on physical capital to depending on 'intellectual property' protected by patents and copyrights. Thus, defining the international application of intellectual property rights has also become a major pre-occupation of the WTO. The WTO tries to take this issue with its Agreement on TRIPS.

The basic purpose of TRIPS is to allow for the creation of domestic laws which concern the protection of intellectual property rights, as well as the enforcement of such laws in violating countries. TRIPS established minimum levels of protection that each WTO member government must provide to the intellectual property of fellow WTO member countries. TRIPS cover the following types of intellectual property:

(i) Copyrights,
(ii) Trademarks (including service marks),
(iii) Geographical indications: such as 'Champagne', 'Scotch' and 'Tequila',
(iv) Industrial designs,
(v) Patents,
(vi) Layout designs of integrated circuits, and
(vii) Undisclosed information, including trade secrets.

TRIPS provide guidelines for how basic principles of the trading system and other international intellectual property rights agreements should be applied. It also spells out how various WTO member governments must provide adequate protection of intellectual property rights in their domestic laws and set intellectual rights within their own borders. TRIPS also provide a means of settling disputes regarding the intellectual property between the members of WTO.

Developing countries like India, which are technologically backward, face difficulties in importing modern sophisticated technology from developed countries. The transfer of such technology to developing countries was held in check due to protection given by intellectual property rights. In addition, developing countries face difficulties in implementing public health programmes because they cannot derive the benefits of developments in medical science which can make lifesaving drugs readily available to people of such countries at affordable prices.

As a part of India's commitment to WTO on TRIPS, the Patents (Amendment) Act was passed in March 1999. The basic objective was to protect such intellectual property rights as invention and innovations and to ensure diffusion of technological progress.

However, the WTO rules allow for certain exceptions to reduce trade barriers, such as allowing countries to continue to provide support for domestic agriculture and for developing countries to protect infant industries.

In retrospect, it appears that the TRIPS features of the WTO agreement hurt the developing countries through the payments that were expected to be made by them in the future to the developed countries for the use of intellectual property.

- **Comments:** The WTO has failed to solve all global trade problems. Various legal and regulatory differences often impede trade expansion. And a wide gap separates developing nations like India from industrialised nations like the USA. The WTO trade talks in Doha, Qatar, began in 2001 to address dismantling protection of manufactured goods, elimination of subsidies on farm (agricultural) products and overturning temporary protectionist measures. However, the sad truth is that the Doha Round ended in 2008 with hardly any agreement.

One of the major complaints of developing countries during the Doha negotiations was the continuing existence of large agricultural export and production subsidies in rich countries. For instance, the US cotton subsidy depresses world cotton prices and, therefore, hurts cotton growers in West Africa. In addition, some farmers in the Third World countries are hurt by low prices of subsidised food exports from Europe and the USA.

4. Trade-related Investment Measures (TRIMs)

Some trade-related investment measures (TRIMs) such as local content requirements for foreign investors are to be eliminated within two years by the developed countries, five years by the developing countries, and seven years by the 'least developed countries'. It may be noted that the local content rule or the rule of origin refers to the stipulation by a country that for a product to qualify as an authentic domestically manufactured product (that is, originating in that country) the product must be manufactured predominantly from locally supplied as opposed to imported components. Local content rules are used by governments mainly to prevent the operation of the so-called 'screwdriver' plants (plants producing final products from mainly imported CKDs/sub-assemblies and components) established to circumvent tariffs, quota, and anti-dumping duties dumping on imported final goods.

22.7 SUCCESSES AND FAILURES OF WTO

From the above, it is evident that although the principles and objectives of WTO are quite laudable, in reality, power politics have restrained it from achieving the desired goals. It is quite obvious, as reconciling multi-lateral trade agreement clauses with domestic economic compulsions of more than 100 countries is a gigantic task. And, it will take years to resolve all the issues to the satisfaction of all. We now enumerate below certain achievements and failures (for which WTO has faced criticisms of various groups and third world countries) of the world body.

22.7.1 Successes of WTO

1. WTO has enhanced international trade through removal of trade and non-trade barriers. Being a member of the WTO is a significant step towards a country being able to enjoy the benefits of globalised world trade. A case in point is China's entry into the WTO and consequent rapid rise in export of manufactured goods.
2. It has brought trade in services in the ambit of multilateral system.
3. It has helped in the settlement of trade-related disputes and also paved the way for improving monitoring by introducing Trade Policy Review.
4. WTO has been instrumental in ushering in bold trade and exchange reforms in developing countries leading to efficiency in resource use, and opened up with new investment opportunities thereby promoting economic growth.
5. Special concession for the Third World countries with emphasis on the least developed countries.
6. WTO has developed a bilateral approach of multilateral bargaining.

22.7.2 Failures of WTO

1. WTO is highly biased towards the developed and rich nations.
2. WTO rules put the "rights" and "interests" of corporations over local concerns and policies.
3. Liberalisation process is incomplete — e.g. liberalisation of trade in services has not been fully achieved, high tariffs in some areas still remain on which negotiations are going on at various levels.
4. WTO has not been able to remove non-tariff barriers imposed by developed countries to imports from Third World countries. For instances, EU and US agricultural markets for some crops continue to be highly protected with extensive subsidies to farmers.
5. Implementation issues are source of concern in the areas of anti-dumping, correcting asymmetries in TRIPS, TRIMS, movement of people, etc.

22.8 IMPACT OF THE WTO ON INDIAN ECONOMY

The WTO was established to deal with all the major aspects of international trade and it has far-reaching effects not only on India's foreign trade but also on its internal economy. The benefits and adverse effects of the WTO on the Indian economy are discussed below.

22.8.1 Benefits of the WTO on Indian Economy

1. *Increase in exports:* India's exports of goods and services witnessed considerable growth. India also hopes to benefit from higher agricultural exports due to reduction in domestic subsidies and barriers to trade. Phasing out of MFA will help in the export if textiles and clothing.
2. *Boost in FDI:* With the withdrawal of restrictions in foreign investments as per TRIMS agreement, developing countries like India would benefit from higher inflow of FDI, FII, etc.
3. *Predictability:* The agreements of safeguard, subsidies and anti-dumping measures will provide greater security and predictability in international trade. Arbitrary changes in the laws governing trade and investments will not be made under the WTO regime. Removal of non-tariff barriers and quantitative restrictions often is expected to promote competition and give India an edge in export of goods where it has got competitive advantages like services, labour-intensive goods, etc.
4. *Policy assistance:* As a member of the WTO, India can get assistance from the International Trade Centre in formulating and implementing export promotion programmes.
5. *Multilateral trade links:* India has market access to all nations. It is thus saved from the trouble of entering into multiple bilateral trade agreements with so many countries.
6. *Easier dispute settlement:* WTO provides a forum for settlement of disputes among member countries. The agreements are legally binding on member countries.
7. *Special concessions:* There are several provisions extending to developing countries which would benefit India.
8. *Sustainable development:* WTO seeks to uphold and safeguard an open and non-discriminatory multilateral trading system for promoting sustainable development. Tariff and non-tariff barriers for environment goods and services shall be reduced and eliminated. No country is prevented from taking measures for the protection of its environment.
9. *Policy review mechanism:* Members of WTO need to undertake reviews of policies and programmes periodically.

22.8.2 Adverse Effects of the WTO on Indian Economy

1. *TRIPS:* Protection of intellectual property rights has been one of the major concerns of the WTO. Although as a member of WTO, India has to comply with the TRIPS standards, the agreement on TRIPS goes against the Indian Patent Act, 1970 in the pharmaceutical sector and agriculture. These will have a severe adverse effect on public health programmes and livelihood of majority of the population.
2. *TRIMS:* WTO benefits the developed countries more. TRIMS undermines our strategy of self-reliant growth based on locally available resources and technology. TRIMS favour the multinational corporations as there are no rules in the agreement to formulate international rules for controlling business practices of foreign investors.

3. *Price rise:* WTO agreements are likely to cause a hike in the prices of drugs and agricultural inputs, due to MNCs control over patents, etc.
4. *GATS:* The agreements on GATS will also favour the developed countries more, as India's is rapidly growing services sector will have to compete with very big foreign firms.
5. *Barriers to trade:* Reduction of tariff and non-tariff barriers has adversely affected the exports as various Indian goods have been hit by non-tariff barriers imposed by the developed countries. These include: textiles, marine products, floriculture, pharmaceuticals, basmati rice, etc. Free movement of labour is also not allowed.

Key Points

1. **GATT:** General Agreement on Tariffs and Trade (GATT) was established in 1948 (after World War II) to foster international economic cooperation and growth by lowering tariff barriers to international trade. Eight rounds of trade negotiations took place under GATT in its nearly seven decades of existence. In the eighth or Uruguay Round, negotiations extended to include trade in services and intellectual property.
2. **WTO:** The World Trade Organisation (WTO) was founded in 1995, after 8 year "Uruguay Round" of talks. Succeeding GATT; WTO has wider scope which includes services, agriculture and intellectual property, not just trade in goods. Headquartered in Geneva, it has 164 member nations and 20 observer governments at present.
3. **Principles and key functions of WTO:** Five fundamental principles underlying all the WTO agreements are: Non-discrimination, Reciprocity, Transparency, special and differential treatment, and safety values. These lay the foundation of multilateral trading system. Key functions of WTO are: (i) it acts as a forum for all multilateral trade negotiations among members, (ii) it facilitates settlement of disputes among members to ensure smooth trade flow.
4. **Major WTO Agreements:** The bulk of WTO's current work comes from the eight-year Uruguay Round of negotiations under GATT. WTO oversees about 60 different agreements, four major of them are: (i) Agreement on Agriculture (AOA) which seeks to evolve an equitable reforms programme on trade in farm products among the member countries: (ii) GATS which calls for rational treatment in services by member countries, (iii) TRIPS which calls for creation of domestic laws for protection of intellectual property rights (viz., copyrights, patents, etc.) in WTO member countries, and (iv) TRIMS which calls for phase-wise elimination of local content requirements.
5. **Success and Failures of WTO:** WTO has succeeded in enhancing global trade through gradual reduction in trade barriers and also brought trade in services in the ambit of multilateral trading system besides providing a platform for settlement of trade-related disputes among member countries. It has also provided for special concession to third world countries in elimination of trade barriers.

However, WTO has yet been able to fully remove non-tariff barriers imposed by developed countries to imports from third world countries. Also, it is seen to be biased towards the developed and rich member nations. WTO's favouritism towards MNCs is reflected in its rules which overrides local concerns and policies of developing countries. Further, liberalisation of trade in services has not yet been completed.

6. **WTO and Indian Economy:** India has benefited in certain areas — viz. multilateral trade links, increased export volumes, earlier dispute settlement etc. India also hopes to benefit from higher agricultural exports consequent upon reduction in trade barriers in developed countries. However like other developing countries, India is also adversely impacted due to TRIPS, TRIMS, GATS and other barriers of trade imposed by the developed countries.

KEY Terms	
GATT	Tariff barriers
WTO	Non-tariff barriers
GATS	Intellectual property rights
TRIPS	WTO agreements
TRIMS	Policy review mechanism
Most Favoured Nation	Non-discrimination

Assignments

SHORT ANSWER-TYPE QUESTIONS

1. What is the full form of WTO?
2. What is GATT? [ISC 1992]

ESSAY-TYPE QUESTIONS

1. What exactly is the role of WTO in the arena of International Trade?
2. Examine the effect of the setting up of WTO on the Indian economy.

QUESTION BANK

1. *What are the functions of WTO?*

Ans. See text.

2. *What is the role of WTO in settling trade disputes and promoting foreign multilateral trade?*

Ans. See text.

23 BUSINESS RISKS AND INSURANCE

SYLLABUS

- *Meaning, objectives and purpose of insurance; Concept of reinsurance and double insurance. Risks in business — insurable and non-insurable — meaning and examples of both. Characteristics of insurable risks.*
- *Principle of insurance.*
  *Fundamental principles to be **explained: utmost good faith; insurable interest; indemnity; contribution**; doctrine of subrogation; **causaproxima. Mitigation of loss.***

> *Insurance is gambling in reverse.* — Anon

LEARNING OUTCOMES

On completion of this chapter, you will be able to understand the following:

23.1 Types of Business Risks
23.2 Insurable and Non-Insurable Risks
23.3 Meaning of Insurance
23.4 Objectives and Purpose of Insurance
23.5 Principles of Insurance
23.6 Reinsurance and Double Insurance
23.7 Vocabulary of Insurance

Business firms operate in an uncertain environment because they are exposed to different types of risks. The term 'risk' refers to the measurable possibility of losing or not gaining value or the state in which a number of possible future events exceeds the number of events which will actually occur; and in which some measure of probability can be attached to each possible outcome. Risk is different from uncertainty which is not measurable and in which there are multiple possible future events, but in which probability is attached to each are too vague to have numbers attached to them.

The term 'risk' rather than 'uncertainty' is used to describe business situations where large amounts of information are available about the extent of possible losses and the likelihood of such losses occurring. For example, an insurance company dealing with fire insurance policies and claims from large numbers of manufacturers will be able to compile detailed statistics about numbers of fires and amount of damage done by each, and can use this information to predict the likelihood of a business experiencing a fire. This detailed statistical information allows the insurance company to charge manufacturers premiums for indemnifying them against the fire losses, and thereby to make a profit. By contrast, a single manufacturer would find it very difficult to predict the likelihood of his premises being damaged by fire and the amount of damage, since such an event would probably be a unique experience for him. Faced with a possibility of fire, the manufacturer can either choose to bear the risk of losses resulting from a serious fire or can avoid the risk of fire damage by paying an insurance company a premium to bear the risk.

It is normally assumed that economic agents dislike risks. And they try to avoid or, at least, minimise it. One way of doing it is to take insurance policies which are of different types.

23.1 TYPES OF BUSINESS RISKS

The most common types of business risks are the following:

1. **Actuarial risk:** Risk is an insurance underwriter covers in exchange for premiums, such as the risk of premature death.
2. **Exchange risk:** Chance of loss on foreign currency exchange.
3. **Inflation risk:** Chance that the value of assets or income will be eroded as inflation shrinks the value of a country's currency.
4. **Interest rate risk:** Possibility that a fixed-rate debt instrument will decline in value as a result of a rise in interest rates.
5. **Inventory risk:** Possibility that price changes, obsolescence, or other factors will shrink the value of inventory.
6. **Liquidity risk:** Possibility that an investor will not be able to buy or sell a commodity or security quickly enough or in sufficient quantities because buying or selling opportunities are limited.
7. **Political risk:** Possibility of nationalisation or other unfavourable government action.
8. **Repayment (credit) risk:** Chance that a borrower or trade debtor will not repay an obligation as promised.
9. **Risk of principal:** Chance that invested capital will drop in value.
10. **Systemic risk:** Risk affecting an entire business or industry, not just one company.
11. **Underwriting risk:** Risk taken by an investment banker that a new issue of securities purchased outright will not be bought by the public and/or that the market price will drop during the offering period.
12. **Unsystemic risk:** One-time occurrence that may affect a single property of business, such as fire.

23.2 INSURABLE AND NON-INSURABLE RISKS

All risks are not insurable. An uninsurable risk is one which is not covered by any insurance company. Examples of such risks are market risks (e.g., losses which occur because of price changes, style changes, or appearance of new products which may make a company's existing products obsolete); political risks (e.g., losses from war or government restrictions on trade); some personal risks (such as loss of a job); and some risks of operation (e.g., strikes or break-down of inefficient machines and equipment which may lead to work stoppage).

An uninsurable risk is one which an insurance company will cover by using the following guidelines:

(i) The policyholder must have an insurable interest. This means that the policyholder is the one at risk to suffer a loss. An individual cannot buy fire insurance for his neighbour's house and realise the compensation money if it burns out.

(ii) The loss must be measurable.

(iii) The chance of loss must be measurable.

(iv) The loss must be accidental.

(v) For the insurance company the risk should be dispersed. This means that it must be spread among different geographical areas so that a flood or a hurricane in one area does not make the insurance company totally bankrupt.

(vi) The insurance company must be able to set standards for accepting the risks.

What is not relevant for analysing the pros and cons of insurance is non-insurable risk. Such risk cannot be anticipated with reasonable accuracy by making probability calculations. This type of risk comes under the heading uncertainty. A few examples of such uncertainties are the following:

(i) A sudden fall in the demand for a company's product due to appearance of a better (cheaper) product (or, a close substitute item) in the market.

(ii) A sudden disappearance of a critical raw material from the market such as paper at the beginning of the school season.

(iii) A sudden change in technology which makes a company's existing machines obsolete.

(iv) A sudden change in government policy such as nationalisation of an industry such as sugar or tea or its state take-over.

(v) Natural calamities such as frequent earthquake in Nepal, severe flood in Assam and drought in Maharashtra.

23.3 MEANING OF INSURANCE

Insurance is a method of protecting a person or a firm against financial loss resulting from damage to, or theft of, personal and business assets (general insurance) and death and injury (life and accident insurance). It is essentially a contract to pay for others' losses — a legally binding arrangement in which individuals or companies pay the insurance company to guarantee them compensation if they suffer loss resulting from risks such as fire, theft, or accidental damage.

'To insure' means 'to agree to compensate in declared circumstances' and to make a contract to pay compensation if a particular loss or event occurs. Insurance breaks large risks into small pieces and then sells these small pieces in return for a small risk premium. Insurance may be obtained directly from an insurance company or through an intermediary such as an insurance broker/agent.

Insurance is a essentially a contract to pay compensation in certain eventualities (e.g., death, fire, theft and motor accident) in return for a premium. The premiums are so calculated that on average, in total, they are sufficient to pay compensation for policyholders who are likely to make a claim, together with a margin to cover administrative costs and profit. In effect, insurance pools risk so that loss by an individual is compensated for at the expense of all those who insure against risk.

BUSINESS FOCUS: MEANING OF INSURANCE

An insurance is a "legal contract in which an insurer promises to pay a specified amount to another party, the insured, if a particular event (known as the peril) happens and the insured suffers a financial loss as a result : The insured's part of the contract is to promise to pay an amount of money, known as the premium, either once or at regular intervals." **The Oxford Dictionary of Business**

The term insurance tends to be used interchangeably with assurance in practice but, technically, an insurance policy is taken out against what might happen while an assurance policy covers what is bound to happen (e.g., death and therefore payment of life cover) but at an unknown time.

H. Johansen and T.G. Page

Four Key Terms

Four key terms associated with insurance business are the following:

- **Insurance premium:** In return for an insurance premium the person or firm obtains insurance cover against financial risk. Insurance premium is a regular payment made by a person or a company to the insurance firm for a specific insurance policy.
- **Insurance coverage:** It refers to the type and amount of compensation against a specific risk which is guaranteed by an insurance policy.
- **Insurance policy:** It is a contract specifying terms of insurance — a document which sets out the terms and conditions for providing compensation against specific risks.
- **The insurer and the insured:** The insurance provider is known as 'insurer' or the insurance company. It provides insurance protection against various types of risks. The person who is protected by insurance is known as 'insured'. He is covered for specific risks such as loss, damage, illness, or death.

COMMENTARY: INSURANCE AND RISK SPREADING

Insurance is the major form of risk spreading. It is a kind of gambling in reverse. An insurance company spreads risks by pooling many different risk. It may insure millions of house or lives or cars. The speciality of a insurance company is that what is unpredictable for one individual is highly predictable for a population. Insurance helps reduce individual risks by spreading them out.

Insurance and Assurance

It is necessary to know at the outset the distinction between insurance and assurance. Normally, the term insurance is used to cover events (such as fire) which may or may not occur. By comparison, assurance refers to an event such as death which must happen at some time.

23.3.1 Characteristics of Insurance

The basic features of an insurance contract are the following :

1. *Involvement of two parties:* Two parties are involved in an insurance contract, viz., the 'insured' and the 'insurer'.
2. *Utmost good faith:* An insurance contract is essentially a contract requiring utmost good faith from both the parties. As Abraham Lincoln said long ago, " Faith earns faith." It is the

duty or moral obligation of the insured to disclose all material facts concerning or relating to the specific type of insurance so as to enable the insurer to estimate the risk that he is undertaking as accurately as possible.

3. *Insurable interest:* The insured must have an insurable interest. without an insurable interest, an insured person is unable to enforce an insurance contract as it is the insurable interest which distinguishes insurance from a bet or a wager.
4. *Uncertainty of risk:* The risk to be insured must not be imminent or a certainty at the time of insurance. For example, a person who is on deathbed cannot get insurance protection or a factory which has already caught fire cannot be insured.
5. *Indemnification:* An insurance contract (other than for life, personal accident and sickness insurance) is essentially a contract of indemnity. An indemnity is an arrangement whereby an insurance company agrees to compensate a client for any financial loss suffered as a result of damage, theft or destruction of the client's property.

BUSINESS FOCUS: INDEMNITY INSURANCE

Indemnity insurance refers to insurance policy which seeks to reimburse any damage or loss—an insurance contract in which the insurer agrees to cover the cost of losses suffered by the insured party. Most insurance contracts are like this except personal accident and life insurance policies, where fixed sums are paid as compensation, rather than reimbursement, for a loss which cannot be measured in terms of money.

23.4 OBJECTIVES AND PURPOSE OF INSURANCE

Insurance companies, like banks, are in the financial intermediation business, i.e., the business of transforming one type of asset into another for the public. Insurance companies use the premiums paid on policies to invest in assets such as government bonds, corporate stocks, mortgages, and mutual fund; the earnings from these assets are then used to pay out claims on the policies. In effect, insurance companies transform assets such as bonds, stocks and housing loans into insurance policies that provide a set of services (for example, claim adjustments, salary savings plans and group insurance).

If the insurance company's process of transformation of assets efficiently provides its customers with adequate insurance services and coverage at low cost and if it can earn high returns on its investments, it will make profits; if not, it will suffer losses.

By performing the following functions insurance offers a number of benefits to both the insured persons and the society at large:

1. **Transfer of risk:** By taking a suitable insurance policy, a business person can shift the risk of loss due to theft or fire or any other untoward event such as accident to the insurance company. To quote Oxford Dictionary of Economics, " In every insurance contract the insured pays to achieve a reduction in risk. without insurance there is a small chance of a large loss; with insurance there is a certain small loss, that is, the premium, and possibly some further loss if the damage done by the event insured against exceeds the sum insured. Insurance both reduces overall risk, and transfers risk from the insured to the insurer."
2. **Protection:** Insurance ensures safety of goods in transit or lying in warehouse as also of property such as house or office building. So the insured person (or the firm) feels secured

since he gets full protection in case of any loss or damage which has been covered by insurance. Life insurance business, because of its long-term contractual nature, is especially conducive to offering long-term investment returns to policyholders as well as the insurance company. So a win-win situation is created.

3. **Risk spreading:** Insurance helps in reading unavoidable risks as widely as possible. The burden of compensation payable to an affected party is virtually borne (shared) by all the policyholders.
4. **Risk pooling:** An insurance company operates by pooling risk among a large number of policyholders. Premiums are based on the probability of a particular event occurring and the average financial loss associated with each.
5. **Contractual savings:** In addition, many insurance companies offer contractual savings schemes. One such scheme is salary saving. Another is group insurance.
6. **Financial investment:** A life insurance policy is also a source of income in old age for investment made during an individual's working life. The assured gets a bonus every year under 'with profits policy.' A with-profits life-assurance policy is one which has additional amounts added to the sum assured, as a result of a profit made on the investing of the fund or funds of the life insurance company in which the policy holder is entitled to share1. So insurance benefit is combined with profit-sharing.
7. **Capital formation:** Insurance companies use the premiums they receive not only to settle day-to-day claims but also to generate additional income and profit by investing their funds in financial securities particularly fixed-interest beating government bonds and corporate stocks and shares. Their portfolios attempt to maintain a judicious mix of highly liquid assets and long-term investment returns. In truth, insurance companies are institutional investors, i.e, the financial institutions which collect savings and other deposits and invest these in long-term financial instruments. Through such activities insurance companies promote capital formation in the country.
8. **Growth of business:** Insurance facilitates growth of industry and commerce by covering various different types of risks to which businesses are often exposed. Examples of such risks are fire, theft, flood, accident and deterioration of product quality due to delayed arrival.
9. **Social benefits:** Finally, the society as a whole derives various benefits from insurance by being able to avoid various types of losses. People also feel secured through old-age, accident, whole life, child's education and marriage and other types of policies. Such policies also give protection to the dependants of the policyholders. Life insurance policies linked to the provision of mortgage finance for house purchase are another socially useful innovation.

23.5 PRINCIPLES OF INSURANCE

The fundamental principle of insurance is that it is available only for those risks which are insurable. Insurability of any risk is contingent upon the following factors:

1. **Possibility of quantification of loss:** It must be possible to measure the loss in terms of money by making probability calculations. In other words, the loss must be predictable and accurately measurable.

2. **Uncertainty:** Insurance coverage is given only for those losses which are uncertain. If the possibility of loss is almost certain no insurance coverage can be given.
3. **The law of large numbers:** By the law of large numbers the total of the premiums collected can be made to equal at least the total compensation paid out. The law says that if a large number of people or organisations are exposed to the same risk, a predictable number of losses will occur during a given period of time. Once the insurance company predicts the number of losses likely to occur, it can determine the appropriate premium for each policy it issues against that loss. The premium may be high enough in some cases to cover expected losses and yet earn a profit for the insurance company.
4. **Scattered location of policyholders:** If the policyholders remain scattered over a wide geographical area, then any natural calamity such as an earthquake or crop loss due to flood or drought in a small area may not impose any undue pressure on the insurance company. And the law of averages can apply.
5. **Monetary value:** Insurance policy is issued only in terms of pecuniary (monetary) benefits in case of loss or damage. Nonpecuniary factors (such as sorrows, anxieties, happiness, prestige and self-esteem) cannot be covered through insurance.
6. **Contribution:** The term 'contribution' refers to the right of an insurer who has settled claim under an insurance policy to call upon other insurers to make necessary contributions to the payment or compensatory adjustment. Suppose a person (the insured) has taken more than one policy on the same property such as a factory. However, he will not be entitled to claim from each insurance company more than the rateable proportion of the loss which he has incurred due to say, fire. This means that if he has incurred a loss of ₹10 lac, he cannot make a claim of more than this amount from all insurers taken together.

The principle of contribution applies only when the following conditions hold:

(a) The insured has to be the same individual.

(b) All the policies must cover a common risk.

(c) All the policies have to remain valid when the loss is incurred.

(d) The total amount of compensation under all policies taken together must not exceed the total amount of loss.

Calculation of the Contributions Payable

The contributions payable by different insurance companies for a common policy is calculated by using the following formula:

$$\frac{\text{Sum insured with an insurance company}}{\text{Total sum insured with all the insurance companies}} \times \text{Amount of loss}$$

Suppose, for example, *A* gets an insurance policy of ₹ 1,00,000 from *X* & Co., ₹ 60,000 from *Y* & Co. and ₹ 40,000 from *Z* & Co. He suffers a loss of ₹ 80,000 due to fire. *A* cannot claim more than ₹ 40,000 from *X* & Co., ₹ 24,000 from *Y* & Co. and ₹ 16,000 from *Z* & Co. If *X* & Co. compensates him fully for the loss of ₹ 80,000, *Y* & Co. will pay ₹ 24,000 and *Z* & Co. will pay ₹ 16,000 to *Y* & Co. This is the essence of the principle of contribution.

(a) Liability of *X* & Co. $= \frac{100,000}{1,00,000+60,000+40,000} \times 80,000 =$ ₹ 40,000

(b) Liability of Y & Co. $= \dfrac{60{,}000}{1{,}00{,}000 + 60{,}000 + 40{,}000} \times 80{,}000 =$ ₹ 24,000

(c) Liability of Z & Co. $= \dfrac{40{,}000}{1{,}00{,}000 + 40{,}000 + 40{,}000} \times 80{,}000 =$ ₹ 16,000

23.6 REINSURANCE AND DOUBLE INSURANCE

Reinsurance

Reinsurance refers to the passing of all or part of an insurable risk which has been covered by an insurer to another insurer in return for a premium. The contract between the parties is usually known as reinsurance treaty. The policy-holder is not usually aware that reinsurance has been arranged as no mention is made of it in the policy. More often than not an insurer will always accept a risk with a high pay-off if a total loss occurs (e.g., for a jumbo jet) in the sure knowledge that the potential loss can be reduced by reinsurance.

Double Insurance

When an insured person feels that he has insured for a lesser amount than the value of his property, he may purchase another insurance policy for the same property with a different company to get full or more than full coverage of the market (notional) value of his property. This is known as double insurance which means insurance with two insurance companies for getting adequate (full) protection against the same risk and same subject matter but for different amounts so as to get extra (full) protection. Double insurance is usually possible in case of life insurance as also in case of medical insurance. But there is no benefit of double insurance in case of fire and marine insurance due to the application of the principle of indemnity.

A person may take two or more policies on his life and claim the amount of all the policies if the policies mature during his life time. In case he dies before maturity of any policy, his nominees will get the full benefit of insurance.

23.7 VOCABULARY OF INSURANCE

Since various technical terms have been introduced in this chapter, some common terms are defined at the end of this chapter for enabling the students to recapitulate a fairly technical and complex subject.

1. **Insurability:** Circumstance in which an insurance company can issue life or health insurance to an applicant based on standards set by the company.
2. **Insurable interest:** Relationship with a person or thing that supports issuance of an insurance policy. A person having an insurable interest can derive financial advantage from preservation of the subject matter insured or suffer loss from its destruction. An insurable interest in the life of another requires that the continued life of the insured is of real interest to the insuring party.
3. **Insurable risk:** Risk situation meeting an insurance company's standards in that it: (i) is measurable; (ii) is accidental; (iii) meets a standard classification; and (iv) has a premium proportional to a possible loss.
4. **Insurable title:** Title that can be insured by a title insurance company. In some contracts for the sale of real estate the buyer must receive insurable title or he is not obligated to purchase the property.

5. Insurable value: The cost of total replacement of destructible improvements to a property; may be based on replacement cost rather than market value.
6. Insurance: System whereby individuals and companies concerned about potential hazards pay premiums to an insurance company, which reimburses (in whole or part) them in the event of loss. Some common forms of insurance cover business risks, automobiles, homes, boats, workers' compensation and health. Life insurance guarantees payment to the beneficiaries when the insured person dies. In a broad economic sense, insurance transfers risk from individuals to a larger group, which is better able to pay for losses.
7. Insurance agent: Representative of an insurance company who sells the firm's policies. Independent agents sell the policies of many companies.
8. Insurance broker: Independent broker who searches for the best insurance coverage at the lowest cost for the client. Insurance brokers do not work for insurance companies but for the buyers of insurance products. They generally compare the merits of competing insurance policies to find the best policy for their customers.
9. Insurance business: Issuing an insurance policy by a company to give protection against risk by accepting a fixed premium per period.
10. Insurance claim: Request for payment from an insurance company by the insured. For example, a home owner files a claim after suffering damage from a fire, theft, or other loss. Survivors submit a life insurance claim when the insured dies.
11. Insurance company (Insurer): Organisation that sees insurance policies. There are two principal types of insurance companies — mutual and stock.
12. Insurance contract: Legally binding unilateral agreement between an insured and an insurance company. In exchange for premium payment(s) the company covers stipulated perils.
13. Insurance coverage: Total amount and type of insurance carried.
14. Insurance policy: Insurance contract specifying what risks are insured and what premiums must be paid to keep the policy in force. The policy is the written document that both insured and insurance company refer to determining whether or not a claim is covered.
15. Insurance premiums: Amounts paid to an insurance company to cover potential hazards. Most insurance premiums are tax deductible to a business, except life insurance premiums when the company is the beneficiary. Most insurance premiums are not deductible by an individual, except that medical insurance premiums may be considered an itemised medical expense or self-employed individuals may deduct a portion.
16. Insurance settlement: Receiving proceeds of an insurance policy. Settlements terms are stated in the policy.
17. Insured: Person whose interests are protected by an insurance policy; person who contracts for a policy of insurance that indemnifies him against loss of property, life, health, etc.
18. Insured account: Account at a bank, that belongs to a state, or private insurance organisation.
19. Insured mail: Parcels sent via Postal Service that are insured for loss or possible damage by paying an insurance fee. A claim is then filed if the package fails to arrive at its destination.

20. Coinsurance: It refers to an insurance plan in which the insurer provides indemnity for only a certain percentage of the insured's loss, reflecting the relative division of risk between insured and insurer. A coinsurance clause of 80%, for example, requires the property owner to keep property insured to at least that percentage of the property value. If the insured fails to keep that much insurance, he will not be reimbursed (compensated) for the full loss.
21. Deductible: The term 'deductible' refers to the portion of a loss which must be borne by the insured. In other words, it is the initial amount of an insurable expense which the insured is required to pay, up to the limits of the policy, before insurance reimbursement is made for a claim. It has the effect of reducing the total sum insured. Thus, a deductible of ₹ 10 crore in a contract of ₹ 100 crore puts the insurer under an obligation to pay a claim, if made, of ₹ 90 crore. The higher the absolute rupee amount of the deductible, the lower the premium.

Key Points

1. Insurance: Insurance is a method of compensating for financial loss arising from case of death, illness, injury, accident, theft, destruction or damage of property through fire and other hazards, negligence or incompetence, and other eventualities. The method is the creation of a fund out of payments, or premiums paid by those who are exposed to the risk, from which compensation is paid to those to whom the eventuality ultimately occurs. The party to benefit under an insurance contract is called the 'insured' and a company engaged in the business of insurance is called an 'insurer'.
2. Principles of insurance. Six main principles of insurance are the following:
   (a) principle of utmost good faith,
   (b) principle of insurable interest,
   (c) principle of indemnity,
   (d) principle of subrogation,
   (e) principle of causa proxima and
   (f) principle of minimisation of loss,
   (g) principle of contribution.
3. Main types of insurance. Insurance business is divided broadly between life insurance and general insurance, which is of different types such as:
   (i) fire insurance,
   (ii) marine insurance and
   (iii) various other types of insurance such as health insurance, fidelity insurance, motor vehicle insurance and crop insurance.
4. Reinsurance and double insurance. Reinsurance refers to the passing of all or part of an insurable risk which can been covered by an insurer to another insurer in return for a premium. When an insured person feels that he has insured for a lesser amount that the value of his property, he may purchase another insurance policy for the same property with a different company to get full or more than full coverage of the market (notional) value of his property. This known as double insurance.

KEY Terms	
Insurance	Utmost good faith
Insured	Life insurance
Insurable interest	General insurable
Subrogation	Fire insurance
Insurance policy	Marine insurance
Uninsurable risk (uncertainty)	Internet
Rule of indemnity	Claim
Surrender value	Insurable risk
Market value	Risk
Insurability	Law of large numbers
Contribution	Double insurance
Reinsurance	Deductible

Assignments

SHORT ANSWER-TYPE QUESTIONS

1. Explain in brief the principle of contribution as a corollary of the doctrine of Indemnity. [ISC 1987]
2. Name the general principles of insurance. [ISC 1988]
3. Insurance is a contract of Indemnity. Explain. [ISC 1989]
4. What is the principle of 'utmost good faith' in insurance? [ISC 1990]
5. What is the term used for the insurance of goods carried by a ship? [ISC 1990]
6. Give the term used for risks which do not occur fairly regularly or in which the person asking for insurance has no insurable interest. [ISC 1990]
7. What is the type of insurance under which an insurer enters into a contract with another insurer for the assumption of part of or all, the risks taken by the first insurer? [ISC 1991]
8. Explain the principle of 'utmost good faith' in a contract of insurance. [ISC 1990]
9. Give two advantages of reinsurance. [ISC 1985]
10. What is meant by the term insurable interest? Explain the applicability of the concept in life insurance.
11. (a) Define insurance. What are the fundamentals principles of insurance?
    (b) Describe insurable and non-insurable risks.

ESSAY-TYPE QUESTIONS

1. Distinguish between risk and uncertainty.
2. Make a brief review of different types of risks to which a business firm is exposed.
3. What is meant by insurance? Make a brief review of the fundamental principles of insurance.
4. "Insurance is a method of spreading risks." In the light of this statement, explain how does insurance help in minimising business risks.
5. "Insurance is a contract of indemnity." Explain.
6. "The principle of contribution is a corollary to the principle of indemnity." Comment.
7. Explain the concept of insurable interest.
8. Distinguish between reinsurance and double insurance.
9. Explain the principle of utmost good faith in a contract of insurance.
10. What is insurable interest? Is it necessary any type of insurance contract?
11. Write short notes on:
    (a) Insurable interest
    (b) Doctrine of subrogation
    (c) Causa proxima
    (d) Reinsurance.
12. Highlight the characteristics of insurance contract.
13. Explain the advantages of Insurance to businessmen and the general public.

QUESTION BANK

1. *What is reinsurance?*

Ans. Reinsurance refers to the practice of insurers of passing on the some of the risks they assume to other parties in return for a proportional share of the premium income.

2. *Answer the following statements True or False:*
   (a) In life insurance, insurable interest must exist at the time of signing a contract.
   (b) In fire insurance, insurable interest must exist both at the time of agreement and at the time of loss.
   (c) In marine insurance, insurable interest is supposed to exist at the time of incurring loss.
   (d) Coinsurance is the same as double insurance.

Ans. True: (a), (b), (c)
False: (d).

3. *Fill in the blanks:*
   (a) A creditor is supposed to have ________ in the life of his debtor.
   (b) In case of life insurance, insurable interest is supposed to exist at the time of ________
   (c) In marine insurance, insurable interest has to exist at the time of ________
   (d) Life insurance ________ a contract of indemnity.
   (e) ________ is a contract between two insurance companies.

Ans. (a) insurable interested
(b) signing a contract
(c) incurring loss
(d) is not
(e) Reinsurance.

24 TYPES OF INSURANCE

SYLLABUS

- *Types of insurance: life and non-life.*
- *Types of insurance — life, health, fire, marine, motor, social and fidelity insurance (Meaning and importance only).*

> *One of the things young people think about is the idea that they may become sick, get injured or die. It is not a pleasant thought but the unexpected does happen every day. To protect your loved ones from the loss of your income, you should buy life insurance.* — W.G. Nickels and others

LEARNING OUTCOMES

On completion of this chapter, you will be able to understand the following:

24.1 Types of Insurance
24.2 Life Insurance — Meaning and Definition
24.3 Health Insurance
24.4 Fire Insurance
24.5 Marine Insurance
24.6 Motor Vehicle Insurance
24.7 Fidelity Insurance
24.8 Social Insurance

Different types of insurance facilities (policies) are available to meet the diverse needs of individuals and companies who (which) want protection against risks. The traditional form of insurance are general insurance (e.g., marine and other property insurance against theft, fire and accident) and life insurance (strictly assurance, because the cover is given against the occurrence of an event which is inevitable). There are also many other kinds of insurance including public or professional liability, sickness and unemployment insurance, some of which (like national insurance and private health care) are not, or not always, carried out by the traditional insurance companies. Life insurance is a popular way of providing for old age and house purchase as well as protecting the financial position of dependents. In endowment insurance, policyholders benefit from a share in the appreciation of the life fund. The lumpsum payable is increased by bonuses, called reversionary bonuses, annually plus a terminal bonus on death or termination of the policy.

24.1 TYPES OF INSURANCE

As shown in Fig. 24.1, insurance policies are of two broad types. viz., life insurance (or life assurance) and general (non-life) insurance. Life assurance consists of provision for paying compensation against an inevitable occurrence; that of death, and in this respect differs from any other type of insurance, which offers compensation against an eventuality which may or may not occur.

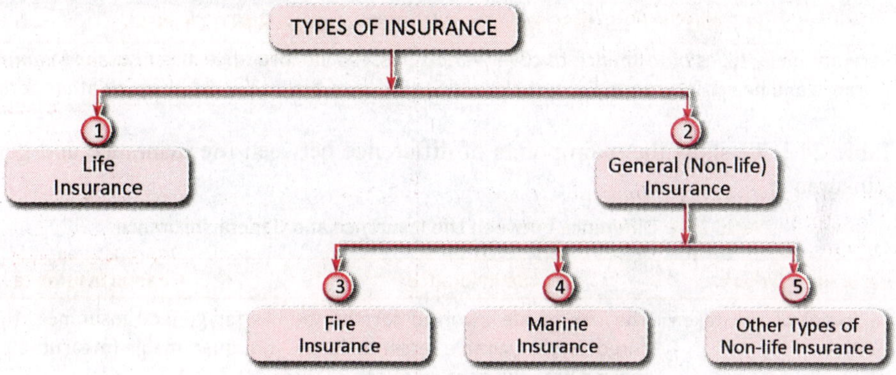

FIGURE 24.1: Main Categories of Insurance

General insurance contracts or policies are normally for a risk of specified monetary value and for a specified period of time. Life assurance policies are for a specified monetary amount and are necessarily indeterminate in time; however, life policies may also be taken out for a specified period of years, in which case they are known as term policies.

1. **Life Insurance:** Life insurance refers to an insurance policy which pays a specified amount of money on the death of the life assured, or, in the case of an endowment policy at the end of an agreed period, whichever is the earlier. Life assurance is a means of saving for oneself or one's dependents, with certain tax advantages. With-profits policies provide sums of money in excess of the sum assured by the addition of bonuses. Unit-linked policies invest the premium in funds of assets, by means of buying units in the funds.

   Life insurance is insurance which pays a specified sum to the insured person's beneficiaries after his (her) death.

2. **General Insurance:** General (non-life) insurance refers to insurance cover against the occurrence of certain specified events or insurance against loss excluding life insurance. The most common types of general insurance (discussed next) relate to the risks of fire, auto-mobile damage or loss, or theft.

   General insurance relates to various potential losses such as theft or damage, but excluding life insurance.

However, of two main types of such insurance are the following:

(i) *Fire insurance:* Fire insurance protects an individual or a company against loss due to fire. If there is damage to the property of the insured due to fire, he (it) will get compensation equal to the value of damaged property. However, to get this compensation only annual premium (depending upon the coverage of loss) has to be paid.

FOCUS OR TERMINOLOGY: ASSURANCE

Assurance is a contractual saving arrangement through which a persons pays premiums at regular intervals to an insurance company in return for a sum of money to be received at a later date. With life assurance a lumpsum payment and/or an annuity becomes due to the dependents of the person assured. With endowment assurance a lumpsum payment and/ or an annuity is payable to the person assured at an agreed future date.

(ii) *Marine insurance:* Marine insurance provides protection to business people (exporters and importers) against risk of loss of goods during sea voyage. The shipping company can also get its ship insured by paying a fixed premium to the insurance company.

BUSINESS FOCUS: INSURANCE COVER FOR VARIOUS KINDS OF RISKS

There are many types of insurance to cover various losses : life insurance, fire insurance, marine insurance and health insurance. Property losses occur due to fire, accidents, theft, or other perils.

In Table 24.1 we show the main points of difference between life insurance and general (or non-life) insurance.

TABLE 24.1: Difference between Life Insurance and General Insurance

Basis of Comparison	Life Insurance	General Insurance
1. Nature (type) of risk taken (covered)	The risk of life involved for the insured is measurable essentially by making probability calculations.	As for general insurance, the risk is not quantifiable (measurable).
2. Type of contract	Life insurance is usually contract of certainty since a payment is guaranteed in case of death of the policyholder.	It is essentially contract of indemnity.
3. Time period covered	Life insurance is usually taken for a long period ranging from 5 to 25 years or even longer.	Such insurance is normally taken for one year and has to be renewed every year.
4. Presence of insurable interest	Insurable interest has to be present at least at the time of taking the policy.	It must exist both at the time of making the contract as also at the time of suffering loss.
5. Need for medical test(s)	A medical test of the insured person is a must.	No medical examination is needed for taking it.
6. Right to pre-mature surrender of the policy	The assured has the right to surrender the policy before maturity.	The insured is not required to surrender for taking it.
7. Surrender value	The policyholder gets the surrender value.	Nothing is paid under general insurance.
8. Benefit of double (triple) insurance	A person can get insured with two or more companies and thus derive multiple benefits.	There is no benefit of double insurance under the scheme.

24.2 LIFE INSURANCE — MEANING AND DEFINITION

Life insurance is perhaps the most important and popular form of insurance. It is an insurance policy which pays a specified amount of money on the death of the life assured or, in the case of an endowment assurance policy, on a certain maturity date, whichever is earlier.

As mentioned earlier life insurance not only protects a family from the uncertainty associated with the sudden death of the bread-earner[1], it is also a means of saving for oneself or one's dependants, with certain tax advantages. With-profits policies provide sums of money in excess of the sum assured by the addition of bonuses. The insurance company gives protection to the injured person against a premium (which may be paid annually, half-yearly, quarterly or even monthly as in the case of salaried persons) by paying a certain sum of money either on the death of the insured or on the maturity of the policy.

The person whose life is insured is called the assured. The money paid to the insurer (insurance company) at periodic intervals is called the premium. The nonpayment of premium within a certain period makes the insurance contract invalid.

Five essential elements of a life insurance contract are the following:

(i) *Intangibility:* The first thing to note about an insurance contract is that the product sold is intangible. It cannot be seen or felt.

(ii) *Good faith:* The whole concept of life insurance is based on good faith. In any insurance contract, there is an implied condition that each party must disclose every material fact known to him[2]. Utmost good faith can be defined as a positive duty to disclose accurately and fully all facts relating (or relevant) to the risk involved whether requested or not.

(iii) *Insurable interest:* Insurable interest has to be present while taking-up an insurance policy. As the Insurance Institute of India has put it, "All risks are not insurance. In order to be insurable, the risk must be capable of financial measurement, there must be sufficient number of similar risks and the risk must be capable of statistical (actuarial) estimation".

(iv) *Contractual obligation:* The amount payable by thc insurance company after a certain number of years (i.e., on the maturity date) or on the death of the assured, whichever is earlier, remains contractually fixed.

(v) *Valid contract:* An insurance contract should have all the essential elements of a valid contract, e.g., offer and acceptance, premium, legal binding and free consent.

24.2.1 Different Kinds of Life Insurance Policies

Life insurance policies are of the following types:

1. *Term insurance:* The simplest and least expensive form of life insurance is term insurance. It is pure insurance protection for a fixed number of years which normally costs less the younger is the buyer of the policy.
2. *Whole (of) life policy:* It is a life assurance policy which pays a specified amount on the death of the policyholder. The cover continues until the death of the insured person, provided the premiums continue to be paid, either for life or until a specified date. If the premia are payable throughout life, the policy is called 'Ordinary Life Policy'. If the premia have to be paid just for a certain limited number of years, the policy goes by the name 'Limited Payment Life Policy'. Whole life insurance combines pure insurance and savings. So a person buys both insurance and a savings plan.

1 The reason is that like taxes, death is one of the certainties of life.

2 This type of contract is called Uberrimal Fides, i.e., contract of utmost good faith.

3. *Endowment life assurance policy:* It is a life assurance policy which pays a specified amount of money on an agreed date or on the death of the life assured, whichever is the earlier. This policy makes a guaranteed payment (either to the policyholder or his or her dependents) and offers both life coverage and a reasonable investment. A with-profits policy also provides bonuses in addition to the sum assured. These policies are often used as a form of savings. The premium for such policy is slightly higher than that of whole life policy.

Whole life insurance combines pure insurance and savings.

4. *Joint life policy:* A joint policy involves insurance coverage of two persons at the same time such as a policy on the lives of a husband and his wife, payable to the survivor on the death of either of the policyholders. The policy money is payable upon the death of one of the policyholders to the other person and the assured sum will be payable to the survivor.

An annuity is a contract to make regular payments to a person for life or for a fixed period.

5. *Annuity policy:* Life insurance companies recognised people's desire to earn higher returns on their insurance (and to protect themselves against cash shortage before they die) and began selling annuities. An annuity is a contract to make regular payments to a person for life or for a fixed period. With an annuity, an individual is guaranteed to have an income until his death. So it does have a maturity date.

   There are two kinds of annuities: fixed and variable. Fixed annuities are investments which pay the policyholder a specified interest rate. Variable annuities provide investment choices identical to mutual funds. But buyers have to be careful in selecting an insurance company and choosing the investments made with their money. To quote the Insurance Institute of India, "Annuities start where life insurance ends. It is called the 'reverse' of life insurance. In annuity contract, a person agrees to pay to the insurer a specified capital sum, maybe, by installments, in return for a promise from the insurer to make a series of payments to him so long as he lives."

6. *Children's endowment policy:* This policy is taken to cover the cost of children's education or the expenses of daughters' marriages. The insurer agrees to pay a certain sum when the children reach a certain age. Premium is payable by the policyholder. But if he dies before the maturity of policy, no further premium is payable.

7. *With profit and without profit policies:* A life assurance policy which has additional amounts added to the sum assured is called with-profits policy. Under this policy the policyholder is entitled to the profit made on the investment of funds raised (through premium) by the insurance company. By comparison a without-profit policy is one under which the insurance company does not share its profits with policyholders.

   Under 'with profit' policies, a major part of the surplus earned by an insurance company through portfolio investment, (i.e., investment of funds in various financial assets) is distributed to policyholders as bonus. For getting bonus a policyholder has to pay a little extra premium. No bonus is paid to holders of 'without profit' policies.

8. *Variable life insurance:* A variable life insurance is a form of whole life insurance which invests the cash value of the policy in stocks or other high-yielding securities (mainly blue-chips, which are first class equity shares carrying little risk of capital loss even in times of recession). Death benefits may thus vary, depending on the performance of the investment.

   Variable life insurance is a comparatively new policy and has not gained much acceptability or popularity till date. In fact,it is not yet known to most people.

24.2.2 Importance of Life Insurance

Of all forms of insurance, life insurance is no doubt the most important. It offers the following advantages.

(i) *Protection against risk:* Since in case of premature death, insured sum of money is handed over to the nominee(s) of the policyholder. His family gets necessary income protection.

(ii) *Provision after retirement:* Through life insurance, an individual can make a living after retirement. He continues to enjoy economic independence if he lives enough and get the insured sum of money along with bonus.

(iii) *Development of savings habit:* To be able to pay insurance premium at periodic intervals, an individual is to save some money. Thus life insurance helps to develop the habit of saving and thriftiness among people.

(iv) *Financial investment:* By paying small amounts as premium over a number of years a person can build a fund through insurance for making real investment (such as building a house), or investment in human capital (such as higher education of his/her children) or even marriage of daughters.

(v) *Collateral:* Life insurance policy can also be used as a collateral for taking loans in times of financial need.

(vi) *Tax savings:* The premium paid on life insurance policy enables a person to reduce his tax liability. The reason is that the premium paid is deducted from a person's taxable income.

(vii) *Capital formation:* The money collected by life insurance companies is invested in industry and various other developmental activities. Such investment promotes faster economic development of the country and thus enhances social welfare. Life insurance companies also increase personal wealth by giving housing loan.

(viii) *Generation of employment opportunities:* Life insurance companies provide not only direct employment to millions of people but also self-employment opportunities to many people who act as agents or sub-agents.

24.3 HEALTH INSURANCE

Businesses and non-profit organisations may offer their employees an wide range of health care benefits to choose from. Everything from hospitalisation to doctor's fees, eye exams, dental exams, and prescriptions can be covered by health insurance. General insurance companies provide special and, often attractive, health insurance policies such as Mediclaim. Under health or medical insurance policy, the insurance company charges a certain sum as premium on an annual basis and provides certain stipulated amounts for the treatment of specific diseases such as heart ailments, cancer, tumour, asthma, etc. in exchange.

Under mediclaim, the insurance company pays up to ₹ 5 lacs to enable the insured meet the costs of treatment mentioned above against the diseases covered by the insurance contract. in India health insurance is very popular among professionals, business people as also self-employed persons due to low premium, multiple options and wide choice.

Health insurance was not very popular in the early 1990s. However, due to two main advantages offered by most health insurance scheme, these have gained much popularity of late. Firstly there is provision for cashless treatment. Secondly the insurance premium is tax-deductible.

24.3.1 Importance of Health Insurance

Health insurance offers the following advantages:

(i) By paying a small premium the insured person gets a large insurance coverage for various diseases such as heart attack, tumour, cancer, kidney failure, etc. The treatment of such diseases involves huge cost which most person cannot bear.

(ii) The premium paid for health insurance is treated as a deductible expense from one's tax-able income up to a certain amount.

(iii) In case of sudden hospitalisation, the insured and his (her) family is not required to bear the burden of heavy expenditure because most insured person now get cashless treatment.

(iv) Since health is wealth, health insurance conduces to a country's economic development by improving health of active population and thereby raising their productivity.

(v) The health insurance industry promotes social welfare by improving the quality of life of people.

24.4 FIRE INSURANCE

A fire insurance policy covers financial losses caused by damage to property by fires. Most fire insurance policies also include cover for other types of damages such as those caused by lightning and explosion of boilers in factories or cooking gas used by households. If additional premium is paid, then fire insurers are often ready to widen the cover all to include such special perils as those arising from various weather-related and man-made causes.

Under a fire insurance policy, the insurer undertakes, on receipt of a premium and subject to the conditions of the contract, to compensate the insured either fully or partly for any loss or damage caused to his property by fire during the period covered by the policy, up to the amount mentioned (quoted) in the contract. The contract specifies the period during which the indemnity is to last as also the maximum compensation the insurer is bound to pay in case of an eventuality.

The essential features of a fire insurance contract are the following:

1. **Utmost good faith:** It is a contract of *uberrimal fides*, i.e., utmost good faith. This means that it is a duty of both the parties — the insured and the insurer — to disclose fully and accurately all facts related to the risk involved, whether requested or not.
2. **Indemnity:** It is a contract of indemnity. An indemnity is an arrangement whereby an in-surance company agrees to compensate a client for any financial losses suffered as a result of damage, theft or loss of the client's property.
3. **Insurable interest:** As noted earlier in this chapter the insured must have an insurable interest. Insurable interest refers to the legal right to enter into an insurance contract. An individual is said to have an insurable interest if the event insured against could cause that person a financial loss. For example, anyone may like to insure his house or property since he would incur a loss if it was destroyed, or damaged by fire. If no financial loss is likely to occur, no insurance can be arranged. The limit of an insurable interest is the value of the item concerned such as a property or a factory. without an insurable interest, an insured person is unable to enforce a fire insurance contract.
4. **Causa proxima:** The insurer is liable to compensate for the loss if and only if fire is the proximate cause of loss or damage to a property (i.e., causa proxima).

5. **Validity subject to annual renewal:** A fire insurance contract is valid for only one year. It remains valid and effective if and only if it is renewed year after year.
6. **Enforcement:** To be enforceable a fire insurance contract must have the following essentials: (a) offer and acceptable, (b) consideration, (c) capacity to contract, (d) consensus 'an idem', and (e) legality of object. The contract should also be capable of being operational and both parties should have an intention to create legal relationship.

24.4.1 Types of Fire Insurance Policies

Four important types of fire insurance policies are the following:

1. *Valued policy:* Under this policy, the insurer has to pay the full value declared in the policy to get insurance benefit to the extent of loss of the value of property which is insured irrespective of the market or notional value of the property at the time of loss. This means that the policy violates the principle of indemnity. So such an insurance policy is a rarity. It is issued only in case of rare goods such as works of art and antiques whose market value cannot be accurately determined or calculated.
2. *Specific policy:* Under this policy, the insurer pays compensation to the insured in case of loss or damage up to the amount specified in the policy. Suppose, a house worth ₹ 10 lacs is insured against fire for only ₹ 5 lacs. If the damage to the property is ₹ 2 lacs or even if the loss is ₹ 5 lacs the insured will get full compensation and if the loss is more than ₹ 5 lacs, the insured will get ₹ 5 lacs only. So in this case the value of property is not taken into consideration in determining the amount of indemnity.
3. *Floating policy:* A floating policy is issued for large business firms whose stock of goods lie in different railway stations, sea ports, and warehouses. Firms dealing in multiple products take out such a policy for all the goods lying at different places by paying a single premium.
4. *Reinstatement policy:* In case of such a policy, the insurer has the legal right to reinstate or replenish the property partly lost or fully destroyed. No cash is paid to the insured as compensation for the damage suffered.

24.4.2 Importance of Fire Insurance

By protecting an individual or a company against risk of loss by fire the insured person or company is placed in almost the same financial position as he/it was before incurring loss due to fire. Fire can cause huge loss to a person if his house is gutted. In case of a company, its entire factory, office or godown may be destroyed by fire. This may make a business person virtually penniless. Fire insurance helps him to restart his business all over again with the money he receives as compensation.

24.5 MARINE INSURANCE

Marine insurance is the insurance of ships and other cargo against specified cases of loss or damage which might be encountered at sea. Over the years the scope of such insurance has been widened to include the transit of cargo over land at each end of the voyage. In addition, the term 'vessel' now includes ships under construction or repair and drilling rigs. Under this policy, the insurer undertakes to indemnify the insured for marine losses against the premium paid by the latter. The marine insurer is also known as 'underwriter'.

24.5.1 Features of Marine Insurance

Five characteristic features of a marine insurance contract are the following:

1. Like life insurance it is also based on utmost good faith.
2. It is essentially a contract of indemnity.
3. Insurable interest in the subject-matter of insurance must be present at the time of incurring loss and not necessarily at the time of taking the insurance policy.
4. Like fire insurance marine insurance is subject to the doctrine of causa proxima.
5. It must contain all the essential requirements of a valid contract.

All these points have been discussed in detail under life assurance and fire insurance and need not be repeated.

24.5.2 Types of Marine Insurance

Marine insurance is of three main types:

(a) *Ship insurance:* Ship insurance seeks to indemnify the insured for losses during the voyage. Such insurance policy is taken by traders since a vessel is exposed to many dangers or risks at sea.

(b) *Cargo insurance:* The cargo transported at the port by sea is often subject to various types of risks at the port as also during the voyage. Such risks are covered through cargo insurance.

(c) *Freight insurance:* A shipping company is not legally entitled to receive freight on the cargo if it fails to reach the destination safely for any reason. And a freight insurance policy is issued to reimburse the loss to the insured.

24.5.3 Importance of Marine Insurance

Shipping involves different types of risks some of which are very serious due to such perils as shinking of ships after being hit by a rock, loss of cargo due to storms at sea or ocean, collision with another ship, looting of a ship by pirates, etc. A ship and its cargo may be lost/damaged/destroyed due to accident, storm, piracy, etc.

Since the journey/dispatch of goods by a ship is a time-consuming process, the chance of loss is usually much higher than that associated with other modes of transport.

A marine insurance policy provides protection against different types of risks. Since the cost of a ship is very high, the ship-owners always take insurance policies for the whole ship (called hull insurance policies).

Marine insurance promotes export-import trade by giving protection against the perils of the sea such as piracy, capture by enemies, seizure, restrain, jettison and barratry.

Jettison refers to deliberately throwing of goods over board in order to avoid sinking of ships.

Barratry refers to fraudulent breach of duty by master or staff of the sea. Marine insurance provides protection against all possible risks to both traders (importers and exporters) as also the shipping company.

In case of marine insurance, all parties concerned such as owner of goods/ship, captain and employees of the ship must have insurable interest both at the time of taking insurance policy and at the time of suffering marine loss.

Table 24.2 we make a comparison among the above three types of insruance.

Table 24.2: A Comparison of the Three Main Types of Insurance — Life, Fire and Marine Insurance

Basis of comparison	Life Insurance	Fire Insurance	Marine Insurance
1. Indemnity or compensation for any financial losses suffered by a client as a result of damage, theft or loss of property.	The principle of indemnity is not applicable to life insurance. The assured, if he (she) survives, is entitled to maturity value of the policy or the same sum is paid to his dependents or legal heirs in case of his (her) death.	The principle of indemnity applies. The insured can claim compensation amounting to the actual market value of property if it is damaged or destroyed by fire.	It is based on the principle of indemnity. This means that the insured can claim the full market value of the ship and the cost of goods destroyed by perils of sea voyage plus a certain amount for anticipated (potential) profits, by giving adequate proof or documentary evidence.
2. Presence of insurable interest	Insurable interest must be present at the time of taking the policy.	Insurable interest has to be present both at the time of taking the policy as also at the time of suffering loss or fire-related damage.	Insurable interest has to be present only at the time of suffering loss, and not at the time of making the policy.
3. Permission of the insurance company	Life insurance policy can be made by an agent or a representative without taking prior permission of the insurance company.	Fire insurance policy cannot be made without taking prior permission of the insurance company.	Marine insurance policy can be made without taking prior permission of the insurance company. So it is flexible in nature.
4. Time period of policy	Life assurance is usually for a period of from 5 to 30 years. Sometimes whole life policy is also taken.	Fire insurance policy is made for one year, and has to be renewed every day.	Marine insurance policy can be made either for a particular voyage or for just one year. A mixed policy can also be taken.
5. Measurement of loss	Loss cannot be measured.	Loss can be measured.	Loss can be measured or quantified.
6. Double (multiple insurance)	The benefit of double or even multi-insurance can be derived by the policy-holder.	The benefit of double insurance is not offered.	The benefit of double insurance is not available.
7. Realisation of surrender value	Both surrender value and paid-up value can be realised.	No such provision exists.	No such provision exists.
8. Inevitability (certainty) of risk	Since every policyholder makes a claim sooner or later, there is always an element of risk.	Since every policy-holder does not make a claim, the presence or risk is not inevitable.	Since every policyholder does not make a claim, the presence of risk is not inevitable.

24.6 MOTOR VEHICLE INSURANCE

A motor vehicle insurance is a form of insurance covering loss or damage to motor vehicles and any legal liabilities for physical injury or damage to other peoples' property. Drivers have a legal obligation to be covered against third-party claims, but most drivers or owners of vehicles have a comprehensive insurance, providing wide coverage of all types of risks involved in owning a motor vehicle. It is an insurance policy of motor car, motor cycle, or scooter. It covers the following types of risks:

(a) Loss or damage to the vehicle, i.e., car, motor cycle, or scooter;

(b) Physical injuries to or death of any passenger;

(c) Damages done to the third party by the owner of the vehicle in case of an accident.

Motor vehicle insurance is of two types:

(a) **Third party insurance:** In case the insured vehicle inflicts damage or causes injury to any vehicle or person the owner of the vehicle will compensate the third party and insurer will, in turn, reimburse the same amount the insured.

FOCUS ON TERMINOLOGY: THIRD PARTY INSURANCE

Third party insurance refers to insurance of a prson's legal liability to others. Since the insurer and the policyholder are the two parties to the insurance contract, any other person to whom there is a legal obligation from either of the two parties is, therefore, a third party. Some forms of third-party insurance are compulsory. For example, motorists must have third-party cover for any loss or damage suffered by members of the public as a result of their rash/careless driving.

(b) **Comprehensive insurance:** This type of insurance covers all types of risks which cause damage or loss to the insured vehicle.

24.6.1 Importance of the Motor Vehicle Insurance

The owner of motor vehicles receives the current market value of the vehicle in case of any loss due to fire, theft, or accident. With the compensation received from the insurance company, he/she can buy another motor vehicle. This is of considerable help to a person who makes his living from taxi, auto or bus. He can restart his business with the compensation he gets from the insurance company. The owners of motor vehicle are under the legal obligation to insure against the risk of liability to third parties as per the Motor Vehicles Act, 1939. The objective is to mitigate the financial hardship caused to the people who suffer injury or are killed by motor vehicles. The reason is that the compensation payable to a third party in case of accident or death can also be recovered from the insurance company.

24.7 FIDELITY INSURANCE

Fidelity insurance is an insurance policy covering employees for any financial losses they may suffer due to the dishonesty of employees. policies can be arranged to cover all employees or some specific persons. Under such policy, the insurance company compensates the insured business firm against any loss arising from misappropriation of funds or theft of goods by its employees. Such a policy is most suitable for those employers who often suspect or apprehend stealing companies' money, forgery, fraudulent activities and dishonesty of various types on the part of their employees. Due to the nature of the cover, insurers need full information or complete details of the procedure(s) adopted by an organisation in recruiting and vetting new employees as insurers usually reserve the right to refuse to cover a particular person without giving any reason.

24.7.1 Importance of Fidelity Insurance

Fidelity insurance protects an employer from any financial loss suffered due to dishonesty like fraud and embezzlement by his employees. The employer is protected against loss suffered up to the insured amount by the insurance company.